T0332747

Building a Scalable Data Warehouse with Data Vault 2.0

Building a Scalable Data Warehouse with Data Vault 2.0

Daniel Linstedt

Michael Olschimke

ELSEVIER

AMSTERDAM • BOSTON • HEIDELBERG • LONDON
NEW YORK • OXFORD • PARIS • SAN DIEGO
SAN FRANCISCO • SINGAPORE • SYDNEY • TOKYO

Morgan Kaufmann is an Imprint of Elsevier

Publisher: Todd Green
Editorial Project Manager: Amy Invernizzi
Project Manager: Paul Prasad Chandramohan
Designer: Matthew Limbert

Morgan Kaufmann is an imprint of Elsevier
225 Wyman Street, Waltham, MA 02451, USA

British Library Cataloguing-in-Publication Data
A catalogue record for this book is available from the British Library

Library of Congress Cataloging-in-Publication Data
A catalog record for this book is available from the Library of Congress

ISBN: 978-0-12-802510-9

For information on all Morgan Kaufmann publications
visit our website at www.mkp.com/

Contents

Please refer the companion site for more details — http://booksite.elsevier.com/9780128025109

Authors Biography

DANIEL LINSTEDT

Daniel has more than 25 years of experience in the Data Warehousing and Business Intelligence field and is internationally known for inventing the Data Vault 1.0 model and the Data Vault 2.0 System of Business Intelligence. He helps business and government organizations around the world to achieve BI excellence by applying his proven knowledge in Big Data, unstructured information management, agile methodologies and product development. He has held training classes and presented at TDWI, Teradata Partners, DAMA, Informatica, Oracle user groups and Data Modeling Zone conference. He has a background in SEI/CMMI Level 5, and has contributed architecture efforts to petabyte scale data warehouses and offers high quality on-line training and consulting services for Data Vault.

MICHAEL OLSCHIMKE

Michael has more than 15 years of experience in IT and has been working on business intelligence topics for the past eight years. He has consulted for a number of clients in the automotive industry, insurance industry and nonprofits. In addition, he has consulted for government organizations in Germany on business intelligence topics. Michael is responsible for the Data Vault training program at Dörffler + Partner GmbH, a German consulting firm specialized in data warehousing and business intelligence. He is also a lecturer at the University of Applied Sciences and Arts in Hannover, Germany. In addition, he maintains DataVault.guru, a community site on Data Vault topics.

Foreword

I met Daniel Linstedt during a speech at Lockheed Martin in the early 1990's for the first time. By the time, he was an employee of the company, working for government projects. He approached me because he wanted my opinion about a concept that he had invented at the Department of Defense, in order to store large amounts of data. Back then, the term Big Data was not invented yet. But from what Daniel explained to me, the concept to deal with such huge amounts of data, was born.

Because back then, the end user had cried for "give me my data!". But over time the end user became more sophisticated. The end user learned that it was not enough to get one's data. What a person needed was the RIGHT data. And then the sophisticated end user cried for "give me my accurate and correct data!"

The data warehouse represented the architectural solution to the issue of needing a single version of the truth. The primary reason for the existence of the data warehouse was the corporate need for integrity and believability of data. As such the data warehouse became the major architectural evolutionary leap beyond the early application systems.

But the data warehouse was not the end of architecture. Indeed, the data warehouse was only one stepping stone – architecturally speaking – in the progression of the evolution of architecture. It was Daniel's idea that followed the data warehouse. In many ways the data warehouse set the stage for him.

Daniel used the term common foundational modeling architecture to describe a model based on three simple entities, focusing on business keys, their relationships and descriptive information for both. By doing so, the model closely followed the way business was using the data in the source systems. It allowed to source all kinds of data, regardless its structure, in a fully auditable manner. This was a core requirement of government agencies at the time. And due to Enron and a host of other corporate failures, Basel, and SOX compliance auditability was pushed to the forefront of the industry.

Not only that, the model was able to evolve on changing data structures. It was also easy to extend by adding more and more source systems. Daniel later called it the "Data Vault Model" and it was groundbreaking.

The data vault became the next architectural extension of the data warehouse. But the data vault concept – like all evolutions – continued to evolve. He asked me what to do about it and, as a professional author, I gave him the advice to "publish the heck out of it." But Daniel decided to take it to the long run. Over multiple years, he improved the Data Vault and evolved it into Data Vault 2.0. Today, this *System of Business Intelligence* includes not only a more sophisticated model, but an agile methodology, a reference architecture for enterprise data warehouse systems, and best practices for implementation.

The Data Vault 2.0 System of Business Intelligence is ground-breaking, again. It incorporates concepts from massively parallel architectures, Big Data, real-time and unstructured data. And after all the time, I'm glad that he followed my advice and has started to publish more on the topic.

This book represents that latest, most current step in the larger evolution of the Data Vault that has been occurring. This book had been carefully and thoughtfully prepared by leaders in the thought and implementation of the Data Vault.

Bill Inmon
June 29, 2015

Preface

When I was asked by the Department of Defense to build a scalable data warehouse, I was confronted with a problem. Back then, before the term Big Data was invented, there was no approach for building such systems – systems that could accommodate large data sets, delivered at high frequencies, and in multiple structures.

I started intensive research to come up with a viable solution for this challenge. The analysis was based on patterns from nature, because I expected that a partial solution would already exist somewhere. Over more than 10 years, from 1990 to early 2000, I tested the applicability of these natural patterns in data warehousing. By doing so, I reduced the initial list of 50 potential entities down to three. These remaining entity types were based on a hub-and-spoke architecture that scaled well and was easy to extend. This model is known today as Data Vault modeling. The three entities are: hubs, which provide a unique list of business keys from business processes; links, which integrate the business keys within and over source system boundaries; and satellites, which provide descriptive data.

This model enabled my clients to build the most sophisticated systems and complete their assigned tasks. When I left the government context, the system was storing and processing more than 15 petabytes of data and is still growing today.

However, over the years, Data Vault modeling evolved. It became one of the pillars of the Data Vault 2.0 Standard. The Data Vault 2.0 Architecture and the Data Vault 2.0 Methodology are the other pillars, in conjunction with the Data Vault 2.0 Implementation best practices. Without these other pillars, a Data Vault 2.0 model is just a model. The pillars together provide a set of best practices, standards, and techniques that organizations rely on to build scalable data warehouse systems by using agile practices. Data Vault 2.0 enables data warehouse teams around the world to exploit the Data Vault as a system of business intelligence. This is what I teach: how to take advantage of the Data Vault 2.0 Standard, in rapid, small steps; and it is what this book is all about.

Daniel Linstedt
Inventor of Data Vault modeling and the Data Vault 2.0
System of Business Intelligence
St. Albans, Vermont, USA

This book is the result of my own evolution regarding the Data Vault. When I heard of the concept for the very first time in 2011 or 2012 from Oliver Cramer, I remained very skeptical. This was due to the fact that, at that time, Data Vault was seen primarily as a model. It was different, but the model by itself was not enough for me to become convinced of the value of it.

But Christian Haedrich, CEO of Dörffler, wanted to find out what's behind Data Vault and decided to go for a training in 2013 with the inventor, Daniel Linstedt, in Vermont. To be honest, my first thought was: "what a waste of time." I was not very happy to board a plane for six or more hours, head over to Vermont, sit in a training class for four days, and spend another six hours on the return trip.

And because I hate to waste time, I decided to take advantage of it. My goal became not to waste my time during the flight or in Vermont. Instead, I wanted to seriously understand what the Data Vault is, but certainly not to use it in business. Instead, I wanted to rule it out with confidence. That's not a lot of value, honestly, but at least you lose the uncertainty that you might miss some great technology because you don't understand it.

That was the plan, and I failed miserably at it. In fact, Daniel convinced me that the Data Vault was the technology you don't want to miss if you're building data warehouse solutions. Most people in the industry are unaware that he had further developed the concept and integrated best practices for implementation and methodology, as well as a reference architecture. These were the pieces that were missing for me. This now explained to me why the model is as it is, along with all the background information that described why some designs are fundamentally different in Data Vault.

Since then, I have asked Daniel many questions, because I wanted to fully understand the Data Vault, the concepts behind it and what his intentions are behind his design decisions. Our discussions back then started a work relationship and learning experience that I have truly enjoyed. This book is the outcome of this time spent.

I might have failed when I tried to rule out Data Vault as a viable solution for business intelligence projects. But I always try to make mistakes only once in life. I'm glad that I changed my mind. Since that time, the Data Vault has become part of daily work and success in the industry.

My personal wish is that this book becomes part of your success, too.

The file name of the source code file is provided in the companion site, please refer the site for more details: *http://booksite.elsevier.com/9780128025109*

Michael Olschimke
Hannover, Germany

Acknowledgments

DANIEL LINSTEDT

I would like to acknowledge my wife and family for granting me the support and love I needed to finish this book. I would also like to acknowledge my co-author Michael Olschimke for working extremely hard at trying to understand my writing, and spending countless hours on Skype calls with me in order to discuss my ideas. Furthermore, I would like to personally thank Scott Ambler for all his contributions over time (especially to my last book); many of these ideas have made it into the foundations of Disciplined Agile Delivery embedded in the Data Vault 2.0 methodology. I am also pleased to thank Bill Inmon (the father of the data warehouse) for not only writing the foreword but also creating the industry I earn a living in. Without the "Data Warehouse" I would not have been able to create the Data Vault 2.0 System of Business Intelligence.

In addition, I would like to thank Roelant Vos for kick-starting the Australian Data Vault market, as well as my partners: Doerffler & Partner, and Analytics8, who assist me with training in the Data Vault 2.0 space. I also would like to thank AnalytixDS, for their brilliant work on Automation of Data Vault 2.0 templates through their incredible product, Mapping Manager. Without their assistance, we could not generate much of the work that goes into Data Vault 2.0 systems worldwide.

In addition, there are some customers I would like to thank for trying out the Data Vault 2.0 ideas as I refined them over the past several years. This includes Commonwealth Bank in Australia, QSuper in Australia, Intact Financial in Canada, and Microsoft – not only for creating the wonderful technology we have applied in this book, but also for utilizing Data Vault Modeling in-house for their own solutions.

MICHAEL OLSCHIMKE

My acknowledgements go to Dörffler + Partners who have financed my contributions to this book and gave me a safe harbor to be able to focus on writing. This certainly includes the management team around Werner Dörffler, Christian Hädrich and Siegfried Heger, but also the current and former employees of the firm, especially Timo Cirkel, Dominik Kroner, and Jens Lehmann. I would also like to thank our customers, especially the team of Gabriela Goldner at SwissLife and the team of Marcus Jacob at DEVK for giving me some valuable opportunities and feedback.

Furthermore, I'd like to thank all those who have helped me become what I am today. This includes my parents Barbara and Paul Olschimke, for obvious reasons; Udo Bornschier who encouraged me to take an academic career; Prof. Cornelius Wille (Bingen) who promoted my scientific interest and encouraged me to continue my academic career; Dr. Betty Robbins (OU) who taught me how to write, with the help of large amounts of red ink, which I deserved; Dr. Albert Schwarzkopf (OU) who helped me to discover my interest for data warehousing; Udo Apel who supervised my bachelor's thesis at Borland and gave me some valuable advice when I started my graduate studies at Santa Clara University; Prof. Manoochehr Ghiassi (SCU) who taught me how to organize a research team, among other valuable things (such as data mining and the value of taking notes); Oliver Cramer who discovered the Data Vault for me; and Daniel Linstedt for explaining it to me. The faculty at Santa Clara University deserves credit for helping me to understand the value of the Data Vault and see the glory in the service to others.

But the most life-changing person, and the one who enabled me to make my contribution to this book, is Christina Woitzik, my partner for the last ten years. We strayed through darkness and went all the way through hell. But in the early light of dawn, our love is still there.

By the time this book is published, she should be my lovely wife.

INTRODUCTION TO DATA WAREHOUSING

Information has become a major asset to any organization. Corporate users from all levels, including operational management, middle management and senior management, are requesting information to be able to make rational decisions and add value to the business [1, p334f]. Each level has different requirements for the requested information, but common dimensions include that the information be accurate, complete and consistent, to name only a few [2, p133]. A rational manager will use available and trusted information as a basis for informed decisions that might potentially affect the bottom line of the business.

When we use the terms *data* or *information*, we often use them interchangeably. However, both terms and the terms *knowledge* and *wisdom* have significant and discrete meanings. But they are also interrelated in the information hierarchy (Figure 1.1).

Data, at the bottom of the hierarchy, are specific, objective facts or observations. Examples could be expressed as statements such as "Flight DL404 arrives at 08:30 a.m." or "LAX is in California, USA." Such facts have no intrinsic meaning if standing alone but can be easily captured, transmitted, and stored electronically [4, p12].

Information is a condensed form of the underlying data. Business people turn data into information by organizing it into units of analysis (e.g., customers, products, dates) and endow it with relevance and purpose [5, p45-53]. It is important for this relevance and purpose that the information is considered within the context it is received and used. Managers from one functional department have different information needs than managers from other departments and view the information from their own perspective. In the same way, these information needs vary across the organizational hierarchy. As a rule of thumb, the higher an information user sits in the organizational hierarchy, the more summarized (or condensed) information is required [4, p12f].

Knowledge, towards the top of the information hierarchy, is information that has been synthesized and contextualized to provide value. Managers use information and add their own experience, judgment and wisdom to create knowledge, which is richer and deeper than information and therefore more valuable. It is a mix of the underlying information with values, rules, and additional information from other contexts.

The highest level of the pyramid is represented by wisdom, which places knowledge from the underlying layer into a framework that allows it to be applied to unknown and not necessarily intuitive situations [6]. Because knowledge and wisdom are hard to structure and often tacit, it is difficult to capture them on machines and hard to transfer [4, p13]. For that reason, it is not the goal of data warehousing to create knowledge or wisdom. Instead, data warehousing (or business intelligence) focuses on the aggregation, consolidation and summarization of data into information by transferring the data into the right context.

Due to the value that information provides to users within the organization, the information assets must be readily available when the user requests them and have the expected quality. In the past, this

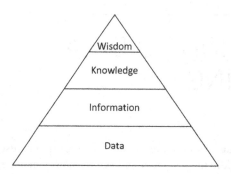

FIGURE 1.1

The information hierarchy [3, p3-9].

analysis has been conducted directly on operational systems, such as an e-commerce store or a customer relationship management (CRM) system. However, because of the massive volumes of data in today's organizations, the extraction of useful and important information from such raw data becomes a problem for the analytical business user [7, p1]. Another problem is that there are often isolated databases, called "data islands," in a typical organization. The only connections between these data islands and other data sources are business keys, which are used to identify business objects in both systems. Therefore, the integration of the disparate data sources has to be done on these business keys at some point but often exceeds the capabilities of the ordinary business analyst.

Users in operations often query or update data of a specific business object in their daily work. These operations are performed using transactional queries. Examples include the issue of a support ticket, the booking of an airplane ticket or the transmission of an email. In these cases, the operational user works on business objects that are part of their business processes. Users within the middle or senior management often have other tasks to complete. They want to get information from the business or business unit that they are responsible for. They use this information to make their managerial decisions. For that purpose, they often issue analytical queries against the database to summarize data over time. By doing so, they transform the raw data, for example sales transactions, to more useful information, e. g., a sales report by month and customer. Such analytical queries are different from transactional queries because the first often aggregate or summarize a lot of raw data. If a business user issues an analytical query against an operational database, the relational database management system (RDBMS) has to retrieve all underlying records from disk storage in order to execute the aggregation.

1.1 HISTORY OF DATA WAREHOUSING

Before the emergence of data warehousing, users had to query required information directly from raw data stored in operational systems, as described in the introduction of this chapter. Such raw data is often stored in relational databases serving the user's application. While querying an operational database has the advantage that business users are able to receive real-time information from these systems, using analytical queries to transform the raw data to useful information slows down the operational database. This is due to the aggregation that requires the reading of a large number of records on the fly to provide a summary of transactions (e.g., sales per month, earnings per year, etc.). Having both operational and analytical users on the same database often overloads the database and impacts the usability of the data for both parties [7, p1].

1.1.1 DECISION SUPPORT SYSTEMS

In order to allow quick access to the information required by decision-making processes, enterprise organizations introduced decision support systems (DSS). Such systems combine various expandable and interactive IT techniques and tools to support managers in decision-making by processing and analyzing data.

To achieve its goals, a DSS is comprised of an analytical models database that is fed with selected data extracted from source systems. Source systems are the operational systems that are available within an organization, but can include any other source of enterprise data. Examples might include exchange rates, weather information or any other information that is required by managers to make informed decisions. The raw data is aggregated within the analytical models database or on the way into the system [1, p57]. ETL (extract, transform, load) tools that have been developed to extract, transform, and load data from data sources to targets do the loading:

The analytical models database in Figure 1.2 is loaded by an ETL process with data from five data sources. The data is then aggregated either by the ETL process (in the data preparation process) or when the business user queries the data. Business users can query the analytical models database with ad-hoc queries and other complex analysis against the database. In many cases, the data has been prepared for their purpose and contains only relevant information. Because the decision support system is separated from the source systems, interactions with the DSS will not slow down operational systems [7, p1].

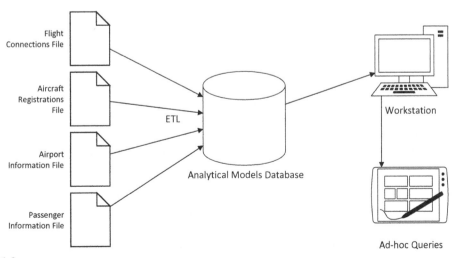

FIGURE 1.2

Decision support system.

The next section discusses data warehouse systems that are covered in this book. These systems were introduced in the 1990s and have provided the data backend of decision support systems since then [7, p3].

1.1.2 DATA WAREHOUSE SYSTEMS

A data warehouse system (DWH) is a data-driven decision support system that supports the decision-making process in a strategic sense and, in addition, operational decision-making, for example real-time analytics to detect credit card fraud or on-the-fly recommendations of products and services [8]. The data warehouse provides nonvolatile, subject-oriented data that is integrated and consistent to business users on all targeted levels. Subject orientation differs from the functional orientation of an ERP or operational system by the focus on a subject area for analysis. Examples for subject areas of an insurance company might be customer, policy, premium and claim. The subject areas product, order, vendor, bill of material and raw materials, on the other hand, are examples for a manufacturing company [9, p29]. This view of an organization allows the integrated analysis of all data related to the same real-world event or object.

Before business users can use the information provided by a data warehouse, the data is loaded from source systems into the data warehouse. As described in the introduction of this chapter, the integration of the various data sources within or external to the organization is performed on the business keys in many cases. This becomes a problem if a business object, such as a customer, has different business keys in each system. This might be the case if a customer number in an organization is alphanumeric but one of the operational systems only allows numeric numbers for business keys. Other problems occur when the database of an operational system includes dirty data, which is often the case when invalid or outdated, or when no business rules are in place. Examples for dirty data include typos, transmission errors, or unreadable text that has been processed by OCR. Before such dirty data can be presented to a business user in traditional data warehousing, the data must be cleansed, which is part of the loading process of a data mart. Other issues include different data types or character encodings of the data across source systems [9, p30f]. However, there are exceptions to this data cleansing: for example, if data quality should be reported to the business user.

Another task that is often performed when loading the data into the data warehouse is some aggregation of raw data to fit the required granularity. The granularity of data is the unit of data that the data warehouse supports. An example of different granularity of data is the difference between a salesman and a sales region. In some cases, business users only want to analyze the sales within a region and are not interested in the sales of a given salesman. Another reason for this might be legal issues, for example an agreement or legal binding with a labor union. In other cases, business analysts actually want to analyze the sales of a salesman, for example when calculating the sales commission. In most cases, data warehouse engineers follow the goal to load at the finest granularity possible, to allow multiple levels for analysis. In some cases, however, the operational systems only provide raw data at a coarse granularity.

An important characteristic of many data warehouses is that historic data is kept. All data that has been loaded into the data warehouse is stored and made available for time-variant analysis. This allows the analysis of changes to the data over time and is a frequent requirement by business users, e.g., to analyze the development of sales in a given region over the last quarters. Because the data in a data warehouse is historic and, in most cases, is not available anymore in the source system, the data is nonvolatile [9, p29]. This is also an important requirement for the auditability of an information system [10, p131].

The next section introduces enterprise data warehouses, which are a further development of data warehouses, and provides a centralized view of the entire organization.

1.2 THE ENTERPRISE DATA WAREHOUSE ENVIRONMENT

Enterprise data warehouses (EDW) have emerged from ordinary data warehouses, which have been described in the last section. Instead of focusing on a single subject area for analysis, an enterprise data warehouse tries to represent all of an organization's business data and its business rules. The data in the warehouse is then presented in a way that all required subject areas are available to business users [11].

The next sections present common business requirements for enterprise data warehouses.

1.2.1 ACCESS

Access to the EDW requires that the end-users be able to connect to the data warehouse with the proposed client workstations. The connection must be immediate, on demand and with high performance [12, pxxiii]. However, access means much more for the users than the availability, especially the business users: it should be easy to understand the meaning of the information presented by the system. That includes the correct labelling of the data warehouse contents. It also includes the availability of appropriate applications to analyze, present and use the information provided by the data warehouse [12, p3].

1.2.2 MULTIPLE SUBJECT AREAS

Because every function or department of an enterprise has different requirements for the data to be analyzed, the enterprise data warehouse must provide multiple subject areas to meet the needs of its individual users. Each subject area contains the data that is relevant to the user. The data is requested and the data warehouse provides the expected version of the truth, which means that it follows the required definition of the information [11].

In order to achieve this goal, all raw data that is required for the subject areas is integrated, cleansed, and loaded into the enterprise data warehouse. It is then used to build data marts that have been developed for a specific subject area. Such data marts are also called dependent data marts because they depend on the data warehouse as the source of data. In contrast, independent data marts source the data directly from the operational systems. Because this approach requires the same cleansing and integration efforts as building the data warehouse, it is often simpler to load the data from a central data warehouse [13].

1.2.3 SINGLE VERSION OF TRUTH

The integration of all business data available in an organization serves the goal of having a single version of truth of its data [11]. There are many operational systems, or even ordinary data warehouses, available in a typical organization. While some of these systems are integrated, there is often a disparity of the data stored within the operational databases. This might be due to synchronization delays or errors, manual inputs or different raw data sources for the operational data. The effect is that there are different versions of the truth within the organization, for example about the shipment address of a customer. It is up to the business to decide how to cleanse the data when loading it into the enterprise data warehouse and this often requires the selection of leading systems or data source priorities. In some cases, an automatic selection and validation based on business rules is sufficient; in other cases, a manual selection is required to achieve a validated, single version of truth.

The consistent, single version of truth of an enterprise data warehouse is an important goal for the consumers of data warehouses [12, pxxiv; 14, p23]. However, different departments often require a unique version of the truth because of a different definition of "what is the truth" [15]. That is why an enterprise data warehouse provides multiple subject areas, as covered in the previous section. Each subject area provides the required information for its individual users in the required context.

1.2.4 SINGLE VERSION OF FACTS

While the goal of the "single version of truth" is to provide an integrated, cleansed version of the organizational *information*, that is, the aggregated and condensed data in a given context, "the single version of facts" goal is to provide all the data, all the time. In such case, the EDW should store and potentially provide all raw data that is critical for the mission of the organization (see next section). The lead author of this book was one of the first people in the data warehousing industry to promote this idea, especially due to compliance issues. Eventually, it led to the invention of Data Vault and is a key principle in Data Vault 2.0 modeling and is implemented in the Raw Data Vault.

The single version of facts is also important under auditing and compliance requirements, which is covered in section 1.2.10. We will learn later in this book that Data Vault based EDWs provide both versions: the single version of truth and the single version of facts.

1.2.5 MISSION CRITICALITY

Due to the importance of the data warehouse as the basis for strategic business decisions, the central data warehouse has become a mission-critical corporate asset. Furthermore, data warehouses not only provide aggregated data for business decisions; they also feed enriched information back to operational systems to support the processing of transactions, to create personalized offers and to present upsell promotions [16, p9].

Mission criticality also requires a specific level of quality of the data warehouse data [12, pxxv]. If source systems don't provide the raw data in the required quality, it is the job of the data warehouse to fix any data quality issues and improve the data quality by means of data cleansing, data integration or any other useful methods.

1.2.6 SCALABILITY

Scalability is the ability of the data warehouse architecture to adapt to higher data volumes and an increasing number of users' requests that have to be met [17, p7]. The architecture should be built in a way that supports adding more data, not only more data volume, but also more complex data. If the data volume grows over the capabilities of the hardware, it should be possible to distribute the data warehouse across multiple machines and fully use the capabilities of the added hardware. This concept is called massively parallel processing (MPP). If the architecture is not scalable, adding more hardware has no or only minimal effect when reaching a certain level of build-out.

Another problem in data warehousing is that changing the data warehouse is often complex because of existing dependencies. While building the first version of the data warehouse was easily done, the second version takes more time. This is because the architecture of the data warehouse was not built with those changes in mind.

Section 1.4 discusses several data warehouse architectures. We will propose an alternate architecture in Chapter 2, Scalable Data Warehousing Architecture. The advantage of this architecture lies in its scalability regarding the absorption of changes to the data model, among other advantages.

1.2.7 BIG DATA

Big data is not only "a lot of data" or "more data that I can handle." We define big data as data having three characteristics: volume, velocity and variety.

The first characteristic is volume. What someone calls "big data" often means that the data is much more than this person is used to handling. However, this statement is highly subjective. Big data for one person or one company might be one gigabyte of raw data but this is rather small data for a person who loads terabytes or even petabytes of data. Loading data in real-time has different requirements and therefore a different definition of big data than loading data in nightly batches or near real-time (near real-time means that the data from operational systems is available in the data mart within a time frame of typically 15 minutes). The definition of big data also depends on the hardware available to the data warehouse.

The second characteristic of big data is velocity. It is not only that there is a lot of static data available in the source systems. Loading this data can become a complex task. However, data stored in an operational system is changing frequently. The more data that is available in a source system, the more changes are applied to it. Therefore, the typical big data project has to deal with lots of updates, data changes or new data that is added to the source system.

The third characteristic is variety. Big data often doesn't have the same structure. Instead, the data structures of big data might change over time or, such as in "unstructured" datasets (e.g., texts, multimedia), has no ordinary structure at all: instead of using columns and rows as relational tables, unstructured datasets use other types of structures, such as linguistic structures. From a computing standpoint, these structures are considered unstructured because the structure is not as obvious as in relational tables. In other cases, there are data from so many different small data sources that the sum of this data is "big data" with high variety in data structures.

Because there is more and more data available nowadays, a data warehouse structure must not only be able to scale (which refers to the volume), it should also be able to deal with velocity and variety of the incoming data. In other cases, data is always in motion: by that we mean that it is currently processed or transferred in packets that are smaller than the actual data asset. Consider for example the transfer of data over a TCP/IP network: the data which needs to be transmitted is usually divided in smaller chunks and stored in IP packets, which are then transmitted over the network. This adds other problems to big data because data is flowing into and out of the network device. In order to analyze the data, it has to be collected, combined, and aggregated – in some cases at real-time. This raises the bar on what and how big data is architected and planned for and leads us to performance issues, which are covered in the next section.

1.2.8 PERFORMANCE ISSUES

Another issue in data warehousing is the performance of the system. Performance is important when loading a new batch of source data into the data warehouse because the load process includes cleaning and integrating the data into existing data within the timeframe available. Often, this timeframe is limited to the time when no users are working with the system, usually during the night. Another reason for performance is the usability of the data warehouse, which depends on the response time of the system to analytical user queries.

The performance of data warehouse systems is influenced by the way a database system stores its data on disk: data is stored in pages with a fixed data size. For example, a Microsoft SQL Server allocates 8 KB disk space for each page [18]. Each page holds some records of a particular table. The wider a table is and the more columns a table has, the fewer rows fit into one page. In order to access the contents of a given column for a given row, the whole page where this piece of data exists must be read. Because analytical queries, which are often used in data warehousing, typically aggregate information, many pages must be read for accessing the contents of only one row. A typical example of an aggregation is to sum up the sales of a given region; this could be the sum of an **invoice_total** column. If there are many columns in the table, a lot of data must be read that is not required to perform the aggregation. Therefore, a goal in data warehousing is to reduce the width of columns in order to improve performance. Similar concepts apply to the loading of new data into the data warehouse.

Other ways to improve the performance of data warehouse systems include (1) the parallelization of loading patterns and (2) the distribution of data over multiple nodes in MPP settings like in the NoSQL databases. Instead of loading one table after the other, the goal of the first option is to load multiple tables at once. The second option increases performance by the distribution of data to multiple nodes. Both ways are critical to the success of Data Vault 2.0 in such environments and have influenced the changes in Data Vault modeling compared to the initial release (Data Vault 1.0).

1.2.9 COMPLEXITY

Data warehouse systems often have complexity issues due to many business requirements. Technical complexity issues arise from three areas: sourcing issues, transformation issues, and target issues.

Sourcing issues are problems that arise from the system from which the data is extracted. The following are typical examples of problems [19, p16f]:

- Limited availability of the source systems.
- Cross-system joins, filters or aggregates.
- Indexing issues in the source data.
- Missing source keys or even missing whole source data sets.
- Bad or out-of-range source data.
- Complexities of the source system's data structures.
- CPU, RAM, and disk load of the source system.
- Transactional record locks.

Transformation issues arise during the transformation of the data to meet the expectations of the target. Often, the following operations are performed directly within the transformation:

- Cleansing.
- Data quality management and data alignment.
- Joins, consolidation, aggregation, and filtering.
- Sequence assignments that often lead to lack of parallelism.
- Data type corrections and error handling.
- Sorting issues, including the need for large caches, frequent disk overflows, and huge keys.
- Application of business rules directly within the transformation of the source data.

- Multiple targets or sources within one data flow.
- Single transformation bottlenecks.

The last area of issues is located at the target. These issues arise when loading the data into the target and include:

- Lack of database tuning.
- Index updates which lead to deadlocks.
- Mixing insert, update, and delete statements in one data flow. This forces the execution of these statements in specific orders, which hinders parallelization.
- Loading multiple targets at once.
- Wide targets, as discussed in section 1.2.8.
- Lack of control over target partitioning.

A common reason for these issues is that many data warehouse systems are trying to achieve too much in one loading cycle instead of splitting up the work. The result is that many loading processes become too complicated, which reduces overall performance and increases maintenance costs. In the end, it also affects the agility and performance of the whole team because they have to fix these issues instead of implementing new features.

1.2.10 AUDITING AND COMPLIANCE

A typical requirement for a data warehouse is the ability to provide information about the source and extraction time of the data stored within the system. There are various reasons for this requirement:

- Data warehouse developers are trying to trace down potential errors and try to understand the flow of the data into the system.
- The value of data depends on the source or age of data. This information might be used in business rules.
- Compliance requires the traceability of data flows and processes for information that is used as the basis of business decisions. It must be clear where the data comes from and when it has been loaded into the data warehouse [20, p4f].

Inmon, however, presents reasons for not adding auditability in the data warehouse [9, p61]:

- Auditing requires data to be loaded into the data warehouse that would not be loaded without such requirement.
- It might change the timing of data to be loaded into the data warehouse. For example, if the data warehouse would be the only place that provides auditing, it could require loading all changes to the operational data instead of the daily batch loads typical in many data warehousing projects.
- Backup and restore requirements change drastically when auditing capabilities are required.
- Auditing the source of data forces the data warehouse to load source data with the very lowest granularity.

It is our opinion that auditability should be limited to answering questions such as:

- From where is this particular data asset extracted?
- When has the data been extracted?

- What was the process that extracted the data?
- Where was this data used?

The data warehouse should not answer the question of how the data was acquired by the operational system. This answer can often only be provided by the source system itself. Only in some cases, the data warehouse will receive information about the user and time when the record was created or modified. If this data is available to the data warehouse, we tend to store this information for informational purposes only.

To support the auditability of the data warehouse, we add meta-information to the data to track the data source and load date and time. However, it is more complicated to answer the question of where the data was used because data marts often aggregate data to create information to be used by the business users. In order to enable data warehouse maintainers to answer such questions, the data warehouse processes should be simple and easy to understand.

1.2.11 COSTS

Another challenge in data warehousing is to keep the costs as low as possible because IT in general is considered as a cost factor by management. The cost of a data warehouse is influenced by many factors, starting from cost of storage to cost of low quality and bad planning. Another cost factor is that business requirements change over time, requiring the data warehouse to adapt to these changed requirements.

The cost of storage is an often unaccounted for cost factor in data warehousing. At the beginning of a data warehouse project, the costs are typically low. If the data warehouse started as a *shadow IT* project, i.e., projects driven by the business, implemented by external IT consultants and bypassing internal IT, the costs might have even been hidden in the budget of another project or activity. However, when some time has passed and the amount of data that is processed by the data warehouse has increased, the storage cost increases as well. In some cases, this happens exponentially and does not only include the costs for adding new disks. If more data is added to the data warehouse, faster network access is required to access the data; more computing power is required to process the data; and better (and more expensive) hard disk controllers are required to access the disks [9, p335ff].

However, ever-increasing storage costs are not the big cost factor in data warehousing. Cost factors include:

- Cost of storage [21, p47]
- Cost of low quality
- Cost of bad planning
- Cost of changing business requirements (see next section as well)

The cost of low quality and bad planning is an even bigger factor: even if the project team has carefully planned the data warehouse and ensured the quality, there is nothing it can do against changing business requirements, except anticipatory planning [21, p335].

This is particularly evident when the business requirements are located upstream of the data warehouse. As introduced earlier, this not only negatively affects performance, but it also drives up the cost of maintenance. Business requirements should not be embedded in the data warehouse loading cycle but rather should be moved downstream to the data mart loading – closer to the business users. This allows the team to be agile and control maintenance and development costs (through auto-generation) and provides better, more rapid response to changing business requirements. In other words, it controls costs of data mart production as well.

The agility of the team is directly proportional to the amount of complexity built into the data handling processes. By separating the complex business requirements into respective components, multiple loading sections of the architecture become streamlined; to a point where a majority of the implementation can actually be generated. The mechanics of this separation provide for extreme agility when responding to business requirement changes.

1.2.12 OTHER BUSINESS REQUIREMENTS

Today's business environment is characterized by rapidly changing conditions and uncertainty. Therefore, it is common that business requirements change quite frequently. Data warehouse developers try to prevent changes to the data warehouse by careful planning and anticipatory design. This approach often follows traditional waterfall software development methods. In such approaches, there are often four phases [22, p162f]:

1. Setting up the requirements for the data warehouse.
2. Architectural planning and design of the data warehouse.
3. Development of the data warehouse.
4. Testing of the data warehouse.

In contrast, agile software development methods have been designed to improve software by using customer feedback to converge on solutions [23]. To support this requirement, the data warehouse must be adaptive and resilient to change [12, p3]. A change to the existing data warehouse structures should not invalidate existing data or applications. One of the major advantages of agile methods is the ability to quickly react on business changes, as we will learn in Chapter 3, Data Vault 2.0 Methodology.

To support both the data warehouse engineers as well as the data warehouse business users, a set of tools to query, analyze and present information is required [12, pxxiv]. Examples include reporting tools, query analyzers, OLAP (on-line analytical processing) browsers, data mining tools, etc. Microsoft SQL Server 2014 includes these tools out-of-the-box.

Another business requirement is the ability of the project team to cope with the natural fluctuation of team members. An important success factor in data warehousing is to keep the knowledge and skills of the data warehouse members within the team, regardless of the retirement or withdrawal of key members. Solutions for this include a well-documented data warehouse system and an easily understandable design. Another solution is to use business intelligence (BI) solutions from a major vendor, such as Microsoft, that is well known in the industry and supported by other vendors and consultancy firms [20, p9].

These are major components of Data Vault 2.0, and the innovation contained within. DV2.0 addresses Big Data, NoSQL, performance, team agility, complexity, and a host of other issues by defining standards and best practices around modeling, implementation, methodology, and architecture.

1.3 INTRODUCTION TO DATA VAULT 2.0

Data Vault really represents a *system of business intelligence*. The true name of the **Data Vault System** is: Common Foundational Warehouse Architecture. The system includes a number of aspects that relate to the business of designing, implementing, and managing a data warehouse. A bit of historical research into Data Vault 1.0 shows that Data Vault 1.0 is highly focused on Data Vault Modeling, that is to say, a dedication to the physical and logical data models that construct the raw enterprise data warehouse. Data Vault 2.0, on the other hand, has expanded, and includes many of the necessary components for success in the endeavor of data warehousing and business intelligence. These components are:

- Data Vault 2.0 Modeling – Changes to the model for performance and scalability
- Data Vault 2.0 Methodology – Following Scrum and Agile best practices
- Data Vault 2.0 Architecture – Including NoSQL systems and big-data systems
- Data Vault 2.0 Implementation – Pattern based, automation, generation CMMI level 5

Each of these components plays a key role in the overall success of an enterprise data warehousing project. These components are combined with industry-known and time-tested best practices ranging from CMMI (Capability Maturity Model Integration), to Six Sigma, TQM (total quality management) and PMP (Project Management Professional). Data Vault 2.0 modeling now includes changes that allow the models to interact seamlessly with (or live on) NoSQL and Big Data systems. Data Vault 2.0 Methodology focuses on 2 to 3 week sprint cycles with adaptations and optimizations for repeatable data warehousing tasks. Data Vault 2.0 Architecture includes NoSQL, real-time feeds, and big data systems for unstructured data handling and big data integration. Data Vault 2.0 Implementation focuses on automation and generation patterns for time savings, error reduction, and rapid productivity of the data warehousing team.

1.4 DATA WAREHOUSE ARCHITECTURE

To meet technical expectations, data warehouse engineers can use various architectures to build data warehouses. Common data warehouse architectures are based on layered approaches, which is often the case in information systems. Two of these typical architectures are described in the next sections.

1.4.1 TYPICAL TWO-LAYER ARCHITECTURE

Kimball has introduced an often-used, two-layer architecture [24, p114]. In this architecture, which is presented in Figure 1.3, there are only two layers that are part of the data warehouse system itself.

The raw data from the source systems is loaded into the stage area. The goal is to have an exact copy of all data that should be loaded into the data warehouse. The main purpose of the stage area is to reduce the number of operations on the source system and the time to extract the data from it. The tables in the stage area are modeled after the tables in the source system. A stage area is required when the transformations are complex and cannot be performed on-the-fly or when data arrives from multiple source systems at different times [17, p33].

Once the data has been loaded to the stage area, Kimball suggests loading the data into the data warehouse. This data warehouse has been modeled after the dimensional model and is made up of data marts (representing the business processes), "bound together with [...] conformed dimensions" [25]. It was first proposed by Kimball in 1996. The dimensional model is a de-facto standard that is easy to query by business users and analytical tools, such as OLAP front-ends or engines. Because it is a logical association of conformed data marts, business rules have to be implemented before the data warehouse layer in order to conform and align the datasets. We will discuss dimensional modeling in Chapter 7, Dimensional Modeling. Data access applications use the dimensional model to present the information to the user and allow ad-hoc analysis.

The advantage of a two-layered architecture is that it is easy to build a dimensional store from the source data as compared to other architectures. However, the disadvantage is that it is more complex to

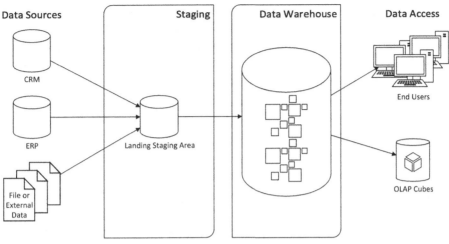

FIGURE 1.3

The Kimball Data Lifecycle [25].

Figure adapted by author from [25]. Copyright by IAS Inc. Reprinted with permission.

build a second dimensional model from the same source data because the data needs to be loaded again from the staging. It is not possible to reuse existing ETL packages [17, p34f].

1.4.2 TYPICAL THREE-LAYER ARCHITECTURE

To overcome the limitations of a two-layer architecture, another commonly found architecture is based on three layers (Figure 1.4).

This architecture has been introduced by Inmon and introduces an atomic data warehouse, often a normalized operational data store (ODS) between the staging area and the dimensional model. The stage area in this architecture follows that of the two-layer architecture. The data warehouse, however, holds raw data modeled in a third-normal form. It integrates all data of the enterprise, but is still based on physical tables from the source systems. By doing so, it acts similarly to a large operational database.

On top of the normalized view of the business data, there is a dimensional model. Business users can access and analyze the data using subject-oriented data marts, similar to the two-layer architecture. However, it is much easier to create new data marts from the data available in the operational data store because the data is already cleaned and integrated. Therefore, it is not required to perform data cleaning and integration for building new data marts [17, p38]. In practice, two-layer data warehouses often have multiple data marts, serving the requirements by heterogeneous user groups, by providing different subject areas to its users.

However, it is more complex and requires more data processing to build the entire data warehouse, including the operational data store and the dependent data marts. Another problem is that changes to the data model can become a burden if many data marts depend on the operational data store. We will discuss an alternate, three-layer architecture to enable faster changes to the data warehouse in the next chapter.

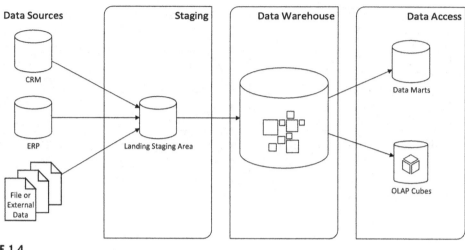

FIGURE 1.4

The Inmon Data Warehouse [25].

Figure adapted by author from [25]. Copyright by IAS Inc. Reprinted with permission.

REFERENCES

[1] Laudon KC, Laudon JP. Essentials of Management Information Systems. 11th ed. Prentice Hall; 2014.

[2] Loshin D. The Practitioner's Guide to Data Quality Improvement. Morgan Kaufmann; 2010.

[3] Ackoff, Russell. From data to wisdom. Journal of Applied Systems Analysis 1989;16:3–9.

[4] Pearlson KE, Saunders CS. Managing and Using Information Systems. 5th ed. Wiley; 2012.

[5] P. F. Drucker, The Coming of the New Organization, *Harvard Business Review* (January-February 1988).

[6] Jennex Murray E. Re-Visiting the Knowledge Pyramid. In: Proceedings of the 42nd Hawaii International Conference on System Sciences – 2009; January 5-8, 2009Waikoloa, Hawaii.

[7] Golfarelli M, Rizzi S. Data Warehouse Design: Modern principles and methodologies. McGraw-Hill Education; 2009.

[8] D. Power, Data-Drive DSS Resources, website, available from http://dssresources.com/dsstypes/ddss.html.

[9] Inmon. Building the Data Warehouse. 5th ed. John Wiley and Sons; 2005.

[10] Rick Sherman: Business Intelligence Guidebook: From Data Integration to Analytics, p131.

[11] What Is Enterprise Data Warehouse, GeekInterview website, 2007, available from http://www.learn.geekinterview.com/data-warehouse/data-types/what-is-enterprise-data-warehouse.html.

[12] Kimball R, Ross M. The Data Warehouse Toolkit. 2nd ed. John Wiley & Sons; 2002.

[13] Oracle, Data Mart Concepts, 2007, website available from http://docs.oracle.com/html/E10312_01/dm_concepts.htm.

[14] Imhof C, Galemmo N, Geiger JG. Mastering Data Warehouse Design. John Wiley & Sons; 2003.

[15] J King, Business intelligence: One version of the truth, Computerworld, Dec 22, 2003, available from http://www.computerworld.com/s/article/88349/Business_Intelligence_One_Version_of_the_Truth.

[16] N Goyal: Real-Time Data Warehousing, PowerPoint presentation available online from http://www.scribd.com/doc/269892533/Real-Time-Data-Warehousing#scribd.

[17] V Rainardi: Building a Data Warehouse. Apress; 2007.

[18] Microsoft, SQL Server, Understanding pages and extents, 2015, available online from http://technet. microsoft.com/en-us/library/ms190969%28v=sql.105%29.aspx.

[19] Linstedt D, Graziano K. Super Charge your Data Warehouse. Createspace Independent Pub; 2011.

[20] Kimball R, Caserta J. The Data Warehouse ETL Toolkit. Wiley Publishing, Inc., Indianapolis; 2004.

[21] Inmon W, Strauss D, Neushloss G. DW 2. 0: The Architecture for the Next Generation of Data Warehousing. Morgan Kaufmann; 2008.

[22] Yu Beng Leau, Wooi Khong Loo, Wai Yip Tham, Soo Fun Tan, Software Development Life Cycle AGILE vs Traditional Approaches, 2012 International Conference on Information and Network Technology, Singapore, p. 162f, available from http://www.ipcsit.com/vol37/030-ICINT2012-I2069.pdf.

[23] Szalvay, Victor. An Introduction to Agile Software Development. Danube Technologies Inc; 2004.

[24] Kimball R, Ross M. The Data Warehouse Lifecycle Toolkit. 3rd ed John Wiley & Sons, Indianapolis; 2013.

[25] Abramson, I. Data Warehouse: The Choice of Inmon vs. Kimball. IAS Inc. (PowerPoint slides). Available from http://www.scribd.com/doc/253618546/080827Abramson-Inmon-vs-Kimball#scribd.

SCALABLE DATA WAREHOUSE ARCHITECTURE

2

Today's data warehouse systems make it easy for analysts to access integrated data. In order to achieve this, the data warehouse development team had to process and model the data based on the requirements from the user. The best approach for developing a data warehouse is an iterative development process [1]. That means that the functionality of the data warehouse, as requested by the business users, is designed, developed, implemented and deployed in iterations (sometimes called a sprint or a cycle). In each iteration, more functionality is added to the data warehouse. This is opposite to a "big-bang" approach where all functionality is developed in one large process and finally deployed as a whole.

However, when executing the project, even when using an iterative approach, the effort (and the costs tied to it) to add another functionality usually increases because of existing dependencies that have to be taken care of.

Figure 2.1 shows that the effort to implement the first information mart is relatively low. But when implementing the second information mart, the development team has to maintain the existing solution and take care of existing dependencies, for example to data sources integrated for the first information mart or operational systems consuming information from existing tables. In order to make sure that this previously built functionality doesn't break when deploying the new functionality for the second information mart, the old functionality has to be retested. In many cases, the existing solution needs to be refactored to maintain the functionality of the individual information marts when new sources are added to the overall solution. All these activities increase the effort for creating the second information mart and, equally, any subsequent information mart or other new functionality. This additional effort is depicted as the rise of the graph in Figure 2.1: once the first information mart is produced, the solution falls into a maintenance mode for all existing functionality. The next project implements another information mart. To implement the second information mart, the effort includes adding the new functionality and maintaining the existing functionality. Because of the dependencies, the existing functionality needs to be refactored and retested regularly.

In other words, the extensibility of many data warehouse architectures, including those presented in Chapter 1, Introduction to Data Warehousing, is not optimal. Furthermore, typical data warehouse architectures often lack dimensions of scalability other than the described dimension of extensibility. We discuss these dimensions in the next section.

2.1 DIMENSIONS OF SCALABLE DATA WAREHOUSE ARCHITECTURES

Business users of data warehouse systems expect to load and prepare more and more data, in terms of variety, volume, and velocity [3]. Also, the workload that is put on typical data warehouse environments is increasing more and more, especially if the initial version of the warehouse has become a success with its first users. Therefore, scalability has multiple dimensions.

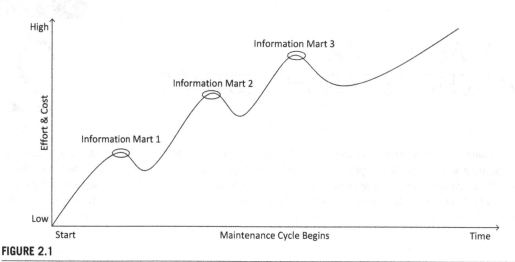

FIGURE 2.1

The maintenance nightmare [2].

2.1.1 WORKLOAD

The enterprise data warehouse (EDW) is "by far the largest and most computationally intense business application" in a typical enterprise. EDW systems consist of huge databases, containing historical data on volumes from multiple gigabytes to terabytes of storage [4]. Successful EDW systems face two issues regarding the workload of the system: first, they experience rapidly increasing data volumes and application workloads and, second, an increasing number of concurrent users [5]. In order to meet the performance requirements, EDW systems are implemented on large-scale parallel computers, such as massively parallel processing (MPP) or symmetric multiprocessor (SMP) system environments and clusters and parallel database software. In fact, most medium- to large-size data warehouses could not be implementable without larger-scale parallel hardware and parallel database software to support them [4].

In order to handle the requested workload, there is more required than parallel hardware or parallel database software. The logical and physical design of the databases has to be optimized for the expected data volumes [6–8].

2.1.2 DATA COMPLEXITY

Another dimension of enterprise data warehouse scalability is data complexity. The following factors contribute to the growth of data complexity [9]:

- **Variety of data:** nowadays, enterprise organizations capture more than just traditional (e.g., relational or mainframe) master or transactional data. There is an increasing amount of semi-structured data, for example emails, e-forms or HTML and XML files and unstructured data, such as document collections, social network data, images, video and sound files. Another type of data is sensor- and machine-generated data, which might require specific handling. In many cases, enterprises try to derive structured information from unstructured or semi-structured data to increase the business value of the data. While the files may have a structure, the content of the files doesn't have one. For example, it is not possible to find the face of a specific person in a video without fully processing all frames of the video and building metadata tags to indicate where faces appear in the content.

- **Volume of data:** the rate at which companies generate and accumulate new data is increasing. Examples include content from Web sites or social networks, document and email collections, weblog data and machine-generated data. The increased data volume leads to much larger data sets, which can run into hundreds of terabytes or even into petabytes of data or beyond.
- **Velocity of data:** not only the variety and volume of data increases, but the rate at which the data is created also increases rapidly. One example is financial data from financial markets such as the stock exchange. Such data is generated at very high rates and immediately analyzed in order to respond to changes in the market. Other examples include credit card transactions data for fraud detection and sensor data or data from closed-circuit television (CCTV), which is captured for automated video and image analysis in real-time or near-real-time.
- **Veracity (trustworthiness) of data:** in order to have confidence in data, it must have strong data governance lineage traceability and robust data integration [10].

2.1.3 ANALYTICAL COMPLEXITY

Due to the availability of large volumes of data with high velocity and variety, businesses demand different and more complex analytical tasks to produce the insight required to solve their business problems. Some of these analyses require that the data be prepared in a fashion not foreseen by the original data warehouse developers. For example, the data that should be fed into a data mining algorithm should have different characteristics regarding the variety, volume and velocity of data.

Consider the example of retail marketing: the campaign accuracy and timeliness need to be improved when moving from retail stores to online channels where more detailed customer insights are required [11]:

- In order to determine customer segmentation and purchase behavior, the business might need historical analysis and reporting of customer demographics and purchase transactions
- Cross-sell opportunities can be identified by analyzing market baskets that show products that can be sold together
- To understand the online behavior of their customers, click-stream analysis is required. This can help to present up-sell offers to the visitors of a Web site
- Given the high amount of social network data and user-generated content, businesses tap into the data by analyzing product reviews, ratings, likes and dislikes, comments, customer service interactions, and so on.

These examples should make it clear that, in order to solve such new and complex analytical tasks, data sources of varying complexity are required. Also, mixing structured and unstructured data becomes more and more common [11].

2.1.4 QUERY COMPLEXITY

When business intelligence (BI) vendors select a relational database management system (RDBMS) for the storage and management of warehouse data, it is a natural choice. Relational databases provide simple data structures and high-level, set-oriented languages that make them ideal for data warehouse applications. The SQL language processors within the database engine map SQL statements into parallel low-level operations to achieve improved query performance (speedup) and enable incremental growth for increased workloads while meeting required levels of performance (scale-up) [12]. Many RDBMSs, such as Microsoft SQL Server, are optimized for data warehouse applications, for example by applying heuristic methods to identify star schema query patterns that are used by the SQL optimizer to improve the query performance of data warehouse applications [13]. Microsoft SQL Server also uses advanced filter techniques to improve query performance by using features such as the bitmap showplan operator [14]. However, some of these features are only available when query statements follow some guidelines (such as using equi-join conditions on INNER joins only) [15].

However, in some cases, queries against the data warehouse can become complex and, given the sheer size of the data warehouse, can take a very long time to complete. Examples include time-series analysis and queries against relational OLAP cubes. For the business analyst, slow response times from the data warehouse are not acceptable because this severely limits productivity [16].

2.1.5 AVAILABILITY

The data warehouse team is responsible for the availability of the whole data warehouse, including the data marts, reports, OLAP cubes and any other front-end that is used by the business users. In most cases, both parties sign a service level agreement (SLA) that documents the requirements of the business and is the basis for any availability planning of the data warehouse team [17].

The availability of a data warehouse system might be affected by added functionality. One example is the addition of new data sources that have to be loaded and integrated into a new data mart. This, however, would extend the time needed to load all data sources and build the data marts. Parallelization of loads is one solution to the problem because adding more computing resources might ensure the availability of the system. However, the capability to "just add new computing power" must be designed into the data warehouse.

In addition, all major relational database management systems, including the Enterprise edition of Microsoft SQL Server 2014, offer many features, such as partitioning and snapshots, that can help you to meet the availability requirements of the business users. Another option is to create a fail-over cluster to provide an alternative server in the event of an emergency [18].

2.1.6 SECURITY

As data sets grow, the need to secure the data also grows – in fact, the need to secure the data grows exponentially relative to the data set size and variety of data. Security increases the complexity of the system, both in storing the data and in retrieving the data. The larger the data set, the more likely someone can breach the security unnoticed by the rest of the world. The proper and most scalable data warehouses of today and tomorrow will have the right level of security applied from the start of the project. Simply throwing NoSQL at this space doesn't solve these issues; in fact, it exacerbates them.

The Data Vault 2.0 system of business intelligence aims to assist in solving security, by providing direct integration points in the data model, through the implementation layers, all the way to the architecture and the project components.

2.2 **DATA VAULT 2.0 ARCHITECTURE**

The Data Vault 2.0 architecture addresses the extensibility and dimensions of scalability as defined in the previous section by modifying a typical three-layer data warehouse architecture, which has been introduced in the previous chapter.

As we have outlined in Chapter 1, the primary purpose of an enterprise data warehouse is to provide and present information – that is, aggregated, summarized and consolidated data put into context. To emphasize this ultimate EDW goal, we prefer the term *information mart* over data mart (which is the term typically used in the BI community).

Other modifications to the typical architecture from Chapter 1 include:

- A staging area which does not store historical information and does not apply any changes to the data, except ensuring the expected data type.
- A data warehouse layer modeled after the Data Vault modeling technique.
- One or more information mart layers that depend on the data warehouse layer.
- An optional Metrics Vault that is used to capture and record runtime information.
- An optional Business Vault that is used to store information where the business rules have been applied. In many cases, the business rules change or alter the data when transforming it into useful information. This is another type of information mart.
- An optional Operational Vault that stores data fed into the data warehouse from operational systems.
- Capabilities for managed self-service BI to allow business users to perform their own data analysis tasks without involvement of IT, including write-back of information into the enterprise data warehouse layer.

All optional Vaults – the Metrics Vault, the Business Vault and the Operational Vault – are part of the Data Vault and are integrated into the data warehouse layer. The reference architecture in the Data Vault 2.0 standard is presented in Figure 2.2.

The Data Vault 2.0 architecture is based on three layers: the staging area, which collects the raw data from the source systems; the enterprise data warehouse layer, modeled as a Data Vault 2.0 model; and the information delivery layer, with information marts as star schemas and other structures. The architecture supports both batch loading of source systems and real-time loading from the enterprise service bus (ESB) or any other service-oriented architecture (SOA). But it is also possible to integrate unstructured NoSQL database systems into this architecture. Due to the platform independence of Data Vault 2.0, NoSQL can be used for every data warehouse layer, including the stage area, the enterprise data warehouse layer, and information delivery. Therefore, the NoSQL database could be used as a staging area and load data into the relational Data Vault layer. However, it could also be integrated both ways with the Data Vault layer via a hashed business key. In this case, it would become a hybrid solution and information marts would consume data from both environments.

However, real-time and NoSQL systems are out of the scope of this book. Therefore, we will concentrate on the relational pieces of the architecture.

One of the biggest differences from typical data warehouse architectures is that most business rules are enforced when building the information marts, and by that are moved towards the end-user. In the Data Vault, there is a distinction between hard and soft business rules. This distinction is discussed in the next section.

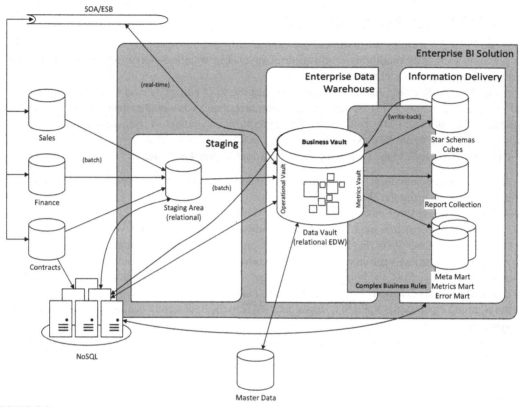

FIGURE 2.2

Data Vault Architecture [19].

2.2.1 BUSINESS RULES DEFINITION

In Data Vault 2.0 we distinguish between hard and soft business rules. Generally stated, business rules modify the incoming data to fit the requirements of the business. The distinction between hard and soft business rules is that hard business rules are the technical rules that align the data domains, so-called data type matching. For example, a typical hard business rule is the truncation of source strings that are longer than defined in the stage table. Hard business rules are enforced when the data is extracted from the source systems and loaded into the staging area. These business rules affect only the enforcement of data types (such as string length or Unicode characters) but don't convert any values to fit the analytical requirements of the business (such as converting between US units and metric units). Other examples of hard business rules include the normalization of hierarchical COBOL copybooks from mainframe systems or XML structures. Also system column computations are examples of hard business rules. As a rule of thumb, hard business rules never change the meaning of the incoming data, only the way the data is stored.

Opposite from hard business rules, soft business rules enforce the business requirements that are stated by the business user. These business rules change the data or the meaning of the data, for example by modifying the grain or interpretation. Examples include the aggregation of data, e.g. allocating the data into categories like income-band, age groups, customer segments, etc., or the consolidation of data from multiple sources. Soft business rules define how the data is aggregated or consolidated. They also define how the data is transformed to meet the requirements of the business.

2.2.2 BUSINESS RULES APPLICATION

Because we have to align the data types of the source system to those of the staging area tables, we have to enforce hard business rules when loading the staging area (Figure 2.3). This is performed at the latest when inserting the data into the staging area tables because the database management server will check the data types of the inserted data and raise an exception if it is not possible to convert the incoming data to the data type specified in the data definition of the column. This is the case if we try to insert an alphanumeric customer number into an integer-based column, for example, because we expected customer numbers of type "integer." We can support this process by adding data type conversion logic into the ETL data flow that loads the data into the staging area. By doing so, we're also implementing hard business rules.

Hard business rules pose a risk to our ETL routines because if the data violate the rule and this case has not been accounted for, the ETL routine will stop and break the loading process. This is different from soft business rules, which only change the data or the data meaning. Therefore, we need to treat hard business rules differently from soft business rules. We achieve this by separating both rule types from each other.

In typical data warehouse systems, for example the two- and three-layer architectures described in the previous chapter, soft rules are also applied early in the loading process of the data warehouse. This

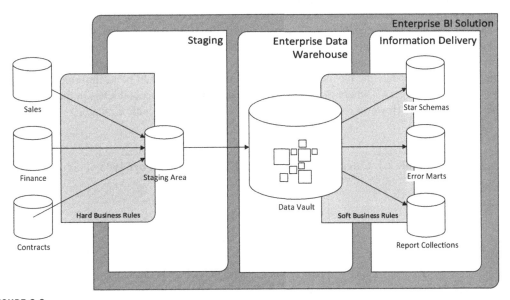

FIGURE 2.3

Application of hard and soft business rules in a Data Vault enterprise data warehouse.

is due to the fact that the data warehouse layer is either a Kimball style star-schema or a normalized data warehouse in third-normal form. In order to fit the data into such structures, the loading ETL data flows have to transform the data to meet the business requirements of the user. This transformation is in effect the implementation of the soft business rules, including required aggregations or consolidation of incoming data. The early implementation of business rules improves the common application of the rules and generally improves the data quality [20].

The problem, however, arises with changes to those business rules. The earlier the business rules are implemented in the architecture of a data warehouse, the more dependencies it has in higher layers of the data warehouse.

Consider the following example from the aviation industry: the aircraft registration number is a standardized alphanumeric identifier for aircraft and is used world-wide. Each number has a prefix that indicates the country where the aircraft is registered. For example, the registration number "D-EBUT" originates from Germany (because of the prefix "D"). Numbers from Germany are actually "smart keys," a concept that is described in more detail in Chapter 4, Data Vault Modeling. In the case of the German aircraft with the registration "D-EBUT", the second character indicates that the plane is a single-engine aircraft. In the US, the prefix "N" is common. Until December 31, 1948, there was also a second prefix (the second letter in the number) that was used to indicate the category of the aircraft (see Table 2.1).

For example, the aircraft with the registration number N-X-211 is registered in the experimental category.

However, the FAA decided to stop using the second prefix and now issues numbers between 3 (N1A) and 6 characters (N99999) without any other meaning, except for the first prefix which indicates the origination country. In fact, the second letter is always a number between 1 and 9.

Now, consider the effect of this change on your data warehouse. If the category has been extracted from the (now historic) N-Number, the second letter would be used to identify the aircraft category just after loading the data from the stage area into the normalized data warehouse, where the category would most probably be a column in the aircraft table. Once the numbers change, however, there would be only a number between 1 and 9 in the second position of the registration number, which has no meaning. In order to update the business rule, the easiest approach would be to introduce a new category ("Unknown category") where those aircraft are mapped to if the second letter in the registration number is from 1 to 9. However, because there will be no new aircraft with a category other than the

Table 2.1 Category Prefixes in the USA until December 1948	
	Category
C	Commercial and private airline
G	Glider
L	Limited
R	Restricted (e.g., cropdusters and racing aircrafts)
S	State
X	Experimental

unknown, it is reasonable to remove the category completely (unless you focus on the analysis of historic aircraft). That makes even more sense if you consider that today's aircraft are categorized by the operation code, air-worthiness class, and other categories at the same time, making the categorization in Table 2.1 obsolete.

Therefore, this change in the business rule requires the replacement of the category by multiple new categories. In the normalized data warehouse, we would have to remove the old category column and add multiple category references to the aircraft. After changing the ETL jobs that load the data from the stage into the normalized data warehouse, we can change the information mart that is built on top of the data warehouse layer and modify the data mart ETL routines. A couple of questions arise when using this approach:

- How do we deal with historic data in the normalized data warehouse?
- Where do we keep the historic data for later analysis (if required by the business at a later time)?
- How do we analyze both historic aircraft and modern aircraft (a business decision)?
- Will there be multiple dimensions (for the historic category and the modern categories) in the same information mart or multiple information marts for historic and modern aircraft?
- What is the default value for the historic category in modern aircraft?
- What are the default values for the modern categories in ancient aircraft?

In the Data Vault 2.0 architecture, the categorization of an aircraft would be loaded into a table called a satellite that contains descriptive data (we explain the base entities of Data Vault 2.0 modeling in Chapter 4 in detail). When the logic in the source system changes – in this case, the format of the N-Number – the old satellite is closed (no new data is loaded into the current satellite). All new data is loaded into a new satellite with an updated structure that meets the structure of the source data. In this process, there are no business rules implemented. All data is loaded. Because there are now two tables, one holding historic data and the other new data, it is easy to implement the business rule when loading the data from the Data Vault into the information mart. It is also easy to build one information mart for the analysis of historic, older aircraft and another information mart for the analysis of modern aircraft that have been built after 1948.

But the real advantage of separating hard and soft rules becomes clear when thinking about the ETL jobs that need to be adapted to fit the new categorization: none. The ETL jobs that load the historic data remain unchanged and are ready to load more historic data if required (for example, to reload flat files from the archive). The new data is loaded to another target (the second satellite) and is therefore a modified copy of the "historic" ETL routine. Nothing needs to be changed, except the information mart (and its loading routines).

2.2.3 STAGING AREA LAYER

The staging layer is used when loading batch data into the data warehouse. Its primary purpose is to extract the source data as fast as possible from the source system in order to reduce the workload on the operational systems. In addition, the staging area allows the execution of SQL statements against the source data, which might not be the case with direct access to flat files, such as CSV files or Excel sheets.

Note that the staging area does not contain historical data, unlike the traditional architectures described in the previous chapter. Instead only the batch that has to be loaded next into the data warehouse layer is present in the staging area. However, there is an exception to this rule: if there are multiple batches to be loaded, e.g., when an error happened on the weekend and the data from the last couple of days has to be loaded into the data warehouse, there might be multiple batches in the staging area. The primary purpose of having no history in the staging area is not to have to deal with changing data structures. Consider the fact that a source table might change over time. If the staging area kept historic data, there would have to be logic in place for defining the loading procedures into the data warehouse. This logic, in fact business rules, would become more and more complex over time. As we have described in the previous section, the goal of the Data Vault 2.0 architecture is to move complex business rules towards the end-user in order to ensure quick adaption to changes.

The staging area consists of tables that duplicate the structures of the source system. This includes all the tables and columns of the source, including the primary keys. However, indexes and foreign keys, which are used to ensure the referential integrity in the source system, are not duplicated. In addition, all columns are nullable because we want to allow the data warehouse to load the raw data from the source system, including bad data that might exist in the source (especially in flat files). The only business rules that are applied to the incoming data are so-called hard business rules. It is common practice to keep the original names from the source system for naming tables and columns; however, this is not a must.

In addition to the columns from the source system, each table in the stage area includes:

- A sequence number
- A timestamp
- A record source
- Hash key computations for all business keys and their combinations

These fields are metadata information that is required for loading the data into the next layer, the Data Warehouse layer, later on. The sequence number identifies the order of the data in the source system. We can use it when the order within the source is important for loading the data into the data warehouse, e.g., RSS news feeds or transactional data without timestamp information included. The timestamp is the date and time when the record arrives in the data warehouse. The record source indicates the source system from which the data record originates and the hash key is used for identification purposes. A detailed description of these columns is provided in Chapter 4.

2.2.4 DATA WAREHOUSE LAYER

The second layer in the Data Vault 2.0 architecture is the data warehouse, the purpose of which is to hold all historical, time-variant data. The data warehouse holds raw data, not modified by any business rule other than hard business rules. Therefore, the data is stored in the granularity as provided by the source systems. The data is nonvolatile and every change in the source system is tracked by the Data Vault structure. Data from multiple source systems, but also within a source system, is integrated by the business keys, discussed in Chapter 4. Unlike the information mart, where the information is subject-oriented, the data in the Data Vault is function-oriented.

In batch loading, the data is fed from the staging area, but in real-time loading the data is fed directly from the enterprise service bus (ESB) into the data warehouse. However, as stated before, real-time data warehousing is beyond the scope of this book. We cover the loading of operational data in Chapter 12, which is also applied directly to the data warehouse and follows similar patterns.

The data warehouse layer is modeled after the Data Vault 2.0 modeling technique, which is examined in Chapter 4 to Chapter 6. This layer is often called the Raw Data Vault layer, as it holds raw data, modeled using the Data Vault 2.0 model.

2.2.5 INFORMATION MART LAYER

Unlike traditional data warehouses, the data warehouse layer of the Data Vault 2.0 architecture is not directly accessed by end-users. Typically, the end-user accesses only the information mart which provides the data in a way that the end-user feels most comfortable with. Because the goal of the enterprise data warehouse is to provide valuable information to its end-users, we use the term *information* instead of *data* for this layer. The information in the information mart is subject oriented and can be in aggregated form, flat or wide, prepared for reporting, highly indexed, redundant and quality cleansed. It often follows the star schema and forms the basis for both relational reporting and multidimensional OLAP cubes. Because the end-user accesses only this layer of the data warehouse, having a Data Vault model in the data warehouse layer is transparent to the end-user. If the end-user requires a normalized data warehouse in third-normal form, we can also provide an information mart that meets those needs. Front-end tools are also able to write-back information into the enterprise data warehouse layer.

Other examples for information marts include the Error Mart and the Meta Mart. They are the central location for errors in the data warehouse and the metadata, respectively. Being the central location of this data is also the difference of these two special marts from standard information marts: unlike information marts, the Error and Meta Marts cannot be rebuilt from the Raw Data Vault or any other data source. However, they are similar because end-users, such as administrators, use these marts to analyze errors in the loading process or other problems in the data warehouse, or the metadata that is stored for the data warehouse, its sources and transformations that lead to the information presented in the information marts. Chapter 14, Loading the Dimensional Information Mart, provides an extensive discussion about how to load the information mart for dimensional OLAP cubes from the Data Vault 2.0 structures in the data warehouse.

2.2.6 METRICS VAULT

While the three previous layers (the staging area, the data warehouse layer, and the information marts) are mandatory in the Data Vault 2.0 architecture (except for real-time cases which are not covered in this book), the Metrics Vault (covered in this section), the Business Vault (covered in section 2.2.7) and the Operational Vault (covered in section 2.2.8) are optional extensions to the Data Vault 2.0 architecture.

The Metrics Vault is used to capture and record runtime information, including the run history, process metrics, and technical metrics, such as CPU loads, RAM usage, disk I/O metrics and network throughput. Similar to the data warehouse, the Metrics Vault is modeled after the Data Vault 2.0 modeling technique. The data is in its raw format, system or process driven and nonauditable. It might include technical meta-data and technical metrics of the ETL jobs or the data warehouse environment. On top of the Metrics Vault, the Metrics Mart provides the performance metrics information to the user.

Chapter 10, Metadata Management, includes an example of how to track audit information during ETL loads and store the data into a Metrics Vault.

2.2.7 BUSINESS VAULT

Because some business rules that are applied to the Data Vault 2.0 structures tend to become complex, there is the option to add Business Vault structures to the data warehouse layer. The Business Vault is a sparsely modeled data warehouse based on Data Vault design principles, but houses business-rule changed data. In other words, the data within a Business Vault has already been changed by business rules. In most cases, the Business Vault is an intermediate layer between the Raw Data Vault and the information marts and eases the creation of the end-user structures.

Figure 2.4 shows the Business Vault on top of the Data Vault enterprise data warehouse. This is because the Business Vault is preloaded before the information marts are loaded and eases their loading processes. The complex business rules (the soft rules) source their data from both the Raw Data Vault and the Business Vault entities.

While the Business Vault is modeled after Data Vault 2.0 design principles, it doesn't have the same requirements regarding the auditability of the source data. Instead, it is possible to drop and re-generate the Business Vault from the Raw Data Vault at any time. The Business Vault provides a consolidated view of the data in the Raw Data Vault to the developers who populate the information marts.

Similar to the Metrics Vault, the Business Vault is not stored in a separate layer. Instead, it is stored as an extension to the Data Vault model within the data warehouse layer. Chapter 14, Loading the Dimensional Information Mart, shows how to use a Business Vault to populate an information mart.

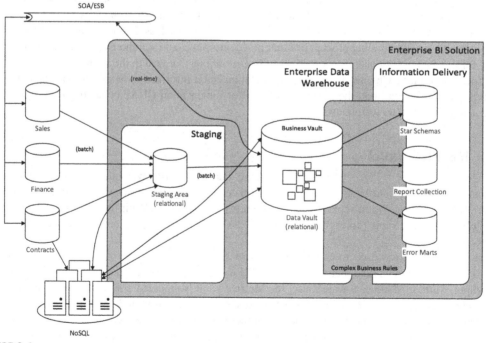

FIGURE 2.4

Business Vault is located within the Data Vault enterprise data warehouse.

2.2.8 OPERATIONAL VAULT

The Operational Vault is an extension to the Data Vault that is directly accessed by operational systems (Figure 2.5). There are occasions when such systems need to either retrieve data from the enterprise data warehouse or when they need to write data back to it. Examples include master data management (MDM) systems, such as Microsoft Master Data Services (MDS) or metadata management systems. In both cases, there is an advantage of directly operating on the data warehouse layer instead of using an information mart or staging area. Other cases include data mining applications that directly analyze the raw data stored within the data warehouse layer. Often, whenever the interfacing application requires real-time support, whether reading or writing, direct access to the Operational Vault is the best option.

For that reason, integration of real-time data from a service-oriented architecture (SOA) or enterprise service bus (ESB) directly writes into the Operational Vault. While we have defined the Operational Vault as an extension to the Data Vault in the opening of this section, interfacing applications read directly from existing Data Vault structures. Thus, the Data Vault structures become, to some extent, Operational Vault structures.

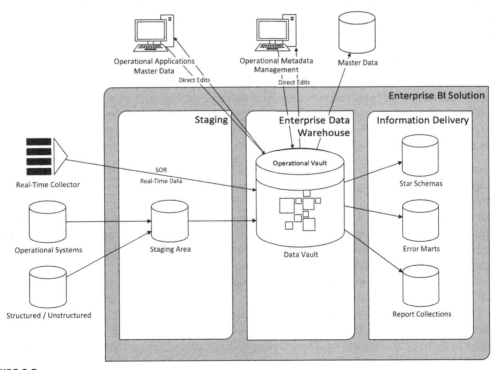

FIGURE 2.5

Operational Data Vault [21].

2.2.9 MANAGED SELF-SERVICE BI

A common experience in data warehousing projects is that, after initial success of the data warehousing initiative, business demands more and more features. However, due to limited team resources in IT, not all requests by the business can be met. In many cases, the requested functionality is only important or applicable to a limited number of business users or has a low business impact. Yet, it is important for those who demand it. But IT has to prioritize their requests in order to use their own IT resources responsibly, with the effect of delayed or completely discarded new features. This low responsiveness to business requests increases discomfort among business users.

An approach called *self-service BI* allows end-users to completely circumvent IT due to its unresponsiveness. In this approach, business users are left on their own with the whole process of sourcing the data from operational systems, integration, and consolidation of the raw data. There are many problems with this self-service approach that lacks the involvement of IT:

- **Direct access to source systems:** end-users should not directly access the data from source systems. This exposes raw data that is potentially private and allowing access to this data might circumvent security access, which is implemented in access control lists (ACLs).
- **Unintegrated raw data:** when sourcing data from multiple source systems, business users are left alone with raw data integration. This can become a tedious and error-prone task if performed manually (e.g., in Microsoft Excel).
- **Low data quality:** data from source systems often have issues regarding the data quality. Before using the data for analysis, it requires clean up. Again, without the right tools, this can become a burden to the end-user. Or, and that is the worst case, it just doesn't happen.
- **Unconsolidated raw data:** in order to analyze the data from multiple source systems, the data often requires consolidation. Without this consolidation, the results from business analysis will be meaningless.
- **Nonstandardized business rules:** because end-users are dealing with only the raw data in self-service BI, they have to implement all business rules that transform the raw data into meaningful information. But who checks whether this implementation is consistent with the rest of the organization?

In many cases, end-users – even if they are power users with knowledge of SQL, MDX, and other techniques – don't have the right tools available to solve the tasks. Instead, much work is done manually and is error-prone.

But from our experience, it is not possible to completely prevent such power users from obtaining data from source systems, preparing it, and eventually reporting the data to upper management. What organizations need is a compromise between IT agility and data management that allows power users to obtain the data they need quickly, in a usable quality.

To overcome these problems, the Data Vault 2.0 standard allows experienced or advanced business users to perform their own data analysis tasks on the raw data of the data warehouse. In fact, a Data Vault 2.0 powered IT welcomes business users to take the data that is available in the enterprise data warehouse (either in the Raw Data Vault or in the Business Vault) and use their own tools to transform the data into meaningful information. This is because IT just cannot deliver the requested functionality in the given time frame. Instead, IT sources the raw data from operational systems or other data sources and integrates it using the business key for the Raw Data Vault. IT might also create Business Vault structures to provide a consolidated view on parts of the model or precalculate key performance indicators (KPIs) to ensure consistency among such calculations.

The business user then uses the raw data (from the Raw Data Vault) and the business data (from the Business Vault) to create local information marts using specialized tools. These tools retrieve the data from the enterprise data warehouse, apply a set of user-defined business rules and present the output to the end-user.

This approach is called *managed self-service BI* and is part of the Data Vault 2.0 standard. In this approach, IT evolves to a service organization that provides those power users with the data they want, in the timeframe they need. The data is integrated by its business key, and, if the end-user wants it, can be consolidated and quality checked. Consolidation and quality checks occur on the way into the Business Vault, as we will show later in this book. The Business Vault also implements some of the most important business rules. The power user has direct access to both the Raw Data Vault and the Business Vault and can, depending on the task at hand, select the raw data or the consolidated, cleaned data. In fact, both types of data are already integrated, so the business user can also join consolidated data with raw data from specific source systems.

This book will demonstrate that loading the raw data into the Raw Data Vault is very easy, including integration using the business keys. In fact, it can be accomplished in short sprint iterations, as we will explain in Chapter 3, Data Vault 2.0 Methodology. When users ask for more data, and this data is not available in the data warehouse, it is possible to source and integrate the data into the Raw Data Vault to provide it to the power user for a managed self-service BI task.

2.2.10 OTHER FEATURES

The Data Vault 2.0 architecture offers additional capabilities to support real-time (RT) and near-real-time (NRT) environments, unstructured data and NoSQL environments. However, a description of these options is out of the scope of this book.

This chapter introduced the Data Vault 2.0 architecture, a fundamental item in the Data Vault 2.0 standard. The next two chapters will focus on the project methodology and Data Vault modeling, two other fundamental pillars of the Data Vault 2.0 standard.

REFERENCES

[1] Inmon: Building the data warehouse, 4th edition, p. 91ff.
[2] Dan Linstedt: Data Vault 2.0 Training Slides, p. 12.
[3] Splunk – "Splunk for Big Data" in Philip Winslow et al. Does Size Matter Only?, p. 32.
[4] Mark Sweiger: Scalable Computer Architectures for Data Warehousing, p. 1.
[5] http://student.bus.olemiss.edu/files/Conlon/Others/Others/BUS669/ResearchPapers/From%20ACM/The%20IBM%20data%20warehouse%20architecture%20-bontempo.pdf.
[6] Golfarelli and Rizzi: Data Warehouse Design, p. 199.
[7] Vassiliadis 2000: Gulliver in the land of data warehousing: Practical experiences and observations of a researcher. In Proceedings 2nd International Workshop on Design and Management of Data Warehouses, Stockholm.
[8] Gupta et al. 1997b: Index selection for OLAP. In Proceedings 13th International Conference on Data Engineering, Birmingham, UK, p. 208-219.
[9] Mike Ferguson: Architecting a big data platform for Analytics, p. 5.

[10] James Kobielus: Living the Big Data Dream: Confidence, Confidentiality and Continuous Automation in the 21st Century: http://www.ibmbigdatahub.com/blog/living-big-data-dream-confidence-confidentiality-and-continuous-automation-21st-century.

[11] Mike Ferguson: Architecting a big data platform for Analytics, p. 5f.

[12] Bontempo, C. and Saracco, C. Database Management: Principles and Products. Prentice Hall, Upper Saddle River, N.J., 1995 in Charles Bontempo and George Zagelow: The IBM Data Warehouse Architecture, p. 44.

[13] https://technet.microsoft.com/en-us/magazine/2008.04.dwperformance.aspx.

[14] https://technet.microsoft.com/en-us/library/bb522541(v=sql.105).aspx.

[15] Dayong Gu, et al. "Using Star Join and Few-Outer-Row Optimizations to Improve Data Warehousing Queries," https://msdn.microsoft.com/en-us/library/gg567299.aspx.

[16] Harinarayan et al. Implementing Data Cubes Efficiently, p. 1.

[17] Joy Mundy, Warren Thornthwaite: "The Microsoft Data Warehouse Toolkit", Second Edition, p. 603f (System and Availability Management).

[18] Joy Mundy, Warren Thornthwaite: "The Microsoft Data Warehouse Toolkit", Second Edition, p. 114f (Setting up for High Availability).

[19] Dan Linstedt: Data Vault 2.0 Training, p. 9.

[20] Zaki, A. Business Rules and the Data Warehouse, http://altis.com.au/business-rules-and-the-data-warehouse/, August 19, 2011.

[21] Dan Linstedt: Data Vault 2.0 Training, p. 37.

THE DATA VAULT 2.0 METHODOLOGY

3

The Data Vault 2.0 standard provides a best practice for project execution, which is called the "Data Vault 2.0 methodology." It is derived from core software engineering standards and adapts these standards for use in data warehousing. Figure 3.1 shows the standards that have influenced the Data Vault 2.0 methodology.

By combining these standards, the Data Vault 2.0 methodology becomes a best-of-breed standard for project management in data warehousing. Scrum is used for team coordination and to apply to the project day-to-day tasks. Within a two- to three-week-long Scrum iteration (sprint), the team executes a mini-waterfall which is based on the software development life cycle (SDLC). The goal is to have completed deliverables after this iteration, which can be put into production.

Project management techniques from the PMI Project Management Body of Knowledge (PMBOK), as recognized in the Project Management Professional (PMP) designation is applied to define and execute the project plan at the physical level of the project. Capability Maturity Model Integration (CMMI) is used for overall management and project oversight and applied for review and improvement sessions.

A continuous improvement of the process and the underlying data is done using Total Quality Management (TQM) in a closed loop approach. When business users are involved in aligning the data sets across the sources and correcting errors in the source systems, they follow TQM principles. We will discuss in section 3.3.2 that this requires more activities than in commonly used approaches focusing on data quality (DQ) only.

Six Sigma rules and principles are applied in order to achieve maximum optimization in agility of the process of building and implementing Data Vault 2.0 styled data warehouse initiatives. This process relies on measurements (estimates vs. actuals), or key performance indicators (KPIs), covered in section 3.1.4.

The Data Vault 2.0 methodology consists of three major activities in which the methods shown in Figure 3.1 are applied:

1. Project planning, which includes the management, definition, and estimation of the project;
2. Project execution, which includes sprint definition, team organization, and technical numbering for artifact organization;
3. Review and improvement, which includes review and improvement activities.

The remaining sections in this chapter describe these activities and the application of the methods in detail.

3.1 PROJECT PLANNING

Because a data warehouse is a piece of software, many academic researchers and professionals from industry agree to the fact that methodologies from the software engineering discipline can be applied to data warehousing projects [1]. We have already discussed some well-known methodologies for project planning.

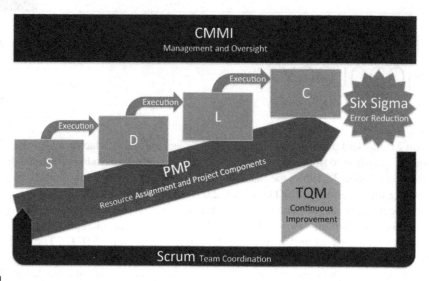

FIGURE 3.1

Components of the Data Vault 2.0 methodology.

The Data Vault 2.0 methodology derives its project planning capabilities from PMP. And unlike the agile Scrum methodology, there is an emphasis on having a formal project plan within a sprint. Each project has a project plan: that includes the tasks to be accomplished, outcomes to be expected as the output of the task and roles that will execute the task. Depending on the project type, there are different types of roles that perform the project. The following list presents the roles and their responsibilities:

- **Business Sponsor:** Business sponsors should create alignment between the project and business and cultural goals; communicate on behalf of the project, especially towards senior management; be the key advocate of the project and gain commitment among other key stakeholders; arrange resources to ensure the success of the project; facilitate problem solving by ensuring the escalation of issues to be solved effectively at the organizational level; support the project manager by offering mentoring, coaching and leadership; and build durability to make sure that project outputs are sustainable [2].
- **Technical Business Analyst:** They establish standards and access control lists; prioritize change requests; establish new requirements; create new reports for the general business user audience; help the team debugging alpha releases; participate in the development and design of information marts; and create user training material. The Technical Business Analyst is a power user who reports to the business but has a level of technical skills including the ability to understand data models, and leverage or write SQL directly.
- **Project Manager:** This role is responsible to make sure that the project team completes the project. The project manager develops the project plan, manages the team's performance of project tasks and secures acceptance and approval of deliverables from the project sponsor and other stakeholders. In addition, this role is responsible for communication, such as status reporting, risk management and escalation of issues that cannot be solved within the project team [3].

- **IT Manager:** Information technology (IT) managers ensure the business continuity and success of the business. For that reason, they oversee projects and make sure that they use resources effectively. IT managers advise the management team objectively on where IT might make a difference to business; agreeing on costs, timescales, and standards to be met and monitoring them throughout the project; helping the organization to transition smoothly from legacy systems to new systems; and keeping management updated on the progress of current projects [4].
- **ETL Developer:** Team members who are assigned to this Extract, Transform, Load (ETL) role implement the data or control flows that load the data from source systems to staging, from staging to Data Vault structures and from there to the Business Vault and to information marts. They are also responsible for creating virtual marts, or implementing soft business rules in ETL as requested by the business.
- **Report Developer:** Report developers implement business-driven reports based on information marts, Business Vault tables, or directly on the Raw Data Vault (in rare circumstances). In most cases, they don't need to implement any business rules for this purpose; however, in rare cases, implementing a business report might require implementing a limited number of business rules directly within the report. This should be avoided in most cases as performance will drop and reusability is at risk.
- **Data Architect / Information Architect:** Information architects (known as data architects in the industry, but we think the term is misleading given the fact that they should deal with information instead of data; see Chapter 2, Scalable Data Warehouse Architecture) are responsible for the information architecture and data integration [5].
- **Metadata Manager:** This role is responsible for the planning of metadata design; facilitates a framework for metadata development; coordinates activities and communication with other roles and projects; administrates access levels to metadata for all members and external staff who need to work with the metadata [6].
- **Change Manager:** The change manager ensures that new functionality will not disrupt other IT or business services on roll-out. This role is also responsible for making sure that roll-outs are possible in the environment and not hindered by other projects.

Many organizations make the mistake of assigning the responsibilities to persons instead of defined roles. The advantage of having defined roles in a team is that it is possible to replace the person who fulfills the role by another, skilled person – for example, if the current person leaves the organization or changes the project. Defined roles help the organizations in many ways: these role definitions help the human resource department to find the right people for the job in the free market; it is possible for new hires to quickly identify their responsibilities and deliver what they are expected to deliver; and finally clear responsibilities help the team to decide who does what when working on issues that naturally arise in development projects.

Most of the presented roles are already known to project teams in data warehousing. The exception is the technical business analyst. This role serves an intermediate function between business and IT. The characteristics and more information about the responsibilities of this role are given in Figure 3.2.

Due to the role's location between business and IT, the job of the technical business analyst is to mitigate between both parties and prevent an "over-the-fence-throwing" mentality between them. Such a mentality, where both parties don't work together with a mutual understanding and mutual support of each other, is oftentimes a root cause for failing projects. Such projects are characterized by unclear business requirements, technical artifacts that don't meet the business requirements nor those that IT

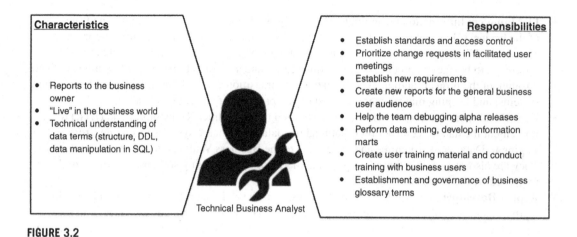

Characteristics

- Reports to the business owner
- "Live" in the business world
- Technical understanding of data terms (structure, DDL, data manipulation in SQL)

Technical Business Analyst

Responsibilities

- Establish standards and access control
- Prioritize change requests in facilitated user meetings
- Establish new requirements
- Create new reports for the general business user audience
- Help the team debugging alpha releases
- Perform data mining, develop information marts
- Create user training material and conduct training with business users
- Establishment and governance of business glossary terms

FIGURE 3.2

Characteristics and responsibilities of a technical business analyst.

has understood, and unreliable software due to untested or incomplete testing (from a business perspective). Oftentimes, finger pointing is involved and each party is very confident that mistakes are the sole responsibility of the other side.

This is also why it is a recommended practice for Data Vault 2.0 teams not to separate business from IT roles. Instead, both groups should work together, with each role focusing on their responsibilities. If possible, the team should be co-located to be more efficient. It is important to create a level of collaboration and mutual understanding between business and IT and each individual role, to prevent situations as outlined in the previous paragraph. This is the responsibility of the project manager and requires continuous actions if the groups start separating from each other during the course of the project.

Part of the understanding that needs to be established from the business side is to understand that IT needs a way to work relatively uninterrupted from day-to-day issues during their two-week sprints. Issues that arise in operations have to be scheduled for one of the next sprints. In order to achieve this, IT has to change their thinking as well: their job should be the enabling of business to solve some if not most of their problems on their own without the involvement of IT. That is where "managed" self-service business intelligence (BI) comes into play. The Data Vault 2.0 standard gives guidelines to IT as to how to provide the data in a way that it can be consumed by business users on their own. This requires shifting responsibilities to business. For example, it should not be the responsibility of IT to fix data in the enterprise data warehouse in order to compensate for errors in operational systems. It is the responsibility of business to get these errors fixed in order for IT to deliver the data through the data warehouse back to business, where they can apply business rules to transform data into information. IT will use this knowledge to institutionalize those information marts that are used on a frequent basis.

To prevent interruptions from either side, an established process is required for requested changes to the system. Figure 3.3 shows this communication channel.

New change requests often have their origin on the business side of the project. IT is required to assess the risks and the impact to the system currently in production. That is why the change requests are funneled from business users through the sponsor (who decides about the prioritization of their change requests) through the technical business analyst (who helps to translate the business requirements into technical

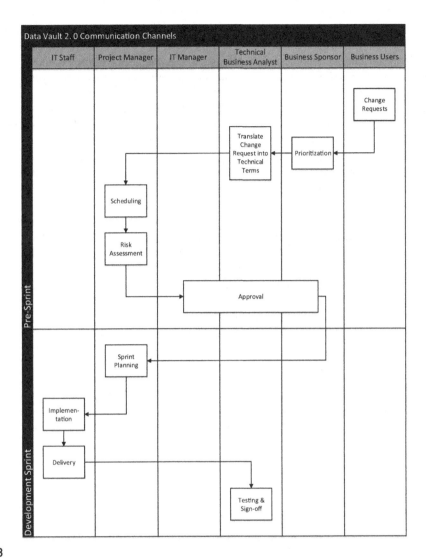

FIGURE 3.3

Defined processes showing the communication channels in the Data Vault 2.0 methodology.

terms) to the IT manager and the project manager, who are responsible for scheduling. When IT is done with the risk assessment, it returns this information to the business so they can make a final decision whether the change request should be implemented given the risk and impact assessment. If business decides to go ahead with the change request, it is scheduled by IT in one of the next sprints, depending on the previous prioritization by the business. They are then responsible for the development and subsequent delivery of the new artifact. After business has tested the change (in addition to development testing) and accepted the change, the formal sign-off releases IT from more duties on this change request.

When new releases of the data warehouse system are being developed, development teams use the same approach as teams in traditional software development. They use Alpha releases to test the new release early in the development process, Beta releases to test it against a limited business audience and Gamma releases for production. Alpha releases should only affect technical team members up to the technical business analyst, as Figure 3.4 shows.

It is very common that three to five technical business analysts are involved in the Alpha release, in addition to the technical IT team. When IT releases new reports to the analysts, it should be made clear that these reports are not intended for circulation towards business, because the information on the reports or in the multidimensional cubes might be wrong or even bad. Technical business analysts receive these reports nevertheless, in order to help them to spot those errors or identify miscalculations. It is very common that an Alpha release is distributed to technical business analysts after the first two or three sprints of the data warehouse project.

Once the new release achieves Beta status, the release is shown to more technical business analysts, the business sponsor and a selected number of business managers and other users with a vested interest in the functionality of the new release. Figure 3.5 shows the roles that are involved in the Beta release.

The Beta release has been tested thoroughly by IT and business representatives and no longer contains any obvious or known errors. However, the generated reports are still not good for circulation because of the nature of the release state. Instead, the reports are used by the limited team to identify issues that have not been identified by development and technical business analysts so far. If the limited team agrees to the readiness of the release for production, the data warehouse system enters Gamma state, as shown in Figure 3.6.

FIGURE 3.4

Data Vault 2.0 methodology Alpha release reach.

FIGURE 3.5

Data Vault 2.0 methodology Beta release reach.

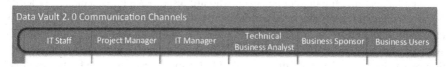

FIGURE 3.6

Data Vault 2.0 methodology Gamma release reach.

The Gamma or production release is deployed and made available to all business users. This approach closely follows CMMI, which is part of the Data Vault 2.0 methodology.

3.1.1 CAPABILITY MATURITY MODEL INTEGRATION

The Capability Maturity Model Integration (CMMI) is a process improvement framework developed more than 20 years ago and governed by the Software Engineering Institute (SEI) at Carnegie Mellon University (USA). CMMI is sponsored by the U.S. government (especially the U.S. Department of Defense) and is in use by organizations of all sizes world-wide. It has helped to streamline costs, reduce rework and defect rates and improve timelines and quality [7].

CMMI by itself is a process improvement framework that has been developed to address a broad range of application environments. There are three different models based on the CMMI framework [7]:

- **CMMI for Development**, a process model for process management and improvement in software development organizations
- **CMMI for Acquisition**, a model for organizations that have to initiate and manage the acquisition of products and services
- **CMMI for Services**, a process model for organizations to help them to deploy and manage services

By its nature, CMMI for Development is the right choice for process improvement in data warehouse development. It can be used to increase the efficiency of development processes for software products (such as a data warehouse), including processes for planning, management, and control of development activities [7]. The CMMI for Development standard provides best practices from successful development organizations and experiences from software quality experts [7]. The idea is to set organizations on a track of process improvement by enabling them to predict the outcome of their (defined and managed) processes. The prediction of process outputs (including the time-frame and quality of the product) results in a lower risk of exceeding budget, encountering quality problems and going over schedule [7].

It is possible to integrate CMMI with other frameworks and best practices, such as agile development, PMP and Six Sigma. That is because CMMI doesn't define how the software development has to be done. Instead, it defines what must be done in order to improve development processes. Therefore, the CMMI framework supports agile principles by providing a reference framework for successful development environments [8]. It supports the integration of Six Sigma with the option of implementing CMMI process areas as Six Sigma (e.g., DMAIC) projects [9]. PMP is also supported due to an overlapping between Project Management's Body of Knowledge (PMBOK's) knowledge areas and CMMI process areas [7].

There are two different representations of CMMI: the continuous representation and the staged representation. These representations exist to provide organizations with different requirements and a unique set of tools for process improvement [10]. The staged model is focused on the overall organization and provides a road map as a series of stages (hence the name). These stages are called *maturity levels* and indicate the maturity of the organization regarding a set of process areas. While the organization is advancing on the maturity levels, it implements more and more practices from various process areas. As soon as the organization has satisfied the goals of all process areas in a maturity level, it can advance to the next level to further improve its processes [10]. The continuous model is different from the staged model as it provides less guidance on the order of the process areas that should be implemented and improved. Instead, the focus is on the individual process area and how it can be improved. Each process area is on its own capability level. The grouping of process areas is not followed in the continuous model [10].

The next sections present the capability and maturity levels of CMMI in more detail.

3.1.1.1 Capability Levels

Organizations that are working with the continuous representation of CMMI are using capability levels to measure their process improvement efforts. The following capability levels exist in CMMI [10]:

0. Incomplete
1. Performed
2. Managed
3. Defined
4. Quantitatively Managed
5. Optimizing

An organization starts with the **capability level 0: incomplete**. It indicates that processes are not, or only partially, performed. It also indicates that at least one specific goal of the process area is not satisfied. There are no generic goals for this capability level because partially performed processes should not be institutionalized [11].

The organization can proceed to **capability level 1: performed** if all generic goals of level 1 are satisfied. This level requires that processes are performed and produce the needed output. However, this level doesn't require that the process itself be institutionalized, which means that process improvements can be lost over time [11].

The **capability level 2: managed** requires a process that is planned and executed in accordance with policy. This managed process employs skilled people who have access to the right resources and are able to produce controlled outputs. All relevant stakeholders are involved in the process, which is monitored, controlled, reviewed and evaluated on a regular basis.

The next capability level an organization can accomplish is **capability level 3: defined**. It is characterized by a defined process which is a managed process derived from the organization's set of standard processes and derived to the needs of the circumstances. The process has been tailored according to the tailoring guidelines of the organization and maintains a process description. In addition, it contributes process-related experiences back to the overall process organization.

Capability level 4: quantitatively managed is a defined process (see capability level 3) that uses statistical and other quantitative methods to control selected subprocesses. These methods are used to identify processes that produce a higher number of defect outputs or outputs with a lower quality [10].

The highest capability level that an organization can reach is **capability level 5: optimizing** which focuses on the institutionalizing of an optimizing process. This process requires that the organization constantly measures its (quantitatively managed) processes, analyzes trends, surveys technical practice, addresses common causes of process variation and then adapts the processes to changing business needs [10].

3.1.1.2 Maturity Levels

Maturity levels are different from capability levels as they are applied to sets of process areas where a combined set of goals has to be achieved (compare this to capability levels, which are applied to individual process areas). The following maturity levels are used in CMMI and are explained in this section [12]:

1. Initial
2. Managed
3. Defined
4. Quantitatively managed
5. Optimizing

The first **maturity level 1: initial** indicates an organization with ad-hoc and chaotic processes. There is no stable process environment provided by the organization. The success of the organization depends on the skills and engagement of individuals rather than defined and established processes. Organizations at maturity level 1 can deliver working products. However, they often exceed the budget and original delivery schedule. These organizations usually overcommit, abandon their processes in times of stress and have problems in repeating past successes [12].

Organizations at **maturity level 2: managed** have processes that are planned and executed in accordance with policy and that involve all relevant stakeholders. Skilled people with adequate resources produce controlled outputs under a monitored, controlled, and reviewed process that is evaluated on a regular basis. Existing processes are retained during times of stress [12].

Maturity level 3: defined indicates well-characterized and understood processes which are described in standards, procedures, tools, and methods. Organizational standard processes are established and improved over time. The major difference between maturity levels 2 and 3 is that standards, process descriptions and procedures at maturity level 2 can be different at each specific process instance. However, in maturity level 3, standards, process descriptions and procedures are tailored from the standard processes of the organization [12].

At **maturity level 4: quantitatively managed**, organizations use quantitative objectives for quality and process performance for managing their projects. Selected subprocesses are measured by collecting and statistically analyzing specific measures of process performance [12].

Organizations at **maturity level 5: optimizing** continually improve their processes using a quantitative approach to understand the variation of their processes and their process outcomes. The focus is on the continual improvement of process performance by incrementally improving processes and used technology [12].

3.1.1.3 Advancing to Maturity Level 5

Organizations who want to comply with maturity level 5 should focus on achieving capability levels for selected process areas first and then control the most advanced level – organization-wide performance management and continuous process improvement. The achievement is performed using an incremental undertaking. With each achieved maturity level, the organization achieves generic and specific goals for the set of process areas in a maturity level and increases its organizational maturity. Because maturity levels are based on their lower levels, the organization can leverage its past accomplishments when advancing to the next maturity level. For these reasons, it is often counterproductive for organizations to try to skip maturity levels [12].

3.1.1.4 Integrating CMMI in the Data Vault 2.0 Methodology

The Data Vault 2.0 methodology enables organizations to reach CMMI level 5 by addressing the following goals:

- **Measurable**: Section 3.1.4 will describe how the estimation process in the Data Vault 2.0 methodology is based on the comparison of estimated and actual effort. This requires capturing this information along the way.

- **Repeatable:** In order to estimate future effort, it is important to have repeatable processes. The Data Vault 2.0 model helps in this regard due to repeatable, pattern-based processes for modeling and loading data into the enterprise data warehouse.
- **Defined:** Data Vault 2.0 promotes defined standards, rules, procedures and prebuilt templates, including project documentation. An example of this definition of processes is presented in Figure 3.3. The definition also promotes repeatable processes.
- **Flexible:** The methodology is the enabler for rapid succession deployments (two to three weeks, depending on the capabilities or preferences of the organization). It is also possible to grow and shrink the team, depending on demand. This falls in line with the defined patterns in Data Vault 2.0. They help new team members to rapidly understand the processes and get involved in the implementation or testing.
- **Scalable:** Once a data warehouse based on Data Vault 2.0 has been deployed to part of the enterprise, it is possible to add more functionality required by other parts of the organization. This is due to the potential of Data Vault 2.0 models to grow organically, a characteristic that is not only unique to Data Vault, but has been designed into the modeling approach from its beginning.
- **Monitored:** Consistent team reviews as in Scrum (for example in the retrospective meeting) and constant releases in each sprint make sure that business users don't lose interest in the project and its activities. Instead, it keeps attention levels high, which means that business reacts quicker when IT is not delivering the expected results.
- **Governed:** Monitoring also involves governance. If the releases don't meet (or exceed) documented standards, the project is halted and reassessed to make sure it will in the future. This is done between the two- or three-week sprints.
- **Optimized:** The Data Vault 2.0 processes improve the opportunity for optimization due to low complexity: the lower the complexity of development processes, the fewer dependencies that have to be taken into consideration when continually improving processes.

Table 3.1 shows the activities and tasks of the Data Vault 2.0 methodology and how they relate to the maturity levels of CMMI.

Organizations can use this table to focus on the given Data Vault activities when they try to advance through the maturity levels. For example, parallel teams should only come into the focus of the organization when they have already achieved CMMI maturity level 4 (quantitatively managed) and try to achieve level 5 (optimizing). This follows the recommended practice as outlined earlier in this chapter, to advance through the maturity levels instead of directly trying to become an optimizing organization from the onset. While the first approach requires more time and a careful development of organizational capabilities, the risk is much lower than going directly after maturity level 5.

3.1.2 MANAGING THE PROJECT

As section 3.1 described, the Data Vault 2.0 methodology promotes the development processes of defined, repeatable, and governed, among other characteristics. However, it doesn't mean that the goal is to overdefine or overrestrict the development process. The goal is to use a structured yet agile approach to the development of business intelligence solutions. Business agility is defined by the ability to rapidly adapt to changes in the business environment. To support this ability, the data warehouse development team has to cope with these rapid changes as well. IT should avoid long-term project planning as much as possible and focus on iterative and incremental development instead. They need to be

Table 3.1 Mapping the Data Vault 2.0 Methodology to CMMI Maturity Levels		
Level	**Maturity Level**	**Data Vault 2.0 Methodology**
1	**Initial chaos**	N/A
2	**Managed**	Predefined Document Templates
		Implementation Standards
		Pattern Based Architecture
3	**Defined**	Defined Project Process
4	**Quantitatively managed**	Estimates and Actuals Captured
		Measured Lead Times
		Measured complexity
		Measured defects
5	**Optimizing**	Automation tools
		Rapid delivery
		Reduced cost
		Parallel teams

able to adapt to changing business requirements within two-week boundaries. An exception to this rule is the long-term (or overall) planning required at the program or enterprise level of the organization.

In order to achieve this goal, cross-functional teams are required, as already described in the previous section. Collaboration between each single team member, between business and IT is required at all times. If the business decides to change requirements (because external factors force them to do so or because they have changed their mind along the way for whatever reason), the development team has to know this as soon as possible. Changing direction should not be avoided, but promoted in order to deliver the right product that meets the user's expectations. However, this requires adaptive planning and an evolutionary approach to the development of the data warehouse. By deriving the Data Vault 2.0 model from a hub-and-spoke network model (this will be described in Chapter 5, Intermediate Data Vault Modeling), it was designed to support such an evolutionary approach from the onset.

Building a Data Vault model is a natural evolution. The best approach for implementing a Data Vault 2.0 based data warehouse is to focus on a well-defined small-scoped problem, where the business keys cross multiple functional areas. Attempting to model the whole enterprise at once should be avoided, as is common in the typical architectures and the approaches to build them, presented in Chapter 1, Introduction to Data Warehousing. Modeling the whole enterprise at once is required in these *legacy* architectures, because the effort to modify the initial model (either a third-normal-form or star schema) is too high. Therefore, developers try to implement as many features into the initial model as possible to minimize future changes. However, given changing business environments, this approach is not realistic. Data Vault 2.0 has been designed to quickly absorb changes to the model, among other design characteristics. Organizations who have decided to use Data Vault 2.0 should leverage this characteristic by organically growing their model in order to fully gain the advantages from Data Vault modeling.

But agility doesn't only depend on the Data Vault model or the architecture. It also depends on the people: the project members in the team and external people who support the core development team. A successful agile project requires people who are properly trained and follow a disciplined, collaborative approach (as described in the previous section). It is also important to involve all parties that have an interest in the data warehouse to be delivered. That is not only the business user. Development teams often forget to involve operations and support people early in the process.

Operations and support people need to support the solution in production. Thus, they have specific requirements for configuration, documentation, and roll-out of the solution. The evolutionary approach of the Data Vault 2.0 methodology helps in this regard as well: because the data warehouse is delivered in increments, operations and support can give early feedback in addition to the feedback provided by the business users. Development should leverage this potential feedback to the maximum by delivering working software on a frequent basis. In the end, frequent testing isn't only performed by IT during a sprint, but also by business users (the technical business analyst), operations and support.

Ultimately, the goals for the agile delivery are [12]:

- **Scaling agile:** This is not only about scaling the team size, but also location-wise (scale the distribution of your team), compliance, complexity (domain, technical, and organizational) and into an enterprise environment [13].
- **Avoid chaos:** Poorly run and managed projects run into the same problems as unmanaged projects. Don't "be agile" without agile discipline. Learn from mistakes made in past sprints and continuously improve your processes [13].
- **Effectively initiate:** Before actually building the system, the business problems should be clarified, a viable technical solution identified, the approach planned and the work environment and team set up. It is also import to gain stakeholder commitment for the chosen approach and implementation strategy [13].
- **Transition from individuals to agile teams:** The focus of every individual in your team should be on collaboratively working towards the goals of the project, not on individual benefits [13].
- **Build incrementally:** Every sprint should produce a solution that can be consumed by its business users. Only then can they give realistic and valuable feedback on the current solution. The goal is not to preview something – it is to put it into actual production [13].
- **Deploy agile solutions:** Today's business and technology environments are of complex nature. The agile solution has to be deployed into such an environment [13].
- **Leverage enterprise disciplines:** The Data Vault 2.0 methodology already leverages established and proven enterprise methodologies such as CMMI, Scrum, Six Sigma, PMP, etc. There are other enterprise disciplines that help you to deploy, maintain and support the solution, such as the Information Technology Infrastructure Library (ITIL). Make use of these proven disciplines, especially if they are already used within your organization [13].
- **Adapt governance strategy:** Governance of agile projects should fall in line within the sprints. As the solution is delivered towards the end of the sprint, adherence to standards and rules set by the organization should be reviewed [13].

These goals are from Disciplined Agile Delivery (DAD), which is used in enterprise organizations to ag- ilely deliver software. It is a hybrid approach that extends Scrum with proven strategies from Agile Modeling (AM), Extreme Programming (XP) and Unified Process (UP). Therefore, it follows a similar strategy to the Data Vault 2.0 methodology, with a clear focus on data warehousing and business intelligence.

3.1.2.1 Scrum

The traditional software development life-cycle, also known as the waterfall approach, has several advantages and disadvantages. If everything goes well (and as planned), the waterfall approach is the most efficient way to carry out a project. Only the required features are implemented, tested and deployed. The process produces a very good set of documentation, especially during the requirements and design phase of the project. However, it is almost impossible to carry out larger projects where the customer is not very concrete with requirements and ideas and where the business requirements evolve over time [14].

As a result, agile methodologies have been developed to make software development more flexible and overall more successful. Scrum is one example of such agile methodology and is described in the following sections. It was introduced in the late 1990s [15,16] and has become *"the overwhelming [agile] favorite."* [17]

User requirements are maintained as user stories in a product backlog in Scrum [18]. They are prioritized by business value and include requirements regarding customer requests, new features, usability enhancements, bug fixes, performance improvements, re-architecting, etc. The user stories are implemented in iterations called "sprints" which last usually two to four weeks. During a sprint, user stories are taken off the product backlog according to the priority of the item and implemented by the team [19]. The goal of Scrum is to create a potentially shippable increment with every sprint, which is a new release of the system that can be presented to the business user and potentially put into production [20] (Figure 3.7).

This requires that a user story be implemented and tested as a whole, including all business logic that belongs to this story. All stakeholders, such as business users and the development team, can inspect the new, working feature and provide feedback or recommend changes to the user story before the next sprint starts. Scrum supports the reprioritization of the product backlog and welcomes changing business requirements between the sprints [20] (Figure 3.8).

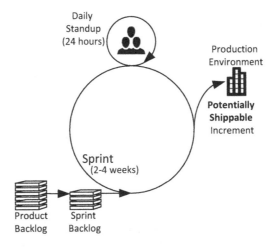

FIGURE 3.7

The flow of requirements in the Scrum process [20].

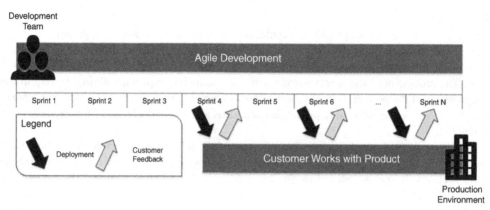

FIGURE 3.8

Quick turns in Scrum [21].

This helps to improve the outcome of the project in a way that meets the expectations of the business user. To ensure this, the customer should become as much a part of the Scrum team as possible [21].

The next sections explain the elements of Scrum in more detail.

3.1.2.2 Iterative Approach

The previous section has already discussed that Scrum uses an iterative approach for developing the final system. Each iteration is a small step towards the final solution and adds more value to the product [20]. The idea behind this approach is that most initial plans need to be corrected over time because of changing or roughly specified business requirements. Therefore, it should be possible for the team and the business users to take corrective action while the project is ongoing. However, this requires that business users receive value from the project as early as possible [20]. Figure 3.9 shows this concept.

In the first project base course, each iteration is only one day long. After the iteration, all stakeholders review the current "potentially shippable" system and check whether it still meets the expectations. If one of the stakeholders of the project identifies an issue in the project that requires correction, this correction will be relatively quick. For example, a business requirement can be modified and the system changed in the next iteration. In many cases, the change will be relatively small because it was identified early in the process. In the worst case, the whole iteration needs to be rolled back and performed again. In this case, only one day of work is lost.

If the iteration cycle (the sprint) is longer, for example a month, more requirements, expressed as user stories, will be implemented. Because there are often requirements that depend on each other, changing a requirement with many dependencies will take much more corrective effort than in the first case with a shorter sprint length.

3.1.2.3 Product and Sprint Backlog

The primary artifact in Scrum projects is the user story. User stories describe features from a user's perspective and are kept in the product backlog until a team member selects a user story for implementation. At the beginning of the project, user stories tend to be more general, roughly describing the primary features of the business users. They are primarily used to begin a discussion between the product

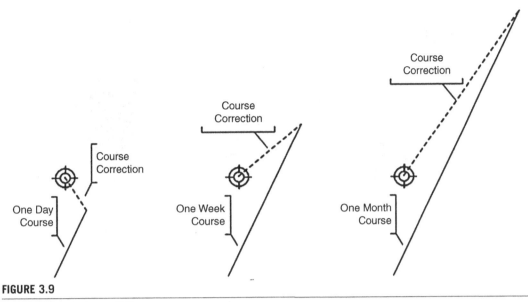

FIGURE 3.9

Project control in Scrum [21].

owner (a project role that we discuss in a following section) and the development team. As the team learns more about the features and the customer learns more about the product, new and more detailed user stories are added to the product backlog [18].

Each user story is prioritized before adding it to the product backlog. Developers strictly have to pick up user stories from the backlog in the order of priority [14]. At the beginning of each iteration, the user stories that should be implemented are taken off the product backlog and moved to the sprint backlog (see Figure 3.7 for details) [18]. The user story is designed, implemented, tested and integrated into the product as a whole. Problems are fixed immediately in order to maintain a "potentially shippable" product [14]. Figure 3.10 shows how team members work off the product backlog.

The work items that have a high priority (and therefore will be picked next by a team member) have to be detailed and well-defined because they describe the upcoming task for the developer. On the other hand, user stories with lower priority can be less detailed. These user stories are often not well elaborated by the business user and require more definition. The typical process is to remove such a user story, split it up into multiple stories, define them in more detail and put them, prioritized, back into the product backlog [18]. It is also possible to reprioritize existing user stories between sprints to adapt the project to changing demands by the business. A common practice is to derive (at least the initial) user stories from a requirements specification written by the product owner using traditional methods [22].

3.1.2.4 Integrating Scrum with the Data Vault 2.0 Methodology

In order to become an agile project team and to achieve the goals presented in the beginning of this section, the team has to evolve through the different levels of CMMI. Too many teams and too many organizations just decide to be "agile" without correctly applying the principles of the chosen methodology. All agile approaches, including Scrum, follow a set of principles that are required to enable

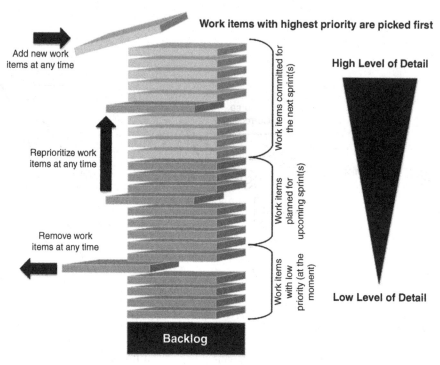

FIGURE 3.10

Backlog and priority [14].

a team to be agile. Without following these principles properly, the team joins the many teams that pretend to "do agile development" but have decided to forego most project management activities in reality. But agile project management doesn't mean "no project management." It is a different approach to project management and requires that team members know the principles and how to perform them. Team members who have never worked on an agile project often don't know the principles. They have to learn these principles from training or more experienced team members in order to be successful agile team members.

Not only that – running agile projects also requires an agile organization. If the organization thinks waterfall with "over-the-fence" throwing of artifacts between departments (e.g., from development to test to business) and putting changes into production requires a minimum of 3 weeks, your team will not perform very well from an agile perspective. As already stated in this chapter, the goal is to put the changes that are being developed in one iteration into production in the same sprint. That goal might not hold true at all times, for example if it is not possible to scope a change down to a manageable piece that can be developed and deployed within one sprint. In this case, multiple sprints might further develop the artifact until it is ready to deploy. However, the standard should be to deploy within the sprint where the artifact is being developed. There is no "agile big-bang" – that is, developing the data warehouse over sprints and deploying it at the end of the project in two years.

CMMI can help to evolve both the team and the organization to achieve agility. When following the recommendations outlined in section 3.1.1 (subsection titled "Advancing to Maturity Level 5"), organizations develop these skills over time, leaving team members time to learn, use and improve their agile skills. In fact, Scrum builds on CMMI level 5 (optimizing) where teams have the goal of improving their abilities over time. We will discuss this in more detail in section 3.3.

Most agile projects have in common the understanding that, to achieve the presented goals, the business intelligence (BI) team has to assume several responsibilities:

- **Customer satisfaction:** To meet this responsibility, the team has to rapidly and continuously deliver not only working software, but useful software. By that, we mean the increment should provide value to the user (and work).
- **Deliver frequently:** To show progress to business users and other stakeholders, it is the responsibility of the BI team to deliver working software on a frequent basis (in weeks rather than months).
- **Measure progress:** Oftentimes, development teams measure their progress by the person hours invested and compare it to the initial or updated plan. In agile development approaches such as the Data Vault 2.0 methodology, progress is measured in working software: the features that have been implemented.
- **Welcome changes:** Agile BI teams should not avoid late changes to the initial requirements. To meet business requirements and keep business users satisfied with the outcome, requirements gathering is a continuous approach in Data Vault 2.0.
- **Close cooperation:** Business people and developers should work on new features of the data warehouse daily. However, the goal is not to quick-fix any problems in production. They should collaborate to implement new features as planned for this sprint. Quick-fixing should be done by the operations department, which is why the data warehouse should be developed in such a way that it is maintainable by the business itself, without the need to integrate IT into this process.
- **Communicate face-to-face:** BI teams should avoid sending emails back and forth and instead meet face-to-face in order to solve any current issues.
- **Motivate individuals:** Motivation often comes from trust and is a bidirectional relationship.
- **Technical excellence:** To make business users satisfied in the long run, a technically excellent product is required. However, IT should avoid achieving this in the first try. Instead, they should focus on a good design that allows them to ultimately achieve the excellent product in an agile fashion. The Data Vault 2.0 model helps in this regard, because the design makes sure that the model is extensible to implement more features in later sprints.
- **Simplicity:** True engineers love simple solutions. Avoid adding features that are not needed by the business. Avoid modifying the Data Vault 2.0 model by system attributes if there is no actual need. Whenever complexity is added to the solution, there must be a good reason for it. This makes it easier to maintain the final solution.
- **Self-organizing teams:** Team members are responsible for self-organizing themselves around the associated tasks.
- **Adapt regularly:** It's the responsibility of the BI team to review past decisions, and make sure that they are still valid if the environment or other circumstances have changed. This responsibility might be the hardest, because people don't want to admit mistakes. But it was not a mistake to make a decision six months ago under the circumstances back then. It would be a mistake to keep going if the circumstances have changed.

The presented responsibilities are directly derived from Scrum principles but apply to all agile projects. Therefore, the Data Vault 2.0 methodology can only be successful if the development teams adhere to these responsibilities.

3.1.3 DEFINING THE PROJECT

One of the discussed responsibilities was to create simple yet extensible solutions. This responsibility is required in order to allow an iterative approach to the development of the data warehouse. Instead of planning the complete solution from the onset, only the next couple of sprints are planned. This doesn't mean that we don't have a general idea or an overall goal of the data warehouse. It only means that we're not immediately planning every task to get there, or modeling every available source or information mart that is required to deliver the final solution. The development team has to ask the customer what is required first, what has the most value for the business. That is what is delivered first, given that the dependencies of the deliveries are met.

Sometimes, this requires building some dependencies first, such as setting up the initial data warehouse infrastructure. However, building the final data warehouse infrastructure initially should be avoided. Start small, but make it extensible. Grow the infrastructure with growing requirements.

Oftentimes, architects try to create the data warehouse solution layer by layer: they decide on an initial set of source systems to deliver all the required reports or OLAP (online analytical processing) cubes. Then, they implement the whole stage layer to capture all source tables, including the ETL to load the tables. Once they are done with the stage layer, they start modeling the enterprise data warehouse to its maximum extent, because touching it later is too expensive. After the ETL load jobs are implemented, the data marts are created to finally satisfy the business users. This approach usually takes months if not years to complete, including several phases of debugging and error fixing. However, the problem arises when the requirements change (the architects in this example would say "too often") or business demands additional features (in many cases when the initial architects already have left the organization).

Given the extensible model and architecture and the agile methodology in the Data Vault 2.0 standard, data warehouse architects don't need to follow this approach any longer. Instead of building the data warehouse in a horizontal fashion, layer for layer, the data warehouse is built feature by feature, in a vertical fashion. The overall goal of the data warehouse initiative is the same, but it is now achieved in incremental deliveries of functionality. The goal of the BI team becomes to deliver the required functionality in rapid and frequent releases as described in the previous sections of this chapter. In order to do so, the functionality has to be scoped to individual features that are separated as much as possible from other features.

The recommended approach for achieving this goal is to use a scoped approach to requirements engineering and implementation of the single feature, as shown in Figure 3.11.

The feature to be implemented in the example shown in this figure is a report, but might be any other artifact required by the user. For example, it could be a new dimension or attribute in an OLAP cube, a new OLAP cube by itself (with the minimum number of dimensions), or a corpus for text mining. Once this artifact has been scoped and described by the business, IT starts to identify the sources (tables in the source system) that are required to build this single report. Next, the information mart targets are identified to assess what is already in place to deliver the required report (or other feature). Once this identification has been performed, engineers can stage the required data, build and load the Data Vault

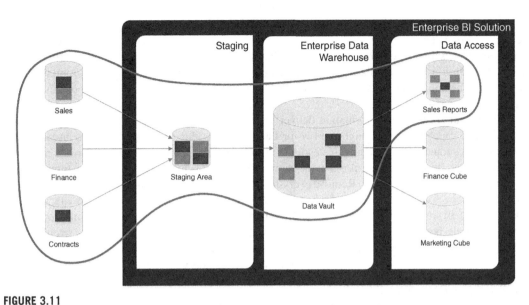

FIGURE 3.11

Scoping the report.

entities, and build the marts. When following this procedure, all the data in the source tables is loaded and modeled in the Data Vault, not partial attribute sets. Therefore, the source table has to be touched only once and not multiple times. In order to assess the availability of data, it should be possible to track what data is already loaded into the enterprise data warehouse. Partially loaded data makes this assessment more complex, which we want to avoid. Also, loading only partial data from source tables creates more complex Data Vault satellites.

Scoping the artifact to be developed in the iteration (that is, the change request) is an important prerequisite for success of the iteration. Proper scoping reduces the risk that the team is unable to complete and deploy the change within the timeframe of one sprint. Without scoping down a required change, it is also impossible to achieve short sprints of two, or even one, week duration. Furthermore, because of the Data Vault 2.0 model, the teams are now enabled to build their solution incrementally across lines of business – so they can be flexible in the scope of implementation.

Two common objections should be noted: the first one is to implement all tables from a source to keep the costs of integrating source systems low – in this case, loading data that is not required by the current solution. Loading this data requires additional ETL capacity, which requires a larger initial infrastructure. Also implementing all source tables from one source system might not be completed in one sprint and binds manpower that could be used to implement the feature to be delivered to the business. The effort often outweighs the complexity to assess the data already in the Data Vault (which is easy when focusing on tables). Another issue is that when implementing source tables into the staging area, it is a good practice to integrate the data in the Data Vault as well. Otherwise, additional complexity to assess the current state of the data warehouse is required when both systems are potentially out-of-sync. Loading all source tables completely requires complete modeling and loading of the corresponding Data Vault tables if this practice should be followed.

The second objection is that it is costly to touch the target multiple times in order to implement the final solution. This might be true, but the ultimate goal is to deliver working and useful features to the business within one sprint because it reduces the risk of failure: that the business doesn't accept the solution, for example because written requirements are not met, the requirements have changed in the meantime or the solution turns out to be the wrong one, once business users have actually used it.

This vertical approach to information delivery is performed within one sprint. Depending on the organizational capabilities, this might be two or three weeks in duration. Therefore, the modeling of the Data Vault shouldn't take months. Instead, the model should be created within the sprint's duration. If it takes longer, it is a good indicator that the scope of the sprint is too large. In that case, functionality should be removed from the sprint. Remove everything that is not required to be delivered with the single feature that is the focus of this sprint. Make sure that business users understand that this functionality is still to be delivered – but in later sprints. Oftentimes, business users think that the functionality is removed entirely because it is removed from the sprint under planning. However, this is wrong as the missing functionality will be delivered shortly, in the next or after-next iteration. Once business users have seen the progress of the project, they will naturally accept this procedure.

3.1.3.1 Agile Requirements Gathering

Before new functionality can be implemented in a sprint, it needs to be defined. However, the requirements-gathering process is very similar to the implementation process. Usually, business has a general idea about a function to be implemented in the data warehouse. But IT has many more questions that need to be answered, such as questions regarding the data source, business rules to aggregate or convert the data, data types, use cases, etc. To answer these questions, requirements gathering is used.

To support an agile approach to requirements gathering, requirements are gathered along the way, unlike classical data warehousing where these requirements are gathered at the beginning of the project. The approach that has worked best in our projects is to use *Raw Marts* and quickly roll out data into the requirements meeting for review. These Raw Marts are used for creating reports or cubes to a limited number of business users who attend the requirements meeting and are not intended for distribution. This is because the Raw Marts contain raw data with or without incomplete implementation of business rules. The exercise is to show these reports to the users and ask them: "what is wrong with this report?" It turns out that business users can easily point to the problems within the report and, by doing so, provide all the business rules IT needs to implement the final report.

The procedure for this approach to requirements gathering is as follows:

1. **Identify the required data:** As described in the previous section, the first step is to identify the sources for the Raw Mart and its report. Again, only the data which is in the scope should be loaded into the staging area and into the enterprise data warehouse. If possible, the data should be even reduced for rapid output. For example, data that is only needed for the final report, but not the intermediate raw report, should be left out in this first step.
2. **Produce the Raw Mart:** Once the data has been loaded to the Raw Data Vault, a Raw Mart is created from this raw data. There are no business rules implemented when loading the Raw Mart. Instead, the format of the data is simply changed from the Data Vault model to the dimensional model. Virtual views work best for this approach because they can be easily built.

3. **Produce Raw Reports:** As soon as the data is in the dimensional Raw Mart, it is possible to create Raw Reports. Because no business rules have been applied to the data, the report contains the good, the bad, and the ugly data.

Up to this point IT is in control of the time-to-deliver. They are responsible for being agile to this point. The next steps are driven from the business side of the project:

4. **Post Raw Reports on wall:** When the Raw Reports have been created from the Raw Mart, the reports are presented to the attendees of the requirements meeting. A good way is to print them and post them on one side of the room. If that is not possible or feasible, it is also possible to use an LCD projector to show the reports to the group. However, the advantage of printed reports on the wall is that attendees can take the time they need to review the report and add their comments or corrections directly to the printout. Most of the issues the report has become easily available to them. They can explain to IT what issues the reports have and why they can't use them in this state.

5. **Gather business rules and other requirements:** IT should directly ask the attendees what makes the report unusable and how this report can be made useful to the business. What modifications to the data are required to make the data correct? The answers of the business side are the missing business rules that need to be documented in the requirements document and applied to the data that goes into the Raw Report. Note that there should be less focus on the layout of the report, because this discussion should be driven by the business side, in the best case without dependency from IT.

As soon as the requirements have been gathered, at least partially, IT drives the project again, by implementing the business rules and other requirements:

6. **Translate business rules and other requirements:** The last step in this turn is to translate the business rules and other requirements, given by the business and documented in the requirements document, into program logic. This can be either done in ETL flows or virtually in SQL views. The business rules turn the raw data into information on the way from the Raw Data Vault to the Business Vault or the Information Mart.

After these business rules have been implemented by IT, the business side of the project can review and test the outputs and ask for further modifications if they are not yet satisfied with the end result. However, these modifications become change requests and are implemented in subsequent sprints. The described agile requirements-gathering process helps business users to express their business rules. For many of them, the traditional focus on requirements documents is too abstract and prevents the required identification from identifying issues with draft reports.

A recommended practice is to record these requirements meetings and set up a Wiki or other Web 2.0 enabled Web site that is available to everyone in the organization. The recordings from the meeting, including a description of the found business rules, should be posted on the Web site to ensure the transparency of the requirements-gathering process. Web 2.0 mechanisms enable participants to post comments or even modify the business rules according to their understanding. This approach makes sure that the requirements are correct in the first place. If a lot of discussion occurs on the Web site, another requirements meeting may be necessary to clarify any open issues before implementation should begin. Having these discussions before the actual implementation has taken place means a huge benefit and productivity boost to the organization and is a contributing factor to the overall success of the project. In order to make the right assumptions about the functionality that the team is able to complete in one sprint, which is important for scoping, the team has to be able to make correct estimates about the effort it takes to complete certain functionality. This topic is covered in the next section.

3.1.4 ESTIMATION OF THE PROJECT

The estimation process in the Data Vault 2.0 methodology depends on function point analysis (FPA). This approach is recommended over other estimation techniques, because it is based on the disaggregation of the functionality into individual items, which is fairly easy in Data Vault 2.0 (due to standardized artifacts). By using FPA, team members assess the required functionality of the data warehouse by calculating the function points of individual items and estimating the required hours to deliver the function points.

3.1.4.1 Function Point Analysis

Successful data warehouse projects require a realistic planning of the efforts to be done in the upcoming project. In order to perform a realistic planning, an accurate estimation technique is required. In order to estimate any piece of software, such as a data warehouse, metrics are used to measure the units of work that have been performed in the past and that will be performed in the future. Function points are the measure and are the key elements in function point analysis, an estimation technique widely used in software estimation [23].

With the use of function points, FPA is independent from technology-dependent metrics, such as lines of code (LOC) or other metrics that require a specific tool or platform to be measured [24]. Lines of code measures penalize high-level languages [25]. For example, the same functionality requested by a business user might require 100 lines of code in C# but 500 lines of code in C. Function points, however, measure the functionality that has been delivered to an end user or will be delivered in the future [23].

Figure 3.12 shows the functional characteristics of a software system in the airline industry.

The functional characteristics of software are made up of **external inputs (EI)**, which is the data that is entering a system; **external outputs (EO)** and **external inquiries (EQ)**, which is data that leaves the system one way or another; **internal logical files (ILF)**, which is data manufactured and stored within the system; **external interface files (EIF)**, which is data that is maintained outside the system but necessary to perform the task. The assessment of function points also includes the complexity of the general system.

In function point analysis, systems are broken into smaller components for better analysis [26]. The next section introduces the high-level steps to count function points and perform a function point analysis.

3.1.4.2 Measuring with Function Points

In order to measure the size of a software system, each of its components is analyzed for the characteristics outlined in the previous section. The International Function Point User Group (IFPUG), the organization behind function point analysis, recommends the following procedure of steps to perform the measurement [27,24]:

> **Step 1: determine function point count type.** Because the effort is counted differently for new or existing projects, the estimator has to pick one of the following three options:
> - Development project function point count
> - Enhancement project function point count
> - Application function point count.

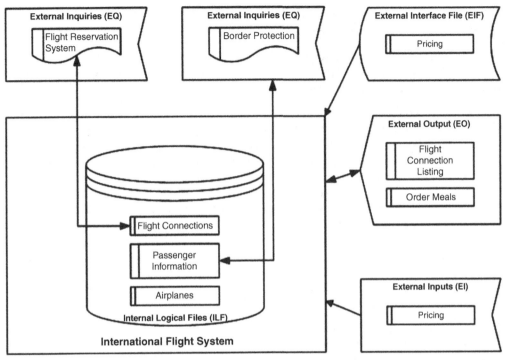

FIGURE 3.12

Functional characteristics of software [23].

Step 2: identify the counting boundary. Identify and define the boundary of the component to be measured. This is required to make a decision as to which functions are included in the count and which aren't. Also, it is required to distinguish internal from external files as well as inputs and outputs to the component.

Step 3: identify and count data function types. The previous section introduced two data function types: internal logical files (ILF) and external interface files (EIF). These functions represent the user functionality to meet the internal and external data requirements.

Step 4: identify and count transactional function types. Transactional function types represent the functionality of the system to meet user requirements regarding the processing of data. It includes external input (EI), external output (EO) and external inquiries (EQ).

Step 5: determine unadjusted function point count. The number of function types from step 3 and 4 are adjusted according to complexity.

Step 6: determine value adjustment factor. The value adjustment factor (VAF) indicates the overall value of the general system to the user by assessing the general functionality of the system. There are 14 general system characteristics that make up the factor.

Step 7: calculate final adjusted function point count. This is done using one of the following formulas, depending on the function point count type selected in step 1.

The described series of steps is valid for all software development efforts, including data warehousing projects. The next sections describe how this procedure can be applied in such projects.

3.1.4.3 Function Point Analysis for Data Warehousing

In order to apply function point analysis to data warehousing, estimators have to cope with a number of challenges that are specific to these types of projects [28]:

1. Data warehouse projects often depend on various technologies and tools to handle business problems. Each tool has advantages and limitations that have to be considered when estimating the effort.
2. The backend processes, such as the ETL for loading the data warehouse layer, often has many interlinked processes that are required to gather the required information. The result is an increased complexity that makes estimation complex in return.
3. The frontend, which consists primarily of OLAP cubes, reports, dashboards and other graphical user interfaces, has its own set of aspects that have to be taken into consideration when estimating the effort. Examples include the performance of the interfaces, understandability, etc.
4. When new functionality is added to the system, the project team has to ensure that existing functionality is not affected in a negative way by breaking it or introducing errors. Therefore the effort for regression tests on the data warehouse has to be considered.
5. Because data warehouses can load a large amount of data on a daily basis, the effort to perform load testing for new requirements has to be considered in the estimation process.

These challenges make the previously described process, which is used extensively in classical software engineering, a tough, if not impossible, task. This is due to the process orientation of software versus a subject-oriented view of data warehouses [28]. As a result, the process has to be adapted to be used in data warehousing.

3.1.4.4 Boundaries in Data Warehousing

The first transformation for the adaptation is to define the boundary of a "component" in data warehousing. Due to the layered approach in this field, every function has to be implemented in various layers of the system. The component is made up of all these changes (Figure 3.13).

Figure 3.11 shows that each capability is composed of staging tables, objects in the core data warehouse and the data mart. That includes all logic implemented in ETL, such as business rules. Also included are graphical elements such as reports, dimensions and measures in the OLAP cube and items on the dashboard.

3.1.4.5 Estimating Size

The second transformation is to define the function types that are used for estimation in data warehousing projects. Because data warehouse architectures often follow some form similar to the architectures described in Chapter 2, the mapping table shown in Table 3.2 is used during the estimation process.

The reason why **staging tables**, which are actually within the boundary of the data warehouse functionality, are considered as external interface files (as opposed to internal logic files) is that they primarily hold external data as a direct copy (enriched with some simple metadata). However, if internal processing is applied to these tables, they are considered as internal logic files [28].

For the same reasons, **target tables** are considered as internal logic files and not external to the boundary: they are updated with data processed within the boundaries of the data warehouse function [28].

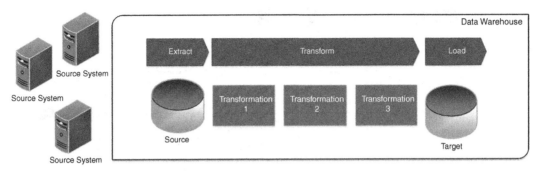

FIGURE 3.13

Data warehouse application boundary [28].

Figure adapted by author from Function Points Based Estimation Model for Data Warehouses, by Karthikeyan Sankaran. Copyright by Enterprise Warehousing Solutions, Inc. (www.EWSolutions.com). Reprinted with permission.

Mappings in the data warehouse implement the required logic by extracting data from source tables, transforming it, and loading it to the target tables. They are considered as external input (EI) because they alter the system's behavior by implementing the business rules [28].

Data warehouse mappings usually make extensive use of **lookup tables** which map codes with more descriptive data. For example, surrogate keys are mapped against business keys to support the understandability for end-users. Because they provide such data, these tables have more value to the business user than providing technical advantages. Therefore, they are considered as internal logic files (ILF) [28].

Process alerts notify external entities of the ETL process statuses and are considered as external output (EO) [28].

3.1.4.6 Assessing ETL Complexity Factors

The third transformation is to identify the factors that have an effect on the complexity of ETL processes. Typical complexity factors are provided in Figure 3.14.

Table 3.2 Mapping Data Warehouse Components to Function Point Types [58]	
DWH Component	**Function Point Type**
Staging tables	External interface file (EIF)
Target table	Internal logic file (ILF)
Fact table	Internal logic file (ILF)
Dimension table	Internal logic file (ILF)
Lookup table	Internal logic file (ILF)
Mapping	External input (EI)
Process alert	External output (EO)
Table adapted by author from "Function Points Based Estimation Model for Data Warehouses," by Karthikeyan Sankaran. Copyright by Enterprise Warehousing Solutions, Inc. (www.EWSolutions.com) Reprinted with permission.	

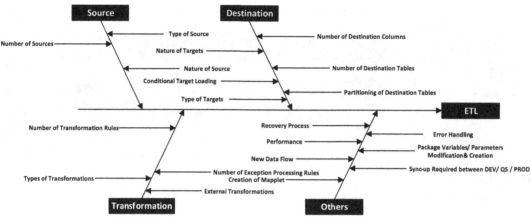

FIGURE 3.14

Cause and effect diagram for ETL complexity factors [29].

Figure adapted by author from "Function Points Based Estimation Model for Data Warehouses," by Karthikeyan Sankaran.
Copyright by Enterprise Warehousing Solutions, Inc. (www.EWSolutions.com). Reprinted with permission.

The figure shows the causes and effects of complexity factors on typical ETL projects. However, not all these factors are in correlation with the actual effort. They depend on the organization and project teams. To find out the factors that have an effect, a correlation analysis, for example using a step-wise forward regression analysis, is required.

A sample equation for a specific data warehouse project regression analysis could look like the one presented in Equation 3.1:

Sample equation for regression analysis [58]:

$$Actual\ Effort = A + B(x_5) - C(x_9) + D(x_{15}) - E(x_{16}) + F(x_{19}) + G(x_2x_4) + H(x_3x_4)$$

where x_5: Number of target columns

x_9: Type of transformation

x_{15}: Parameter file to be modified or created

x_{16}: New mapping

x_{19}: Unadjusted function points

x_2x_4: Amount of data processed * Number of transformations (interrelated factors)

x_3x_4: Performance criteria * Number of transformations (interrelated factors)

The actual equation for the project's regression analysis would also contain the regression coefficients that are depicted as characters A to H in Equation 3.1.

3.1.4.7 Applying Function Point Analysis to Data Warehousing

The overall goal of the estimation process is to standardize the business information system development by making the effort more predictable: because the development team estimates the required functionality using a systematic approach, it is possible to compare the estimated values with the actual values once the functionality has been delivered. When both values are compared against each other, team members can learn from those previous estimates and improve their future estimations.

The estimation process should support the IT team when the business asks for an estimated timeframe or effort for the requested functionality to be delivered. The ability to provide a profound answer is a core requirement from CMMI, in order to achieve capability levels higher than the initial/performed capability level. For example, FPA can be applied in capability level 2 (managed) in order to quantify the size of functional requirements in requirements management, estimate the effort and cost in project management, report function point data to management, etc [30].

In order to perform an estimation process using FPA, it is required to keep accurate metrics about past data warehouse development efforts to be able to use the experience from the estimation process for future estimations. This information is used to adjust the level of effort to the organization. The person hours depend on the complexity of the functionality. It should be clear that difficult functionalities will take longer to implement than easy functionalities (per calculated function point). Table 3.3 shows an example that is valid within one particular project.

Note that Table 3.3 has to be adjusted to each project under estimation and these values also change over time as developers are becoming more experienced or, due to turnover, lose experience in the team.

As we have seen in the previous discussion, the number of function points depends on the functional characteristic of the software to be built. To use FPA in the Data Vault 2.0 methodology, the functional characteristics of software (external inputs, external outputs, external inquiries, internal logical files, and external interface files) had to be adapted to reflect Data Vault projects. The following functional characteristics of data warehouses built with Data Vault are defined:

- Stage load
- Hub load
- Link load
- Satellite load
- Dimension load
- Fact load
- Report build

In the same way, it is possible to define other functional characteristics, e.g. for point-in-time (PIT) tables, bridge tables, Business Vault entities or OLAP cubes. In general, Data Vault 2.0 loading routines are EtL patterns (small-capital "t" for transform): there is only minimal transformation of the raw data required to load the Raw Data Vault. Therefore, the function points for those transformations should be low, leading to high levels of optimization, low levels of complexity, and simple function point counts.

Consider the exemplary list of function points per work item shown in Table 3.4, used to calculate the levels of effort.

Table 3.3 Person Hours per Function Point

Complexity Factor	Person Hours per Function Point
Easy	0.1
Moderate	0.2
Difficult	0.7

The example shows that each type of functionality has to be estimated independently from the other types. Column *Item* indicates the type of functionality. The second column indicates the complexity factor of the item. The shown values are typical. However, it is also possible that there are satellites in the easy and the moderate category (some satellites have a low number of attributes, which makes the load process much easier than the average). For that reason, multiple rows are added for satellites with varying complexity factors. The estimated function points indicate the number of function points counted for the item type. The *Estimated Total Hours* column is the product of the *Estimated Function Points* column in Table 3.4 and Person Hours per Function Point in Table 3.3.

Note that there is a distinction made between thin and wide satellites. This distinction refers to the number of columns and not the physical width of the table, which depends on the number of columns and the width of each column in bytes. In general, the more columns a satellite has, the more complex load logic is required, the more spelling errors might occur, and the more chances to load the wrong fields to the wrong targets or miss a column comparison occur. This is why this table distinguishes between such loads.

Similarly, the same concept is applied to unit tests in the second part of Table 3.4. For each item and the complexity for testing, the function points are estimated and enhanced with the total estimated

Table 3.4 Function Points and Level of Effort

Item Build Outs	Complexity Factor Build Outs	Estimated Function Points Build Outs	Estimated Total Hours Build Outs
Stage Load	Easy	2	0.2
Hub Load	Easy	2	0.2
Link Load	Easy	3	0.3
Thin Satellite Load	Easy	3	0.3
Wide Satellite Load	Moderate	4	0.8
Dimension Load	Difficult	4	2.8
Fact Load	Moderate	4	0.8
Report Build	Difficult	5	3.5
Unit Tests	**Unit Tests**	**Unit Tests**	**Unit Tests**
Stage Load	Easy	1	0.1
Hub Load	Easy	1	0.1
Link Load	Easy	1	0.1
Satellite Load	Easy	2	0.2
Dimension Load	Moderate	2	0.4
Fact Load	Easy	2	0.2
Report Build	Moderate	4	0.4

person hours, which are based on Table 3.3 again. Therefore, the second part of the table turns out to be very similar to the first part. However, it adjusts for different efforts between implementation and testing. Remember that this table has to be built individually for each project and updated over time. There might be additional differentiation required between less or more complex work items (such as the satellite loads in the example in Table 3.4). To get the process started, it is important to follow the general procedure as outlined before to come up with function point estimates that relate to the actual effort behind the items being built and to track the person hours required for implementation and testing behind these function points. Therefore, tracking the hours per function point becomes an important step in the first cycle of your development effort, before you can actually estimate effort in the future. This is due to the fact that estimates are driven from past experiences within a given context. It is not possible (without complex transformation) to use the experience from one context (e.g., one organization) to estimate the effort in another context, because there are many differences between organizations – for example, the maturity level, the experience levels of development staff and management, and the ratio between internal and external staff (who bring specialized experiences to the firm).

3.1.4.8 Function Points for Enterprise Data Warehouse

While the estimated hours per function point can be drawn directly from past projects or sprints, function points per item have to be decided differently (but this can be done organization-wide and needs less maintenance). There are some general rules for deciding how many function points should be associated with various items:

- **Staging tables:** The number of function points depends on the amount of required normalization. Consider the case of comma-separated values (CSV) flat files that require no normalization (for staging) because all columns can be added directly to staging. Compare this to XML or COBOL files that are not as easy to load into relational tables as CSV files, because of the substructures. In order to load such data, some normalization effort is required to transform the data from its structured format to a set of relational tables. You can avoid this normalization effort when loading the data into hierarchical tables (such as the XML data type), accepting a (serious) performance drop.
- **Staging and Data Vault loads:** Depending on the ETL complexity required for loading stage tables or Data Vault entities (such as hubs, links, satellites, etc.), the number of function points are different. Function points for hubs are generally the same, regardless of the size or composition of the business key. In all other cases, this is not true: the more hubs are connected to a link, the more function points should be associated, due to a slightly more complex ETL data flow (but again, all links connecting two hubs should have the same function points associated). Also the number of satellite attributes, satellite overloading and splitting makes a difference. However, focus on the complexity of the mapping itself for this functional characteristic. As a general rule: hubs are the easiest to load, links are easy to moderate, and satellites often moderate to difficult to load.
- **Information mart loads:** For these functional characteristics, the number and complexity of business rules and the number of additional columns that are implemented in the ETL load are the key factor. It is also a difference if you implement the business rules in ETL and or virtually in SQL views. In addition, there should be different function points for fact tables, dimensions, OLAP cubes, relational reports, etc.
- **Business Vault loads:** They are similar to information marts because they also implement business rules.

These general rules should provide guidance to development teams when deciding on the function points associated with individual functional characteristics. Note that the estimated person hours for development but also for maintenance are drastically reduced when automating the Data Vault loading process, a concept that is beyond the scope of this book.

When organizations advance through CMMI maturity levels, they will recognize that estimation based on function points becomes easier over time. This is due to consistent and repeatable business processes which are easier to predict because experiences from the past can be actually applied to such processes. Without such consistent execution, the estimates are not well founded because the circumstances of process execution change all the time. Well-defined standards help organizations to achieve such consistent and repeatable business processes. FPA also helps to promote measurable and optimizable components, which are required to perform estimates. This goal is supported by separation of the individual components that have to be delivered to business. Without this separation, estimates would overlap functionality and therefore make the estimates less accurate. Identifying the components also reduces the confusion over what is delivered and when. Because each component has to be identified and described, it is also possible to schedule the delivery of each component.

The overall goal of the estimation process is to make the data warehouse development effort more predictable. It helps to justify the costs of the data warehouse project and secure further funding from the business. Because correct estimates build trust into the development team and the business, they are therefore a central part of the Data Vault 2.0 methodology.

Once the team has decided what and how much it is going to deliver in the upcoming sprint, the focus goes over to project execution, which is covered in the next section.

3.2 PROJECT EXECUTION

Being agile, the Data Vault 2.0 methodology follows Scrum for team organization and uses an evolutionary and iterative approach similar to Scrum. The following guidelines help to make this approach a success:

1. **Envision initial architecture:** Because there is no time within a sprint to develop the final architecture in one step, an initial architecture is required that allows an evolutionary approach.
2. **Model details just-in-time:** Instead of modeling the whole enterprise data warehouse upfront, model only those areas that are required to deliver the functionality in the scope of the sprint.
3. **Prove architecture early:** Make sure that the architectural decisions are proven early. It is better to fail early in the process and make appropriate changes to the architecture than fail later (and hard); late changes to the architecture are very costly.
4. **Focus on usage:** Only implement functionality with direct business value.
5. **Avoid focusing on "the one truth":** Focus on the facts and the data (more details can be found in Chapter 1, sections 1.2.3 and 1.2.4).
6. **Organize work by requirements:** Because requirements are easier to document and modify than implementing them or modifying the implementation, there is great value for project execution having those requirements documented.
7. **Active stakeholder participation:** Follow Scrum by having a daily standup meeting. Make sure that stakeholders come to these meetings and participate.

The iterative approach is implemented in Data Vault 2.0 by two- to three-week sprints. The sprint length depends on the abilities of the organization. Usually, organizations start with longer cycles, such

Table 3.5 Agile Delivery Objective

Week	Activities
Week 1	Design & Develop
Week 2	Manage & Test
Week 3	Deployment & Acceptance

as three to four weeks, when beginning with agile methodologies but quickly try to reduce the sprint length in favor of more rapid deployments. The same applies in the Data Vault 2.0 methodology and confirms what we have seen in practice. A good start for organizations is to start with a three-week sprint and divide it into the activities shown in Table 3.5.

Table 3.5 shows that the team executes a "mini-waterfall" within the sprint. This waterfall follows the traditional software development life-cycle (SDLC) which is briefly outlined in section 3.2.1. The application of these concepts in the Data Vault 2.0 methodology is described in section 3.2.2.

3.2.1 TRADITIONAL SOFTWARE DEVELOPMENT LIFE-CYCLE

Traditionally, data warehouse projects have followed one variant of a software development life-cycle model, called the waterfall model [31]. While there are multiple versions of it in the literature, with different numbers and names of the phases, they all follow a phased approach. In addition, these models have an extensive planning in common, followed by comprehensive design, implementation, and testing. User input is given at the beginning of the process, and then transferred into the technical system during implementation and testing. Some of these phased models allow steps backward in the process, for example if system tests have uncovered issues that require additional user input. Figure 3.15 shows a representative version of the original waterfall method.

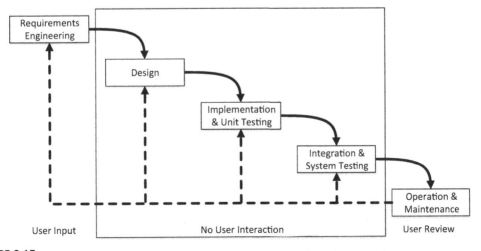

FIGURE 3.15

Waterfall model.

The figure shows that this particular model consists of five phases [32]:

1. Requirements engineering
2. Design
3. Implementation and unit testing
4. Integration and system testing
5. Operation and maintenance

The project team starts with the requirements engineering phase and advances through the pre-defined phases. In order to advance to the next phase, the team has to fully complete the current phase because there is no way back to the previous phase. In the waterfall methodology, the project usually fails if the results of a previous phase need to be modified. This inability to cope with changes during the life-cycle of the project is the major drawback of the waterfall model in data warehousing projects (similar to projects which deliver online transaction processing systems).

Despite its drawbacks, such as long project cycles [33], the waterfall model is the predecessor for many modern methodologies in data warehousing. Therefore, the next sections will cover the individual phases of the waterfall model in more detail.

3.2.1.1 Requirements Engineering

In this phase, the project team gathers and collects all business and technical requirements from the organization. The primary output of this phase is the "Data Warehouse Definition" document, which is the equivalent of the "Software Requirements Specification (SRS)" document in operational software engineering. The document fully describes all required features and limitations of the data warehouse to be built. That includes the following requirements:

- Business area data requirements
- Architecture requirements
- Audit requirements
- Archive requirements

The major challenge in this phase is to consolidate an unambiguous collection of the user requirements, which is often difficult because different user classes often have contradicting requirements. Therefore, this phase is often the most difficult and time-consuming phase in the waterfall model [32]. In order to collect system requirements, analysts use various traditional and modern methods. Traditional methods include the following [34]:

- **Interviewing individuals** with deep knowledge of the operations and business processes of the current and future system.
- **Observations of workers** at selected times to understand how data is handled and collect the information needs of those workers.
- **Analysis of business documents** to identify reported issues, policies, rules, and directions. In addition, specific examples of data and data usage within the organization are identified.

Modern methods include the following [34]:

- **Joint Application Design** that brings together key users, managers, and system analysts to collect system requirements simultaneously from key people.
- **Prototyping** to augment the requirements determination process.

These methods have in common to identify and gather the requirements from business users in order to provide them to the next process steps, which are described in the following sections.

3.2.1.2 Design

During the design phase, the data warehouse designers design the architecture of the data warehouse, such as the layers and each module of the system. The definition is based on the "Data Warehouse Definition" document and includes the database definitions of each layer, such as the structure of the staging area tables, the tables in the data warehouse layer and the star schema in the data mart. For each database, the names and columns of each table are defined [32]. Often, the database definition is performed using entity-relationship (ER) tools which are used to define and document the database. Microsoft SQL Server 2012 includes SQL Server Management Studio, which can be used to quickly create and populate each layer [35] using the Visual Database Tool Designer [36].

Another area of interest is the selection of the required hardware and software which is based on the performance, security and storage requirements of the whole system. In some projects, there is an existing infrastructure for data warehousing available. In such cases, new databases have to be created for the new project and the infrastructure provider will check whether there is enough capacity in the existing infrastructure to serve the new project. In other projects, where data warehousing is introduced to the organization, new infrastructure has to be created. This task should not be underestimated and often becomes an independent project with the procurement of hardware and supporting services, such as maintenance of the future data warehouse (think of backup and restore services, deployment of new features, bug tracking, end-user support, network maintenance, etc.).

3.2.1.3 Implementation and Unit Testing

Once the data warehouse has been described (in the requirements engineering phase) and designed (in the design phase), the individual modules of the system are implemented by the data warehouse developers. While they develop the modules, they also test the modules and remove errors found in this process [32].

There are various tools included in Microsoft SQL Server 2012 to build the data warehouse. Most of these tools can be found in Microsoft Business Intelligence Development Studio. This development environment includes the following tools [37]:

- SQL Server Integration Services for data integration
- SQL Server Analysis Services for developing multidimensional data warehouses (OLAP cubes) and performing data mining tasks
- SQL Server Reporting Services for developing reports based on relational and multidimensional data sources.

In addition, most teams use additional tools from Microsoft or third-party application vendors. Tools often used include:

- OLAP front-ends to easily browse OLAP cubes or provide advanced reporting capabilities
- Data mining environments to provide advanced analytical options to end-users
- ER tools for defining and documenting databases
- Tools for automating the data warehouse population, such as Data Definition Language (DDL) generators

- Data profiling tools to better understand the raw data
- Data quality tools for data cleansing and assessment.

3.2.1.4 Integration and System Testing

While the data warehouse developers have implemented and tested the modules of the data warehouse in individual units, the integration of each unit takes part in this phase. The individual units are connected to each other and integrated. This integration process starts with some modules at the bottom of the architecture which are fully integrated and tested (Figure 3.16).

Once the tests have passed, the modules are added to the system by integration. After the integration of these units has been completed, the whole system is tested again. When all units at the bottom that can be integrated with each other are integrated, the integration team moves to the next level and integrates the larger parts. The new larger unit is tested again to check whether all subunits work together seamlessly [32].

Because such a testing approach requires running many tests over and over again, tools for test automation are often used in this phase.

3.2.1.5 Operation and Maintenance

In the last phase of the waterfall model, the data warehouse is handed over to operations where the system is installed at the end-user premises for regular use. If end-users find bugs in the data warehouse, the operations team is responsible for correcting those bugs and handling other modifications of the data warehouse. This continuous process is performed until the data warehouse retires or is replaced by a new data warehouse [32].

In order to support the operations and maintenance team, the data warehouse team which develops the solution has to provide both an end-user and administration documentation, including specific instructions for the maintenance of the data warehouse (such as loading new data deliveries or customizing existing reports).

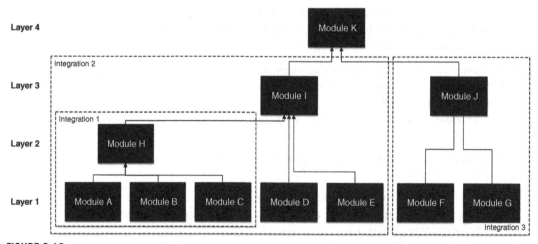

FIGURE 3.16

Bottom-up testing [38].

3.2.2 APPLYING SOFTWARE DEVELOPMENT LIFE-CYCLE TO THE DATA VAULT 2.0 METHODOLOGY

The Software Development Life-Cycle is applied within a sprint of the Data Vault 2.0 methodology, as a mini-waterfall. To execute this mini-waterfall, a project plan is used. Table 3.6 shows an example for implementing a new report.

The *ID* identifies the task in the project management tool, such as Microsoft Project. It is primarily used internally, such as in the *Predecessors* column, which provides information about dependencies between individual tasks. The *WBS* column is used to add a project-wide reference string to the task. The next section discusses how to utilize this identifier. Column *Task Name* provides a user-readable name and *Duration* the estimated amount of time that is needed in order to complete the task. In addition

Table 3.6 Agile Project Plan

ID	WBS	Task Name	Duration	Predecessors
1	3	**Agile Delivery of Single Requirements**	**58 hrs**	
2	3.1	Choose Report to Produce (Scope)	0.5 hrs	
3	3.2	Estimate Work Effort	0.5 hrs	2
4	3.3	Fill in Risk Assessment	0.5 hrs	3
5	**3.4**	**Identify Source/Stage Tables for Report**	**4 hrs**	**4**
6	3.4.1	Source to Requirements Matrix	4 hrs	
7	3.5	Design ER Data Vault Model	2 hrs	3
8	3.6	Add Attributes to ER Data Vault Model	6 hrs	7
9	**3.7**	**Create ETL Data Vault Loads**	**4 hrs**	**8**
10	3.7.1	Create Hub Loads	1 hr	
11	3.7.2	Create Link Loads	1 hr	
12	3.7.3	Create Satellite Loads	2 hrs	
13	3.8	Design Data Mart Model for Report	4 hrs	3
14	**3.9**	**Create ETL Data Vault to Information Mart**	**16 hrs**	**13**
15	3.9.1	Build Dimension Loads	8 hrs	
16	3.9.2	Build Fact Loads	8 hrs	15
17	3.10	Build Report and Produce Output	8 hrs	13
18	3.11	Create Source-to-Target Report for Project Documentation	2 hr	5;8;13
19	3.12	Unit Test	4 hrs	17
20	3.13	Record Actual Effort	0.5 hrs	
21	3.14	Sign-off	1 hr	20
22	3.15	Deploy to Test Environment	2 hrs	
23	3.16	Run User Acceptance Test	2 hrs	
24	3.17	Deploy to Production	1 hr	22;23

to the duration, many projects add a *Work* column that is used to estimate the work effort. This is required, because there is a difference between the work required and the duration when more than one full-time employee can work on a task. This can be used in addition to the estimates from Function Point Analysis (refer to section 3.1.4). Most project management tools, including Microsoft Project, support an optional *Notes* column, not shown in Table 3.6, which can be used to include references to additional dependencies (using their technical number) in order to identify the remainder of the artifacts. This concept is equal to the project-wide reference string in the WBS column and is described in one of the next sections, as well.

Note that the project plan in Table 3.6 shows durations that are calculated for a two-week sprint, with 58 hours total. This example also assumes that automation tools are used for creating the ETL Data Vault loads (item 3.7). If this is not the case, it is recommended to add detail tasks for hub, link, and satellite loads (beneath items 3.7.1, 3.7.2, and 3.7.3). If the length of the sprint is different (either three weeks or a different number of work hours per week), it is possible to recalculate the durations accordingly. Recalculating the sprint lengths might be required if you don't use automation tools, because it will be difficult to achieve a two-week sprint without automation. Note that some task durations should keep the times depicted in Table 3.6 because the duration is static (the sign-off procedure is such an example). It makes no sense to add 50% to the duration when transforming this table into a three-week sprint. At any rate, it is required to adjust the durations to the needs of the project. And while scoping (task ID 2 to 4) is critical to the success of the project, it should be noted that the task should not require more than two hours.

There are variations to this project plan for sprints that focus on other activities than implementation, for example for requirements gathering, user acceptance testing, or infrastructure setup.

The project plan also shows that there are certain deliverables produced over the course of the project. This is not only limited to database models or ETL data flows. A focus of the Data Vault 2.0 methodology is to produce documentation valuable for both the business and IT. Necessary documentation includes:

- **Business glossary:** This document helps building information marts because business objects and terms that are related to them are identified and documented.
- **Requirements documentation:** This document describes the information marts and reports in detail. There should be no functionality in the data warehouse solution that has no corresponding requirement recorded in this document. This document should be kept rather short, e.g., by using user stories around one page per requirement.
- **Project plan:** The project plan focuses only on tasks that need to be executed during one sprint.
- **Abbreviations glossary:** Common abbreviations in the business or in the technological field of data warehousing are provided in this document.
- **Scope or statement of work document:** This document describes the scope of the sprint and reflects what was agreed upon. It is an important source for the sign-off procedure at the end of the sprint.
- **Change request document:** Each request to change requirements that have already been implemented requires a documented process that is based on a change request document.
- **Delivery and sign-off document:** When the project team delivers new functionality at the end of the sprint, it requires a sign-off from the business before it can get rolled out. This document states that the delivery meets or exceeds expectations as outlined in the requirements documentation or change request document.

- **Roles and responsibilities:** This document identifies the roles in the project team and the responsibilities that are associated with them.
- **Work breakdown structure:** Breaks down the overall deliverable (the data warehouse solution) into manageable components.
- **Process breakdown structure:** Each business process supported by the data warehouse should be described using a business process diagram. It should be modeled to a level of detail in which data sets and their business keys can be identified.
- **Data breakdown structure:** For each (scoped) business report, there are two tables: one that maps the report to source tables, and the other that maps the report to the Data Vault source for the information mart output.
- **Organizational breakdown structure:** This structure displays organizational relationships and can be used to assign resources to the project. It is created in conjunction with the work breakdown structure. It also links individual team members to the roles as defined in the roles and responsibilities document.
- **Data model standards:** The data model standards document provides naming conventions for Data Vault entities, facts and dimensions, and attributes of those entities. It provides information about agreed standards to model specific entities, system attributes, etc.
- **ETL standards:** This document describes how control or data flows are implemented, such as naming conventions, documentation requirements, and physical design issues, among others.

Above list shows that some of these documents reference each other. To maintain this process, it is recommended to use project-wide technical numbering (a concept described in section 1.2.4) to identify each artifact in the documentation and in the implemented solution. Otherwise, it is not possible to uniquely cross-reference these artifacts within the project. Figure 3.17 shows an organizational breakdown structure example.

In this structure, each role is associated with a team member whose name is given in the diagram. Project management standards such as the project management professional (PMP) require that project plans track roles instead of individual people because individuals can play only a partial role in a project, but each role must be filled to 100% effort. Otherwise the project schedule cannot be met. The same is true for CMMI. In addition, each role is identified by using technical numbering. Note that if there were two ETL developers, both would have the same technical number, because the technical number is a cross-reference to the roles and responsibility document, described in the previous list. It is not uncommon that an individual person fills multiple roles. We have seen individuals filling more than four roles!

3.2.3 PARALLEL TEAMS

Having defined roles and responsibilities helps to scale the project up by adding more team members and entire teams to the project. Each team operates on small scoped deliveries, with no dependencies to other teams. All work is done in parallel with little or no synchronization required. They use the same templates as defined in this chapter, and produce documentation that follows the same guidelines. When implementing and delivering business requirements, the teams who work in parallel synchronize their data models using the link entity, which is discussed in Chapter 5, Intermediate Data Vault Modeling.

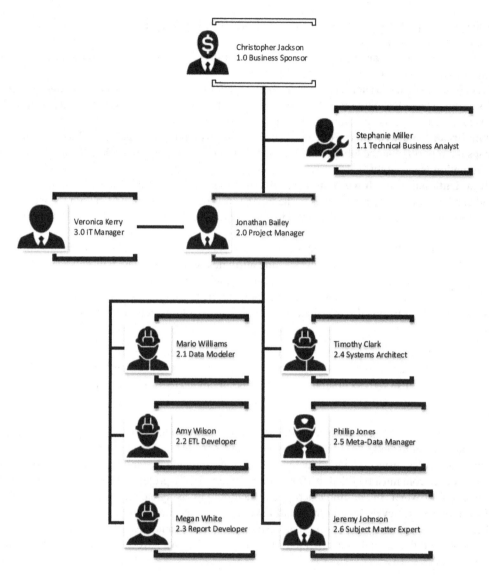

FIGURE 3.17

Example of an organizational breakdown structure.

With an existing Data Vault team, new team members are not required to have a lot of prior knowledge or Data Vault skills. In order to add new human resources to a running project, the following skills, besides the knowledge of the development environment and development rules, are required (by task):

- **Source to stage loading:** New team members need to know how to create new stage tables and load the data from source tables. In the best case, this requires only a CREATE TABLE and an INSERT INTO … SELECT FROM construct in SQL.

- **Stage to hub and link loading:** Again, very similar and simple. It requires only a SELECT DISTINCT, some filtering to handle only nonexisting records, and INSERT INTO statement to load hubs and links.
- **Stage to satellite loading:** When using only SQL statements, only a SELECT DISTINCT, row comparison, and an INSERT to store the actual data.

This list should make it clear that it is not required to have a lot of Data Vault skills to add *additional resources* to a project where Data Vault experts are already existent. The more experienced developers and modelers can guide new team members to accomplish these tasks. Note that these skills are applicable for teams without using ETL tools. In addition to these skills, knowledge is required in the selected ETL tool, such as Microsoft SQL Server Integration Services. Chapter 12, Loading the Data Vault, shows how to actually load the data into the Data Vault using Microsoft SQL Server.

In addition to parallel implementation of business requirements, there are other teams that are focused on different activities in the project, such as requirements gathering, data mining, managed self-service BI, etc. These activities are also run in parallel to the implementation.

3.2.4 TECHNICAL NUMBERING

Section 1.2 introduced a concept called technical numbering that was used in project documentation to identify individual artifacts. Technical numbering is the assignment of decimal point based numbers to text documents and paragraphs that describe artifacts and other pieces of important information. It is also called scientific numbering. The goal is to identify each artifact in the documentation and in the implemented solution uniquely within the project. It should be applied to *every* document or artifact produced or utilized within *every* project or sprint.

Examples for artifacts are:

- **One single role** in the roles and responsibilities document
- **One change request** in the change request document
- **One single requirement** in the requirements document
- **One task** in the project plan
- **One business object** in the business glossary
- **One abbreviation** in the abbreviation glossary

When assigning technical numbers to these artifacts, a hierarchical and incremental approach is used. The numbering is incrementally assigned to each artifact, reflecting the hierarchy as well. Table 3.6 has shown this approach by assigning dot-separated numbers to each task. Each subtask was assigned a number that was prefixed with the WBS number of the parent task, separated by a dot from the incremented number of the subtask.

If technical numbering is applied in document processing software, such as Microsoft Word, it is a good practice to manually assign the numbers and avoid using automated numbering of headings, because these automatic numbers are reassigned when a heading is inserted in between two other headings or they get rearranged. It is important to avoid changing technical numbers once they have been assigned to an artifact. There should be no renumbering of these artifacts in order to support cross-referencing between applications.

There are different applications where these artifacts are cross-referenced by their technical numbers:

- **Requirements to source tables:** This is probably the most powerful cross-reference mapping because it identifies the source tables and the attributes that are used by a specific requirement.

There should be one line per requirement to identify the sources for all requirements. This is one of the *data breakdown structures* as mentioned in the previous section.

- **Source tables to Data Vault tables:** This mapping is created before the ETL jobs to load the Data Vault tables are created and indicate the source table and Data Vault targets.
- **Data Vault tables to information mart tables:** Similar to the previous mapping, this document shows how the data is mapped from the Data Vault tables to the information mart. This document should be a simple matrix without indication to business rules. They are supposed to be documented in the requirements documentation.
- **Requirements to information mart tables:** This matrix is similar to the first mapping and indicates the information mart tables that are used by specified requirements. Again, there should be one line per requirement. This is the second *data breakdown structure* as mentioned in the previous section.

The best approach is to provide these mappings as cross-reference matrix tables in a modeling tool or (if no better option is available) in a spreadsheet program, such as Microsoft Excel. Table 3.7 exemplifies how a data breakdown structure should look.

Table 3.7 shows *requirements to target map*, also known as *requirements to information mart tables*. It describes which information mart dimension or fact tables are used by a given report or OLAP item. There are three reports in this example: *Passenger*, *Airplane Utilization* and *Connections*. While the *Passenger* report uses only the *Passenger Information* table in the information mart, the *Connections* report uses the *Connections* and the *Airplanes* table. These entity names are the logical names; the physical names are also provided as a reference. In addition, this table references the requirements document where the reports are defined in more detail (there might be multiple requirements documents in a project if the team decides to split the requirements up, e.g. per function, etc.).

It is a good practice to use acronyms as a prefix to the technical number, to provide an easy indicator of the artifact type that is being numbered.

Table 3.7 Requirements to Information Mart Tables Example

Requirements to Target Map XREF

Requirement Document: MyDoc

Table

Logical Name	Physical Name	Business Key	Passenger	Airplane Utilization	Connections
Passenger Information	PASSENGER		X		
Connections	CONNECTION				X
Airplanes	AIRPLANE			X	X

Table 3.8 Example Acronyms for Artifact Types

Document Type	Acronym
Business Requirements	B2.2
Technical Requirement	T5.1
Organizational Breakdown Structure	O3.3
Process Breakdown Structure	P2.4
Data Breakdown Structure	D23.2
Work Breakdown Structure	W9.9
Change Requests	C25.5

Table 3.8 shows only examples for such acronyms. Usually, organizations already have a set of acronyms in place, which should be utilized.

The ability to identify single documents and artifacts is a prerequisite for measuring them. Without proper identification, this is not possible because actual efforts cannot be correctly associated with them. And without the ability to measure the actual effort, it is not possible to compare it to the planned effort and, in turn, not possible to optimize the development processes. This optimization of development processes is performed in the review and improvement phase of the sprint. The required concepts are described in the next section.

3.3 REVIEW AND IMPROVEMENT

Before the team completes a sprint and starts with the next one, the team goes into two relatively short meetings:

- **Sprint review meeting** [39]: during this meeting, the produced artifacts are reviewed by the team, the product owner, and other stakeholders, such as the end-user.
- **Retrospective meeting** [40]: just after the sprint review meeting, the development team meets to identify those activities during the sprint that need improvement.

The first meeting focuses on the product: participants review whether the features meet the expectations and the documented requirements. For that reason, the participants in the meeting are relatively broad and include everyone who has a stake in the features under review. If the attendees in the meeting identify problems or variations from the defined requirements, a change request has to be created and implemented in a subsequent sprint. In order to perform this review meeting, the team must be able to identify the features that are expected and trace them all the way back to the initial requirements. This is why technical numbering, outlined in section 1.2.4, plays such an important role in the Data Vault 2.0 methodology. Improving the project outcomes is not possible if the team is unable to fully identify the source of issues, but this is a requirement for successful optimization of the project.

The optimization of the project also requires reviewing the process itself. This is done during the retrospective meeting. The team reviews the activities that have been performed during the iteration and decides how to improve them in order to improve the overall project execution. The process review also includes a review of the initial estimates for the change requests of the iteration. This is performed for the very same motivation: to identify the causes for under- or overestimation and stop them. Sometimes, agile teams argue that agile development doesn't require estimation of change requests. But this is a problem in enterprise organizations, as overall project management needs estimates in project controlling and budgeting.

3.3.1 SIX SIGMA

Six Sigma plays an important role in this process improvement effort. The principles from Six Sigma are applied in order to achieve maximum optimization in agility of the process of building and implementing enterprise data warehouse systems with the Data Vault 2.0 standard. Six Sigma relies on measurements (estimates vs. actuals), or KPIs to determine what went wrong at the project level, how badly out of alignment the sprint is, and what needs to be done to the process to bring it back into compliance.

This is the process side of Six Sigma as applied to "error correction" or "optimization" of the process of building business intelligence systems. Note that these measurements and KPIs should measure teams, not individual team members. By doing so, the Data Vault 2.0 methodology puts people first, as in other agile methodologies, including Disciplined Agile Delivery (DAD) [13]. If people realize that they are in fact being measured, they will find ways to subvert such measurements. It is also illegal to measure the productivity of individuals in certain legislations [13]. Consider metrics as potential indicators for performance. To find out what the real causes of the problems in a project are, talk to the people in the project, because they most probably know what's going on [13].

Six Sigma also applies to the data itself, when we turn data into information and deploy it to the business and test environments. How many "bugs" were found in testing is a metric that indicates how "bad" the data is and how many errors have been found. Measuring the errors using Six Sigma provides metrics around the quality of the processes being built within the business intelligence system. The fewer errors that are made (over time) and the more optimized and streamlined the processes become, the better, faster and cheaper the team can execute, and the more agile the team will be.

Six Sigma is a very popular program to eliminate defects from process and products [41]. It is "a strategic initiative to boost profitability, increase market share and improve customer satisfaction through statistical tools that can lead to breakthrough quantum gains in quality."[42] The program is a "new strategic paradigm of management innovation" and fosters "statistical measurement, management strategy and quality culture."[43] The advantage of Six Sigma is that it provides information about the quality of products and services and creates quality innovation and total customer satisfaction. In addition, Six Sigma maintains a quality culture [44].

The key concept behind Six Sigma is to improve the performance of processes to attempt three targets [44]:

1. Reduce the costs of the processes
2. Improve customer satisfaction
3. Increase revenue and thereby increase profits.

A process in Six Sigma is defined as in most other disciplines of management. It is an activity or series of activities that transform inputs to outputs by using a repetitive process.

There are many types of inputs to processes that apply to data warehousing projects: labor, material (such as office supplies), decisions, information and measurements. While a product is the predominant output for the processes of most companies in manufacturing, it could also be a process or other deliverable as in R&D-centric organizations [44].

It is common that the results of a process execution vary in terms of quality, even if the process itself is of a repetitive nature. No two products are the same and the differences might be large or immeasurably small. But they are always present. It is possible to analyze the variation of the process outcome and then measure and visualize the outcome. There are three characterizations that describe the variation [44]:

- Location (the average value of the quality)
- Spread (the span of values)
- Shape (the variation's pattern).

The more variation a process has, the lower the quality of the output. Hence, it is the number one enemy of quality control [44]. However, the variation depends on other factors in the organization or project, which are depicted in Figure 3.18.

The variation in Six Sigma is equivalent to the standard deviation, a statistical measurement of variation. In statistics, this variation is denoted by the Greek sigma letter: σ. Six standard deviations is the definition of outcomes as close as possible to perfection. As Figure 3.18 shows, the other factors are cycle time and yield. The yield is the success rate of the process outcomes, expressed as a percentage, indicating the percent of outputs with an acceptable quality [45]. Table 3.9 provides an overview of the performance levels that can be reached with various levels of standard deviations (hence variations) [45].

Sources for variation are manifold. The types of variation are classified into common causes and special causes.

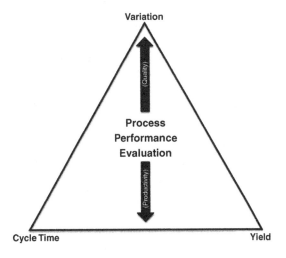

FIGURE 3.18

Process Performance Triangle [44].

Table 3.9 Sigma Table [55]

Sigma	Defects per Million	Yield
0.0	933,193.0	6.7 %
0.5	841,345.0	15.9 %
1.0	691,462.0	30.9 %
1.1	655,422.0	34.5 %
1.2	617,911.0	38.2 %
1.3	579,260.0	42.1 %
1.4	539,828.0	46.0 %
1.5	500,000.0	50.0 %
2.0	308,538.0	69.1 %
2.5	158,655.0	84.1 %
3.0	66,807.0	93.32 %
4.0	6,210.0	99.379 %
5.0	233.0	99.977 %
6.0	3.4	99.9997 %

Common causes happen in every repetitive process that has a stable and repeatable distribution over time. It is not easy to remove common causes. Only if the design of the process itself is changed, it is possible to reduce common causes (but also the redesign might introduce new variation). There-fore, variations that are classified into common causes are found everywhere. The upper part of Figure 3.19 shows the variation of a stable and predictable process with variation resulting from com-mon causes.

The second type is the **special causes**, also called assignable causes. This is displayed in the second part of Figure 3.20. These factors refer to causes that are uncommon to the typical process and change the process distribution. If these factors are left unaddressed in the process, they will affect the process output in an unpredictable way. The existence of special causes prevents stable processes [32].

3.3.1.1 Applying Six Sigma to Software

Six Sigma was originally designed and developed for manufacturing and other processes that are more mature than software engineering processes. However, because it is a domain-independent initiative, it is possible to apply the concepts of Six Sigma to other, less mature disciplines as well. That is because software engineering follows a process model somewhat similar to processes in manufacturing. How-ever, software engineering processes often include innovative and creative tasks, but that is actually similar to other engineering processes. To the process definition given in this chapter, it doesn't matter if a process is ad-hoc, different every time, or highly repetitive. In any case, it is a process that follows our definition [46].

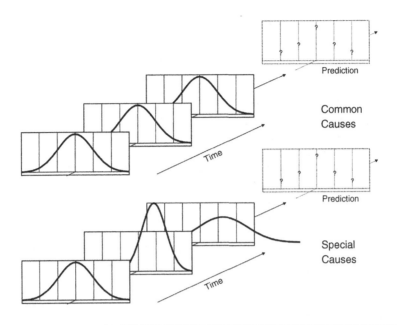

FIGURE 3.19

Common and special causes for variation [32].

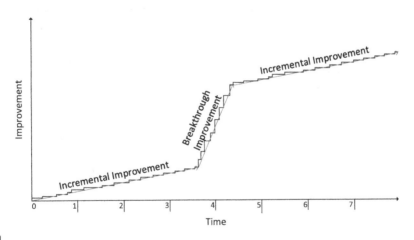

FIGURE 3.20

Breakthrough results in Six Sigma [47].

It is possible to collect a large number of measures regarding the processes in software engineering [46]:

- the time between start and end of a process step
- the number and quality of outputs
- the estimated product performance
- etc.

And because the owners of the processes have the same interests as the ones in their manufacturing counterparts, e.g., improving the quality of the process output, improving performance, better meeting customer needs, etc., Six Sigma can be applied to software engineering processes as well. However, because of differences between software engineering and other engineering disciplines, additional thought is required [46].

Often, the **overall process cycle time is much longer** in software engineering than in creating machine-manufactured goods. Therefore, Six Sigma projects might take longer or might have a greater risk, due to less data for statistical analysis [46].

The **intensity of human interaction** is much higher than in many other manufacturing areas. It also involves creative elements throughout the project life-cycle. Six Sigma teams might focus on the repetitive tasks within the project (such as inspections) or they might focus on the human factors. In any case, it is important to carefully normalize the data to make sure that the comparisons are valid [46].

In software engineering, there is only one master copy produced. The duplication of this master copy is simple and can be easily made without variation of the produced output. However, developing the subcomponents of the software is done only once and there might be **variation between the individual subcomponents** of the final product. Another source of variation is the implementation of the software into the user's environment [46].

3.3.1.2 Six Sigma Framework

Corporations that decide to implement Six Sigma in their organizations rely on a Six Sigma framework with several important components. There are three major elements that drive the framework: top management commitment, stakeholder involvement and the improvement strategy. The latter consists of the five DMAIC steps (define, measure, analyze, improve, and control; see next section for details) and is based on training schemes, project team activities and the measurement system [32]. All these components drive the three different Six Sigma functions: Design for Six Sigma, Manufacturing Six Sigma, and Transactional Six Sigma [32].

Top level management commitment is required because Six Sigma is a strategic management decision that has to be initiated by top-level management. In order to become a success, all elements of the framework, including the improvement strategy, require top-level management commitment [32]. Special attention by the top management should be given to the training program and project team activities, because they are seldom successful without strong top-level commitment. It should be clear that true commitment is required and not just empty promises. Instead, pragmatic management is required that drives the initiative for several years [32].

However, not only is the top management committed to the Six Sigma initiative success. Instead, full **stakeholder involvement** is required. All employees, suppliers, customers, owners and parts of the close society should become involved in the Six Sigma improvement process. The majority of activities are performed by employees who need support by top management, for example in the availability of training courses, project team activities and evaluation of process performance. Key suppliers to the organization are encouraged to start their own Six Sigma initiatives and are supported by information sharing and participation at in-house trainings. Financial support to smaller companies is also not uncommon [32].

The success of any Six Sigma initiative depends on skilled stakeholders, such as employees. A comprehensive knowledge of the improvement methodology, the process performance and statistical tools is required. It is also important to understand the processes of the project team activities and how to deploy customer requirements. It should be clear that this skillset is not readily available within the organization and has to be built using training schemes and other knowledge transfer. For this purpose, Six Sigma provides standardized training courses with various levels. These levels are denoted by the belt rank system from martial arts: there are White Belts, Green Belts, Black Belts, Master Black Belts and Champions [32]. Importance is given to Black and Green Belts because they become the center of the Six Sigma team.

The job of the Black and Green Belts is to keep the project focused [47]. The following procedure is recommended for **project team activities** [32]:

1. Set up the Six Sigma team and establish the long-term management vision for the organization.
2. Educate Six Sigma champions first.
3. Select the business areas of the first introduction of Six Sigma processes.
4. Educate Six Sigma Green Belts and Black Belts.
5. Appoint Black Belts as full-time project managers to process areas in order to focus on critical quality problems.
6. Strengthen the infrastructure towards Six Sigma, for example by introducing knowledge management, statistical process control, and database management systems.
7. Make sure that top management checks the progress of Six Sigma project teams. Introduce a regular "Six-Sigma" day and organize presentations or awards for accomplishments.

To uncover new areas for process improvement, Six Sigma depends on a pragmatic **system for measuring** performances. It reveals poor process performance and helps to identify future problems that have to be dealt with. The measurement depends on characteristics of the product that are tracked over time and consolidated. Results are typically visualized in trend charts and other graphical illustrations [32].

As already indicated, the improvement strategy is based on the DMAIC steps for improvement. The next section covers them in detail.

3.3.1.3 DMAIC Improvement

The improvement strategy introduced in the last section is based on the DMAIC steps, an approach that is also called the *Breakthrough approach*.

The first step in the approach is to **define** the problem and clearly describe the impact on customer satisfaction stakeholder's employees, and profitability. The project members define the following [48]:

- Requirements that are critical for the customer
- Project goals and objectives
- Team roles and responsibilities
- Project scope and resources
- Process performance baseline
- Process map, including the supplier, input, process, output, and customer.

It is important in this step to gather and document the customer requirements and, once understood, send them towards the operational level where project goals and objectives are set. There are several techniques that support the project team, including [48]:

- Project charter
- Stakeholders' commitment analysis

- Affinity diagrams
- Voice of the customer
- Quality analysis
- Force field analysis
- Pareto analysis
- Process mapping

The second step is to **measure** the current performance to identify opportunities for improvement. After changes have been done, the business can measure its success by comparing the new performance with the past performance baseline. Several statistical tools are available for the measurement: including averages, standard deviation and probability distributions.

After having identified issues in the process, the next step is to search for the root cause during the **analyze** phase. Opportunities for improvement are prioritized by two dimensions: their contribution to customer satisfaction and the impact on profitability [48].

The **improvement** step implements the opportunities identified in the previous step. Project members develop solution candidates and select the solution with the best results and performance. While other improvement frameworks develop solutions by varying one variables of the process at a time, Six Sigma is using statistically designed experiments to vary multiple variables simultaneously and obtain multiple measurements under the same experimental conditions [48].

The last step of DMAIC improvement is the **control** step. Its goal is to control the improved processes and to make sure that the Six Sigma initiative sustains. If, however, the results of the improvements made in the last steps are at risk, the DMAIC improvement can start again, as Figure 3.21 shows.

3.3.1.4 Applying Six Sigma to Data Warehousing

Both meetings, the sprint review meeting and the retrospective meeting, are required if the organization aims to reduce the iteration length from four to three weeks or from three to two weeks. Without constant improvement of both the ability to deliver the right features in the expected quality and the

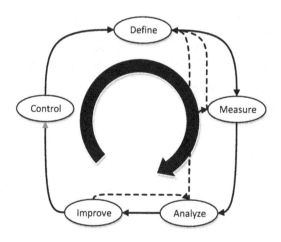

FIGURE 3.21

DMAIC improvement methodology [49].

activities that lead to these artifacts (the process perspective), the team will not be able to achieve such goals. If teams want to reduce the iteration lengths, they have to review the activities themselves and check how much time is spent on each individual activity. The team then decides where too much time is spent (e.g., on documentation, implementation, etc.) and has to figure out how to reduce the time for these activities. In some cases, technology might help, for example blue-green-deployment, which we will describe in Chapter 8, Physical Data Warehouse Design, or ETL automation. In other cases, scoping is key to achieving shorter sprint durations by removing the functionality that is not required in the first deployment of a feature. Another factor is the people themselves: additional training can help to achieve such improvements regarding the duration, or more and better resources (technology, organizational and human resources).

With this approach in mind, there is not much difference between software development and data warehouse development in respect to Six Sigma. Therefore, the same concepts as regarding the application of Six Sigma to software apply (see previous section titled "Applying Six Sigma to Software").

3.3.2 TOTAL QUALITY MANAGEMENT

In order to achieve superior quality, management and teams often refer to Total Quality Management (TQM), a set of theories, methods, techniques and quality strategies for achieving quality to compete against world-wide competition. TQM is a management process, with the emphasis on continuous quality improvement. The term *Total* in TQM refers to the fact that everyone in the organization and every organizational function should participate in the continuous improvement of quality. In that sense, *Quality* means to meet or exceed user expectation on a product's or service's quality. *Management* means to improve and maintain business systems, including their related processes and activities [50]. Typical activities include [50]:

- Design of experiments
- Quality circles
- Value engineering
- Cost of quality
- Information systems
- Taguchi methods
- Total productive maintenance
- Statistical process control
- Quality assurance
- Robust design
- Computer-integrated design
- Quality function deployment
- Continuous improvement
- Participative management

Not included are activities that are primarily of interest in the manufacturing industry, such as Manufacturing Resource Planning. However, some of the activities can be transferred to data warehouses, especially for DWH systems built with the Data Vault standard. Also, there are activities that are already described in other concepts in this chapter (or will be described in subsequent sections). For example, **participative management** is already applied in Scrum: instead of making decisions at the top of the project organization, decision authority is delegated further down the organizational line. The same is true for TQM: responsibility is extended to the lowest possible level. Project members must be empowered to make an informed decision to improve the quality of the product or service. They make decisions in this regard without prior approval from superiors [50].

Typical TQM implementation efforts follow a phased approach that consists of the five phases as presented in Figure 3.22.

As the figure shows, the five phases are the **preparation phase** where considerable time, thought, resources, and energy are expended *before* the implementation of TQM to reduce the risk of failure [50]; the **planning phase** where people get together and set up time tables and objectives [50]; the assessment phase that is used to better understand the internal organization, external products or services provided,

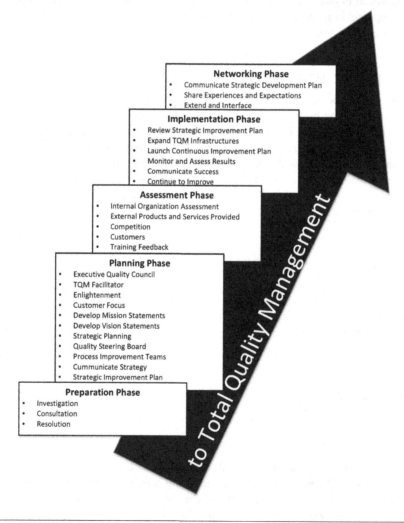

FIGURE 3.22

Successful TQM implementation in five phases [50].

competition, and customers [50]; the **implementation phase** in which quality practices and their support systems are deployed within the organization [50]; and the **networking phase** where participants of the TQM effort get connected with similar efforts within the rest of the organization to form stronger linkages and alliances [50]. However, you should not become confused by Figure 3.22. Only the preparation phase is implemented once in the organization. The other phases are continuous and evolving activities that are repeated in the TQM implementation to further improve quality [50].

3.3.2.1 Data Quality Dimensions

Because the focus of the Data Vault 2.0 methodology is on the data quality management aspects of TQM, it is worth looking at two methodologies that can become part of a TQM effort in data warehousing.

Both methodologies rely on objective assessments of the data quality. Data quality on the other hand, has many dimensions that are of interest for business users, and therefore can be used to classify the quality of data (or information). Table 3.10 lists common data quality dimensions.

Table 3.10 Data Quality Dimensions [51–53]

Dimension	Definition
Accessibility	Indicates the extent to which the data is available or easily and quickly retrievable by the business user
Appropriate Amount of Data	Provides information about the appropriate volume of data for the business user's task
Believability	Indicates the extent to which the data is believed to be true and credible by the business user
Completeness	Defined by the extent of available data, that is, not missing data and if the data is available in sufficient breadth and depth for the task of the business user. It is defined as expected comprehensiveness. Optional data that is missing doesn't affect the completeness of the data.
Concise Representation	Indicates if the data is represented in a compact format
Conformity	Indicates if the data is represented in the same, consistent format if available at multiple locations. It ensures that standard data definitions are met, including data type, size and format
Ease of Manipulation	Determines if the data is easy to manipulate and apply to different tasks
Free-of-Error	Indicates if the data is free of errors and therefore correct and reliable
Integrity	Indicates if the data is valid across data relationships
Interpretability	Indicates if the data is using the right language, symbols, definitions, and units
Objectivity	Defines the extent to which the data is unbiased, unprejudiced, and impartial
Relevancy	Indicates if the data is applicable and helpful for the business user's task
Reputation	Provides information about the reputation of the data source or content
Security	Indicates if the data is properly secured in terms of properly restricted access
Timeliness	Provides information about the business user's perception regarding the up-to-dateness of the data
Understandability	Indicates if the data is easily to comprehend by the business user
Uniqueness	Ensures that data is not stored redundantly
Value-Added	Provides information about the benefit and advantage of the data for the business user

The assessment of these data quality dimensions can be task-independent or task-dependent. Task-independent assessments require no knowledge about the context of the application and can be applied to any data set. Task-dependent dimensions on the other hand require knowledge about the business rules of the organization, regulations of the company or legal authorities [54].

3.3.2.2 Total Data Quality Management
The first methodology is Total Data Quality Management (TDQM), which applies human resources and quantitative resources to improve products and services, similar to TQM. TDQM supports database migration, promotes the use of data standards, and the use of business rules to improve databases [55]. There are four cyclic phases in TDQM, which are shown in Figure 3.23.

The first phase is the **definition phase**, where the data is analyzed and business requirements are gathered. The information manufacturing system which processes the information is also defined. The output of the phase is a logical and physical design of the information product with attributes related to quality and a quality E/R model which defines the information product and the information quality. The second phase is the **measurement phase** that defines the metrics for the information quality and uncovers problems in information quality after an analysis. The third phase is the **analysis phase** that analyzes the information quality problems found in the previous phase and identifies the root cause of errors. The fourth phase is the **improvement phase** where key areas for improvement are selected along with strategies and techniques. These strategies and techniques are applied within the definition phase of the TDQM when the cycle starts over again [56].

3.3.2.3 Data Warehouse Quality
The second methodology is the Data Warehouse Quality (DWQ) methodology that has been developed by the European Data Warehouse Quality project [67]. While the same phases are used as in the Total Data Quality Methodology as described in the previous section, the meaning and connection of the phases are different. Figure 3.24 shows the process flow of the DWQ methodology.

The input to the **definition phase** is the data definition from the operational systems, stakeholder perspectives and project and context information from the data warehouse. Relevant data quality dimensions of the data warehouse are identified including to relations to objects in the data warehouse. Business users and other stakeholders weight the quality dimensions. The **measurement phase** uses

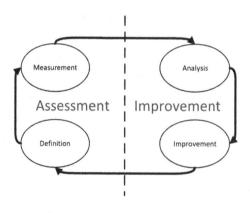

FIGURE 3.23

TDQM Phases [56].

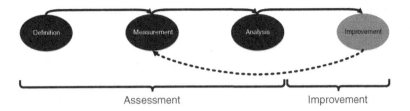

FIGURE 3.24

DWQ Phases [57].

the quality dimensions from the definition phase and identifies dependencies among them. In the next phase, the analysis phase, the results from the measurement phase are used to identify critical areas by comparing the data quality values and the data quality requirements of the business users. The list of data quality dimensions that require improvement are used in the **improvement phase** to improve the data [57].

3.3.2.4 Integrating TQM with the Data Vault 2.0 Methodology

In the Data Vault 2.0 methodology, TQM serves as a governance mechanism for the application of agile methodologies, CMMI and Six Sigma. By doing so, it connects the improvement elements of these methods in order to continually improve and exceed the expectations of business users, the business sponsor, and other stakeholders.

TQM has several primary elements that are important when implementing a customer-focused continual improvement process [58]:

- **Customer focus:** the quality in the context of TQM is ultimately determined by the customer. In the case of data warehousing, the business user determines the quality of the artifacts by the data warehouse project. Therefore, those users decide if the effort made by the data warehouse team, the training, the continual process and quality improvement were worthwhile.
- **Total employee involvement:** to achieve superior quality of data warehouse artifacts, every employee has to be involved in the continual improvement efforts. Management has to provide the required environment to support these efforts. Continuous improvement efforts need to be integrated into normal business operations.
- **Process-centric:** similar to Six Sigma, TQM is focused on processes. This is perfect for Data Vault 2.0, where defined processes with defined process steps produce the desired outcomes. Performance measures are monitored continually. If unexpected variations from the expected outcomes occur, they are reported to project management.
- **Integrated:** TQM doesn't occur within one functional team. TQM requires the integration of many different functional units, interconnecting them in order to achieve total quality.
- **Strategic and systematic:** total quality doesn't happen by accident. It is the result of strategic planning and strategic management and includes the integration of quality into the strategic plan of the organization.
- **Continual improvement:** total quality cannot be achieved without continual improvement of the organizational capabilities. TQM manages these continuing efforts.

- **Fact-based decision making:** decision-making in the improvement process is based on performance measurements. In order to provide these measurements, the organization has to continually collect and analyze data.
- **Communication:** effective communication is required to maintain the motivation of employees at all levels of the organization.

The meetings discussed in the introduction to this section should integrate these elements in order to be successful from a TQM perspective.

Sometimes, when erroneous information is found in reports or OLAP, the organization decides not to follow the recommended TQM approach to identify the root cause of the error and fix it, probably in the source system or the business processes. Instead, the organization decides to fix the error somewhere between the source system and the front-end reports. If such an approach is followed, the only acceptable way to fix the error in the data warehouse is to apply soft business rules on the way out of the Raw Data Vault, for example using the Business Vault or when providing the information mart. Chapter 13, Implementing Data Quality, demonstrates how to implement data quality in the data warehouse. However, in the light of TQM, the goal of the effort is to achieve a closed loop process. This is done by involving the business user in aligning the data set across the source systems and correcting the error in the source system instead of in the data warehouse.

But TQM is more than just fixing data quality (DQ). While it involves data quality activities, it is the ability to see the error in the error marts, take the data into question, and then issue change requests back to the source systems in order to correct the process, or the data, or both. Without closed loop processing (as described previously: users fix and align the data sets in the source), it is nothing more than pure DQ. Instead, TQM requires that people are involved and the loop between source system and presentation layer is closed by providing feedback and removing the errors, thus closing the gaps that are found in the system as a whole.

Chapter 9 will discuss master data management (MDM), which is used to enable business users and requires that "management" and governance work together. The same principles apply to closing the gaps and aligning all the source systems to the vision of master data that the business users designate. The same chapter covers how managed self-service BI is used by business users to directly interact with the data in the enterprise data warehouse, making corrections in real-time, with the feedback loop becoming a publication of the messages (resulting from managed self-service BI), directly from the data warehouse and feeding back to the operational systems through the Service Oriented Architecture (SOA) and the Enterprise Service Bus (ESB). This requires write-back capabilities to enable business users to make corrections in source systems.

REFERENCES

[1] Kimball: "The Data Warehouse Lifecycle Toolkit," p. 542.
[2] http://blogs.pmi.org/blog/voices_on_project_management/2012/04/what-does-a-project-sponsor-re.html
[3] http://www2.cit.cornell.edu/computer/robohelp/cpmm/Project_Roles_and_Responsibilities.htm
[4] http://www.cwjobs.co.uk/careers-advice/profiles/it-manager
[5] The DAMA Guide to The Data Management Body of Knowledge (DAMA-DMBOK Guide), 1st edition, page 33.
[6] Li Sun: "A Metadata Manager's Role in Collaborative Projects: The Rutgers University Libraries Experience".

[7] James Persse: Project Management Success with CMMI, pp. 14f–15f, 17–18, 55.

[8] Paul E. McMahon: Integrating CMMI and Agile Development, p. 277.

[9] Jeannine M. Siviy, M. Lynn Penn, Robert W. Stoddard: CMMI and Six Sigma, p. 95.

[10] Dennis M. Ahern, Aaron Clouse, Richard Turner: CMMI Distilled, pp. 83f, 84f, 85f, 98f, 102, 102f.

[11] Mary Beth Chrissis, Mike Konrad, Sandy Shrum: CMMI for Development, pp. 35, 41f, 42–43, 43f, 44–45.

[12] http://www.ambysoft.com/books/dad.html

[13] Scott W. Ambler, Mark Lines: Disciplined Agile Delivery, pp. 22f, 87, 311ff, 111ff, 273ff, 267f, 309ff, 441ff, 465.

[14] Stober, Hansmann: Agile Software Development, pp. 27f, 119–120.

[15] Schwaber K, Beedle M. Agile software development with scrum. Englewood Cliffs, NJ: Prentice Hall; 2001.

[16] Hirotaka Takeuchi, Ikujiro Nonaka. The new new product development game. Harvard Business Review 1986.

[17] Dave West and Tom Grant, "Agile Development: Mainstream Adoption Has Changed Agility Trends in Real-World Adoption of Agile Methods," available from www.forrester.com/rb/Research/agile_development_mainstream_adoption_has_changed_agility/q/id/56100/t/2, 17

[18] Resnick, Bjork, de la Maza: Professional Scrum with Team Foundation Server 2010, pp. 13, 14.

[19] Greg Cohen: Agile Excellence for Product Managers, p. 22.

[20] Sam Guckenheimer, Neno Loje: Agile Software Engineering with Visual Studio, p. 7.

[21] Kim H. Pries, Jon M. Quigley: Scrum Project Management, pp. 11, 66, 67.

[22] Beyer: User-Centered Agile Methods, p. 5.

[23] David Garmus, David Herron: Function Point Analysis, pp. 28–29.

[24] Varun Barthwal, Jaydeep Kishore, Bhagawati Prasad Joshi: Estimation of Software Metrics using Function Point Analysis, pp. 5, 11.

[25] Minerva Softcare: Function Point Analysis and Data Warehousing, p. 4.

[26] David Longstreet: Function Point Analysis Training Course, p. 7.

[27] Harput V, Kaindl H. Kramer S. Extending Function Point Analysis to Object-Oriented Requirements Specifications, Proceeding on 11th IEEE International Software Metrics Symposium (METRICS 2005).

[28] Karthikeyan Sankaran: Function Points Based Estimation Model for Data Warehouses: retrieved from http://www.ewsolutions.com/resource-center/rwds_folder/rwds-archives/issue.2008-03-01.6090544414/document.2008-03-01.9435972766

[29] Karthikeyan Sankaran: Function Points Based Estimation Model for Data Warehouses: retrieved from http://www.ewsolutions.com/resource-center/rwds_folder/rwds-archives/issue.2008-03-01.6090544414/document.2008-03-01.9435972766 (modifed from its original version to reflect SSIS terminology).

[30] Carol Dekkers, Barbara Emmons: How Function Points Support the Capability Maturity Model Integration, http://www.crosstalkonline.org/storage/issue-archives/2002/200202/200202-Dekkers.pdf

[31] Ken Collier: Agile Analytics, p. 30.

[32] Dr. K.V.K.K. Prasad: "Data Warehouse Development Tools", pp. 25f, 26, 26f, 27, 25ff.

[33] Inmon et al. DW2.0 The Architecture for the Next Generation of Data Warehousing, p. 124.

[34] Valacich et al. "Essentials of Systems Analysis and Design", pp. 122ff, 133ff.

[35] http://technet.microsoft.com/en-us/library/ms174173%28v=sql.110%29.aspx

[36] http://technet.microsoft.com/en-us/library/ms190415.aspx

[37] http://technet.microsoft.com/en-us/library/ms173767%28v=sql.105%29.aspx#AnalysisServices

[38] http://ditakurniawaty.blogspot.de/2012/06/software-testing.html

[39] http://www.mountaingoatsoftware.com/agile/scrum/sprint-review-meeting

[40] http://www.mountaingoatsoftware.com/agile/scrum/sprint-retrospective

[41] Tomkins, R. (1997). GE beats expected 13% rise, Financial Times, (10 October), p.22.

[42] Harry, M.J. (1998). The Vision of Six Sigma, 8 volumes, Phoenix, Arizona, Tri Star Publishing.

[43] Park SH, Lee MJ, Chung MY. Theory and Practice of Six Sigma. Seoul: Publishing Division of Korean Standards Association; 1999.

[44] Sung H. Park: "Six Sigma – For Quality and Productivity Promotion", pp. 1ff, 5, 5f, 6f, 7, 8, 8f, 30, 30f, 31, 33, 34, 37, 41.

[45] Michael C. Thomsett: Getting Started in Six Sigma, pp. 6–7.

[46] Jeannine M. Siviy, M. Lynn Penn, Robert W. Stoddard: CMMI and Six Sigma – Partners in Process Improvement, pp. 37f, 38, 38f.

[47] Craig Gygi, Neil DeCarlo, Bruce Williams: Six Sigma for Dummies, pp. 42, 54.

[48] Praveen Gupta: Six Sigma Business Scorecard, pp. 25, 31, 36.

[49] George Eckes: Six Sigma fo Everyone, p. 29.

[50] Terry L. Richardson: Total Quality Management, pp. 51, 55, 57, 137, 138ff, 144, 149, 170, 186, 200.

[51] Leo L. Pipino, Yang W. Lee, Richard Y. Wang: Data Quality Assessment, p. 212.

[52] DAMA UK Working Group: "The Six Primary Dimensions for Data Quality Assessment", p. 7ff.

[53] http://smartbridge.com/data-done-right-6-dimensions-of-data-quality-part-1/

[54] Leo L. Pipino, Yang W. Lee, Richard Y. Wang: "Data Quality Assessment", p. 211

[55] Phil Cykana, Alta Paul, Miranda Stern: DOD Guidelines on Data Quality Management, p. 154.

[56] Carlo Batini, Cinzia Cappiello, Chiara Francalanci, Andrea Maurino: Methodologies for Data Quality Assessment and Improvement, pp. 16:35–16:37 (figures 6 and 7).

[57] Manfred A. Jeusfeld, Christoph Quix, Matthias Jarke: Design and Analysis of Quality Information for Data Warehouses.

[58] http://asq.org/learn-about-quality/total-quality-management/overview/overview.html

DATA VAULT 2.0 MODELING

This chapter introduces the Data Vault model, including the base entity types used when modeling data warehousing based on the Data Vault. The model is oriented toward scale-free networks that are often observed in nature; therefore, we briefly discuss such networks before defining the entity types. Each definition includes examples of the discussed entity type. Note that this chapter is partially based on the book *Super Charge Your Data Warehouse* by Dan Linstedt [1].

Also note that this chapter uses a logical modeling language called Visual Data Vault. More information, including a white paper and a Microsoft Visio stencil, can be found at http://www.visualdatavault.com [2].

4.1 INTRODUCTION TO DATA VAULT MODELING

The Data Vault model was invented by Dan Linstedt in the 1990s and is oriented on complex networks that are often found in nature. Many of these natural systems can be described using models of complex networks, which are structures consisting of nodes or vertices connected by links or edges. Examples include the human brain, which is a network of neurons. Another example from nature is an organization, which is a network of people. The global economy is another example; it is a network of national economies, which consist of networks of markets. In turn, these markets consist of networks of producers and consumers. What these networks have in common is that they have hubs, such as persons or other objects, links between those objects, and information that describes the context of the objects.

In the past, scientists assumed that these networks were of random nature; i.e., that the placement of links between the hubs was random and that most hubs had approximately the same number of links. This type of random network is presented in Figure 4.1.

In a random network, such as the U.S. highway system, most hubs have only a few connections. This characteristic is the outcome of numerous historical decisions, arising from geographical, political, and economic factors. For example, the cost of building a highway generally limits the number of highways added to the system. The same is true for the U.S. airline system presented in Figure 4.2. But the difference is that it is much easier to extend the network by adding new connections between airports, which are the hubs in this network. The overall structure of the network is mostly determined by the concurrent actions of airline companies, who try to maximize their profits. Therefore, the air transportation network is self-organized by the objects in the network.

We will learn that a data warehouse built using the Data Vault model is as easy to extend as any other scale-free network.

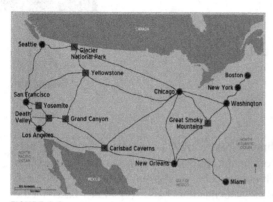

FIGURE 4.1

The U.S. highway system: a random network.

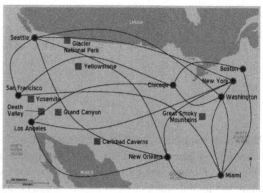

FIGURE 4.2

The U.S. airline system: a scale-free network.

4.2 DATA VAULT MODELING VOCABULARY

The Data Vault model represents the transformation of the natural model described in section 4.1 into a business-centric model for data warehousing. The model represents business processes and is tied to business through business keys. This is an important property of the Data Vault model because business keys indicate how businesses integrate, connect, and access information in their systems. With the orientation of the Data Vault model on business keys, we inherit the ability to integrate, connect, and access information in the same manner as the business does in its daily operations.

The goal of the Data Vault model is to represent the business as closely as possible. With that goal in mind, think about critical characteristics of businesses:

- The ability to react to rapidly changing business requirements, also known as **agility**.
- The **integration** of various information sources to create new knowledge.
- The **complexity** of the business environment and, sometimes, the organization itself.
- The **flexibility** to jump on new market opportunities.
- The need for **transparency** and **accountability**, at least to the auditor of the firm.
- The ability to respond to information requests with **specialized** and **tailored** reports.
- The ability to **scale** a business once it is successful.

These key characteristics allow a company to sustain in today's competitive markets. The Data Vault model is designed in such a way that it supports all these key characteristics when users build a data warehouse system. When you use the Data Vault model, you will be able to adjust the data warehouse as closely as possible to the business and to leverage the Data Vault to your advantage.

To achieve the goals of the Data Vault model, the model is based on three basic entity types, which are derived from the natural model described in the previous section. These entity types are *hubs*, *links*, and *satellites*. Each entity type serves a specific purpose: the **hub** separates the business keys from the rest of the model; the **link** stores relationships between business keys (and/or hubs); and **satellites** store the context (the attributes of a business key or relationship).

We describe the entity types in more detail in the following sections.

4.2.1 HUB ENTITIES

When business users access information in an operational system, they use a business key to refer to the business objects. This might be a customer number, invoice number, or a vehicle identification number. Sometimes the system requires the user to provide a combination of keys, e.g., a customer number and a region code, such as a country code. In other cases, no business key is defined for business objects, but the user is able to find the right object by searching for it by name or by using another identifying attribute. Due to the central importance of these business keys in identifying business objects, the Data Vault model separates them from the rest of the model. The purpose of a hub entity is to store the business keys of business objects along with some other information, which is called the metadata.

In a Data Vault model, there are hubs for each type of business key. In an aviation scenario, there are separate hubs for storing airport codes, carrier codes, and flight numbers, among other hubs. Because they contain the business keys for the business, hubs are the foundation of the Data Vault model. We provide a more detailed description of hubs in section 4.3.

Comparing a Data Vault hub with the air transportation example from section 4.1, it is clear that the airports are the hubs. They are the central elements in the network. In the Data Vault, the business keys are central and are therefore located in the hubs.

4.2.2 LINK ENTITIES

In the same way that airports are linked by flight connections in Figure 4.2, business objects are connected in business. No business object is entirely separate from other business objects. Instead, they are connected to each other through the operational business processes that use business objects in the execution of their tasks. The Data Vault models these relationships with links that connect two or more hubs. Typical business processes are purchasing, manufacturing, advertising, marketing, and sales. Because these processes often (but not always) represent transactions, a link often represents a transaction as well. Therefore, it often provides the basis for creating the facts of the dimensional model (refer to Chapters 7 and 14 for more details). However, this is only a rule of thumb, as you will learn at the end of this section.

In the aviation scenario from the previous section (presented in Figure 4.3), there is a link between the carrier, the airport, and the flight number hubs to represent a flight. In addition, this link could include a reference to the tail number. Other links could track available security events, on-board sales, or seat reservations. Other possible links might not represent transactions (thus voiding the rule of thumb from the introduction to this section.) For example, there could be a link for indicating that a connection is available between two airports (Figure 4.4).

The logical diagram shows a link between the Airport and Carrier hubs. Note the two references to the hub airport, which reflect the origin and destination of the connection. Without any further information, we only know which connection between given airports existed at any time in the past. We will see in the next section why such a nontransactional link is useful.

4.2.3 SATELLITE ENTITIES

A Data Vault model with hubs and links alone would not provide us with sufficient information. As we saw in section 4.2.2, they only provide information about the relationship between business objects. The missing piece is the context of these business objects and the context of these links. For a flight transaction, this might be the air time of the plane or the security delay of a flight.

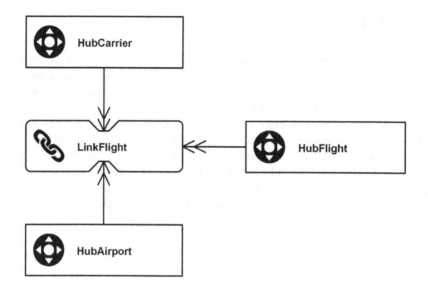

FIGURE 4.3

A link connecting three hubs (logical design).

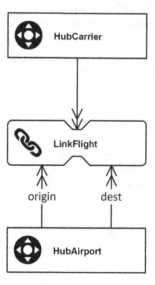

FIGURE 4.4

A link representing a connection between only two hubs (logical design).

Satellites add this functionality to the Data Vault model. They store the attributes that belong to either a business key (in a hub), relationship or a transaction (in a link) (Figure 4.5).

We have added satellites to hubs and links to store the information that is required to understand the context of the data stored in the Data Vault. Notice the satellite on the connection link between the two airports. The satellite tracks the distance and the number of connections between

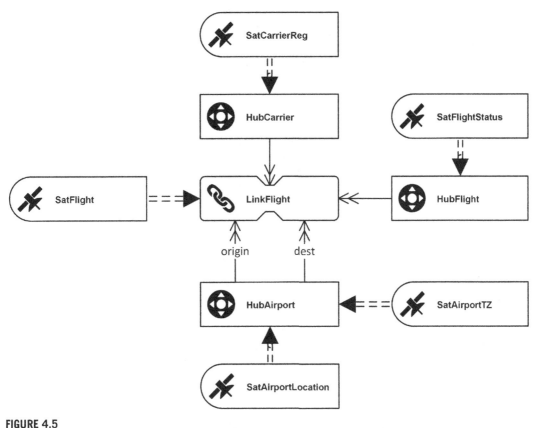

FIGURE 4.5

Satellites on hubs and links (logical design).

the airports. The satellite also stores the history of the attribute data. Every attribute change is logged to the satellite.

As you can see with the airport hub, there can be multiple satellites on a hub or link. Reasons for distributing the attributes of a hub or satellite include multiple or changing source systems, different frequency of changes, or functional separation of attribute data. We provide a more detailed description of satellites in section 4.5 and throughout the book.

4.3 **HUB DEFINITION**

As described in section 4.2.1, hubs are the main pillars of the Data Vault model. The next sections review the hub entity type and describe how to define a business key. In addition, you can find examples of hubs and their business keys in section 4.3.3.

Hubs are defined using a unique list of business keys and provide a soft-integration point of raw data that is not altered from the source system, but is supposed to have the same semantic meaning. Therefore, business keys in the same hub should have the same semantic granularity. That means that

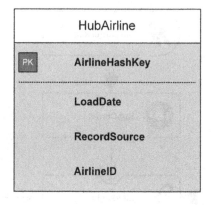

FIGURE 4.6

A Data Vault hub entity (physical design).

a contact person that is an individual should be in a different hub than a customer that is a corporation (there might be more than one contact in a corporation). The business key can be a composite key. One example of a composite key is a vehicle identification number (VIN), which includes information about the manufacturer (the first three characters, called the WMI code) and vendor-specific information, such as the manufacturing plant and a serial number. These composite keys are also known as smart or intelligent keys, and are covered later in this chapter in more detail.

A hub tracks the arrival of a new business key in the data warehouse. It uses the metadata to track the source system (called the record source) and the arrival date and time of the business key in the data warehouse (called the load date). In addition, a hash key is generated for each business key in the hub. The hash key is used to reference the business object in other Data Vault entities, such as links and satellites. In addition, it improves the performance of data warehouse loads and joining business keys within the model. We discuss hash keys in section 4.3.2. Figure 4.6 presents a typical physical entity structure of a hub for airlines.

This hub uses the required metadata discussed in the previous paragraph. More options for hub metadata are discussed in section 4.3.2.

The metadata from the hub (in this case, the **LoadDate** and **RecordSource** attributes) should be placed at the beginning of the entity. That keeps the design clean (because all hubs start with the same attributes) and makes the maintenance of Data Vault entities easier.

We will use the symbol shown in Figure 4.7 for hubs in the remainder of this book.

FIGURE 4.7

A Data Vault hub (logical symbol).

4.3.1 DEFINITION OF A BUSINESS KEY

Before digging deeper into the hub entity structure, let's review the business key definition provided in section 4.2.1 and discuss how to identify a business key in operational systems.

Business keys are used to identify, track, and locate information. By definition, a business key should have a very low propensity to change and should be unique. That means that in one operational system, only one business object is identified by a given business key and this business key doesn't change. To be clear: there might be different business objects in different operational systems with the same business key, but they will not be in the same operational system. In many cases, natural keys can be used as business keys, as long as they are unique and populated. Business keys are supposed to have meaning to the business. Some examples of business keys are:

- Customer numbers
- Product numbers (also UPC, EAN, or ISBN bar codes, depending on the business case)
- Account numbers
- Vehicle identification numbers (VINs)
- Part numbers
- Invoice numbers
- Auto license plate numbers
- Portfolio numbers
- Employee badge numbers
- Support ticket numbers
- Driver's license numbers
- Work order numbers

Some of these business keys are smart keys (or intelligent keys). Examples include vehicle identification numbers, UPCs, or EAN bar codes. These keys are made up from other keys that identify other business objects (for example, the manufacturer in the vehicle identification number). In other cases, businesses have failed to keep the business key truly unique. A guitar manufacturer used the following systematic for its serial numbers: *"the first digit is the year being reproduced, the 2nd digit is the year of production"* [3]. That allows duplicates for any year with similar last digits (e.g., 1996/2006). In order to have a truly unique business key, a composite of the serial number and the production year is required. Other businesses decide to introduce a surrogate key to overcome the problem of duplicate business keys. They combine the serial number with an artificially generated key or replace the serial number completely when referencing the business object. The surrogate key becomes the business key. However, all these definitions of a business key are valid because the business uses these keys to identify business objects.

4.3.1.1 Composite Keys (aka Smart Keys, Intelligent Keys)

We have introduced vehicle information numbers (VINs) as examples for composite keys, also known as smart keys or intelligent keys. Composite keys comprise multiple parts. For example, every VIN in the world is composed of three sections: a world manufacturer identifier (WMI) code, a vehicle descriptor section (VDS), and a vehicle identifier section (VIS). WMI codes are unique and are assigned to only one car manufacturer. However, a car manufacturer can have multiple WMI codes assigned. The VDS code identifies the vehicle type and includes information about the model and the body style. The VIS identifies individual vehicles (Figure 4.8).

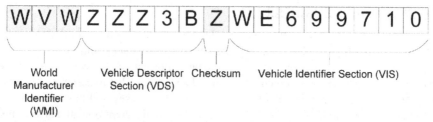

FIGURE 4.8

Individual sections of a vehicle identification number.

Composite keys are also known as smart or intelligent keys because the keys are given business meaning through position values and formats. Other examples for composite business keys include:

- Bar codes (UPC, EAN, etc.)
- IMEI number used for mobile device identification
- MAC numbers for identifying network equipment
- ISBN codes for books
- ISSN codes for periodicals
- Phone numbers
- Email addresses
- Credit card numbers

In Visual Data Vault, the logical modeling language for Data Vault modeling, we distinguish between composite keys and smart keys: while they have the same goal to capture the required grain of the business key, a composite key is made up of an unique combination of columns [4]. A smart key is only a single column where the individual parts of the business key are combined (such as the vehicle identification number in Figure 4.8).

4.3.1.2 Business Key Identification Process

A business key can be identified from various sources. We wrote in the previous chapter that "business keys are used to identify, track, and locate information." With that in mind, the analyst should focus on source system applications, online lookup screens, and report headers. Wherever a business user can search for a business object with a reference code, there is a good chance that the business user is using business keys for that purpose. Interviewing the business user is a great source of information as well. The key question that the analyst needs to ask the user is: "How do you identify, track, or locate information?" This sentence represents a key concept for identifying business keys.

Another good strategy for identifying business keys is to analyze the business processes of the firm (or between firms). Businesses often identify and track their information sets through business keys. Users communicate to each other via business processes and translate, send, or attach information to the business process flow. Therefore, analyzing these business processes helps to identify the business keys used to process the tasks.

Other sources of information include source system data and data models and XML or XSD schemas. There is often a unique index on the business key, and this is a first indicator for identifying a business key. The analyst can also find business keys in spreadsheets, OLAP cubes, and software documentation.

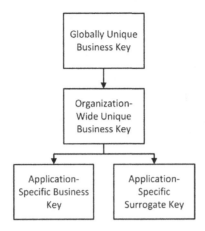

FIGURE 4.9

Scope of business keys.

4.3.1.3 Scope of Business Keys

It is important to understand that a business key has a scope in which the key is valid. For example, business keys from an operational system might be valid only in this specific operational system. They are not used in any other system or in any other business process. Other business keys are used in a local context, for example an organizational unit (e.g., sales). Some business cases have been defined to be valid for one organization but are not valid between organizations. Figure 4.9 shows this relationship.

It is important to understand the scope of the business key in order to select the most applicable identifier in the business context. The larger the scope, the better it can represent the business object. For example, a car might have a surrogate key in an operational system for car manufacturers. This surrogate key is only valid within this specific operational system. When a vehicle is produced in a manufacturing plant, it receives a serial number that is unique for all vehicles of the same make, model year, and factory. Therefore, this serial number is unique for this context. Usually, the serial number is used as a part of vehicle identification numbers, which are globally unique identifiers for vehicles. There should be no duplicate vehicle identification number for two different cars. However, the car manufacturer might decide to use only the last 14 characters of a vehicle identification number in order to save storage in operational systems. This is due to the fact that all vehicle identification numbers should start with the same three characters – the WMI code of the manufacturer. However, large car manufacturers usually have more than one assigned WMI code; therefore it is not a good business practice to assume that the serial number of a vehicle is unique.

4.3.1.4 Difference between Business Keys and Surrogate Keys

Surrogate keys are often used by operational systems to identify the business object. However, they are not good candidates for a business key if the business itself is not using them. As soon as the business uses the surrogate key to uniquely identify (and track) data in the source system, the surrogate key becomes a business key.

We have taught students of computer science to use surrogate keys as primary keys in database development because it can speed up joins between tables. Instead of using a character string (the business key) to join two records, they started to use integer-based surrogate keys to reduce the complexity (think of composite keys) and improve the speed of joins. It was a rule of thumb and it went much further than anticipated. Software developers often use surrogate keys to business users to identify records. They are displayed on screens and printed on reports. However, surrogate keys are meaningless. They serve no purpose, except to technically identify a record uniquely in one source system.

4.3.2 HUB ENTITY STRUCTURE

Every Data Vault entity type contains standard attributes that assist with construction of the model, as well as tracking and querying it. The hub entity type is no exception to this rule. The following attributes are common for all Data Vault hubs:

- Hash key
- Business key(s)
- Load date
- Record source

In addition, the following attribute is optional:

- Last seen date

4.3.2.1 Hash Key

Querying the final Data Vault model requires many more joins than in a traditional data warehouse. Therefore, we have to prepare the Data Vault model to increase the processing speed of the joins while the model is being created. This is when the **hash key** comes into play: the key, which is based on the business key, becomes the primary key of the hub entity and is used as a foreign key to reference entities such as links and satellites.

The **hash key** in a Data Vault hub is used to improve the lookup performance within a data warehouse built with the Data Vault. When the ETL job loads a Data Vault hub with data from a stage table, it checks whether the business keys in the source already exist in the target hub. Because lookups on variable length strings tend to be slower than those with fixed length strings, a **hash key** can be calculated and added to the hub. The performance is also improved because of the shorter character sequence of a **hash key** for long business keys. A safe method for calculating the **hash key** for a hub's business key is discussed in Chapter 11, Data Extraction.

Each unique business key in the Data Vault hub must have a unique **hash key**. Hash keys should be either calculated using MD5 (the recommended practice) or any other hash algorithm, such as SHA-1. Note that the **hash keys** should never be exposed to the business users and must not be used outside the Data Vault. Like surrogate keys, they are meaningless character strings and are intended only for speeding up and simplifying the joins.

Note that the **hash key** replaces the sequence number from the Data Vault 1.0 standard. The sequence number was replaced by the hash key in order to support linking to other data sources, such as NoSQL databases. In addition, it is cross-platform compatible and can be regenerated (the same business key will always provide the same hash key, if no errors are made in the hash value calculation). Joining data based on hash keys might be slower compared to integer-based sequence numbers, but the advantages outweigh the disadvantages. The proof of this statement is left to the coming chapters.

4.3.2.2 Business Key

The **business key** attribute in the Data Vault hub stores the business key as identified in the business key identification process described in section 4.3.1. This attribute is the main purpose of a Data Vault hub. Therefore, it is the central element in a hub.

The data type is oriented to the source data. Some business keys are integer numbers; in many other cases, the **business key** is a character string. Therefore the data type and length of the attribute should be closely modeled after the source system.

There should be a unique index on the **business key** in order to indicate this characteristic in the model. We will follow this practice throughout this book.

When composite keys are used by a business, they must be kept together in a single hub within the Data Vault. This is consistent with the definition and context of the business processes that search and index this key for the purpose of discovering additional context.

Hubs are not required to keep their business keys within a single field. If the data is a well-defined composite key, its sections can be split into separate fields within the hub. In such a case, the unique key should span all fields that are part of the composite key. It is also possible to store both the composite business key as a single field and the separated keys in separated fields within the same hub. In this case, the hub should have two unique keys, one on the single field that contains the composite business key, and one on the group of individual fields for the composite key.

It is also possible to create multiple hubs for each individual part of the composite business key. For example, there could be one hub for vehicle identification numbers, another for WMI codes (the manufacturer identifier within the VIN), another for the vehicle descriptor section (VDS), and yet another hub for the vehicle identifier section (VIS). But because the VIN is used as a whole by the business, there also has to be a hub that contains the VIN number as a whole.

4.3.2.3 Load Date

The **load date** indicates when the business key initially arrived in the data warehouse. It is a system-generated and system-maintained field. The **load date** should be the same for all data that arrived in the same batch (refer to Chapter 11, Data Extraction, for more details). When the same **load date** is used, it becomes possible to trace errors and find technical load problems that affected the data that was loaded in a batch. Load cycles become repeatable, consistent, and restartable for any given load cycle over time.

The **load date** is generated by the data warehouse (or the ETL process that is loading it). It represents a consistent time-stamped view of the data as it appears to the data warehouse and should never be altered once it is set. All load dates for a single load cycle should be set to the same timestamp.

4.3.2.4 Record Source

In addition to a batch being given a timestamp, the originating **record source** is also tracked. The **record source** is hard-coded and applied to maintain traceability of the arriving data set. If a given **business key** has multiple data sources, the **record source** should indicate the master data source. If the **business key** is not available in the master data source (but is available in other data sources), it should contain the origination source of the actual key.

The **record source** is a key attribute for maintaining auditability of the data warehouse. It allows the identification of the source application and enables traceability from the information marts all the way back to the source system to comply with regulatory standards. Developers, auditors, and business users benefit from having a **record source** attribute in each row of data over the entire model.

It is best to refrain from using a generalized **record source**, such as "SAP" for all SAP data. Instead, use the lowest level of granularity, for example "SAP.FINANCE.GL" to indicate the general ledger module in the financial application of SAP.

4.3.2.5 Last Seen Date

In an optimal scenario, a source system would indicate the records that have been inserted, modified or deleted to the data warehouse. This concept is known as Change Data Capture (CDC) and is supported by many relational database management systems, including Microsoft SQL Server. However, many operational systems don't provide us such *delta load*. Instead, source systems provide a full table dump of all the records currently available in the operational system, known as a *full load*. It is oftentimes easier to implement for the operations team or the application developer.

In order to detect deleted data in such full loads, the ETL process that sources the data into the data warehouse has to perform a table scan over all rows in the target tables (e.g., the hub table) and check for existence of the record in the source data. If a record doesn't exist in the data source anymore, it means that it *might* have been removed from the source. For example, mainframe systems might not export a record if it is currently locked for editing.

If your source system behaves in this manner, you need the **last seen date**, which is optional for the Data Vault model and meant for such a purpose. It gives business the power to decide when a record should be considered as being deleted by the source system, by defining the number of days required to pass before the record is considered as being deleted.

The **last seen date** indicates when the **business key** was "last seen" in the source system. Every **business key** in the current batch is updated with the batch date as the **last seen date**. If a **business key** is not in the current batch, its **last seen date** is not modified. All business keys that have a **last seen date** that is below a configured threshold are considered to be deleted. The threshold is configured by the business and depends on the source system and the business case. Note that a **last seen date** should only be used if there is no audit trail or CDC information.

Chapter 11 discusses the reasons for this problem and how to populate **last seen dates** in more detail.

4.3.3 HUB EXAMPLES

The hubs shown in Figure 4.10 exemplify the use of the different attribute options.

The first example, **HubAirline**, uses the airline identification number (**AirlineID**) assigned by the US Department of Transportation (US DOT) to identify a unique airline. The business key is identified by the hash key **AirlineKey** which hashes the **AirlineID** business key. The **HubCarrier** example uses the IATA-assigned carrier code that is more commonly used to identify a carrier than is the **AirlineID**. The problem with the carrier code is that it is not always unique, because the same code might have been assigned to different carriers over time.

The **HubFlight** uses a composite business key to represent the business object, which is a flight. The composite key is made up of two independent business keys, **Carrier** and **FlightNum**. Having a hub for the flight number alone makes no sense, because it is not possible to identify a flight using only the flight number (a flight number is assigned by the airline, hence the same flight number might be used to identify a different flight from a different carrier). The primary key hashes the composite business keys into a single attribute for identification and better performance. As with all Data Vault hubs, the hub contains no other information, such as the flight date. This type of information is stored in satellites. **HubFlightCode** is another way of representing the composite business key in a hub. In this example, the composite key is provided as a combined key in the **FlightCode** field, and the individual sections of the flight code are contained in **Carrier** and **FlightNum**.

FIGURE 4.10

Example of Data Vault hubs (physical design).

The last example is **HubAirplane**, which uses the **LastSeenDate** in the hub. This makes sense because the data source only provides information about the airplane that is used for a flight, but does not include information as to whether the airplane was discharged by the carrier. Using the **LastSeenDate**, it is possible to identify airplanes that are no longer being used by the airline.

4.4 **LINK DEFINITION**

The link entity type is responsible for modeling transactions, associations, hierarchies, and redefinitions of business terms. The next sections of this chapter define Data Vault links more formally. A link connects business keys; therefore links are modeled between hubs. Links capture and record the past, present, and future relationships between data elements at the lowest possible granularity. They don't capture time-lines or temporality because these concepts, including the *active* status of a relationship, are an expression of context, which is not the goal of links. For that reason, it is important that links not be end-dated and contain no other time or context information, except a *Load Date* attribute for technical and informative reasons. Links represent a relationship that currently exists or one that existed in the past.

Adding temporality to link structures, for example by adding a *Begin* and *End Date*, bounds the relationship to a single timeline and forces the data warehouse to start and stop this relationship only

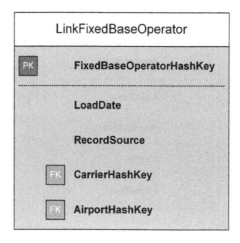

FIGURE 4.11

A Data Vault link entity (physical design).

once. This limitation should always be avoided because it will not hold true. For example, even if this limitation is acceptable for the organization right now, business might change. In addition, a relationship might be deleted in the source system by accident (or temporarily) and recovered in a later source extract. The Data Vault model should capture this temporary deletion for audit purposes, but the context information (the business side) should capture the reversed action.

Data Vault links are implemented by tables that represent many-to-many relationships. They connect two or more hubs (or the same hub at least twice by using multiple hub references). A link contains the hash key of each connected hub along with some metadata, which is explained later in this chapter. A typical Data Vault link entity is presented in Figure 4.11.

The primary key of the entity is a hash key that identifies the link within the data warehouse. It is used by satellites that add context to the link or by other links that reference this link. The hash key also improves lookups when loading new records into the table and is based on the **CarrierCode** and **AirportSeqID** business keys, which are stored in the referenced hubs. The Load Date and Record Source attributes provide information about the time when the record was loaded and where it comes from.

Throughout the book, we will use the logical symbol shown in Figure 4.12 for Data Vault links.

The shape of the entity is similar to a link in a chain, in order to increase the recognition of this basic entity. In addition, a chain icon is used for the same purpose.

A Data Vault link connects two or more hubs (hub references); therefore it is always drawn in conjunction with them (Figure 4.13).

FIGURE 4.12

A Data Vault link (logical symbol).

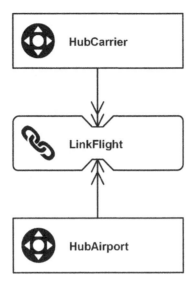

FIGURE 4.13

A link connecting two hubs (logical design).

Links ensure the scalability of the Data Vault model. It is possible to start with a relatively small Data Vault model for the data warehouse and extend this model (to scale it out) by adding more hubs and links to create a larger model.

4.4.1 REASONS FOR MANY-TO-MANY RELATIONSHIPS

Many-to-many relationships provide some benefits to the model. First, they provide flexibility because changes to the business rules don't require re-engineering the links. We will cover this advantage in more detail in the next section. Another advantage is that the granularity is expressed by the number of referenced hubs (or business keys) and is thus well documented. We discuss the granularity of links in section 4.4.3 in more detail.

Because relationships are modeled in link entities, these entity types help the physical model to absorb data changes and business rule changes with little to no impact on either existing data sets (history) or existing processes (load and query). Links help to mitigate required changes to the Data Vault model that are introduced due to relationship changes in the business model. The following example clarifies this characteristic: if a business defines today that "one carrier can handle multiple airports, but each airport must be handled by one and only one carrier," that relationship would be modeled in traditional third normal form with a foreign key in the airport child table that references the primary key in the carrier table, as shown in Figure 4.14.

While this is well designed, problems occur when the business decides to change the business rule: "now, an airport may be handled by multiple carriers." This would require a many-to-many relationship in the traditional data warehouse (Figure 4.15).

The problem is that this change of business rule requires a redesign of existing structures. Every redesign requires re-engineering all processes and models downstream (towards the business user)

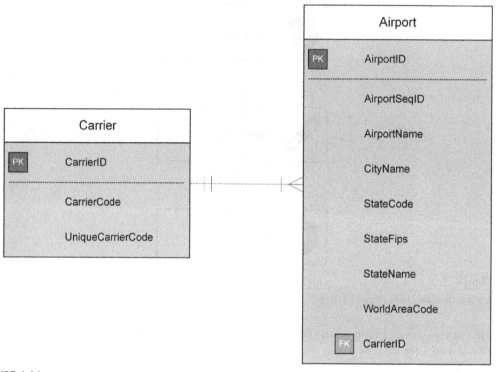

FIGURE 4.14

One-to-many relationship (physical design).

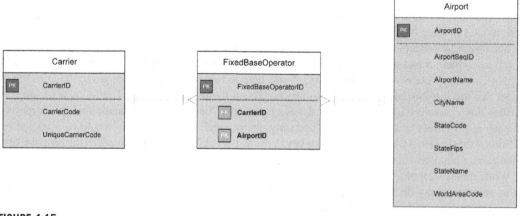

FIGURE 4.15

Many-to-many relationship (physical design).

because they are depending on the selected model. Such re-engineering has an impact on the agility of the data warehouse project, because every small change requires not only a large amount of re-engineering, but also to test existing functionality that was not touched. Also, it might require that downstream functionality that should not be changed (from a business perspective) needs to be modified to support the new many-to-many relationships. Without these modifications, current functionality would just break because it still expects a one-to-many relationship.

In the Data Vault model, only many-to-many relationships exist due to the use of link entities. Link entities can model 1:m, m:n, m:1, and 1:1 relationships without any change to the definition of the link entity table. Re-engineering is not required for the ETL loading routines. This would not be the case for traditional data warehouses, where a change to the definition of the relationship requires re-engineering the ETL loading routines. By doing so, the Data Vault model tries to reduce the re-engineering effort down to zero.

4.4.2 FLEXIBILITY OF LINKS

Links greatly improve the flexibility of the Data Vault model. Because it is easy to add links or modify the relationship type of existing links, it takes less time for IT to respond to changes in the business. To add new functionality, IT only needs to add new hubs and connect them via links to existing hubs. For example, the Data Vault shown in Figure 4.16 represents our aviation example from the last section.

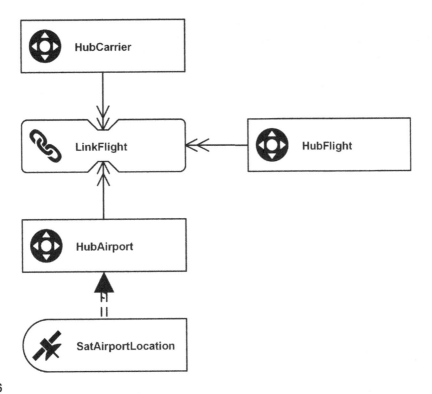

FIGURE 4.16

Starting model before changes (logical design).

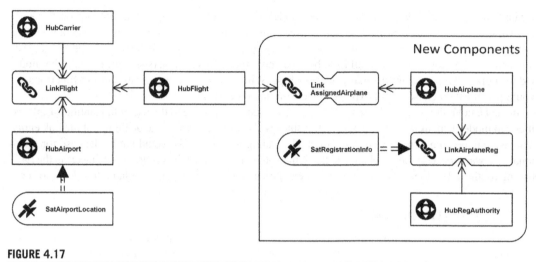

FIGURE 4.17

Data Vault after modification (logical design).

If the business decides to add information about the plane, the Data Vault gets a new hub and the hub is linked to the existing Data Vault with a new set of links (Figure 4.17).

The existing model has not changed. Therefore, the ETL jobs that depend on it do not need to be refactored. The impact of the change to the existing data warehouse is zero. That is the clear advantage of Data Vault modeling. Further modifications to add more data to the data warehouse are performed in the same way.

Links can also be used to connect distributed data warehouses, where some parts of the model are stored in one location and other parts in other locations (Figure 4.18).

The drawing shows a Data Vault for flight information for the USA, another Data Vault for Europe and a traditional data warehouse for the Asia-Pacific region. As you can see, it is even possible to connect a Data Vault-based data warehouse to traditional data warehouses that were not built with the Data Vault modeling technique. We can also connect to unstructured data sources, such as Hadoop or ordinary flat files on a file system, in a similar fashion.

4.4.3 GRANULARITY OF LINKS

The granularity of links is defined by the number of hubs that they connect. Every time a new hub is added to a link, a new level of grain is introduced. The more hubs a link connects to, the finer the granularity becomes. When we add a new hub, we lower the granularity of the link. In this way, links behave like facts in a dimensional model. When a new dimension is added to a fact table, the granularity is lowered as well.

If the Data Vault link is already in production and the business requires a change of grain, there are two options for refactoring the Data Vault model. First, we could modify the existing link and add a reference to another hub. However, this would require re-engineering existing ETL jobs and the way that historic data is handled in the new link must also be determined (which has a different grain). It also puts the auditability of the data at risk, because the source system never delivered a NULL value (Figure 4.19).

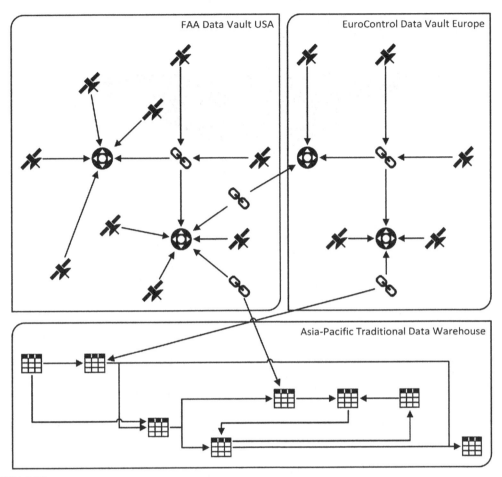

FIGURE 4.18

Distributed data warehouse connected by Data Vault links.

Carrier	SourceAirport	DestAirport	Airplane
8fe9... {UA}	3de7... {DEN}	62a1... {SFO}	(Null)
29ad... {DL}	62a1... {SFO}	1aab... {JFK}	(Null)
8fe9... {UA}	388b... {OKC}	3de7... {DEN}	(Null)
3af7... {LH}	887b... {FRA}	62a1... {SFO}	384b... {D-AZUH}
3af7... {LH}	224c... {LAX}	4cca... {MUC}	784c... {D-ECCH}

FIGURE 4.19

Manipulating historic data in a Data Vault link.

Carrier	SourceAirport	DestAirport
8fe9... {UA}	3de7... {DEN}	62a1... {SFO}
29ad... {DL}	62a1... {SFO}	1aab... {JFK}
8fe9... {UA}	388b... {OKC}	3de7... {DEN}

Carrier	SourceAirport	DestAirport	Airplane
3af7... {LH}	887b... {FRA}	62a1... {SFO}	384b... {D-AZUH}
3af7... {LH}	224c... {LAX}	4cca... {MUC}	784c... {D-ECCH}

SELECT Carrier, SourceAirport, DestAirport, 0 AS Airplane
FROM LeftTable AS Connection
UNION ALL
SELECT Carrier, SourceAirport, DestAirport, Airplane
FROM RightTable AS Flight

Carrier	SourceAirport	DestAirport	Airplane
8fe9... {UA}	3de7... {DEN}	62a1... {SFO}	0 {Unknown}
29ad... {DL}	62a1... {SFO}	1aab... {JFK}	0 {Unknown}
8fe9... {UA}	388b... {OKC}	3de7... {DEN}	0 {Unknown}
3af7... {LH}	887b... {FRA}	62a1... {SFO}	384b... {D-AZUH}
3af7... {LH}	224c... {LAX}	4cca... {MUC}	784c... {D-ECCH}

FIGURE 4.20

Merging historic data (upper left) with new data (upper right) from individual Data Vault links.

For this reason, the modification of existing link structures is no longer an acceptable practice in Data Vault 2.0 modeling.

Note that, in Figure 4.19, every reference to other business objects (hubs) is provided by a pseudo hash key and the business key in curly brackets (e.g., "8fe9… {UA}").

The better option is creating a new link for new incoming data and "closing" the old link. Closing the link means that no new data is added to the link table. Instead, new data is added to the new link. When the new business builds the information mart, it must define how the links with different grains are to be merged. By doing so, we can ensure the auditability of the incoming data and meet the requirements of the business.

The SQL statement in the middle of Figure 4.20 represents a business rule that describes how to handle old data. For example, the rule specifies that the airport in the old data be set to *unknown*, as represented by the hash key 0 (simplified). The resulting table is used to create a Business Vault table, as is discussed in Chapter 14, Loading the Dimensional Information Mart, or a dimension in the information mart.

The second option also works when a level of grain needs to be removed (a reference to a hub) (Figure 4.21).

Carrier	SourceAirport	DestAirport	Airplane
8fe9... {UA}	3de7... {DEN}	62a1... {SFO}	2821... {N-4XDU}
29ad... {DL}	62a1... {SFO}	1aab... {JFK}	18af... {N-ERTD}
8fe9... {UA}	388b... {OKC}	3de7... {DEN}	49ff... {N-9ZGC}
3af7... {LH}	887b... {FRA}	62a1... {SFO}	384b... {D-AZUH}
3af7... {LH}	224c... {LAX}	4cca... {MUC}	784c... {D-ECCH}

FIGURE 4.21

Removing historic data in a Data Vault link.

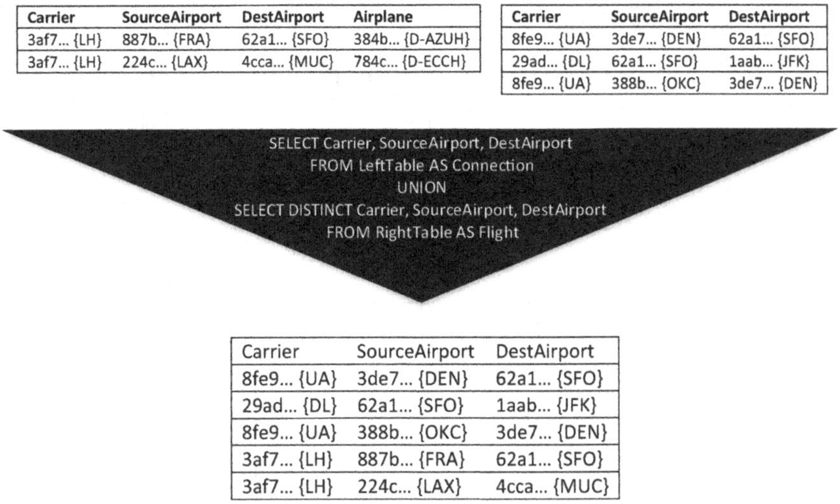

Carrier	SourceAirport	DestAirport	Airplane
3af7... {LH}	887b... {FRA}	62a1... {SFO}	384b... {D-AZUH}
3af7... {LH}	224c... {LAX}	4cca... {MUC}	784c... {D-ECCH}

Carrier	SourceAirport	DestAirport
8fe9... {UA}	3de7... {DEN}	62a1... {SFO}
29ad... {DL}	62a1... {SFO}	1aab... {JFK}
8fe9... {UA}	388b... {OKC}	3de7... {DEN}

```
SELECT Carrier, SourceAirport, DestAirport
FROM LeftTable AS Connection
UNION
SELECT DISTINCT Carrier, SourceAirport, DestAirport
FROM RightTable AS Flight
```

Carrier	SourceAirport	DestAirport
8fe9... {UA}	3de7... {DEN}	62a1... {SFO}
29ad... {DL}	62a1... {SFO}	1aab... {JFK}
8fe9... {UA}	388b... {OKC}	3de7... {DEN}
3af7... {LH}	887b... {FRA}	62a1... {SFO}
3af7... {LH}	224c... {LAX}	4cca... {MUC}

FIGURE 4.22

Merging historic data (upper left) with new data (upper right) from individual Data Vault links.

If we simply removed the Airplane column from the old link, we would lose the data due to the removal of the reference from the link. This is the worst case for an auditable data warehouse. The data reduction works similarly to a GROUP BY statement without any measures.

Figure 4.22 shows the reduction of a level of grain. Note the SELECT DISTINCT in the SQL statement.

4.4.4 LINK UNIT-OF-WORK

A similar issue related to the granularity of links exists when violating the link's unit-of-work. The unit-of-work is a correlated set of data that keeps key sets together. It enforces query on link data later by establishing consistency between arriving data and data stored in the Data Vault links. In some cases, data warehouse modelers try to split a link into multiple, smaller links in order to normalize the link information for modeling purposes. Table 4.1 shows an example of a simplified source system table that will become the basis for a Data Vault link.

The data in the source table identifies the connections between airports serviced by carriers. Each carrier (in this case there are two carriers) identified by the sequence numbers 222 and 729 serves

Table 4.1 Unit-of-Work in Source System

Carrier ID	Source Airport ID	Destination Airport ID
222	12	96
222	12	93
729	15	87
222	17	93

Table 4.2 Normalized Source System

Carrier ID	Source Airport ID	Carrier ID	Destination Airport ID
222	12	222	96
222	17	222	93
729	15	729	87

Table 4.3 Denormalized Source System

Carrier ID	Source Airport ID	Destination Airport ID
222	12	96
222	12	93
222	*17*	*96*
729	15	87
222	17	93

various source airports and connects them with destination airports. If the data is being normalized, the following two tables (Table 4.2) would be the result:

To test the validity of this normalization, it is a good practice to check if the source system data can be recovered from this data. Table 4.3 would be created after denormalizing the data from the data in the previous tables.

By rejoining the data, a record has been created that doesn't exist in the original source system. This is because the unit-of-work was broken when normalizing the data in the previous step, making the data captured by the two normalized tables invalid. In relational data modeling, this problem is also known as multivalued dependencies.

4.4.5 LINK ENTITY STRUCTURE

The main structure of a Data Vault link comprises the hash keys of the business keys stored in referenced hubs. In addition, a Data Vault link has the following required metadata:

- Hash key
- Load date
- Record source

These attributes are the same as those in hubs and were discussed extensively in section 4.3.2 of this chapter. It is also possible to use an optional

- Last seen date

in a Data Vault link. The **last seen date** was discussed in section 4.3.2 as well.

In addition to these required attributes, a Data Vault link might have the following optional attribute:

- Dependent child key

4.4.5.1 Hash Key

Similar to Data Vault hubs, a link must have a **hash key**. When the link is loaded with data from a stage table, the ETL job has to check whether the relationship or transaction is already present in the link table because there should be no duplicate link entries that represent the same relationship or transaction. To achieve this, the ETL job has to compare the business keys of all linked business objects. Because a relational database engine is slow in comparing strings with variable length (a common characteristic of business keys), the lookup performance is often slow. The problem becomes more serious if the business keys are not stored in the Data Vault link and have to be joined with those from the referenced hubs before they can be compared. The **hash key** replaces the subsequent joins to referenced hubs when data is loaded from staging tables. To enable joins, a hash code is calculated for the combination of all business keys in the link. Because there is a great potential for errors when calculating hash codes on business keys, we will discuss a safe method in Chapter 11, Data Extraction.

Hash keys might also be used to join unstructured data from external data stores, such as a Hadoop distributed file system (which uses MD5 hash keys for identifying data).

4.4.5.2 Dependent Child Key

A link might have a **dependent child key** (such as a line-item number) that is used under some circumstances, for example to represent an invoice transaction in a link. The line item number on an invoice is a sequential index that is only valid within the scope of the invoice. It is not unique on its own, but rather it is unique only in combination with the invoice number. This type of number is called a *degenerate field* and affects the grain and uniqueness of the data set in the link. The following rules apply to degenerate fields:

- They cannot stand on their own (like hubs).
- They have no business meaning.
- They are "dependent" on another context in order to be valid.
- They give meaning and uniqueness to additional relationship information.
- They have no "descriptors" of their own.

   Examples of degenerate fields include:

- Line-item numbers on invoices
- The sides of a cassette tape (side A and side B)
- The page number in a book
- The sequence number in a TCP frame
- The timestamp of an email message

The examples show that degenerate fields don't need to be number values. They can be characters (as with the cassette tape) or dates (as with the timestamp of an email message). However, dates should be used with caution because not all dates (such as start/stop, begin/end and other descriptive dates) might end up part of the link. Most of the time these descriptive attributes of business objects become part of satellites. The dependent child key is also used as an identifying element of the link structure, so the hash key is derived from the business keys of the referenced hubs and the dependent child key.

4.4.6 LINK EXAMPLES

Figure 4.23 presents some examples of Data Vault link entity tables.

The first link, LinkConnection, connects a total of four hubs: the carrier airports, the source airports, the destination airports, and the flight number. Note that the airport hub was referenced twice, once by

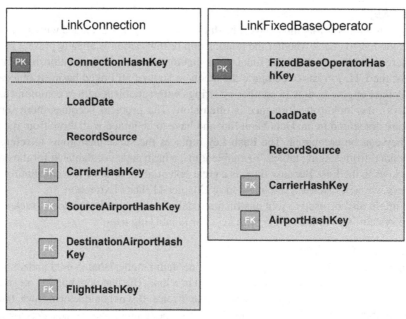

FIGURE 4.23

Data Vault link examples (physical design).

SourceAirportHashKey and another time by DestinationAirportHashKey. In addition, the link includes the required metadata LoadDate and RecordSource.

The second link references only two other hubs: HubCarrier and HubAirport.

4.5 SATELLITE DEFINITION

Satellites store all data that describes a business object, relationship, or transaction. They add context at a given time or over a time period to hubs and links. However, this context often changes in a business – thus the descriptive data in a satellite also changes over time. The purpose of a satellite is to track those changes as well.

A satellite is attached to only one hub or link. Therefore, it is identified by the parent's hash key and the timestamp of the change (Figure 4.24):

In addition to the known standard metadata, a satellite stores the attributes that describe the context of the business object or relationship. To achieve this goal, attributes capture the nonidentifying business elements of the business objects or relationships. These elements are often known in the source system as descriptions, free-form entries, or computed elements. Examples for descriptive data include:

- Exterior color of a car
- First and last name of a person (e.g., a customer or employee)
- Shipment address of an order
- Number of available seats on an airplane

FIGURE 4.24

A Data Vault satellite entity (physical design).

- Business name of an airline carrier
- Product descriptions in a product catalog
- Start and end date of a car rental

The last example shows that the end date of a relationship (in this case: the end date of a car rental) is captured by a satellite. There is no other concept of end-dating Data Vault links. As with other Data Vault entity types, the metadata comes first in the column order. Descriptive attributes are located at the end of the satellite. Because one of the primary objectives of the Data Vault is to capture the source systems, the descriptive attributes should use data types that are as close as possible to the source systems, from a technical perspective. This includes NULL values.

Not all attributes of a business object, relationship, or transaction are stored in one satellite. Instead, attributes are organized by business classification or type of data and are stored in individual satellites by category. A common practice is to store all attributes from one source system in one satellite, but separate them by the frequency of change. Section 4.5.2 discusses best practices for splitting the attributes of a satellite by classification or type of data. It also discusses the separation by frequency of change.

We will use the logical symbol shown in Figure 4.25 for drawing satellites throughout the book.

Note that satellites are never dependent on more than one parent table (that means, they are never dependent on more than one hub or one satellite). They also can't be parents to any other table (no snow flaking). For this reason, they don't introduce their own hash keys.

FIGURE 4.25

A Data Vault satellite (logical symbol).

4.5.1 IMPORTANCE OF KEEPING HISTORY

Providing a historic view of the data is one function that data warehouse performs in a business. The Data Vault uses its satellites to store every change to the raw data. It is possible, however, to change, alter, or redesign a satellite's structure. When doing so, make sure to preserve 100% of the historic data stored in the satellite that is being changed. Otherwise, your data warehouse loses its auditability and will not be able to pass an audit.

Due to the Data Vault architecture, the data warehouse becomes the one and only place where historic data is stored. There is no historic data in the stage area of the data warehouse. Data in the information mart might change depending on the business requirements. The only place where data is kept unchanged is the data warehouse. Therefore, it is important to understand that the data warehouse is the system of record. Business users might have a different opinion about the system of record, but: the Data Vault becomes the system of record whenever operational systems are retired, changed, or redesigned. In such a case, Data Vault satellites might be closed (as we discuss in the next section), but the data still remains in an auditable raw data format.

Because the history of the data needs to be preserved, you are not allowed to update or modify the data in the satellite. The only exception to this rule is the Load End Date attribute of the previous version of the data. Chapter 12, Loading the Data Vault, shows how to modify this attribute. In addition, only those source records with at least one change are added to the satellite. Therefore, a satellite is delta driven, comparable to a Type II dimension in dimensional modeling.

4.5.2 SPLITTING SATELLITES

It is not our goal to recommend that all descriptive information of a business object be kept in attributes of one satellite. Instead, it is recommended to distribute the data among various satellites. The recommendation is to split the raw data first by source system and second by rate of change.

4.5.2.1 Splitting by Source System

It is recommended practice to split the incoming data first by the source system. That means that each incoming data set is kept in individual satellites, which are in turn dependent on their parent (either a hub or link). Therefore, the raw data from a denormalized source data set would be distributed to different satellites in order to be kept dependent on the appropriate business object, relationship, or transaction. The advantages of such practice are the following:

- It allows the designer to add new data sources without changing existing satellite entities.
- It removes the need to alter the incoming data so that it fits existing structures (for example, by casting data into another data type or split, concatenating, lengthening, shortening, or otherwise manipulating the incoming data).

Airplane Hash Key	Load Date	Load End Date	Record Source	Avail Seats	Kitchen	Max Cargo	Flown Miles
384b... {D -AZUH}	2013-07-13 03:12:11	9999-12-31 24:00:00	FAA.OT	290	Y	1900	24750

FIGURE 4.26

Satellite before update of flown miles.

- It enables the Data Vault model to keep the history of the source system and therefore keep an audit trail for the system. Consider a satellite that keeps data from multiple systems: a change in one system would create a new record in the satellite. From the number of rows, it would not be immediately clear which system caused the change.
- It maximizes load parallelism because there is no competition (at the I/O or database level) for the target resource (the satellite). The data can be inserted into the satellite immediately without taking the arrival of data from other systems into account (which might try to insert their data immediately as well).
- Allows for the integration of real-time data without the need to integrate it with raw data loaded from batches. There are no dependencies across multiple systems that could force the system to have both types of data ready at the same time.

Even when the satellites are arranged by source system, a Record Source attribute is still required. The Record Source attribute can be used to identify the data source geographically or by application. For example, the source might be an SAP source system that is distributed across more than one physical machine. Depending on the requirements of the data warehouse, we track the individual physical machine in the Record Source attribute.

4.5.2.2 Splitting by Rate of Change

Once the data is split by source system, it is also best practice to further split the data by rate of change. Consider a satellite that holds information about an airplane. A number of attributes don't change very often: for example, the number of available seats, equipment, maximum possible cargo, etc. Some attributes might change more often, for example, the total number of flown miles (Figure 4.26).

Because the last attribute changes every time the airplane operates, it would produce a new record in the satellite to track the change. In order to do so, the current state of the other attributes has to be tracked as well. But because they have not changed, they just consume storage in the new record (Figure 4.27).

Airplane Hash Key	LoadDate	LoadEndDate	Record Source	Avail Seats	Kitchen	Max Cargo	Flown Miles
384b... {D -AZUH}	2013-07-13 03:12:11	2013-07-14 03:10:14	FAA.OT	290	Y	1900	24750
384b... {D -AZUH}	2013-07-14 03:10:15	9999-12-31 24:00:00	FAA.OT	290	Y	1900	27225

FIGURE 4.27

Satellite after update of flown miles.

To overcome this problem, the best approach is to split the data. Those attributes that are frequently changed are stored in one satellite, and those attributes that change less frequently are stored in another. If there are more than two frequencies, there should be more than two satellites (e.g., one satellite for nonchanging attributes, one satellite for those attributes that change monthly, one satellite for those attributes that change daily, etc.).

Throughout the book, we will use both practices when loading data into the Data Vault satellites.

4.5.3 SATELLITE ENTITY STRUCTURE

In addition to the attributes that store descriptive data in a satellite, the following metadata is required:

- Load date
- Record source

These attributes are discussed extensively in section 4.3.2 of this chapter. In addition, the following attributes are required in Data Vault satellite entities:

- Parent hash key
- Load end date

The following attributes are optional to Data Vault satellites:

- Extract date
- Hash diff

The next sections discuss all of these attributes in detail.

4.5.3.1 Parent Hash Key

The required **parent hash key** is part of the primary key that identifies the row of the satellite. The other part of the identification is the **load date**; together they provide the context and the date and time of the change. The **parent hash key** references hub or link's primary key of the parent business object (the one that the hub or link adds context to). As mentioned, every satellite entity must depend on only one hub or satellite entity. It is not possible to have a satellite that depends on more than one hub or link.

There should be at least one satellite entry for every hub or link key. Otherwise you have to use outer joins, which should be avoided for performance and complexity reasons.

4.5.3.2 Load Date

The required **load date** is the second part of the satellite's primary key. It indicates the date and time of the change captured by the satellite entry. Note that this is the time when the data warehouse saw the record for the first time. It is not the timestamp provided by the source system. Such a timestamp would be added as an ordinary satellite attribute that describes the data. The reason behind this is that timestamps from source systems are often unreliable or come from a different (or unspecified) time zone that is beyond the control of the data warehouse. Therefore, it captures this information as descriptive data.

There is an exception to this rule: when loading historical data, for example during the initial load of the data warehouse, the *Load Date* has to be set artificially in order to capture the historical loads. The problem is that the *Load Date* is used by the Data Vault model to identify changes in the source system.

If the historic data would be loaded with a *Load Date* set to the actual date and time of the initial load, all changes that have been made in history override each other on the same day (the day of the initial load) and cannot be captured by the Data Vault. In order to capture the changes as they would have happened in the past, we pretend that the data has been loaded in the past and set the load date to the date of the extraction from the source system.

A similar problem occurs when source systems provide multiple changes to the descriptive information of a business key (in a hub), relationship or transaction (both captured by a link): in this case, a mini-delta is provided, that provides the changes as they occurred by the operational system. To capture such sources, subsequence numbers are used, similar to multi-active satellites, which are covered in Chapter 5, Intermediate Data Vault 2.0 Modeling.

4.5.3.3 Load End Date

The required **load end date** indicates the date and time when the satellite entry becomes invalid. It is the only attribute that is updated in a satellite. The update occurs once a new entry is loaded from the source system. While the new entry has a current **load date**, the last satellite entry that was valid just before the loading of the new entry is updated to reflect the new **load end date**, which is the **load date** of the new record. The load end date is required to achieve the necessary physical performance when retrieving the data from the Data Vault, as demonstrated in Chapter 14, Loading the Dimensional Information Mart. It is not required from a logical modeling perspective.

4.5.3.4 Hash Difference

The optional **hash difference** attribute is similar to the **hash key** in a Data Vault link. It is a hash value of all the descriptive data of a satellite's entry. Having this hash value helps you to compare row values quickly and efficiently. **Hash difference** helps you identify differences in descriptive attributes quickly and add new satellite entries only when a change has been made to the satellite. It is possible to ignore some of the descriptive attributes by leaving them out of the hash value calculation for the **hash difference** attribute. This is required if some of the changes in the source system are to be ignored by the Data Vault. Note: the abbreviation often used in Data Vault models to represent a hash difference is **hdiff** or **hash diff**.

Chapter 11, Data Extraction, shows how to calculate the **hash diff** attribute when using it in satellite loads.

4.5.3.5 Extract Date

The optional **extract date** attribute captures the date and time when the data was extracted from the source system. It helps to understand historic load processes and is of most use if data is provided by flat files and pulled from sources around the world. When you use direct SQL access, the **extract date** is often not available. However, the ETL jobs typically log their activities, including the date and time at which data was extracted from source systems. Therefore, the **extract date** is available as metadata in the process logs of the ETL tool and doesn't need to be included in the Data Vault.

Because the **extract date** depends on the source system, it is treated as an unreliable timestamp. The data could be extracted from a source system in which the clock and system time zone are in question because it might not have been properly set up. In other cases, the data is extracted from another server (not the data source) with a different time zone than that of the source system or the data warehouse, without adding this information to the timestamp. In either case, the **extract date** is just reference data and becomes a descriptive attribute in a Data Vault satellite.

There are lots of other "dates" and "times" arriving on the source data, i.e. create dates, planned dates, actual dates, and so on. Any and all of these dates should be stored as descriptive attributes in the satellite tables; however, they should *never, ever* be used to populate the load-date or load-end-date values.

4.5.4 SATELLITE EXAMPLES

Figure 4.28 presents some examples of Data Vault satellites.

The first example, SatAirport, depends on HubAirport via the AirportSeq. The identifying primary key is a combination of the AirportSeq and the LoadDate (the date and time this record was seen by the data warehouse for the first time). In addition, the satellite uses the LoadEndDate and RecordSource

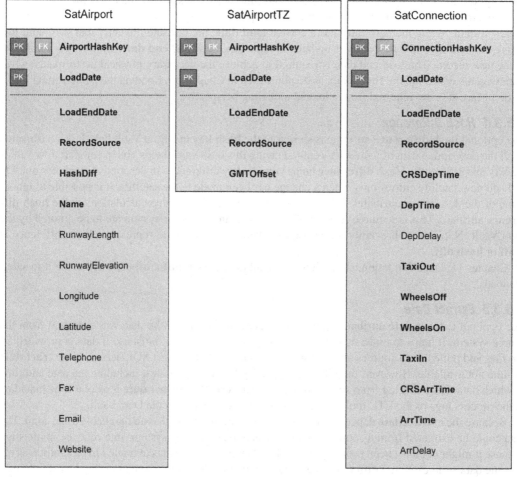

FIGURE 4.28

Data Vault satellite examples (physical design).

metadata attributes. To speed up lookups on the satellite for detecting changes to the rows, the satellite also uses the optional HashDiff attribute. The rest of the satellite comprises descriptive attributes from the source system.

SatAirportTZ was separated from SatAirport because it stores an attribute that changes more often than the descriptive attributes in SatAirport. While those attributes change very rarely (less than once in ten years), the GMT offset of a location changes twice a year (when the airport's region observes daylight savings time). If the GMTOffset attribute were to be stored in the SatAirport, all descriptive attributes would be copied over to a new row, even though there was no change to the descriptive data.

The last satellite is a satellite on a Data Vault link, LinkConnection. It stores all descriptive data to the connection. Because the information is provided in delta loads (the source system only provides new connection information), there is no need to look up which data already exists, hence no need for the HashDiff attribute.

4.5.5 **LINK DRIVING KEY**

The SatConnection example in Figure 4.28 depends on a link, as described. The model in Figure 4.29 shows this relationship.

The satellite SatConnection is attached to LinkConnection. The link itself depends on four hubs, which are shown in Figure 4.29, as well. If a new link entry is added, there will be one or more satellite entries, describing the context of the link.

Table 4.4 shows two entries describing the same connection. Apparently, the descriptive information was updated in the source system and was captured as a change by the satellite. Both records reference the same connection, by using the same *Connection Hash Key*. The *Load Date* attribute gives information when the data was loaded from the source system. However, the link in Figure 4.29 doesn't cover the reality of the data in Table 4.4. In fact, the key of the link consists of two parts. The first part

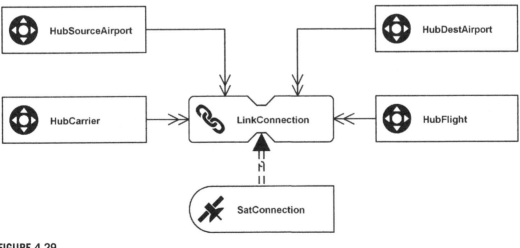

FIGURE 4.29

Link attached to four hubs (logical design).

Table 4.4 Satellite Data in SatConnection

Connection Hash Key	Load Date	Load End Date	Record Source	Dep Time	Dep Delay	Taxi Out	Taxi In
28db...	2013-07-13 03:12:11	2013-07-14 02:11:09	BTS	06:03	12	25	23
28db...	2013-07-14 02:11:10	9999-12-31 24:00:00	BTS	06:07	2	27	21

identifies the carrier and the connection served, which is the source airport and the hub airport. The second part of the key is the flight number. In reality, the carrier might change the flight number that is serving the connection. Nevertheless, it is still the same connection. The connection is identified by the three hub references that are marked by the bold arrows in Figure 4.30, which is a modified version of Figure 4.29.

Such a set of hub references is called a driving key in Data Vault 2.0 modeling. It is often referred to as the primary key of the source structure. Table 4.5 shows the data within the link structure.

The populated data in LinkConnection shows that United Airlines has changed the flight code from UA4711 to UA123 on the connection from Denver (DEN) to New York (JFK). Because the hash key is calculated on all parent business keys, each link entry has a different identifying hash key.

From a modeling perspective, the driving key is not visible. It is a logical construct that needs to be implemented in the loading procedures, especially when loading the satellite data. If a key in the link changes which is not part of the driving key, it triggers a new satellite entry, describing the changed context of the driving key (Table 4.6).

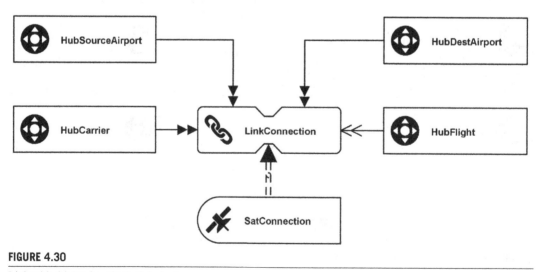

FIGURE 4.30

Link with driving key (logical design).

Table 4.5 LinkConnection with Populated Data

Connection Hash Key	Load Date	Record Source	Carrier Hash Key	Source Airport Hash Key	Destination Airport Hash Key	Flight Hash Key
28db...	2013-07-13 03:12:11	BTS	8fe9... {UA}	3de7... {DEN}	1aab... {JFK}	8df7... {UA4711}
9de7...	2013-07-14 02:11:10	BTS	8fe9... {UA}	3de7... {DEN}	1aab... {JFK}	9eaf... {UA123}

Table 4.6 Satellite Data in SatConnection with Driving Key

Connection Hash Key	Load Date	Load End Date	Record Source	Dep Time	Dep Delay	Taxi Out	Taxi In
28db...	2013-07-13 03:12:11	2013-07-14 02:11:09	BTS	06:03	12	25	23
9de7...	2013-07-14 02:11:10	9999-12-31 24:00:00	BTS	06:07	2	27	21

The driving key ties the different hash keys together, as shown in the link in Table 4.5. Without the driving key concept, the hub entries would be completely independent from each other. The satellite entries would depend on these independent link entries, having nothing to do with each other. Using the driving key, the satellite entries have a relationship, and the link entries in **LinkConnection** are tied together. The identification of link entries that belong together is done using the driving key information. The result of this relationship is that the first record for **connection hash key** 28db... is end-dated by using the **load date** of the next record (minus a second or less).

REFERENCES

[1] Linstedt, D, *Super Charge Your Data Warehouse: Invaluable Data Modeling Rules to Implement Your Data Vault*, 2012, available as pdf ebook from http://learndatavault.com/books/super-charge-your-data-warehouse/.
[2] Dörffler & Partner GmbH, Visual Data Vault (website), 2015, available at http://www.visualdatavault.com.
[3] Gibson Guitar, Community Forum website, 2008, available at http://forum.gibson.com/index.php?/topic/765-duplicate-serial-number/
[4] Michael Olschimke, Daniel Linstedt: "Visual Data Vault", http://www.visualdatavault.com

INTERMEDIATE DATA VAULT MODELING

5

The entity types presented in the previous chapter are the foundation for other Data Vault entities presented in this chapter. Many of these examples are just applications of existing link or satellite entities without changing the structure of the entity. These are often used in the Business Vault that was described in Chapter 2, Scalable Data Warehouse Architecture. In addition, this chapter discusses some important issues that often come up when designing and implementing a Data Vault based data warehouse. Note that this chapter is partially based on the book *Super Charge Your Data Warehouse* by Dan Linstedt [1].

5.1 HUB APPLICATIONS

Chapter 4, Data Vault 2.0 Modeling, has presented Data Vault hubs as the central entity used for storing business keys that identify business objects. In theory, an enterprise should have one leading operational system that keeps track of a specific business object. Customer relationship management (CRM) systems are good examples of such operational systems that are the main source for all customer-related information. In reality, however, business objects, such as customers, are stored in multiple operational systems, for example in retail databases, e-commerce applications, invoice management systems, and so on. Enterprises try to consolidate this information with a concept called *master data management*, which we briefly discuss in Chapter 9, Master Data Management.

Figure 5.1 shows that all data, including the business keys, is first loaded into the Data Vault layer via the staging area. The consolidation happens when the complex business rules are being processed and the information marts are being built. Data warehouse practitioners have to deal with multiple sources for a given business object. The major problem with having multiple sources is that each source has different capabilities for defining each business object. That is due to the different requirements that have been expressed by the business when these source systems have been built in the past. The result is that even the business key data types might be different: in some cases, the alphanumeric customer number (e.g., US4317 for a customer in the United States) that is defined on an enterprise level doesn't fit into some other operational system because it won't allow alphanumeric characters into the customer number. In that case, the business will rely on some sort of mapping tables that map customer US4317 in the CRM system to customer 132842 in the e-commerce application. (See section 5.2.2 for a more detailed discussion and an example of such a mapping table.)

Because this situation is more than common, the Data Vault has a solution to it. The recommended best practice is to load all business keys, regardless of their specific format, to one common hub (in this case the customer hub) and create a special link, called a same-as link (or SAL), to indicate the business keys that identify the same business object. The next section discusses hub consolidation with same-as links in more detail.

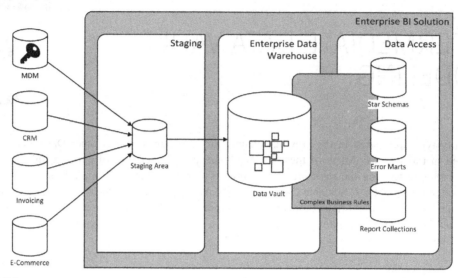

FIGURE 5.1

Consolidation of various sources in the data warehouse.

5.1.1 BUSINESS KEY CONSOLIDATION

As described in Chapter 2, Scalable Data Warehouse Architecture, the Business Vault is an extension to the raw Data Vault and allows data warehouse developers to add computed data to the Data Vault layer. This chapter will introduce computed aggregate links, exploration links, and computed satellites as examples of entity types that are part of the Business Vault. These entity types are modeled similarly to the core Data Vault entity types by following Data Vault modeling concepts, especially for links and satellites.

However, it is possible to customize every standard Data Vault entity in order to meet the needs of the organization. These modifications, which become part of the Business Vault, are sourced from the raw data in the standard Data Vault entities (hubs, links, and satellites) and are often optimized to improve the performance when querying the data from the Data Vault. A common use case is to consolidate business keys from various sources, as shown in Tables 5.1 and 5.2 and Figure 5.2.

Table 5.1 Passenger Hub			
Passenger HashKey	**Load Date**	**Record Source**	**Passenger Number**
8473d2a...	2014-06-26	DomesticFlight	1234
9d8e72a...	2014-06-26	DomesticFlight	1257
1a4e2c2...	2014-06-26	InternationalFlight	C21X9
238aaff...	2014-06-26	InternationalFlight	C43Z8

Table 5.2 Same-as-Link for Passenger				
SALPassenger HashKey	Load Date	Record Source	Master Passenger HashKey	Duplicate Passenger HashKey
38dfa8...	2014-06-26	Dedupe	238aaff...	8473d2a...
937aae...	2014-06-26	Dedupe	1a4e2c2...	9d8e72a...

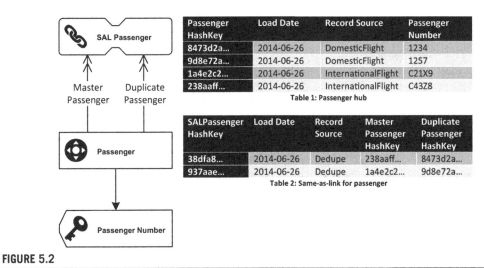

Passenger HashKey	Load Date	Record Source	Passenger Number
8473d2a...	2014-06-26	DomesticFlight	1234
9d8e72a...	2014-06-26	DomesticFlight	1257
1a4e2c2...	2014-06-26	InternationalFlight	C21X9
238aaff...	2014-06-26	InternationalFlight	C43Z8

Table 1: Passenger hub

SALPassenger HashKey	Load Date	Record Source	Master Passenger HashKey	Duplicate Passenger HashKey
38dfa8...	2014-06-26	Dedupe	238aaff...	8473d2a...
937aae...	2014-06-26	Dedupe	1a4e2c2...	9d8e72a...

Table 2: Same-as-link for passenger

FIGURE 5.2

Hub with same-as link structure to de-duplicate passenger business keys.

In this case, there is a *Passenger* hub in the Raw Data Vault that has been sourced from multiple source tables providing passenger numbers. In too many organizations, source systems are used which are not integrated. Therefore, the same passenger exists in multiple operational systems, having different passenger identification numbers (such as driver license number or passport number) assigned. Another reason for this problem is that source systems can sometimes support different formats for the same business key.

In this example, source system *Domestic Flight* allows (and uses) numeric driver license numbers only, while system *International Flight* allows alphanumeric business keys. This situation is far from optimal but often arises when two organizations merge together and continue to use their old systems without proper integration. The problem is solved by attaching a same-as link structure to the hub to indicate which customer numbers are used for the same customer. There are multiple options to compute the records for the same-as link, and could result from customer de-duplication algorithms, as in this example. The corresponding entity-relationship (ER) diagram is presented in Figure 5.3.

This approach, based on a same-as link and a hub with a single business key, only works as long as the number ranges of both systems don't overlap. If that is the case, the same business key can identify multiple business objects in different systems. Instead of using one hub for all business keys from all source systems in the Raw Data Vault, there are two options to deal with this situation. First, the hub

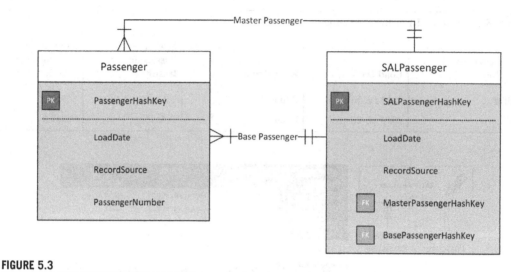

FIGURE 5.3

ER diagram for same-as link structure to de-duplicate passenger business keys (physical design).

could be extended by another business key, identifying the source system. This artificial key becomes part of the hub's composite business key. This solution has the drawback that it won't integrate the source systems. Another solution is to create multiple hubs and link them using a link table. This solution documents the different business key usages in the model but requires more entities in the Raw Data Vault.

From a modeling standpoint, both solutions are far from being optimal, but this reflects the actual use of business keys in the source systems, by the business. However, in both cases, this is the correct approach, because Data Vault 2.0 modeling is oriented to the business. If an organization is using a suboptimal way to run their business, it is therefore reflected in the Data Vault model as well. When the data is transformed to the Business Vault, it is still possible to merge the business keys into one business hub, including a same-as link structure as shown in Figure 5.3. In fact, a same-as-link is actually a Business Vault entity, as long as the information is not pulled from the source system, instead of being maintained by human intervention or algorithms. However, if the business keys are merged into a business hub, they should not overlap and identify only one business object. This follows the Data Vault 2.0 standard and can be achieved by the use of pre- or postfixes (or formatting elements) for those business keys that are not from the leading source system. For example, if the leading system is a CRM application and doesn't provide a business key for a specific business object, the identifying business key is taken from a secondary source system and loaded into the business hub. An example of such a secondary source system might include a ticketing system where a customer is added but has never been synchronized or replicated to the CRM application. To indicate this suboptimal case and prevent confusion, the business key from the ticketing system is enclosed by brackets, e.g. "(4711)". This business key is then used in analytical reports and it is apparent for the business user that the key is not a key from the CRM application and cannot be found there. It is also possible to add the source system to the business key, e.g., "(TCK:4711)" to provide the business user an indication where the key is coming from.

The query from such two tables could be relatively complex in some cases. In addition, the consolidated view of customer numbers is required in many cases, because business is interested in a consolidated list of customer keys instead of the raw data, except for some data quality reports. Therefore, it makes sense to provide the consolidated list, resulting from the complex query, in a new, materialized hub. This hub has the same structure as the hub in the Raw Data Vault, but with different data. Therefore, the statement from the beginning of this section remains valid: there is no special hub entity for the Business Vault. However, it makes sense to have Business Vault hubs in order to provide different sets of business keys to improve later querying. In such a case, the record source attribute is changed to "SYSTEM" or "SYS" to indicate that the value has been generated by the data warehouse system.

This example is a typical case where business rules are applied in the Business Vault. While business rules are typically implemented when loading the information marts, it is a good practice to implement them if they are generally used in more than 80% of the reports, or if heavy lifting is necessary. In this case, heavy lifting equates to long-running or complex business rules. By doing so, reimplementing the business rules for every information mart can be avoided. This becomes even more important with complex and time-consuming business rules that are used in multiple information marts.

The other Business Vault entities in this chapter on links and satellites are used in similar cases and with the same reasoning as described in this section.

Chapter 6, Advanced Data Vault Modeling, discusses two other Business Vault entities (the PIT table and the bridge table) that are used in order to make querying the data from the Raw Data Vault easier and to increase the query performance. For that reason, they are also called query assistant tables.

5.2 LINK APPLICATIONS

The next sections present frequent link structures and applications that Data Vault practitioners often use in their projects.

5.2.1 LINK-ON-LINK

One question that is often raised in the Data Vault design phase is whether it is possible to create links that reference other links (link-on-link structures). Consider the example of a flight diversion in the airline industry. Instead of reaching the original airport, the flight is diverted due to severe weather conditions or a security incident. The first idea to model the Data Vault model for this concept is represented in the logical model shown in Figure 5.4.

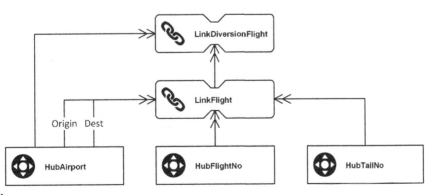

FIGURE 5.4

Link-on-link Data Vault model (logical design).

The link in the center of the model, **LinkFlight**, represents the original flight information as planned by the carrier. Each flight has a source and a destination airport (thus the two connections between **LinkFlight** and **HubAirport**), a reference to the flight number and another to the tail number. Note that there are no satellites modeled in this drawing.

The flight diversion is modeled as another link, **LinkDiversionFlight**. It references the original flight in **LinkFlight** and adds a reference to the new destination airport. While this model seems to be very efficient, it introduces an unwanted dependency between both links in this model. This dependency *does not scale* nor perform well in a high volume, high velocity (big data) situation. The more link-to-link structures are required to resolve at the DBMS level, the more exponential the work the DBMS needs to do. It needs to be reengineered at the start in order to achieve maximum flexibility in the future and ensure scalability with large datasets.

We have discussed in Chapter 3, The Data Vault 2.0 Methodology, how the functionality requested by the business user is delivered within separate sprints. The goal is to deliver small increments of the data warehouse and deploy these changes into production at the end of each sprint. The problem with link-to-link entities is that a change to the parent link (in this case **LinkFlight**) requires changes to all dependent child links (e.g., **LinkDiversionFlight**).

These cascading changes increase the time to modify parts of the data warehouse for change requests and can prevent the full implementation of the request within a sprint's length. Thus, these links should be avoided to secure the agility of the IT team. The recommended practice is to abstain from using link-to-link references and implement the links independently (Figure 5.5); this is known in data modeling circles as *denormalization*.

Now, each link is independent and can be modified independently when a change to its structure is required in the future.

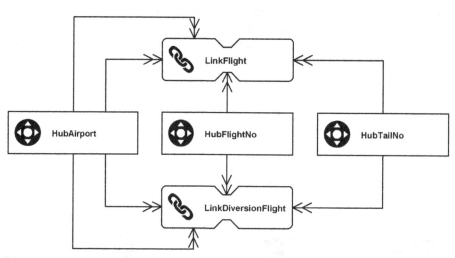

FIGURE 5.5

Independent links (logical design).

Table 5.3 Customer Hub				
#	**CustomerHashKey**	**LoadDate**	**RecordSource**	**CustomerNo**
1	**b7b0a554b9...**	**2014-01-17 08:20:15.000**	CRM	DE4711
2	**dd2c1f2d8d...**	**2014-01-17 08:20:15.000**	CRM	US4317
3	**e138c1d3c9c...**	**2014-01-17 08:20:15.000**	CRM	UK8876
4	**d1360901d7...**	**2014-01-17 09:05:43.000**	SHOP	764912
5	**74f33a3c01...**	**2014-01-17 09:05:43.000**	SHOP	124784
6	**a11593aeaa...**	**2014-01-17 09:05:43.000**	SHOP	132842

5.2.2 SAME-AS LINKS

As we have already seen in section 5.1.1, same-as links are used to indicate duplicate business keys within a Data Vault hub entity. This is required when the same business objects are identified by more than one business key. For example, Table 5.3 provides an extract from a customer list that has been loaded from multiple source systems.

The hub has been loaded from multiple sources, which have different options for storing a customer number. While the CRM system stores customer numbers as a composite key (a "smart-key" as described in Chapter 4, Data Vault 2.0 Modeling), the online shop is only able to store numeric values for customer numbers. Therefore, the business provides the mapping table between the customer numbers from the CRM system and the shop system (Table 5.4).

With that information, it is possible to create the link structure shown in Figure 5.6.

The link is loaded with the records shown in Table 5.5.

From a loading perspective, the hash keys in column **CustomerMasterHashKey** should come from the leading source system. That way, it is possible to look up the SHOP customer number by selecting the record from the same-as link table where **Customer1HashKey** is equal to the CRM customer number as the leading source system.

5.2.3 HIERARCHICAL LINKS

Hierarchical links are used to model parent-child hierarchies using Data Vault links. One example of such parent-child hierarchy is the bill of material (BOM) hierarchy that describes the parts required

Table 5.4 Customer Number Mapping Between Source Systems	
CRM Customer Number	**SHOP Customer Number**
DE4711	124784
US4317	132842
UK8876	764912

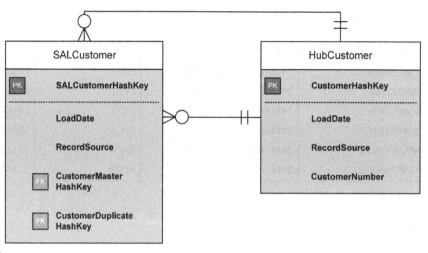

FIGURE 5.6

Same-as link for customers (physical design).

to build an airplane component. For example, an airplane consists roughly of the parts displayed in Figure 5.7.

Each part of the aircraft is made up of other, smaller parts. The components of a typical turbojet engine are displayed in Figure 5.8. The parts and subcomponents of an aircraft are recorded in a bill of material (BOM) structure displayed in Figure 5.9.

Each item on the bill of material is named, identified by a part number, and it is indicated how many items are required to create the component. In addition, the source of the item is given.

The Data Vault model to represent this so-called parent-child hierarchy is presented in Figure 5.10.

Instead of modeling each level of the hierarchy as separate hubs, the definition of one hub is preferred. It is true that the level itself, when analyzing it from a technical perspective, has a different

Table 5.5 Same-as Link for Customer Numbers

#	SALCustomerHashKey	LoadDate	RecordSource	CustomerMaster HashKey	CustomerDuplicate HashKey
1	c5cd634e4a… {DE4711;124784}	2014-01-17 09:08:27.000	MDM	b7b0a554b9… {DE4711}	74f33a3c01… {124784}
2	69777c1b5b… {US4317;132842}	2014-01-17 09:08:27.000	MDM	dd2c1f2d8d… {US4317}	a11593aeaa… {132842}
3	ae7324fa23… {UK8876;764912}	2014-01-17 09:08:27.000	MDM	e138c1d3c9… {UK8876}	d1360901d7… {764912}

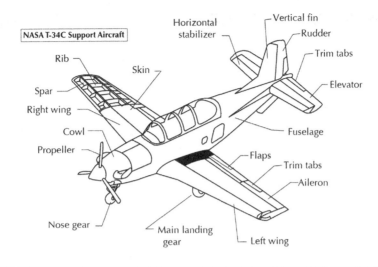

FIGURE 5.7

The parts of an airplane [2].

grain: the engine: for example, consists of the cowl and the propeller and therefore has a different grain than the individual parts that make up the engine. However, the business treats the hierarchy levels as *levels*. The grain of the levels is the same, considering this logical modeling perspective, because each level is made up of one or more sublevels. The level is a super-type in this regard and maintains the grain of the data as it exists in the source system.

In fact, the hierarchical link is just an application of the standard Data Vault link. It doesn't have a different structure, or violate the rules outlined in the previous chapter regarding links in any way.

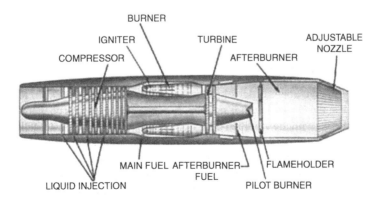

FIGURE 5.8

Sectional view of a turbojet engine [3].

Item	Level 0	Level 1	Level 2	Level 3	Part Number	Required	Source
Airplane	.				XJET-2000	2	Stock
Fuselage		.			10-0001	1	Stock
Vertical fin			.		20-0001	1	Stock
Rudder			.		20-0002	1	Stock
Elevator			.		20-0003	2	Stock
Horizontal stabilizer				.	30-0001	1	Stock
Trim tab				.	30-0002	1	Stock
Wing			.		20-0004	2	Stock
Spar				.	40-0001	3	Stock
Rib				.	40-0002	5	Stock
Skin				.	40-0003	2	Stock
Flaps				.	40-0004	1	Stock
Trim tab				.	40-0005	1	Stock
Aileron				.	40-0006	1	Stock
Main landing gear			.		20-0005	1	Stock
Engine			.		20-0006	1	Just in time
Cowl				.	50-0001	1	Just in time
Propeller				.	50-0002	1	Just in time

FIGURE 5.9

A bill of material [4].

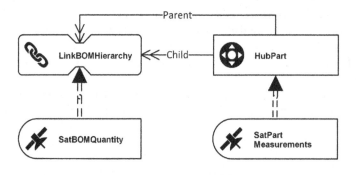

FIGURE 5.10

Hierarchical link representing a bill of material (logical design).

5.2.4 NONHISTORIZED LINKS

The links presented in the previous sections have one thing in common: they keep the relationship between business objects in the Data Vault. It is possible to capture data that has changed in the source system by adding a new record with the modified descriptive attributes to a standard satellite hanging off the Data Vault link. However, the updates from the source systems, implemented as inserts into the satellite, are not intended in all cases. For example, in some cases, Data Vault links store transactional data or data from sensors. This data should not be modified at any time. This is where nonhistorized links (also known as transactional links) come into play. This modified link is not updateable. If, for example, a transaction needs to be cancelled, a reverse transaction has to be created in the source system and loaded into the nonhistorized link. Other corrections, for example in case of error, should be avoided in the Data Vault.

FIGURE 5.11

Nonhistorized link (logical design).

Note that the former term "transactional link" is misleading: the link structure can also store relationships that cannot be updated, such as photos that are generated by a CCTV and stored as an incoming stream of data. The video surveillance system will not update the data that it has once written into the Data Vault model. Therefore, this link type is called a nonhistorized link today.

The logical symbol for nonhistorized links is shown in Figure 5.11.

The symbol is similar to the standard link, except for the indicator next to the icon to make clear that this is a nonhistorized link. For historical reasons, the indicator is a T as in transactional link. Note that it is not possible to add satellites to nonhistorized links in the logical design (even though there are options to add satellites in the physical implementation, as we will learn a little later in this section). Attributes that are part of the transaction are added directly to the nonhistorized link.

There are two options to physically model nonhistorized links in the Data Vault. The first involves a standard link entity and a satellite without a **LoadEndDate** attribute. Thus it is not possible to insert new versions of the records in this satellite because it is not possible to end-date the record and replace it by another version. Figure 5.12 shows an electronic invoice for a flight, a typical transaction in the aviation industry.

The transaction is identified by the invoice number 0198536 and was issued on January 21, 2014. Other information is also given, such as the customer and the sales person. Note that it is not possible to update flight reservations. If the information given during the reservation is wrong, for example because a wrong destination airport was given, the only way to change the reservation is to pay a change fee and buy a new flight reservation. The old reservation will be cancelled. Therefore, updating the old invoice is not possible without creating a new invoice.

Electronic Invoice

Prepared For:
OLSCHIMKE/MICHAEL MR   Ref: DOB110581

SALES PERSON	W1
INVOICE NUMBER	0198536
INVOICE ISSUE DATE	21 Jan 2014
RECORD LOCATOR	ZREJEY

Bill Address

DATE: Wed, Mar 19

Flight: **UNITED AIRLINES 9409** Operated by: **LUFTHANSA**

From	HANNOVER, GERMANY	Departs	7:00am
To	MUNICH, GERMANY	Arrives	8:15am
		Arrival Terminal	2
Duration	01hr(s) :15min(s)	Class	United Economy
Type	AIRBUS INDUSTRIE A320 JET	Meal	
Stop(s)	Non Stop		

FIGURE 5.12

Electronic invoice for flight.

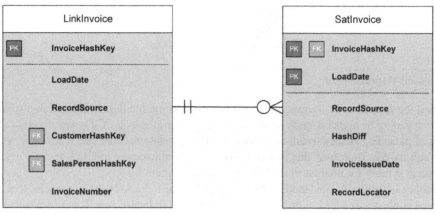

FIGURE 5.13

Nonhistorized link (physical design).

The logical Data Vault model in Figure 5.13 captures the electronic invoice transaction.

The link **LinkInvoice** captures the core transaction with a customer reference, a sales person reference and the transaction identifier **InvoiceNumber**. By definition, this transaction identifier is added to the nonhistorized link itself. The hash key of nonhistorized is derived from the business keys of the referenced hubs and the transaction identifier. The satellite **SatInvoice** contains all descriptive attributes such as the record locator and the issue date of the invoice. Note that the invoice issue date is different from the load date of the record, which is why it has to be added to the model. However, it is possible to use the transactional date as the load date if the time at which the transaction is loaded to the Data Vault is relatively close (within seconds) of the actual transaction date itself. Note that the entities in Figure 5.13 do not show all the descriptive attributes shown in the invoice displayed in Figure 5.12.

In some cases, it is possible to abstain from using a **LoadDate** attribute in the satellite entry, because both records (the link record and the accompanying satellite record) will have the same load timestamp. Therefore, the **LoadDate** attribute in the satellite stores duplicate data that consumes disk space. However, there are cases where the data for both entities comes from different sources and the data is delivered from both sources sequentially, just milliseconds apart. This often happens, for example, in real-time cases, which are not covered in this book. Anyway, in such a case, the **LoadDate** attribute should be modeled in both entities to capture the different arrival timings. Another reason for modeling the attribute in both entities is that of standardization, which makes it easier to understand the entities for new project members.

The second option, which should be avoided in most cases, is to add the attributes of the transaction directly to the link structure and abstain from using a satellite structure at all. Figure 5.14 presents an example of such a nonhistorized link.

The attributes **InvoiceIssueDate** and **RecordLocator** have been moved from the satellite into the **LinkInvoice** link. The satellite **SatInvoice** from Figure 5.13 has been removed completely, as it is not needed anymore.

This option is not recommended, because it changes the architectural design of the Data Vault model by introducing decisions to the design process. By doing so, it increases the complexity of the

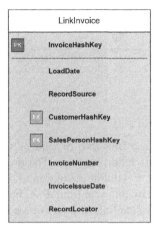

FIGURE 5.14

Nonhistorized link alternative without satellite (physical design).

model and increases the maintenance costs. In addition, it makes it more complicated to automatically load nonhistorized links. Nevertheless, there are times when the second option is valuable: if performance is an important issue, by which we mean that it is required to load data within milliseconds or faster, it might be necessary to model the nonhistorized link as in Figure 5.14. However, keep in mind that the width of the link table can do harm to your performance optimizations. If the data within a row becomes too wide, it will cut down the number of records per database page (at least in row-oriented database management systems, such as Microsoft SQL Server). The physical implementation may vary based on the physical platform chosen for implementation. As a result, the performance of both loading and querying the link structure will decrease. While the same could happen in the first option, it is possible to split the data into multiple satellites to keep the row size small.

Figure 5.15 shows that the attributes from the transaction are distributed over the satellites. Both satellites follow the definitions for nonhistorized satellites as outlined in this section. Moving the

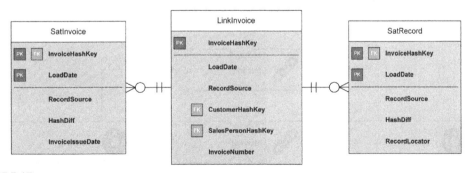

FIGURE 5.15

Nonhistorized link with multiple satellites (physical design).

FIGURE 5.16

Low-value link (logical design).

descriptive data from the nonhistorized link into dependent satellite should be considered if the number of attributes to be captured is relatively high. The problem is that Microsoft SQL Server stores its data in file pages of 8 KB size without the option to reconfigure this setting. The potential width of the link is primarily limited by this size limitation. For that reason, only a limited number of descriptive fields should be added to the link structure of a nonhistorized link in order to maintain performance.

Note that the Data Vault 2.0 is independent of the actual database system used. The examples in this book are based on Microsoft SQL Server, but can be transferred to other database systems easily.

5.2.5 NONDESCRIPTIVE LINKS

In many cases, Data Vault links will have one or more satellites to provide the context of the link. In some cases, however, links will not have any satellites. This might be the case if only the relationship between two business keys should be indicated, for example if an airline customer has expressed interest in a specific offering by clicking an advertisement on the Web site of the airline.

In Figure 5.16 the low-value link **Interest** connects hubs **Customer** and **Offering** without providing additional context.

Nondescriptive links are also used to store single states in a multistate relationship or in a role-playing relationship. If we extend the previous example, we could create another link to model another state – that a customer has been selected for a marketing campaign.

Figure 5.17 shows that this second state is added to the model by another link, **Mailing**. Note that there are other options to model multistate relationships, for example using a combination of a satellite and a code table.

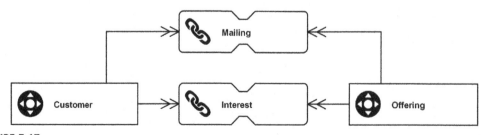

FIGURE 5.17

Multistate low-value link (logical design).

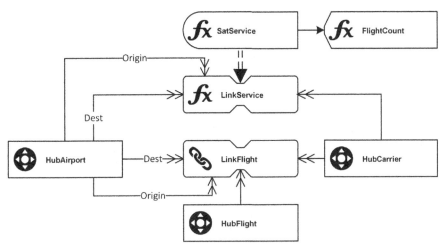

FIGURE 5.18

A computed aggregated link with computed satellite (logical design).

5.2.6 COMPUTED AGGREGATE LINKS

This type of Business Vault link removes one hub from a link and aggregates the data by the remaining relationships. For example, consider the Data Vault model shown in Figure 5.18.

The original link, **LinkFlight**, connects three hubs: **HubAirport**, **HubFlight** and **HubCarrier**. It denotes a flight that has been scheduled by a carrier between two connecting airports with a given flight number. When the flight number is removed from the link, the new link, **LinkService**, loses flight information because it doesn't contain a reference to **HubFlight** anymore. The link only indicates which carriers serve which airport connections. The number of individual flight numbers is aggregated into attribute **FlightCount** in satellite **SatService**. Both the **LinkService** and the associated satellite **SatService** are not from the source system. Instead, the data stored in the entities is calculated based on the aggregation functions.

Because this data is calculated and not raw anymore, computed aggregate links are part of the Business Vault. The entity is not auditable but can be regenerated from the source data in **LinkFlight** at any time. In this regard, the computed aggregate link is an application of the bridge table, covered in Chapter 6, Advanced Data Vault Modeling.

Because the computed aggregated link in this example is part of the Business Vault, it is also possible to modify the structure if needed, for example, by moving the computed attribute into the link structure, as shown in Figure 5.19.

This option is only available if the computed aggregate link is a Business Vault entity – that is, the link itself is calculated from raw data using a business logic, for example a GROUP BY statement. If the link data of the computed aggregated link is from the source system, the link entity remains in the Raw Data Vault (Figure 5.20).

In this case, the aggregation, which is still calculated from other data in the source system, is stored in computed satellites and attached to the raw link. This situation can happen if the link itself is available in the source system, but the aggregation is not. In this case, the aggregation is based on other raw

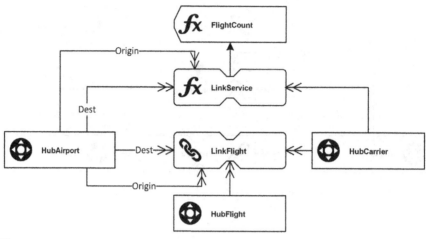

FIGURE 5.19

A computed aggregate link with computed attribute in the link (logical design).

data and attached to the right grain, which is the **LinkService** in the example in Figure 5.20. Therefore, the distinguishing characteristic of both modeling options is where the link data is coming from: is it from the source system or is the link data already calculated? In the first case, the data is modeled as a raw link with an attached computed satellite, as in Figure 5.20. If the link is already calculated from raw data, for example by a GROUP BY statement, the link entity becomes part of the Business Vault, as in Figure 5.18.

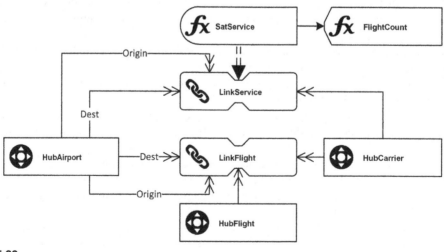

FIGURE 5.20

Computed aggregation on a Raw Data Vault link (logical design).

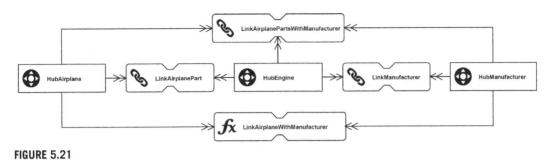

FIGURE 5.21

Exploration links (logical design).

5.2.7 EXPLORATION LINKS

Exploration links are computed links that have been created for business reasons only. Therefore, they are part of the Business Vault (see Chapter 2, Scalable Data Warehouse Architecture, for details). While the link between two hubs doesn't exist in the source system, the business might decide to create an exploration link to investigate the data (Figure 5.21).

The three hubs (**HubAirplane**, **HubEngine**, and **HubManufacturer**) in Figure 5.19 are interconnected to each other by two links (**LinkAirplanePart**, **LinkManufacturer**). The business might decide to analyze the relationship between those three hubs by adding **LinkAirplanePartsWithManufacturer**, which is a denormalized version of both links. In other cases, the business might decide to analyze the relationship between two hubs that are only indirectly connected, in this case **HubAirplane** and **HubManufacturer**. The resulting link **LinkAirplaneWithManufacturer** provides such an opportunity as shown in the figure.

The links, which are standard Data Vault links, are manually generated and maintained, even though the business can decide to automate the process of creating the link. Exploration links are part of the business vault and therefore not auditable. Reasons to create exploration links include:

- Determine relationships and dynamic networks between business entities (hubs) that are not in the source system
- Represent relationships that would be only indirect in the model otherwise
- Consolidate links between business objects if one of the referenced hubs contains duplicate entries (see same-as link)
- Identify clusters of similar entries within hubs (again, using same-as links)
- Automated discovery of patterns, for example in fraud detection

5.3 SATELLITE APPLICATIONS

After completing the discussion on specific purpose links, the next sections discuss similar cases for Data Vault satellites.

5.3.1 OVERLOADED SATELLITES

We have recommended in Chapter 4, Data Vault 2.0 Modeling, that for each data source there should be an individual satellite tracking the attributes from the source. In some cases, Data Vault implementers try to combine data from multiple sources into one satellite. While there are sometimes valid reasons for doing so, it introduces inherent risks as well.

The first problem occurs if the data format of each individual source is different, for example the character length of the name or address attribute. If the data is different, and there is a good chance that it is, the data becomes dirty very quickly.

Other problems become clear when analyzing Table 5.6, which shows a data extract from an overloaded satellite.

According to the **RecordSource** attribute, the data is from five different data sources. Because each source had the same structure and was using the same data types, the business decided to load all data into the same satellite. When analyzing the data, the following questions arise:

- Which source system should be the master system if data is contradicting each other (as in Table 5.6)?
- Are there any rows that supersede other rows?
- Which of the rows is the most current one?
- The primary key of this satellite should be a combination of **PassengerHashKey** and **LoadDate** (as discussed in Chapter 4). However, the field combination in this satellite is not unique. Should we include the **RecordSource** attribute to the primary key in order to make this a valid primary key?
- If some of the data sources provide NULL values or no values at all for some of the attributes, how do we handle them?
- Should we combine or merge the data from the source systems on loading or should we leave the data as is?

Some of these questions lead us to another problem, which lies in the delta-detection of the satellite. Remember that satellites should only store attribute changes, not the attribute state of each loading cycle. However, due to the problems we discussed above, the change detection becomes very complicated (because we want to keep every change of each source system, not only the one from the master system).

Table 5.6 Overloaded Satellite with Data from Multiple Sources

#	Passenger HashKey	LoadDate	Load EndDate	Record Source	HashDiff	Name	Addr	Phone
1	86f8sa7b3c...	2014-01-17 09:05:43.000		TICKETING	10daeb8564...	Dan Linstedt	26 Prospect St	802-524-8566
2	86f8sa7b3c...	2014-01-17 09:05:43.000		ONLINE	00ebf10b9e...	Daniel L	28 Root Beer	827-295-1212
3	86f8sa7b3c...	2014-01-17 09:05:43.000		BILLING	ef843ac01e...	Dan Linste	26 Prospect	999-111-1111
4	86f8sa7b3c...	2014-01-17 09:05:43.000		SECURITY	a7c8a5e9f1...	Dan Linstedt	26 Prospect St	802-555-152
5	86f8sa7b3c...	2014-01-17 09:05:43.000		BAGGAGE	a723cca93f...	Dan Linstedt	1 Richland	802-555-1215

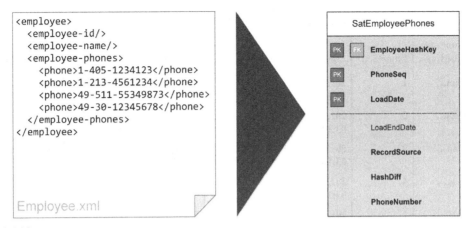

FIGURE 5.22

Multi-active satellite example.

5.3.2 MULTI-ACTIVE SATELLITES

Multi-active satellites are similar to overloaded satellites: they store multiple entries per parent key. However, these records don't come from different sources, but from a denormalized data source, such as COBOL copybooks or XML files. There are many examples of valid use cases. For example, employees might have an unlimited number of phone numbers, as in Figure 5.22.

The XML file on the left of Figure 5.22 represents an employee with a number of phone numbers. The structure of the XML file is translated to the Data Vault satellite entity on the right. The structure of the satellite is very similar to the one described in Chapter 4. The descriptive attribute (the phone number) is the PhoneNumber attribute, which is the only descriptive attribute in this example. The only difference from the proposed structure in Chapter 4 is the PhoneSeq, a sequence number which is the index that identifies the phone number within the left structure. The resulting satellite data is presented in Table 5.7.

	Table 5.7 Multi-Active Satellite Data						
#	Employee HashKey	PhoneSeq	LoadDate	LoadEndDate	RecordSource	HashDiff	PhoneNumber
1	33aa…	1	2013-07-14 03:10:15	(Null)	Employee.xml	12fb…	1-405-1234123
2	33aa…	2	2013-07-14 03:10:15	(Null)	Employee.xml	76ca…	1-213-4561234
3	33aa…	3	2013-07-14 03:10:15	(Null)	Employee.xml	8cb1…	49-511-55349873
4	33aa…	4	2013-07-14 03:10:15	(Null)	Employee.xml	9944…	49-30-12345678

Table 5.8 Multi-Active Satellite Data with Changed Source Order

#	Employee HashKey	PhoneSeq	LoadDate	LoadEndDate	RecordSource	HashDiff	PhoneNumber
1	33aa...	1	2013-07-14 03:10:15	2013-07-20 02:54:04	Employee.xml	12fb...	1-405-1234123
2	33aa...	2	2013-07-14 03:10:15	2013-07-20 02:54:04	Employee.xml	76ca...	1-213-4561234
3	33aa...	3	2013-07-14 03:10:15	2013-07-20 02:54:04	Employee.xml	8cb1...	49-511-55349873
4	33aa...	4	2013-07-14 03:10:15	2013-07-20 02:54:04	Employee.xml	9944...	49-30-12345678
5	8321...	1	2013-07-14 03:10:15	(Null)	Employee.xml	93ca...	1-205-1234123
6	8321...	2	2013-07-14 03:10:15	(Null)	Employee.xml	328a...	49-40-12345678
7	33aa...	1	2013-07-20 02:54:05	(Null)	Employee.xml	12fb...	1-405-1234123
8	33aa...	2	2013-07-20 02:54:05	(Null)	Employee.xml	8cb1...	49-511-55349873
9	33aa...	3	2013-07-20 02:54:05	(Null)	Employee.xml	76ca...	1-213-4561234
10	33aa...	4	2013-07-20 02:54:05	(Null)	Employee.xml	9944...	49-30-12345678

The data shows that there is one record for each phone number in the XML source file. Each record is identified by **EmployeeHashKey**, the hash key of the satellite parent; **PhoneSeq**, the phone number's position in the XML source file; and **LoadDate**, the timestamp of the first occurrence of the data within the source file.

However, there are issues involved with multi-active satellites because there is an order-dependency of the detail records. If the order of phone numbers in the XML source file changes, the whole employee's data will be seen as a delta, even if only two numbers switched positions without a phone number change. Table 5.8 shows an example of such data.

The first four records (records #1 to #4) represent the first order in the source system, while the last four records (records #7 to #10) represent the order of the same and unchanged records at the second batch load. However, the old records in the first batch are marked as deleted due to the **LoadEndDate**, which is not null in these cases (remember that this means that they have been replaced).

To solve this issue, it is possible to use the phone number itself as the sequence number. Subsequencing, as in Table 5.7, should be only the architectural fallback and used with active table-compression only. Table 5.9 provides an example. This removes the order dependency during delta checking but destroys any chance of reproducing the data set in the proper order as it arrived. If that is important, subsequencing as shown in the previous example is the only way. Another option is to include the

Table 5.9 Multi-Active Satellite Data with Alternative Sequence Attribute

#	Employee HashKey	PhoneSeq	LoadDate	LoadEndDate	RecordSource	HashDiff	PhoneNumber
1	33aa...	1-405-1234123	2013-07-14 03:10:15	(Null)	Employee.xml	12fb...	1-405-1234123
2	33aa...	1-213-4561234	2013-07-14 03:10:15	2013-07-20 02:54:04	Employee.xml	76ca...	1-213-4561234
3	33aa...	49-511-55349873	2013-07-14 03:10:15	2013-07-20 02:54:04	Employee.xml	8cb1...	49-511-55349873
4	33aa...	49-30-12345678	2013-07-14 03:10:15	(Null)	Employee.xml	9944...	49-30-12345678
5	33aa...	1-213-4561235	2013-07-20 02:54:05	(Null)	Employee.xml	776a...	1-213-4561235

existence of the phone number in the satellite as a currently active row before inserting. However, this option doesn't check the deleted phone numbers that may have disappeared from the incoming data set.

The table shows that record #2 has been updated by record #5 in the second batch. Record #3 was deleted and did not exist anymore. Therefore, it has been end-dated in the satellite. Note that the **PhoneNumber** descriptive attribute is duplicated into the primary key of the satellite (attribute **PhoneSeq**) instead of simply moved. This makes it easier to understand the satellite for the next user, who needs to extract descriptive attributes from the satellite for the business.

If the described solution is used, two issues could occur: first, the alternative attribute has to be NOT NULL and unique in the context of the parent and, second, performance could become a great problem. The performance problem arises if the sequence column alternative is a character string and not a number. However, a sequence number made up of characters is the better solution of two bad ones (the best worst-case scenario).

5.3.3 STATUS TRACKING SATELLITES

Status tracking satellites are used to load audit trails or data from change data capture (CDC) systems. These techniques track information on CRUD (also SCRUD) operations within the source system. The information has to be provided by the source system and includes information about the creation (C), reading (R), updating (U), deleting (D) and searching (S) of the data within the source system. Often, this information is stored by the operational system whenever a user executes one of these operations in the application. Table 5.10 provides an example for such a SCRUD table. It is the result of a CDC function and shows all the changes in the source table.

The __**$operation** column indicates the type of operation on the data. The CDC implementation of Microsoft SQL Server allows the following values [5]:

1. Delete
2. Insert
3. Update (old values)
4. Update (new values).

Table 5.10 Change Data Capture (CDC) Table for Employees

#	__$start_lsn	__$seqval	__$operation	__$update_ mask	Employee ID	First Name	Last Name
1	0x0000001C 000000610004	0x0000001C 000000610002	1	0x07	5	Chris	Miller
2	0x0000001C 000000620004	0x0000001C 000000620003	2	0x07	3	Jane	Brown
3	0x0000001C 0000006D0004	0x0000001C 0000006D0002	4	0x02	1	Mike	Freeman
4	0x0000001C 0000006E0004	0x0000001C 0000006E0002	4	0x02	1	Michael	Freeman

Note that, depending on the application, logging of reads (which is not supported by the CDC implementation of Microsoft SQL Server) might require a lot of storage. The same might be true for searches (again, not supported). However, some environments require this for security reasons to provide information about who accessed which data.

The status tracking satellite is defined as in Figure 5.23.

The status tracking satellite in Figure 5.23, **SatEmployeeStatus**, consists of only one descriptive attribute, the **Status** attribute where the __$operation data is stored. Other than that, there is only metadata which is not captured in logical Data Vault diagrams. The data in the table, derived from the data in Table 5.10, is presented in Table 5.11.

Note that the descriptive data (e.g., the business key) is not stored in the status tracking satellite. Only the status and the timestamp of the status change are tracked. In addition, the original values for these records are not displayed (they are outdated). The descriptive data is loaded to the respective standard satellites that are designed to capture this data. Other than that, the data in status tracking satellites should be normalized and follow the standard satellite layout and rules. Compression should be active on these tables in order to preserve disk space.

If multiple source systems provide status information, only the information from the master system (the leading system) should be tracked. Another good practice is to use multiple status tracking satellites for the business key or relationship, thus splitting the status tracking satellite by source system, a practice similar to the one described in Chapter 4.

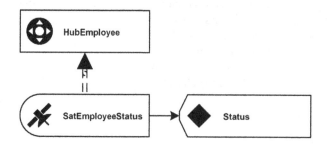

FIGURE 5.23

Status tracking satellite (logical design).

Table 5.11 Status Tracking Satellite Data

#	EmployeeHashKey	LoadDate	LoadEndDate	RecordSource	Status
1	5af3...	2013-07-14 03:10:15	(Null)	Employee	D
2	389a...	2013-07-14 03:10:15	(Null)	Employee	C
3	1121...	2013-07-14 03:10:15	2013-07-20 02:54:04	Employee	U
4	1121...	2013-07-20 02:54:05	(Null)	Employee	U

5.3.4 EFFECTIVITY SATELLITES

Effectivity satellites are often found hanging off Data Vault link entities and are presented in Figure 5.24. They track the effectivity of a relationship between two business objects among other applications (for example, it might be useful to track the effectivity of a business key in a hub). Its purpose is to track when the link is active according to the business and provides begin and end dates for this purpose. This data often represents the organizational-wide perspective, i.e., when the relationship (or business key) is considered as deleted in the organization.

The **LinkMembership** link in Figure 5.24 connects the two hubs in the model. While the link consists only of default attributes that capture the metadata of the relationship between airline and alliance, such as **LoadDateTime** and **RecordSource**, the link is not end-dated within the link structure itself (other sections in this chapter explain why this is not possible). The airline's membership start and end is captured by the **SatMembership** satellite, which depends on the link. The attributes **Membership-Begin** and **MembershipEnd** are added for this purpose.

The begin and end dates are not system generated. Instead, they have to be provided from a data source, for example the audit trail of Microsoft Master Data Services, effectivity dates within the master data, change data capture (CDC) or any other audit trail from operational systems. In order to pass an audit of the data warehouse, it must be possible to trace back the dates to the source system.

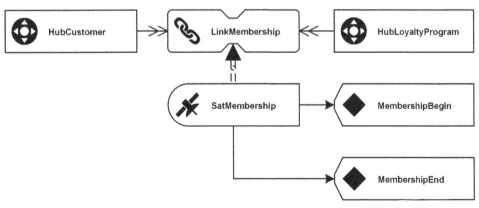

FIGURE 5.24

Effectivity satellite (logical design).

FIGURE 5.25

Effectivity satellite (physical design).

Effectivity satellites are only reasonable if the source system provides the effectivity dates. Avoid creating artificial effectivity dates unless the source system provides the data. Usually this is only true for a subset of data tables or feeds. However, the more sources provide effectivity dates, the better. Make sure to capture them in the Data Vault because they can often be used for data mining purposes.

The relational structure shown in Figure 5.25 implements the example from Figure 5.24 and is used to track the effectivity of airline memberships in airline alliances.

For each entry in the link table, there is one record active in the effectivity satellite. It is also possible to insert updated records, for example if memberships are extended.

Note that effectivity satellites don't track the availability of data in the source system. This is tracked by record tracking satellites, which record the status of data in source systems. They are described in the next section.

5.3.5 RECORD TRACKING SATELLITES

Sometimes, it is required to track which source applications are feeding which keys and associations on what load cycles. For example, many systems provide data in full dumps every day. In some cases, not all records are included every day. Instead, they appear and disappear from day to day without any fixed rule. This is especially true for legacy mainframe systems, because they're often locked records when they are being edited by the business user. If the records are dumped into the export file at the same time as the business user is locking the record for editing, the record is skipped and therefore not exported. In the export file, the record just doesn't exist at all.

Another problem is that these systems only rarely provide change data capture (CDC) information. Therefore, it is not possible to positively identify deleted records. However, in order to load the Data

Vault, we need to figure out which records have been deleted from the source system (in order to end-date them using the **LoadEndDate** attribute in satellites) and which only have disappeared from the exported file but will appear in one of the next exports. The latter should not be end-dated. This is similar to the **LastSeenDate** of hubs and links (see Chapter 4 for details) where the last timestamp is marked when the business key or relationship was last found in the source system – for the very same reasons.

In order to identify the difference between *"missing for a few days"* and *"was deleted,"* businesses usually set up a business rule to distinguish both classes. For example, the business could decide that all records that have not appeared for 7 consecutive days should be treated as deletes. The number of dates is often different for various types of data and data sources. This is also similar to the handling and update procedures of the **LastSeenDate** of hubs and links. Figure 5.26 presents the logical diagram of a record tracking satellite.

In this example the hub **HubPassenger** is extended by the record tracking satellite **SatPassenger-Track**. The diagram shows that the following record sources are watched for the occurrence of the customer key: flights, finance, loyalty program, and reservations.

For the existence of each business key or relationship in the source system at a given point in time, an insert is made into the record tracking satellite if one is available (for the hub or link). Therefore, the satellite indicates that the given key or relationship was present at the satellite record's time of tracking (the **LoadDate**). Table 5.12 shows an example of the data in the satellite from Figure 5.26.

Unlike other satellites, the record tracking satellite has no **RecordSource** and no **LoadEndDate** attribute. This is due to the fact that all records are system generated (thus no **RecordSource** attribute) and records are never updated (thus no **LoadEndDate** attribute). Instead of updating the records on each load cycle, a new entry is inserted every time. A value of 1 in the descriptive attributes indicates that the customer key was present in the source system, and a value of 0 indicates that the business key was not present. As a result of these modifications, record tracking satellites are nonauditable. However, this is not a problem because it allows us to bend the rules of Data Vault entities without breaking the whole model.

The record layout is optimized for partitioning, filtering and querying. It provides fast access to these components and the discovery as to which data sources *"appear and disappear."* However, the disadvantage is that it introduces an insert followed by an update for every new record source added to this table.

Table 5.12 Denormalized Record Tracking Satellite Data

#	CustomerHashKey	LoadDate	Manufacturing	Finance	Contracts	Sales
1	5af3...	2013-07-14 03:10:15	1	1	1	0
2	5af3...	2013-07-15 03:10:15	1	1	0	0
3	5af3...	2013-07-16 03:10:15	1	0	1	0
4	5af3...	2013-07-17 03:10:15	1	1	0	1

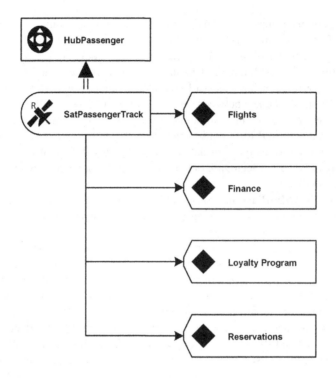

FIGURE 5.26

Record tracking satellite (logical design).

Note that, in order to avoid data explosion, each column or the whole table should be compressed. It is also advisable to summarize old data and remove it from the record tracking satellite in order to save more disk space. Old data is defined by the business again and should include all data that is not required for the initial purpose of the record tracking satellite – that is, identifying deleted data in the source system. An alternative to deleting this data is to move the data to slower (thus cheaper) disk space or backup tapes. Partitioning might help in this case again.

The structure in Table 5.12 shows that the record tracking satellite is not driven by data as all entities in the Data Vault should be. Instead, it is driven by the structure of the source systems: every time a source system is added to the data warehouse and feeds the parent table of this satellite, a new column has to be added for tracking purposes. This could be the right approach for your Data Vault if you are willing to accept these frequent structural changes. If it is not an option, it is also possible to normalize the data as shown in Table 5.13.

In this case, the record source is provided in the **RecordSource** attribute and the appearance of the business key or relationship under watch is tracked in **Appearance**. This design requires no structural changes to add new record sources because a new record source only requires inserts into the record tracking satellite. However, analyzing the satellite data is more complex but can be handled using the PIVOT SQL operator, which is available in Microsoft SQL Server and other database systems.

Table 5.13 Normalized Record Tracking Satellite Data

#	CustomerHashKey	LoadDate	RecordSource	Appearance
1	5af3…	2013-07-14 03:10:15	Manufacturing	1
2	5af3…	2013-07-14 03:10:15	Finance	1
3	5af3…	2013-07-14 03:10:15	Contracts	1
4	5af3…	2013-07-14 03:10:15	Sales	0
5	5af3…	2013-07-15 03:10:15	Manufacturing	1

If the business is providing detailed record sources (a practice that we try to follow in this book as much as possible), it is also possible to track the movement of data within the source system: where did the business key or relationship first occur in the system, where did it go from there, etc.). A detailed record source indicates the source as much as possible. For example, the record source *"CRM/Contact/ Lead"* identifies the **Lead** entity within the **Contact** area of Microsoft CRM [6]. Compare this implied information with the nondetailed record source *"CRM"* where no detailed information regarding the source of data is provided. To get the most out of the record source and thus provide as much value to the business as possible, try to use record sources as detailed as possible. The use of a hierarchical system is also advised in order to aggregate the data on the individual levels for analysis.

5.3.6 COMPUTED SATELLITES

By the definition in Chapter 2, Scalable Data Warehouse Architecture, the Data Vault stores raw data. However, in some cases, it might be useful to store computed data. In the Data Vault model, there is a place available for this, which is the Business Vault. In section 2.2 of Chapter 2 we have introduced the Business Vault as a set of tables that follow the Data Vault model and house business-rule changed data. These tables are called computed satellites and have the purpose of storing computed data, which is data that is the result of aggregation, summarization, correction, evaluation, etc. It might be the outcome of data quality routines, cleansing routines or address correction routines.

Usually, the business wants to perform such operations only once before distributing to the information marts to save computing resources. The computed satellite is exactly for this purpose: it stores the data before it is distributed. By doing so, the structure of a computed satellite follows that of a standard satellite. The only difference is that the record source indicates that it is system generated. It is also possible to provide the function, operation, or application that is computing the data for the satellite, especially if multiple sources for the data within the computed satellite exist and feed the very same satellite.

Because there is no direct raw data source for the computed data, it is not auditable by its very nature. However, it could be possible that an auditor would want to review the computational logic or at least see how, when, and what the data was before it went downstream to the information marts. The computed satellite is the place to show this.

The logical symbol for computed satellites is presented in Figure 5.27.

Other than the icon on the shape, there is no difference from standard satellites. As already mentioned, the structure is the same. Again, the difference is the source of data, because it is calculated data that is stored in this entity type.

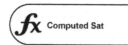

FIGURE 5.27

Computed satellite (logical symbol).

REFERENCES

[1] Linstedt, D. Super Charge Your Data Warehouse: Invaluable Data Modeling Rules to Implement Your Data Vault, 2012. available as pdf ebook from http://learndatavault.com/books/super-charge-your-data-warehouse/.

[2] NASA. Aeronautics Educator Guide – Parts of an Airplane, 2014. available at http://www.nasa.gov/audience/foreducators/topnav/materials/listbytype/Aeronautics_Parts_of_Airplane.html.

[3] NASA. Liquid Hydrogen as a Propulsion Fuel, http://history.nasa.gov/SP-4404/app-b5.htm.

[4] U.S. Department of Transportation, Federal Aviation Administration: "Aviation Maintenance Technician Handbook", p. 2–6.

[5] Microsoft SQL Server, Technet Library, 2015. available at http://technet.microsoft.com/en-us/library/bb500305.aspx.

[6] Microsoft MSDN Library website, Contact Entities, 2015. available at http://msdn.microsoft.com/en-us/library/bb928236.aspx.

ADVANCED DATA VAULT MODELING

The previous chapter has introduced applications and special versions of the core entities in Data Vault 2.0, such as same-as links (a basic application of the link structure) and computed satellites (a special version of the satellite, used in the Business Vault). This chapter introduces more entity types that are not directly based on these core entities but are commonly used in Data Vault 2.0 modeling. The structures presented in section 6.1 and 6.2 have in common that their primary use case is to make querying the data out of the Data Vault easier, and therefore to increase the query performance. This is of great value when using virtual information marts to present the information to business users. The concept of virtual information marts has already been introduced in Chapter 2 and will be demonstrated in Chapter 14, Loading the Data Information Mart, using SQL views. Section 6.3 shows how to deal with reference data in the Data Vault.

6.1 POINT-IN-TIME TABLES

A problem that can occur when querying the data out of the Raw Data Vault happens when there are multiple satellites on a hub or a link (Figure 6.1).

In this example, there are multiple satellites on each hub and link included in the diagram. This is a very common situation for data warehouse solutions, because they integrate data from multiple source systems. However, this situation increases the complexity when querying the data out of the Raw Data Vault. The problem arises because the changes to the business objects stored in the source systems don't happen at the same time. Instead, a business object, such as a passenger, is updated in the *Domestic Flight* system at a given time, then updated in the *International Flight* system, etc. Note that the PIT table is already attached to the hubs, as indicated by the ribbon. Tables 6.1, 6.2, 6.3 and 6.4 show data views of the updates to the passenger hub and related satellites.

The example shows two passengers and the changes to their data over time. For example, Amy Miller probably married a Mr. Freeman and subsequently changed her name to Amy Freeman (see Table 6.2). She also changed her preferred dish over the time, from vegetarian food to meat and back to vegetarian food (see Table 6.3). Both passengers moved (or at least gave changing addresses) over time (see Table 6.4).

Changes came in at various times, not related to each other. Most updates would be added when bookings were performed, but they did not affect all operational systems at the same time. And as a consequence, a change did not affect all satellites. Instead, it affected only the satellite that was supposed to cover the change, an advantage that we have already discussed in Chapter 4.

In addition, satellites do not cover all changes that occur in a source system. Instead, the changes or deltas captured by the satellites are only as frequent as the feeds that supply them. Satellites track only those changes that are delivered to the data warehouse. If the warehouse needs to keep records of all changes on the source system, the source system needs to supply an audit log, such as the one produced by Microsoft SQL Server 2014 with Change Data Capture (CDC) turned on. The other option is to provide the data in real-time using an Enterprise Service Bus (ESB) or Message Queue (MQ). If these options are not used, only those changes included in the source extracts are loaded. For example, if the batch loads run every six hours, then the deltas in the satellites will only track the record as it stands every six hours.

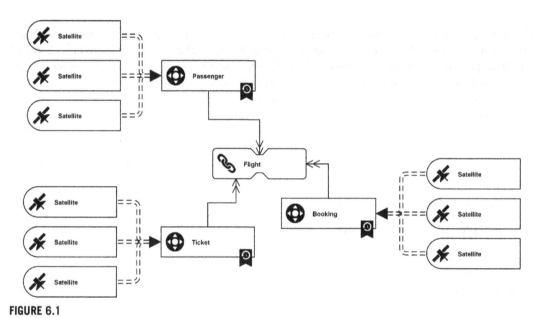

FIGURE 6.1

Hubs with multiple satellites and PIT ribbon (logical design).

Table 6.1 Passenger Hub Data

Passenger HashKey	LoadDate	Record Source	Passenger Number
8473d2a...	1995-06-26	DomesticFlight	1234
9d8e72a...	2001-06-03	DomesticFlight	1257

Table 6.2 Passenger Name Satellite Data

Passenger HashKey	LoadDate	LoadEndDate	Record Source	Title	First Name	Last Name
8473d2a...	1991-06-26	2003-03-03	DomesticFlight	Mrs.	Amy	Miller
9d8e72a...	2001-06-03	9999-12-31	DomesticFlight	Mr.	Peter	Heinz
8473d2a...	2014-06-20	9999-12-31	DomesticFlight	Mrs.	Amy	Freeman

Table 6.3 Satellite with Preferred Dish Data

Passenger HashKey	LoadDate	LoadEndDate	RecordSource	Preferred Dish
8473d2a...	1995-06-26	1997-03-21	InternationalFlight	Vegetarian
8473d2a...	1997-03-21	2001-04-01	InternationalFlight	Meat
8473d2a...	2001-04-01	9999-12-31	InternationalFlight	Vegetarian
9d8e72a...	2001-06-03	9999-12-31	InternationalFlight	Vegetarian

Table 6.4 Satellite with Address Data for Passenger

Passenger HashKey	Load Date	Load End Date	Record Source	Address Line 1	Address Line 2	City	Zip	State	Country
8473d2a...	1995-06-26	2000-05-20	Domestic Flight	31 Main St.		Norman	30782	OK	USA
8473d2a...	2000-05-20	2007-04-21	Domestic Flight	9612 Lincoln Road	Apt. #3	Santa Clara	70831	CA	USA
9d8e72a...	2001-06-03	2014-08-21	Domestic Flight	Am Platz 3		Berlin	10872		Germany
8473d2a...	2007-04-21	9999-12-31	Domestic Flight	2050 1st street		San Francisco	94114	CA	USA
9d8e72a...	2014-08-21	9999-12-31	Domestic Flight	Auf dem Hofe 9		Stadt Oldendorf	98472		Germany

When building an information mart from this raw data, querying the passenger state on a given date, e.g. January 5th, 2006, becomes complicated: the query should return the customer data as it was active according to the data warehouse delta process on the selected date. It requires OUTER JOIN queries with complex time range handling involved to achieve this goal. With more than three satellites on a hub or link, this becomes complicated and also slow. The better approach is to use equal-join queries for retrieving the data from the Raw Data Vault. To achieve this, a special entity type is used in Data Vault modeling: point-in-time tables (PIT) and a set of ghost records in satellite tables attached to fixed primary keys.

This entity is introduced to a Data Vault model whenever the query performance is too low for a given hub or link and surrounding satellites. In the model, point-in-time tables are added to each hub or link where the PIT table should be calculated. Because the data in a PIT table is system-computed and is not originating from a source system, the data is not to be audited. The purpose of this table is to provide performance only.

6.1.1 POINT-IN-TIME TABLE STRUCTURE

A Point-In-Time structure is a query assistant structure, and is geared towards query performance. One can and should consider the PIT structure to be part of the Business Vault or Information Mart layer.

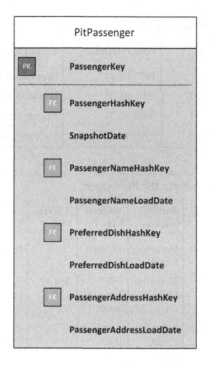

FIGURE 6.2

Physical PIT table for passenger (physical design).

In this manner, the structure can be modified to include computed columns as necessary to achieve maximum query performance.

To achieve this goal, a PIT table creates snapshots of data for dates specified by the data consumers upstream. For example, some businesses require the current state of data each day, others every second. To accommodate these requirements, the PIT table includes the date and time of the snapshot, in combination with the *PassengerHashKey*, as a unique key of the entity. For each of these combinations, the PIT table contains the load dates and the corresponding hash keys from each satellite that corresponds best with the snapshot date. A physical representation of the PIT table for the example in the previous section is presented in Figure 6.2.

Each entry in the point-in-time table is identified by a hash key. This hash value can be used downstream when loading the Type 2 dimension tables of the information mart. This is discussed in more detail in Chapter 14, Loading the Dimensional Data Mart. Once the PIT table of the previous example is populated with data, it looks like Table 6.5.

As this figure shows, there should be one load date column for each available satellite. For each *PassengerHashKey* and *SnapshotDate* combination, the corresponding *Load Dates* are given per satellite. In addition, the hash key is copied over from the satellite. In most cases, this value will be the same value as the hash key in the identifying key (in this example, PassengerHashKey). However, in some cases, there is no corresponding satellite entry for a given snapshot date: either the business key was not known by the source system at the given snapshot date or it was deleted from the source system. In the

Table 6.5 Data View on PIT Table for Passenger

Passenger Key	Passenger Hash Key	Snapshot Date	Passenger Name Hash Key	Passenger Name Load Date	Preferred Dish Hash Key	Preferred Dish Load Date	Passenger Address Hash Key	Passenger Address Load Date
1a8d2ef...	8473d2a...	1995-01-01	8473d2a...	1991-06-26	NULL	NULL	NULL	NULL
234def9...	8473d2a...	2000-01-01	8473d2a...	1991-06-26	8473d2a...	1997-03-21	8473d2a...	1995-06-26
39834fa...	8473d2a...	2005-01-01	8473d2a...	2001-06-03	8473d2a...	2001-04-01	8473d2a...	2000-05-20
4fafa90...	9d8e72a...	2005-01-01	9d8e72a...	2001-06-03	9d8e72a...	2001-06-03	9d8e72a...	2001-06-03
501ab9f...	8473d2a...	2010-01-01	8473d2a...	2001-06-03	8473d2a...	2001-04-01	8473d2a...	2007-04-21
6c0429b...	9d8e72a...	2010-01-01	9d8e72a...	2001-06-03	9d8e72a...	2001-06-03	9d8e72a...	2001-06-03
7ab9233...	8473d2a...	2015-01-01	8473d2a...	2014-06-20	8473d2a...	2001-04-01	8473d2a...	2007-04-21
81298bb...	9d8e72a...	2015-01-01	9d8e72a...	2001-06-03	9d8e72a...	2001-06-03	9d8e72a...	2014-08-21

PIT shown in Table 6.5, this is the case for entry number 1. Unlike the satellite for storing passenger names, the satellites **Preferred Dish** and **Passenger Address** don't provide an entry for the snapshot date 1995-01-01. If the source system doesn't provide a corresponding record from the source system, the PIT table should point to an unknown record. In Data Vault 2.0 modeling, this record is called the ghost record. This record should be added to each satellite (Table 6.6).

The advantage of this entry is that it is valid at all times (thus the earliest load date and latest load end date available in the selected data type). The record source has been set to SYSTEM to indicate that the record is artificially generated. The PIT table from Table 6.5 would be modified by replacing NULL references with references to the ghost record in the satellite table (Table 6.7).

The NULL values from the previous version of this PIT have been replaced by references to the ghost record in each satellite. By providing the ghost record in each satellite referenced by the PIT table, it is possible to use equi-joins instead of outer joins when querying data from it. Because NULL values do not exist in the PIT table references to the satellites anymore, they don't need to be accounted for.

The PIT table doesn't contain any other system-generated attributes such as the record source. That is because the data is system generated and has no record source or load date by itself. However, it is possible to add additional computed attributes as seen fit. For example, a load end date could be added to support queries with a BETWEEN clause. Other attributes could provide aggregations or computations to improve the query performance even further. However, special attention should be paid to the

Table 6.6 Satellite for Passenger Data Utilizing the Ghost Record

Passenger Hash Key	Load Date	Load End Date	Record Source	First Name	Last Name
0000000...	0001-01-01	9999-12-31	SYSTEM	?	?
8473d2a...	2001-06-03	2014-06-19	Passenger DB	Daniel	Linstedt

Table 6.7 Data View of PIT with Referenced Ghost Records

Passenger Key	Passenger Hash Key	Snapshot Date	Passenger Name Hash Key	Passenger Name Load Date	Preferred Dish Hash Key	Preferred Dish Load Date	Passenger Address Hash Key	Passenger Address Load Date
1a8d2ef...	8473d2a...	1995-01-01	8473d2a...	1991-06-26	0000000...	0001-01-01	0000000...	0001-01-01
234def9...	8473d2a...	2000-01-01	8473d2a...	1991-06-26	8473d2a...	1997-03-21	8473d2a...	1995-06-26
39834fa...	8473d2a...	2005-01-01	8473d2a...	2001-06-03	8473d2a...	2001-04-01	8473d2a...	2000-05-20
4fafa90...	9d8e72a...	2005-01-01	9d8e72a...	2001-06-03	9d8e72a...	2001-06-03	9d8e72a...	2001-06-03
501ab9f...	8473d2a...	2010-01-01	8473d2a...	2001-06-03	8473d2a...	2001-04-01	8473d2a...	2007-04-21
6c0429b...	9d8e72a...	2010-01-01	9d8e72a...	2001-06-03	9d8e72a...	2001-06-03	9d8e72a...	2001-06-03
7ab9233...	8473d2a...	2015-01-01	8473d2a...	2014-06-20	8473d2a...	2001-04-01	8473d2a...	2007-04-21
81298bb...	9d8e72a...	2015-01-01	9d8e72a...	2001-06-03	9d8e72a...	2001-06-03	9d8e72a...	2014-08-21

width of the PIT table. If the width becomes too large, the performance will decrease again, losing the advantage of the PIT table. This recommendation is especially important with Microsoft SQL Server 2014 as it only supports database page sizes with 8 KB. If database servers support database pages with more than 32 KB and a corresponding block size of the physical storage, it alleviates this issue.

To keep the performance of PIT tables high, there are two recommendations. The first one is to turn on compression on the database level. Microsoft SQL Server supports data compression for database tables. Compressing the data in the table has multiple advantages:

- Compression reduces the size of the database
- It improves the I/O performance because the compressed data is stored on fewer database pages which need to be read from disk

However, data compression also requires more CPU resources to compress and decompress the data.

The second solution to keep the performance high on PIT tables is to delete unused snapshots. The next section describes this approach in more detail. Chapter 14 also demonstrates how this structure can be used to improve the query performance when building information marts. The standard PIT table is based on a regular snapshot and forced to be built based on business user service level agreements and provisioning requirements. Note that there may be times when full history is required and that it is possible to derive the snapshot date from all load dates stored in the satellites hanging off the parent. This way, the snapshot date is not based on a regular interval but on the actual changes in the source system, covering the full history of the data. However, full history should be the exception rather than the rule.

6.1.2 MANAGED PIT WINDOW

It is a good practice to introduce managed windows in PIT tables to prevent uncontrolled storage consumption for them. In most situations, there is only need for PIT table snapshots within a limited time. Older data should be deleted because it is not used anymore.

In Figure 6.3, the PIT table only keeps history for the last three months and removes all snapshots that are older than these three months. Having older, unused data in PIT tables decreases the query

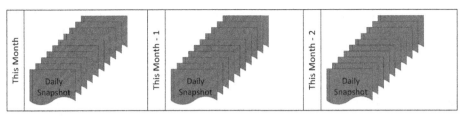

FIGURE 6.3

Managing the PIT Window.

performance if no additional optimization is done, such as partitioning the table. It is required that the business state how much of the old snapshots should be kept in PIT tables, thus available in virtual dimensions. In fact, this "designation of old data" is specified differently for each PIT table.

The other option to prevent a decrease of performance is to introduce another concept that doesn't delete all historic snapshots from PIT tables. Instead of deleting all data in the PIT table that is older than a given number of days or months, *most* old data is removed. This concept is called logarithmic PIT table and is shown in Figure 6.4.

All snapshots from the current month are kept. In addition, one snapshot per week is stored for the current year. After that, the PIT table stores only one snapshot per month, but only for the last five

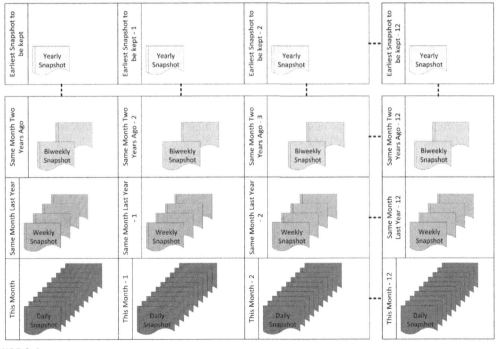

FIGURE 6.4

Logarithmic PIT table snapshots.

years. Older data is deleted. Such a table is a compromise between storage consumption and query performance. It helps to query older data relatively easy. If additional snapshots are required, they could be rebuilt using the same algorithm that has built them in the past.

6.2 BRIDGE TABLES

There is another type of query assistant table in the Data Vault 2.0 standard: the bridge table. Similar to PIT tables, their purpose is to improve the performance of queries on the Raw Data Vault by reducing the number of required joins for the query. They are also part of the Business Vault, because the data in bridge tables are system generated and cannot be audited for this reason. Bridge tables should only be constructed if the queries on the Raw Data Vault experience performance issues.

Unlike PIT tables, which span across multiple satellites of a hub or link, a bridge table spans across multiple hubs and links. By doing so, it is similar to a specialized link table. It doesn't contain any information from satellites, primarily because the table width would become too large. Figure 6.5 shows a logical model of a bridge table in Data Vault 2.0.

In the above scenario, there is *Passenger* data linked with the *Sales Agent* via the *Booking* link. Satellites are used for most hubs and links in this example. The *Passenger Bridge* doesn't span over *Flight* and *Airline*. The model doesn't show the business keys or any other attributes that are part of the Data Vault entities. The bridge table acts as a higher-level fact-less fact table and contains hash keys from the hubs and links it spans.

Another performance improvement can be achieved by adding computations to the bridge table that take much time. This is especially important when creating virtual information marts on the Data Vault because these require some computing, which slows down the access to the virtualized information mart entities. Using bridge tables, the query performance can be drastically improved.

Bridge tables are not required to have the same grain as the links that they are covering. In these cases, the bridge table might contain aggregated values that are added to the structure and loaded using GROUP BY statements. The resulting bridge table has a higher grain than the links that are included in the table. By doing so, the bridge table becomes very similar to an exploration link which has been covered in Chapter 5, Intermediate Data Vault Modeling.

Note that loading the bridge table will cause the Cartesian product of all business keys involved in associated hubs. Therefore, the query should be limited by a WHERE clause in the statement. Instead

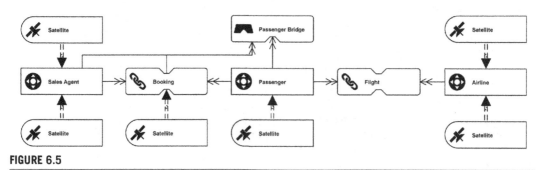

FIGURE 6.5

Bridge table to improve the query performance on passenger data (logical design).

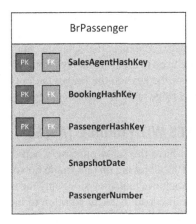

FIGURE 6.6

Physical design of a bridge table (physical design).

of loading all possible combinations, the statement should focus on the grain required for the fact table, that is, based on the bridge. If there are multiple fact tables with different grains in the information mart, there should be multiple bridge tables (at least one bridge table per grain definition).

6.2.1 BRIDGE TABLE STRUCTURE

A bridge table contains all hash keys from hubs and links that are part of the bridge table, in addition to the snapshot date and a hash key for each entry. Business keys, computed or aggregated fields are optional. Figure 6.6 shows an example of a bridge table.

Each entry in the bridge table *BrPassenger* is identified by the hash keys of the referenced hubs and links. The *SnapshotDate* attribute shows when the individual record was loaded into the bridge table. In some cases, the SnapshotDate is included in the primary key, for example when creating fact tables for inventory tracking: in this case, the stock is tracked per product, per store, and per day.

Table 6.8 contains example data for the bridge table.

While it is possible to add business keys, such as the passenger number in Table 6.8, to the bridge table, it should be done carefully because it increases the width of the table. If the width becomes too large, the performance will drastically drop, especially in large data sets. It also introduces fragmented data

Table 6.8 Bridge Table Information				
Sales Agent Hash Key	Booking Hash Key	Passenger Hash Key	Snapshot Date	Passenger Number
912cd73…	9ef749c…	8473d2a…	2010-01-01	1234
8bca7f0…	91234cc…	9d8e72a…	2010-01-01	1257
f843de9…	43f8e9a…	a8c7678…	2010-01-01	3587

and overindexing of rows. These effects neutralize the advantages of a bridge table and in fact cause it to lose performance. Therefore, it is important to keep the width of the bridge table as small as possible.

In some cases, bridge tables can also contain actual satellite data, such as key performance indicator (KPI) values or other values that are used to create measures in the fact table. However, the grain of the satellite data must match the grain of the keys in the bridge table. Otherwise, facts can be double and triple counted when the data in the bridge table is further aggregated.

6.2.2 COMPARING PIT TABLES WITH BRIDGE TABLES

While PIT tables and bridge tables have the same purpose when they assist querying the Raw Data Vault, they have some differences. PIT tables are on one single hub or link only. They are used to create a snapshot of satellite load dates. To achieve that, they store only the hash key of the hub (or link) and the load dates of the corresponding satellite load dates, in addition to the snapshot date of the PIT table. It is possible to add more computed attributes, such as the hubs business key, which is a common practice.

Bridge tables, on the other hand, are created from multiple hubs and links. They contain the hash keys from all hubs and links that they span. In addition, it is common practice to add their business keys, as well. Computed fields are allowed in addition. They are also identified by a snapshot date.

Both entities have in common that they are system-generated entities that are not part of the core architecture. System-generated fields make them nonauditable. Both of them can contain computed fields. They are used to improve the query performance on the Data Vault, especially if a virtualized information mart is used upstream. In that case, they can drastically improve the query performance and are a key enabler for virtualization. However, in reality, if the right hardware is used, there should be no need for them.

6.3 REFERENCE TABLES

These next sections cover another type of entity, which is not part of the core architecture but used often in the Data Vault.

We have introduced the hub in Chapter 4 as a unique list of business keys, identifying objects that are used in business. However, there are more keys and codes in enterprise data that don't necessarily qualify as business keys because they don't reference business objects. For example, ISO country codes, such as USA for the United States or DEU for Germany, are codes that are used in business, but the countries themselves are not used as business objects within the organization. Instead, they are used as descriptive reference data that delineate a specific state of information. In the case of country codes, the ISO code could describe the country where a sale had taken place. This description usually includes the official name of the country and some other more descriptive information, such as the continent or the capital. Often, this reference data is not controlled by the organization, but by an external body. On the other hand, the very same country code could be a business key in another organization, such as the United Nations Organization (UNO).

Reference data is not purely descriptive. It lives in the context of other information. The country information without the context of the sales transaction would be of no value to the business. Or to rephrase this statement: what is the value to the business of an *unused* list of country codes with their corresponding official names? It's zero. But if the country code is used in other data, such as the sales transactions, it provides value by adding additional descriptive data to the business. But they don't qualify as business keys because they are not used by business objects; therefore, they usually don't go into hub structures.

This is where reference tables come into play. Reference tables are used to store information that is commonly used to set up context and describe other business keys. In many cases, these are standard codes and descriptions or classifications of information.

The next sections describe some options for reference tables.

6.3.1 NO-HISTORY REFERENCE TABLES

The most basic reference table is just a typical table in third or second normal form. This basic table is used when there is no need to store history for the reference data. That is often the case for reference data that is not going to change or that will change very seldom. Typical examples include:

- Medical drug prescription codes and definitions
- Stock exchange symbols
- Medical diagnosis codes
- VIN number codes and definitions (such as manufacturer codes)
- Calendar dates
- Calendar times
- International currency codes
- US state code abbreviations

Note that it depends on the actual project: e.g., in some countries other than the USA, there might be frequent changes in the medical diagnosis codes, for whatever reason.

The simple no-history reference table has no begin-date and no end-date because there are no changes in the data. Therefore, the structure is very simple, as Figure 6.7 shows.

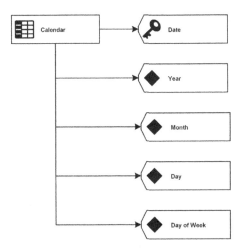

FIGURE 6.7

A nonhistorized reference table for calendar (logical design).

FIGURE 6.8

A nonhistorized reference table for calendar (physical design).

This logical model shows a reference table to store a simple calendar in the Business Vault. The data is identified by the *Date* key, which is a Date field in the database. Other attributes in this example are the *Year*, *Month*, and *Day,* which store the corresponding whole numbers. *Day of Week* is the text representation of the week day, e.g. "Monday." There is no need for keeping a history of changes because there will be no need to track those in most businesses. It doesn't mean that there are no changes to the data in this structure. However, most changes are bug-fixes or should update all information marts, including historical data. Examples for the latter include translations of the *Day of Week* attribute or abbreviating the text. Figure 6.8 shows the ER model for this reference table.

The descriptive business key is used as the primary key of the table. The reason for this is that the key is used in satellites and Business Vault entities to reference the data in this table. That way, it becomes more readable and ensures auditability over time. If a business key is used as the primary key of the reference table, it has the advantage that it can be used in ER models or in referential integrity, if turned on, for example for debugging purposes.

Table 6.9 shows an excerpt of the reference data in the calendar table.

Table 6.9 Calendar Data in Nonhistory Reference Table

Date	Load Date	Record Source	Year	Month	Day	Day of Week
2000-01-01	2014-06-20 04:30:21.333	MDS	2000	1	1	Saturday
2000-01-02	2014-06-20 04:30:21.333	MDS	2000	1	2	Sunday
2000-01-03	2014-06-20 04:30:21.333	MDS	2000	1	3	Monday
2000-01-04	2014-06-20 04:30:21.333	MDS	2000	1	4	Tuesday
2000-01-05	2014-06-20 04:30:21.333	MDS	2000	1	5	Wednesday
2000-01-06	2014-06-20 04:30:21.333	MDS	2000	1	6	Thursday
2000-01-07	2014-06-20 04:30:21.333	MDS	2000	1	7	Friday

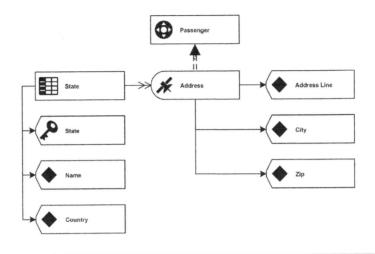

FIGURE 6.9

Satellite with reference data (logical design).

This example uses a *RecordSource* attribute again because the data is sourced from Master Data Services (MDS). If the data in MDS is changed by the user, it will overwrite the content of the reference table because there is no history tracking. In other cases, the data is not sourced from anywhere. Then, the *LoadDate* and the *RecordSource* attributes are not needed. However, it is good practice to source the data from analytical master data because it becomes editable by the business user without the need for IT. This is a prerequisite for managed self-service business intelligence (BI), a concept that is covered in Chapter 9, Master Data Management.

Once the reference table has been created in the model, it can be integrated into the rest of the model by using the primary key of the reference table wherever appropriate: the biggest use is in satellites, but they are also used in Business Vault entities. Figure 6.9 shows a typical use case where a satellite on a *Passenger* hub is referencing the primary key of a reference table.

The satellite *Address* references the reference table *State* via the USPS state abbreviations. That way, the reference indicates that there is more descriptive information for *State* in the reference table. By doing so, we don't use readability in the satellite and keep the basic usage of Data Vault entities intact.

6.3.2 HISTORY-BASED REFERENCE TABLES

The last section introduced simple reference tables that hold no history. However, there are cases when reference data needs to be historized, similar to satellite data. To provide an alternative to Data Vault satellites when dealing with reference data, there is an option for history-based reference tables. If it is important to the business to reprint reports or go back in time and look at the historic reference data, these tables can be used to meet this requirement.

The way that Data Vault deals with this requirement is by adding standard satellites to the reference table presented in the previous section. While the base table holds only nonhistorized attributes, the satellite holds the reference data that requires history.

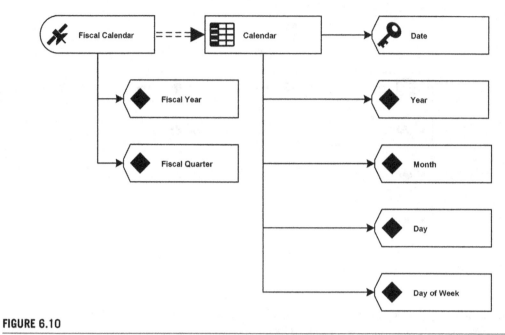

FIGURE 6.10

History-based reference table for calendar (logical design).

Figure 6.10 shows an extended version of the reference table in the last section. It is extended by satellite *Fiscal Calendar* which adds two historized attributes to the reference table: *Fiscal Year* and *Fiscal Quarter*. By having them historized, the business is capable of changing it in the future or addressing a change in the past. This could be a requirement if two organizations with different fiscal calendars merged in the past and the business wants to be able to work with historic reports.

By adding a satellite to the reference table to enable historization, it is possible to follow the basic concepts of Data Vault 2.0 modeling to extend the simple reference table introduced in the previous section. This is a great example of how these basic entities can be used by combining them into advanced entities.

Figure 6.11 shows the physical model derived from the logical model in Figure 6.6.

Satellite *SatFiscalCalendar* is attached to the reference table by using its primary key *Date*. We don't use a hashed version of the key in favor of readability of the reference table. If we preferred a hashed Date, it would require the use of the hash as the primary key, which in turn would affect the usage of the reference table. Other than that, the satellite is very similar to standard Data Vault 2.0 satellites, especially the use of the *LoadDate* in the primary key and *LoadEndDate* for end-dating satellite entries.

6.3.3 CODE AND DESCRIPTIONS

Often, there are standard codes in a business that require a description to be used by end-users effectively. One example is the state codes that were used in the previous sections. However, there are more

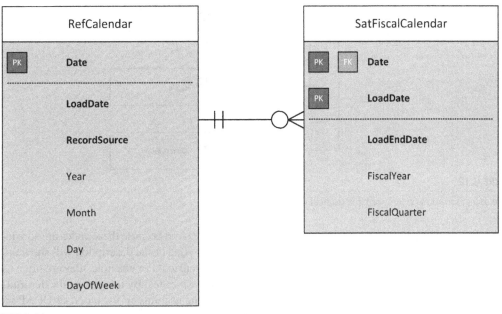

FIGURE 6.11

Physical model of historized calendar by using Data Vault satellite (physical design).

cases for abbreviations or other codes that are enriched with descriptions. For example, the FAA uses the operation codes in Table 6.10 to classify aircrafts regarding their intended use:

The Standard Operations Code is used in all business processes of the FAA, both with internal and external interfaces. Everyone in the airline industry who deals with the FAA knows about the meaning of these codes. But there are also glossaries that translate the codes into descriptions, providing more

Table 6.10 List of FAA Standard Operations Codes	
Standard Operations Code	**Description**
N	Normal
U	Utility
A	Acrobatic
T	Transport
G	Glider
B	Balloon
C	Commuter
O	Other

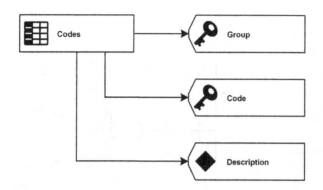

FIGURE 6.12

Code and descriptions reference table (logical design).

meaning to those users who are not using these codes every day. And because these codes are so widely used in the business processes, there is a 100% chance that the code or the description will show up on a user-interfacing component, such as a report or an OLAP dimension. For example, they are often used to group information on a report or aggregate measures over these codes. By integrating the description into the user interface (in addition to or instead of the code), the usability of the report or OLAP view is drastically increased for casual users of the presented information.

It should be clear that there are many of these lists with codes or abbreviations and their corresponding description. Instead of creating a reference table, with or without history, for each of these lists, we introduce a code and description table that groups these lists into one categorized table (Figure 6.12).

Figure 6.12 shows a minimal reference table for code and descriptions. Usually, there will be additional descriptive attributes in such table, for example:

- **Short description**: for use in charts and other diagrams, because there is only limited room for captions in bar charts, pie charts, etc.
- **Sort order**: most of the reference data is not sorted alphabetically when used in a report. Instead, the business wants to decide how to order entries in dimensions.
- **External reference**: oftentimes, this is a URL where more information about the reference data entry can be found. Useful to integrate your reference data with Wikis on the Intranet.
- **Owner**: indicates the functional unit that is responsible for maintaining the record.
- **Comment**: free text to describe the reference data entry to the business user who maintains the record.

The ER model of the code and descriptions reference table is presented in Figure 6.13.

The layout of the entity follows the layout of the other reference tables by using the descriptive business key combination as the primary key for the table.

Note that this approach is only applicable if the reference data uses the same data types and the same attributes that describe the code. If the structure of the reference data is different, individual reference tables are used.

The FAA data presented in Table 6.10 would be stored using the following data in the physical table, as shown in Table 6.11.

Table 6.11 includes data from two groups: standard operation codes (StdOpCode) and restricted operation codes (RstOpCode) by the FAA. Both groups are identified by the *Group* attribute and have

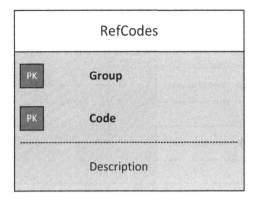

FIGURE 6.13

Code and descriptions reference table (physical design).

one or more records identified by a unique *Code* attribute. Therefore, the primary key of the table has to be on both columns (*Group* and *Code*).

There are two options to use the code and descriptions reference table in satellites. It is possible to use the combined primary key, consisting of attributes *Group* and *Code* as a foreign key (with or without referential integrity) in the satellite. Or, if foreign keys are not used in the model, it could also be possible to use only a *Code* attribute in the satellite and identify the *Group* implicitly using the satellites

Table 6.11 Code and Descriptions Table

Group	Code	Description
StdOpCode	N	Normal
StdOpCode	U	Utility
StdOpCode	A	Acrobatic
StdOpCode	T	Transport
StdOpCode	G	Glider
StdOpCode	B	Balloon
StdOpCode	C	Commuter
StdOpCode	O	Other
RstOpCode	0	Other
RstOpCode	1	Agriculture and Pest Control
RstOpCode	2	Aerial Surveying
RstOpCode	3	Aerial Advertising
RstOpCode	4	Forest
RstOpCode	5	Patrolling
RstOpCode	6	Weather Control
RstOpCode	7	Carriage of Cargo

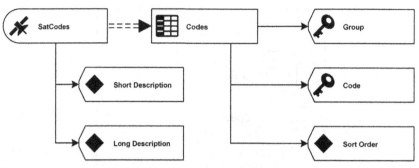

FIGURE 6.14

Codes and descriptions reference table with history-tracking satellite (logical design).

attribute. This means adding hard-coded filters to WHERE clauses when the data is retrieved or joined for resolution. This is an acceptable practice – as the model is "type-coding" codes and descriptions, allowing all codes to exist in a super-typed table at a subtype level grain. However, the second approach requires documentation in order to know which *Group* belongs to which satellite attribute, without the need to analyze the code from virtual facts and dimensions or ETL code.

6.3.3.1 Code and Descriptions with History

It is also possible to store history with the code and descriptions reference table. This is done similar to the history-based reference table, presented in section 6.3.2. The logical model for such a table is presented in Figure 6.14.

As the figure shows, this concept is again based on a satellite that holds the attributes that require tracking of history. In this example, this is the case for *Short Description* and *Long Description*. If there are attributes where the history should not be tracked, they can be added to the reference table itself. The attribute *Sort Order* follows this approach.

The ER diagram for this history-based code and description table is shown in Figure 6.15.

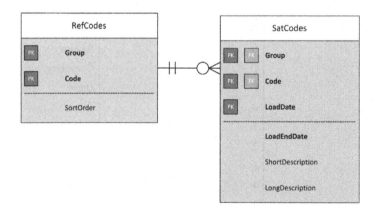

FIGURE 6.15

Codes and descriptions reference table with history-tracking satellite (physical design).

Having a composite primary key in the reference table requires that the satellite references both primary key attributes. The attributes without history tracking, in this case *SortOrder*, is added to the parent table and the attributes with history tracking are added to the satellite: attributes *ShortDescription* and *LongDescription* are such fields.

Chapter 9 describes in more detail how to create such entities in Master Data Services and how to load them into the Data Vault 2.0 model.

REFERENCE

[1] Microsoft Developer Network, MSDN Library, Data Compression. available at http://msdn.microsoft.com/en-us/library/cc280449.aspx.

DIMENSIONAL MODELING

7

The best application for Data Vault 2.0 modeling is in the enterprise data warehouse layer. It has been specifically developed for this purpose and is the optimal choice when an extensible, functionally oriented model is required that allows history tracking and auditability and can be integrated into real-time and NoSQL environments. Chapters 4 to 6 have covered Data Vault modeling in detail.

However, most business users are not familiar with Data Vault 2.0 modeling. In many cases, end-users need proper training first, in order to directly access the Raw Data Vault or the Business Vault, which is modeled after the same principles. They also need to understand how to join the many entities in order to get valuable and usable raw data that can be used for processing into usable information. Therefore, direct access to the enterprise data warehouse layer is limited to power users, who want to use their own queries and need raw data for this purpose. Most end-users will use an information mart to access prepared information that they can directly use for their job at hand.

Another issue is that most front-end tools, which are used by the business to analyze the information provided by the data warehouse, cannot directly use the Data Vault structures. For example, building an OLAP cube in Microsoft SQL Server Analysis Services (SSAS) works best if the data source is modeled in a star schema, which is the relational version of a dimensional model.

Dimensional modeling was introduced to a broad audience in the data warehouse industry by Ralph Kimball in 1997 [1]. However, he did not invent it. The terms *dimensions* and *facts*, which are elementary constructs in dimensional modeling, date back to the 1960s when a joint research project between Dartmouth University and General Mills was conducted [2]. The first dimensional model was introduced by AC Nielsen and IRI to describe early dimensional data marts for retail sales data [2]. But Ralph Kimball's series of books have helped to promote dimensional modeling within the data warehousing industry and it has become a standard for modeling. As a result, dimensional modeling is supported by many front-end tools today. Therefore, it is well known and understood by end-users and is the optimal choice for modeling the information marts, which serve as front-end layers.

7.1 INTRODUCTION

Data warehouse systems support the business by helping to solve analytical problems – that is, the answering of questions regarding business processes. For example, business users in the airline industry might want to analyze questions such as:

- How has the degree of capacity utilization on specific connections evolved over the last financial year?
- What is the impact of our frequent flyer reward system on sales?
- Who are our frequent flyers? What is their average sales volume?

Such questions don't deal with individual transactions but with measurements from the overall process. Usually, the measurements from individual transactions are aggregated (e.g., summed or

Table 7.1 Proportion of Passengers, Workers, Visitors, and Senders/Greeters at Selected Airports (with Artificial Data) [4]

Airport	Number Passengers	Number of Senders and Greeters	Number of Workers	Number of Visitors
Amsterdam	0.421	0.263	0.298	0.086
Atlanta	0.397	0.26	0.089	0.236
Bogota	0.231	0.423	0.363	Negligible
Curacao	0.25	0.642	0.089	0.032
Frankfurt	0.602	0.065	0.279	0.045
JFK	0.375	0.5048	0.125	Not included
Los Angeles	0.412	0.486	0.125	Not included
Melbourne	0.476	0.312	0.124	0.187
Mexico City	0.354	0.512	0.123	Negligible
Paris	0.621	0.079	0.231	0.078
Singapore	0.232	0.612	0.164	Negligible
Tokyo	0.676	0.131	0.197	0.056
Toronto	0.4038	0.545	0.087	Not included
Vienna	0.501	0.202	0.2119	0.089

averaged) for this purpose. Another characteristic of analytical questions is that no modification of data in the operational systems is required in order to answer the questions [3].

For all these reasons, it makes sense to organize the data within the information mart layer in a way that allows business users to quickly aggregate the information instead of quickly modifying it. That is why the dimensional model is modeled in the way the data is measured. Because measurement is often based on a business process, the business process should be the center of modeling as well. In addition, context is required to provide meaning to the measurements, for example to arrange the measurements by airport in Table 7.1 [3].

In this table, there is one measure presented, which is the number of individuals that have either been passengers, senders or greeters, workers or visitors to an airport, expressed as a ratio between these four roles. The four roles are the first dimension, while the airport is the second. Both dimensions span the data and provide the level of detail for the counting of individuals.

These two fundamental concepts, measurements and context, are the foundation of dimensional modeling [3].

7.2 STAR SCHEMAS

When a dimensional model is expressed on a relational database, it is called a star schema. This is due to the fact that the dimensional model of relational tables looks like a star from an overview (Figure 7.1).

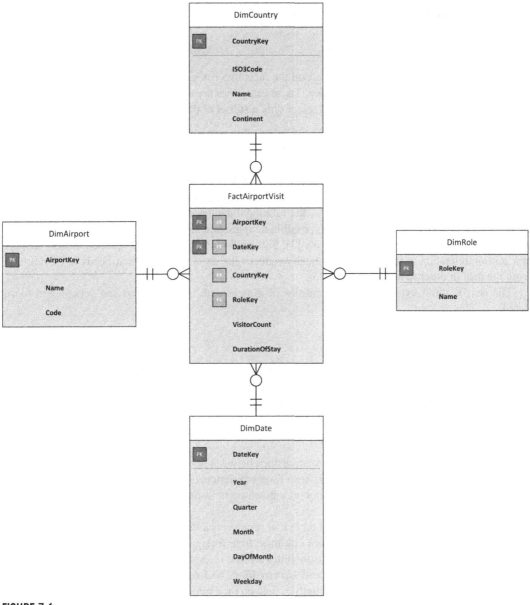

FIGURE 7.1

Sample star schema for airport visits (physical design).

The model in Figure 7.1 represents the model underlying the data in Table 7.1. There is a fact table in the center of the model, surrounded by four dimension tables.

The major difference between the star schema in Figure 7.1 and a normalized model in third-normal form (3NF), which is often used in operational systems, is that the dimensional model typically uses denormalized tables, especially:

- **Fact tables:** the table in the center of this figure holds the measures of the business, which in the case of Figure 7.1 are flight transactions. These measures are typically metrics which the business wishes to put through further analysis.

- **Dimension tables:** dimension tables group the facts into categories and provide additional descriptive attributes to these categories. These categories are called dimensions and help the end-user to navigate in the model and select only a subset of data for analysis.

In addition to these major tables, there are other table types often used in dimensional modeling, for example bridge tables. In most cases, it is possible to create a dimensional model that contains the same content as the 3NF model. However, expressed as a star schema, it is easier to understand for business users and is tuned for query performance. This is due to the denormalization that typically occurs when transforming a 3NF model into a dimensional model. Hierarchies and lookup tables are prejoined, which requires the optimizer of the relational database server to consider fewer joins and requires fewer temporary tables. It is also possible to aggregate data very easily, because all measures are already included in the central fact table [2]. Some editions of Microsoft SQL Server also support star join optimization, a feature that drastically reduces the amount of data that needs to be returned from the disk in order to answer queries [5].

The next sections explain the basic entities of dimensional modeling and star schemas in more detail.

7.2.1 **FACT TABLES**

Fact tables contain information about specific business processes or events within these processes. Examples for such business processes and events are flights, orders, phone calls, or Web site hits. Each record in the fact table represents one of these events and provides the measures that are associated with the business event. Usually, these are numerical values that quantify how long the flight was, the time to take-off, the number of diversions, or how many items were ordered, at which price [2]. These values are called the facts of the table.

In other cases, fact tables can contain relationships between business objects, for example inventory levels at given days. These inventory levels are a form of relationship because they indicate which product is available at which warehouse location at a given point in time. Each relationship is represented in the fact table as one record.

Figure 7.2 shows an example of a fact table that represents a flight.

The fact table has two different types of columns: first, foreign key references to dimension tables which are covered in the next section. This includes all four references that are part of the primary key, but also *TailNumberKey*, *CancelledKey*, and *DivertedKey*. And second, the measure values, the facts themselves. Many of them indicate the length of delays, for example *DepartureDelay*, *WeatherDelay*, or *SecurityDelay*. Others indicate the length of subprocesses, for example the time to taxi in and out, airtime and the traveled distance.

Not all facts are numeric values, but they are of most value to business users, because they can be easily aggregated by dimension. The fact table is identified by a subset of foreign key references to dimension tables. This subset becomes the composite key that represents the primary key of the table. Not all foreign keys are required to be included in the primary key, because many times the dimension only describes the fact but does not identify it. In other cases, it might be required to add another identifying fact into the fact table's primary key to guarantee uniqueness, for example a transaction number, such as an invoice number or a booking reference code [2].

Introducing keys for uniquely identifying the rows as the primary key of the fact table should be avoided, because of the storage space required for storing the key value but also for maintaining the

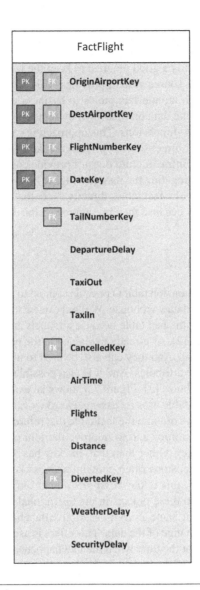

FIGURE 7.2

Fact table for flights (physical design).

index. The index itself is of no use, because it cannot be used by the end-user to identify individual facts. Only in some limited cases, mostly for technical reasons, a generated or derived key used as primary key actually makes sense. One example for such a reason is when it is required by the business to load identical rows into the fact table (for example, when dealing with history) or when other fact tables should be cross-referenced [2].

7.2.1.1 The Grain of a Fact Table

The number of dimension references in the fact table represents the fact table's level of detail. This level of detail is called the *grain*. It is a good practice to keep the level of detail as low as possible, in the best case at the lowest level the source system provides. This original level of detail is also known as the atomic level. Providing such atomic fact tables to business users offers the most flexibility to them, because they can aggregate the data on their own by removing a dimension from the query and grouping the data by the remaining dimensions. This approach is called a roll-up and is used to summarize the data on a subset of fact dimensions [6]. However, keeping fact tables on the lowest grain is not always feasible if the server infrastructure doesn't provide enough resources to keep the lowest level of detail. In this case, pre-aggregating the data to a higher level of detail offers faster responses to the business users when they query the fact tables directly. Note that this is not true anymore when using multidimensional OLAP cubes because they pre-aggregate the data within the cube, transparently for the end-user.

7.2.2 DIMENSION TABLES

Dimensions (thus the relational dimension tables) provide context to the facts [3]. They are very important to the understandability of the data warehouse. Without dimensions, it would not be possible to understand the measures provided by the fact table because all labels and other descriptive information is sourced from the dimension tables [2]. As already explained in the previous section, they are also used to specify how facts will be rolled up. And they can also be used to filter facts according to a dimension entry itself or one of its descriptive attributes. And it is also possible to sort aggregated measurements by the dimension or one of its attributes [3]. Figure 7.3 shows an example dimension table.

Unlike fact tables, a dimension table uses a *PassengerKey* key value as the primary key of the table. This is because this key is used quite often in the fact table that references the dimension table. In order to reduce the amount of required storage and to improve the join performance, it makes sense to do so and avoid the use of a natural key. Other than that, the key has no meaning to the business [3]. In addition to this technical key, dimensions often contain business keys that identify the entries in the dimension table [3]. In Figure 7.3, this is the *PassportNumber* attribute. The entries often represent business objects and the changes to these objects in the operational system. While the natural key for the same business object remains the same, even if descriptive data has been changed in the operational system, the key changes for each change of the data. This effect is used by the fact table to reference the version of the data that was active at the time when the fact happened in the business [3]. The hash key from the Data Vault 2.0 model is used as the key in the dimensional model. This simplifies the loading process and helps to virtualize information marts. The loading of information marts, both materialized and virtualized, is demonstrated in Chapter 14, Loading the Dimensional Information Mart.

Despite the keys in the table, the dimension table holds the descriptive data that describe the dimension entry. It is very common that dimension tables consist of many descriptive attributes. They can range up to 50 or 100 columns. On the other hand, they often don't have many rows in the table. There are some dimensions, such as the Passenger dimension presented in Figure 7.3, that might hold many records, but most dimensions are rather small, holding maybe a hundred records at most [2].

Not all numeric attributes should be measures in the fact table. For example, the row number of seats within an airplane is not used in any calculations. It might be used as a natural key, but it is not aggregated by the business user. The same applies to the age of the passenger, as long as the business

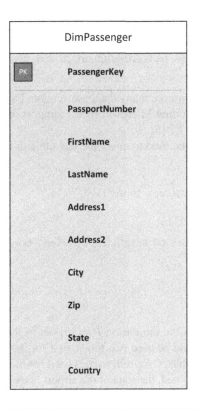

FIGURE 7.3

Passenger dimension table (physical design).

doesn't want to calculate the average age of the airplane's passengers. There are different types of measures in the fact table of a dimensional model [2]:

- **Fully additive measures:** are fully additive in the sense that the values, such as amounts and quantities, can be added up to a valid total.
- **Semi-additive measures:** can be added up along some of the available dimensions, but not all.
- **Nonadditive measures:** cannot be added up.

Therefore, it also depends on the business needs whether an attribute becomes a measure in the fact table or a descriptive attribute in one of its dimension tables [2].

7.2.3 QUERYING STAR SCHEMAS

End-users who are familiar with star schemas often follow a simple pattern when directly querying data from a dimensional model:

- **Selection of required facts:** first, the end-user decides which facts should be selected by identifying the fact tables to be used.
- **Selection of required dimensions:** by joining dimensions to the query, end-users add required context.

- **Limiting scope of facts:** the facts are filtered according to dimensional values (either from the fact table or from joined dimensions).
- **Summarization of facts:** the raw facts are summarized with aggregate functions, such as SUM() or COUNT().

Because this approach is so common, many database vendors have optimized their relational database engines to such requests, including Microsoft by the support of star join optimization, which we have already mentioned in section 7.2 [5].

The following statement could be used to query the fact table in Figure 7.2:

```
SELECT
        OriginAirport.Code, AVG(DepartureDelay)
FROM
        FactFlight
INNER JOIN
        DimAirport OriginAirport ON OriginAirport.AirportKey = FactFlight.OriginAirportKey
WHERE
        OriginAirport.State = 'CA'
GROUP BY
        OriginAirport.Code
```

This statement would first join the dimension *DimAirport* to the fact table, using the *OriginAirportKey*. Note that *DimAirport* could be used two times: first for the origin airport, and second for the destination airport. Therefore, an alias, *OriginAirport*, is used for the dimension table in the statement.

Once the dimension has been joined, the state of the airport is used to filter the data to all airports in California. The airport's state is a descriptive attribute in the dimensional table. In addition, the airport code is used to group the data in order to present the user a list of known airports in California with the average departure delay of that airport.

The statement also shows how the individual clauses of the statement are used in dimensional queries:

- The **SELECT clause** identifies the measures and dimensions that should be presented to the end-user. It also describes any formulas, including aggregate functions, that should be used to modify the presented result.
- The **FROM clause** identifies the fact table that is queried. In many cases, this includes only one fact table. However, it is also possible to query data from multiple fact tables.
- The **JOIN clause** joins the context of the facts to the end-result. There are multiple join clauses in many cases, each clause joining a different dimension table.
- The **WHERE clause** limits the scope of the facts to be used in the end-result. In many cases, there is data from more dimensional entries available (such as sales regions), which are of no interest for the given task at hand. Therefore end-users typically limit the data to the dimension entries of interest.
- The **GROUP BY clause** defines how the data is grouped before aggregation and presentation to the end-user. The aggregation in the SELECT clause is based on this GROUP BY clause. By doing so, the GROUP BY clause is used to change the grain of the result from the fact table.

While the GROUP BY clause can be used to change the grain of the facts to a higher level, it is not possible to produce a lower grain level [3]. Consider a fact table that stores data about flight totals: how many passengers were on the plane, origin and destination airport, flight date, etc. If the fact table doesn't store any information on the passenger level, it is not possible to analyze this information. Therefore, it is important to select the appropriate fact table grain when designing the dimensional model.

7.3 MULTIPLE STARS

The statement in the previous section used only one fact table as the basis for the result. However, we have already mentioned that it is also possible to use multiple fact tables as the source of the query. This behavior is supported by conformed dimensions, which are used by multiple stars (a fact table with its dimension tables) and therefore connect these individual stars via the conformed dimension itself.

7.3.1 CONFORMED DIMENSIONS

Conformed dimensions are dimensions that are shared by multiple stars. They are used to compare the measures from each star schema [3]. The reuse of conformed dimensions is very common in order to *"support true, cross-business process analysis"* [6]. This is only possible if all star schemas that should be analyzed in cross-business process analysis use exactly the same dimension, with exactly the same key values (primary keys). By using the hash keys from the Data Vault 2.0 model, meeting this requirement is simplified (see Chapter 14, Loading the Dimensional Information Mart, for details). Such analysis is called drill-across and brings the information from multiple business processes or events together [3]. Only then is it possible to analyze data from different fact tables by using the conformed dimension. Figure 7.4 shows an example.

In this example, there are two star schemas, with their fact tables in the center: *FactConnection* on the left and *FactAirportVisit* from Figure 7.1 on the right. Each of them has a number of connected dimensions. Both share two conformed dimensions, *DimAirport* and *DimDate*, which are shown in the center of the diagram. In order to support cross-process analysis between *FactConnection* and *FactAirportVisit*, it is crucial that both conformed dimensions have exactly the same structure and data.

To support such conformed dimensions, it is required that any change to a conformed dimension should not break one of the dimensional stars which uses the conformed dimension. This might and probably will occur in later sprints of the project. Whenever the structure of the content of a conformed dimension is modified, the impact on each dependent star schema has to be reviewed and properly tested. Therefore, the use of conformed dimensions incurs a change impact that might limit the agility of the development team. This overhead of maintaining conformed dimensions often leads to the practice that developers don't touch existing conformed dimensions in order to avoid testing. Instead, they create new, additional conformed dimensions to avoid the reengineering costs, leading to nonconformed dimensions. In other cases, they copy the structure and data of existing conformed dimensions into new stars and extend them with new features, leaving the conformed dimension in the old model untouched (therefore, no testing is required) and adding nonconformed dimensions again. We call this practice "dimension-itis," which leads to an unmanageable number of dimensions that are all the same, somehow… nonconformed.

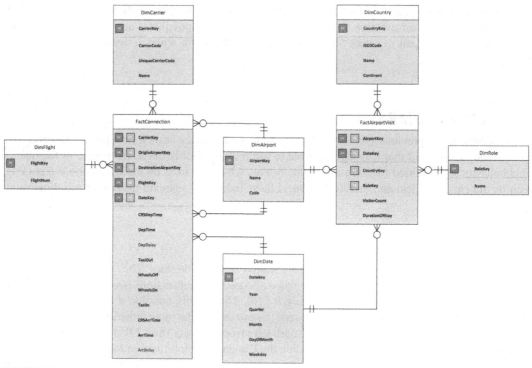

FIGURE 7.4

Two star schemas connected by conformed dimensions (physical design).

The opposite practice is to add more attributes and data into existing conformed dimensions in order to avoid adding new dimensions. This approach is practiced when developers want to avoid creating new conformed dimensions due to the amount of required testing of existing facts and dimensions. The end result of this approach is that the "conformed" dimension cannot sustain any further changes due to unclear and unmanageable changes to the structure and unclear or complex dependencies, and it becomes a "deformed" dimension: a nightmare requiring huge reengineering costs when touched in the future. Teams that produce such deformed dimensions often are likely to avoid documenting them, adding more headaches for their successors.

We don't recommend preventing the use of conformed dimensions. What we need is a way to quickly create and change them, with low maintainability costs. Our recommendation is to use virtual information marts, which we describe in Chapter 14.

7.4 DIMENSION DESIGN

The last section of this chapter covers some additional concepts from dimensional modeling that are used in later chapters of this book, including slowly changing dimensions, hierarchies, and a short introduction to snowflake design, which is a more extended dimensional model.

7.4.1 SLOWLY CHANGING DIMENSIONS

So far, we have discussed dimensions as entities providing the context of facts. This is true, but it is important to understand that this context changes over time. For example, the home address of passengers changes due to relocation, the last name changes due to marriage and the salutation might change due to an error correction. Because the connection between the star schema and the dimension is based on key values, it is possible for the model to absorb the source system changes in the best way to satisfy analysis requirements: changes can be either tracked within the dimension or they might also overwrite the existing data in the dimension [3].

Slowly changing dimensions are used to handle changes in dimensional tables. This is because the pace at which dimensions change is relatively slow, especially compared to fast-changing fact tables [3]. Because there are multiple ways to track history in a dimension, Kimball introduced a classification for the dimensional tables [7].

A slowly changing dimension **type 0** preserves the initial dimensional attribute values. If a change occurs in the source system, the value in the dimension is not changed. While this type is less common than the next three, it can be used to retain the initial credit score of a customer or any other initial value [7].

Changes in the source system overwrite the data in the slowly changing dimension **type 1**. The dimension's attribute always reflects the most current value. Therefore, no history is tracked [2]. If there are aggregations based on this attribute (e.g., in the GROUP BY clause of the statement), the results of those aggregations change due to the new value [2]. Table 7.2 shows an example of a Type 1 dimension.

The dimension table presented in Table 7.2 holds address information about passengers. Each passenger is identified by a key, which is the primary key that is used by the fact table, and a natural key, the passport number. All other attributes in the dimension are of descriptive nature and describe the current address in detail.

When a passenger moves, the current record is overwritten. Therefore, no history is kept in the dimension table. The table only reflects the current address and no past addresses of the passenger.

Instead of overwriting existing data, changes in the source system add a new row to the **type 2** dimension table. By using this approach, it is often possible to correctly keep track of history. Therefore, it is the predominant technique to track history in information marts [2]. An example of a Type 2 dimension is presented in Table 7.3.

The table (modified from Table 7.2 and fit for purpose) shows how changes are tracked in a slowly changing dimension type 2: each new version of the record is added as an additional row to the

Table 7.2 Slowly Changing Dimension Type 1

Passenger Key	Passport Number	First Name	Last Name	Address 1	Address 2	City	Zip	State	Country
1b3ba82...	1234567	Amy	Miller	31 Main St.		Norman	30782	OK	USA
28ab342...	8473621	Peter	Heinz	9612 Lincoln Road	Apt. #3	Santa Clara	70831	CA	USA
39934aa...	9482612	Jennifer	Freeman	Am Platz 3		Berlin	10872		Germany

Table 7.3 Slowly Changing Dimension Type 2

Passenger Key	Passport Number	First Name	Last Name	Address	City	Zip	Country	Load Date	Load End Date
1b3ba82...	1234567	Amy	Miller	31 Main St.	Norman, OK	30782	USA	0001-01-01	2015-08-22
28ab342...	8473621	Peter	Heinz	9612 Lincoln Road	Santa Clara, CA	70831	USA	0001-01-01	9999-12-31
39934aa...	9482612	Jennifer	Freeman	Am Platz 3	Berlin	10872	Germany	0001-01-01	9999-12-31
444bbaa...	1234567	Amy	Heinz	9612 Lincoln Road	Santa Clara, CA	70831	USA	2015-08-22	9999-12-31

dimension table. In this example, Amy Miller, with key 1b3ba82..., has married Peter Heinz, with key 28ab342..., and moved to his place in California. Therefore, her new record with key 444bbaa... reflects these changes. The old record remains untouched to keep the historical information. Old facts keep using the record with key 1b3ba82..., but new facts reference the dimension entry with key 444bbaa....

Changes in a slowly changing dimension **type 3** don't add additional rows but track history in additional columns. For each attribute that should be historized, a new column is added per change that occurred in the source system *and* should be displayed to the business user. This makes it easier to analyze the changes over time. Table 7.4 shows an example.

This example shows how a business keeps track of the passenger's previous state using an additional column. When the passenger moves, as is the case with Amy Miller (now Amy Heinz) in the entry with key 1b3ba82..., the old address is overwritten and the attributes that should be historically tracked are copied into additional columns. In this case, the *Previous State* column is updated to reflect the previous state of the passenger. History is not limited to only one entry. It is common to use a limited number of columns to keep a couple of changes – in most cases only the actual and the previous value. In other cases, key performance indicators (KPIs) are tracked over time, as in the example in Table 7.5.

Table 7.5 shows a dimension that keeps track of available flights, where they start from and their destination airport. In addition to this basic information, the dimension table provides three KPI values

Table 7.4 Slowly Changing Dimension Type 3

Passenger Key	Passport Number	First Name	Last Name	Address 1	Address 2	City	Zip	State	Previous State
1b3ba82...	1234567	Amy	Heinz	9612 Lincoln Road	Apt. #3	Santa Clara	70831	CA	OK
28ab342...	8473621	Peter	Heinz	9612 Lincoln Road	Apt. #3	Santa Clara	70831	CA	CA
39934aa...	9482612	Jennifer	Freeman	Am Platz 3		Berlin	10872		

Table 7.5 Slowly Changing Dimension Type 3 with Multiple Columns

Flight Key	Flight Number	Origin Airport	Destination Airport	Avg No Passengers (current year)	Avg No Passengers (last year)	Avg No Passengers (year before last year)
1ba45fa...	DL123	SFO	JFK	130	85	103
23498bb...	UA8734	LAX	FRA	507	604	620
323cb8f...	LH4711	FRA	LHR	140	121	105

that show how the average number of passengers has evolved over the last three years (including the current year).

In addition to the presented dimension types, the following ones are found in some cases [7]:

- **Slowly changing dimension type 4:** this type puts volatile attributes into a separate mini-dimension table.
- **Slowly changing dimension type 5:** a hybrid between type 4 and type 1 dimensions (4 + 1 equals 5). It allows access of the currently assigned mini-dimension attributes along with the base dimension's others without linking through a fact table.
- **Slowly changing dimension type 6:** this type adds current attributes to a type 2 dimension.
- **Slowly changing dimension type 7:** this type achieves the same functionality as type 6 dimensions but with dual foreign keys added to the fact table: one that references a type 2 dimension with the tracked attributes, while the other one references the current row.

7.4.2 HIERARCHIES

Hierarchies are another important concept in dimensional modeling. They allow drilling down of data in order to analyze the data in more detail. Consider the following example: An Excel PivotTable presents worldwide passenger revenue of several years in total values (Figure 7.5).

The columns in Figure 7.5 show the financial years (FY) from the *Date* dimension that are available in the PivotTable. The rows show the geographic regions from the Geographic dimension. In addition, there are grand totals that show the overall value for each column or row. For example, the passenger revenue of FY 2008 in the United States was $19,471.989.04.

Passenger Revenue	Column Labels			
Row Labels	⊞ FY 2006	⊞ FY 2007	⊞ FY 2008	Grand Total
⊞ Australia			$1.594.335,38	$1.594.335,38
⊞ Canada	$3.079.806,81	$5.615.169,14	$5.682.949,64	$14.377.925,60
⊞ France		$1.428.020,38	$3.179.517,56	$4.607.537,94
⊞ Germany			$1.983.988,04	$1.983.988,04
⊞ United Kingdom		$1.406.491,96	$2.872.516,87	$4.279.008,83
⊞ United States	$13.208.634,95	$19.471.989,04	$20.927.177,22	$53.607.801,21
Grand Total	$16.288.441,77	$27.921.670,52	$36.240.484,70	$80.450.596,98

FIGURE 7.5

Passenger revenue per year and region.

The geographic hierarchy is made up of the following levels:

1. Country
2. State-Province
3. City
4. Postal Code

It is possible to drill-down to any level that is available in the PivotTable (which is based on an OLAP cube), but not any further. Figure 7.6 shows a logical model that shows the *Geography* dimension with its hierarchy.

The notation follows the ADAPT™ modeling methodology for dimensional databases [8]. The methodology is frequently used in the industry to model and document dimensional models. The first element depicts the Geography dimension itself. The dimension includes one hierarchy, also called Geography. The other elements are the individual levels of the hierarchy and have to follow in the given order. We are going to the ADAPT modeling methodology throughout the book.

Similar to the *Geography* hierarchy, the *Fiscal Calendar* hierarchy consists of multiple levels:

1. Fiscal Year
2. Fiscal Semester
3. Fiscal Quarter
4. Month
5. Date

This hierarchy is very common in data warehouse systems and is frequently used by end-users. It uses a different start date for the year, a practice often performed by commercial organizations. For example,

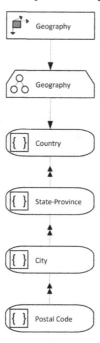

FIGURE 7.6

Geography dimension (logical design).

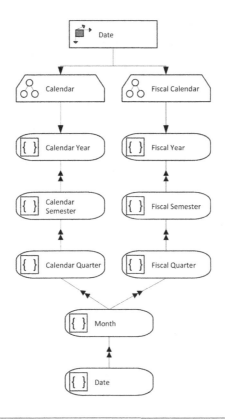

FIGURE 7.7

Date dimension (logical design).

businesses in commerce and trade often start their fiscal year on another day than December 31. This is often due to the frequent post-Christmas returns made by customers who are not happy with their gifts. Because the volume of these returns is relatively high, it has an impact on the year's total revenue. However, in most cases, the returns happen in January of the following calendar year. If the company closes the books by the end of December, the returns would account to the following fiscal period and skew the financial results. Therefore, these companies often choose another month as the end of the fiscal period. One example is Best Buy, an electronics retailer in the US. The company's fiscal year ends on February 1 [9]. Figure 7.7 shows the logical model of the Date dimension.

Note that there are two hierarchies available in the dimension: *Calendar* and *Fiscal Calendar*. Both have their own *Year*, *Semester* and *Quarter* levels but share their *Month* and *Date* levels. Both hierarchies use all attributes of the dimension, but they are organized in a different way. Depending on the business analyst's need, one or the other hierarchy is used. Nothing is wrong with either; the value of each hierarchy depends on the context of the business analysis.

To analyze the information in Figure 7.5 in more detail, it is possible to click the plus sign next to the row label and drill-down into the *Geography* hierarchy, as shown in Figure 7.8.

The total passenger revenue that is still displayed in the row marked bold is broken up by state, the next geographic level below the country level. For each state, the passenger revenue is displayed per year. It is possible to further break down this data, by drilling-down to the next level (Figure 7.9).

Passenger Revenue	Column Labels ▼			
Row Labels ▼	⊞ FY 2006	⊞ FY 2007	⊞ FY 2008	Grand Total
⊞ Australia			$1.594.335,38	$1.594.335,38
⊞ Canada	$3.079.806,81	$5.615.169,14	$5.682.949,64	$14.377.925,60
⊞ France		$1.428.020,38	$3.179.517,56	$4.607.537,94
⊞ Germany			$1.983.988,04	$1.983.988,04
⊞ United Kingdom		$1.406.491,96	$2.872.516,87	$4.279.008,83
⊟ United States	$13.208.634,95	$19.471.989,04	$20.927.177,22	$53.607.801,21
⊞ Alabama		$15.497,20	$29.931,83	$45.429,03
⊞ Arizona	$20.796,25	$448.353,42	$963.435,90	$1.432.585,57
⊞ California	$2.339.427,00	$3.860.128,46	$3.564.715,24	$9.764.270,71
⊞ Colorado	$303.695,32	$1.071.753,62	$1.020.464,90	$2.395.913,84
⊞ Connecticut	$189.168,60	$498.866,74	$437.665,07	$1.125.700,41
⊞ Florida	$909.510,29	$515.173,61	$875.204,97	$2.299.888,87
⊞ Georgia	$348.112,74	$345.141,06	$351.324,00	$1.044.577,80
⊞ Idaho		$8.724,01	$218.577,74	$227.301,75
⊞ Illinois	$427.689,00	$103.451,65	$76.799,32	$607.939,97
⊞ Indiana	$219.501,56	$671.294,92	$182.592,11	$1.073.388,59
⊞ Kentucky	$12.306,57	$16.857,89	$134.549,38	$163.713,84
⊞ Maine		$388.169,48	$91.696,05	$479.865,53
⊞ Massachusetts	$57.433,93	$12.826,06	$37.093,88	$107.353,87
⊞ Michigan	$247.457,01	$590.727,99	$609.697,21	$1.447.882,21
⊞ Minnesota	$615.723,87	$216.514,67	$121.132,82	$953.371,36
⊞ Mississippi	$378.003,31	$145.196,69		$523.200,00
⊞ Missouri	$266.431,77	$641.459,81	$896.949,92	$1.804.841,51
⊞ Montana	$1.445,19	$5.309,34	$20.580,42	$27.334,95
⊞ Nevada	$568.607,77	$205.796,56	$336.414,67	$1.110.819,00
⊞ New Hampshire	$172.421,18	$1.040.864,22	$596.902,63	$1.810.188,04
⊞ New Mexico	$260.307,23	$169.296,22	$185.380,19	$614.983,64
⊞ New York	$243.977,78	$488.777,96	$637.839,32	$1.370.595,07
⊞ North Carolina	$102.642,94	$220.213,67	$508.631,33	$831.487,94
⊞ Ohio	$287.553,68	$250.958,89	$413.579,04	$952.091,61
⊞ Oregon	$271.035,29	$268.243,36	$974.421,46	$1.513.700,11
⊞ Rhode Island	$12.863,74	$469,79	$325,37	$13.658,90
⊞ South Carolina	$136.474,72	$53.434,82	$22.259,36	$212.168,90
⊞ South Dakota	$2.566,42	$7.942,41	$196.690,08	$207.198,91
⊞ Tennessee	$760.533,35	$900.332,75	$426.251,21	$2.087.117,32
⊞ Texas	$1.268.708,99	$2.964.247,72	$2.421.662,16	$6.654.618,87
⊞ Utah	$442.778,97	$559.546,19	$747.586,29	$1.749.911,46
⊞ Virginia	$209.463,86	$268.340,99	$182.027,68	$659.832,53
⊞ Washington	$1.714.588,67	$2.032.833,85	$3.207.292,53	$6.954.715,04
⊞ Wisconsin	$160.612,41	$178.736,52	$149.511,46	$488.860,38
⊞ Wyoming	$256.795,54	$306.506,49	$287.991,66	$851.293,69
Grand Total	$16.288.441,77	$27.921.670,52	$36.240.484,70	$80.450.596,98

FIGURE 7.8

Passenger revenue in the United States per year.

Passenger Revenue	Column Labels ▾			
Row Labels ▾	⊞ FY 2006	⊞ FY 2007	⊞ FY 2008	Grand Total
⊞ Australia			$1.594.335,38	$1.594.335,38
⊞ Canada	$3.079.806,81	$5.615.169,14	$5.682.949,64	$14.377.925,60
⊞ France		$1.428.020,38	$3.179.517,56	$4.607.537,94
⊞ Germany			$1.983.988,04	$1.983.988,04
⊞ United Kingdom		$1.406.491,96	$2.872.516,87	$4.279.008,83
⊟ United States	$13.208.634,95	$19.471.989,04	$20.927.177,22	$53.607.801,21
⊟ Alabama		$15.497,20	$29.931,83	$45.429,03
⊞ Birmingham		$9.015,49	$11.495,24	$20.510,74
⊞ Florence		$1.772,43		$1.772,43
⊞ Huntsville		$4.709,28	$18.436,58	$23.145,86
⊞ Arizona	$20.796,25	$448.353,42	$963.435,90	$1.432.585,57
⊞ California	$2.339.427,00	$3.860.128,46	$3.564.715,24	$9.764.270,71
⊞ Colorado	$303.695,32	$1.071.753,62	$1.020.464,90	$2.395.913,84
⊞ Connecticut	$189.168,60	$498.866,74	$437.665,07	$1.125.700,41
⊞ Florida	$909.510,29	$515.173,61	$875.204,97	$2.299.888,87
⊞ Georgia	$348.112,74	$345.141,06	$351.324,00	$1.044.577,80
⊞ Idaho		$8.724,01	$218.577,74	$227.301,75
⊞ Illinois	$427.689,00	$103.451,65	$76.799,32	$607.939,97
⊞ Indiana	$219.501,56	$671.294,92	$182.592,11	$1.073.388,59
⊞ Kentucky	$12.306,57	$16.857,89	$134.549,38	$163.713,84
⊞ Maine		$388.169,48	$91.696,05	$479.865,53
⊞ Massachusetts	$57.433,93	$12.826,06	$37.093,88	$107.353,87
⊞ Michigan	$247.457,01	$590.727,99	$609.697,21	$1.447.882,21
⊞ Minnesota	$615.723,87	$216.514,67	$121.132,82	$953.371,36
⊞ Mississippi	$378.003,31	$145.196,69		$523.200,00
⊞ Missouri	$266.431,77	$641.459,81	$896.949,92	$1.804.841,51
⊞ Montana	$1.445,19	$5.309,34	$20.580,42	$27.334,95
⊞ Nevada	$568.607,77	$205.796,56	$336.414,67	$1.110.819,00
⊞ New Hampshire	$172.421,18	$1.040.864,22	$596.902,63	$1.810.188,04
⊞ New Mexico	$260.307,23	$169.296,22	$185.380,19	$614.983,64
⊞ New York	$243.977,78	$488.777,96	$637.839,32	$1.370.595,07
⊞ North Carolina	$102.642,94	$220.213,67	$508.631,33	$831.487,94
⊞ Ohio	$287.553,68	$250.958,89	$413.579,04	$952.091,61
⊞ Oregon	$271.035,29	$268.243,36	$974.421,46	$1.513.700,11
⊞ Rhode Island	$12.863,74	$469,79	$325,37	$13.658,90
⊞ South Carolina	$136.474,72	$53.434,82	$22.259,36	$212.168,90
⊞ South Dakota	$2.566,42	$7.942,41	$196.690,08	$207.198,91
⊞ Tennessee	$760.533,35	$900.332,75	$426.251,21	$2.087.117,32
⊞ Texas	$1.268.708,99	$2.964.247,72	$2.421.662,16	$6.654.618,87
⊞ Utah	$442.778,97	$559.546,19	$747.586,29	$1.749.911,46
⊞ Virginia	$209.463,86	$268.340,99	$182.027,68	$659.832,53
⊞ Washington	$1.714.588,67	$2.032.833,85	$3.207.292,53	$6.954.715,04
⊞ Wisconsin	$160.612,41	$178.736,52	$149.511,46	$488.860,38
⊞ Wyoming	$256.795,54	$306.506,49	$287.991,66	$851.293,69
Grand Total	$16.288.441,77	$27.921.670,52	$36.240.484,70	$80.450.596,98

FIGURE 7.9

Passenger revenue in Alabama per year.

| Passenger Revenue | Column Labels | | | | | | | FY 2007 Total | Grand Total |
Row Labels	July 2006	August 2006	September 2006	Q1 FY 2007 Total	Q2 FY 2007	H1 FY 2007 Total	H2 FY 2007		
⊞ Canada	$638.115,20	$658.166,94	$564.052,73	$1.860.334,87	$1.396.216,98	$3.256.551,84	$2.358.617,30	$5.615.169,14	$5.615.169,14
⊞ France	$97.496,29	$262.815,13	$163.687,81	$523.999,23	$333.123,94	$857.123,18	$570.897,20	$1.428.020,38	$1.428.020,38
⊞ United Kingdom	$80.686,69	$182.735,99	$208.360,54	$471.783,23	$369.974,53	$841.757,76	$564.734,20	$1.406.491,96	$1.406.491,96
⊟ United States	$1.577.391,34	$2.497.472,65	$1.949.258,12	$6.024.122,11	$4.941.868,30	$10.965.990,41	$8.505.998,63	$19.471.989,04	$19.471.989,04
⊟ Alabama	$367,88	$393,19		$761,07	$2.348,97	$3.110,04	$12.387,16	$15.497,20	$15.497,20
⊞ Birmingham		$209,26		$209,26		$209,26	$8.806,24	$9.015,49	$9.015,49
⊞ Florence		$183,94		$183,94	$939,59	$1.123,53	$648,91	$1.772,43	$1.772,43
⊞ Huntsville	$367,88			$367,88	$1.409,38	$1.777,26	$2.932,02	$4.709,28	$4.709,28
⊞ Arizona	$82.641,73	$4.364,27	$60.890,18	$147.896,18	$109.285,93	$257.182,11	$191.171,31	$448.353,42	$448.353,42
⊞ California	$72.027,27	$527.771,09	$677.857,76	$1.277.656,12	$949.107,75	$2.226.763,87	$1.633.364,59	$3.860.128,46	$3.860.128,46
⊞ Colorado	$62.510,31	$193.123,20	$36.291,24	$291.924,75	$267.763,13	$559.687,88	$512.065,74	$1.071.753,62	$1.071.753,62
⊞ Connecticut	$69.865,70	$69.729,76	$11.526,44	$151.121,90	$123.477,86	$274.599,76	$224.266,98	$498.866,74	$498.866,74
⊞ Florida	$130.942,18	$17.568,62	$5.275,27	$153.786,07	$116.258,43	$270.044,50	$245.129,11	$515.173,61	$515.173,61
⊞ Georgia	$37.141,13	$42.329,13	$28.053,60	$107.523,86	$90.982,64	$198.506,49	$146.634,57	$345.141,06	$345.141,06
⊞ Idaho	$1.626,47		$2.112,54	$3.739,01	$4.109,62	$7.848,64	$875,38	$8.724,01	$8.724,01
⊞ Illinois	$18.088,56	$7.001,77	$14.211,50	$39.301,84	$27.824,93	$67.126,76	$36.324,89	$103.451,65	$103.451,65
⊞ Indiana	$134.437,94	$61.987,63	$379,47	$196.805,04	$162.571,75	$359.376,78	$311.918,14	$671.294,92	$671.294,92
⊞ Kentucky		$9.803,57	$684,03	$10.487,60	$3.272,20	$13.759,80	$3.098,10	$16.857,89	$16.857,89
⊞ Maine		$105.539,94		$105.539,94	$104.193,59	$209.733,53	$178.435,95	$388.169,48	$388.169,48
⊞ Massachusetts		$4.254,45		$4.254,45	$4.610,74	$8.865,19	$3.960,87	$12.826,06	$12.826,06
⊞ Michigan	$92.201,65	$73.392,78	$39.494,48	$205.088,90	$158.435,05	$363.523,95	$227.204,04	$590.727,99	$590.727,99
⊞ Minnesota	$30,28	$794,25	$64.178,40	$65.002,92	$58.252,61	$123.255,53	$93.259,14	$216.514,67	$216.514,67
⊞ Mississippi	$1.308,94	$47.413,72		$48.722,65	$36.401,13	$85.123,79	$60.072,91	$145.196,69	$145.196,69
⊞ Missouri	$98.996,58	$39.373,22	$48.087,93	$186.457,73	$155.788,08	$342.245,81	$299.214,00	$641.459,81	$641.459,81
⊞ Montana		$209,26		$209,26	$2.574,64	$2.783,89	$2.525,45	$5.309,34	$5.309,34
⊞ Nevada		$56.887,54	$9.020,69	$65.908,23	$48.341,55	$114.249,78	$91.546,78	$205.796,56	$205.796,56
⊞ New Hampshire	$115.741,21	$49.220,16	$146.154,57	$311.115,94	$248.979,40	$560.095,34	$480.768,88	$1.040.864,22	$1.040.864,22
⊞ New Mexico	$59.238,96			$59.238,96	$43.386,80	$102.625,77	$66.670,45	$169.296,22	$169.296,22
⊞ New York		$87.721,04	$72.350,96	$160.072,01	$130.764,74	$290.836,75	$197.941,22	$488.777,96	$488.777,96
⊞ North Carolina		$63.404,00		$63.404,00	$58.753,09	$122.157,09	$98.056,59	$220.213,67	$220.213,67
⊞ Ohio		$41.865,44	$11.415,91	$53.281,35	$72.268,28	$125.549,63	$125.409,26	$250.958,89	$250.958,89
⊞ Oregon		$50.022,43	$36.370,68	$86.393,11	$72.907,87	$159.300,99	$108.942,38	$268.243,36	$268.243,36
⊞ Rhode Island		$469,79		$469,79		$469,79		$469,79	$469,79
⊞ South Carolina		$22.381,50		$22.381,50	$14.288,71	$36.670,20	$16.764,61	$53.434,82	$53.434,82
⊞ South Dakota		$2.342,45		$2.342,45	$1.998,43	$4.340,88	$3.601,52	$7.942,41	$7.942,41
⊞ Tennessee	$7.213,76	$116.746,78	$140.152,42	$264.112,96	$221.627,98	$485.740,94	$414.591,81	$900.332,75	$900.332,75
⊞ Texas	$282.309,58	$356.464,81	$287.104,58	$925.878,96	$757.893,26	$1.683.772,22	$1.280.475,50	$2.964.247,72	$2.964.247,72
⊞ Utah	$6.709,57	$118.320,67	$39.972,13	$165.002,37	$146.161,92	$311.164,29	$248.381,90	$559.546,19	$559.546,19
⊞ Virginia	$7.370,84	$33,77	$103.299,68	$110.704,30	$81.959,68	$192.663,98	$75.677,01	$268.340,99	$268.340,99
⊞ Washington	$205.512,88	$326.542,42	$70.359,90	$602.415,19	$537.466,51	$1.139.881,70	$892.952,15	$2.032.833,85	$2.032.833,85
⊞ Wisconsin			$44.013,75	$44.013,75	$48.509,99	$92.523,74	$86.212,78	$178.736,52	$178.736,52
⊞ Wyoming	$91.107,94			$91.107,94	$79.301,04	$170.408,98	$136.097,50	$306.506,49	$306.506,49
Grand Total	$2.393.689,53	$3.601.190,71	$2.885.359,20	$8.880.239,44	$7.041.183,75	$15.921.423,19	$12.000.247,33	$27.921.670,52	$27.921.670,52

FIGURE 7.10

Passenger revenue in Alabama per year in detail.

In Figure 7.9, the passenger revenue for the state of Alabama is further analyzed. Each city in Alabama is displayed and the passenger revenue for each city is presented per year. The date column represents a similar hierarchy. It is possible to drill-down this hierarchy, too.

Figure 7.10 shows only data from FY 2007, but in more detail. Note that the first three months of the financial year, which starts in July, are being displayed. For each month, quarter and half-year, the table

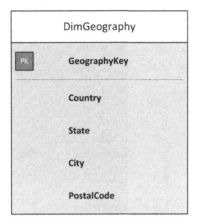

FIGURE 7.11

Geography dimension (physical design).

shows total values in the columns on the right. By using this approach, business analysts are enabled to understand the information in the table in great detail.

The *Geography* hierarchy is implemented physically from the dimension table, as shown in Figure 7.11.

Each level of the hierarchy is based on one of the physical attributes of the dimension table. The association between the attribute and the hierarchy level is done in Microsoft SQL Server Analysis Services and is discussed in more detail in Chapter 15, Multidimensional Database. Similar hierarchies will be implemented in the chapter when the OLAP cube is being built and a date dimension is added as a hierarchy.

7.4.3 SNOWFLAKE DESIGN

This chapter has introduced the star schema, which is based on a fact table in the center, and accompanying dimension tables that provide context for the facts. These dimension tables are directly joined to the fact table. An indirect joining of dimension tables – that is, a dimension table that is referenced by another dimension table – is not possible in a true star schema. This is also true if there is a relationship between dimension attributes. Consider the example of corporate groups in the airline industry and individual carriers. Each airline is part of a larger group, which owns the carrier. For example, United Continental Holdings, Inc. owns both United Airlines and Continental Airlines, among other, smaller carriers.

If a star schema should express this relationship, both dimensions, *DimGroup* and *DimCarrier*, have to be directly referenced by the fact table, as shown in Figure 7.12.

This example follows the one presented in Figure 7.4. However, it shows only one star schema. Note the two dimensions *DimGroup* and *DimCarrier* which are independently referenced by the fact

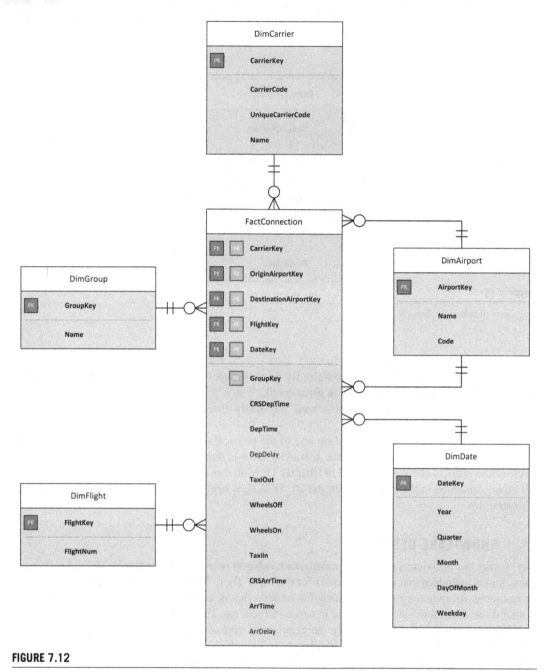

FIGURE 7.12

Star schema with fact table in the center and directly referenced dimensions only (physical design).

table. However, there is an implicit relationship between these two dimensions. The relationship is implemented in the ETL job that loads the table. The ETL job makes sure that only valid *CarrierKey* and *GroupKey* combinations are loaded into the fact table. The model does not implement any rule that prevents the loading of invalid combinations. On the other hand, this model is easy to use by business users, because they can directly join all required context information. This is why, on the first hand, the star schema allows only directly referenced dimension tables. For example, in order to return the average delay of a group, the following statement could be used:

```
SELECT
      DimGroup.Name, AVG(DepDelay)
FROM
      FactConnection
INNER JOIN
      DimGroup ON DimGroup.GroupKey = FactConnection.GroupKey
GROUP BY
      DimGroup.Name
```

As the statement shows, there is not much effort required to join the group into the result set. The join is performed directly using the *GroupKey* field in the fact table.

A snowflake schema, on the other hand, allows indirect dimension tables. This is useful if the relationships between dimension attributes should be modeled explicitly. If the model in Figure 7.12 were modeled as a star schema, it would look similar, as in Figure 7.13.

As you can see from the diagram, the term "snowflake" comes from the appearance of the model. Dimension tables emerge from the fact table in the center, similar to the branches of a snowflake [3]. Instead of directly referencing *DimGroup* from *FactConnection*, the group is indirectly referenced using *DimCarrier*. The *GroupKey* which identified the group in the fact table has moved into *DimCarrier*. In order to return the average delay of a group, as similar to the previous statement, it is required to first join *DimCarrier* in order to join *DimGroup*:

```
SELECT
      DimGroup.Name, AVG(DepDelay)
FROM
      FactConnection
INNER JOIN
      DimCarrier ON DimCarrier.CarrierKey = FactConnection.CarrierKey
LEFT JOIN
      DimGroup ON DimGroup.GroupKey = DimCarrier.GroupKey
GROUP BY
      DimGroup.Name
```

This is not a problem if you are used to writing SQL statements and have no problem with indirectly joining tables as in this statement. For an experienced database developer, this statement poses no threat at all. However, if business analysts with less knowledge and experience with SQL statements have to deal with snowflake designs, they might become overwhelmed and not be able to cope with the database anymore. Despite this problem, snowflake designs are actually used very frequently.

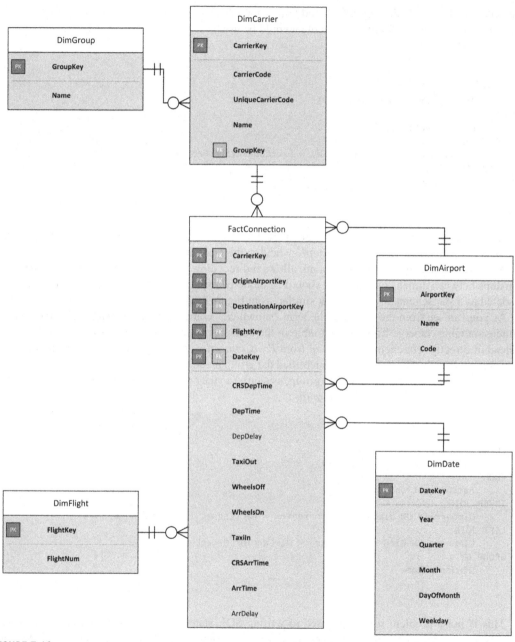

FIGURE 7.13

Snowflake schema with fact table in the center indirectly referenced dimensions (physical design).

REFERENCES

[1] Ralph Kimball: The Data Warehouse Toolkit, first edition 1997.

[2] Ralph Kimball and Margy Ross: The Data Warehouse Toolkit, 2nd edition, page 16, 16ff, 17, 20, 30f, 31f, 19, 95f, 97.

[3] Christopher Adamson: Star Schema – The complete reference, p. 4f, 5f, 6, 10f, 11, 12, 13, 86f, 87, 44, 45f, 157.

[4] Norman J. Ashford, et al., Airport Operations", 3rd edition, p. 415.

[5] http://technet.microsoft.com/en-us/library/cc278097(v=sql.100).aspx.

[6] Joy Mundy and Warren Thornthwaite: The Microsoft Data Warehouse Toolkit, 2nd Edition, pp. 33, 36.

[7] http://www.kimballgroup.com/2013/02/design-tip-152-slowly-changing-dimension-types-0-4-5-6-7/.

[8] http://www.symcorp.com/tech_expertise_design.html.

[9] Best Buy, Fiscal 2014 Annual Report.

PHYSICAL DATA WAREHOUSE DESIGN

8

Data warehouse projects have special requirements for the physical architecture of the database system. These requirements distinguish data warehouse projects from operational data stores and are often underestimated. This chapter covers topics such as hardware options, optimization of the underlying hardware and the operating system, and some background information on table partitioning and file-groups for database tables, among other topics.

This chapter also shows how to set up the databases required for following chapters in Microsoft SQL Server 2014.

8.1 DATABASE WORKLOADS

Relational databases are used for different purposes. For example, business applications use them to store and retrieve operational data in **online transaction processing (OLTP)**. When processing trans-actional data, database management systems have to deal with many read and write requests. In most cases, the required workload for read outnumbers the workloads for writes in OLTP scenarios: a ratio of 80% to 20% is common [1]. However, compared to **business intelligence (BI)** applications, the number of reads is very low.

Also, there is a different work load pattern: transactional systems have reads and writes all through the (working) day, as long as business users are working with the data: for example, open-ing screens in applications (which require SELECT statements), performing transactions (requires SELECTs and INSERT statements) and modifying product data (requires UPDATE statements). The operations in OLTP applications are typically performed on individual records, or only a few records.

Business intelligence applications are different in this regard: usually, they are loaded in inter-vals, for example in the early morning of the day, and the batch loads are finished before the office opens. These batches involve much larger data sets than in transactional systems. The data in a data warehouse is optimized for fast reads because SELECT statements make up the majority of the workload throughout the day. Quick response times are not as important as in OLTP applications (where users are not willing to wait for some seconds to open a product description). However, a fast response time from the business intelligence application is still desired. Another type of work-load is the one experienced when dealing with **online analytical processing (OLAP),** which is not only read intensive but also requires lots of computations and aggregations. Tools in this field, such as Microsoft SQL Server Analysis Services, often access whole datasets in order to perform their calculations [2–4].

8.1.1 WORKLOAD CHARACTERISTICS

In addition to this read-write mix, there are additional characteristics that pose challenges to the infrastructure [2]:

- **Data latency:** this characteristic is the lag between data creation and data consumption. Some applications, such as many OLTP applications, require a short latency in order to use new data in upstream business processes. Batch-driven data warehousing applications have a higher tolerance for longer latency, because the data is often loaded overnight, long before it is used by the business user. Therefore, the database management system has enough time to store the data and make it retrievable. This gives data warehouse architects the freedom to use database resources in a more efficient way, for example by using bulk data processing and set operations. Exceptions to this truly analytical use case are real-time data warehouse systems, where short latency is required. These systems have special requirements and constraints and are not covered by this book.
- **Consistency:** the immediate consistency of data is very critical for OLTP systems because the data is being accessed as soon as it is written to disk. The data consumers expect to find a consistent view of the data when using the data in subsequent business processes. The same is true for data warehousing, but, depending on the use case, an eventual consistency [5] might be enough to satisfy the business users. This is often experienced when massively distributing the data among many nodes. Many Big Data technologies such as Apache Cassandra [6], MongoDB [7] and others provide eventual consistency. However, this is not a perfect solution, which is strict consistency where any change to the data is atomic and is taken into effect instantaneously [8]. Instead it is a pragmatic approach that follows the CAP theorem [9] by ensuring that the network partitioning is ensured, availability is high and consistency is a little loose in overall terms (i.e., eventually) [10].
- **Updateability:** there are different options available if data is not updateable but permanent. While OLTP systems often perform updates on existing data (such as updating product descriptions), business intelligence and OLAP applications often assume that data is written to disk permanently. For example, transactions are often permanent, e.g. Web logs from a Web server such as Microsoft Internet Information Services (IIS). Because this data never changes, it is possible to optimize the data collection procedures for this behavior. This is a great advantage given the fact that UPDATE operations are much slower than INSERT operations on most relational database management systems (RDBMS).
- **Data types:** the fastest option is to deal with tabular sets of data. However, not all data is in tabular form. Sometimes, a data warehouse needs to absorb hierarchical data or, in other cases, unstructured data such as texts or audio files. In order to deal with such data in a RDBMS, the data needs to be flattened or structured. If that is not the desired goal, the data warehouse can also be put on NoSQL databases or can integrate NoSQL databases for parts of the data. Data Vault 2.0 provides provisions for both cases, but a lengthy discussion is out of the scope of this book. Some details are provided in Chapter 2, Scalable Data Warehouse Architecture.
- **Response time:** the response time is the time it takes the RDBMS to return the results from a user query. The challenge is to read all required data and return the aggregated or otherwise computed data to the user. To satisfy the user requests, it is often required to read large volumes from disk in order to summarize it. For that reason, many OLAP engines, such as Microsoft SQL Server

Analysis Services, try to prestage the data and perform most calculations and aggregations ahead of time. That way, they can return the results for predicted calculations and aggregations much faster. The other response time that should be noted is the response time for writing data into the data warehouse, including achieving an eventual consistency of the data.

- **Predictability:** in some cases, the expected workloads are highly predictable: for example, most OLTP systems have a highly predictable workload over the day. The same applies for relational reporting and dashboards in data warehousing because the same queries are executed over and over. In other cases, the workload is less predictable. This is true for some OLTP scenarios, for example small Web servers with unexpected Web traffic peaks. Ad-hoc queries and data exploration tasks are another example from data warehousing where the workload is not predictable.

Due to the different characteristics of each workload, it is important to understand that the hardware configuration needs to be optimized differently for OLTP, BI and OLAP applications. It is not recommended to use the same infrastructure for OLTP and OLAP applications, for example. Instead, an infrastructure should be used to house data warehouse applications and another to house transactional systems. This separation allows IT to optimize the infrastructure according to the described characteristics.

However, even having two sets of infrastructure is not enough, as discussed in the following section.

8.2 SEPARATE ENVIRONMENTS FOR DEVELOPMENT, TESTING, AND PRODUCTION

While the separation of OLTP systems from data warehouse systems is necessary because of the different workload characteristics of both applications, it is also required to distinguish between a development environment, a test environment and a production environment, following standard principles from software development. Chapter 3, The Data Vault 2.0 Methodology, explains why and how software development approaches are used in the data warehousing and business intelligence field. This is due to different requirements regarding the stability of the system and the loaded data and due to security requirements. There are business areas where the developers and testers must not have access to production data.

Business intelligence developers need a test bed to run their code and their tests against. Usually, these tests are executed against extreme cases of data and random samples of production data. Regardless of the actual testing method, whether it is test-driven development or something else, business intelligence developers need a **development environment** to develop their solutions.

Once developers have implemented all planned features of the sprint and have tested their code with their means, the goal becomes to deploy the functionality to the business user. In order to do so, a standardized deployment process is required, and such a process requires testing the new functionality against production data without putting the production system at risk. This is where the **test environment** comes into play: it provides a copy of the actual production data with all functionality currently in productive use. In fact, it is a copy of all functionality and as much production data as possible. If possible, the test environment should contain a full copy of the data that is currently being used by the business users. However, it is not always possible to have a full copy of the data in the test environment, for example because of storage limitations (apart from legal requirements, which complicate these matters). As a general guideline, at least 50% of the production data should be used for testing. The test environment is not only used to test new functionality against production data [11], but it is also used to test the deployment procedures, such as any installation or other setup routines against a realistic copy of the production environment [12]. And, as soon as the new functionality has been successfully installed in the test environment and, therefore, passed all technical tests, the test environment provides the basis for acceptance tests performed by business users [13].

Without the successful completion of these tests, it is not possible to deploy the new functionality into the **production environment**. This environment provides the data and the current functionality to all business users, and therefore has a much higher workload than the development or test environment. While the development and test systems are primarily used by team members and a limited number of business users and other stakeholders, the production environment is mission-critical and is used by a much higher number of users and might be integrated into subsequent business processes or to the public. Therefore, running any tests or development activities against the production environment is highly debatable (this is the diplomatic version of "don't do this!"). Also, the production environment should be physically separated from the development and test environments. This is important to prevent any side effects on the production environment while new functionality is being developed or tested. Also, sometimes these activities require extra workload, which might affect the production environment if all environments run on the same infrastructure [14].

8.2.1 BLUE-GREEN DEPLOYMENT

One problem with the deployment approach described in the last section is that the deployment must be performed two times within the sprint: first, all changes are deployed into the test environment to test the features and the deployment procedure itself and to perform user acceptance testing. Once all these tests have been performed successfully, the deployment into the production environment is performed in order to get the new functionality to the business user and bring the current sprint to a successful end [14].

The drawback of this approach is that these deployments have to be performed in sequence: without the first deployment successfully passing, it is not possible to start the second deployment. This could pose a serious bottleneck to organizations trying to achieve a two-week sprint cycle [14].

To speed up the deployment procedure, without compromising any established test standards, a concept from the mainframe world is used: blue-green deployment. In this scenario, there is a development environment and two production environments, shown in Figure 8.1.

Business users use only one production environment. A router between them and the two environments routes user requests to the one that is currently active. In the case of Figure 8.1, the active environment is the green environment. The other remains in sync but is not used in actual production – hence the connection to the blue environment is dashed out (not active). As soon as the development team is ready to test new functionality against production data, the passive environment is used as the test environment. The team uses it as the test environment, deploys all new functionality and performs all tests that are required for production deployment.

Once the business users have successfully completed the user acceptance tests, there are two production environments: the currently active one, representing the old version before the sprint and the inactive one with new functionality as developed in this sprint. By hot-switching the router from the old

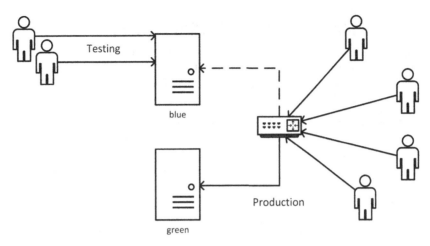

FIGURE 8.1

Blue-green deployment.

production environment to the new one, the new functionality is immediately deployed into active use [14]. In order to make this scenario work, it is required that both environments be synchronized before tests start. Because this will usually happen towards the end of the sprint, the QA team has enough time from the beginning of the sprint to synchronize both environments before one of the systems is required for testing.

By using this approach, organizations can speed up the deployment into production. However, it imposes multiple disadvantages: first, there are two infrastructures required to run the production environments. Both have to be able to handle the workload that is required by the business. In the previous scenario, the test environment is often less powerful than the production environment, but serves the designated purpose very well. In the blue-green scenario, both infrastructures for production have to meet the requirements for full productive workloads, including all required software licenses [14].

The second challenge is that this approach requires a disciplined team: while the tests are performed against the passive production environment, this exact environment becomes active once the tests have been successfully completed. The same deployment has to be performed against the other production environment in order to get them synchronized again. There are other options for handling this synchronization, however. For example, it is possible to use database replication in Microsoft SQL Server and use Distributed File System replication to synchronize the ETL code [15].

Another challenge is that if new features require changes in the ETL processes, then the resulting ETL might have to be executed in both environments, which is not always possible. This challenge can be mitigated if the extraction of data follows a standard pattern and business logic is implemented using virtualized views which require no materialization of data. Both are true for the Data Vault loading patterns, presented in Chapter 12, Loading the Data Vault. It is possible to generate standard patterns, which are easy to deploy in replicated environments. Absorbing the changes is done in a single meta-data layer.

8.3 MICROSOFT AZURE CLOUD COMPUTING PLATFORM

Before describing traditional data warehouse infrastructure within the premises of the enterprise, another emerging option should be introduced: Microsoft SQL Azure, which is part of the Microsoft Azure cloud computing platform. The Microsoft Azure platform consists of three scalable and secure solutions [16]:

- **Microsoft Azure** (formerly known as **Windows Azure**): A collection of Microsoft Windows powered virtual machines which can run Web services and other program code, including .NET applications and PHP code.
- **Cloud Services:** A set of services that provide a service bus for handling messages in a subscriber/publisher topology and other core capabilities, such as federated identity for securing applications and data.
- **SQL Database:** A transactional database in the cloud, based on Microsoft SQL Server 2014. It is possible to consume the data in this database from applications within the Azure cloud.

In addition, other services have been released, including HDInsight, which is Microsoft's implementation of Hadoop for Azure [16]. Figure 8.2 presents the HDInsight ecosystem of Microsoft Azure.

Without going into much detail regarding the individual components, it becomes obvious that HDInsight provides a powerful and rich set of solutions to organizations that are using Microsoft SQL

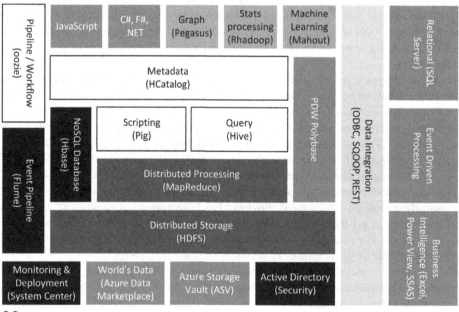

FIGURE 8.2

Hadoop/HDInsight Ecosystem [17].

Figure adapted by author from Getting Started with Azure HDInsight, *by Vipul Patel. Copyright 2015 QuinStreet Inc.*

Reprinted with permission.

Server 2014. The cloud platform enables organizations from small startups to large enterprises to scale their business intelligence solutions without any actual limitations.

In a cloud platform such as Microsoft Azure, the software solution is decoupled from the actual physical storage and implementation details. Developers who deploy their solutions to the Azure cloud don't know the actual hardware being used; they don't know the actual server names but only an Internet address that is used to access the application in the cloud [16]. While this is a nice architectural design on its own, it helps organizations to [16]:

- **Provide seasonal applications and database solutions:** data warehouse solutions that load only a small number of source systems, but with large amounts of data, often have peak times over the day. Some data warehouse systems source data only once a month, for example for calculating a monthly balance. In this case, the peak occurs only once a month as well. Providing large infrastructure for such cases might be financially unattractive.
- **Provide solutions with short lifespan:** some data warehouse systems are specifically built for prototypes. Setting up the infrastructure for such applications is already a burden, apart from maintaining it (or tearing it down) after the prototype is finished. However, due to the Data Vault 2.0 model, it is also possible to integrate the data into the Enterprise Data Warehouse and later archive the entities of the prototype. The integration would follow the standard patterns, such as satellites hanging off hubs and links, providing data from the prototype application.
- **Separate storage:** because the data in the cloud is separated from the local SQL Server on premise, the cloud can be used as a safe backup location.
- **Reduce fixed costs of infrastructure:** smaller companies can take advantage of the lower fixed costs to set up a SQL Azure database in the cloud and grow their cloud consumption with their business.

These business scenarios and advantages are behind the growing demand for cloud services. They also drive demand for business intelligence solutions in the cloud, at least partially (for now). Another driver for moving business intelligence into the cloud is the growing volume, velocity and variety of data that needs to be sourced for the data warehouse. Cloud services, such as Microsoft Azure, provide the storage and the compute power to process and analyze the data.

Hadoop, an open source framework, is the de-facto standard for distributed data processing. It provides MapReduce "for writing applications that process large amounts of structured and semi-structured data in parallel across large clusters of machines in a very reliable and fault-tolerant manner." There are also many related projects that use the Hadoop core distributed storage and MapReduce framework [18].

MapReduce itself is a programming model that is used to process large amounts of data on a Hadoop cluster. These programming models are written in Java and split the raw data on the Hadoop cluster in independent chunks which are processed by independent and parallel map tasks. The advantage of using MapReduce is that the data is no longer moved to the processing. Instead, the processing is moved to the data and performed in a distributed manner. As a result, the processing of data is speeded up significantly. The output of these map tasks is then used as an input to reduce tasks which are stored in the Hadoop file system for further processing. Other projects, such as Hive or Pig, provide higher-level access to the data on the cluster [18].

With HDInsight, Microsoft provides a service that allows easily building a Hadoop cluster whenever it is required and tearing it down as soon as MapReduce jobs are completed. It also supports

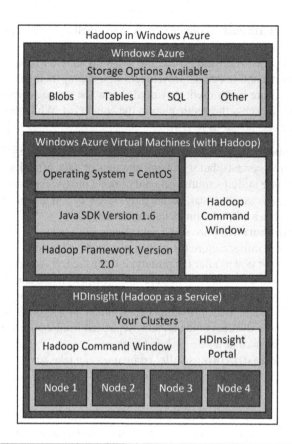

FIGURE 8.3

Hadoop in Microsoft Azure [18].

Figure adapted by author from Hadoop and HDInsight: Big Data in Windows Azure, *by Bruno Terkaly and Ricardo Villalobos. Copyright 2015, Microsoft Corporation. Reprinted with permission.*

Microsoft Azure Blobs, which are mechanisms to store large amounts of unstructured data in the Azure cloud platform. The breadth and depth of Hadoop support in the Microsoft Azure platform (formerly Windows Azure platform) is presented in Figure 8.3 [18].

The first level on top of the diagram in Figure 8.3 is the Microsoft Azure Storage system, which provides secure and reliable storage, including redundancy of data across regions. A number of storage mechanisms are supported, for example Tables (NoSQL key-value stores), SQL databases, Blobs, and other storage options. Microsoft Azure provides a REST-ful API that is used to create, read, update, or delete (CRUD) text or binary data. The API allows clients with support for HTTP to directly access the data in the Microsoft Azure Storage system if they have granted access [18].

The data itself is transparently stored in custom virtual machines providing single-node or multi-node Hadoop clusters; or in a Hadoop cluster provided by HDInsight. The first option, which is the second layer in Figure 8.3, requires setup of your own Hadoop infrastructure in Microsoft Azure virtual machines. However, setting up a multinode cluster by hand isn't a trivial task. The second option is to use HDInsight, and directly set up a Hadoop cluster with a specified number of nodes and a geographic location of the storage using the HDInsight Portal [18]. In both cases, the underlying hardware is invisible to the developer because the infrastructure is managed by the Microsoft Azure cloud computing platform.

However, if an enterprise decides to set up its own infrastructure, the various hardware options are worth a deeper look, because they can drastically affect the performance and reliability of the data warehouse system. The remaining sections of this chapter describe the hardware options and how to set up the data warehouse on premise.

8.4 PHYSICAL DATA WAREHOUSE ARCHITECTURE ON PREMISE

The physical architecture describes the hardware components of the data warehouse and depends on a number of factors, including [19]:

- **Data size:** the data size that needs to be stored in the data warehouse depends on the number of functional units from the enterprise to include in the data warehouse, the number and size of input sources, and the business problems to solve (which influences the number of information marts).
- **Volatility:** because the raw Data Vault tracks all changes to the data sources, the volatility of these source systems affects the data warehouse in two dimensions: first, the data size is higher, and second, the data warehouse will be much more frequently updated.
- **Number of business processes:** the more business processes that should be included in the data warehouse, the more source systems have to be loaded. This also affects the required resources to load them and run the data warehouse.
- **Number of users:** the more users are using the data warehouse, the more resources are required in order to handle their requests. The required resources also depend on how active these users are, how many are using the system at the same time, and what kind of peaks are in their usage patterns (for example, month-end reporting).
- **Nature of use:** the front-end tools also have influence on the required hardware resources. In some cases, virtualized Information Marts are applicable which require less storage but sometimes more CPU power. In other cases, more data has to be materialized which requires more storage for the Information Marts.
- **Service level agreements:** the performance and availability requirements set by the business can become a major influence factor for the physical data warehouse architecture. If users are accessing the data warehouse from all over the world, a 24×7 availability is standard. This also affects your loading cycles of the data warehouse. In other cases, the response time of your reports should be in the subsecond range. In such cases, more computing power is required.

These factors drive the requirements that are established by the business and have a direct influence on the selected hardware for the data warehouse. The next sections describe some of the hardware options that are available for the data warehouse.

8.4.1 HARDWARE ARCHITECTURES AND DATABASES

The Data Vault 2.0 standard is based on a model that allows an incremental build-out of the data warehouse. Data Vault 2.0 is also based on an architecture that incorporates NoSQL and Big Data Systems.

Organizations that follow such an incremental build-out of the enterprise data warehouse benefit from rapid delivery of new features and are able to quickly integrate new source systems and deploy new information marts. Over time, the data warehouse will outgrow the initial hardware, such as the acquired disk storage or the CPU power. If this process is left unmanaged, only one system element is exceeded or out of balance – for example, because the data warehouse architecture requires many I/O reads. For optimum performance, the system elements should be in balance at most if not all times.

In order to ensure the growth of the data warehouse in the future, a scalable architecture is required. There are multiple options for data warehouse architectures, offering more or less scalability [5]:

The simplest architecture uses only a **single server**. In this scenario, presented in Figure 8.4, there is only one Microsoft SQL Server 2014 installation that uses its own single disk. Scalability is limited to the server box, e.g. the mainboard limits the number of CPUs by the number of available CPU sockets, and the number of hard disks is limited by the number of drive slots. It is possible to scale the hardware to some extent, for example by replacing the chassis with a larger one, offering more hard disk slots, or by adding more disk controllers in order to utilize more hard disks in the system. But at some point, the cost to add more hardware is too high and scalability become infeasible.

Microsoft SQL Server offers **scalable shared databases**, which allow use of a read-only database in multiple server instances. They can be used in reporting environments to distribute the workload among those instances. The database can be accessed by these instances over a storage attached network (SAN), which is discussed in section 8.4.4. Each instance uses its own memory, CPU and tempdb database. While queries run on only one instance (thus they cannot be executed across multiple

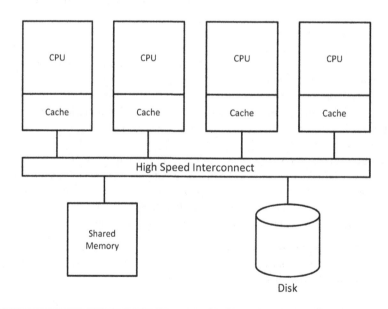

FIGURE 8.4

Single server architecture [20].

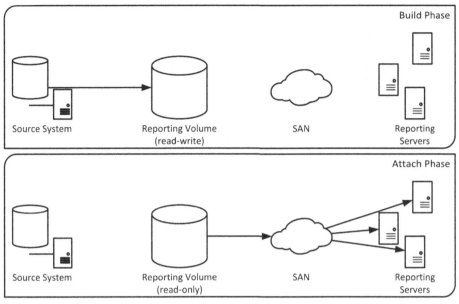

FIGURE 8.5

Building and scaling out a reporting database [21].

Figure adapted by author from "Scalable Shared Databases Overview," by Microsoft Corporation.

Copyright 2015 Microsoft Corporation. Reprinted with permission.

instances), they cannot block the execution of queries on other instances [21]. Figure 8.5 shows how such databases are loaded.

This solution requires a refresh phase, as Figure 8.5 shows. During this refresh phase of the displayed reporting servers, a stale copy of the database is updated and, once the update has been completed, attached to the reporting servers (multiple instances). Due to the read-only limitation, scalable shared databases should be used for materialized information marts only. They should not be used for the Raw Data Vault layer, especially not if real-time or near-real-time data is loaded.

A more sophisticated option is Microsoft SQL Server 2014 Parallel Data Warehouse (PDW) edition. It is a **massively parallel processing (MPP)** platform, implementing a SQL Server grid. This allows the distribution of data to multiple nodes on the grid. Each node has only a subset of data and user queries are answered by all nodes together. Microsoft SQL Server PDW supports two table types for this purpose: *replicated* tables that are actually copied to each node and *distributed* tables where the content of the table is distributed among the nodes. Figure 8.6 shows an example of an MPP architecture.

The first option is best suited for relatively small dimension tables. The data in the table is replicated to each node in order to have the data locally available. This improves the queries' join performance because no data has to be collected from multiple nodes. The second option, which is shown in Figure 8.6, distributes the content of the table among nodes in order to improve the query performance by utilizing the resources of all nodes when handling user queries [22]. In Figure 8.6, the data is distributed according to a key which can be defined when setting up the distribution of the table. In this simple figure,

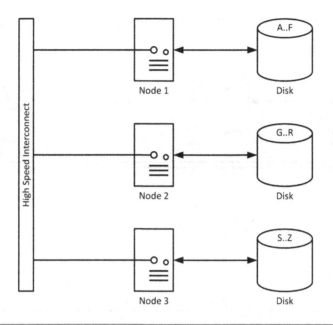

FIGURE 8.6

Massively parallel processing (MPP) architecture [20].

Figure adapted by author from "Transitioning from SMP to MPP, the why and the how," by the SQL Server Team.
Copyright 2015 Microsoft Corporation. Reprinted with permission.

all records with a key starting with A, B, C, D, E, or F are stored on the first node. Records with keys starting with a letter between G to R are stored on the second node and the remaining records are stored on Node 3. Note that, in practice, the data is often not well distributed because the data distribution in Figure 8.6 depends on the key distribution, which is often skewed. Hashing the key helps in this regard, because it creates hash values that are very random and distributed [20].

User queries are performed against a control node and executed by active servers. These servers use dedicated storage systems to store a particular set of data. Data loading and backups are performed using other nodes, specifically added to the control rack for this purpose.

Note that Data Vault 2.0 doesn't require a specific architecture. But due to the incremental build-out of the enterprise data warehouse, the initial hardware specifications will only last for a limited time. The objective is to scale the data warehouse over time and extend the original architecture as soon as the architecture becomes a bottleneck.

As soon as the hardware architecture for the data warehouse has been selected, the individual components must be selected. The next sections introduce some general guidelines for better hardware utilization if financial resources are limited.

8.4.2 PROCESSOR OPTIONS

While some SQL Server editions require a per-core licensing, which can make CPUs with multiple cores very expensive, data warehousing, especially those who implement Data Vault loading patterns, can greatly benefit from multiple cores. We will demonstrate in Chapter 12, Loading the Data Vault, how hubs, links, and satellites can be loaded in parallel, using individual cores for each loading process. Having multiple cores also allows more users to issue queries against the data warehouse. Therefore, the data warehouse server should be equipped with as many cores as (financially) possible. For the same reason, Hyper-Threading Technology, a proprietary technology by Intel®, should be activated. Another factor that should be considered is the cache size of the processor as it also affects the performance of the data warehouse. Similar to the next hardware option, the general guideline is: the more the better if financial resources are not very limited. In all other cases, a properly balanced system is the best solution.

8.4.3 MEMORY OPTIONS

The database server uses physical memory for caching pages from disk. While operational database systems often deal with small transactions, data warehouse systems deal with large queries (referring to the amount of data being touched by the query). In addition, a query often requires multiple passes to deal with large tables; having the table already in memory can greatly improve the performance [23]. If SQL Server doesn't have enough memory available to complete the operation, it uses hard disk storage, for example by using page files, tempdb or re-reading database pages from disk. Therefore, the more RAM the data warehouse system provides to Microsoft SQL Server, the better.

8.4.4 STORAGE OPTIONS

There are several storage options available for the data warehouse. This section introduces various storage options that are used in data warehousing, including RAID levels, local connectivity such as SCSI and Fibre Channel, and local versus network attached storage.

Most setups use one RAID level or another:

- **RAID-0** is an unprotected disk stripe combining the access rates and the capacity of individual disk drives. A RAID-0 array appears to the operating system as one logical disk. For example, if four 100 GB disks are added to the RAID-0 disk array, a logical disk with a capacity of 400 GB is available in the system. The speed is also combined, as the data is written to all four disks simultaneously. Therefore, it is the fastest RAID option available. However, there is no failure protection. In fact, if one of the disks fails, the whole disk array becomes invalid, leaving unreadable data on the remaining disks [24]. To add failure tolerance, either RAID-1, RAID-5, or RAID-6 are often used.
- **RAID-1** is a simple disk mirror, copying the data to all the disks in the RAID array. Therefore, the disk array has the same logical size as each of the individual disks: combining two 100 GB disks results in one 100 GB logical disk. If one of the disks fails, an exact copy of the data remains on the second disk [3].
- **RAID-5** uses a more advanced approach to add failure tolerance to the disk array. It requires at least three disks [25] and calculates parity bits for the data that are distributed over all disks in the array. The parity bits are spread over the disk array. In total, the capacity of one disk is used for these distributed parity checks, resulting in a total capacity of the combined capacity of all drives minus one drive worth of space. If one drive fails, it is possible to replace the disk and rebuild the data from this disk using the distributed parity checks (and the data on the other drives).

If more than one disk fails at the same time, all data in the disk array is lost [3]. This option is slower than RAID-1 but more cost effective as more capacity is available than in a similar setup with RAID-1 [26].

- **RAID-6** overcomes the limitation of RAID-5 to handle only one failed disk. It requires at least four disks in the array and allows two failed disks at the same time by calculating and distributing two parity bits [31]. This RAID level is recommended for physical disks with a capacity higher than 1 TB or with disk array with more than five physical disks [27].

In addition to these RAID levels, there are more advanced levels that often combine multiple RAID levels, e.g. RAID-50 combines two RAID-5 arrays in a disk stripe (RAID-0). We suggest a review of those RAID levels in more detail before building the data warehouse infrastructure. Table 8.1 summarizes the presented RAID levels.

Note that the last row of Table 8.1 introduces some use cases for each RAID level. They apply only to data warehouse infrastructures following the Data Vault 2.0 standard. Note that it is also possible to store the stage area, information marts, and the Metrics Mart on another RAID level than the indicated 0 level. However, it is possible to accept the intolerance to failures, because the data that lives in these layers only exists for a limited time or can be reproduced from the Raw Data Vault. Section 8.6 will discuss the use cases in more detail.

For the best performance, it is advised to use multiple disk controllers for the data warehouse server. Section 8.5.3 will discuss the fact that row data should be separated from index data (and both from log files). Each set of data should be stored on separate physical disks or disk arrays. In order to maximize the parallelization and bandwidth of SQL Server's data access, the best strategy is to use separate disk controllers as well [29].

Another option for data warehouse systems is the use of memory-based disks, for example solid-state disks (SSDs). While consumer SSDs only allow a very limited number of writes during their device life cycle, enterprise-grade SSDs allow many more program and erase cycles [30]. Enterprise SSDs can be used in some cases in data warehousing [3]. One example is to store some indices on SSDs: indices are often updated only after batch loading the data into the table. However, they are accessed very frequently and, even more importantly, in random order. For that reason, indices can utilize the random access mode of SSDs very well [31].

Table 8.1 RAID Level Comparison [28]				
Feature	**RAID-0**	**RAID-1**	**RAID-5**	**RAID-6**
Minimum # Drives	2	2	3	4
Fault Tolerance	None	1 disk	1 disk	2 disks
Read Performance	High	High	High	High
Write Performance	High	Medium	Low	Low
Capacity Utilization	100 %	50 %	67 % – 94 %	50 % – 88 %
DWH Use Case (with Data Vault)	Stage Area, Info Marts, Metrics Mart	Raw Data Vault, Meta Mart, Error Mart	Raw Data Vault, Meta Mart, Error Mart	Raw Data Vault, Meta Mart, Error Mart

It is also possible to use storage networks in data warehousing. In fact, many organizations actually use technologies such as Fibre Channel to attach storage to the data warehouse server. The advantage is that it is possible to share storage resources with other applications and extend it relatively easily when required. Other options include iSCSI which is used to transport data frames via IP traffic [3]. The advantages of such Storage Area Networks (SANs) are the following [31]:

- **Higher availability:** in many cases, SAN storage is more reliable than local storage. Therefore, SAN has the potential to reduce downtime of the data warehouse server.
- **Better recovery from disaster:** SANs are backed up centrally. This reduces operational costs and speeds up the time to restore files from a backup.
- **Central management:** instead of managing each server's local storage, it is possible to manage the storage for all servers centrally. It's even possible to increase available storage capacity to a server without opening the server. Instead, more space is assigned to the server remotely, often not requiring a reboot of the server.
- **Space utilization:** local storage is often underutilized because more disk space is added to the server than actually (or currently) required.

When using these options, make sure to understand that the bandwidth on these technologies is limited by the transport protocol. This limitation can affect the performance of your data warehouse applications [3]. The next section covers some networking options that should be considered.

8.4.5 NETWORK OPTIONS

Another key component of a data warehouse server is the network interface [31]. It is used in several ways:

- **Transfer data into the data warehouse:** when data is loaded from source systems, it is transferred via the network interface.
- **Transfer data out of the data warehouse:** some tools, such as SQL Server Analysis Services (SSAS), pull out a great deal of data from the data warehouse to process it in a tool-specific way. If these tools are not installed on the same machine, a lot of traffic has to go over the network.
- **Receive application queries:** tools such as SQL Server Reporting Services (SSRS) or data mining tools access the data in the data warehouse using queries. These queries often ask the database server to perform aggregations or computations. Similar to the previous case, the query is transmitted over a network if the application is not installed on the same machine. However, these queries tend to be very small, as these queries are expressed in text format.
- **Receive user queries in ad-hoc reporting:** in some cases, users directly access the data warehouse to retrieve data. In order to do so, they have to submit queries to the data warehouse. Usually, the queries go through the network, as most users work from their local workstations. But again, these queries are small compared to the other traffic to and from the data warehouse.
- **Respond to application or user queries:** both types of queries have to return a result set with some amount of data. However, in most cases, this data is often aggregated or reduced to a limited number of records. But the traffic has to be transmitted over the network if the application is not installed on the same machine.
- **Access data on SAN:** if the data warehouse is using SANs, the data which are written by Microsoft SQL Server into database pages have to be transmitted over a network interface as well.

While receiving and responding to application or user queries should not be a problem for modern network interfaces, transferring data into and out of the data warehouse, or accessing a SAN, can become a problem. Organizations try to mitigate this challenge by using multiple network interfaces to improve the fault-tolerance of the system and allow for the separation of duties. SANs take advantage of such separation of duties when dedicated Fibre Channel networks are used to provide the required speed for this type of storage. But depending on the actual workload it might be worthwhile to review the use of additional network interfaces (many servers today have two cards) to separate sourcing from information access. In addition, reviewing the networking components between source system and data warehouse might identify bottlenecks that limit the actual bandwidth on the network.

This concludes our brief discussion of hardware components for data warehousing. Section 8.5 covers some general database options that should be considered additionally when setting up the infrastructure for the data warehouse.

8.5 DATABASE OPTIONS

Before we present how to set up each individual data warehouse layer, a discussion on general database options is required. These options, which are covered in the next sections, help to improve the performance of the data warehouse.

8.5.1 TEMPDB OPTIONS

Microsoft SQL Server 2014 maintains a database for holding various internal database objects or version stores. This includes [32]:

- **Temporary user objects:** these objects are explicitly created by the database user, for example temporary tables, temporary stored procedures, cursors, or table variables.
- **Internal objects:** the SQL Server database engine creates internal objects, for example to store intermediate results for spools or sorting.
- **Row versions from read-committed transactions:** row version isolation or snapshot isolation transactions create row versions that are temporarily stored in tempdb.
- **Row versions from database features:** some features create row versions in tempdb as well, for example Multiple Active Result Sets (MARS), online index operations, and AFTER triggers.

The database is not only used in operational databases, but also heavily in data warehousing. As described in the previous list, indices and sort operations, which are used very frequently in data warehousing, are all performed with help of tempdb. Therefore, its usage should be optimized. Some guidelines should be considered when setting up the initial data warehouse infrastructure [33]:

- **Set recovery model to SIMPLE:** the database will automatically reclaim log space to keep the size of the database small.
- **Move tempdb to a very fast disk:** it should be the fastest option available.
- **Put tempdb to a different disk:** don't put it on the same disk as other data or log files.
- **Create multiple data files:** the recommendation is to create one data file per CPU core.
- **Allow the database to grow automatically:** the database should only be limited by the physical disk, not any logical limits.

- **Pre-allocate database if required:** often, the production environment should not be interrupted for the allocation of new space for tempdb. In this case, pre-allocate as much space as expected for the workload of the data warehouse.
- **Set reasonable growth increment:** if the database needs to be expanded, make sure the growth increment is not too small in order to prevent frequent expansions of tempdb.

It is also recommended to monitor the size of the tempdb in order to identify bottlenecks due to space restrictions or changed usage patterns. The following query can be used [26]:

```
SELECT
        SUM(u.internal_object_reserved_page_count)*8 AS internal_objects_kb,
        SUM(u.user_object_reserved_page_count)*8 AS user_objects_kb,
        SUM(u.version_store_reserved_page_count)*8 AS version_store_kb,
        SUM(u.unallocated_extent_page_count)*8 AS freespace_kb
FROM
        sys.dm_db_file_space_usage u
LEFT JOIN master..sysdatabases d ON (d.dbid = u.database_id)
WHERE
        d.name = 'tempdb'
```

This query identifies and shows the space used by internal objects, user objects, and version store. It also shows how much space is left in the database. The query should be run regularly, for example on a weekly interval.

8.5.2 PARTITIONING

Partition is used when the data in a table or index becomes too large to manage by SQL Server 2014. If the data is too big, the performance of maintenance functions, such as backup or restore, can drop [26]. For this reason, data is often archived in operational systems, but this is not an option in data warehousing where we try to keep all history if possible. Also, the tables in data warehousing are often much larger than in operational systems, making this problem even more serious.

Partitioning splits the data into smaller pieces, called partitions. Rows that are added to the table are redirected into one partition during INSERT, resulting in partitions with subsets of data. It is possible to transfer or access each partition individually, thus applying the operation on the subsets of data in this partition. For example, it is possible to load the data from a source system directly into a partition, without affecting the data in other partitions. It is also possible to individually compress the records of a partition or partially rebuild a database index, based on partitions. Database partitions also improve the query performance because it is possible to directly join partitions, which the query optimizer can use to improve the performance of equi-join queries [34].

Table and index partitioning in Microsoft SQL Server 2014 is based on the following components [34]:

- **Partition function:** this function is used to distribute the rows of the table or data in the index to the partitions. It also defines the number of partitions to be used and how the boundaries of the partition are defined. Often, the distribution of data is based on a datetime column, for example the sales date of sales order data. In this case, the data could be distributed into 12 or 365 partitions, based on the month or day of the sales date.

- **Partition scheme:** this database object maps the partitions of the given partition function to filegroups. This allows the placement of partitions on separate disk drives. It also allows independent backups of filegroups holding one or more partitions.
- **Partitioning column:** the partition function is based on this column to distribute the data (the sales date in the previous example).

Loading patterns in data warehousing and queries can take great advantage from partitioning. This is especially true if partitions are distributed over multiple physical disks. However, this requires the use of filegroups, which is discussed in the next section.

8.5.3 FILEGROUPS

Filegroups are used in order to distribute the partitions in a partition scheme (as described in the last section) to multiple physical disks or RAID arrays. Each filegroup is associated with a specific logical disk drive and accessed independently from other filegroups by Microsoft SQL Server. It is possible to backup and restore the filegroup independently from other filegroups as well.

Filegroups can also be used to separate row data from indices. Such a strategy can improve the performance if the data is distributed to different physical drives with their own disk controllers. It allows the database server to read row and index data independently from each other in parallel because multiple disk heads are reading the pages [29]. Because indices are very read-intensive, consider placing the index filegroup on a SSD for faster and random access [31].

For the same reason, different physical disks should be used to separate row data from log data. When SQL Server (or any other database management system) maintains the log files, it writes all the database transactions to the separate disk, which should be optimized for write operations. On the other hand, the disk that stores the data pages should support many read operations from queries [31].

8.5.4 DATA COMPRESSION

Another database feature that can increase the performance of queries is the use of data compression. Microsoft SQL Server supports compression on the page level, offering the following benefits [26]:

- **Better I/O utilization:** because the page is compressed, more data can fit into a page. The page itself is read and written to disk in compressed form; it is uncompressed only when used by the CPU. Therefore, more data can be read and written to and from disk when compressed pages are used. This improves the I/O performance.
- **Reduced page latching [35]:** because more data fits into a page, it requires less latching to safely retrieve the data.
- **Better memory utilization:** compression also increases the amount of data that will fit into the buffer cache, similar to better I/O utilization.

While data compression consumes more CPU power, it uses less I/O to store and retrieve the same amount of data. Therefore, it is the better option to turn data compression on where possible. Exceptions are servers where computing power is limited or workloads that require many writes (and less reads) of database pages. However, the latter should not be the case in data warehousing.

8.6 **SETTING UP THE DATA WAREHOUSE**

The following sections describe a data warehouse setup that represents the best case possible. By describing this best case, our goal is to focus your attention on the desired options per data warehouse layer. Therefore, we describe RAID levels that should be used per layer and the reasoning behind this decision. However, in many cases, the data warehouse only has one logical drive, which is fine, too – at least as long as some kind of failure protection is available to protect the data in the Raw Data Vault.

If you're experiencing performance bottlenecks in such a solution, refer back to this chapter to find options for a better setup than having the whole data warehouse only on one disk or disk array. It also gives you alternatives to using the most expensive hardware for the whole data warehouse infrastructure and directs you to some alternatives where money can be saved. This helps to find an economical setup for the data warehouse.

In many cases, it is a good approach to start with a RAID 5 or 6 storage setup and extend it as soon as the single disk array becomes a performance bottleneck. This strategy follows the incremental build-out that should be used when building an enterprise data warehouse. Don't plan ahead for multiple years. Get the data warehouse initiative started, planning ahead only a limited number of years. Nobody can foresee the success of the enterprise data warehouse and you don't want to stop the project early on, due to high costs for infrastructure setup. Instead, build out the system, once you have shown success and the user demands more functionality.

The same applies to CPU and memory options. When purchasing the components, make sure that you can extend the initial hardware setup, for example by replacing the initial CPU with a more powerful one or adding another CPU to a dual-socket mainboard. Similarly, add more RAM modules when needed. For that reason, spend more money to buy an extensible hardware platform.

In order to support the incremental build-out of the data warehouse, use filegroups as described in the following sections. If all database objects are placed in the same filegroup (e.g. row data and index data), it becomes more complex and therefore more time-consuming to move the database objects later on.

This chapter assumes that Master Data Services (MDS) and Data Quality Services (DQS) have been set up and already integrated to each other. The installation of these components is out of the scope of this book. If you are having trouble setting these components up, please refer to Books Online or your systems administrator.

8.6.1 **SETTING UP THE STAGE AREA**

We have already discussed in Chapter 2 that the goal of the stage area is to stage incoming data in order to reduce the workload on the operational systems and shorten the access time to them. The stage area is defined as a temporary storage of the incoming data. It can be a relational database system or a NoSQL storage. The first option is often the best choice if the incoming data is coming from relational sources and fully typed. For example, if the source data is extracted directly from its operational database and loaded into the stage area, a relational stage area is the best choice.

In other cases, data is delivered as flat files or even unstructured information. If that is the case, a NoSQL storage such as Hadoop might be the better option for staging the incoming data. In fact, a NoSQL stage area is often a better choice when data arrives with high volume or high velocity. This is true for both unstructured data and strongly typed, i.e., structured data. The reason is that NoSQL has an advantage when absorbing the data as big and fast as it arrives, because storing data in NoSQL requires only a file-copy operation. Once the data has been absorbed by the NoSQL stage area, the data is extracted and loaded into the Raw Data Vault for further analysis.

No matter which option you choose, the requirements for each option remain the same (as in the intro to this section): to pull out the data from the source system as fast as possible in order to reduce the amount of time that the data warehouse is using CPU and network resources on the source system. Therefore, the goal of the stage area is to collect the incoming data as fast as possible. This depends on a number of other elements, such as the network interface, but the selected disk storage remains one of the most important options that we can deal with.

8.6.1.1 Hardware Considerations for Stage Area

As we have described in section 8.4.4, RAID level 0 provides the highest performance by distributing the data to multiple disks, combining the I/O performance of the individual disks. RAID level 0 is superior to all other RAID levels in terms of read and write performance. The number of disks in the RAID array depends on the performance of the selected bus.

Having no fault-tolerance on RAID 0 can become a problem, but not so much for the stage area, due to its temporary nature. If the underlying disk stripe fails, the worst-case scenario is that only the unloaded data that was currently residing in the stage area is lost. However, it is often possible to reload the data from its original source in such a case. Depending on such options for reloading the stage data, RAID level 0 can become a viable solution.

Because the stage area contains only direct copies of the source data for one or a limited number of loads, but no history, the storage space requirements for a relational stage area are not very high, compared to the rest of the data warehouse. For that reason, fast disks (such as SAS disks with 15,000 rpm) should be favored over large but slow disks. If the stage area uses disk striping with RAID level 0, the capacity of the disks is combined, lessening the storage limitations of those fast disks.

Microsoft SQL Server 2014 also introduces in-memory tables which could be used in staging. However, this option is more expensive because it requires that the infrastructure provides enough RAM to stage the incoming data in memory.

Note that this discussion holds true for relational stage areas. When using a NoSQL staging area, storage and reliability requirements are much higher.

8.6.1.2 Stage Database Setup

The stage database is created in Microsoft SQL Server Management Studio 2014. The name of the database should give an indication of the purpose. In many enterprise settings, there are naming standards in place that need to be considered as well. Figure 8.7 shows the database creation.

In order to ensure the scalability of the later solution, it was decided to create four filegroups. When starting small, there is no need to have four or more physical disk arrays to put these filegroups on, but these filegroups help to distribute the data to multiple disks later on. Figure 8.7 shows that Full-Text Indexing is used on the server. You should consider removing this feature from your data warehouse if it is not being used in queries. SQL Server uses system memory for creating the full-text index [49]. If it is turned on, as in this case, it has to be disabled on a per-table basis. Another option is to turn off the feature using the following SQL command:

```sql
IF (1 = FULLTEXTSERVICEPROPERTY('IsFullTextInstalled'))
begin
EXEC [StageArea].[dbo].[sp_fulltext_database] @action = 'disable'
end
GO
```

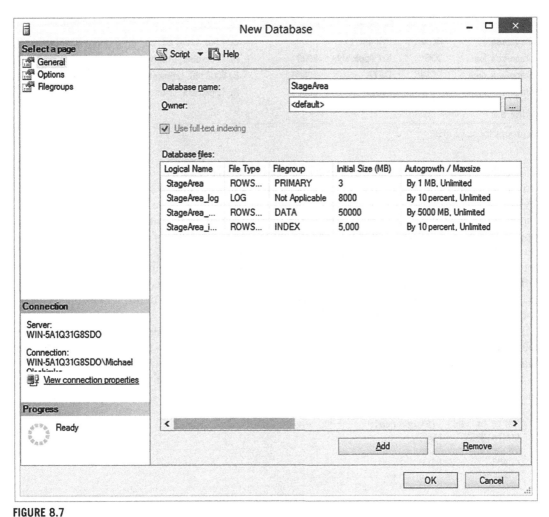

FIGURE 8.7

Create new stage area database.

In this example, the data was actually put onto different disks in order to increase performance from the onset. Figure 8.8 shows the filegroups and their locations in detail.

The **PRIMARY** filegroup will contain only system objects. It is expected to stay relatively small and is left on the direct attached storage disk (DASD) of the data warehouse. The log files are separated from the data. In addition, the indexes are also separated and put on a very fast disk, for example a solid-state drive (SSD). The initial sizes are chosen to meet the expected storage requirements of the stage area. This size depends on the size of the source data, multiplied by the maximum number of loads that should be potentially kept in the stage area. Although the stage area doesn't keep history (see Chapter 2), it might keep multiple batches of source data. This is due to the fact that, in some cases, the stage is not loaded into the enterprise data warehouse immediately, for example because of maintenance work or other reasons for downtime.

Logical Name	File Type	Filegroup	Initial Size (MB)	Autogrowth / Maxsize		Path
StageArea	ROWS...	PRIMARY	3	By 1 MB, Unlimited	...	C:\Program Fil
StageArea_log	LOG	Not Applicable	8000	By 10 percent, Unlimited	...	E:\
StageArea_data	ROWS...	DATA	50000	By 5000 MB, Unlimited	...	D:\
StageArea_index	ROWS...	INDEX	5000	By 10 percent, Unlimited	...	F:\

FIGURE 8.8

Filegroups for stage area.

The filegroups in Figure 8.8 might not fit larger installations, but are a good start and serve the purpose of this book. In reality, performance should increase when distributing data and logs to more physical drives [36]. Consult your database administrator for better options that meet the specific requirements of your project. Another issue is the selected auto growth values, as they might not be applicable to huge databases where 10% can become multiple gigabytes of data. Instead, it is recommended to limit the auto growth setting to 1 to 5 gigabytes per filegroup. Another important setting that drastically affects the performance of the stage area is the recovery model. The default option is **Full** recovery [37]. However, it is recommended practice to use **Simple** recovery in data warehousing because data can be reloaded manually instead of using the log files [36]. For this reason, the recovery model is changed, as Figure 8.9 shows.

It is also recommended to select the same database collation in all databases to avoid problems with character conversion between the collations. The best option is to leave it to the default collation of the data warehouse server and make sure that it has been properly selected during installation.

When selecting the OK button, the following statement is executed on SQL Server to create the database [38]:

```
CREATE DATABASE [StageArea]
 CONTAINMENT = NONE
 ON  PRIMARY
( NAME = N'StageArea',
  FILENAME = N'C:\Program Files\Microsoft SQL
Server\MSSQL12.MSSQLSERVER\MSSQL\DATA\StageArea.mdf' ,
  SIZE = 3072KB , MAXSIZE = UNLIMITED, FILEGROWTH = 1024KB ),
 FILEGROUP [DATA]
( NAME = N'StageArea_data',
  FILENAME = N'D:\StageArea_data.ndf' ,
  SIZE = 51200000KB , MAXSIZE = UNLIMITED, FILEGROWTH = 5120000KB ),
 FILEGROUP [INDEX]
( NAME = N'StageArea_index',
  FILENAME = N'F:\StageArea_index.ndf' ,
  SIZE = 5120000KB , MAXSIZE = UNLIMITED, FILEGROWTH = 10%)
 LOG ON
( NAME = N'StageArea_log',
  FILENAME = N'E:\StageArea_log.ldf' ,
  SIZE = 8192000KB , MAXSIZE = 2048GB , FILEGROWTH = 10%)
GO
```

Chapter 11, Data Extraction, shows how to extract data from source systems and load it into the staging area.

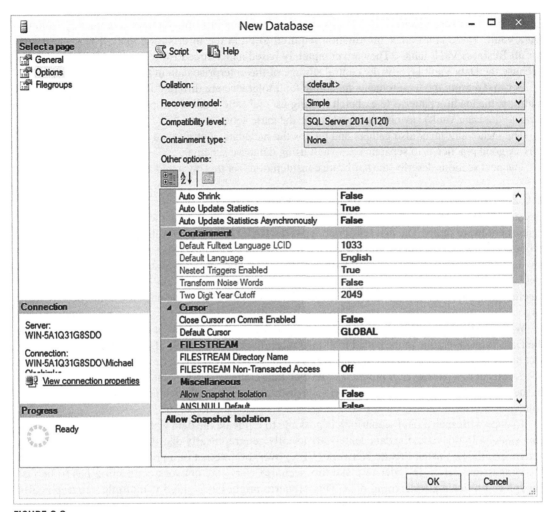

FIGURE 8.9

Setting the recovery model.

8.6.2 SETTING UP THE DATA VAULT

The purpose of the Data Vault layer is to permanently store the enterprise data with all its history. This is different from the stage area where the data was stored only temporarily. As we have outlined in Chapter 2, the goal of the Data Vault layer (the data warehouse layer) is to keep a nonvolatile copy of every change of data in multiple source systems, integrated using the business key. This layer is, unlike all other layers in the data warehouse, not easily recoverable from other data sources, if possible at all. For example, it is possible to recover the data in the stage area from the operational source systems, if the recovery is started promptly (to make sure that the data in the operational system has not yet changed very much). It is also possible to rebuild the information marts completely from the Data Vault. There is no other information required to build the information mart. The same is true for all Business Vault tables. They are completely based and sourced from Data Vault tables. That is because the Data Vault layer is the central storage of the enterprise data in the data warehouse.

For that reason, the requirements regarding fault tolerance are different for the Data Vault layer. In addition, the loading patterns (e.g., batch loading vs. real-time loading or operational-style access patterns to the Data Vault) have implications to the database setup.

The Data Vault layer also gathers and retains the metadata, metrics data and information about errors. A good practice is to separate each vault using database schemas.

The next sections describe the hardware considerations for this layer and how to set up the database.

8.6.2.1 Hardware Considerations for Data Vault Layer

Because the Data Vault is the permanent storage for the enterprise data, the data needs to be secured against hardware faults. The first set of options is the RAID setup used for the physical drive. The best economical options should be either RAID-1 for disk mirroring or RAID-5 for adding parity bits to the data written to disk. The second option is often favored because it presents a compromise between available disk space and fault tolerance. Keep in mind that the Data Vault layer stores the history of all enterprise data that is in the data warehouse. Therefore, the size of the database could become very large.

While RAID-1 and RAID-5 are not the fastest available RAID options, it is worth favoring them for the Data Vault layer, due to the added fault tolerance of the physical disk. If one disk fails, it might affect the availability of the data warehouse (because the RAID array might be rebuilt), but the data is not necessarily at risk. However, if more than one disk fails at the same time, this is not the case any longer. In such a case, for example during a large-scale disaster that affects the whole server infrastructure, the collected enterprise data is still at risk.

To cope with such a fatal scenario, it is possible to replicate the data warehouse between multiple data centers. In this case, the data centers are usually geographically distributed and connected via a network (either a Virtual Private Network (VPN) over the Internet or a private network using satellite connections, etc.). In order to make this scenario work, the network connection has to be fast enough to replicate all incoming data. This scenario might be required if multiple geographically distributed enterprise data warehouses (EDWs) should be made available around the world and a central EDW is not sufficient. Note, however, that the requirements for replicated data warehouses are high.

8.6.2.2 Backing Up the Data Vault

In order to achieve the highest data reliability, database backups should be used for all layers. However, the Data Vault layer is the one that has highest priority among all layers, again, because the stage area holds only temporary data and the information marts can be rebuilt from the Data Vault. Due to the central function, being the single point in the data warehouse that holds the data including all history requires that this layer be fully backed up.

Often, the Data Vault is loaded in daily batches overnight. In this case, the backup should be scheduled just after the Data Vault has been loaded, to make sure that the backup contains the last version of data as soon as possible. Also, make sure to test the database backup, by actually restoring it at frequent intervals.

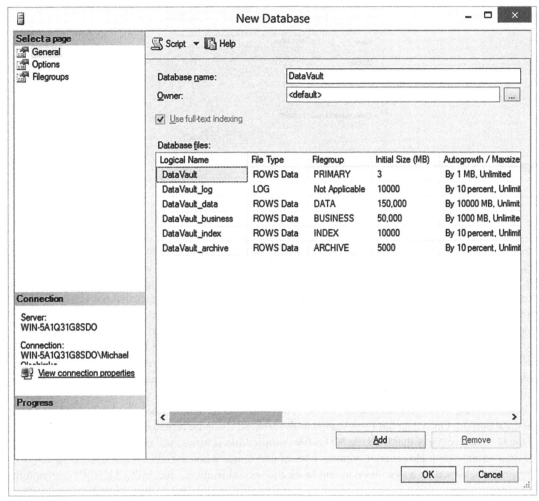

FIGURE 8.10

Create new Data Vault database.

8.6.2.3 Data Vault Database Setup

The Data Vault database is again created in Microsoft SQL Server Management Studio 2014. For the same reasons that we used to come up with the name of the stage database, we use the name *DataVault* for the database (Figure 8.10).

Another option for the database name would be *EnterpriseDataWarehouse* or any other desired name (the database names in this chapter are examples only). Figure 8.10 shows that a set of database files has been created, similar to the stage area. However, the initial sizes are larger to adjust to the fact that the Data Vault stores the history of all changes to the enterprise data. In your actual project, these

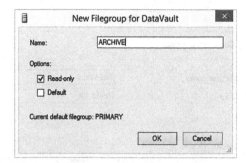

FIGURE 8.11

Creating the archive filegroup for the Data Vault layer.

sizes might be even larger. There are two additional filegroups, compared to the stage area setup from the last section. The first file is *DataVault_business* which will be stored within the filegroup *BUSI-NESS*. This filegroup will be used for storing Business Vault tables and might be on another physical drive with more tolerance to potential hardware faults. This is due to the fact that the Business Vault can be fully recreated from the DataVault, similar to an information mart. For that reason, another RAID level, such as RAID 0, could be used to take advantage of higher performance.

The second filegroup, *DataVault_archive*, can be used to keep historical Data Vault entities that are being closed and not loaded with new data anymore. This file will be stored on a compressed NTFS volume to save storage or use built-in compression from the database management backend. The underlying filegroup has been selected as read-only [39] (Figure 8.11).

However, the NTFS volume should not be compressed yet. It needs to be turned off in order to create the filegroup. Once data has been loaded to the archive, it can be turned on. Adding tables and data to the filegroup requires that both the NTFS file compression is turned off and the filegroup is enabled for read-write access. However, it requires a lot of disk space when the file compression is turned off. The first is achieved on a system operating level, the second using the following ALTER command in SQL [40]:

```
ALTER DATABASE DataVault MODIFY FILEGROUP ARCHIVE READWRITE
```

Another optional filegroup for the Data Vault layer is an in-memory filegroup to house Data Vault entities that are loaded in real time. However, real time is not covered in this book.

The recovery model of the Data Vault database should be set to **Bulk-logged** because ETL batch loading might not be used for all Data Vault entities. Real-time scenarios present the biggest challenge for a **Simple** recovery model, but any operational system writing back data into the Data Vault requires log backups maintained by SQL Server [37]. Therefore, a simple recovery model is not sufficient for data warehouses if data is coming in more ways than simple batches. We were able to turn it off for stage loading, because it was possible to rerun the ETL for loading the operational data from the source systems. The same is true for the Data Vault layer as long as data is loaded in batches, followed by a backup. However, as soon as real-time or operational systems write directly into the

Data Vault, this is not possible anymore, at least without restarting the processes in the operational systems.

There is no need for the **Full** recovery model if the backup strategy, as outlined in the previous section, is used. Bulk operations from ETL are not required to log, because the database backup is started just after ETL for loading the Data Vault layer has been finished. Therefore, there *should* be no bulk operations after over the day. Real-time and operational systems should only write using singular statements. For that reason, the Bulk-logged recovery model is turned on during database creation (Figure 8.12).

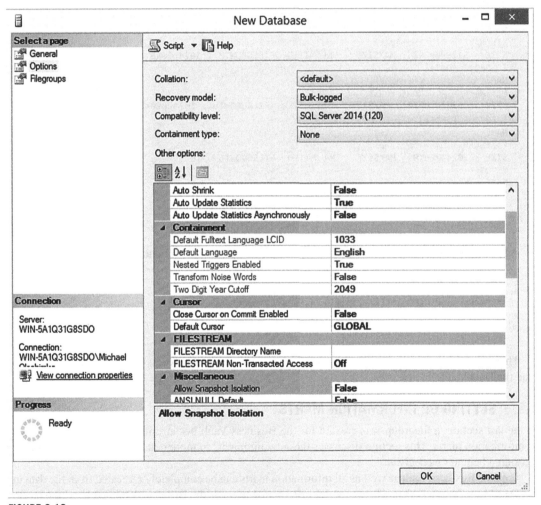

FIGURE 8.12

Options of the Data Vault database.

The following command is generated and executed against the database server when selecting the OK button:

```
CREATE DATABASE [DataVault]
 CONTAINMENT = NONE
 ON  PRIMARY
( NAME = N'DataVault',
  FILENAME = N'C:\Program Files\Microsoft SQL
Server\MSSQL12.MSSQLSERVER\MSSQL\DATA\DataVault.mdf' ,
  SIZE = 3072KB , MAXSIZE = UNLIMITED, FILEGROWTH = 1024KB ),
 FILEGROUP [ARCHIVE]
( NAME = N'DataVault_archive',
  FILENAME = N'G:\DataVault_archive.ndf' ,
  SIZE = 5120000KB , MAXSIZE = UNLIMITED, FILEGROWTH = 10%),
 FILEGROUP [BUSINESS]
( NAME = N'DataVault_business',
  FILENAME = N'D:\DataVault_business.ndf' ,
  SIZE = 51200000KB , MAXSIZE = UNLIMITED, FILEGROWTH = 1024000KB ),
 FILEGROUP [DATA]
( NAME = N'DataVault_data',
  FILENAME = N'D:\DataVault_data.ndf' ,
  SIZE = 153600000KB , MAXSIZE = UNLIMITED, FILEGROWTH = 10240000KB ),
 FILEGROUP [INDEX]
( NAME = N'DataVault_index',
  FILENAME = N'F:\DataVault_index.ndf' ,
  SIZE = 10240000KB , MAXSIZE = UNLIMITED, FILEGROWTH = 10%)
 LOG ON
( NAME = N'DataVault_log',
  FILENAME = N'E:\DataVault_log.ldf' ,
  SIZE = 10240000KB , MAXSIZE = 2048GB , FILEGROWTH = 10%)
GO
```

Again, consider turning off full-text search using the following command:

```
IF (1 = FULLTEXTSERVICEPROPERTY('IsFullTextInstalled'))
begin
EXEC [DataVault].[dbo].[sp_fulltext_database] @action = 'disable'
end
GO
```

That way, there is no need to deal with full-text search on a table level. Chapter 12 shows how to load the Data Vault.

8.6.3 SETTING UP INFORMATION MARTS

In the last section, a filegroup was created for the Business Vault because it has similar requirements to information marts. This section discusses these requirements in more detail to better understand the reasoning behind this decision.

Both the Business Vault as well as all information marts can be completely recreated from the data in the Data Vault. The only dependency for the information marts is the Business Vault itself, which has to be created before the information marts are created. That is due to the fact that the Business Vault provides consolidated, precomputed data, and implements business rules that are used by many information marts. But as a matter of fact, all data is housed by the Data Vault in its raw format. Information marts use this data in two ways: virtualized, which means that no data is actually copied to the information mart database; or materialized, which means that data is actually copied to the information mart for performance reasons. Both the Business Vault and information marts have much more tolerance to hardware faults than the Raw Data Vault. That doesn't mean that we welcome hardware faults in the information marts, as it would be a lot of work to replace the disks and rebuild the databases used by the information marts. However, our statement is that it is *possible* to recreate them without any data loss.

But be aware that these statements are only valid as long as the write-back feature of SQL Server Analysis Services isn't used. Once this SQL feature is turned on, it needs to store the data that is written back into the cube in relational tables somewhere. If you select the information mart as the target for the write-back data, it should be considered as an operational system and meet the requirements for such systems. There are other, more viable destinations for the write-back data, but this is out of the scope of this book.

8.6.3.1 Hardware Considerations for Information Marts

For that reason, it is possible to use disk setups with less fault tolerance than RAID 1 or RAID 5. The best option is RAID level 0 due to performance. As a matter of fact, the information marts have fewer requirements on fault tolerance than the stage area.

In some cases, business users directly use information marts, unlike the usage pattern when SQL Server Analysis Services is involved and loads the data from the information marts into a multidimensional database. Examples of a direct use of information marts includes relational or ad-hoc reporting, relational OLAP, or data mining. These use cases have in common that performance becomes key to ensure an acceptable user experience. Therefore, information marts should be optimized for reading. This is done using indexing, but also by using fast disk setups that house the database files. RAID 0 combines the read performance of multiple disks and represents the fastest RAID option available. Another option might be the use of SSDs for this layer.

However, if SQL Server views are used to implement virtual marts, no data is actually copied to the information mart. Instead, the SELECT query is performed against the raw data in the Data Vault. Therefore, virtualized marts will gain no performance benefit from SSDs or another RAID level beyond that used by the Data Vault layer.

8.6.3.2 Information Mart Database Setup

There are some considerations that need to be made before setting up the database or the databases for the information marts. Having one database for all information marts is easy to set up and maintain, but reduces the flexibility of the usage. For example, when each information mart uses its own database, the individual information marts are isolated from each other. Each business user sees only the schemas and tables that it is supposed to see. Security is maintained much more easily. It is also possible to move a large information mart to another database server in order to distribute the workload among multiple servers. Separating information marts in such a manner becomes impossible if they are all deployed into the same database.

Therefore, our recommendation is to use individual databases for information marts. In this book, we're going to use only one information mart, called *FlightInformationMart*, which is used by the flight operations department. The setup is shown in Figure 8.13.

Three filegroups have been set up for this information mart, in addition to the *PRIMARY* filegroup which is only used for system tables. *FlightInformationMart_log*, which stores the database log and is

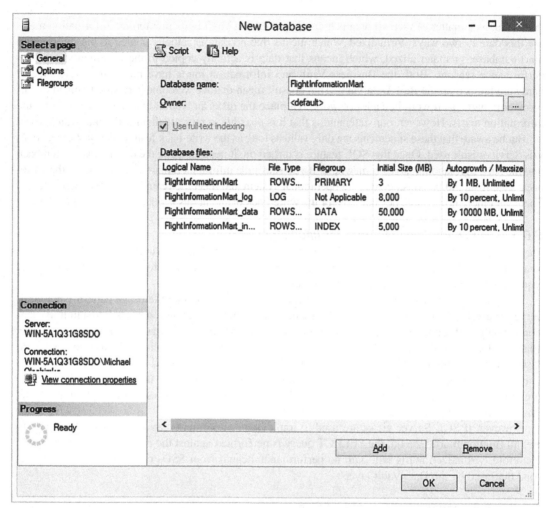

FIGURE 8.13

Create new database for the flight information mart.

separated from the rest of the database; *FlightInformationMart_data*, which stores the data pages; and *FlightInformationMart_index*, which stores the indexes of this information mart. Figure 8.14 shows the created filegroups in more detail.

The initial sizes accommodate the expected volume for initial load and subsequent loads over the next couple of months. Again, these sizes have been set relatively arbitrarily for this book and have to be adjusted for the expected volume in the actual project.

The figure also shows that all database files are distributed to various drives which represent the individual RAID arrays, as described in the opening of section 8.6.

Similar to the previous databases, the recovery model has been adjusted to the expected load behavior of the database (Figure 8.15).

Logical Name	File Type	Filegroup	Initial Size (MB)	Autogrowth / Maxsize		Path
FlightInformationMart	ROWS Data	PRIMARY	3	By 1 MB, Unlimited	...	C:\Program Files\Microsoft SQL Server\MSSQL\
FlightInformationMart_log	LOG	Not Applicable	8000	By 10 percent, Unlimited	...	E:\
FlightInformationMart_data	ROWS Data	DATA	50000	By 10000 MB, Unlimited	...	D:\
FlightInformationMart_in...	ROWS Data	INDEX	5000	By 10 percent, Unlimited	...	F:\

FIGURE 8.14

Filegroups for the flight information mart.

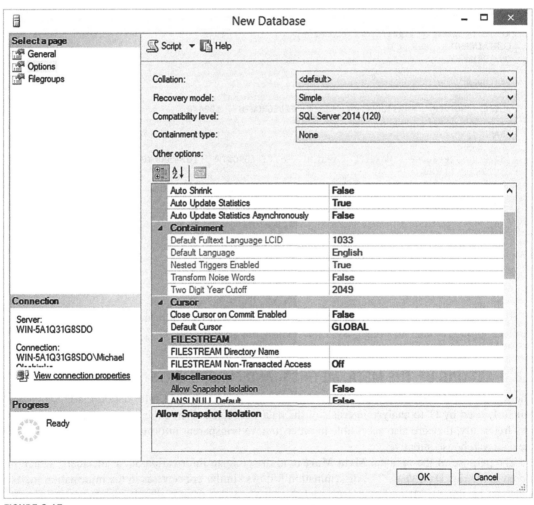

FIGURE 8.15

Options of the information mart database.

We have already discussed that there are two methods to populate the data into the information mart: either virtually, which means no data is loaded into the information mart at all, or using batched ETL processes that load the data in batches. Both methods can be restarted at any time, because all underlying data is stored in and protected by the Data Vault layer. Therefore, we go with the fastest recovery model possible, which is the **simple** option. It provides no safety if data is added or updated in the information mart, but that is not the goal of the information mart. It should be used by the business user for read-only access.

Again, if you plan to use the write-back capabilities of SQL Server Analysis Services, you need to adjust this setting to either **bulk-logged** or **full** recovery model.

Once the OK button is selected, the following SQL statement creates the database on the server backend:

```
CREATE DATABASE [FlightInformationMart]
 CONTAINMENT = NONE
 ON  PRIMARY
( NAME = N'FlightInformationMart',
  FILENAME = N'C:\Program Files\Microsoft SQL
Server\MSSQL12.MSSQLSERVER\MSSQL\DATA\FlightInformationMart.mdf' ,
  SIZE = 3072KB , MAXSIZE = UNLIMITED, FILEGROWTH = 1024KB ),
 FILEGROUP [DATA]
( NAME = N'FlightInformationMart_data',
  FILENAME = N'D:\FlightInformationMart_data.ndf' ,
  SIZE = 51200000KB , MAXSIZE = UNLIMITED, FILEGROWTH = 10240000KB ),
 FILEGROUP [INDEX]
( NAME = N'FlightInformationMart_index',
  FILENAME = N'F:\FlightInformationMart_index.ndf' ,
  SIZE = 5120000KB , MAXSIZE = UNLIMITED, FILEGROWTH = 10%)
 LOG ON
( NAME = N'FlightInformationMart_log',
  FILENAME = N'E:\FlightInformationMart_log.ldf' ,
  SIZE = 8192000KB , MAXSIZE = 2048GB , FILEGROWTH = 10%)
GO
```

Remember to turn off full-text search if you don't need it in your information marts by following a similar approach to the one already described in previous sections.

8.6.4 SETTING UP THE META, METRICS, AND ERROR MARTS

The Meta Mart, Metrics Mart, and Error Mart are special instances of information marts which are primarily used by IT to analyze internals of the data warehouse. While the business uses these marts less frequently, they are also accessible in order to have transparent information about the success of the data warehouse initiative.

The purpose of the optional **Meta Mart** is to disseminate information about metadata, which is stored in the raw Data Vault. The dissemination follows similar concepts as in the information marts, which means that the Meta Mart is structured in such a way that front-end tools can query the information as effectively as possible. If the Meta Mart is queried using OLAP tools, a dimensional model is the best approach to model this mart.

The following information is presented to the end-user (typically administrators, power users, or team members from the data warehouse initiative) [4]:

- Metadata about data and information, from all layers
- Metadata about processes, primarily, but not limited to, the loading processes in ETL
- Metadata about performed backups
- Metadata about source systems and interfaces to other systems (e.g., information consumers)
- Definition of hard and soft business rules
- Definition of access control lists (ACLs) and other security measures
- Definition of retention times for privacy related data

This list is not complete. The Meta Mart makes all information accessible that is not directly used by the business user, but describes what kind of data and information is available, where it comes from, how it is processed, who is using it for what purpose, etc. In more sophisticated environments, the Meta Mart might be replaced by a Meta Data Warehouse solution.

The **Metrics Mart** presents the information captured by the Metrics Vault to the end-user. This was discussed in more detail in Chapter 2 and includes information about run history, process metrics, and technical metrics.

Finally, the **Error Mart** stores and presents statistics and detailed information about errors in the loading processes and other functions of the data warehouse.

8.6.4.1 Hardware Considerations for Meta, Metrics, and Error Marts

While the Metrics Mart is sourced from the Metrics Vault, the other two marts are a single point of data. Therefore, there are different reliability requirements for each database that holds the marts:

- **Metrics Mart:** this mart derives its reliability requirements from the Information Mart discussion in section 8.6.3.1. Because it can be rebuilt and reloaded very easily, it can be stored on less reliable RAID configurations, such as RAID-0.
- **Meta Mart:** This optional mart contains all metadata of the data warehouse. Because it is the central place of storage, it has higher reliability requirements than other information marts. Instead, the requirements are comparable to the raw Data Vault layer, where a RAID-5 or RAID-1 level is typically used.
- **Error Mart:** This optional mart is comparable to the Meta Mart, regarding the reliability requirements. It is the central location of all error information in the data warehouse. Therefore, it should be kept on RAID-5 or RAID-1.

It is also important to include the Meta Mart and the Error Mart in the backups, as it is not possible to recreate them from the Data Vault or any other layer. The backup for the Metrics Mart is optional, because it can be recreated from the Metrics Vault.

8.6.4.2 Meta, Metrics, and Error Marts Database Setup

Due to space limitations, this book will not cover the creation of these technical marts. However, there are two options for them. First, create information mart to hold all three marts in separate schemas. The other option is to follow the same approach as with all other information marts, that is to create individual databases in the data warehouse in order to separate them physically. That way, it is possible to distribute the marts to separate hardware (either on the same server or among multiple servers) much easier. If you put all marts into the same database, you should make sure to meet the highest reliability requirements of all included marts.

REFERENCES

[1] http://technet.microsoft.com/en-us/library/hh393556(v(sql.110).aspx.

[2] Soumendra Mohanty, Madhu Jagadeesh, Harsha Srivatsa: Big Data Imperatives, p. 83, 83ff, 92f.

[3] Christian Bolton, et al. "Professional SQL Server 2012 – Internals and Troubleshooting", pp. 31f, 81, 84ff, 104ff.

[4] http://sqlmag.com/database-administration/data-warehouse-workloads-and-use-cases.

[5] http://www.allthingsdistributed.com/2007/12/eventually_consistent.html.

[6] http://wiki.apache.org/cassandra/ArchitectureOverview.

[7] http://blog.mongodb.org/post/498145601/on-distributed-consistency-part-2-some.

[8] Lars George: "HBase: The Definitive Guide," p. 9.

[9] http://dl.acm.org/citation.cfm?id(564585.564601.

[10] http://blog.mongodb.org/post/475279604/on-distributed-consistency-part-1.

[11] Doug Vucevic: "Testing Data Warehouse Applications", p. 99.

[12] Scott W. Ambler, Mark Lines: "Disciplined Agile Delivery", p. 425.

[13] Vincent Rainardi: "Building a Data Warehouse", p. 486, 487.

[14] Ken Collier: "Agile Analytics" p. 169f.

[15] http://technet.microsoft.com/en-us/library/jj127250.aspx.

[16] Scott Klein, Herve Roggero: "Pro SQL Database for Windows Azure", pp. 3, 4.

[17] http://www.developer.com/services/getting-started-with-azure-hdinsight.html.

[18] http://msdn.microsoft.com/en-us/magazine/dn385705.aspx.

[19] Kimball: The Data Warehouse Lifecycle Toolkit, p. 157f.

[20] http://blogs.technet.com/b/dataplatforminsider/archive/2014/07/30/transitioning-from-smp-to-mpp-the-why-and-the-how.aspx.

[21] http://technet.microsoft.com/en-us/library/ms345392(v(sql.105).aspx.

[22] http://sqlmag.com/sql-server-2008/getting-started-parallel-data-warehouse.

[23] Ralph Kimball: "The Data Warehouse Lifecycle Toolkit, 2nd Edition", p. 164.

[24] Adam Jorgensen et al. "Professional Microsoft SQL Server 2012 Administration", p. 259f.

[25] Peter M. Chen, et al. "RAID: High-Performance, Reliable Secondary Storage".

[26] Adam Jorgensen et al. "Professional Microsoft SQL Server 2012 Administration", pp. 260, 260f, 262f, 252, 277, 279f, 290ff.

[27] http://www.zdnet.com/blog/storage/why-raid-6-stops-working-in-2019/805.

[28] http://www.adaptec.com/en-us/_common/compatibility/_education/raid_level_compar_wp.htm.

[29] http://technet.microsoft.com/en-us/library/ms190433(v(sql.105).aspx.

[30] HP: "Understanding endurance and performance characteristics of HP solid state drives," http://h20565.www2.hp.com/hpsc/doc/public/display?docId(emr_na-c03312456.

[31] http://sqlmag.com/storage/sql-server-storage-best-practices.

[32] http://msdn.microsoft.com/en-us/library/ms190768.aspx.

[33] http://technet.microsoft.com/en-us/library/ms175527(v(sql.105).aspx.

[34] http://msdn.microsoft.com/en-us/library/ms190787.aspx.

[35] http://technet.microsoft.com/en-us/library/aa224727(v(sql.80).aspx.

[36] Rainardi: "Building a Data Warehouse. With Examples in SQL Server", pp. 122, 125, 126.

[37] http://msdn.microsoft.com/en-us/library/ms189275.aspx.

[38] CreateStageArea.sql.

[39] http://technet.microsoft.com/en-us/library/ms190257(v(sql.105).aspx.

[40] http://msdn.microsoft.com/en-us/library/bb522469.aspx.

[41] http://www.inmoncif.com/registration/whitepapers/ttmeta-1.pdf.

MASTER DATA MANAGEMENT

Master Data Management (MDM) enables organizations to create and use a "single version of the truth" [1]. This is especially helpful when using conformed dimensions, as discussed in Chapter 7, Dimensional Modeling, which require a defined set of attribute values. In some organizations, the source for such conformed dimensions comes from a leading source system, but in many other cases, the data comes from multiple systems. It is not only required to combine the data from those multiple systems. Often, the data contradicts and overlaps. Therefore, the data has to be conformed in some way [2].

Conformity is not required by dimensional models. They represent only one modeling method that allows data to be aligned and produced as information for business. In some cases, the master data is delivered in a cube, while in other cases it may be delivered in flat and wide denormalized table structures (otherwise known as first normal form). The notion of conformity is truly what Master Data cares about.

This chapter discusses how to use master data and MDM as an enabler for business users to take control of data warehousing, getting them closer to true managed self-service BI (a concept discussed in Chapter 2). It also shows how to set up a database in Microsoft Master Data Services (MDS), an MDM solution included in Microsoft SQL Server 2014. Finally, it will show how to integrate master data from MDS with the Data Vault. Because MDS as a feature is often not very well known to users of Microsoft SQL Server, we have dedicated a lot of space to MDS in this book.

9.1 DEFINITIONS

The next sections provide introductory definitions of the core components of MDM to better distinguish between the terms used throughout this chapter and the rest of the book.

9.1.1 MASTER DATA

The definition of master data is the business's answer to the chaos of reference data in source systems. Master data describes the business entities, which are part of the business processes implemented in operational systems of the organization. While master data, at first glance, look very similar to data warehouse dimensions, they should be much closer to operational systems. However, master data become a source for data warehouse dimensions and can provide a great source of such data if the master data have been implemented well [2].

Master data is commonly distinguished by operational master data and analytical master data.

Please refer the companion site for more details — http://booksite.elsevier.com/9780128025109

9.1.2 DATA MANAGEMENT

Data management includes the development and execution of architectures, practices, procedures and policies which are required to effectively manage an enterprise information life cycle [3]. Its purpose is to plan, control and deliver the data and information assets required by the organization. Data management is a shared responsibility between both IT and business: data management professionals within the IT organization and business data stewards within the business organization have a shared interest to produce data and consume information [4].

Data management involves people, processes, and technology. Included in data management are ideas around governance, process control and management, data quality, total quality management, and the human act of identifying and blessing the appropriate records as *the* corporate standard. Master data mixed with good data management principles really are about gap analysis: understanding the gaps between the perception of how the business is run, what the raw data / source system processes are collecting, and how well that data set meets the *conformed* or consolidated view at the enterprise level.

9.1.3 MASTER DATA MANAGEMENT

Master data plays an important role in business organizations, and so does data management. Both components represent a separate and independent set of definitions, processes and activities. When put together, they merge into master data management.

Figure 9.1 shows that master data plays a vital role in master data management, so does data management. However, in order to achieve true master data management, people and processes are also required; they bind both components together and enable TQM and gap analysis activities.

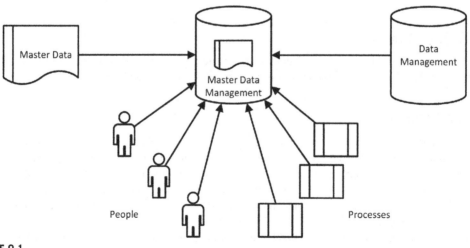

FIGURE 9.1

Master data management.

MDM is the creation of a single, well-defined version of all the data entities in the enterprise, the so-called "golden records" – in other words, a single copy of a record representing a single business concept like customer, or product, or order, or sale and so on.

9.2 **MASTER DATA MANAGEMENT GOALS**

The final step in true MDM is the ability to reconcile the *source systems* and close the data gap, or the process gap, by applying the principles of Six Sigma and Total Quality Management (TQM). This means that once the golden copy of the data has been selected and identified, it needs to be fed back to all the source systems – overwriting any of the data which is out of balance. This notion in TQM is called *data harmonization*. The harmonization of disparate data especially improves the data interoperability but has several other advantages [5]:

- **Improve the quality of the data:** when source systems should be integrated that implement different sets of master data, mapping or other business rules are required to enable the integration of these systems. As a general guideline, adding new mapping or business rules requires testing them, because they add new functionality to the system. They also affect the data that is generated as a result from these rules.
- **Facilitate receiving, processing and checking of information:** process gaps often prevent the information exchange between business processes. If source systems use the same set of master data, they understand each other and integration of business processes becomes much easier.
- **Facilitate exchange of data:** the integration of source systems that use the same set of master data can easily be automated as no human input to resolve master data conflicts or manual deduplication is required.
- **Reduce information requirements:** in order to produce useful information from the source data, fewer business rules are required to eliminate redundancies or duplications.

Data harmonization is only the first step. The next step is to figure out what processes are currently producing "mismatched" or unbalanced data sets. The focus, then, is in correcting (Six Sigma error reduction) the improperly applied source system process in order to stop the flow of *bad data* at the start of the stream. When MDM is done right, the end-result is an enterprise information system holding the "single version of the truth" or the "golden copy."

The Data Vault 2.0 methodology decrees that MDM become a part of the standard operating procedures for the enterprise business intelligence teams. Good governance, and data control, along with total quality management procedures are baked into the application of Software Engineering Institute/ Capability Maturity Model Integration (SEI/CMMI) principles. These principles are applied at the implementation level to achieve the highest level of MDM that a business is willing or capable of providing.

It is difficult to determine the correct set of attributes from the data in such an environment on the fly. For that reason, the business has to make a decision about the values in the conformed dimension. This problem is not limited to conformed dimensions, though. It applies to most dimension entries, regardless whether they are conformed or not.

MDM helps in this regard to create and maintain reference data that can be used in many ways in a data warehouse: to define dimension entries, as already stated; to conform data, for example customer records from multiple systems; or to set up parameters for the calculation of business rules. The data is very similar to the reference data discussed in Chapter 6, Advanced Data Vault 2.0 Modeling. However, it is not only external data that should be managed in MDM. Both internal and external business entities should be centrally managed within an MDM initiative. Such business entities participate in business transactions and include [2]:

- **People**, such as customers, passengers and employees
- **Locations**, such as airports, countries, states and cities
- **Physical entities**, such as airplanes, seats, products, and other assets
- **Logical entities**, such as brands, organizational units, functional departments, and project roles.

You will recognize that this list does not include any transactional data, such as flights, sales, or maintenance actions. Master data is the data that provides context information to transactions, usually implemented in business processes [6].

9.3 DRIVERS FOR MANAGING MASTER DATA

Organizations who carefully manage master data benefit from it in several ways [6]:

- **Consistent master data:** MDM provides a consistent set of business entities and their attributes, even if they are used across different operational systems. The decision how to handle contradicting attribute values or otherwise conflicting data has been made by the business as part of the master data management process. Another typical problem exists if the same semantic attribute value is expressed differently across systems, for example a Boolean attribute indicating the gender of a passenger: the ticketing system could use the values "Male" and "Female" while the flight system uses "M" and "F", respectively.
- **Complete master data:** Some operational systems allow NULL or blank values for specific attributes that are missing in the particular operational system. Other systems could calculate a default value instead. The decision as to which value should be used by other systems that use the master data is again part of the master data management process.
- **Correct format of master data:** Many systems, especially mainframe systems, allow only uppercase attribute values. In many other cases, the data should use a proper case, such as title case, for example when using the first name in the salutation of a letter addressing the customer. Algorithms might help to change from upper case to proper casing; however, many nonwestern names are more complicated to handle. That is why business frequently wants to override the results from algorithms.
- **Master data attributes within range:** MDM allows the business to ensure the correctness of numerical attribute values. It can be assumed from downstream systems (applications that use the master data from MDM) that the master data has been verified and processed by data quality routines. An example for this is the horsepower of airplane engines. Usually this value is, except for some powerful engines, below 10,000 HP. Even the powerful engines don't have more than 20,000 HP. If there were an engine with more than 200,000 HP, something is wrong with the data, such as a typo. It is the job of MDM to identify such problems and correct them in the master data and operational sources (if available).
- **Complex data handling:** In some cases, attribute values are, when analyzed independently, within the correct range. However, if analyzed in conjunction with other attributes, the value

might be completely off. An example is the fact that turbo-jets produce thrust and are not measured in horsepower [7]. An MDM application supports such complex business rules to validate complex data.
- **Deduplicated master data:** Oftentimes, personal data contains many duplicates when the data is directly sourced from operational systems. The MDM application provides a set of deduplicated master data that can be used by subscribing applications without taking care of potential duplicates.

The required data cleansing should be performed before the data is loaded into the MDM application. There are tools that support the MDM team with this task, including Microsoft Excel. The MDM application usually validates the incoming data and logs all violations against the business rules.

In addition to these benefits, there are multiple drivers that are the reasons for a fast-growing adoption of MDM within organizations [8]:

- **Regulatory compliance:** today, companies are required to provide, use, and report relevant data about their financial performance in an accurate and verifiable form. This also includes information about significant events that could impact company valuations and shareholder value. The reason for this legislation and regulations, such as the Sarbanes-Oxley Act and Basel II and Basel III, is due to corporate scandals, such as Enron, and several class-action shareholder lawsuits.
- **Privacy and data protection:** federal and state law also forces organizations to protect enterprise data from unauthorized access, use, and editing. This is especially important when dealing with customer data, such as health care records, social security information and credit card data.
- **Safety and security:** the USA Patriot Act and other regulations regarding anti-money laundering to prevent the support and financing of terrorist attacks requires organization to manage their data on customers and financial transactions and maintain the integrity, security, accuracy, and timeliness of corporate operational and customer data.
- **Growing complexity and increased velocity:** MDM helps to improve customer service and customer experience management by providing a "single version of the truth."

These benefits have helped MDM to become a fast-growing discipline in organizations, regardless of data warehousing. And, in fact, most initiatives are focused on these benefits, ignoring additional ones in the analytical domain.

In cases where MDM is not available, the data warehouse can become another driver and the source for master data: data warehouse teams often start developing a new data warehouse without master data available. Over time, the master data management initiative matures from the data warehouse project. Figure 9.2 shows this evolution.

The **first maturity level** is characterized by no MDM system in place. Instead, master data is sourced from operational systems or developed and managed as part of the data warehouse. The master data is only used by the subscribing information marts of the data warehouse; no external applications are using it. Because the enterprise data warehouse is the single version of the facts in the organization, it serves as a central location of facts that are used more and more in other applications, especially when approaches such as managed self-service BI are used. In this approach, many applications consume raw data and preprocessed information from the data warehouse. These applications also need to use a conformed set of master data. In such cases, because there is no organization-wide MDM available, the data warehouse becomes the source for master data as well.

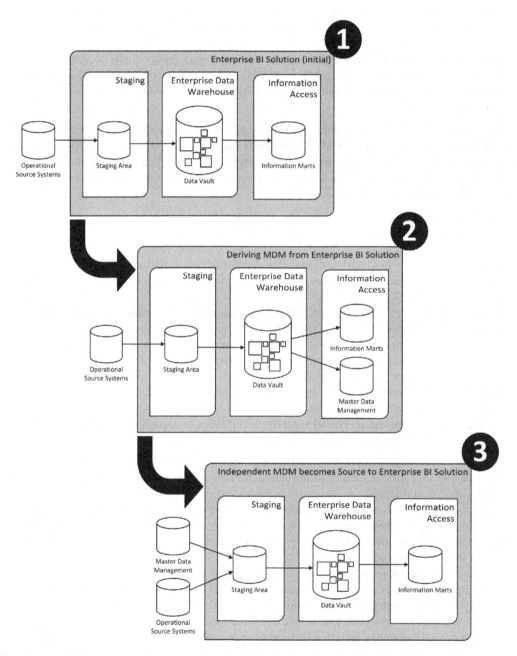

FIGURE 9.2

Master data matures during the data warehouse project.

The **second maturity level** shows this situation by publishing the master data from the data warehouse in an individual information mart, for example an information mart modeled in third normal form, to provide a standardized access to the master data in the data warehouse to other operational systems.

The **third maturity level** is characterized by the ability to modify the master data by the business. The information mart is no longer just a read-only view to the master data in the data warehouse, but becomes an MDM database; business users can directly or indirectly (by using operational systems) modify the master data and feed it back into master data subscribers, such as other operational systems or the data warehouse. The information mart from maturity level 2 can be used as a starting point to build this MDM database. Once business users can modify the master data, the database becomes another source system to the data warehouse.

9.4 OPERATIONAL VS. ANALYTICAL MASTER DATA MANAGEMENT

Master data can be used in two types of organizational systems. First, the data is used by operational systems as common reference data within the application. Then, the application uses the reference data from MDM as business objects within its business processes that are implemented in the operational system. It enriches the data by new information that has been collected during execution of these processes. It also uses business keys from MDM to manage its references to the business data when it stores the transactions within its own database.

However, this means that businesses must decide which departments or functional units are allowed to change the master data in MDM in order to avoid unwanted or unauthorized changes to the reference data used throughout the business [9]. The usage of master data in operational systems is shown in Figure 9.3.

The figure shows master data from an airport that is used by multiple operational systems. Each operational system uses a partial set of master data in the local scope of the application. Such an operational system is called a *master data subscriber*, because it subscribes to the master data, and the changes to its entities. Because operational systems share the master data from its central location, the data within the operational systems becomes integrated, often through a business key that was defined in the MDM application. In some cases, the operational system might update master data with new information. These changes occur within the business processes implemented in the operational system. No system, however, will write transactional information to the MDM application. Instead, the transactional data remains in the operational system only. In order to load it into the data warehouse, it has to be collected independently by ETL routines as part of the data warehouse loading process. We discuss this in more detail in Chapter 11, Data Extraction.

The data warehouse system is another subscriber of master data. Often, operational systems don't use all master data, or modify it locally. Therefore, the data warehouse is interested in the centrally stored version of master data and the master data that is used and enriched in local applications. For that reason, it loads master data from both locations: the central MDM application and all operational source systems. The master data is often used to source dimensional entries, while the transactional data is used to source fact tables. However, there is some master data that is only created and maintained for the data warehouse itself. This case is called analytical master data and includes some of the following master data types:

- **Business rule parameters:** Many business rules that are implemented in the data warehouse to transform raw data into useful information are based on parameters. For example, tax rates

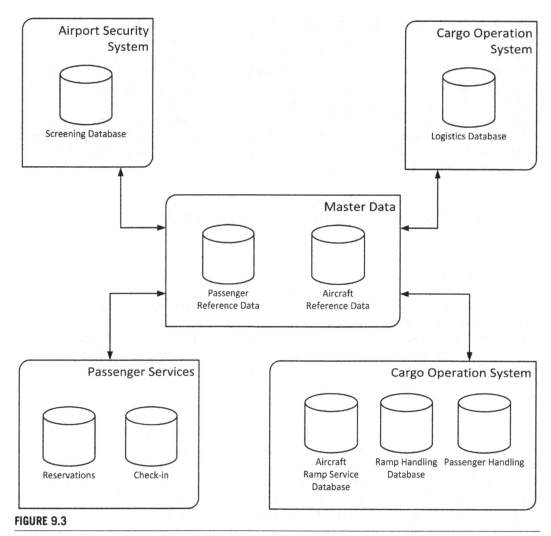

FIGURE 9.3

Use of master data by operational systems [9].

change over time and need to be adjusted frequently. Also, a flight delay is currently defined as a flight which arrives (or departs) the gate at least 15 minutes or more after the scheduled time [10]. Because this definition might change in the future, it is not a good practice to encode such parameter values in the ETL jobs or virtual views directly. Instead, the use of MDM allows business users to modify these definitions on their own, without IT involvement.

• **Defining groups and bins:** In some cases, it is sufficient to identify if a flight is delayed or not (again, if the flight is 15 minutes late). In other cases, a more detailed analysis is required. For that reason, the Bureau of Transportation Statistics (BTS) has defined departure and arrival delay groups that measure the delay in intervals of 15 minutes. Table 9.1 shows their defined delay

Table 9.1 BTS Delay Groups	
Code	**Description**
–2	Delay < -15 minutes
–1	Delay between -15 and -1 minutes
0	Delay between 0 and 14 minutes
1	Delay between 15 to 29 minutes
2	Delay between 30 to 44 minutes
3	Delay between 45 to 59 minutes
4	Delay between 60 to 74 minutes
5	Delay between 75 to 89 minutes
6	Delay between 90 to 104 minutes
7	Delay between 105 to 119 minutes
8	Delay between 120 to 134 minutes
9	Delay between 135 to 149 minutes
10	Delay between 150 to 164 minutes
11	Delay between 165 to 179 minutes
12	Delay ≥ 180 minutes

groups definition. In order to map the actual delay of a flight to this definition, the table needs to be stored in MDM and enriched with numerical limits (minimum and maximum number of minutes) that can be used in ETL to map the value to the definition. For example, if a flight is 65 minutes late, it would be between the 60 and 74 minutes limitation of group number 4 and therefore mapped to this delay group.

- **Codes and descriptions:** Often, source systems use codes that are easily understood by business users. Examples for such cases are IATA airport codes. However, the sheer number of those three-letter codes available makes it complicated or error-prone to handle reports using these codes. Therefore, such codes are often enriched with readable captions and other important attributes, such as a sort order.
- **Hierarchy definitions:** MDM can be used to define organization hierarchies, product definitions (bill of materials) and other frequently used hierarchies. Having them in the MDM application allows business uses to modify these definitions without IT involvement.
- **Date and other calendar information:** Date and other calendar information is another example of a hierarchy that can be defined using MDM. Using MDM allows the end user to modify the names and definitions of signing holidays or business seasons if needed. It is also possible to modify the beginning and ending dates of the financial calendar when required by organizational changes, e.g. a takeover.
- **Technical parameters:** The data warehouse is installed on top of one or multiple servers, as discussed in Chapter 8, Physical Database Design. Some parts of this environment can be

controlled by the business user and technical users, such as systems administrators, by using MDM. For example, it is possible to define external scripts that need to be called during loads, set the name of the environment ("Development," "Test," "Production") that is displayed on technical reports and dashboards, source system names such as FTP address or database names, and date and time formats or time zones to be used. It is also possible to configure users who should be informed if problems during loads occur, such as the business owner or data steward.

Because this information is used only for the data warehouse, it is not fed back into operational systems. However, in some cases, it might actually become used by operational systems, transforming the analytical master data into operational master data.

In addition to these analytical use cases, it is also common practice to enrich operational data with additional attributes that are only required by analytical systems. This could be a classification number or tag that is attached to passengers. Instead of adding the new field, which is only used within the analytical system, to the operational system, which would require substantial time and effort, it is added to a new entity in the MDM application. If new passengers are added to the operational system, they are added to the MDM database using a staging process, similar to those used in data warehousing. Business users can classify those new passengers or other business entities and the added data is used in the data warehouse downstream.

9.5 MASTER DATA MANAGEMENT AS AN ENABLER FOR MANAGED SELF-SERVICE BI

The availability of master data and proper master data management play an important role in the Data Vault 2.0 standard. We have already discussed in the previous section that analytical master data management can be used to store parameters for business rules. These parameters influence how business rules are executed when the ETL process or virtual SQL view process the raw data from the Raw Data Vault and load it into the information mart. This architecture has been described in Chapter 2. Chapters 13 and 14 will show how to implement such business rules.

Because the parameters are stored in the MDM application, authorized business users are able to change the parameter values and therefore influence the results of the business rules. An example for such parameters might be expected earnings ratios or which depreciation rules should be used when calculating the depreciation of organizational assets. In the latter case, the business user would select straight-line depreciation, declining balance method, annuity depreciation or another rule for specific assets of the business. Besides the ability to influence the outcomes of the business rules, there are more advantages of having these parameters in an MDM application:

- **Transparency:** MDM tracks which settings have been used by the business, at which times, who modified them at what time and who did the authorization of taking the change into production. Compare this to a relational table in the data warehouse, without any change tracking or versioning.
- **Compliance:** Regulation bodies require documentation as to how the raw data was transformed into the information that was presented to the business users, in many cases, in upper management. Change tracking of MDM applications ensures compliance to such regulations.
- **Security:** Not everyone in the organization is allowed to modify the business rule definition. MDM applications typically have built-in security controls that safeguard the master data.

- **Reusability:** Having the business rule parameters in the MDM application means that the business rule definition becomes more reusable: consider the reusing of the same business rule implementation for different information marts. Each information mart requires a slightly different execution of the business rule. Because MDM holds the parameter values of the business rule, it is possible to provide different sets of parameter values for each information mart.

Because the business user can, if authorized, fully control the parameter values, the business can implement changes on its own, in a self-service BI sense. However, it is not possible to completely change the business rules, because only parameters are available for modification. Therefore, it also follows the managed self-service BI approach as described in Chapter 2: IT has to set up the business rule parameters and implement the business rules either in ETL or in virtual SQL views in a managed approach. The business, on the other hand, can adjust these parameter values in the boundaries of these parameters, in a self-service approach.

The other aspect of managed self-service BI regarding master data management is by implementing a closed loop between the operational systems and the operational master data. If business users are able to modify the master data that is used by both the operational systems and the data warehouse, the data is first used by the operational system and influences the execution of implemented business processes, which, in turn, has influence on the transactional data that is stored in these systems. Second, it also influences the data warehouse, as both the master data from the MDM application and the transactional data from the operational system is sourced by the data warehouse. Therefore, the business users' modification affects both systems, and influences the results from the analytical application as well. Therefore, this loopback between operational systems, the MDM application, and the data warehouse is an integral part of any successful managed self-service BI approach.

In both described scenarios, master data management becomes an enabling technology for successful managed self-service BI solutions. If reference data is stored in internal database tables only, business users are often not able to modify it without IT support. To allow true managed self-service BI, business users have to take over control of such data, be able to modify it, write it back into the MDM database and apply it to the data warehouse itself, influencing the end results of the business rules that are presented to the end-user as usable information in reports, OLAP cubes and dashboards.

9.6 MASTER DATA MANAGEMENT AS AN ENABLER FOR TOTAL QUALITY MANAGEMENT

When users find errors in reports, they often approach the data warehouse team to fix the error in the output. However, not all errors originate from the loading processes or the business rules implemented in the data warehouse. In many cases, the error is already in the source data, due to wrong data stored in the operational systems.

In order to react to user requests to fix erroneous information in the report, the data warehouse team has two choices:

1. **Modify the loading processes and overwrite erroneous data by corrected values:** this option is actually not modifying the raw data, but implements a business rule that modifies the wrong data in a way that produces the desired outcome in the report.
2. **Modify the raw data in the operational systems directly:** this option modifies the source system data or fixes any errors in the source code of the source system.

Often, the data warehouse team has no control over the operational systems. Therefore, the first option is performed in many cases. However, the goal of total quality management is to fix the error at the source and prevent the use of wrong data in subscribing applications. This is why it should be fixed in the source system.

However, this approach requires that a gap analysis be performed as outlined in the introduction to this chapter. It is important for the enterprise to understand the differences between the perception of the business and the realities in source systems: the business expects certain master data (among other data) to exist in the source system and with the desired quality. On the other hand, IT has a different view on the source systems and sees the data actually available and in the actual quality. Often, there is a gap between the business perception and the IT reality. In order to close the gap, an analysis is required first to assess the differences between both sides (the gap).

Gap analysis frequently focuses on documentation only: product documentation and documented processes are used to identify and perform the gap analysis. In some cases, interviews are conducted in order to understand how people within the organization use the processes. However, traditional IT organizations often have their focus on documentation instead of people during gap analysis. In agile organizations, the focus of gap analysis should be on the latter: structured interviews should be conducted with individuals from the organization to identify gaps in the business processes [11]. Both approaches provide advantages and disadvantages (Table 9.2).

Having a focus on documentation or on agile interviewing doesn't exclude the other approach from the gap analysis. In practice, both approaches should be followed, but, depending on the target organization, not a lot of documentation is available. In that case, agile interviews help to provide input to the assessment. However, even if documentation is available, it doesn't mean that the documentation is up-to-date or correct. The goal of the gap analysis is to find the gaps between the business perception and IT realities. Therefore, both methods should be applied where possible, even if the focus is on one of the approaches.

The findings of the gap analysis are documented in an assessment report. The report identifies the opportunities for improvement, the team's recommendations, and associated benefits. Before the report is delivered to final consumers, it should be validated with the help of key stakeholders and subject matter experts from the business to ensure accuracy as well as promote stakeholder buy-in [12].

The assessment report with its findings and recommendations is used to direct effort to close the gaps between business perception and IT realities. By doing so, the organization is able to realize the associated benefit for each finding and create real business value.

Table 9.2 Gap Analysis Approaches [11]

Gap Analysis Approach	Advantage	Disadvantage	Comment
Focus on Traditional Documentation	Understand the gaps in documented processes (if followed)	Actual processes remain hidden	Difficult to change behavior for process improvement
Focus on Agile Interviews	Understand the actual followed by the people	Requires more effort than traditional approach. Requires more analysis	Helps to uncover the most valuable process improvements

A master data management system, such as MDS, gives business users control over the master data used in operational and analytical systems. However, in order to fully achieve this goal, the master data needs to be integrated into the operational systems, in addition to the analytical use case. This way, business users can correct any errors in the master data on their own instead of relying on IT when improving the data quality in the end-reports. In other words: gaps are closed without IT involvement.

Microsoft Master Data Services (MDS) is an MDM application that is included with Microsoft SQL Server and allows the features discussed in the previous sections. While it is a separate product, it is fully integrated with recent versions of Microsoft SQL Server and Microsoft Excel. The software provides the following MDM features to developers, administrators, and end-users [8]:

- **Model management:** MDS allows administrators to create data models that hold MDM entities.
- **Entity management:** End-users can add, update, and delete members of entities that have been defined within the MDM application.
- **Hierarchy management:** MDS supports the creation of hierarchies between entity members.
- **Version management:** It is possible to copy a complete set of entity data and associated metadata to create different versions, for different applications and use cases, of the same data.
- **Business rules and workflow:** Business rules enforce data quality and help to trigger events within a workflow engine.
- **Security:** MDS prevents unauthorized access to users who have no permission to the master data. This can be done on a model basis, or on an entity basis.

The next section covers the object model of MDS and explains each of the concepts used in the data structure and how the data used in this book is organized.

9.6.1 MDS OBJECT MODEL

MDS organizes its master data within models and around entities, members and attributes. The following sections describe the MDS object model in detail and document the master data that was collected and assembled for the purpose of this book. The models can be found on the companion Web site for this book.

9.6.1.1 Models

MDS organizes master data within a Model that represents a subject area of master data. It is comparable to a database on Microsoft SQL Server by closely collecting the master data that belongs to the subject area of the model and keeping it together. The companion Web site of this book provides three MDS models, which are described in more detail in this section.

The *FAA* **model** provides master data for aircraft registration, including detailed reference data to describe the aircraft, the registrant, and the dealer where the aircraft was bought. Table 9.3 provides a detailed list of the master data included in this model.

There are no entities that can be used to describe flights, such as airlines or airports. Such master data is provided by the *BTS* **model** and includes the entities shown in Table 9.4.

You might have noticed that one set of master data, called *Record Owner*, is used in both models. This entity is referenced by most entities and indicates the organizational department or function that owns the master data record. By using such references, the master data within these models is stored in a normalized form. That means the master data items within a subject area are integrated with each other, as long

Table 9.3 Master Data Entities in the FAA Model

Entity	Description
Aircraft Category	Provides the aircraft categories, e.g. land, sea or amphibian.
Aircraft Model	A list of model and series of the aircraft, as assigned by the manufacturer or the aircraft.
Aircraft Reference	A list of aircraft registered with the FAA.
Aircraft Type	Provides the types of the aircraft, e.g. fixed wing single engine or balloon.
Aircraft Weight	This entity provides groups for the aircraft maximum gross take-off weight in pounds.
Airworthiness Class	The airworthiness certificate class which is reported on the Application for Airworthiness, FAA Form 8130-6.
Builder Certification	Provides the builder certifications.
Collateral Type	Provides a list of collateral types that can be registered with the FAA.
Correction Type	The members in this entity can be used to denote if the registration record has been added or corrected.
Dealer	This entity contains aircraft dealers and aircraft manufacturers who have made application for Dealer's Aircraft Registration Certificates.
Engine	This entity contains all engines registered with the FAA.
Engine Type	Provides the types of the engine, e.g. turbo-jet or ramjet.
Experimental Operation	The approved experimental operations (up to a maximum of six), which are reported on the Application for Airworthiness, FAA Form 8130-6.
Expiration Flag	Can be used to indicate expired records.
Fractional Ownership	Can be used to indicate if the registration is fractional owned.
Light Sport Operation	The approved light sport operations (up to a maximum of six), which are reported on the Application for Airworthiness, FAA Form 8130-6.
Manufacturer	This entity contains manufacturers of aircraft and engines.
Multiple Operation	The approved multiple operations (up to a maximum of six), which are reported on the Application for Airworthiness, FAA Form 8130-6.
Ownership	A list of values describing the ownership status of a dealer, e.g. individual or corporation.
Party	A list of parties that appear on indexed documents.
Provisional Operation	The approved provisional operations (up to a maximum of six), which are reported on the Application for Airworthiness, FAA Form 8130-6.
Record Owner	The record owners who own the record from an organizational perspective. Often, this might be a department or a function of the organization.
Registrant	The individuals or organizations that have registered or reserved an aircraft with the FAA, with the data as it appears on the Application for Registration, AC Form 8050-1.
Registrant Region	Provides the regions of the registrants, e.g. Central USA or Europe.
Registrant Type	Provides the types of the registrants, e.g. an individual or corporation.
Reservation Type	A list of types that describe the reservation of N-Numbers.
Reserved	Contains a list of N-number reservations.

Table 9.3 Master Data Entities in the FAA Model *(cont.)*

Entity	Description
Restricted Operation	The approved restricted operations (up to a maximum of six), which are reported on the Application for Airworthiness, FAA Form 8130-6.
Special Flight Permit Operation	The approved special flight permit operations (up to a maximum of six), which are reported on the Application for Airworthiness, FAA Form 8130-6.
Standard Operation	The approved standard operations (up to a maximum of six), which are reported on the Application for Airworthiness, FAA Form 8130-6.
State	A list of federal states that are used in FAA registrations.
Status	Provides the status codes and their meaning of the registrations, e.g. valid, revoked or retired.

Table 9.4 Master Data Entities in the BTS Model

Entity	Description
Airline	A list of unique airlines (carriers) as defined as one holding and reporting under the same US Department of Transportation (US DOT) certificate.
Airport	A list of unique airports. An identification number assigned by US DOT to identify a unique airport identifies the list.
Airport Size	A list of airport size classifications, for example small or large airports and heliports.
Airport Type	This list is used to classify airports into public or military airport types.
Alliance	Provides a list of major airline alliances.
Alliance Member	Indicates the membership status of airlines within an airline alliance.
Cancellation	A list of cancellation flags.
Carrier History	Historic information on carriers (airlines).
City	A list of cities that are served by airports. This entity is referenced in the *Airport* entity and elsewhere.
Country	A list of countries. This entity is referenced in the *Airport* entity and elsewhere.
Delay Group	This list is used to group departure and arrival delays into value bins.
Distance Group	This list is used to group distances into value bins.
Diversion	Provides a list to indicate the number of flight diversions in textual form.
Group	A list of airline groups. Unlike an airline, the group is an organizational or financial body that owns one or more airlines.
Group Type	Indicates if the group is a major or regional group, among other types.
Record Owner	The record owners who own the record from an organizational perspective. In many cases, this might be a department or a function of the organization.
Region	Indicates the region of the airline or group.
State	A list of federal states. This entity is referenced in the *Airport* entity and elsewhere.
Time Block	This list is used to group times (e.g., arrival or departure time of a flight) into value bins.
Yes No	This entity provides only two Boolean states, which are frequently used in multiple entities.

as the data remains in the same model. It would be great if the master data were more tightly integrated: if master data in one model could reference master data in another model. However, MDS doesn't support the integration of models. And, in reality, not all master data models will be fully integrated. Instead, the subject areas are independently developed and maintained. This is not a problem for operational or analytical systems, because not all master data needs to be completely integrated. Many operational applications only use the master data from one subject area. If they need master data from other subject areas, they integrate the data items with each other in the same way as the data warehouse handles it: via business keys that are included in the master data just as in any other operational database.

Because of the impossibility to integrate master data from one model with another, it is not possible to reuse a set of master data from one model in another. Therefore, it is required to copy the *Record Owner* master data to each model.

The last MDS model, the ***DWH* model**, provides master data that has been primarily created for the data warehouse, including reference data for calendar date, fiscal date, and other general information that is required by the data warehouse. Table 9.5 shows the master data included in this model.

In this case, not only the *Record Owner* entity, but also the *Yes No* entity was copied in order to be used within the MDS model. Figure 9.4 shows a partial entity relationship model of the **Airport** entity in MDS.

The **Airport** entity right of the center references seven other MDS entities, of which only five are displayed due to space constraints. Just like in any other database model in third normal form, the MDS entities referenced by entity **Airport** reference other entities. For example, the Country entity references entity **Region** in its definition. Note that some information has been denormalized into the **Airport** entity: it would not be required to reference the **State** and **Country** entities from the **Airport**

Table 9.5 Master Data Entities in the DWH Model	
Entity	**Description**
Country	A list of countries which are used in the *Holiday* entity.
Date	A list of dates with descriptive information from the standard calendar and the fiscal calendar. It is used to source the Date dimension in the dimensional model.
Fiscal Month	A list of month names for the fiscal calendar. The entity is used by the *Date* entity.
Fiscal Quarter	A list of quarter names for the fiscal calendar. The entity is used by the *Date* entity.
Holiday	A list of holidays. This is required in order to identify holidays on the *Date* entity.
Holiday Type	Holiday types indicate the recurring type of the holiday, e.g. Christmas, Independence Day, etc.
Month	A list of month names for the standard calendar. The entity is used by the *Date* entity.
Quarter	A list of quarter names for the standard calendar. The entity is used by the *Date* entity.
Record Owner	The record owners who own the record from an organizational perspective. In many cases, this might be a department or a function of the organization.
Religion	Holidays in the *Holiday* entity often have a religious reason. This entity provides the reference data for religions as needed.
Weekday	A list of weekday names for both the standard calendar and the fiscal calendar. The entity is used by the *Date* entity.
Yes No	This entity provides only two Boolean states, which are frequently used in multiple entities.

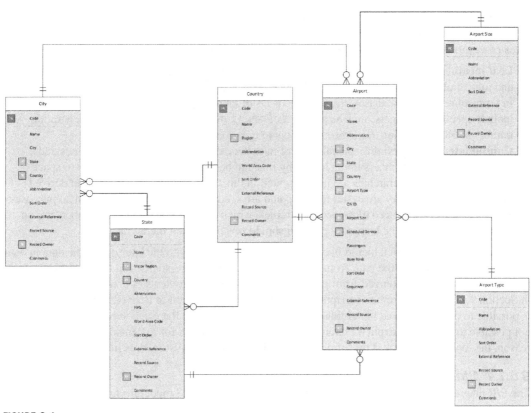

FIGURE 9.4

Partial E/R diagram of the BTS model (physical design).

entity, as it is possible to indirectly retrieve this information from other entities ("each city is located within a state and each state is located within a country"). However, the business decided to model it this way in order to provide an easier interface. What is not displayed here is the use of business rules to copy the redundant state and country information when the city is selected by the user. Section 9.7.2 discusses how to create business rules in MDS.

We have used the term entity throughout this section, assuming that there is a general understanding among the readers of this book regarding this term. The next section provides an MDS-related definition and shows some of the entities in more detail.

9.6.1.2 Entities

The previous section introduced models as a collection of master data. The master data is stored in entities within the model. These entities are very similar to entities in a relational database. They store the master data in a tabular form. Entities can reference other entities, thus following a normalized data model.

The tables in the previous section have listed the master data of the three models prepared for the book. In fact, the tables list the entities of the MDS models.

9.6.1.3 Members

Master data records within an entity are called members in MDS, which distinguishes between two types of members, leaf members and consolidated members [13]:

- **Leaf members:** in most cases, leaf members represent the business objects or other physical and logical objects within the business. They are the most granular items within an MDS entity. In terms of relational databases, the term record is often used [13]. Examples for such members include specific passengers, such as passenger Daniel Linstedt or the aircraft with registration number N-58739. Section 9.7.1 discusses how to create entities with leaf members.
- **Consolidated members:** this special form of member exists only in explicit hierarchies and groups specific leaf members into a hierarchy that can be used for reporting [6]. Due to space restrictions, explicit hierarchies are not presented in this book. Instead, the focus is on derived hierarchies, because they are easier to set up and are used more frequently for analytical purposes. However, if you are in need of ragged hierarchies, which are hierarchies where members are on different levels across the hierarchy [6], you should review explicit hierarchies.

The problem with explicit hierarchies and data warehousing is with the later use of the data in data warehousing. Oftentimes, the data from MDS hierarchies is used to source dimensional hierarchies. However, they are better sourced from plain, flat MDS subscription views (a concept that we discuss in Section 9.9.2) and not from subscription views that provide explicit or derived hierarchies. While it is possible to provide derived hierarchies by a set of such plain and flat MDS subscription views, it is not possible to provide an explicit hierarchy in an easy to use format for dimensional loading. For that reason, the focus of the book is on simple leaf members, which are just records in a master data entity.

9.6.1.4 Attributes

The E/R diagram in Figure 9.4 shows some of the entities in the MDS model for this book and includes the attributes of each entity. Attributes are used to define what kind of data is stored within an entity. This is similar to columns in a relational database. The following attribute types are available in MDS [6]:

- **Free form:** a free form attribute can take any value, for example a numeric value or unstructured text. Table 9.6 shows the data types that are available for this attribute types.
- **Domain attribute:** the domain attribute is used to reference another entity, especially a member within this entity. A member is one entry in a master data table and is explained in the next section.
- **File:** a file attribute can store any file, for example Microsoft Word documents that describe the member in more detail or a photo.

Table 9.6 Data Types for the Free Form Attribute Type in MDS

Data Type	Description
Text	This attribute type allows storing any text with up to 4000 characters in the attribute.
Number	A numeric value with up to 7 decimal positions can be stored in attributes of this type.
DateTime	Regardless of the name, MDS allows storing date values in attributes of this type. Note that storing time information (hours, minutes) is not possible [14].
Link	This attribute type allows the storage of an Internet link in attributes of this type. The string must begin with http:// or an error will be displayed [15].

MDS allows storing additional metadata for each attribute in a member. For example, it is possible to define the display width that is used to arrange the columns in the Explorer Grid or in Microsoft Excel when editing the master data. If a free text attribute is expected to store long text descriptions, this value should be increased in order to adjust the display width to the actual data stored in this attribute.

Each entity in MDS uses two standard attributes. When a new entity is created, these attributes are already included in the entity and it is not possible to delete these attributes:

- **Code:** the *Code* attribute identifies a member within the entity. This attribute is especially important when creating references to other entities using domain attributes, because these domain attributes reference the *Code* attribute of the other entity. Therefore, this attribute is very similar to a primary key in a relational table, while domain attributes are similar to foreign keys. It should be noted that the *Code* attribute is not using a numeric attribute type. Instead, the *Code* attribute uses a text with 250 characters. Therefore, it can be used to store most business keys, as long as they are unique (which they *should* be anyway).
- **Name:** the *Name* attribute provides a more descriptive text, also 250 characters long. A typical use case of this attribute is the name of the business object that is represented by the master data member, for example the name of the airline or the name of the aircraft manufacturer. This attribute is also important in normalized MDS models because it is displayed to the end-user while selecting an entry in a domain attribute.

Note that it is not possible to modify the name or the data type of any of these two standard attributes. The only way to limit the data that is stored in these attributes is by using business rules, which are described in section 9.7.2. This includes defining NOT NULL attributes, which is only possible by using business rules in MDS.

All master data entities in this book use some additional and mandatory attributes that are not required by MDS from a technical perspective but exist for standardization reasons within the DWH or MDM initiative. The following attributes are created on all entities:

- **External Reference:** a link to an external Web page or Intranet page with additional information that describes this member. A good choice to store such additional information resources could be a Wiki or Microsoft SharePoint.
- **Record Source:** indicates where the master data for this member comes from. Could be used when staging data from one or more operational systems or to indicate the third party source if the data has been collected from the Web.
- **Record Owner:** indicates who owns the member from an organizational perspective. This could be used to ensure user authorization on a member level using business rules. Note that it is also possible to create this attribute using metadata [16], but for ease of use, it has been created as a regular attribute.
- **Comments:** a free-form text that can be used to add descriptive comments for information purposes within MDS only. The data is not used in the data warehouse.

In addition, many entities use one or more of the following attributes:

- **Description:** this free form allows storing an additional text that describes the member in more detail.
- **Abbreviation:** this short text can be used for the member when space restrictions exist. Examples include charts and reports with many columns where space is limited.

- **Sort Order:** the sort order can be used to sort the members according to an order defined by the business. Unlike alphabetic ordering, businesses often want to order members according to a custom order, indicating the relative importance of members to their business. An example is the importance of brands, e.g. major brand (with most sales volume) comes first, followed by those with less importance.
- **Valid from:** this attribute indicates the date when the member becomes valid from a business perspective. It can be used to implement temporality in the data warehouse. Chapter 14, Loading the Dimensional Information Mart, shows how to use this information when loading information marts. The **Alliance Member** entity in the BTS model uses such an attribute by providing a **Start Date** attribute.
- **Valid to:** this attribute indicates the date until which the member is valid from a business perspective. Also used to implement temporality in the data warehouse. Chapter 14 shows how to use this information when loading information marts. The **Alliance Member** entity in the BTS model uses such an attribute by providing an **End Date** attribute.

Standardizing these attributes in a MDM project helps to streamline the definition of entities regarding the use of attributes and their names and help business users to quickly identify and recognize the standard attributes and their purpose.

When setting the name of new attributes for an entity, it should be preferred to use readable names, instead of technical names. The name that is defined within MDS for the attribute is displayed to end-users when they edit master data in the Web front-end of MDS or in Microsoft Excel using the MDS add-in, described in section 9.6.3.1. Having a readable name, including spaces where required, improves the user experience. For example, avoid the attribute name "AircraftType" or even worse "T_AIRCRAFT" because it requires end-users to figure out what "T_" means, in the worst case. Instead of using these names, consider using "Aircraft Type." The drawback of such naming is that the attribute name is also used in the SQL Server integration and requires the use of square brackets. Section 9.9.2 shows how to do this. In any case, keep in mind that the data warehouse system is built for the end-user and not for IT.

9.6.1.5 Attribute Groups
Attribute groups can be used to group a number of attributes within an entity. This is a great feature that increases the user experience, especially when dealing with entities with a large number of attributes. They are defined on an entity basis. Therefore, they are not used for reusability purposes. Instead, they are only used in order to group attributes on tabs in the user interface [6].

Another important feature of attribute groups is that they can be used for security reasons: it is possible to grant users access rights to individual attribute groups, easing the management of user security [6]. However, not all front-ends support attribute groups; in particular, Microsoft Excel with the MDS add-in doesn't support them. Therefore, we will not cover attribute groups in this book in more detail. Just note that they are still available, for example in the Web front-end and in the database interface, but just not as convenient for business users as via Excel.

9.6.1.6 Hierarchies
We have already mentioned hierarchies when we described members. MDS supports the definition of derived and explicit hierarchies:

- **Derived hierarchies:** these hierarchies are based on domain attributes within MDS entities. In order to create a derived hierarchy, it is required to have at least one domain attribute that references the parent entity within the hierarchy. For example, the **City** entity in the **BTS** model references the

State entity by using a domain attribute of the same name. In addition, the **State** entity references the **Country** entity, in a similar way. Each entity represents a level in the derived hierarchy. The derived hierarchy is called *derived* because it is *derived* from this information. While entities might have multiple domain attributes, there is only one domain attribute that is used to indicate the parent. When setting up the hierarchy, this domain attribute is selected for each level.

- **Explicit hierarchies:** this hierarchy doesn't rely on the relationship between entities. Instead all members within explicit hierarchies come from the same hierarchy. The hierarchy is built by creating explicit relationships between leaf members and consolidated members, which are defined during design time. The advantage of these hierarchies is that they allow ragged hierarchies where members exist on different levels across the hierarchy. This is not possible with derived hierarchies.

Because the derived hierarchy is based on standard entities using domain attributes for defining the relationship between levels, it is possible to directly import the raw entities into the data warehouse, without modification. In fact, the data is perfectly suited for the definition and sourcing of dimensional hierarchies. That is why we will cover only derived hierarchies throughout this book.

9.6.2 MASTER DATA MANAGER

Most development of master data elements, such as models, entities, and attributes, happens within Master Data Manager, a Web-based front-end of MDS. When installed with default settings, the tool is available under the following URL: http://localhost:8080 where localhost should be replaced by the server name if accessing a remote server. If the Web site doesn't show up, ask your system administrator for advice.

The first Web page that is presented to the user shows five functional areas, as Figure 9.5 shows. The following functional areas are displayed on the front page of Master Data Services:

- **Explorer:** the primary interface of the application and used to add, edit, or delete entity members in master data entities. It is also used to manage hierarchies, view transaction details, and create and manage collections, among other things [6]. Throughout the book, we will use another alternative to create and manage master data: Microsoft Excel and the MDS add-in. In practice, Microsoft Excel and the MDS add-in are more convenient for most business users. The only exception as to when to use the Web-based explorer is when working with hierarchies or collections, because these features are not supported in Microsoft Excel.
- **Version Management:** this area allows copying entities, along with associated data and control access to such version. It is also possible to validate the version and review any issues [6].
- **Integration Management:** in order to import and export data to and from MDS, this area is utilized. It shows information about the batches that load data into MDS, and allows the creation of subscription views to export master data by using Microsoft SQL Server views [6]. We will create staging tables and subscription views in section 9.9.1 and 9.9.2, respectively.
- **System Administration:** this area is used to create the models, entities, hierarchies, and other system objects [6]. We will show how to use this area in section 9.7.
- **User and Group Permissions:** master data should be protected from unauthorized access. Setting up users, groups and their permissions is done in this functional area of MDS [6].

The next sections describe these functional areas in more detail and explain how to use them for the purpose of this book. However, a comprehensive documentation of MDS is not possible within this book, due to space limitations.

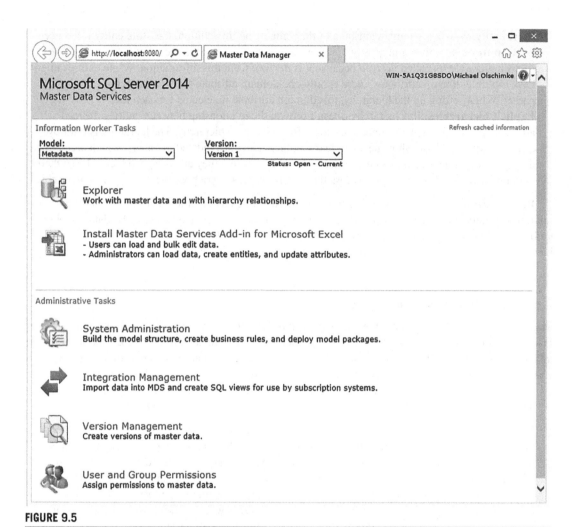

FIGURE 9.5

Front page of Microsoft Master Data Services 2014.

9.6.3 EXPLORER

Data stewards use the **Explorer** to manage the master data in MDS. Because all master data is first organized around a model, the currently selected subject area is displayed in the model view as shown in Figure 9.6.

The model that is selected in the combo box is the one that is active in the Web front-end. When the Explorer functional area is selected, the **Explorer Grid** is shown, which displays all members of an entity in MDS, similar to a table in a relational database (Figure 9.7).

The center of Figure 9.7 shows the explorer grid itself. Note that not all members are displayed if the entity has many records. Instead, the members are divided into multiple pages for performance reasons. The right-hand side of the page shows the detail pane with all attributes of the member selected in the explorer grid. To the top of the explorer grid, there are various action buttons to modify the entity,

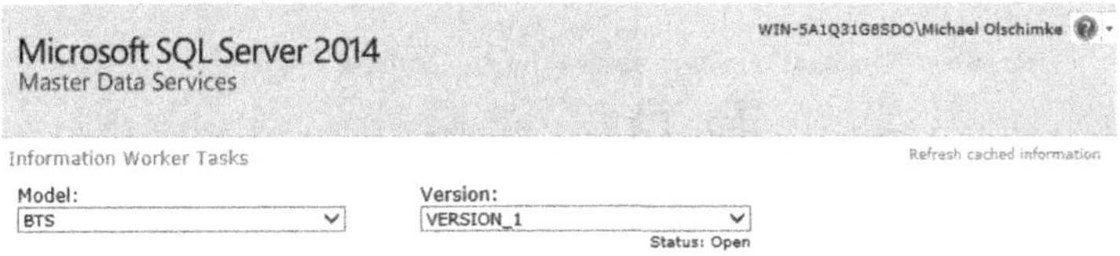

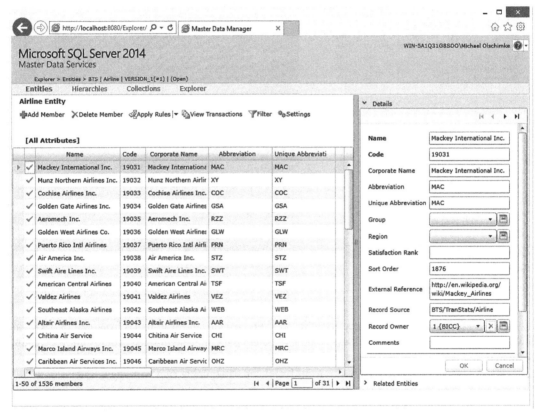

FIGURE 9.6

Selecting the model in MDS.

FIGURE 9.7

Explorer grid.

for example by adding or deleting new members. The main menu can be used to switch the entity or display hierarchies that are available in MDS.

9.6.3.1 Microsoft Excel and MDS

As an alternative to the Web-based front-end to edit master data, Microsoft provides an add-in to Microsoft Excel to allow data stewards to add, update, and delete master data. Figure 9.8 shows the **Region** entity of the **MDS** model loaded to Microsoft Excel.

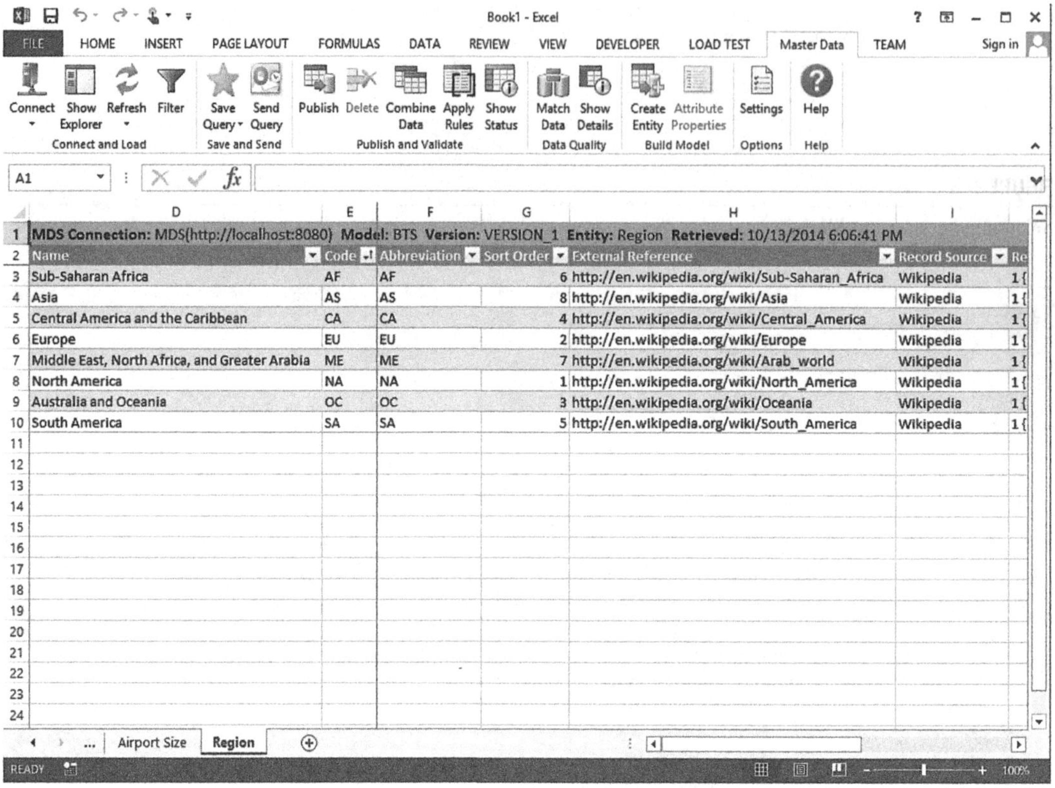

FIGURE 9.8

Microsoft Excel add-in for MDS.

The add-in, which can be installed from the welcome page of the Web-based front-end of MDS, allows inserting new members, as well as updating or deleting them. In addition, it actually allows creating new entities or adding new attributes to existing entities. One of the advantages of the add-in is that business users are very comfortable with Microsoft Excel and can quickly start working with master data. It also allows business users to use built-in Excel functions to set up master data, for example by concatenating cells in order to create the attribute values of the master data and performing other repetitive tasks.

9.6.4 VERSION MANAGEMENT

The version management, which is managed by this functional area, is a powerful feature of MDS. Versions are physical copies of entities and all of their members. They can be used to save snapshots of master data and record historical changes to it or to record major data changes. The version management of MDS is based on copying an old version into a new one. MDS supports protecting old versions from later modification, in order to maintain the old state, for example for audit purposes [30].

Versions can also be used in a defined master data validation process, by allowing subscribing applications (see the next section) to access only validated and released versions. Business rules are used to implement the validation of master data. They are covered in section 9.7.2 [30].

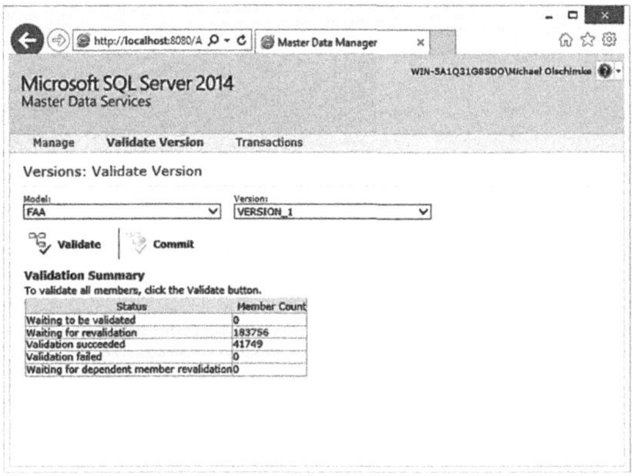

FIGURE 9.9

Validate a version in MDS.

This functional area allows one to [6]:

- **Create copies of entities:** this function copies all members from the selected source version into a new version. The copy includes all required entities, attributes, attribute groups, derived hierarchies, and collections [6].
- **Validate versions:** in order to validate a version, it is possible to run all business rules against the members in associated entities of a version [6]. Creating business rules is covered in Section 9.7.2.
- **Review issues with versions:** it is possible to review summary information of issues in a version. This is presented in Figure 9.9.
- **View and reverse transactions on versions:** this function is used to view and reverse transactions on versions. It is also possible to annotate transactions [6].

By using the versioning functions of MDS, it is possible to create separate versions of master data for different subscribing applications. This allows the business to run applications with different update levels. For example, one application could still use version 1 of the master data, while other applications are already using a more advanced version of the entity. This is not the preferred situation, but in too many cases, not all operational or analytical systems are at the same version. Therefore, this feature of MDS allows the business to cope with such situations.

We will describe a situation of this type in more detail in Section 9.9.2 when we demonstrate how to export a version of master data to subscribing applications.

9.6.5 INTEGRATION MANAGEMENT

MDS is not an isolated system. The master data stored within MDS only provides value to the business if it is integrated with operational and analytical systems. MDS supports the integration of master data with two different approaches, which are discussed in Section 9.9: staging tables and subscription views.

Both options are maintained using the **Integration Management**. Figure 9.10 shows the main page of this functional area.

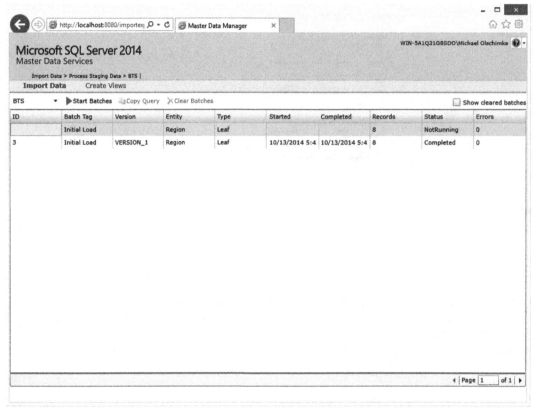

FIGURE 9.10

Integration management of MDS.

This area allows administrative users to start batches that modify current master data, stored in entities. These batches insert new members into entities, update their attributes or delete the members as a whole. It is also possible to create subscription views that can be used by subscribing applications to retrieve master data from MDS and use the data within the application. For example, it is possible to integrate a list of products on an e-commerce platform, such as an online Web store. The list of products is stored and maintained centrally in MDS and the online store updates or directly uses the product list from MDS. That way, all operational systems have the same list of products. Analytical systems, such as the data warehouse, use the list of products in the same manner: they use the master data, which is provided to the data warehouse by the subscription view, to create dimensions that can be used by the business to analyze fact information.

9.6.6 SYSTEM ADMINISTRATION

Administrative users and master data developers create MDS models, entities and their attributes using this functional area. In fact, it is the place where the whole MDS object model, which was described in section 9.6.1, is created and maintained. Figure 9.11 shows the maintenance page of the FAA model.

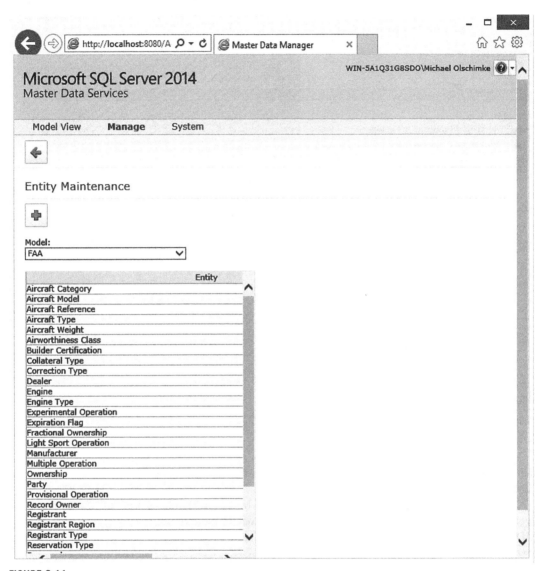

FIGURE 9.11

Entity maintenance.

This page allows the user to create, modify or remove entities. Section 9.7 covers how to create an MDS model, including entities and attributes in more detail.

9.6.7 USER AND GROUP PERMISSIONS

Section 9.3 introduced privacy and data protection as a driver for master data management in organizations. To support this aspect, MDS allows securing the master data by setting up the permissions of

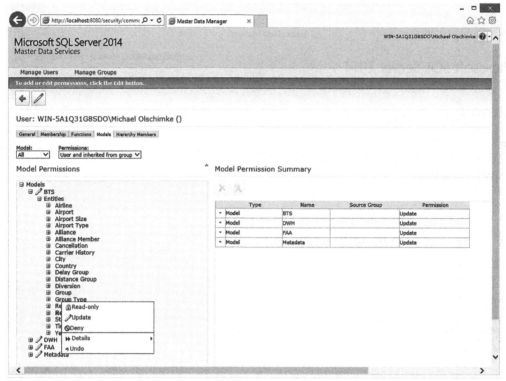

FIGURE 9.12

Managing user permissions in MDS.

individual users and groups who are allowed to access the master data. Figure 9.12 shows how user permissions are managed in MDS.

This functional area is integrated with the standard Microsoft Windows user and user group management. Each user or group can be granted access to one or more of the five functional areas within MDS. In addition, detailed read and write permissions can be granted on an entity, attribute, or single member level of detail [6].

9.7 CREATING A MODEL

In order to create a model in MDS, the **System Administration** of the Web front-end is used. The first menu entry in the main menu of this function area provides the means to manage models by using the first menu entry in the menu. Selecting the menu entry opens the model maintenance page, as shown in Figure 9.13.

The page shows the MDS models that are currently available in MDS. By default, only the **Metadata** model is available in a fresh MDS installation. In order to create a new MDS model, the

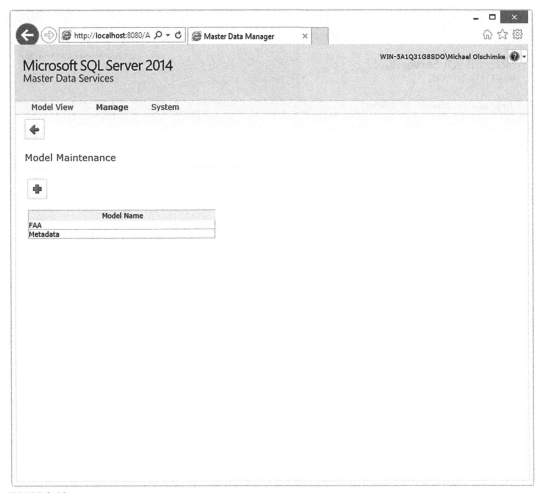

FIGURE 9.13

Model maintenance in MDS.

button with a green plus sign is used. After selecting it, the page shown in Figure 9.14 is presented to the user.

The dialog allows specifying the name of the new model. In addition, it is possible to create the first entity within the model. If the user selects this option, the new model will automatically contain a first entity with the same name as specified for the model. It is also possible to add additional options that are available when creating new entities, which are to create an explicit and a mandatory hierarchy.

After selecting the save button, the new model is created and becomes available in MDS. The next step is to create new entities within the new model.

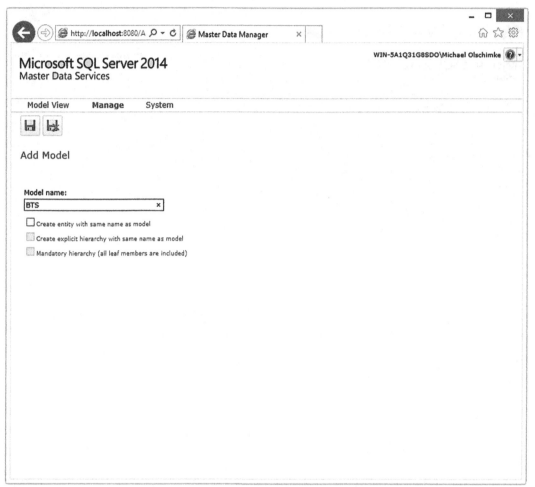

FIGURE 9.14

Add a model to MDS.

9.7.1 CREATING ENTITIES

The model created in the last section contains no entities yet. As an empty model, it does not provide any value to the business. In order to create entities that can be used to manage master data, the second menu item in the **Manage** main menu is used. After selecting the **Entities** menu entry, the entity maintenance page appears (Figure 9.15).

This page displays all the entities in the currently selected model. Note that, for new models, this list is empty. To create a new entity, the button with the green plus sign is used. After selecting this button, the following page, which is shown in Figure 9.16, is used to set up the new entity.

The **entity name** should be unique within the scope of the model. The name of the staging table has to be unique for the whole MDS database. Therefore, it is a recommended practice to add the model

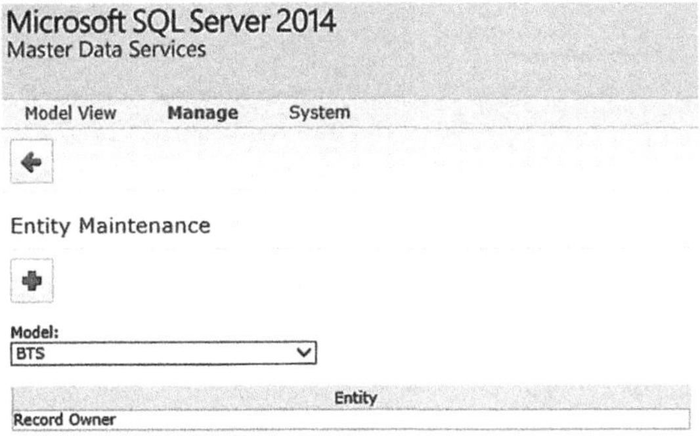

FIGURE 9.15

MDS entity maintenance page.

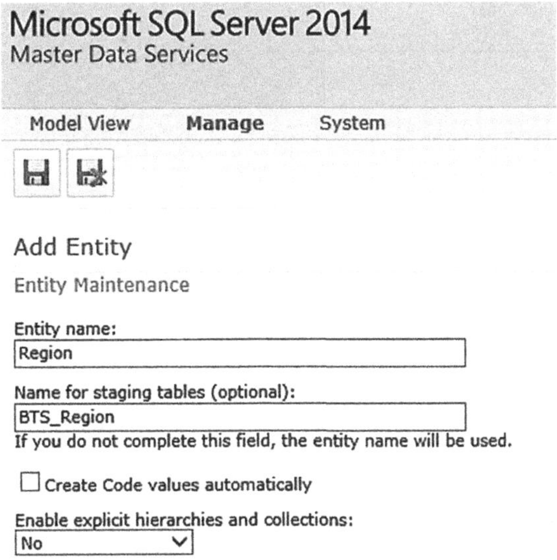

FIGURE 9.16

Add a new entity in MDS.

name to the stage table name in order to prevent name collisions with staging tables for entities of the same name but in different models.

If the option **Create Code values automatically** is selected, the value of the **code** attribute is populated automatically by a sequence generator. However, it is possible to overwrite this value when creating new members in the entity.

For the purposes of this book, we don't create explicit hierarchies and collections.

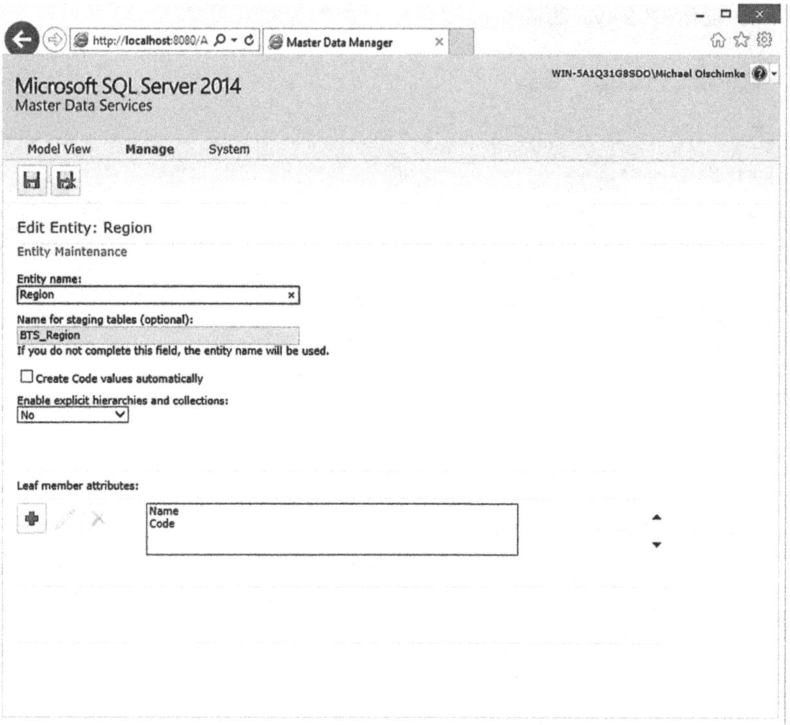

FIGURE 9.17

Edit MDS entities.

Saving the new entity using the save button allows the user to define the attributes of the new entity. In order to do so, select the new entity in the list of entities of the model and select the edit button. The next page (Figure 9.17) allows modifying the entity properties, along with the definition of the entity attributes.

As Figure 9.17 shows, most of the properties that have been set during the entity creation process can be modified, except the name of the staging table. This table was created during the creation of the entity and cannot be modified, as it became an important technical foundation for the entity.

To create new attributes, select the button with the green plus sign, in the **Leaf member attributes** section to the bottom of the page. The next page allows setting up the properties of the new attribute (Figure 9.18).

The page allows selecting one of the attribute types, which have been described in section 9.6.1. In addition, the dialog asks the user to provide an attribute name, and the number of pixels used for displaying the attribute in the Web front-end. Depending on the selected attribute type, additional properties have to be provided by the user to set up the attribute. This includes the data type and length of the value, as shown in Figure 9.17. It is also possible to activate change tracking, a feature that can be used to trigger business rules, which are discussed in the next section.

After saving the new attribute, the same procedure can be used to create additional attributes for the entity. The entity definition is completed when the entity is saved as a whole in the **Edit entity** page.

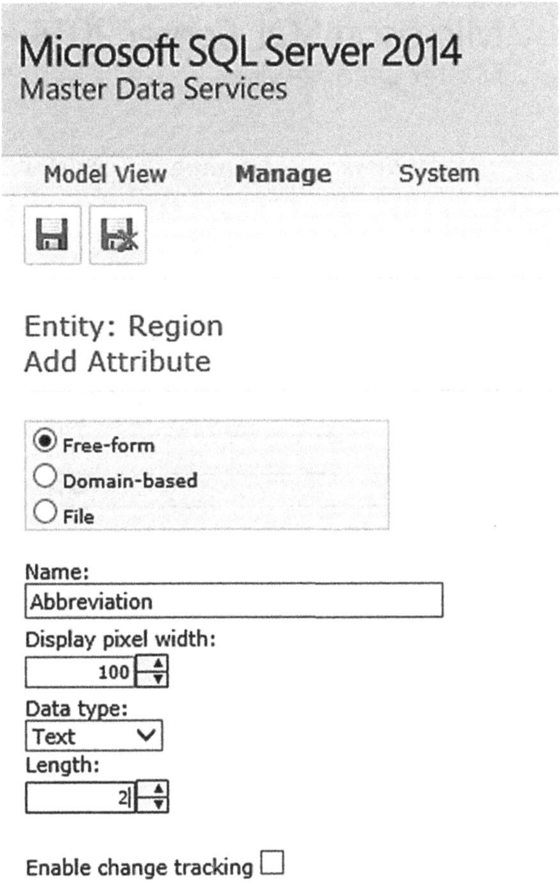

FIGURE 9.18

Add attribute to entity.

9.7.2 CREATING BUSINESS RULES

Business rules are a powerful feature of MDS that help to validate the master data that is created or modified by the business user. They implement logic that is executed when the master data changes and can enforce a given value format for attributes or the existence of data in specified attributes. It is also possible to trigger actions using business rules.

In order to create a business rule in MDS, the **Business Rules** entry in the **Manage** main menu in **System Administration** is used. The following page allows the user to define the entity for which business rules should be created, as shown in Figure 9.19.

The page asks for the model, the entity and the member type to display the current business rules for. In addition, it is possible to filter for business rules that are defined for specific attributes. Note that it is not possible to change the member type for standard entities. Selecting the button with the green plus symbol creates a new business rule on the entity. Figure 9.20 shows the same page as in the previous figure with the newly created business rule.

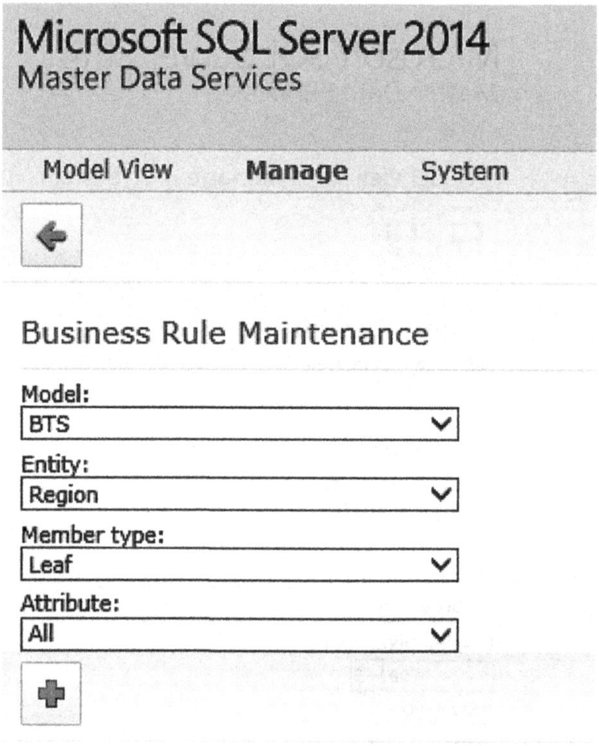

FIGURE 9.19

Business rule maintenance in MDS.

The grid on the page can be used to change the name of the business rule and add a description by double-clicking the respective cell in the grid. It is also possible to modify the selected business rule by selecting the edit button, which is the third button from the left in the icon bar. When creating new business rules, the status is **Rule not defined**, which means that the business rule needs to be modified in order to provide a definition of the business rule.

After selecting the button, the page shown in Figure 9.21 is used to define the business rule. Business rules are expressed in MDS by two elements:

- **Conditions:** a condition selects the members to apply the business rule to. If no condition is set, the business rule affects all members in the entity.
- **Actions:** the action defines what should happen with the member that is included in the condition. In many cases, it defines what should be checked, for example the length of an attribute, as shown in Figure 9.21.

MDS allows changing the value during modification, set default values, validating values or starting external workflows. When validating values, it is possible to check a number of properties, for example string length, uniqueness, or the input range of numeric values. Thus, business rules present a powerful means to ensure the quality and correctness of master data in MDS.

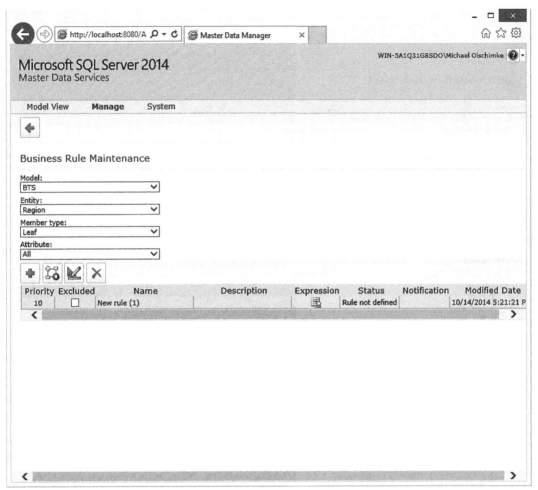

FIGURE 9.20

Managing business rules in MDS.

9.8 IMPORTING A MODEL

As already stated, the companion Web site of this book provides a number of MDS models, which are used throughout the book. In order to load the models to a local MDS installation, it is required to unzip the models and import them into MDS on the server system.

MDS models are imported using the command line tool MDSModelDeploy.exe which is located under `\Program Files\Microsoft SQL Server\120\Master Data Services\Configuration` of the system drive where Microsoft SQL Server 2014 is installed.

The following command is used to identify which MDS installations are available on the server:

```
MDSModelDeploy listservices
```

FIGURE 9.21

Modifying a business rule in MDS.

This command returns a list of installations on the local server, including the service name, Web site and virtual path. By default, the first service name is MDS1, which is used throughout this section. The following commands import the master data models of the book to MDS:

```
MDSModelDeploy deployclone -package BTS.xml
MDSModelDeploy deployclone -package FAA.xml
MDSModelDeploy deployclone -package DWH.xml
```

After running these commands, the MDS models are ready to use for the examples in this book. Addititional information is provided at https://msdn.microsoft.com/en-us/library/ff486956.aspx.

9.9 INTEGRATING MDS WITH THE DATA VAULT AND OPERATIONAL SYSTEMS

MDS stores entity members in internal tables within the SQL Server database assigned to MDS. At first glance, the table structure of MDS is complex because the tables have no semantic meaning. It is not possible to quickly identify the internal table for a given entity of a specified model. But it is possible to find out which internal system table holds the data for a given entity by executing the following statement against the MDS database:

```
SELECT
      e.Model_ID
     ,m.Name AS Model_Name
     ,e.Name AS Entity_Name
     ,e.EntityTable
     ,e.StagingBase
  FROM
      mdm.tblEntity e
  LEFT JOIN
      mdm.tblModel m ON (m.ID = e.Model_ID)
  WHERE
    m.Name = 'BTS' AND e.Name = 'Region'
```

This query will return the name of the internal table that holds the master data for the **Region** entity in the **BTS** model. The name is given column 4 **EntityTable**. This information can then be used to truncate the table, which is required when the data becomes corrupt, which sometimes happens during development. The following statement truncates the data:

```
TRUNCATE mdm.tbl_4_76_EN
```

Note that the name of the entity table differs from installation to installation. You should not execute this statement against your MDS database without modifying the table name appropriately.

The described approach should not be used in production. Instead, there are other options for manipulating or accessing the master data in MDS entities. In fact, the managed master data within MDS is of no value for the business as long as it is not integrated with other systems, for example operational systems and the data warehouse. MDS supports two options for integration:

1. **Staging tables [13]:** staging tables are used to load master data from operational systems to MDS. They can also be used to modify or delete entity members programmatically, for example using T-SQL statements or SQL Server Integration Services (SSIS).
2. **Subscription views [13]:** these views are created within MDS and populate the members of an entity. They can be used to integrate master data stored in MDS with operational or analytical systems, called subscribers.

While the first option is to get master data into MDS, the second option is to get master data out of MDS. The data flow of master data is presented in Figure 9.22.

Master data is loaded from operational systems into MDS using staging tables. The figure shows that business users modify and enrich the master data within MDS. The data warehouse then loads the master data from MDS using subscription views into the staging area. However, the same master data, in its enriched form, is also fed back into the operational systems and follows the Total Quality

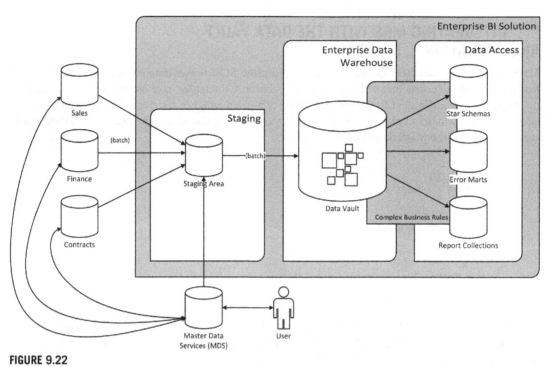

FIGURE 9.22

Closed loop in master data management.

Management (TQM) approach as outlined in section 9.5 and Chapter 3, The Data Vault 2.0 Methodology. Only this closed loop enables business users true self-service because they can now modify the data that is available in both systems, the operational system and the analytical system. In the best case, the master data application should write the master data directly into the Data Vault based EDW layer. However, because the structure of the entities in MDS is fixed and defined by the staging tables and subscription views of MDS, it is treated as just another source system. As a result, the data from MDS is staged and then loaded into reference tables in the Data Vault 2.0 model.

When operational systems deliver master data to MDS, they usually create batches of data within the staging table of MDS. This process is either performed by the operational system itself, if it is aware that MDS is receiving the data and fully supports integration with MDS. In many cases, however, an ETL job, implemented using SSIS, loads the data from the operational source and stages the master data to MDS by creating a new batch in the staging table. Also, there might be multiple source systems that provide master data to MDS, each creating individual batches per load. The batch describes the required modifications to the members within the entity. For example, it describes which members should be added to the entity, which should be updated and which should be deactivated or permanently removed from the entity. Administrative users can apply these batches to MDS by executing them within the Web-based front-end [13] (Figure 9.23).

Each batch is identified within MDS by a batch tag that can be set when the staging table is loaded. The end-user can start selected batches in the **Integration Management** functional area of MDS. The

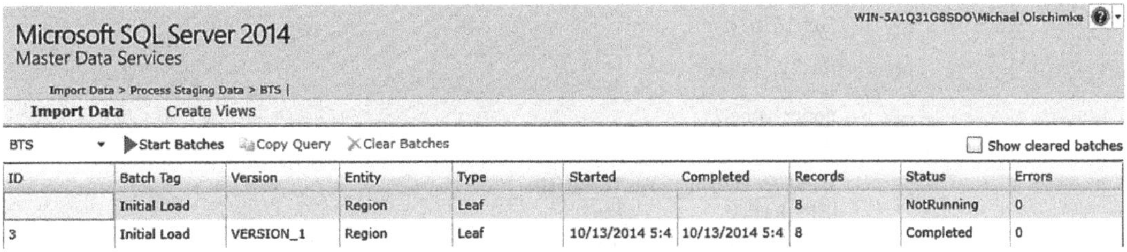

FIGURE 9.23

Manage staging batches in MDS.

Import Data tab serves this purpose, as Figure 9.23 shows. The table on the tab shows the available batches and provides the following columns:

- **ID:** the ID column uniquely identifies a batch by a surrogate key. This key is automatically assigned to the batch by MDS after it has queued to run.
- **Batch Tag:** the batch tag is an alphanumeric identifier that is assigned by the user or process that creates the batch. Examples of such batch tags include "Initial Load" or "CRM 2014-10-08".
- **Version:** this field identifies the entity version to which this batch has been applied.
- **Entity:** the target entity of the batch.
- **Type:** indicates the type of staged data. For the purposes of the book, we will only deal with **Leaf** types, but there are more possible in MDS.
- **Started:** indicates when the staging process has been started.
- **Completed:** indicates when the staging process has been completed.
- **Records:** the number of records within the batch.
- **Status:** indicates the status of the batch, either **NotRunning**, **QueuedToRun**, **Completed** or **Cleared**.
- **Errors:** the number of records that failed to apply. The staging table provides more information on the individual errors on a per-record basis. See section 9.9.1 for more details.

The next sections cover how to create and use staging tables and subscription views in more detail.

9.9.1 STAGE TABLES

While business users can modify master data in MDS using the Web-based front-end or the Microsoft Excel add-in, it is also possible to load new or updated master data from operational systems programmatically, for example using T-SQL or SSIS. It is also possible to delete master data in MDS in the same manner.

The key for programmatic manipulation of master data in MDS is the use of staging tables, which are created within the MDS database when adding new entities. Section 9.7.1 has already covered that it is possible to provide an optional name for the staging table, as shown in Figure 9.24.

The name, in this case **BTS_Region**, can only be set while adding the entity. It is not possible to change the name afterwards. It is a recommended practice to modify the initial name and add the name of the MDS model to the staging table name. The reason for this practice is that MDS uses the provided

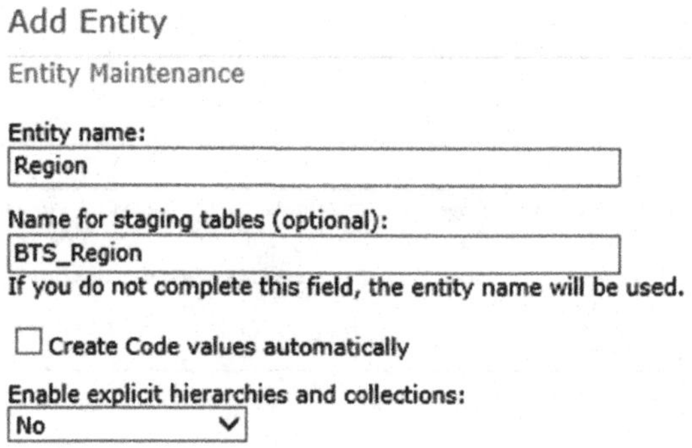

Add Entity

Entity Maintenance

Entity name:

| Region |

Name for staging tables (optional):

| BTS_Region |

If you do not complete this field, the entity name will be used.

☐ Create Code values automatically

Enable explicit hierarchies and collections:

| No ⌄ |

FIGURE 9.24

Providing optional name for staging table.

name and creates staging tables for leaf nodes, consolidated members and relationships. For example, the model distributed on the companion Web site creates many staging tables for leaf notes. By default MDS creates a staging table named **stg.Region_Leaf** for the entity **Region** in the **BTS** model. The issue arises when two different models include an entity called **Region**. In this case, MDS cannot create a staging table with the same name and will warn the user. If the model name is included in the name for the staging tables, this problem cannot arise because all staging table names will be unique.

9.9.1.1 Using T-SQL to Stage Master Data into Microsoft Master Data Services

In order to stage data into MDS using T-SQL only, the following statement can be used to load data into the entity **Region**:

```
INSERT INTO [stg].[BTS_Region_Leaf]
        ([ImportType]
        ,[ImportStatus_ID]
        ,[BatchTag]
        ,[Code]
        ,[Name]
        ,[Abbreviation]
        ,[Sort Order]
        ,[External Reference]
        ,[Record Source]
        ,[Record Owner]
        ,[Comments])
    VALUES
        (0
        ,0
        ,'Initial Load'
        ,'NA'
        ,'North America'
        ,'NA'
        ,1
        ,'http://en.wikipedia.org/wiki/North_America'
        ,'Wikipedia'
        ,'BICC'
        ,'')
```

Table 9.7 Valid ImportType Values [17]

ImportType	Description
0	Create new members. If the staged data is not NULL, existing MDS data will be replaced by staged data. NULL values are ignored. In order to set a NULL value in the target entity, string values in the stage table have to be set to ~NULL~ and number attributes to -98765432101234567890. DateTime attributes have to be set to 5555-11-22T12:34:56.
1	Create new members only. Updating existing MDS data will fail.
2	Create new members and replace existing MDS data with data from the stage table. NULL values in the stage table will overwrite existing MDS values.
3	Deactivate the member with the given Code value in the target entity. The user interface will hide all attributes, hierarchy and collection memberships, and transactions for this member. This action only works if the member is not used as a domain-based attribute value of another member.
4	Delete the member permanently, based on the given Code value. This action deletes all attributes, hierarchy and collection memberships, and the transactions permanently. This action fails if the member is used as a domain-based attribute value of another member.
5	Deactivate the member with the given Code value in the target entity. If the member is used as a domain-based attribute value of another member, this value is set to NULL. This ImportType value works only for leaf members.
6	Delete the member permanently, based on the given Code value. If the member is used as a domain-based attribute value of another member, this value is set to NULL. This ImportType value works only for leaf members.

This statement adds a new member into the staging table for insert. The insert adds the descriptive data for the member and provides some information to the MDS staging process by using one or more of the following MDS columns [17]:

- **ID:** This surrogate key value is assigned by MDS to each member item in the stage table after processing. You should not enter a value in this field.
- **ImportType:** This value determines what will be done if there is already a member in the target entity that has the same **Code** value as the staged entry. Table 9.7 provides a list of valid values for this field.
- **ImportStatus_ID:** This value provides a status of the staging process. When records are inserted into the staging table for processing, this value has to be set to 0. The staging process will use this field to indicate success or failure of the staging process. Table 9.8 provides a list of valid values.

Table 9.8 Valid ImportStatus_ID Values [17]

ImportStatus_ID	Description
0	The entry in the staging table is ready for staging. This value is set by the process that loads data into the staging table.
1	The entry in the staging table was successfully loaded by the staging process. This value is set by MDS after processing.
2	The entry in the staging table was not loaded by the staging process, due to a failure. This value is set by MDS after processing.

- **Batch_ID:** This identifier is assigned automatically by MDS to group staged data into batches. This field is blank if the batch has not been processed.
- **BatchTag:** This is a unique identifier for the batch and is provided by the process that loads the staging table. It is used to execute the batch later and can contain up to 50 characters.
- **ErrorCode:** If the staging process was unable to load the record into the target MDS entity, this field provides an error code that could be used for further analysis.
- **Code:** A unique **Code** value that is used to identify the member in the target entity. This is also required when updating members.
- **Name:** The name of the member.
- **NewCode:** This is only used when updating the **Code** value of the target member.

The following table lists the values which are valid for the **ImportType** field [17]:

The statement at the beginning of this section has staged a record that will eventually insert a new member into the target entity because it used **ImportType** 0. Providing an **ImportStatus_ID** of 0 indicates that the record is ready for staging and the batch tag **Initial Load** is used by the business user to execute the batch in the Web front-end. Similarly, other import types can be executed, for example deactivating members in the target MDS entity. For that purpose, the following statement, which uses **ImportType** 3, can be used to deactivate the created member for North America (NA):

```
INSERT INTO [stg].[BTS_Region_Leaf]
            ([ImportType]
            ,[ImportStatus_ID]
            ,[BatchTag]
            ,[Code])
      VALUES
            (3
            ,0
            ,'Cleanup'
            ,'NA'
)
```

This statement sets the import type and the intial **ImportStatus_ID**. The batch tag **Cleanup** is used to group multiple stage records into one batch that can be executed at once. The **Code** value identifies the entity member that should be deactivated.

In order to execute the batch, an end-user, such as the MDS administrator, can run the batch from the Web front-end, as described in section 9.6.5. However, it is also possible to execute the batch programmatically, by calling a stored procedure in the MDS database:

```
EXEC MDS.stg.udp_BTS_Region_Leaf @VersionName = 'VERSION_1', @LogFlag = 1, @BatchTag =
'Initial Load'
```

There is one stored procedure for each MDS entity. This stored procedure executes the staged data against the target entity. The procedure takes the following parameters [18]:

- **VersionName:** The name of the version that should be updated. Depending on the SQL Server collation setting, this value might be case-sensitive or not.
- **LogFlag:** Determines if the staging process should log transactions. A value of 0 indicates that transactions should not be logged, and a value of 1 indicates that transactions should be logged.
- **BatchTag:** The name of the batch that should be processed by the staging process.

After the batch has been processed, either by manually executing the staging process in the Web front-end or programmatically by calling this stored procedure, the **ImportStatus_ID** field in the stage table is updated from 0 to one of the following values:

If an error has occurred, the **ImportStatus_ID** is set by the staging procedure to the value 2 and the **ErrorCode** is set. In addition, the **Batch_ID** field is updated by a surrogate number that uniquely identifies the batch within MDS.

9.9.1.2 Using SQL Server Integration Services to Stage Master Data into Microsoft Master Data Services

The process shown in the last section can be implemented in SQL Server Integration Services (SSIS) in a similar manner:

Figure 9.25 shows the control flow which consists of the following tasks:

- **Stage BTS_Region (Data Flow Task):** this data flow loads the data from a CSV source (or any operational database) into the MDS staging table, creating a batch as described in the previous section.
- **Initiate Staging Process (Execute SQL Task):** this task calls the stored procedure to execute the batch.

The control flow is intended to load initial data. It is required to modify both the control flow and the data flow to support inserts when master data is already present in the MDS entity; to stage updates to this master data; and to stage deletes. The best approach to support updates and deletes is to modify the provided data flow **Stage BTS_Region** to support inserts and updates at the same time and add an additional data flow to support deletes. We outline a solution at the end of this chapter.

The tasks in the control flow follow the same approach as described in the previous section. The data flow **Stage BTS_Region** is presented in more detail in Figure 9.26.

While this data flow is very basic, it performs all the actions that are required to load the data from an operational system into the MDS staging table. The following components are included in the data flow:

- **BTS_Region (Flat File Source):** this component sources the data from the CSV file *BTS_Region. csv*, provided on the companion Web site. It defines the structure of the file.
- **Add Staging Columns (Derived Column):** this component adds the additional columns required by the staging table.
- **MDS (OLE DB Destination):** this component writes the data in the data flow into the target stage table.

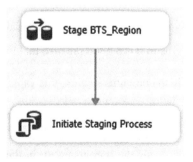

FIGURE 9.25

Control flow for staging master data.

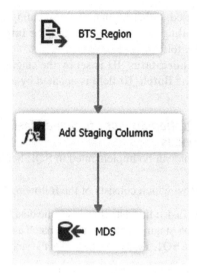

FIGURE 9.26

Data flow for staging master data.

Because the target (as implemented in this book) expects Unicode data, it is required that the data in the data flow use a UTF-8 code page. The package on the companion Web site ensures this by modifying the flat file source **BTS_Region** to provide only text columns that use the data type **Unicode string [DT_WSTR]**. In addition, the code page on the **General** tab has been modified to **65001 (UTF-8)**. Figure 9.27 shows the configuration of columns to meet the requirements of the staging table.

Note that the required data type depends on the code page used by MDS. This setting might differ and requires another data type in the source. Also, there are other ways to change the data type once it has been sourced from the source file or source table: it is also possible to use a **Data Conversion** component to modify the code page.

The component **Add Staging Columns** adds the derived columns which are required by the staging table.

Figure 9.28 shows how the following columns are added to the data flow:

- **ImportType:** setting the import type to 0 is a good practice that works for both the initial load and subsequent loads.
- **ImportStatus_ID:** as described in the previous section, this value is set to 0 to indicate data that has to be loaded from the staging table.
- **BatchTag:** this value is set to Initial Load to identify the loaded master data of the initial load as a group.

Because the data in this data flow loads the regions entity in the BTS model through the **BTS_Region_Leaf** staging table, the OLE DB destination is set to the appropriate target, as Figure 9.29 shows.

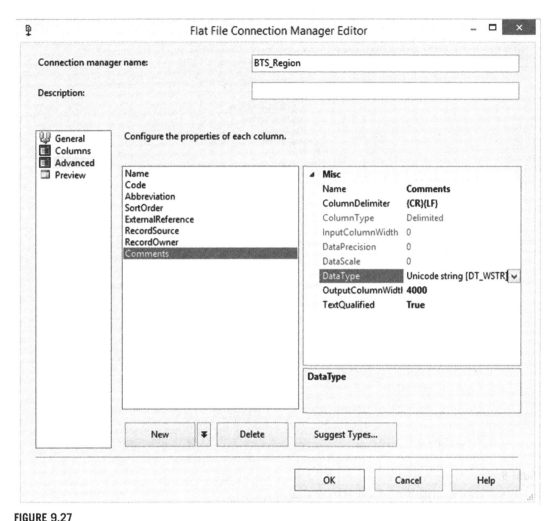

FIGURE 9.27

Setting up the source data types in the flat file connection manager editor.

The name of the destination table is set to **[stg].[BTS_Region_Leaf]**, which is the staging table of the **Region** entity in the **BTS** model. All other values on this tab are left as they are. The **Mappings** tab is used to map the columns in the data flow to the columns in the destination.

Figure 9.30 shows this mapping in more detail. Note that the destination columns **NewCode** and **ErrorCode** have no input column, because **NewCode** is only required during updates (and only if the code of the entity member should be changed) and the **ErrorCode** column is used by MDS to provide any error codes during the staging process.

The control flow in Figure 9.25 included another task to initiate the staging process. This task calls the stored procedure that is responsible for loading the master data in the stage table into the MDS

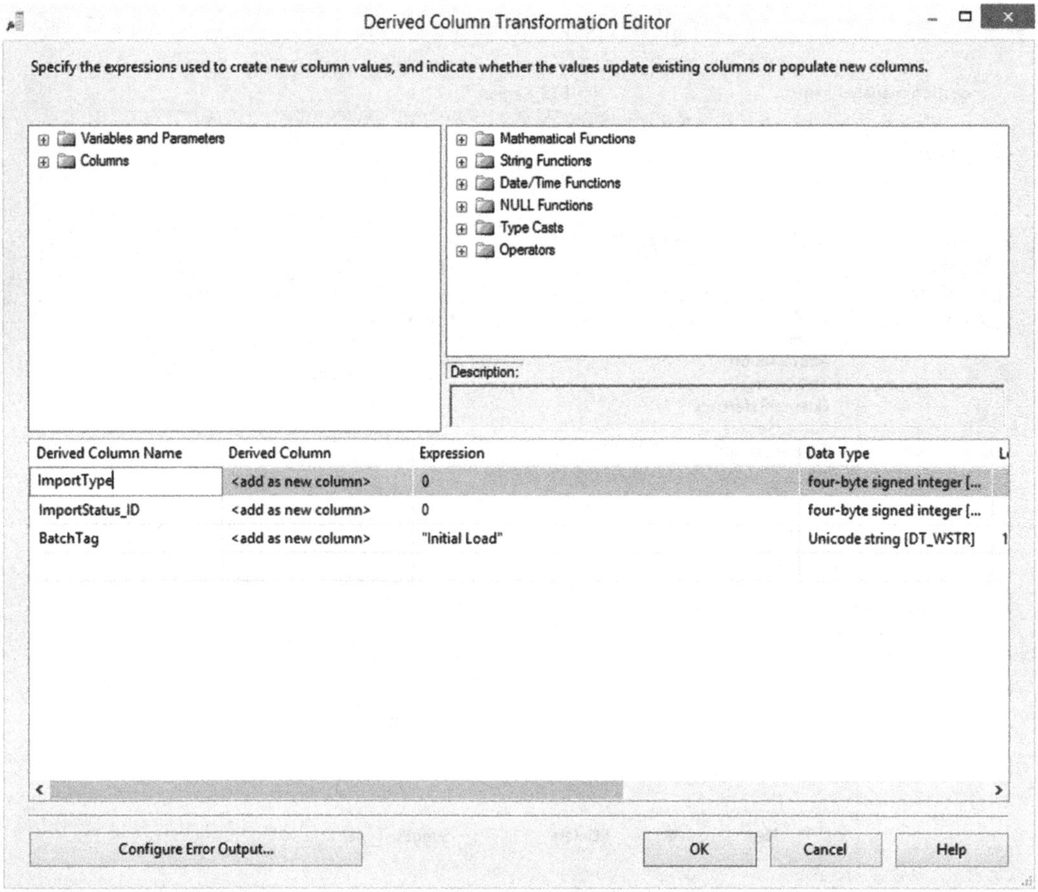

FIGURE 9.28

Adding stage columns in the derived column transformation editor.

entity. This task is executed just after the stage table has been populated with instructions (insert, update, delete). Figure 9.31 shows how this task is configured.

The SQLStatement property of the task is set to the statement that was used in the previous section to initiate the staging process:

```
EXEC MDS.stg.udp_BTS_Region_Leaf @VersionName = 'VERSION_1', @LogFlag = 1, @BatchTag =
'Initial Load'
```

This task completes the basic SSIS control flow for loading master data from operational systems to MDS. In order to use this control flow in production, it needs to be extended in two ways:

- **Support updates and deletes:** in order to support updates and deletes, two additional data flows should be implemented to separate the loading processes from each other. Detecting updates

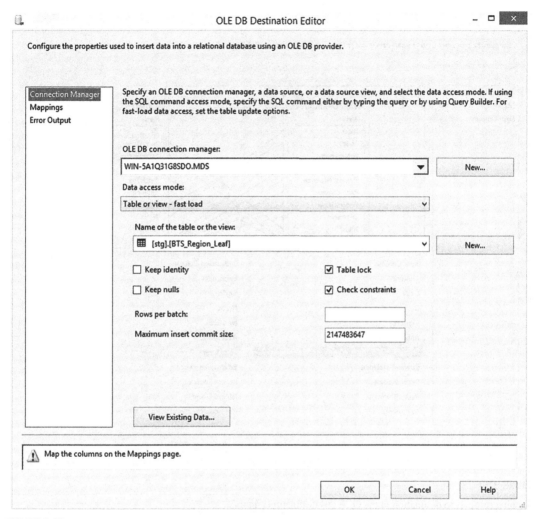

FIGURE 9.29

Setting up the destination in the OLE DB destination editor.

and deletes requires a lookup into the master data in the target entity by using the appropriate subscription view. If there is already a member with the same code as in the source, it should be updated.

- **Log errors to the Error Mart:** this needs to be implemented in the OLE DB destination component, but also in the data flow itself.

Because each source system should be loaded independently from each other, and MDS entities might be sourced from multiple source systems, the data flow should use an **ImportType** setting that

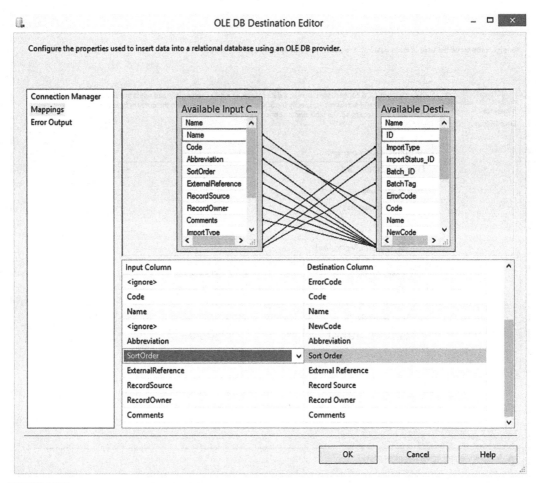

FIGURE 9.30

Mapping columns to destination in the OLE DB destination editor.

allows updating only some of the columns, which is the case with the import type 0: if one of the staging columns is set to a NULL value, the column value is ignored in the staging process. Therefore, only those values are overwritten which are not NULL. Also, not all columns in the MDS entity are sourced from operational source systems. For example, the **sort order** is often set in MDS itself. Using an import type of 2 requires this value to be set in the stage table. Import type 0 allows setting the column to NULL and it will be ignored in the staging process. Therefore, setting **ImportType** to 0 is the preferred method in most cases.

Deleted record detection often requires a lookup to the target entity using the appropriate subscription view, at least if the source system does not provide an audit log that can be used to detect deletes or if the source system does not provide a delta where deletes are marked. If the source

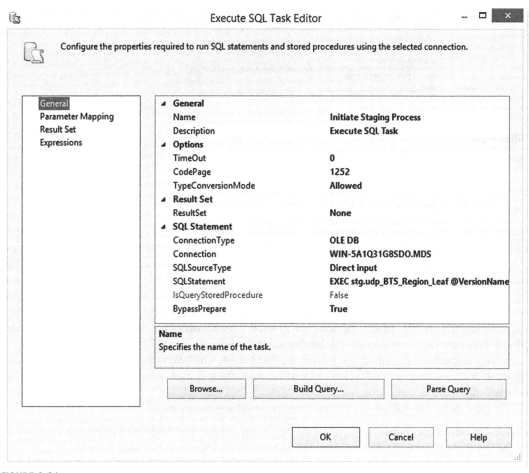

FIGURE 9.31

Setting up the stored procedure.

system provides only full loads of the master data currently used by the operational system, a lookup is required. If the target MDS entity has a member that is not available in the source, the member's **Code** value should be added to the staging table and marked as a delete or deactivation operation by using an import type value between 3 and 6, depending on whether the member in the target entity should be permanently deleted or only deactivated in the user interface and if this operation should also be performed when the member is used as a domain-based attribute value in another entity. The decision how to implement the actual loading of master data depends on these circumstances.

Chapter 10, Metadata Management, shows a modified version of this package that will log errors to the Error Mart.

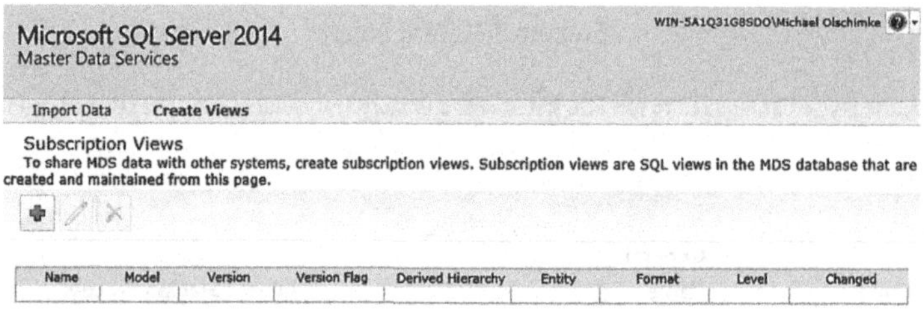

FIGURE 9.32

List available subscription views in MDS.

9.9.2 SUBSCRIPTION VIEWS

As already mentioned in the introduction to section 9.9, subscription views are used to provide master data to external systems, which are called master data subscribers. Thus, the subscription view serves as a tool of master data integration. A subscription view publishes the master data of one entity in the given version. From a technical perspective, the subscription view is just a T-SQL view that populates the data from the internal entity tables covered in section 9.9. However, it is not possible to create the subscription view in T-SQL. Instead, the subscription view is created in the MDS Web front-end. Administrative users use the functional area **Integration Management** for this purpose. The available subscription views are shown on the tab labeled **Create Views** (Figure 9.32).

In order to create a new subscription view, the first button, which shows a green plus button, is used. Figure 9.33 shows the page that follows this action and which is used to set up the subscription view to be added.

The page allows the following options for the new subscription view:

- **Subscription view name:** the name of the new subscription view. Similar to stage tables, the name of the view should be unique throughout MDS. Therefore, the name should include the name of the model. We use the following naming convention throughout this book: <Model name>_<Entity name>_<Subscriber name>.
- **Model:** the model of the entity to be published. The value is set using a combo box that provides a list of available models.
- **Entity:** the entity to be published by the subscription view. A combo box also provides this value.
- **Derived hierarchy:** it is also possible to publish a derived hierarchy. However, for data warehousing, it is often more applicable to publish the individual levels of the hierarchy on its own. This way, the normalized master data becomes available to the data warehouse.
- **Version:** the version of the entity to be published. Each subscription view is created for specific subscribers, which might require an older version of the entity.
- **Version flag:** instead of publishing a specific version, it is also possible to flag a specific version for publication. The advantage of the version flag is that it can be changed when a version gets locked. Therefore, the subscription views that publish the data for a version flag don't need to be updated [19].
- **Format:** for entities, only the option **Leaf members** is available. There are more options available for derived hierarchies, but this is out of the scope for this book.
- **Level:** the level is used for derived hierarchies to indicate the hierarchy level to be published.

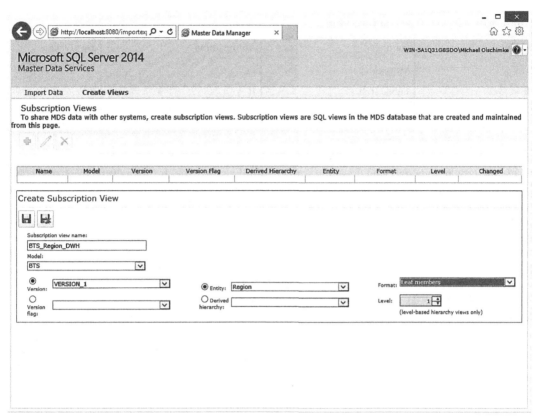

FIGURE 9.33

Create subscription view.

The version is actually an important property for setting up the subscription view. Consider the following issue: multiple operational systems are using the same entity on airport type. One day, the entity is modified by changing the members within the entity to reflect changes in the definition of an airport type (Table 9.9).

Instead of using the two members in Table 9.9, the entity is modified and uses the members in Table 9.10.

However, this modification requires that some operational systems, which subscribe to this entity, be modified as well, in order to make sure that they can actually work with the new members. For

Table 9.9 Airport Types on Day One			
Code	Name	Abbreviation	Sort Order
1	Public	P	1
2	Military	M	2

Table 9.10 Airport Types on Day Two

Code	Name	Abbreviation	Sort Order
1	Military	M	1
2	Public Hub	H	2
3	Public Regional	R	3

example, an operational system might have some business logic built in that distinguishes between public and military airports only and does not support a third airport type. It might even have hard-coded the abbreviations in its business logic. Note that abbreviation P is gone after the modification. To support the third airport type, software developers have to modify the business logic, which also requires testing the modified subscribing application. In some cases, it is not possible to rollout the change to all subscribers at the same time. Instead, some subscribers are updated, and some expect the old master data. Providing both versions of the master data entity can mitigate this problem. In order to cope with this issue, multiple versions of the master data in MDS are created and maintained, as described in section 9.6.4. One subscription view is created per entity version and subscriber. The view returns the master data from the selected entity version to the associated subscriber. This maximizes the independence between subscribing applications because it is possible to set the version that is published to the subscribing application individually.

The T-SQL view is available in the MDS database as soon as the **Save** button is selected on the page. In order to retrieve the master data from the Region entity in the BTS model, the following T-SQL statement can be used:

```
SELECT [ID]
      ,[MUID]
      ,[VersionName]
      ,[VersionNumber]
      ,[VersionFlag]
      ,[Name]
      ,[Code]
      ,[ChangeTrackingMask]
      ,[Abbreviation]
      ,[Sort Order]
      ,[External Reference]
      ,[Record Source]
      ,[Record Owner_Code]
      ,[Record Owner_Name]
      ,[Record Owner_ID]
      ,[Comments]
      ,[EnterDateTime]
      ,[EnterUserName]
      ,[EnterVersionNumber]
      ,[LastChgDateTime]
      ,[LastChgUserName]
      ,[LastChgVersionNumber]
      ,[ValidationStatus]
  FROM [MDS].[mdm].[BTS_Region_DWH]
```

The above statement uses the attribute names that have been set up during entity creation. It is not possible to modify these names when creating subscription views. Remember that they include spaces to improve the usability for business users when they modify master data in the Web front-end or using the Microsoft Excel add-in. T-SQL supports spaces in column names by enclosing the column names with square brackets.

Note that the domain-based attributes are translated into multiple columns. For example, the **record owner** column shows that three columns are created:

- **Record Owner_Code:** this column provides the **code** value of the member that is referenced in the domain-based attribute.
- **Record Owner_Name:** this column provides the name of the member that is referenced in the domain-based attribute.
- **Record Owner_ID:** the internal sequence number that identifies the member which is referenced in the domain-based attribute.

Each domain-based attribute will have a **code**, a **name** and an **ID** column. In addition to the attributes from the entity and these additional columns from domain-based attributes, the subscription view populates metadata columns that provide useful information. The following columns are added [13]:

- **ID:** an internal sequence number that identifies the member. This column is not well documented by Microsoft.
- **MUID:** an internal GUID that identifies the member. This column is not well documented by Microsoft.
- **VersionName:** this column indicates the name of the member's version. This value never changes if the subscription view is based on a given version.
- **VersionNumber:** the number of the member's version. This value never changes if the subscription view is based on a given version.
- **VersionFlag:** this column indicates the current version flag for the displayed member. If the view is based on a version flag, this value will never change. Instead, the version name and number will be updated.
- **ChangeTrackingMask:** this column is used when change tracking is enabled for attributes in this entity. It is not well documented by Microsoft.
- **EnterDateTime:** the date and time when the member was created in the entity.
- **EnterUserName:** the domain and name of the user who has created the member in the entity.
- **EnterVersionNumber:** this column indicates the number of the initial version of the member.
- **LastChgDateTime:** the data and time when the member was updated the last time.
- **LastChgUserName:** the domain and name of the user who has modified the member the last time.
- **LastChgVersionNumber:** this column indicates the number of the version this member was last changed.
- **ValidationStatus:** indicates if the business rules have been completed without any errors. Possible values are listed in Table 9.11.

Derived hierarchies should not be published for data warehousing using the **derived hierarchy** option of this page. This option hides some useful information, such as the validation status, but denormalizes some attributes from domain-based attributes. However, the best place for this denormalization

Table 9.11 Validation Status [20]

Validation Status	Description
Waiting to be validated	This validation status is reserved for new members and indicates that they have not been validated yet.
Waiting to be revalidated	The member values or the associated business rules have changed and the members await revalidation.
Validation succeeded	The members have been successfully validated. There were no errors.
Validation failed	The members have been validated, but not all business rules have passed. At least one business rule has raised an error that needs to be fixed before the data can be committed.
Waiting for dependent member revalidation	This validation status is reserved for consolidated members. In order to validate them, the leaf members have to be validated first.

to take place is when the dimension is being built on the way from the Raw Data Vault to the Business Vault or Information Mart. Therefore, it is recommended to export the levels on an individual basis using subscription views on the leaf member level.

Chapter 11, Data Extraction, will demonstrate how to load master data into Data Vault entities, including reference tables, using the subscription views created within this chapter.

REFERENCES

[1] Alex Berson & Larry Dubov: "Master Data Management and Data Governance, Second Edition", p. 5.
[2] Joy Mundy and Warren Thornthwaite: "The Microsoft Data Warehouse Toolkit, Second Edition," pp. 165, 165f.
[3] http://searchdatamanagement.techtarget.com/definition/data-management.
[4] DAMA International: "DAMA-DMBOK Guide: The Data Guide to the Data Management Body of Knowledge," p. 4f.
[5] Duane Nickull: "A Modeling Methodology to Harmonize Disparate Data Models".
[6] Jeremy Kashel, Tim Kent, Martyn Bullerwell: "Microsoft SQL Server 2008 R2 Master Data Services," pp. 8, 13ff, 34, 37, 38f, 40f, 42, 37f, 126f, 132, 141, 94, 104, 104f.
[7] http://code7700.com/thrust_v_power.html
[8] Alex Berson & Larry Dubov: "Master Data Management and Data Governance, Second Edition", p. 7ff.
[9] Reeves, Laura L.: "A Manager's Guide to Data Warehousing", pp. 241–242.
[10] http://www.transtats.bts.gov/homedrillchart.asp
[11] Paul E. McMahon: "Integrating CMMI and Agile Development," pp. 60f, 61f.
[12] Mary Beth Chrissis, et al. "CMMI for Development," p. 133.
[13] Tyler Graham: "Microsoft SQL Server 2012: Master Data Services," Second Edition, pp. 71, 98, 115, 326ff, 327.
[14] http://msdn.microsoft.com/en-us/library/ff486954.aspx.
[15] http://msdn.microsoft.com/en-us/library/ff487062.aspx.
[16] http://msdn.microsoft.com/en-us/library/ff487016.aspx.
[17] http://msdn.microsoft.com/en-us/library/ee633854.aspx.
[18] http://msdn.microsoft.com/en-us/library/hh231028.aspx.
[19] http://msdn.microsoft.com/en-us/library/ff487013.aspx.
[20] https://msdn.microsoft.com/en-us/library/gg471534.aspx.

METADATA MANAGEMENT

10

In many of our projects, clients ask us how to track metadata, "the data about data." While there are some solutions available to track metadata in data warehouse environments, project teams often work with manual spreadsheets to maintain the metadata required to define the data warehouse, including its artifacts, such as relational tables, information marts, ETL (extract, transform, load) flows, requirements, business rules, etc.

But metadata management, from a Data Vault perspective, also requires the capture of metrics about process execution and errors. This chapter covers the concepts behind capturing metadata, process metrics and error information.

10.1 WHAT IS METADATA?

Our initial definition of metadata as "data about data" is not very helpful. An alternative to this definition is that metadata is all data about other data that is *"needed to promote its administration and use"* [1]. Both definitions are very common definitions from the information technology space but don't provide us with a useful and understandable definition for data warehousing. Another definition, often used in data warehousing, distinguishes metadata by the following two categories [2]:

- **Back room metadata:** this metadata is process related and describes the extraction, cleaning and loading processes. Its main purpose is to help the database administrator (DBA) or the data warehouse team to load the data into the data warehouse. It also helps end-users to understand where data comes from.
- **Front room metadata:** this metadata is more descriptive and is used in query tools and report tools. It primarily benefits end-users and helps them to understand the technical solution when building front-end solutions.

The ultimate goal of metadata management is to describe all artifacts of the data warehouse, not limited to the previous list. There are various examples of metadata that need to be captured in the data warehousing domain, including descriptions of the relational table [1]:

1. **Record layout:** this metadata describes the layout of records in a relational table, including the list of attributes, their relative position and format of data on disk.
2. **Content:** the volume of data within a table or within a load for a particular table (volumetric) [3].
3. **Indexes:** the number and definition of indexes of the table.
4. **Scheduling:** the time schedule when the data in the table is loaded or refreshed.
5. **Usage:** where are the columns in the table being used? What are the dependencies for or on this table?
6. **Referential integrity:** what are the relations from this table to other tables?
7. **General documentation:** usually an unstructured text that describes the purpose of the table.

Often, parts or all of the above metadata is captured in the relational database management system (RDBMS) because database systems provide the means to capture such metadata. In other cases, an entity relationship (E/R) tool is used to capture such information. However, the previous list of metadata isn't even close to being a complete list. Instead, it focuses on only one area of metadata, the metadata about relational structures. However, there is much more metadata in a data warehouse system available, as we have already written in the introduction to this chapter.

Besides the back room and front room categorization of metadata, the metadata in a data warehouse is often categorized into three areas [2,4]:

- **Business metadata:** describes the meaning of data for the business. The Meta Mart covers this metadata and is covered in section 10.2.
- **Technical metadata:** describes the technical aspects of data, including data types, lineage, results from data profiling, etc. This metadata is also covered by the Meta Mart which is covered in section 10.2.
- **Process execution metadata:** provides statistics about running ETL processes, including the number of records sourced and loaded to the destination, number of rows rejected and the time it took to load the data. Collecting ETL process statistics is covered in sections 10.3 and 10.4 when the Metrics Vault and the Metrics Mart are described. In addition, error information is tracked to provide insight into exceptions or stops during ETL process execution. The Error Mart tracks these errors in the Data Vault 2.0 architecture and is covered in section 10.5.

We will follow this definition of metadata through the remainder of this chapter and consequently use this definition throughout this book. The next sections describe the metadata categories in more detail and provide some examples. Note that the list is still only a suggestion and provides only a limited number of metadata examples which we have seen in projects. In practice, each data warehouse team needs to modify the list of metadata that should be tracked to meet the needs of their organization and their project.

It should also be noted that the metadata might change over time because of changes in the underlying definition of the data. This includes all three categories, ranging from changes in the definition of business data (because the business meaning of the data has changed), over technical metadata (because the source systems have changed) to process execution metadata (because the data warehouse has changed).

10.1.1 BUSINESS METADATA

Business metadata describes the meaning of data for the business. Should the business therefore be responsible for business metadata? There are arguments for the assignment of business data to representatives of the business and arguments against it. For example, some argue that business data should be created and maintained during the requirements gathering process by data warehouse business analysts. Others argue that it should be maintained by source system business analysts because most business terms originate from source systems. And another group says that the business metadata should be created and maintained by data modelers when creating logical data models for the data warehouse [2].

The data warehouse team might not be the right party to decide who will be responsible for the business data but, in any case, it needs to decide what business metadata needs to be managed and where.

The list of business metadata that needs to be tracked includes the following metadata related to business definitions [2]:

- **Business column names:** in some cases, the business name might use abbreviations in prefixes or suffixes. Each of these abbreviations should be translated in order to make sense to the business side.
- **Business definitions:** for each attribute, table and other object, including soft business rules of the information mart, there should be a business description of the attribute's, table's or object's business meaning. In some cases, it is not easy to provide a business description for every item. However, this indicates that there is no analytical value of the item for the business and it can be removed from the information mart. If the business demands that the item remain in the information mart, it should be possible for the information consumer to provide a business definition.
- **Ontologies and taxonomies:** these business definitions describe the business objects behind the source data and the relationships to other business objects or the hierarchies that describe the business object itself. It also includes the classification of business objects. Typically, such ontologies and taxonomies are stored in analytical or operational master data management systems. This topic is covered in Chapter 9, Master Data Management.
- **Physical table and column names:** because front-end tools often present information to end-users with references to business names only, the business metadata needs to track the physical names that belong to the business names. Otherwise, the data warehouse team cannot associate business definitions to physical data elements.
- Technical numbering used to identify data elements in the technical model.

This information is required for end-users to understand the information marts they are dealing with; the power users need it in order to find the raw data in which they are interested in the Raw Data Vault; and the ETL developers need this metadata to understand the meaning of the source data when loading the Raw Data Vault and information marts by implementing business rules. In short, these business definitions provide meaning to the source data.

Another set of business metadata includes information about source systems. The following list provides the metadata that needs to be tracked for the data warehouse [2]:

- **Record source:** this metadata describes the record source in business terms, such as "Flight Tracking Database" or "Passenger Information." It should not be a technical reference to the server or database instance. Instead, it should be understandable by the business. In addition, it should include as much detail as possible. For example, instead of using "Passenger Information" for all data sources in the passenger information database, refer to specific data elements, such as "Passenger Information / Personal Module / Home Address Data." Section 10.2.2 describes how to cover such data in the Meta Mart.
- **Table specifications:** In addition to providing the business name of the source system and the detailed data object name, a description should be provided which explains the purpose of the source table, the volume of data in the table and the list of columns and keys (primary and alternate keys). Section 10.2.3 covers how to collect such data in the Meta Mart.
- **(Hard) exception-handling rules:** for each table, there should be a list of potential technical issues provided. This list describes the potential error or data quality issue and how the ETL process should deal with these errors. In Data Vault 2.0, these rules are referred to with the term "hard rule." We describe how to cover such rules in section 10.2.4.

- **Source system business definitions:** this metadata describes the business meaning of source attributes.
- **(Soft) business rules:** source systems implement business rules that modify or generate some of the source data. Other business rules perform data cleansing or prevent the insertion of erroneous data. For example, some business rules aggregate measures as new attributes in the source. When building the data warehouse, ETL developers are interested in these business rules to understand the source system and the business requirements behind it. Some source systems implement business rules within the application itself; others use the RDBMS for this purpose: the use of check constraints, triggers, and referential integrity point to business rule definitions that should be documented. In Data Vault 2.0, these rules are referred to using the term "soft rule." They are covered in more detail in section 10.2.9.

Section 10.2 will demonstrate how to implement these types of metadata with Microsoft SQL Server 2014.

10.1.2 TECHNICAL METADATA

While business metadata describes the meaning of data for the business, technical metadata serves many purposes. The data warehouse team is responsible for creating and maintaining this type of metadata and benefits from it most. Therefore, most technical metadata is around technical components of the data warehouse, such as [2]:

- **Source systems:** this type of metadata provides technical information about the source systems including the source database or flat file location and staging area tables used. See section 10.2.3 for a more detailed description.
- **Data models:** are the physical and logical data models, often presented in a graphical format, and provide information about the relationships between tables. While they are not metadata, they provide an invaluable asset to the data warehouse team.
- **Data definitions:** this list provides technical definitions of all columns in a data source. It including information about the table name, column name, data type, the domain (as enforced by foreign keys, check constraints or the application itself), referential integrity, constraints, defaults, triggers and stored procedures that ensure the data integrity of the source database.
- **Business rules:** the technical definitions of business rules are also considered as technical metadata because they need to be implemented in ETL later on. Similar to business rules in business metadata (refer to section 10.2.8), hard rules should be separated from soft rules. For each rule, there should be a technical description (unlike a more business-oriented description in the business metadata). There are also business rules that describe encryption or decryption requirements, among other data protection and security considerations.
- **Volumetrics:** there should be information about the table size and growth patterns of the source tables to estimate the workload of the data warehouse for this source table. It also helps to predict the growth patterns for hardware acquisition cycles of 6 to 12 months into the future.
- **Ontologies and taxonomies:** technical metadata should also provide information about ontologies and taxonomies, including abbreviations of terms and attributes, relationships, business key designations, peers and parents, hierarchies and re-defines (cross-ontologies matching at a structure level).
- **Data quality:** this kind of metadata provides information about standardization of source data and other data quality metrics.

Section 10.2 will demonstrate how to implement technical metadata in the Meta Mart using Microsoft SQL Server 2014.

10.1.3 PROCESS EXECUTION METADATA

Unlike business or technical metadata, which is provided by the business or source applications, process execution metadata is generated by the data warehouse team and provides insights into the ETL processing for maintenance. The data is used by the data warehouse team or by end-users to better understand the data warehouse performance and results presented in the information marts. There are four different types of process execution metadata, most of them coming from ETL systems such as SQL Server Integration Services (SSIS) [2]:

- **Control flow metadata:** a control flow executes one or more data flows among other tasks. Logging the process execution provides a valuable tool for maintaining or debugging the ETL processes of the data warehouse because it provides information about the data lineage of all elements of the data warehouse.
- **Data flow metadata:** the data flow log provides information about the performance of data flows and how many records have been processed or rejected by each transformation.
- **Package metadata:** a package executes a control flow. The package metadata provides summary information about the running time of the package.
- **Process metadata:** most packages are executed by SQL Server Agent or another scheduling application. The process metadata provides information about the process that has started the package.

While the list uses terminology from Microsoft SSIS, it can be applied to any other ETL tool. This kind of metadata should, on process execution, be held in the Metrics Vault and is usually separated from the business and technical metadata in the Meta Mart. Implementing a Metrics Vault and a Metrics Mart are covered in section 10.3. The next section covers implementing the Meta Mart.

10.2 IMPLEMENTING THE META MART

The Meta Mart is the central piece for collecting business and technical metadata in the Data Vault 2.0 architecture. As outlined in Chapter 2, it is an independent information mart that is not sourced from the Raw Data Vault. Therefore, there is no Meta Vault that could be used as a source for providing a virtual Meta Mart. Instead, the Meta Mart provides a set of tables that are used to collect the metadata of the data warehouse. The Meta Vault is materialized as it actually stores the metadata. Similar to other information marts in the Data Vault 2.0 architecture, the Meta Mart is modeled in such as way that business can make the most use of it. In some cases, this can be a dimensional model, while in others it is a model in third-normal form. In other cases, a metadata tool is used to present the metadata available to the end-user. In that case, the Meta Mart is the database for this metadata front-end.

There is no need for the Meta Mart to be a relational database: many commercial modeling and ETL tools support the customization of their metadata models in order to capture custom metadata, in addition to dedicated metadata management tools. Extending the model can be helpful to capture information about stage tables, such as the record source and the attribute classification (for example if the attribute from the source system is a business key, link information or descriptive attribute). It is also often possible to extend the model with data lineage capabilities especially added for Data Vault purposes. For example, it is possible in many tools to provide the source tables of Raw Data Vault Hubs, Links and Satellites. Some of these tools also support the definition of business rules which can then be linked to the Data Vault model or the information mart model.

The next sections assume that no such tool is in place. Instead, alternative solutions are presented which are based on a relational Meta Mart.

10.2.1 SQL SERVER BI METADATA TOOLKIT

One such front-end tool is the SQL Server BI Metadata Toolkit, available on CodePlex [5]. It is an update of a tool for SQL Server 2005 which was first published on the MSDN Code Gallery. The toolkit is not production ready, but it serves as an example of a metadata front-end. The toolkit[1]:

1. scans SSIS packages, SSAS databases, SSRS reporting services and relational SQL Server databases
2. extracts the metadata from these components
3. stores them in the metadata database (the Meta Mart), and
4. provides a GUI for visually analyzing the metadata elements of the Microsoft BI stack.

By doing so, the toolkit extracts the metadata on its own and populates the Meta Mart of the data warehouse. Features of the toolkit include data lineage, covering business and technical metadata and providing impact analysis [5].

There are three tools included in the toolkit [6]:

1. **Dependency Analyzer:** this tool reads the contents of SSIS packages, SSAS databases and SQL databases and SSRS report collections. When analyzing SSIS packages, it gathers the metadata about all data flows in the package, about all sources and destinations in the data flows and the columns in the data flow. SSAS databases are analyzed for the included data sources, cubes, data source views, and dimensions. The gathered metadata is written to a selected repository database, usually the Meta Mart. Figure 10.1 shows the database tables that are created by the dependency analyzer.
2. **Dependency Executor:** this tool provides a graphical user interface to the dependency analyzer. Figure 10.2 and Figure 10.3 shows the user interface of this application.
3. **Dependency Viewer:** this tool presents the metadata to the end-user. It displays the information gathered by the dependency analyzer and shows metadata about the analyzed SSIS packages, SSAS databases, SSRS reports, and relational SQL Server databases. Figure 10.4 shows its user interface.

The database model which is created by the dependency analyzer is shown in Figure 10.1.

From a modeling perspective, the database model in this figure is not well designed, for example because primary keys are missing. But because it serves only as an example for a Meta Mart, it still presents an acceptable solution. The following tables are present in the database model:

1. **LookupConnectionID:** this table provides internal information about the connection types in SSIS.
2. **Audit:** this table stores run time information about SSIS data flows. We will implement a similar table when implementing the Metrics Vault in section 10.3.
3. **Version:** this table provides version information about the toolkit itself.
4. **RunScan:** this table stores a row for each analysis run (using the dependency analyzer).
5. **ObjectTypes:** this table provides information about the transformations and tasks available in SSIS and other data elements from other components of the Microsoft BI stack.

---

[1]https://sqlmetadata.codeplex.com/

6. **Objects:** this table provides metadata information about objects within SSIS packages, in SSAS or relational databases and in reports.
7. **ObjectDependencies:** this table describes the dependencies of objects within the components of the Microsoft BI stack. Objects might be contained by others, reference other objects, or map to other objects.
8. **ObjectAttributes:** this table provides detailed metadata about the object attributes.

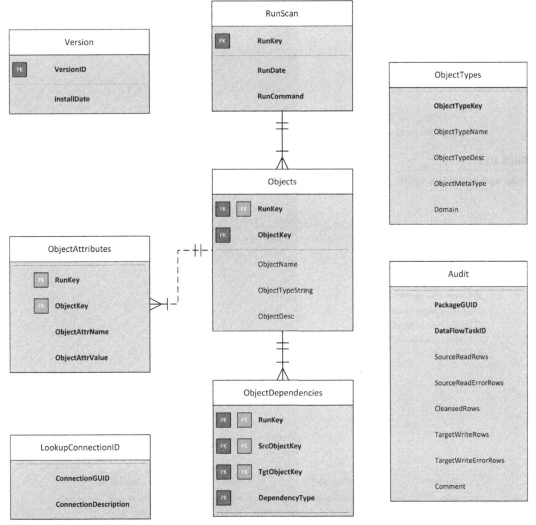

FIGURE 10.1

Database metadata for the SQL Server BI Metadata Toolkit (physical design).

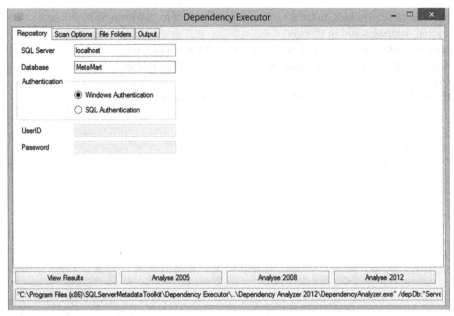

FIGURE 10.2

Setting up the metadata repository in the Dependency Executor.

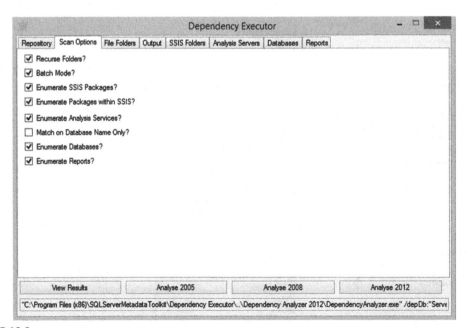

FIGURE 10.3

Setting scan options in the Dependency Executor.

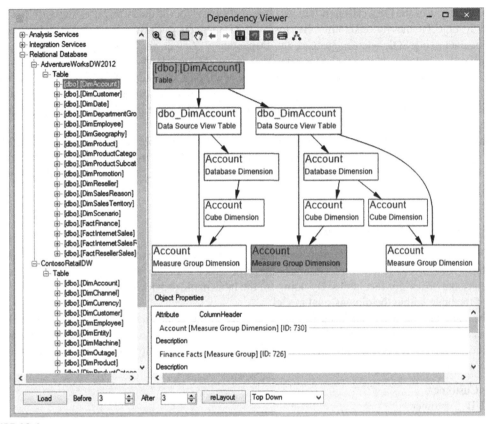

FIGURE 10.4

Dependency viewer of the SQL Server BI Metadata Toolkit.

These tables are populated by the Dependency Analyzer tool which might be run from the command line or using the graphical front-end, the Dependency Executor, as shown in Figure 10.2 and Figure 10.3.

Once the Dependency Executor has performed its analysis, the data is available in the tables presented in Figure 10.1. In order to analyze the dependencies between objects, the following query might be used to receive a readable dependency list:

```
SELECT
    dep.RunKey,
    src.ObjectName AS SrcObjectName,
    tgt.ObjectName AS TgtObjectName,
    dep.DependencyType
FROM
    dbo.ObjectDependencies dep
LEFT JOIN dbo.Objects src
ON dep.RunKey = src.RunKey AND dep.SrcObjectKey = src.ObjectKey
LEFT JOIN dbo.Objects tgt
ON dep.RunKey = tgt.RunKey AND dep.TgtObjectKey = tgt.ObjectKey
```

This query uses the **ObjectDependencies** table as the basis for the query and uses two LEFT JOINS to join the object names for readability. Because of the Dependency Viewer, it is not required to analyze the metadata using SQL queries. Instead, the Dependency Viewer provides a graphical way for the analysis of the metadata stored in the metadata repository (Figure 10.4).

The left tree view of the Dependency Viewer lists all objects found in the Microsoft BI stack. When selecting one of the objects, the object is displayed with all of its dependencies on the central area of the viewer. The bottom area displays the attributes of the selected object for further analysis.

The SQL Server BI Metadata Toolkit provides a powerful example for providing a simple Meta Mart on the technical metadata of the Microsoft BI stack. However, for tracking all artifacts of the enterprise data warehouse, we need to capture more metadata, as described in the previous sections.

10.2.2 NAMING CONVENTIONS

The first step in providing custom metadata is the use of naming conventions. Figure 10.4 from the previous section shows tables from a dimensional information mart that use two prefixes: "Dim" for dimensions and "Fact" for fact tables. By doing so, the table name provides information about the entity type of the table within the dimensional model.

The same approach is often used to denote entities in the Data Vault model. There are multiple options available for abbreviating the various Data Vault 2.0 entities and adding them to the actual identifier of the table. For example, many customers use one of the following abbreviations to name a Data Vault hub:

1. H_Customer
2. HUB_Customer
3. HubCustomer
4. CustomerHub

As you can see, many options exist to use a prefix or a suffix for naming a hub entity. Some customers use a prefix, others a suffix. In some cases, they use Camel Case, while in others they use underscores to separate terms in the table name. Because the options for naming conventions are often limited by development standards already available in the organization [2], project teams who start using Data Vault then only have the choice to decide which prefixes to use for each Data Vault entity. They cannot decide whether they want to use a prefix or a suffix any longer, because this decision has already been made a long time ago, by a prior project or, in larger organizations, a standards committee. In this way, organizations try to standardize their table and attribute namings among multiple projects.

The major question that is left to most project teams is instead: which types of Data Vault entities should have their own prefix? Should there be a prefix for every Data Vault entity type? Or are some entity types the same and should use the same prefix in turn? Table 10.1 lists the Data Vault entity types that should have their own individual abbreviations to be used as a prefix or suffix.

The entity types that should have their own prefix are presented in the first two columns of Table 10.1. Because the Business Vault is modeled after the same principles as the Raw Data Vault, there

Table 10.1 Required Abbreviations for Naming Conventions

Raw Data Vault	Business Vault	Avoid Prefix
Hub	**Business hub**	
Link	**Exploration link**	Nondescriptive links
Same-as-link	Same-as-link	
Hierarchical link	Hierarchical link	
Dependent link	Dependent link	
Nonhistorized link	Nonhistorized link	
Nonhistorized satellite	Nonhistorized satellite	
Satellite	**Computed satellite**	
Multi-active satellites	Multi-active satellites	
Status tracking satellite	Status tracking satellite	
Effectivity satellite	Effectivity satellite	
Record tracking satellite	Record tracking satellite	
Reference table		
Reference table satellite		
	Computed aggregate link	
	PIT table	
	Bridge table	

is often an equivalent of a Raw Data Vault entity in the Business Vault. For example, there might be a nonhistorized satellite in the Business Vault that has reduced the transactions for some reason, thus implementing parts of a business rule or the business rule as a whole. There are some exceptions: reference tables are primarily a concept of the Raw Data Vault, so reference data is usually not modified by a business rule (at least not in our experience). On the other hand, computed aggregate links, PIT tables and bridge tables are concepts of the Business Vault. In other cases, there is an equivalent entity in the Business Vault that follows the same modeling principles as its Raw Data Vault counterpart, but using a different name: for example, an exploration link is a computed link without any other modifications. The only difference is that the exploration link is not sourced from an operational data source, but includes links in the model that have been artificially generated (for example through a data mining algorithm). As a result of these observations, organizations tend to introduce an individual abbreviation for Business Vault entities, especially because it helps them to separate raw data from computed information.

In most cases, a different entity structure demands its own abbreviation. However, there are some exceptions to this rule: the same-as-link or the hierarchical link, for example. While they follow the standard structure of a Data Vault link, they serve a special purpose. Therefore, they should have their own abbreviation. The same applies to status tracking satellites or effectivity satellites which follow standard Data Vault structures for satellites as well. One exception to this rule is the nondescriptive link (or fact-less fact). It is a special link, but only because it has no satellites. The link itself, the relationship between two business keys, is the fact. The reason why this link should not have its own abbreviation is that a satellite could be attached to the link later on. For example when data from a new operational system is sourced and, all of a sudden, this source system provides data that describes this link (thus adding a Raw Data Vault satellite to the link). By doing so, the nondescriptive link transforms into a standard link and should use the same abbreviation as the standard links. The same applies to cases when computed satellites are added to the nondescriptive link.

When naming Raw Data Vault satellites, it is recommended to include an abbreviation for the source system because, in many cases, there are multiple satellites hanging off the parent hub or link. If our recommendation from Chapter 4, Data Vault 2.0 Modeling, is followed, each source system should be loaded to its dedicated satellite or satellites. This avoids the drawbacks of overloaded satellites as described in that chapter. But if each source system creates a new satellite on a hub, they need different names to distinguish them from each other, both in a logical view and in physical implementation. The logical diagram in Figure 10.5 shows this issue.

Three source systems provide descriptive data for the passenger. They are abbreviated as TRV (travel system), CRM (customer relationship system) and SEC (security). Using this simple naming convention makes it clear that the table is a satellite, to which parent hub each satellite belongs, and where the data comes from. The next issue is satellite splitting: if there are source columns that change frequently, the recommendation from Chapter 4 is to split the satellites by rate of change. For example, if the satellite **SatPassengerCRM** in Figure 10.5 is split by rate of change, the logical model shown in Figure 10.6 results from this split.

The preferred dish information was split from the other passenger data because it changes more frequently than, say, the name. In this case, the name of the entity was changed from Sat**Passenger**CRM to Sat**PassengerPreferredDish**CRM because the separated attribute makes it obvious how to name the new satellite. But what if this becomes more complicated because a couple of attributes are separated that don't necessarily belong together? What if you decide to mechanically separate the attributes of a

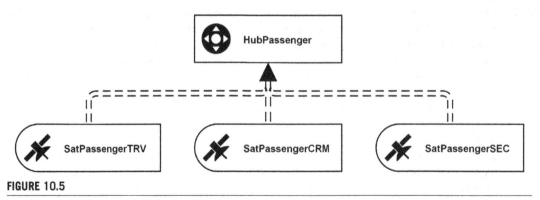

FIGURE 10.5

Multiple satellites on parent hub (logical design).

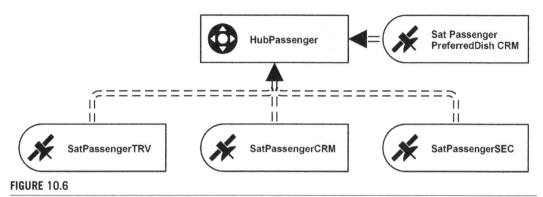

FIGURE 10.6

Multiple satellites after split (logical design).

satellite by some rate of change? To make things more complicated, there are multiple definitions of rate of change as the (incomplete) Table 10.2 demonstrates.

Depending on your understanding of rate of change, one or another (or multiple) definitions might be useful in your project. There should be an abbreviation for each rate of change. For example, if we use the three speed levels slow, medium and fast to denote the rate of change in our satellites, a logical design of our model in Figure 10.5 could look like the design in Figure 10.7.

In this example, the satellite **SatPassengerCRM** has been split into three new satellites: **SatPassengerSCRM**, **SatPassengerMCRM** and **SatPassengerFCRM**. The character before the source system indicates the rate of change for each satellite.

We call this split a mechanical split because it could also be automated: after analyzing the current rate of change for each attribute in a satellite, the algorithm could generate the required DDLs for the new satellites without knowing any business definition of each attribute (thus unable to find a more meaningful name as in the previous example).

Table 10.2 Various Rate of Change Definitions		
Schedule	**Volatility**	**Speed**
Hourly	Low	Very Slow
Daily	Medium	Slow
Weekly	High	Medium
Monthly		Fast
Quarterly		Very Fast
Semiannual		Light
Yearly		Warp

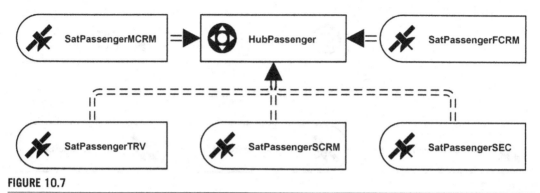

FIGURE 10.7

Multiple satellites after mechanical split (logical design).

The advantage of using naming conventions for the Data Vault tables is that the information about the entity type is encoded in the table name. This information becomes available in all tools that present SQL Server tables to its end-users. The disadvantage, however, is this metadata is not easily retrievable as dedicated metadata, attached to the entity.

10.2.3 CAPTURING SOURCE SYSTEM DEFINITIONS

The purpose of the source system abbreviation in satellites (as described in the previous section) is only to distinguish the table names when multiple source systems provide descriptive data for a business key. It is not a description of the source system.

Instead, much more metadata is required to describe the source system for business and IT usage. For example, the fact that data has been sourced from a source system is important in agile projects, because not all available source system tables are loaded to the data warehouse at once. Instead, only the source systems that provide raw data that is required to build a certain report or other information artifact are sourced into the data warehouse (and only partially, table by table). We source data just in time. Identifying the source system tables that have not been implemented in the data warehouse is required because the data hasn't been loaded in previous sprints. Therefore, these missing source system tables need to be loaded in the current iteration.

Typically, organizations decide to use at least the following metadata attributes to define the source systems sourced by their data warehouse [7]:

- **Source system identifier:** a technical identifier of the source system used to reference the source system in subsequent metadata or other documentation.
- **Source system technical description:** technically describes the source system in a textual format.
- **Source system business description:** describes the source system from a business perspective.
- **Source system version:** the current version of the source system.
- **Source system quality:** describes the quality of the source system (could also use an indicator scale from "poor" to "good" or a percentage value).

- **Data steward:** provides the name and contact information of the data steward responsible for the management of data elements of the operational system.
- **System administrator:** provides the name and contact information of the person who is responsible for administrating the system.

Note that some source systems provide data in separate batches that might not be delivered in the same schedule. For example, some data could be delivered on a daily basis, while other data is delivered in real-time. For that reason, the actual data delivery (a data package) should be defined in another metadata table that includes the following attributes [7]:

1. **Source system identifier:** the technical name of the source system that is providing the data package.
2. **Data package identifier:** the technical name of the data package.
3. **Data package format:** defines how the source system provides its data to the data warehouse: CSV files, XML files, relational access, real-time messages, etc.).
4. **Data package type:** indicates if the package is a full load or delta load.
5. **Delivery schedule:** defines when the data is provided to the data warehouse (e.g., daily between 2 a.m. and 4 a.m.).
6. **Data package technical description:** technically describes the data package in a textual format.
7. **Data package business description:** describes the data package from a business perspective.
8. **Expected data package quality:** describes the quality of the data package (could also use an indicator scale from "poor" to "good" or a percentage value).
9. **Data package refresh type:** indicates the frequency with which the content of the data package are refreshed (e.g., real-time, near-real-time, hourly, daily, monthly, etc.)
10. **Database instance name (relational source):** if the data package is made available using a relational database (for example, if the data warehouse can directly access the operational system to source the data from), the database instance name is required.
11. **Database name (relational source):** if the data package is a relational table, this attribute indicates the database to load the data from.
12. **Delimiter type (flat file source):** if the data package is a flat file, this attribute indicates the delimiter used.
13. **Text delimiter (flat file source):** if the data package is a flat file, this attribute indicates the string delimiter used to separate string elements (usually a double quote).
14. **Header (flat file source):** indicates if a header row is used in a flat file source.
15. **File format (flat file source):** indicates the exact file format, such as CSV, EBCDIC, ASCII, VSAM, etc.
16. **Control flow name:** the name of the control flow that is responsible for loading the data package.

Note that a data package consists of multiple files or relational tables. Depending on the actual source systems and their intended data package formats, there might be need for more metadata attributes. This list should serve only as a starting point. Chapter 11, Data Extraction, lists more potential source systems and data feeds (such as Web sources, social networks, mainframe systems, etc.) and describes the requirements for sourcing them into the data warehouse.

10.2.4 CAPTURING HARD RULES

Hard rules in the data warehouse deal with data type conversions required for loading and technical issues that can arise when staging the data or loading the data from the staging area into the Raw Data Vault. Therefore, they are applied when loading the data into the staging area or loading the data from the staging area to the Raw Data Vault. Examples include:

1. **Assignment of source attribute to target attribute:** in some cases, organizations choose to use a different name in the staging area or in the Raw Data Vault. In this case, the hard rule defines how to map a source field to a target attribute in the staging area or in the Raw Data Vault.

2. **Hard rules that convert a source data type to a target data type:** this practice should be avoided, but in some cases, there is no equivalent data type in the target that directly reflects the source system. For example, an operational system could have been built with Java or .NET types in use, but the data warehouse has decided to use only generic T-SQL data types. A hard rule defines how to perform the required conversion.

3. **Hard rules that ensure how to deal with wrongly sized data:** this type of rule deals with data that is too long to be stored in the destination, for example, because a VARCHAR column in the target is unable to capture the whole source string. Usually, the destination should be able to cover the whole string, but what if the source system was modified and sends more data than expected? In other cases, the incoming data should have an expected number of minimum characters or minimum number of numerical digits. The hard rule defines if and how the data is cut or extended or if the record is rejected.

4. **Invalid data type formats:** because most raw data is not directly sourced from the operational system, but by using comma separated text files (CSV) or other text-based formats. In such a case, the original data is transformed to strings using a predefined format. For example, date data types can be converted from their internal binary representation into UTC strings which present the date using the following format: "YYYY-MM-DD hh:mm:ss[.nnn]" or into a USA style date with the format "mm/dd/yy", omitting the time information and completely changing the structure of the date format. The hard rule does not only define how to convert from a date data type, but also how to deal with strings that don't comply with the expected format. Similar hard rules are required to convert floating numbers, Boolean values, etc.

5. **Unicode:** another practice is to store all string data in the staging area and in the Raw Data Vault using Unicode character sets to make sure that all character data can be stored. The hard rule defines not only the target character set but also any required conversion.

6. **Reformat business keys:** many organizations choose to reformat business keys if there exist multiple formats in operational systems. For example, if a phone number is used as a business key by the business, it might make sense to use a standardized format when loading the hubs to avoid added same-as-links (SAL). Note that the satellites should track the original values as they were stored in the operational systems. This is a hard rule as long as the content of the data doesn't change.

7. **Local smart keys:** In many cases, there are operational systems that are used only in a certain region. In such cases, they often use a local business key, which is extended to a smart key globally. For example, a customer number "12345" for a customer in Germany could be identified as the smart key "DE12345" in the global enterprise. Thus, the business key "DE12345" should

be used in the data warehouse when loading hubs. A hard business rule can be used to convert such local keys into the expected format of the smart key.

8. **Hash keys and hash differences:** the definition of hash keys (on business keys and their relationships) and hash differences (on descriptive attributes) are also defined by hard rules.

Note that the local smart keys should only be used under the described circumstances: to apply the format of the smart key to a local business key. It should be avoided to use a more complicated mapping when applying a hard rule, for example to map the business key "12345" to "XYZ". Because the mapping between these numbers is not a technical mapping but defined by the business (in general), the mapping is actually a soft business rule that should be applied later.

The primary definition of the hard rules for the data warehouse is done using documents that define the hard rules and their applicability. This definition also includes how and where deviations from the expected format and actual errors should be logged. The following metadata attributes should be used to define hard rules:

- **Data flow name (optional):** the data flow that is implementing this hard rule.
- **Name:** a name for the hard rule understandable by the business.
- **Rule identifier:** the technical name of the hard rule.
- **Description:** a technical description of the hard rule.
- **Definition:** the actual definition of the hard rule, using a text-based or graphical notation.
- **Business area:** the functional business area (or business owner) that defines this hard rule.
- **Topic:** a given topic that this hard rule is part of.
- **Task/rule set:** a more detailed task or rule set that this hard rule is part of.
- **Source:** The source of the hard rules definition (for example, project documentation).
- **Implementation type:** Table 10.3 lists the potential rule types.
- **Keywords:** keywords that help to find the hard rule from the business rule collection.
- **Related rules:** relates this hard rule with other hard rules.
- **Example:** provides example inputs and their respective outputs.

The above list provides some commonly used metadata attributes. Not all of them are required in all projects and, in many cases, organizations decide to add additional ones that make sense in their context.

Table 10.3 Hard Business Rule Types [8]	
Hard Rule Type	**Description**
Restriction	These rules define business specific constraints on the data that is allowed or not allowed to use by the business. They state what data is not to enter the staging area or the Raw Data Vault.
Behavior	These rules express how the system should react to given situations, primarily regarding the source systems and their deliveries (such as missing files, etc.).
Deduction	These rules define how to derive corrected data for the staging area or the Raw Data Vault. Note that this rule does not change the data, but fixes data type issues only.
Warning	These rules define what kind of error should be logged and how.
Other	All other rules that don't fit into the standard rule types.

Table 10.4 Hard Rule Definition [9]	
Name:	NULL SAP Date String to DateTime2
Identifier:	HR0012
Description:	SAP provides NULL dates as "00000000" instead of empty strings as Microsoft SQL Server expects it. Therefore, these values are converted to NULL dates instead of direct date representations.
Example:	"00000000" is converted to a NULL date in the target. All other dates are not affected by this hard rule.
Source:	SAP technical interface documentation (Document ID: SAP1234 as of February 3, 2011)
Related Rules:	HR0010: SAP Date String to DateTime2 HR0011: SAP Date String Error Handling

Spreadsheets are often used to define which hard rules apply to which source and target attribute mappings. The form in Table 10.4 can be used to provide a detailed definition of a hard rule.

Because hard rules can be applied when loading the staging area and when loading the Raw Data Vault, the definition is referenced in the mapping table for either or both layers. Section 10.2.5 and 10.2.7 show examples for mapping tables that include such references.

10.2.5 CAPTURING METADATA FOR THE STAGING AREA

We have described in section 10.2.3 that tracking the source systems (that have been loaded into the data warehouse) is important in order to know what raw data is available in the data warehouse and what is still missing. But knowing the source system is not enough: the recommended approach to loading raw data from source systems is to load all the source tables from any source system that provide us the required raw data to build an information artifact, such as a report. For example, if source system A provides required raw data in one table and source system B provides required raw data in two more tables, we source these three tables completely. It is not recommended to source all tables from each source system, because the data contained in these source tables are not required for the current sprint, thus overloading the sprint with unnecessary effort. However, it is also not recommended to source only those attributes in the source tables that provide the required raw data, but load a source table all at once. That way, the overhead for managing the data warehouse contents (the tables already loaded into the data warehouse) is less. It should be clear that managing the data warehouse contents on an attribute level is more effort than on a table level.

For each table in a source system, the following metadata attributes should be managed at a minimum [10]:

1. **Data package identifier:** the technical name of the data package that contains this table or other data structure (for example individual flat file).
2. **Table identifier:** the technical name of the data group, which is a set of data elements (attributes).
3. **Source table schema name:** the name of the source schema.
4. **Source table physical name:** the physical name of the source table.
5. **Table description:** a technical description of the source table.

6. **Table business description:** a detailed textual description of the source table in business terms.
7. **Data quality:** describes the quality of the source table (could also use a indicator scale from "poor" to "good" or a percentage value).
8. **Target table schema name:** the name of the schema in the staging area.
9. **Target table physical name:** the physical name of the staging table.
10. **Data flow name:** the name of the data flow that is loading the table.

Each table consists of multiple source columns and their respective target column mappings, which are described by an additional metadata table [10]:

- **Table identifier:** the technical name of the parent data table.
- **Column identifier:** the technical name of the column in the source table.
- **Source column physical name:** the physical name of the source column in the source table.
- **Source data type:** the data type of the source column.
- **Column description:** the technical description of the column.
- **Column business description:** a detailed textual description of the column in business terms.
- **Column business name:** the common column name that is recognized by business users.
- **Column business alias:** an alternative column name that is recognized by business users.
- **Column acronym name:** a common acronym coding of the column name.
- **Required flag:** indicates if the column is required to have a value (NOT NULL).
- **Computed flag:** indicates if the column is derived from a computed column in the source system.
- **Target column physical name:** the physical name of the target column in the staging area table.
- **Target data type:** the data type of the target column.
- **Is sequence:** indicates if the target column is a sequence column.
- **Is hash key:** indicates if the target column is a hash key.
- **Is hash difference:** indicates if the target column is a hash difference value.
- **Is record source:** indicates if the target column is a record source attribute.
- **Is load date time:** indicates if the target column is a load date time.
- **Hard rules:** references to the hard rules that are applied within the loading process.

It is also possible to denormalize these two tables. While adding redundancy, it is often easier to use.

Note that it should be possible to apply multiple hard rules to a source to stage column mapping. If it is not possible, another option is to define a hard rule that packages multiple hard rules, thus applying multiple hard rules to the referencing mapping. However, such an approach requires more hard rules with fewer chances for reuse.

When sourcing hierarchical files (or tables), additional and more complex metadata is required because the goal of a hierarchical mapping is to map each column (or XML attribute and element) to a relational column in the staging area. Loading hierarchical sources requires normalization for that reason, as Chapter 11, Data Extraction, will demonstrate. One approach to define the metadata for hierarchical sources is to include the hierarchical path in the **source column physical name** and add a **target table physical name** and **target table schema name** (if actually required) to support multiple target tables.

10.2.6 CAPTURING REQUIREMENTS TO SOURCE TABLES

This cross-reference table was introduced in Chapter 3, The Data Vault 2.0 Methodology, and identifies the source tables and optionally the columns that are used by a specific requirement. Table 10.5 shows an example.

Table 10.5 Requirements to Source Tables Cross Reference with Source Attributes

Requirements to
Source Map
XREF

Requirement Document: MyDoc

Table

Source Table	Source Column	Source Table Physical Name	Source Column Physical Name	Passenger Name Dimension (B2.2)	Preferred Dish Attribute (B3.2.1)
Passenger	Passport Number	PAX	NO	X	X
Passenger	First Name	PAX	FNAME	X	
Passenger	Last Name	PAX	LNAME	X	
Passenger	Title	PAX	TITLE	X	
Passenger	Address	PAX	ADDR		
Flight Reservation	Seat	RES	SEAT		
Flight Reservation	Preferred Dish	RES	DISH		X

One row exists per source column. Each source column is described by some additional information, in this case the physical names. Other options are possible and left to the data warehouse team (for example, the business description). For each requirement, one column is added. Note that not only the name of the requirement is provided but also the technical number that uniquely identifies the requirement in the requirements specification. An X in the cell indicates if the source column is used to implement the requirement. In addition to the table itself, the document references the requirements document thata provides the detailed requirements specification (there might be multiple requirements documents in a project if the team decides to split the requirements up, e.g. per function, etc.).

This cross-reference table can be used in two ways:

1. To identify the requirements that are affected by a change of the source system.
2. To identify the source tables and columns that are needed to be sourced in order to implement a requirement.

Following the general recommendation from 10.2.5, that is, to completely load a table into the data warehouse if at least one column is required by a requirement, we can use the cross-reference table to identify those source tables needed by the iteration that implements a specific requirement.

10.2.7 CAPTURING SOURCE TABLES TO DATA VAULT TABLES

In order to capture metadata for mapping from source tables (in the staging area) to Raw Data Vault tables, multiple metadata tables are recommended. The reason lies in the fact that the mapping for a hub entity is fundamentally different from link entities and from satellite entities. For example, in order to map from a staging table to a Data Vault hub, the business key needs to be identified only. However, in order to map from a staging table to a Data Vault satellite, all descriptive attributes need to be mapped in addition to all attributes identifying the satellite's parent. To complicate matters, there are significant differences between satellites on hubs and satellites on links, requiring separate tables for both entity types.

Note that the lists of metadata attributes in the following sections are suggestions only. Before maintaining metadata for the data warehouse, the list should be tailored to the actual needs of the data warehouse team. One problem with metadata management is that it often tends to become outdated because many teams stop maintaining the metadata tables. To overcome this problem and speed up the design and development processes of the data warehouse, it is worth investing in modeling and generation tools.

The following definitions also cover only basic Data Vault entities (as covered in Chapter 4). In order to define the metadata for intermediate or advanced concepts, additional metadata attributes might be required.

10.2.7.1 Metadata for Loading Hub Entities
In order to define the metadata for Data Vault hubs, the following attributes are required:

1. **Data flow name:** the name of the data flow that is loading the target hub.
2. **Priority:** a common practice is to source business keys from multiple sources. In this case, the priority can be used to determine the order of the data sources when loading the hub, which might affect the record source to be set in the target hub.
3. **Hub identifier:** the technical name of the target hub.
4. **Target hub table physical name:** the physical name of the target table in the Raw Data Vault.
5. **Source table identifier:** the technical name of the source data table in the staging area.
6. **Source table physical name:** the physical name of the source table in the staging area.
7. **Source column physical name:** the physical name of the source column in the source table that holds the business key.
8. **Source column data type:** the data type of the source column.
9. **Source column required:** indicates if the source column allows NULL values.
10. **Source column default value:** indicates the default value of the source column.
11. **Source column computation:** if the source column is a computed field, provide the expression that computes the column value for documentation purposes.
12. **Business key column description:** the technical description of the business key column.
13. **Business key column business description:** a detailed textual description of the business key column in business terms.
14. **Business key column business name:** the common business key column name that is recognized by business users.
15. **Business key column business alias:** an alternative business key column name that is recognized by business users.
16. **Business key column acronym name:** a common acronym coding of the business key column name.
17. **Business key physical name:** the physical name of the target business key column in the hub table.
18. **Target column number:** The column number of the business key within composite keys. Otherwise 1.
19. **Target primary key physical name:** the physical name of the target primary key column in the hub table.
20. **Target data type:** the data type of the target business key column.

Table 10.6 Metadata for Capturing Source Tables to Data Vault Hub Entities									
Hub Identifier	Target Hub Table Physical Name	Source Table Physical Name	Source Column Physical Name	Source Data Type	...	Target Column Physical Name	Target Data Type	Last Seen Date Flag	Hard Rules
H001	HubAirline	AIRLINE	ID	Integer	...	AirlineID	Integer	False	HR33.1
H001	HubAirline	AIRX	NUMBER	BigInt	...	AirlineID	Integer	False	HR1.2.3
H002	HubFlight	FLIGHT	CARRIER	VarChar(2)	...	Carrier	VarChar(2)	False	HR33.1,HR33.2
H002	HubFlight	FLIGHT	NUM	BigInt	...	FlightNum	Integer	False	HR33.1,HR33.3

21. **Last seen date flag:** indicates if a last seen date is used in the hub and should be updated in the loading process.
22. **Hard rules:** references to the hard rules that are applied within the loading process for this business key.

In order to support composite business keys in Data Vault hubs, it is required to provide one line per business key part when dealing with composite business keys. Table 10.6 shows examples for both a hub with only one business key and one hub with a composite key consisting of two elements.

The first hub is hub **Airline** that consists of only one business key attribute **AirlineID**. However, the business keys for this hub are loaded from multiple sources: there is a staging table **AIRLINE** present and another staging table **AIRX**. In this case, the source table identifier (which was introduced in the metadata for the staging table) is the same as the source table physical name. Both source tables provide business keys that need to be loaded in order to include all business keys that are used by the business. Therefore, a hub definition is copied per source table in order to fully define the required metadata to load a hub from all sources.

The second hub loads business keys from only one staging table but is defined by a composite business key. Therefore, two metadata rows are required to fully define the composite key. If multiple source tables provided business keys, these two rows would be copied for each source table.

Because copying rows introduces some redundancy, it might be valuable to investigate normalized structures, especially if metadata tools are involved. If no tools are available, a denormalized structure as proposed in this section might be the more user-friendly structure.

Note that this example doesn't display the descriptive metadata attributes due to space restrictions. However, it shows references to hard rules, which are defined in external documents that describe the hard rules in full detail. Technical numbering is used to reference the hard rules.

10.2.7.2 Metadata for Loading Link Entities

Loading Data Vault links follows a similar pattern compared to hubs but with a little more complexity. The additional complexity is due to the fact that a link table references other hubs to store the relationship between the business keys:

1. **Data flow name:** the name of the data flow that is loading the target link.
2. **Priority:** sometimes, link data is sourced from multiple sources. In this case, the priority can be used to determine the order of the data sources when loading the target link, which might affect the record source to be set in the target link.

3. **Link identifier:** the technical name of the target link.
4. **Target link table physical name:** the physical name of the target table in the Raw Data Vault.
5. **Source table identifier:** the technical name of the source data table in the staging area.
6. **Source column physical name:** the physical name of the source column in the source table that holds the business key.
7. **Source column data type:** the data type of the source column.
8. **Source column required:** indicates if the source column allows NULL values.
9. **Source column default value:** indicates the default value of the source column.
10. **Source column computation:** if the source column is a computed field, provide the expression that computes the column value for documentation purposes.
11. **Source data type:** the data type of the source business key column.
12. **Business key driving flag:** indicates if this business key is part of the driving key (if any).
13. **Business key column description:** the technical description of the business key column.
14. **Business key column business description:** a detailed textual description of the business key column in business terms.
15. **Business key column business name:** the common business key column name that is recognized by business users.
16. **Business key column business alias:** an alternative business key column name that is recognized by business users.
17. **Business key column acronym name:** a common acronym coding of the business key column name.
18. **Hub identifier:** the technical name of the referenced hub.
19. **Hub table physical name:** the physical table name of the reference hub.
20. **Hub reference number:** the number of the hub reference within the sort order of the hub references. This is required to calculate the correct hash key.
21. **Hub primary key physical name:** the physical name of the primary key column in the referenced hub table.
22. **Hub business key physical name:** the name of the business key column in the hub.
23. **Hub business key column number:** the number within the column order of the business key in the hub. Required to calculate the correct hash value.
24. **Hub business key data type:** the data type of the business key column in the referenced hub table. Can be used for automatically applying hard rules.
25. **Target column physical name:** the physical name of the target hash key column in the link table.
26. **Last seen date flag:** indicates if a last seen date is used in the hub and should be updated in the loading process.
27. **Attribute flag:** indicates if the column is an attribute instead of a business key. This is required to define degenerated links (refer to Chapter 4).
28. **Hard rules:** references to the hard rules that are applied within the loading process for this business key.

The number of entries per link depends on multiple factors: first, the number of referenced hubs. For each hub reference there is at least one metadata record required to completely define the link. In addition, if a composite business key defines a hub, the dependent link entry in the metadata table for links requires one record per business key part. Table 10.7 shows a simplified example for a link metadata table.

Table 10.7 Metadata for Capturing Source Tables to Data Vault Link Entities

Link Identifier	Target Link Table Physical Name	Source Table Physical Name	Source Column Physical Name	Source Data Type	...	Hub Table Physical Name	Target Column Physical Name	Hub Business Key Column Number	Hard Rules
L001	LinkFixedBaseOp	FB_OPS	CARRIER	VarChar(2)	...	HubCarrier	CarrierHashKey	1	HR22.1
L001	LinkFixedBaseOp	FB_OPS	AIRPORT	VarChar(3)	...	HubAirport	AirportHashKey	1	HR1.2.5
L002	LinkConnection	CONN	CARRIER	VarChar(2)	...	HubFlightNo	FlightNoHashKey	1	HR22.2
L002	LinkConnection	CONN	FLIGHT	Integer	...	HubFlightNo	FlightNoHashKey	2	HR22.2
L002	LinkConnection	CONN	S_AIRPORT	VarChar(3)	...	HubAirport	SrcAirportHashKey	1	HR1.2.1
L002	LinkConnection	CONN	T_AIRPORT	VarChar(3)	...	HubAirport	TgtAirportHashKey	1	HR1.2.1

The table is simplified because some of the metadata attributes are omitted. The first link **Link-FixedBaseOp** references two hubs: **HubCarrier** and **HubAirport**. Both hubs are defined by simple business keys and not by composite business keys. The second link **LinkConnection** also references two hubs, but one hub, **HubFlightNo**, is defined by a composite business key, consisting of two parts: first the carrier ID and second, the flight number. The second hub **HubAirport** is referenced two times: as source airport of the connection and as a target airport of the connection. For that purpose, both references are stored in different hash keys.

Similar to the metadata table for hubs, presented in the previous section, this table contains redundant metadata in favor of usability. Again, it might be valuable to use a metadata tool with normalized metadata tables.

10.2.7.3 Metadata for Loading Satellite Entities on Hubs

The metadata for satellites contains two types of information:

- **Business keys** that identify the entry in the parent hub entity.
- **Descriptive data** that has to be loaded into the Data Vault satellite for data warehousing purposes.

In order to keep the metadata table as simple as possible, both types of information are provided in the same table: first, the business key information, and second the descriptive data mapping. The mapping table consists of the following metadata attributes:

1. **Data flow name:** the name of the data flow that is loading the target satellite.
2. **Satellite identifier:** the technical name of the target satellite.
3. **Target satellite table physical name:** the physical name of the target table in the Raw Data Vault.
4. **Source table identifier:** the technical name of the source data table in the staging area.
5. **Source column physical name:** the physical name of the source column in the source table that holds the business key or the descriptive data.
6. **Source column data type:** the data type of the source column.
7. **Source column required:** indicates if the source column allows NULL values.
8. **Source column default value:** indicates the default value of the source column.
9. **Source column computation:** if the source column is a computed field, provide the expression that computes the column value for documentation purposes.
10. **Business key driving flag:** indicates if this business key is part of the driving key (if any).
11. **Business key column description:** the technical description of the business key column.
12. **Business key column business description:** a detailed textual description of the business key column in business terms.
13. **Business key column business name:** the common business key column name that is recognized by business users.
14. **Business key column business alias:** an alternative business key column name that is recognized by business users.
15. **Business key column acronym name:** a common acronym coding of the business key column name.
16. **Hub identifier:** the technical name of the referenced hub.

17. **Hub table physical name:** the physical table name of the reference hub.
18. **Hub primary key physical name:** the physical name of the primary key column in the referenced hub table.
19. **Hub business key physical name:** the name of the business key column in the hub.
20. **Hub business key column number:** the number within the column order of the business key in the hub. Required to calculate the correct hash value.
21. **Hub business key column data type:** the data type of the business key column in the referenced hub table. Can be used for automatically applying hard rules.
22. **Target column physical name:** the physical name of the target column (for descriptive data) in the satellite table.
23. **Target column data type:** the data type of the target column.
24. **Target column required:** indicates if the target column is nullable.
25. **Target column default value:** the default value of the target column (this should be defined by a hard rule).
26. **Target column description:** a technical description of the descriptive attribute in the target.
27. **Target column business description:** a textual description of the descriptive attribute in the target, using business terminology.
28. **Target column business name:** the common business name of the descriptive attribute that is recognized by business users.
29. **Target column business alias**: an alternative column name of the descriptive attribute that is recognized by business users.
30. **Target column acronym name:** a common acronym coding of the descriptive attribute's column name.
31. **Hard rules:** references to the hard rules that are applied within the loading process for this business key or descriptive attribute.

In order to create a metadata table that fully describes a hub satellite, one record needs to be added per descriptive data attribute and per business key in the parent hub. The latter is required for identification purposes, as Chapter 12, Loading the Data Vault, will discuss. Table 10.8 shows an example of a satellite definition for a hub with a composite business key.

Similar to the other metadata tables in this section, the table in Table 10.8 has been simplified by omitting some attributes that are not required for the explanation. It shows the definition of a satellite **SatPassenger** that is sourced from a source table called **PAX**. Two of the source columns, **COUNTRY** and **PASSPORT_NO**, are used to identify the entry in the Hub, which is defined by the composite business key consisting of **CountryCode** and **Passport ID**. The business keys are used to calculate the hash key, which is used in the satellite as a reference to the hub's primary key. It is possible to retrieve the corresponding hash key columns from the primary key. Naming conventions are not required to identify this column, because there should only be one hash key in the primary key. The other four fields are of a descriptive nature that means they describe the business key. In order to do so, they are being mapped to the attributes in the satellite.

This table clearly distinguishes between the business key definition and the descriptive data mapping. It is important to include the business key definition in this metadata table because of the required mapping between the source data and the business keys, which is used by the hash key computation when loading the data.

Table 10.8 Metadata for Capturing Source Tables to Data Vault Hub Satellite Entities

Satellite Identifier	Target Satellite Table Physical Name	Source Table Physical Name	Source Column Physical Name	...	Hub Table Physical Name	Target Column Physical Name	Hub Business Key Physical Name	Hub Business Key Column Number	Hard Rules
HS001	SatPassenger	PAX	COUNTRY		HubPassenger		CountryCode	1	HR3.4
HS001	SatPassenger	PAX	PASSPORT_NO		HubPassenger		PassportID	2	HR3.5
HS001	SatPassenger	PAX	FNAME			FirstName			HR3.6.1
HS001	SatPassenger	PAX	LNAME			LastName			HR3.6.2
HS001	SatPassenger	PAX	TITLE			Title			HR3.6.3
HS001	SatPassenger	PAX	SEX			Sex			HR3.6.4

10.2.7.4 Metadata for Loading Satellite Entities on Links

Hub satellite entities, which provide descriptive data for Data Vault links, are very similar to hub satellites. However, they are different in the identification of the entry in the parent link entity. The following attributes are used to define the metadata of Data Vault link satellites:

- **Data flow name:** the name of the data flow that is loading the target satellite.
- **Satellite identifier:** the technical name of the target satellite.
- **Target satellite table physical name:** the physical name of the target table in the Raw Data Vault.
- **Source table identifier:** the technical name of the source data table in the staging area.
- **Source column physical name:** the physical name of the source column in the source table that holds the business key or the descriptive data.
- **Source column data type:** the data type of the source column.
- **Source column required:** indicates if the source column allows NULL values.
- **Source column default value:** indicates the default value of the source column.
- **Source column computation:** if the source column is a computed field, provide the expression that computes the column value for documentation purposes.
- **Business key driving flag:** indicates if this business key is part of the driving key (if any).
- **Business key column description:** the technical description of the business key column.
- **Business key column business description:** a detailed textual description of the business key column in business terms.
- **Business key column business name:** the common business key column name that is recognized by business users.
- **Business key column business alias:** an alternative business key column name that is recognized by business users.
- **Business key column acronym name:** a common acronym coding of the business key column name.
- **Link identifier:** the technical name of the referenced parent link.
- **Link table physical name:** the physical table name of the reference link.
- **Link primary key physical name:** the physical name of the primary key column in the referenced link table.
- **Hub identifier:** the technical name of the referenced hub.
- **Hub table physical name:** the physical table name of the reference hub.
- **Hub reference number:** the number of the hub reference within the sort order of the hub references. This is required to calculate the correct hash key.
- **Hub primary key physical name:** the physical name of the primary key column in the referenced hub table.
- **Hub business key physical name:** the name of the business key column in the hub.
- **Hub business key column number:** the number within the column order of the business key in the hub. Required to calculate the correct hash value.
- **Hub business key column data type:** the data type of the business key column in the referenced hub table. Can be used for automatically applying hard rules.
- **Target column physical name:** the physical name of the target column (for descriptive data) in the satellite table.
- **Target column data type:** the data type of the target column.

- **Target column required:** indicates if the target column is nullable.
- **Target column default value:** the default value of the target column (this should be defined by a hard rule).
- **Target column description:** a technical description of the descriptive attribute in the target.
- **Target column business description:** a textual description of the descriptive attribute in the target, using business terminology.
- **Target column business name:** the common business name of the descriptive attribute that is recognized by business users.
- **Target column business alias:** an alternative column name of the descriptive attribute that is recognized by business users.
- **Target column acronym name:** a common acronym coding of the descriptive attribute's column name.
- **Hard rules:** references to the hard rules that are applied within the loading process for this business key or descriptive attribute.

In order to identify the satellite's parent link, it is required to obtain all business keys from the source system that are part of the link. The business keys become input to the hash key calculation. Other than that, the link satellite structure is similar to the hub satellite structure described in the previous section and contains only descriptive attributes. Table 10.9 shows a link satellite on a link that connects two hubs.

The satellite hangs off a link that connects two hubs: **HubCarrier** on one side and **HubAirport** on the other. The metadata information is required in order to map the source data to the business keys, which is required for hash key calculation. For the same reason, the business keys of a hub are ordered using the **Hub Business Key Column Number**. If one of the hubs were defined by more than one business key (or in other words, a composite business key), there would be two entries for this hub in Table 10.9, sequenced using this number. Similar to the metadata for loading satellite entities on hubs, there is no metadata required to identify the hash key column in the satellite because there should be only one hash key in the primary key of the satellite. The remaining three rows at the bottom of the table provide the metadata for the descriptive data attributes in the same manner as in hub satellites.

10.2.8 CAPTURING SOFT RULES

Section 10.2.4 discussed that hard rules only apply technical changes to the data loaded from the source system, for example ensuring that the data type fits the actual data and has the proper size. Hard rules never change the incoming raw data, except for data type alignment. Instead, the modification of data is left to soft rules, which change the value or the grain of the raw data. For example, content is altered by recalculation or is reinterpreted. The grain of the incoming data is changed by required aggregations to modify the source data in such a way that it fits the expected format. In other cases, a lower grain is required than the source system provides. In this case, the raw data needs to be broken up using predefined approximations defined by the business, using soft business rules.

However, the business changes. And so do the definitions of how the raw data should be modified to create information that is useful for the business, because the business rule definitions document the perception of truth by which the business operates on a day-to-day basis. But this truth changes more often than the market changes, for example when the business learns more about the market.

Table 10.9 Metadata for Capturing Source Tables to Data Vault Link Satellite Entities

Satellite Ident.	Target Satellite Table Physical Name	Source Table Physical Name	Source Column Physical Name	...	Link Ident.	Hub Table Physical Name	Hub Ref. No.	Target Column Physical Name	Hub Business Key Physical Name	Hub BK Column No.	Hard Rules
LS001	SatFixedBaseOp	FB_OPS	CARRIER	...	L001	HubCarrier	1		Carrier	1	HR22.1
LS001	SatFixedBaseOp	FB_OPS	AIRPORT	...	L001	HubAirport	2		Airport	1	HR1.2.5
LS001	SatFixedBaseOp	FB_OPS	NAME		L001			Name			HR1.3.4
LS001	SatFixedBaseOp	FB_OPS	DESC		L001			Description			HR1.3.4
LS001	SatFixedBaseOp	FB_OPS	LOC		L001			Location			HR1.3.4

However, modifying any part of the data warehouse requires changing, or at least testing, all parts downstream of the data warehouse that depend on the modified part. That is the major reason why soft rules should be placed in the architecture as close as possible toward the business, downstream in the data warehouse architecture. Because the definitions of how to modify the raw data to retrieve useful information change so frequently, we need to reduce the number of dependencies on these fluid parts of the data warehouse. And that is why the hard rules described in section 10.2.4 should only modify technical aspects of the raw data, but not the data itself.

When capturing business rules, organizations often depend on free-form descriptions, because the soft rule definitions tend to be complex and require verbal explanations in written form. The following sections will describe some approaches to describing soft rules using text or graphical notations that help the business to define the business rules in an easy to interpret format. Regardless whether the business decides to use an unstructured, free-text format for describing the business rules, some text-based or graphical notation, or a combination of both, in any case, metadata should be captured that describes the collection of soft rules in the data warehouse. Such a metadata table should consist of the following attributes [11,8]:

- **Data flow name (optional):** the data flow that is implementing this business rule.
- **Rule identifier:** the technical name of the business rule.
- **Name:** a name for the soft rule understandable by the business.
- **Description:** a technical description of the business rule.
- **Business description:** a textual description of the soft rule in business terms.
- **Definition:** the actual definition of the business rule, using a text-based or graphical notation.
- **Business area:** the functional business area (or business owner) that defines this business rule.
- **Topic:** a given topic that this business rule is part of.
- **Task/rule set:** a more detailed task or rule set that this business rule is part of.
- **Priority:** the priority of the business rule: either "must-have," "should-have," "could-have," or "won't have."
- **Motivation:** defines the motivation why this business rule is defined, for example "data integrity," "security policy," "customer relationship standards," etc.
- **Source:** The source of the soft rules definition (for example, project documentation).
- **Classification:** Table 10.10 lists the potential classifications.
- **Implementation type:** Table 10.11 lists the potential rule types.
- **Keywords:** keywords that help to find the soft rule from the business rule collection.
- **Defined:** the name of the person who has defined the soft rule and the date of definition.
- **Approved:** the name of the person who approved the soft rule and the date of approval.
- **Related rules:** relates this soft rule with other hard rules.
- **Example:** provides example inputs and their respective outputs.

The **data flow name** is an optional metadata attribute because most business rules are implemented in virtual business vault entities or information mart entities. In this case, the record source column is used to refer to the **rule identifier** as Chapter 12 demonstrates. Note the similarity to the metadata attributes for the definition of hard rules in section 10.2.4. The following table lists the possible rule classifications:

The following table provides commonly used rule types:

Again, this table is similar to the hard rule types in Table 10.3. However, Table 10.3 has been condensed to rule types that make sense to hard rules. In contrast, Table 10.11 provides more rule types, because the modification of data is allowed in soft rules.

Table 10.10 Business Rule Definitions [8]

Rule Classification	Description	Example
Term	A noun or noun phrase with an agreed upon definition.	Passenger "female" Preferred dish
Fact	Connects terms into observations relevant for the business.	Passenger's preferred dish is "vegetarian".
Mandatory constraint	Expresses an unconditional circumstance that must be true or not true to complete the business event with integrity.	A flight must have a valid flight number to be included in the **number of flights** measure.
Guideline	Expresses a warning about a circumstance that should be true or not true to complete the business event.	A flight should have a minimum of 2 passengers to be counted as a flight in the **number of flights** measure.
Action enabler	Initiates another business event, message or other activity if the given conditions are true.	If a passenger doesn't show up for a flight, issue a security warning.
Computation	Defines the calculation rule to retrieve the value of a term, including sum, difference, product, quotient, count, maximum, minimum, and average.	The income per passenger is calculated by dividing the total annual income by the number of annual passengers.
Inference	Establishes a new fact if the given conditions are true.	If a passenger has more than 5000 air miles flown, then the customer is of preferred status.

Table 10.11 Soft Business Rule Types [8]

Soft Rule Type	Description
Restriction	These rules define business specific constraints on the data that is allowed or not allowed to use by the business. They state what data is not to leave the Raw Data Vault.
Behavior	These rules express how the system should react to given situations.
Deduction	These rules define how to derive or calculate useful information from the raw data.
Presentation	They define how to present the information to the business user.
Instruction	These rules define how to handle business events, e.g. how to react to passengers not showing up for a flight.
Warning	These rules define what kind of error should be logged and how.
Other	All other rules that don't fit into the standard rule types.

Similar to metadata tables in other sections of this chapter, the metadata attributes and the values in the tables presented in this section are suggestions only. Each project team or organization has to adapt these lists and come up with their own definitions. Use the information given in this section as a starting point.

10.2.9 CAPTURING DATA VAULT TABLES TO INFORMATION MART TABLE MAPPINGS

The mapping between the Data Vault (both Raw Data Vault and Business Data Vault) to information marts is a complex procedure. In many cases, soft business rules with inputs from the Data Vault and outputs in the information mart are defined and documented (refer to section 10.2.8). A soft rule moves the data from the Data Vault into the information mart by transforming, recalculating, aggregating or interpreting the data. To document the inputs and the outputs of the soft rules, the following attributes should be included in the metadata table:

- **Data flow name:** the name of the data flow that is implementing the soft rule.
- **Target table identifier:** the technical name of the target table (such as dimension or fact table if a dimensional model is being built) based on technical numbering.
- **Target table physical name:** the physical name of the target table in the information mart.
- **Source identifier:** the technical name of the source hub, link, or satellite.
- **Source table physical name:** the physical name of the source table in the Data Vault.
- **Source column physical name:** the physical name of the source column in the source table.
- **Source column data type:** the data type of the source column.
- **Source column required:** indicates if the source column allows NULL values.
- **Target column physical name:** the physical name of the target column (for descriptive data) in the satellite table.
- **Target column data type:** the data type of the target column.
- **Target column required:** indicates if the target column is nullable.
- **Target column default value:** the default value of the target column.
- **Target column description:** a technical description of the target column.
- **Target column business description:** a textual description of the target column, using business terminology.
- **Target column business name:** the common business name of the target column that is recognized by business users.
- **Target column business alias:** an alternative name of the target column that is recognized by business users.
- **Target column acronym name:** a common acronym coding of the column name.
- **Soft rule:** references to the soft rules that are applied within the loading process.

Note that this metadata is not only used to describe the detailed metadata for soft business rule execution towards information marts, but also for additional tables in the Business Vault, such as computed satellites.

Table 10.12 shows an example of a Data Vault tables to information mart tables mapping.

Table 10.12 Metadata for Capturing Data Vault Tables to Information Mart Tables

Target Table Identifier	Source Table Physical Name	Source Column Physical Name	Source Data Type	...	Target Table Physical Name	Target Column Physical Name	Target Data Type	Soft Rule
D001	HubAirline	AirlineHashKey	Char(32)	...	DimAirline	AirlineKey	Char(32)	SR443.2.1
D001	HubAirline	AirlineID	Integer	...	DimAirline	AirlineID	Integer	SR443.2.1
D001	SatAirline	Name	VarChar(50)	...	DimAirline	Name	VarChar(50)	SR443.2.1
D001	SatAirline	Abbreviation	VarChar(3)	...	DimAirline	Abbreviation	VarChar(3)	SR443.2.1
F001	BrConnection	FlightNo	Integer	...	FactConnection	FlightNo	Integer	SR221.2
F001	BrConnection	CarrierHashKey	Char(32)	...	FactConnection	CarrierHashKey	Char(32)	SR221.2
F001	BrConnection	SrcAirport	Char(32)	...	FactConnection	SrcAirport	Char(32)	SR221.2
F001	BrConnection	DestAirport	Char(32)	...	FactConnection	DestAirport	Char(32)	SR221.2
F001	BrConnection	Duration	Integer	...	FactConnection	Duration	Integer	SR221.2

There are two dimensional target tables defined: one dimension **DimAirline** and a fact table **Fact-Connection**. The dimension is sourced from a Data Vault hub **HubAirline** and an accompanying satellite **SatAirline**. All three source attributes from the hub and the satellite are directly mapped to a target column in the information mart. The soft business rule, which is further defined in **SR443.2.1**, might change the values from the source before writing the data into the dimension.

The loading process of the fact table, identified as F001, is sourced from a bridge table. In this case, all dimension references, business keys (loaded as dimension attributes) and measures are directly sourced from this source bridge table. The hash keys in the bridge table already reference the later dimension hash keys, which works seamlessly: in the case of Type 1 dimensions, as in Table 10.12, the hash key is directly sourced from the hub. In the case of Type 2 dimensions, it would be sourced from PIT tables. Chapter 14, Loading the Dimensional Information Mart, demonstrates how to load virtual and materialized information mart entities.

Note that there is one set of metadata entries per soft rule. For each soft rule, there are multiple inputs and outputs defined. The relationship between inputs and outputs is multiple to multiple (m:n) with both sides of the relationship being optional. It is possible to define an input to the soft rule that has no direct associated output (for example, because the input is used in a filter condition). Similarly, an output might be defined using a constant value or calculated using a complex formula that might not be traced back to a source column. This is the case for the second Carrier target column of **FactConnection** in Table 10.12.

10.2.10 CAPTURING REQUIREMENTS TO INFORMATION MART TABLES

Chapter 3 has already introduced the requirements for information mart tables cross-reference, which is provided again in Table 10.13.

The cross-reference table describes which information mart dimension or fact tables are used by a given report or OLAP item. There are three reports in this example: *Passenger*, *Airplane Utilization* and *Connections*. While the *Passenger* report uses only the *Passenger Information* table in the information mart, the *Connections* report uses the *Connections* and the *Airplanes* table. These entity names are the logical names; the physical names are also provided as a reference. It also references the requirements

Table 10.13 Requirements to Information Mart Table Example

Requirements to Target Map XREF					
Requirement Document:	MyDoc				
Table					
Logical Name	**Physical Name**	**Business Key**	**Passenger (B3.1)**	**Airplane Utilization (B3.2)**	**Connections (B3.3)**
Passenger Information	PASSENGER		X		
Connections	CONNECTION				X
Airplanes	AIRPLANE			X	X

documentation. It is also possible to add the attributes in the information mart, similar to the requirements to source table in section 10.2.6.

The major value of this cross-reference is:

1. To identify the information mart artifacts which are affected by a change of requirements.
2. To identify the requirements which are affected when changing an information mart artifact.

While these advantages sound interchangeable at first glance, they are important, in both orders. The Data Vault 2.0 methodology embraces change, like other agile methodologies. Requirements are first affected by such change. A change requirement will affect one or more artifacts in the information marts, such as a dimension in an OLAP cube. If this dimension is modified, it affects all requirements that are related to this artifact. Using this cross-reference table, we can track such dependent changes in the data warehouse.

10.2.11 CAPTURING ACCESS CONTROL LISTS AND OTHER SECURITY MEASURES

Most database systems allow the definition of users, roles and access control lists (ACL) on individual databases, tables and views of the data warehouse. However, in order to effectively secure the data in the data warehouse, several actions are required to be performed [12]:

- **Identify the data:** this step is already complete when creating the suggested metadata described in the previous sections.
- **Classify data:** for security purposes, the initial metadata used in step 1 and described in the previous sections should be modified to include a data sensitivity attribute.
- **Quantify the value of data:** in order to estimate the costs of security breaches, the value of data assets needs to be quantified first. It might be hard to determine this value, especially because errors in the data warehouse might lead to erroneous business decisions.
- **Identify data security vulnerabilities:** it is also hard to determine the potential vulnerabilities in a data warehouse, due to the long-lifespan of the data storage and unknown future use of the data.
- **Identify data protection measures and their costs:** for each thread identified in the previous action, the potential remedies are identified and priced.
- **Selecting cost-effective security measures:** the value of the data and the severity of the thread are used to level the identified security measures.
- **Evaluating the effectiveness of security measures:** the effectiveness of the security measures needs to be addressed in the final step.

Without going into more detail regarding these activities, it becomes possible to identify the following metadata attributes that are required to define the security measures:

- **Data sensitivity:** the classification of the data regarding security as defined in step 2. Table 10.14 lists and describes an example of a data classification matrix.
- **Data value:** the value of the data as quantified in step 3.
- **Potential remedies per security vulnerability and data item:** the potential remedies as identified in step 4.
- **Thread severity:** the severity of the thread as identified in step 4.

Table 10.14 provides an example of a data classification matrix that can be used to classify the raw data in the data warehouse:

Table 10.14 Example Data Classifications [13]

	Prohibited	Restricted	Confidential	Unrestricted
Classification Guideline	Data is classified as prohibited if required by law or any other regulation or if the organization is required to self-report to the government or the individual if data has been inappropriately accessed.	Data is classified as restricted if the data would qualify as prohibited but the organization determines that personnel could not effectively work with the data when not stored in the data warehouse.	Data is classified as confidential if it is not classified as prohibited or restricted. Exceptions to this rule are listed under Classification of Common Data Elements.	Data is classified as unrestricted if not classified as prohibited, restricted, or confidential.
Classification of Common Data Elements	Checking account numbers	Export controlled data	Contract data	Data authorized to be available in public
	Credit card numbers	Health information	Emails	Data in the public domain
	Driver license numbers	Passport numbers	Financial data	
	Health insurance policy numbers	Visa numbers	Internal memos	
	Social security numbers		Personnel records	
Access Protocol	Access only with permission and with signed non-disclosure agreements (NDA).	Access restricted only to those permitted under law, regulations or organizational policies and with a need to know for carrying out their assigned work and duties.	Access restricted to user with a need to know and with the permission of the data owner or custodian.	Access to unrestricted data is granted to everyone.
Transmission	Approved encryption is required in order to transmit the data through a network.	Approved encryption is required in order to transmit the data through a network.	Approved encryption is recommended in order to transmit the data through a network.	No encryption is required to transmit unrestricted data through a network.
Storage	It is not allowed to store the data in any computing environment, including the data warehouse, unless especially approved by the organization. If it is explicitly allowed, approved encryption is required. It is not allowed for a third party to process or store the data without explicit approval.	Approved encryption is required to store the data in the data warehouse. It is not allowed for a third party to process or store the data without explicit approval.	Encryption is recommended but not required. The data owner might decide on required encryption. Data might be processed or stored by a third party if a valid contract with the party exists.	No encryption is required.

While Table 10.14 provides a list of data classifications that can be used in data warehouse environments, it is still unclear how these levels can be applied to a Data Vault 2.0 model, among the other metadata attributes.

Classified data might be stored in all Raw Data Vault entities. Business keys might be classified as Table 10.14 shows: a credit card number or social security number by itself is already considered as prohibited and should only be stored in a data warehouse if approved by the organization. In that case, the hub that holds this business key should be elevated to the appropriate sensitivity level, restricted (because the organization allowed the storage of the data in the data warehouse). The same applies to satellites which hold descriptive data that might be classified as restricted or confidential. A best practice is to separate the data by sensitivity level. This can be done using satellite splits. For each resulting satellite, the database engine can enforce separate security controls.

However, the data is not only stored in Raw Data Vault entities. There are dependent entities in the Business Vault and in information marts that provide access to information which is based on the raw data provided by the Raw Data Vault, either in a virtual or materialized form. In both cases, the information should be classified to the same sensitivity level as the underlying raw data. When information is generated from multiple entities in the Raw Data Vault, each of them classified with different sensitivity levels, the most restrictive sensitivity level should be used for the derived information as a whole. For example, if a computed satellite in the Business Vault consolidates raw data from a satellite classified as **unrestricted** and another satellite classified as **confidential**, the computed satellite should be classified as **confidential** as well.

Such a classification of derived entities is not necessary if the grain of data is modified, for example during an aggregation. In this case, the classification of the computed satellite might be actually less restrictive because detailed information is not available anymore [14].

10.3 IMPLEMENTING THE METRICS VAULT

The Metrics Vault is used to capture process metrics from the ETL control and data flows. It is an optional component, not necessary to implement a data warehouse. However, it is very helpful with [15]:

- **Error inspection:** the Metrics Vault is used to identify errors and their causes, which is required to restart the ETL process.
- **Root cause analysis:** using the Metrics Vault, an error can be analyzed in order to find the root cause of the failure and put an improved solution in place in order to prevent the same error from happening again in the future.
- **Performance metrics:** the execution and performance metrics can be used to observe the size and growth rates of data and address negative performance trends before they cause any failure during run-time.

Various metrics are captured in order to support these goals, for example the rows loaded successfully, rows rejected, amount of time to load, etc [2]. Everything related to the following areas should be captured by the Metrics Vault in the highest level of detail:

- **Timing metrics:** the start and end time of the ETL processing, including the elapsed time [2].
- **Performance metrics:** read and write throughput provides information about the ETL performance itself, by reporting the rows per second read from the source or written to the destination [2].

- **Volume metrics:** the total numbers of rows read from the source, written to the destination or rejected during processing provides useful information for debugging and administrative purposes [2].
- **Error metrics:** provide information about the number of rejected or otherwise erroneous records per source or destination. Note that this doesn't include raw data which is left for the Error Mart (refer to section 10.5).
- **Frequency metrics:** involve how often a data source delivers data and how often ETL processes are run.
- **Dependency chains:** dependency chains involve waiting times for dependent ETL processes. These waiting times should be measured as a basis for improvement.

The Metrics Vault should be modeled using the Data Vault 2.0 Model in order to integrate metrics from various sources: while a lot of metrics are sourced from the ETL tool such as SSIS, other metrics might be integrated from the server or network infrastructure. Table 10.15 lists typical metrics of the server and network infrastructure. Often, these sources of metrics data are integrated in an agile fashion, similar to the data warehouse itself. That is due to the fact that, while analyzing errors and performance bottlenecks, more and more potential sources of failure are analyzed during a root cause analysis. Whenever a potential source of failure is analyzed, more and more data needs to be integrated into the Metrics Mart to be available for analysis.

While the process metrics are obtained while the ETL control flow is running, the information from Table 10.15 has to be obtained from the server and network devices. The **WMI Data Reader Task** [20] in SSIS can be used to obtain selected metrics during a running ETL control flow. However, if the infrastructure should be monitored more frequently (for example, to collect CPU usage per second), the database of a monitoring software should be integrated into the Metrics Vault.

Table 10.15 Hardware and Network Infrastructure Metrics [16–18]

Metric Name	Metric Type	Description
Backup Age	Backup	The number of hours a database was last backed up.
Backup Time	Backup	The running time of the last backup.
Log Backup Age	Backup	The number of hours a database log backup was created.
Log Backup Time	Backup	The running time of the last log backup.
Batch Requests	Database	The number of batch requests per second.
Checkpoint Pages	Database	The number of flushed dirty pages per second.
Data Buffer Cache Hit Ratio	Database	The percentage of pages found in the SQL Server buffer pool [19].
Database Online	Database	Indicates if the database is online and accepts queries.
Deadlocks	Database	The number of deadlocks per second.
Free List Stalls	Database	The number of free list stalls per second.
Full Scans	Database	The number of full table scans per second.
Initial Compilations	Database	The number of initial compilations per second.
Latch Wait Time	Database	The average waiting time before a latch request is granted.
Latch Waits	Database	The number of unfulfilled latch-requests per seconds.

(Continued)

Table 10.15 Hardware and Network Infrastructure Metrics [16–18] *(cont.)*

Metric Name	Metric Type	Description
Lazy Writes	Database	The number of lazy writes per second.
Lock Timeouts	Database	The number of lock requests per second, which resulted in a timeout.
Lock Waits	Database	The number of unsatisfied lock requests per second.
Page Life Expectancy	Database	The average time a page is kept in main memory.
Recompilations	Database	The number of recompilations per second.
Total Server Memory	Database	The amount of main memory reserved for the database server.
Transactions	Database	The number of transactions per second.
Availability	Network	The percentage of the time a network resource is available for use.
Delay	Network	The amount of time for a packet to traverse (one-way or round trip) a network, network segment or network device.
Error Rate	Network	The percentage of packets or bits that contain errors on a network link, network segment or network device.
Throughput	Network	The amount of data that can be sent on or through a network resource in a given time period.
Utilization	Network	The percentage of network resource utilization.
Failed Jobs	Scheduler	The number of jobs that did not successfully exist in a given time period.
Free Memory	Server	The total amount of available physical RAM.
Total CPU Usage	Server	The total amount of CPU power currently in use.
Total I/O Usage	Server	The total amount of available I/O currently in use.
Active Users	Session	The total number of active database users.
Average Active Time	Session	The sum of database time over all sessions, divided by the elapsed time.
Connection Time	Session	The total time to login.
Response Time	Session	The response time of a simple query, that is the time it takes to send the query from the client to the database, executing it and returning the result.
Total Users	Session	The total number of users connected to the database.
Data File Auto Growth	Storage	The number of data file auto growth events in a given time period.
Data File Auto Shrinks	Storage	The number of data file auto shrink events in a given time period.
Database File DBCC Shrinks	Storage	The number of DBCC file shrink events in a given time period.
Free Space	Storage	The free space in a database.
Log File Auto Growths	Storage	The number of log file auto growth events in a given time period.
Log File Auto Shrinks	Storage	The number of log file auto shrink events in a given time period.

The next sections demonstrate how to capture ETL and WMI metrics in a running ETL control flow and how to model the underlying Metrics Vault.

10.3.1 CAPTURING PERFORMANCE DATA IN SQL SERVER INTEGRATION SERVICES

When using Microsoft SSIS as the ETL tool, it is easy to capture basic metrics on the processed ETL control and data flows. In order to log messages, select **Logging** in the context menu of the control flow to set up the logging. The dialog in Figure 10.8 will be shown.

By default, there is no logging defined for a SSIS control flow. In order to set up the destination of log events, select one of the following provider types in the selection box [21]:

- **SSIS log provider for SQL Server Profiler:** this provider writes the log events into a trace file that can be imported to SQL Server Profiler. SQL Server Profiler can be used to replay packages in a test environment step by step [15].
- **SSIS log provider for XML files:** this provider writes the log events into a XML file which include schema information that is helpful when importing the events into another application.
- **SSIS log provider for SQL Server:** this provider sends the log events to an OLE DB connection, for example to store the event data in a SQL Server table. When the provider accesses a database

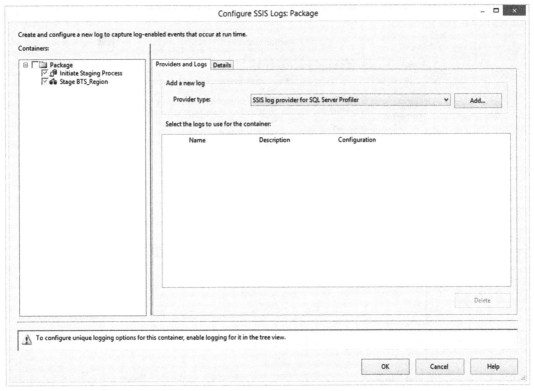

FIGURE 10.8

Configure SSIS logs on package (initial dialog).

for its first time, it checks if a destination table already exists. The destination table (and a stored procedure for writing into it) is created if not [15].

- **SSIS log provider for Windows Event Log:** this provider sends the log events into the Application event store of the Windows Event log. The log is easily accessible by Windows system administrators and can be viewed remotely [15].
- **SSIS log provider for Text files:** this provider writes the log events into a comma-separated file (CSV) which can be easily imported into applications for analysis, including Microsoft Excel or database applications such as Microsoft Access [15].

In addition, it is also possible to develop a custom log provider [22].

To store the log events in a relational Metrics Vault, choose the **SSIS log provider for SQL Server** and select the **Add…** button. A new provider is added to the list below (note that you can configure multiple log providers). Select <**New connection…**> in the selection box behind the configuration column. This will open the dialog to set up a new OLE DB connection (Figure 10.9).

Once the log provider connection has been set up, check the package in the left tree and activate the log provider in the provider list by activating the check mark on the provider (in front of the row), as Figure 10.10 shows.

After setting up the log provider connection to the Metrics Vault, the event types that should be logged have to be selected on the **Details** pane of the dialog (Figure 10.11).

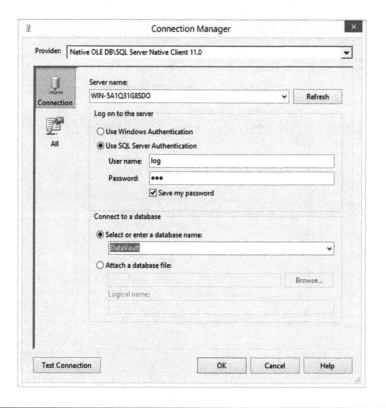

FIGURE 10.9

Connection manager to setup log provider connection.

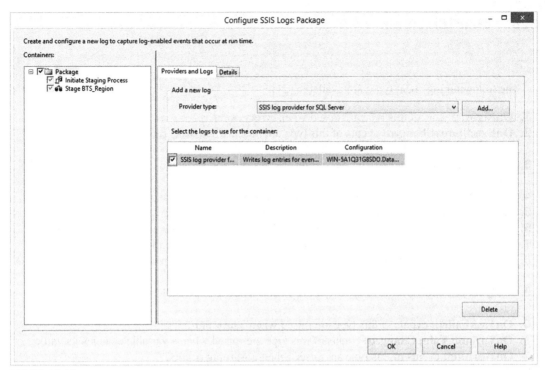

FIGURE 10.10

Configure SSIS logs on package (final dialog).

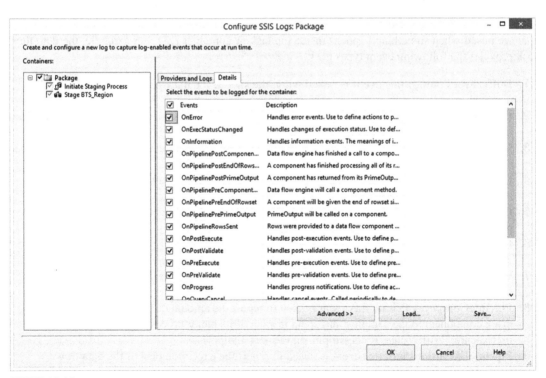

FIGURE 10.11

Log event types available for logging in SSIS.

The following log event types are available [21]:

1. **OnError:** events of this type are raised when errors occur.
2. **OnExecStatusChanged:** events of this type are raised when tasks (not containers) are suspended or resumed during debugging sessions.
3. **OnInformation:** events of this type report the information collected during the validation and execution of executables.
4. **OnPostExecute:** events of this type are raised when executables have finished execution.
5. **OnPostValidate:** events of this type are raised when executables have been validated.
6. **OnPreExecute:** events of this type are raised immediately before executing executables.
7. **OnPreValidate:** events of this type are raised before the validation of executables starts.
8. **OnProgress:** events of this type are raised when executables have progressed in a measurable amount.
9. **OnQueryCancel:** events of this type are raised when it is possible to cancel execution of tasks.
10. **OnTaskFailed:** events of this type are raised when a task fails.
11. **OnVariableValueChanged:** events of this type are raised when a variable changes its value.
12. **OnWarning:** events of this type are raised when a warning occurs.
13. **PipelineComponentTime:** this event type sends a log entry for each phase of validation and execution, including the processing time of each phase.
14. **Diagnostic:** this event type sends diagnostic information.

In addition to these standard event types, many tasks and containers define additional event types that are raised when something happens inside the task or container [21]. For example, the data flow task provides the following event types [23]:

1. **BufferSizeTuning:** this event is raised when the size of the data flow buffer has been changed.
2. **OnPipelinePostEndOfRowset:** events of this type are raised when a component of the data flow has reached the end of the rowset.
3. **OnPipelinePostPrimeOutput:** this event is raised when a component has finished its last prime output.
4. **OnPipelinePreEndOfRowset:** this event is raised before a component of the data flow is reaching the end of the rowset.
5. **OnPipelinePrePrimeOutput:** this event is raised before a component is processing its last prime output.
6. **OnPipelineRowsSent:** this event is raised in order to report the number of rows sent to a component in the data flow task.
7. **PipelineBufferLeak:** this event is raised if a component has not released all buffers, which indicates buffer leaks.
8. **PipelineComponentTime:** this event is used to report the amount of time (in milliseconds) that a component in the data flow has spent in each of its major processing steps (Validate, PreExecute, PostExecute, ProcessInput, and ProcessOutput).
9. **PipelineExecutionPlan:** this event is raised to report the execution plan of the data flow.

10. **PipelineExecutionTrees:** this event is raised to report the execution trees of the layout in the data flow. Execution trees are used to build the execution plan.
11. **PipelineInitialization:** this event is raised to provide initialization information about the data flow task.

Whenever one of the selected events occurs, SSIS will send information about the event to the log provider destination. Using the Advanced button, it is possible to configure the attributes per event that should be logged. The following attributes are logged by default and can be configured (deselected) in the dialog [21]:

- **Computer:** indicates the name of the computer where the event has occurred.
- **Operator:** indicates the user who has launched the package.
- **SourceName:** the name of the container or task in which the event was raised.
- **SourceID:** the unique identifier of the container or task in which the event was raised.
- **ExecutionID:** the GUID of the package instance used for execution.
- **MessageText:** the message text of the logged event.
- **DataBytes:** this byte array stores additional binary data for the event. Used rarely in SSIS logging.

In addition to these optional attributes, the following attributes are always included in the event information [21]:

1. **StartTime:** the start time of the task or container.
2. **EndTime:** the end time of the task or container.
3. **DataCode:** indicates the execution result of the task or container. Possible values are given in Table 10.16.

Note that the **MessageText** attribute is often used to encode other, valuable information, such as the records written to the target. When writing the raw data into the Metrics Vault, the **MessageText** should be split and loaded into separate satellites, following standard Data Vault practices by capturing the raw data in the actual data types of the source system.

Once the event types are selected and the dialog has been confirmed, the selected metrics are captured during execution of the control flow.

In this example, a log user has been created on the database server. When connecting to the database for the first time, SSIS creates two objects in the database:

1. a table named **sysssislog** that becomes the target of all event data [24].
2. a stored procedure **sp_ssis_addlogentry** which is used to write data into the **sysssislog** table.

Table 10.16 Possible DataCode Values

Data Code	Description
0	Success
1	Failure
2	Completed
3	Cancelled

SSIS will call the stored procedure whenever an event occurs that is configured for logging. Interestingly, the table doesn't need to exist; only the stored procedure is required. It is also not required that the table be stored in the **dbo** schema of the database. A modified stored procedure can exist in any schema possible; the only setting that needs to be adjusted is the **default schema** setting of the logging user. That is the reason why another user has been configured in Figure 10.9. The default schema for this user is set to the **log** schema where the stored procedure is located.

The default implementation of the stored procedure just inserts the incoming data into the **sysssislog** table. However, this behavior can be modified to write data into another target or different target structure… the Metrics Vault. The tables shown in Figure 10.12 have been created to capture the events from SSIS.

The central table in the model is a transaction link **TLinkEvent**. It references four hubs: **HubEventType**, **HubComputer**, **HubOperator**, and **HubSource**. In addition, it contains an **id** attribute among some other descriptive attributes that are included in the transaction link. Other descriptive attributes, especially the large attributes such as the **message** and **databytes**, are stored in a transaction satellite **TSatEvent** to keep the transaction link as small as possible. Because the **message** attribute uses a specific format for some event types, additional satellites have been added to capture the message in the best format possible. For example, **TSatDiagnosticExEvent** stores the message in an xml field because this event type is using XML formatted messages. On the other hand, many other SSIS event types are using a text-based format, delimited by colons. To support easy access to the elements of the message, **TSatOnPipelinePreComponentCallEvent** is used to store the separate elements. These satellites are transaction satellites without a **LoadEndDate**, thus not supporting any updates by inserting new versions of the data and end-dating old records. However, for the given task, which is storing unmodifiable events, these entities are the optimal choice. There is one standard satellite in the model, **SatSource,** which allows changing the name of a task or component in SSIS. Referential integrity is implemented using foreign keys but disabled.

The transaction link in the Metric Vault implements the structure described in Chapter 5, Intermediate Data Vault Modeling:

```
CREATE TABLE [log].[TLinkEvent](
        [EventHashKey] [char](32) NOT NULL,
        [LoadDate] [datetime2](7) NOT NULL,
        [RecordSource] [varchar](50) NOT NULL,
        [EventTypeHashKey] [char](32) NOT NULL,
        [ComputerHashKey] [char](32) NOT NULL,
        [OperatorHashKey] [char](32) NOT NULL,
        [SourceHashKey] [char](32) NOT NULL,
        [id] [bigint] NOT NULL,
        [executionid] [uniqueidentifier] NOT NULL,
        [starttime] [datetime] NOT NULL,
        [endtime] [datetime] NOT NULL,
        [datacode] [int] NOT NULL,
 CONSTRAINT [PK_TLinkEvent] PRIMARY KEY NONCLUSTERED
(
        [EventHashKey] ASC
)WITH (PAD_INDEX = OFF, STATISTICS_NORECOMPUTE = OFF, IGNORE_DUP_KEY = OFF,
ALLOW_ROW_LOCKS = ON, ALLOW_PAGE_LOCKS = ON) ON [INDEX]
) ON [DATA]
```

Four hash keys are calculated to reference the hubs in the model. The primary key is on the **EventHashKey**, which is based on the business keys from the referenced hubs and the **id** attribute which

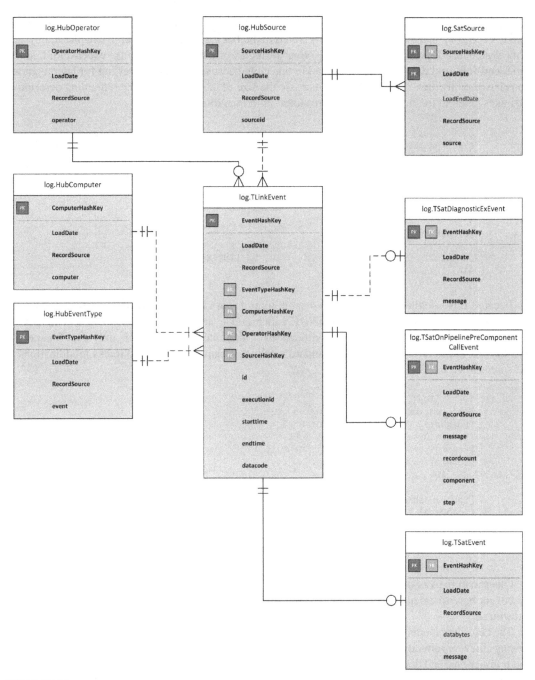

FIGURE 10.12

Metrics Vault for SSIS logging (physical design).

is required for uniqueness of the primary key. The implicit index on the primary key is stored in the **INDEX** filegroup and the data table itself is stored in the **DATA** filegroup. Refer to Chapter 8, Physical Data Warehouse Design, for details. The other attributes of the transaction link (**executionid**, **starttime**, **endtime**, and **datacode**) are included in this table because they are interesting for later aggregations based on the link. Also, they don't increase the size of the row much. The remaining descriptive attributes given to the stored procedure are stored in the satellite **TSatEvent**:

```
CREATE TABLE [log].[TSatEvent](
        [EventHashKey] [char](32) NOT NULL,
        [LoadDate] [datetime2](7) NOT NULL,
        [RecordSource] [varchar](50) NOT NULL,
        [databytes] [image] NULL,
        [message] [nvarchar](2048) NOT NULL,
 CONSTRAINT [PK_TSatEvent] PRIMARY KEY NONCLUSTERED
(
        [EventHashKey] ASC
)WITH (PAD_INDEX = OFF, STATISTICS_NORECOMPUTE = OFF, IGNORE_DUP_KEY = OFF,
ALLOW_ROW_LOCKS = ON, ALLOW_PAGE_LOCKS = ON) ON [INDEX]
) ON [DATA] TEXTIMAGE_ON [DATA]
```

Because this satellite is a nonhistorized satellite, it doesn't contain a **LoadEndDate**. The implicit index on the primary key is stored in the **INDEX** filegroup again, while the data is stored in the **DATA** filegroup. The other satellites are just modifications of this satellite and include only data for specific event types. **SatSource**, however, is a standard satellite, because it allows and tracks modifications in the source system (SSIS in this case):

```
CREATE TABLE [log].[SatSource](
        [SourceHashKey] [char](32) NOT NULL,
        [LoadDate] [datetime2](7) NOT NULL,
        [LoadEndDate] [datetime2](7) NULL,
        [RecordSource] [varchar](50) NOT NULL,
        [source] [nvarchar](1024) NOT NULL,
 CONSTRAINT [PK_SatSource] PRIMARY KEY NONCLUSTERED
(
        [SourceHashKey] ASC,
        [LoadDate] ASC
)WITH (PAD_INDEX = OFF, STATISTICS_NORECOMPUTE = OFF, IGNORE_DUP_KEY = OFF,
ALLOW_ROW_LOCKS = ON, ALLOW_PAGE_LOCKS = ON) ON [INDEX]
) ON [DATA]
```

Other than the **LoadEndDate**, the structure is very similar to the other satellites. The next chapter covers how to calculate the hash keys and how to end-date the satellites, which is required for **SatSource**.

The described model is loaded by modifying the **sp_ssis_addlogentry** stored procedure. Instead of writing all events directly into the **sysssislog** table, the events are split into business keys, relationships and transactions, and descriptive attributes and loaded into the tables of the Metrics Vault. Apart from creating a custom log provider in SSIS, this option is the most feasible one to load the Metrics Vault from SSIS.

One final note on the **LoadDate** in this specific Metrics Vault for SSIS: the recommendation in Chapter 4, Data Vault 2.0 Modeling, is to set the date to a single value for the whole batch in order to identify which records belong together. However, in the case of SSIS logging, each event is reported in a single transaction to the stored procedure. Therefore, each event receives its own load date, following a real-time loading pattern, which is not covered by this book.

In addition to the metrics directly obtained from SSIS using the preceding procedure, more metrics can be retrieved from Integration Services Catalogs, introduced in Microsoft SQL Server 2014. SQL Server maintains this catalog when SSIS packages are deployed to the server, a practice often used in production environments. The following internal views are available and could be integrated into the Metrics Vault [25]:

1. **catalog.catalog_properties:** provides the properties of the Integration Services catalog.
2. **catalog.effective_object_permissions:** provides the effective permissions on all objects in the Integration Services catalog for the current user.
3. **catalog.environment_variables:** provides detailed information about the variables in the environments in the Integration Services catalog.
4. **catalog.environments:** provides details for the environments in the Integration Services catalog.
5. **catalog.execution_parameter_values:** provides the environment variable values in the Integration Services catalog.
6. **catalog.executions:** provides detailed information about package executions in the Integration Services catalog.
7. **catalog.explicit_object_permissions:** provides the explicit permissions assigned to the current user.
8. **catalog.extended_operation_info:** provides extended information for all operations.
9. **catalog.folders:** provides information about the folders in the Integration Services catalog.
10. **catalog.object_parameters:** provides a list of all package and project parameters.
11. **catalog.object_versions:** provides a list of all object versions in the Integration Services catalog. As of Microsoft SQL Server 2014, only project versions are provided.
12. **catalog.operation_messages:** provides logged messages.
13. **catalog.operations:** provides a list of all operations in the Integration Services catalog.
14. **catalog.packages:** provides detailed information about all packages in the Integration Services catalog.
15. **catalog.environment_references:** provides a list of all environment references in all projects.
16. **catalog.projects:** provides a list of all projects in the Integration Services catalog with detailed information.
17. **catalog.validations:** provides a detailed list of project and package validations.

Using the raw data stored in these catalog views, it is possible to create a comprehensive Metrics Vault that integrates metrics from different sources.

However, both sets of metrics are based on SSIS and don't include any information about the hardware and network infrastructure. Such data can be obtained from Windows Management Instrumentation (WMI), provided by Microsoft Windows Server. WMI provides information about the server environment, including the hardware and network infrastructure. Table 10.17 lists the WMI providers currently available.

Table 10.17 Available WMI/MI/OMI Providers [26]

Active Directory	Mobile Device Management Settings	Software Inventory Logging
Application Proxy	MSFT_PCSVDevice	Software Licensing for Windows Vista
BitLocker Drive Encryption (BDE)	MsNetImPlatform	Software License
BITS	NetAdapterCim	Storage Volume
BizTalk	NetDaCim	System Registry
Boot Configuration Data	NetNcCim	System Restore
CIMWin32, Win32, Power Management Events	NetPeerDist	Trusted Platform Module
CIMWin32a	NetQosCim	Trustmon
DcbQosCim	NetSwitchTeam	User Access Logging
Distributed File System (DFS)	NetTCPIP	UserProfileProvider
Distributed File System Replication (DFSR)	NetTtCim	User State Management
Dfsncimprov	NetWNV	View
DhcpServerPSProvider	Network Access Protection	VPNClientPSProvider
Disk Quota	Network Load Balancing (NLB)	WDM
DNS	NFS	WFasCim
Dnsclientcim Provider Classes	Performance Counter	WhqlProvider
DnsClientPSProvider	Performance Monitoring	Win32ClockProvider
DnsServerPSProvider	Ping	Windows Data Access Components (WDAC)
Event Log	Policy	Windows Defender
Formatted Performance Data	Power Meter	Windows Installer
Failover Cluster	Power Policy	Windows Product Activation
Group Policy API	RAMgmtPSProvider	Windows Storage Management
Hyper-V	RAServerPSProvider	Windows System Assessment Tool
Hyper-V (V2)	ReliabilityMetricsProvider	WMI Core
Internet Information Services (IIS)	Remote Desktop Services	Msft_ProviderSubSystem
Internet Protocol Address Management (IPAM) Server	Reporting Services	Win32_Perf
IP Route Provider	Resultant Set of Policy (RSoP)	Win32_PerfFormattedData
Intelligent Platform Management Interface (IPMI)	Security	Win32_PerfRawData
iSCSI Target Server	ServerManager.DeploymentProvider	WMIPerfClass
Job Object	Session	WmiPerfInst
Kernel Trace	Shadow Copy	Work Folders
Live Communications Server 2003	SNMP	
Mobile Device Management Application	SMB Management	

The table also shows the Management Instrumentation (MI) and Open Management Infrastructure (OMI) providers that are available, because they use the same object format. The so-called Management Object Format (MOF) allows querying the data from classes in each provider. Access to the data in these management classes is performed using the WMI Query Language [27]. It is a subset of the ANSI SQL language known from database systems and supported in SSIS by the **WMI Data Reader Task** in the control flow.

10.4 IMPLEMENTING THE METRICS MART

After capturing the raw performance data in the Metrics Vault, the next step is to prepare the data for analysis. To support analysis of performance metrics, a data model is required that provides useful information to end-users. This data model is implemented in the Metrics Mart, which is located downstream towards the user (Figure 10.13).

Figure 10.13 highlights the EDW and the information delivery layer of the data warehouse. The Metrics Vault is implemented as an integral part of the Data Vault model and used exclusively to build the Metrics Mart. By doing so, this approach follows the standard Data Vault 2.0 architecture as outlined in Chapter 2, Scalable Data Warehouse Architectures. The Metrics Mart is an information mart that serves a special purpose and is sourced primarily from the Metrics Vault (instead of the Raw Data Vault and Business Vault). The implementation can use ETL for materializing the Metrics Mart or use virtualization, for example through SQL views. The latter is preferred as the speed to deploy new functionality drastically improves. Both techniques for loading information marts are discussed

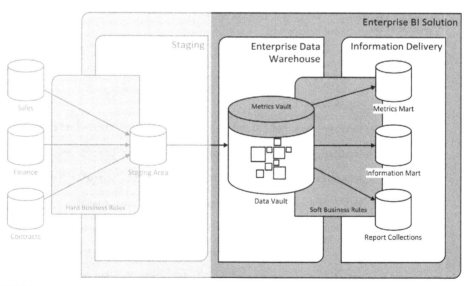

FIGURE 10.13

The Metrics Mart in the Data Vault 2.0 architecture.

in more detail in Chapter 14, Loading the Dimensional Information Mart. Because the Metrics Mart is a special variant of an information mart, the concepts for loading information marts apply for loading the Metrics Mart.

Note that the Metrics Mart can also be sourced from the Raw Data Vault or the Business Vault. In some cases, organizations decide to include business objects into performance measures, for example to measure technical performance metrics related to customers or products. These metrics can help to optimize the data warehouse even further.

The Metrics Mart uses a data model that fits the analysis needs of the end-users the most. This could be a dimensional model, especially if an OLAP cube should be built on top of the Metrics Mart or any other data model. But other data modeling techniques could be used as well, for example if a performance monitoring software is used that expects the data in a different format. It is also possible to feed such a monitoring software package directly from the Metrics Vault or the Metrics Mart, whatever fits the purpose of the task best.

In some cases, it might be helpful to provide the original structure of the SSIS table **sysssislog** in the Metrics Mart. For example, if a third-party tool expects the structure for further analysis. It is easy to provide the original structure by creating a SQL view in the Metrics Mart, sourcing the data directly from the tables in the Metrics Vault. The following T-SQL statement creates such a view:

```
CREATE VIEW sysssislog AS
SELECT
        tle.id,
        het.[event],
        hc.computer,
        ho.operator,
        ss.[source],
        hs.sourceid,
        tle.executionid,
        tle.starttime,
        tle.endtime,
        tle.datacode,
        tse.databytes,
        tse.[message]
FROM
        DataVault.log.TLinkEvent tle
INNER JOIN
        DataVault.log.HubEventType het ON het.EventTypeHashKey = tle.EventTypeHashKey
INNER JOIN
        DataVault.log.HubComputer hc ON hc.ComputerHashKey = tle.ComputerHashKey
INNER JOIN
        DataVault.log.HubOperator ho ON ho.OperatorHashKey = tle.OperatorHashKey
INNER JOIN
        DataVault.log.HubSource hs ON hs.SourceHashKey = tle.SourceHashKey
LEFT JOIN
        DataVault.log.SatSource ss ON ss.SourceHashKey = tle.SourceHashKey
        AND tle.LoadDate >= ss.LoadDate
        AND tle.LoadDate <= ISNULL(ss.LoadEndDate, '9999-12-31 23:59:59.999')
LEFT JOIN
        DataVault.log.TSatEvent tse ON tse.EventHashKey = tle.EventHashKey
        AND tse.LoadDate = tle.LoadDate
```

The statement uses the transaction link TLinkEvent as the primary source because it has the same grain as the original **sysssislog** table. It then joins the business keys from the hubs and other descriptive information to provide the original structure of the table.

In the same manner, another structure required by the end user could be provided. The advantage over the separation of the raw data (in the Metrics Vault) and the information (in the Metrics Mart) is the same as for the Raw Data Vault and information marts: it is possible to integrate other data sources more easily while building required structures in a virtual manner. Thus, it is easy to extend this simple Metrics Vault and Metrics Mart combination by adding additional sources for performance data over the course of the project.

10.5 IMPLEMENTING THE ERROR MART

The Error Mart is another information mart. However, similar to the Meta Mart, the Error Mart is not sourced from the Raw Data Vault or any other source. Instead, it is the primary location to store error information. The error information can come from a variety of sources, but most of it comes from the ETL engine. The Error Mart captures the following types of records:

1. **Records rejected by the staging area:** while the goal of the staging area is to temporarily load all data from the source system, it is not always feasible. In some cases, records have to be rejected because they don't fit into the relational structure of the staging area, for example if transmission errors have occurred.
2. **Records rejected by the Raw Data Vault:** again, the goal of the loading processes for the Raw Data Vault is to capture all raw data, *the good, the bad, and the ugly.* But similar to the staging area, not all data can be captured, especially if it doesn't fit into the relational structure of the Raw Data Vault.
3. **Records not processed by the Business Vault:** the Business Vault processes the raw data from the Raw Data Vault and creates intermediate business rule results. In some cases, soft rules define that the raw data has to comply with given rules, defined by the business. The Error Mart captures which records did not comply with these rules.
4. **Records not processed by the information marts:** because the Business Vault implements business rules only partially, the information marts can reject additional raw records. For that reason, the data rejected by the soft rules implemented in the information mart have to be redirected into the Error Mart as well.

Because soft business rules change over time, the data that is captured by the Error Mart changes over time as well. Interestingly, not all rejected records are bad records. The Error Mart also includes unexpected data that was not expected by the soft rule. In Data Vault, such data is called ugly data. The Error Mart helps to identify ugly data and improve the business rule implementation to capture more data that exists in the operational system and can be processed by some business logic. However, the ultimate goal is to identify the problem as to why the ugly record was not loaded into the Raw Data Vault, fix the issue (e.g., expect it in the loading ETL routines) and load it into the Raw Data Vault.

While the Error Mart can be implemented in the data model preferred by the end-user, many Error Marts are built using a dimension model. Such a model contains the erroneous data in fact tables and includes accompanying dimensions. The next section describes how to set up SSIS to capture erroneous data.

10.5.1 CAPTURING ERRONEOUS DATA IN SQL SERVER INTEGRATION SERVICES

Microsoft SSIS provides the capability to redirect records that have caused a failure in the data flow to an alternative component in the flow. This can include another OLE DB or SQL Server destination. Most data flow components offer an error output that can be used for this purpose.

The error output contains all the columns in the default data flow plus some columns that describe the error. Therefore, all error outputs are different from each other. When building the Error Mart, there are two options:

1. **Create common fact table for all error outputs:** this fact table contains only columns common to all error outputs. It requires the removal of most of the descriptive columns, the raw data, from the fact table.
2. **Create separate fact tables for each error output:** for each error output, a separate fact table is created. It allows the storing of all descriptive data in the corresponding fact table.

The advantage of the first option is that the data model of the Error Mart is fairly simple. However, it doesn't allow us to store the raw data that we might need for error analysis. The second option allows us that but the price is to have a lot of fact tables in the Error Mart which must be analyzed individually. For the sake of this chapter, we will describe a solution that implements option 2 because the goal of the Error Mart is to provide detailed information of the errors in the data warehouse. The production of mere statistics (which is the primary result of option 1) should be left to the Metrics Mart, which can keep error statistics as well.

Consider the staging process for master data in Chapter 9, Master Data Management (Figure 10.14).

Using this process, data on regions was sourced from a flat file and loaded into the Master Data Services (MDS). By doing so, data can be loaded into MDS automatically, without typing it in manually

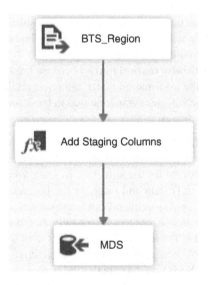

FIGURE 10.14

Data flow for staging master data.

using the Web interface or Microsoft Excel. After adding some columns required by the staging process in the second step, the data is loaded into the appropriate staging table for the **Region** entity in the **BTS** model.

In some cases, the MDS destination might reject records that don't fit into the relational structure. These are technical problems that result from errors in the SSIS implementation, unexpected data or other data-related issues (such as transmission errors in the flat file). On the other hand, MDS business rules which might be defined on the MDS entity could be violated as well. For example, there could be a business rule that requires that the **abbreviation** of the region must be different from the **code** value of the region. If the staged data from the source violates this rule, the record would be marked by MDS after applying the business rules on the entity. MDS would not reject the data. But it is possible to evaluate the result in the subscription view of the target entity and start appropriate measures to deal with invalid data in MDS.

Assuming that the staging table could reject some of the incoming data if there is a hard, technical error, in order to log these erroneous records into the Error Mart, the data flow is extended by redirecting the error output into another destination (Figure 10.15).

All records that have been rejected by the **MDS** destination output in the data flow of Figure 10.15 are redirected into the **Error Mart Destination**. Before doing so, some audit information, gathered from the SSIS engine, is added to the data flow (Figure 10.16).

The **Audit Type** column provides predefined audit information attributes that can be added to the data flow of the error output. On the left side of the table, the corresponding column names are set. In addition to these columns, more audit information can be added using a **Derived Column** component added to the data flow of the error output.

Note that the column names use a readable structure with spaces. In actual projects, the column names should adhere to the standard naming conventions of the data warehouse.

The audit columns should be used as conformed dimensions across the Error Mart. However, to keep things simple, the Error Mart in this example doesn't contain any conformed dimensions, not even

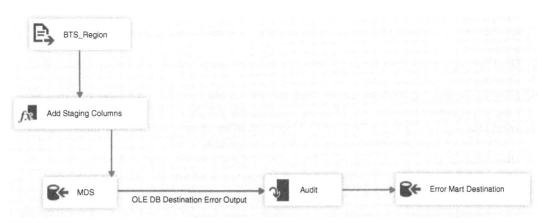

FIGURE 10.15

Data flow for staging master data with Error Mart destination.

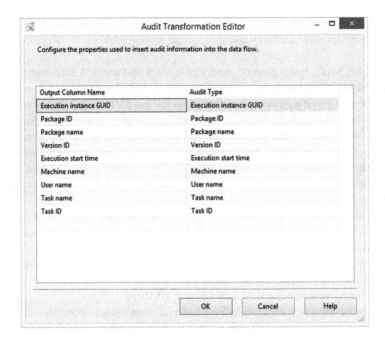

FIGURE 10.16

Audit transformation editor.

dimension tables. All dimensions are directly stored in the fact table, which is not a good practice but works for the purposes of this chapter. A better practice would be to create the following dimension tables:

1. **DimPackage:** containing **Package ID**, **Package name** and **Version ID**. This should be a slowly changing dimension (SCD) type 2 dimension.
2. **DimMachine:** containing **Machine name** and other descriptive information from other sources.
3. **DimUser:** containing **User name** and descriptive information from Active Directory and other sources.
4. **DimTask:** containing **Task name** and **Task ID**. This should be a SCD type 2, because the task name might change (but the task ID doesn't for the same task in SSIS).
5. **DimError:** containing **ErrorCode** and a description of the error. The error description can be obtained by a Script component (refer to [28] for more details).
6. **DimColumn:** providing the **ErrorColumn** and the name of the column. To retrieve the name of the column, a more complicated process is required which is described online (refer to [29]).

The remaining audit columns should be directly added to the fact table in a realistic environment. While using dimension tables is the preferred solution, it would require a more complicated

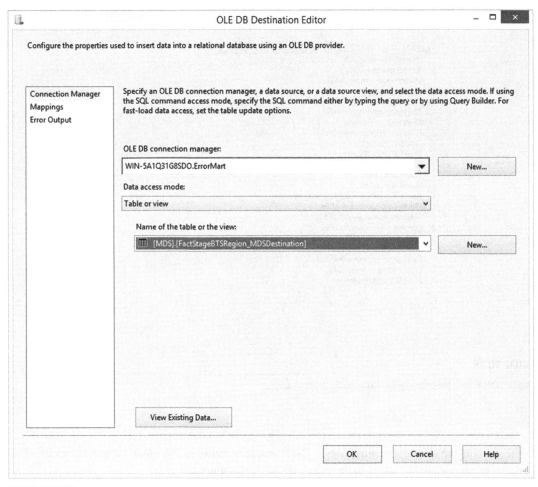

FIGURE 10.17

OLE DB destination editor for the Error Mart destination.

loading process to populate the data in the dimensions as well. Therefore, the Error Mart Destination setup becomes fairly simple. First, the connection to the Error Mart has to be set up (Figure 10.17).

The connection directly accesses the **ErrorMart** database and uses a **table or view** data access mode to the target fact table. The New button in Figure 10.17 allows one to quickly create the target table, based on the data flow of the error output and the added audit columns (Figure 10.18).

Because it is possible to modify the statement directly in the dialog, it is a good place to apply naming conventions to the fact table name. The last step is to map the columns in the data flow to the destination table, which is shown in Figure 10.19.

FIGURE 10.18

Create table editor for creating the Error Mart destination.

Because of the simple structure, only a direct mapping between the input columns from the data flow and the destination columns in the target fact table is required.

To implement this solution with dimension tables (as previously described), multiple options are available:

1. **Extend the SSIS data flow:** the SSIS data flow could be extended to populate the dimension tables by adding additional lookup and database destinations to the error output. Use the **Slowly Changing Dimension** component as a starting point for extending the SSIS data flow. However, this approach requires a large number of components to be added to the data flow, which makes it relatively complex.
2. **Create an INSTEAD OF trigger on a view:** replace the table by a view with an accompanying INSTEAD OF trigger that distributes the data in the fact and dimension tables. This approach is transparent to SSIS but requires programming on the database back-end.
3. **Write into a stored procedure:** instead of using a trigger, write your error output to a stored procedure. Use the **SQL command** data access mode in the **OLE DB Destination** component. By doing so, it is not completely transparent, but easier to understand and more visible than an INSTEAD OF trigger.

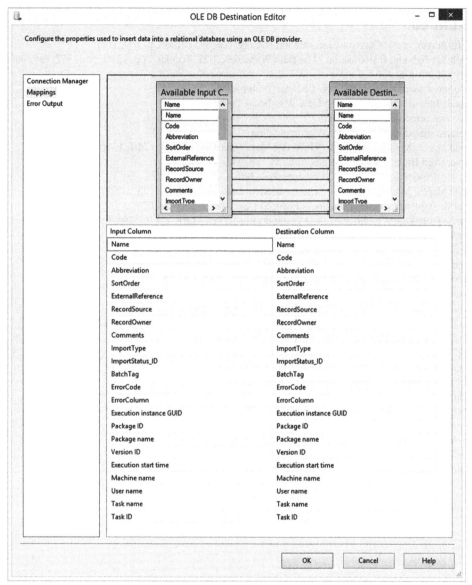

FIGURE 10.19

Column mapping for the Error Mart destination.

Which option you choose depends on a number of factors regarding maintainability and programming requirements. Stick to the solution shown in this chapter if storage is negligible compared to the overhead to maintain the dimension tables. Regardless whether dimension tables are created or if the dimensions are integrated in the fact table, analysis can be performed on the fact tables, either directly or using OLAP cubes in SSAS.

REFERENCES

[1] W. H. Inmon, et al. "Corporate Information Factory," second edition, p. 169, 169f.

[2] Ralph Kimball and Jose Caserta: "The Data Warehouse ETL Toolkit," pp. 124ff, 352, 357, 359, 360ff, 362, 364ff, 367ff, 376, 379.

[3] http://www.merriam-webster.com/dictionary/volumetric

[4] Claudia Imhoff, et al. "Mastering Data Warehouse Design," p. 15.

[5] https://sqlmetadata.codeplex.com/

[6] https://sqlmetadata.codeplex.com/documentation

[7] David Marco, Michael Jennings: "Universal Meta Data Models", pp. 124ff, 134ff.

[8] Barbara von Halle: "Business Rules Applied," pp. 34, 436, 446.

[9] http://agilemodeling.com/artifacts/businessRule.htm

[10] David Marco, Michael Jennings: "Universal Meta Data Models", pp. 125, 126.

[11] Jennifer Stapleton: "DSDM: Business Focused Development," p. 197ff.

[12] Kimmo Palletvuori: "Security of Data Warehousing Server," TKK T-110.5290 Seminar on Network Security.

[13] http://web.stanford.edu/group/security/securecomputing/dataclass_chart.html

[14] Bharat Bhargava: "Security in Data Warehousing".

[15] Brian Knight, et al. "Professional Microsoft SQL Server 2014 Integration Services," p. 622, 622f.

[16] Quest Software: "Spotlight on Oracle 7.6: Getting Started Guide," p. 33ff.

[17] http://labs.consol.de/lang/en/nagios/check_mssql_health

[18] http://www.cse.wustl.edu/~jain/cse567-06/ftp/net_traffic_monitors2

[19] http://logicalread.solarwinds.com/sql-server-buffer-hit-cache-ratio/#.VJ6dOsANA

[20] http://msdn.microsoft.com/en-us/library/ms141744.aspx

[21] http://msdn.microsoft.com/en-us/library/ms140246.aspx

[22] http://msdn.microsoft.com/en-us/library/ms136010.aspx

[23] http://msdn.microsoft.com/en-us/library/ms141122(v(sql.120)

[24] http://msdn.microsoft.com/en-us/library/ms186984.aspx

[25] http://msdn.microsoft.com/en-us/library/ff878135.aspx

[26] http://msdn.microsoft.com/en-us/library/bg126473(v(vs.85).aspx

[27] http://msdn.microsoft.com/en-us/library/aa392902(v(vs.85).aspx

[28] http://msdn.microsoft.com/en-us/library/ms345163(v(sql.120).aspx

[29] http://dougbert.com/blog/post/Adding-the-error-column-name-to-an-error-output.aspx

DATA EXTRACTION

Once the physical environment has been set up (refer to Chapter 8, Physical Data Warehouse Design), the development of the data warehouse begins. This includes master data (as described in Chapter 9, Master Data Management) and the management of metadata (see Chapter 10, Metadata Management). However, the majority of data (regarding the volume and the variety) is periodically loaded from source systems. In addition, more and more data is sourced in real time (not covered by this book) or written directly into the data warehouse (similar to the **sp_ssis_addlogentry** stored procedure in Chapter 10, section 10.3.1).

This chapter covers the extraction from source systems both on premise (such as flat files which provide data extracted from operational systems) and in the Cloud (from Google Drive). Extracting master data from MDS is also covered, both materialized (using SSIS) and virtualized.

Throughout this book, we use example data from the Bureau of Transportation Statistics [1] (BTS) at the U.S. Department of Transportation [2] (DoT). The dataset contains scheduled flights that have been operated by U.S. air carriers. The flights include their actual departure and arrival times. Only those U.S. carriers are covered that account for at least 1% of domestic scheduled passenger revenues [3]. Figure 11.1 shows an overview of the BTS model.

Note that the raw data has been converted into a more usable format for the purpose of this book. For example, the monthly database dumps have been split into daily dumps for ease of use. Also, due to technical issues, some lines have been dropped in some years (for example in 2001 and 2002, among others). You should not conduct research using these files as not all data has been converted – the data sets used in this book are incomplete. If you need files that include all airline data, you should obtain them directly from the BTS Web site [3].

It should also be noted that there are more business keys in the source data that are ignored when building the examples in the book. It is also important to recognize that some of the selected and implemented business keys are far from being optimal; for example, the airport code and the carrier code are not stable because they are reused for new business entities in some cases.

11.1 PURPOSE OF STAGING AREA

When extracting data from source systems, the workload on the operational system increases to some extent. The actual load that is added to the source infrastructure depends on a number of factors, for example how much data is prepared before the extraction or if raw data is exported directly. The required workload is also influenced by the use of bulk exports (i.e., directly exporting the results of a SQL query) or the use of some application programming interface (API). In the worst case (from a

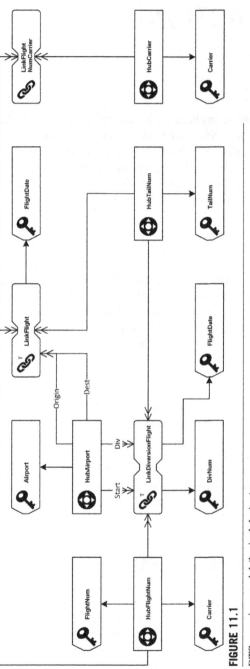

FIGURE 11.1

BTS overview model (logical design).

performance standpoint), all data from the database has to go through an object-relational mapping (ORM) before it is exported into a flat file. In other, similar cases, the relational database is not directly accessible but only some representational state transfer (REST) or Web Service API. Loading the data from such APIs will be a pain on its own, but loading processes for data warehouse systems often involves additional operations, for example lookups to find out the business key for a referenced object or the name of a passenger. If these lookups are directly performed against an operational system, the data warehouse might have an additional burden placed on it. Consider the daily load of 40,000 passenger flight information records for a data warehouse of a midsized airline [4]. Because the business needs detailed information about the aircraft used, a lookup into the aircraft management system with 100 operational aircraft is required. If no lookup caching is enabled, 40,000 lookup operations are required to retrieve the data for the 100 aircraft. Even with lookup caching, more than 100 lookup operations are required to serve all lookups in all data flows.

The primary purpose of the staging area is to reduce the workload on the operational systems by loading all required data into a separate database first. This ingestion of data should be performed as quickly as possible in any format provided. For this reason, the Data Vault 2.0 System of Business Intelligence includes the use of NoSQL platforms, such as Hadoop, as staging areas. Once the raw data has been loaded into the NoSQL platform, it is then sourced and structured once business value and business requirements are established. Due to space limitations, this book will focus on a relational staging area.

The advantage of this staging area is that the data is under technical control of the data warehouse team and can be indexed, sorted, joined, etc. All operations available in relational database systems are available for the staged data. To ensure best usage of the data in the staging area, the data types follow the intended data types from the source system (don't use only varchar data types in the staging area). But another purpose of the staging area is to make data extraction from the operational system easy. We will see in section 11.8 how we violate the recommendation to avoid using only varchars in the staging area in order to retrieve the source data with ease. The data is transformed into the actual data types when loading it into the Data Vault model (refer to Chapter 12, Loading the Data Vault for details).

It is also possible to look up data in a staging area even though, in data warehouse systems built with Data Vault 2.0, this is not often required. Business rules are implemented after the Raw Data Vault and perform their lookups into the Raw Data Vault only. The reason for this is that the staging area provides only a limited history of previous loads. The staging area is transient. It should keep only a limited number of loads in order to deal with erroneous ETL processes downstream (to load the Raw Data Vault). The goal is to prevent data loss if the data cannot be loaded into the data warehouse layer for technical or organizational reasons. For example, not all errors can be fixed within a business day. It is not the goal of the staging area to keep a history of loads. This goal is accomplished by the enterprise data warehouse layer. If the staging area keeps the history for all loads, it requires additional management (consider storage, backup, etc.). As a result, you end up with the management of two data warehouses.

Loading the staging area follows a standard pattern because all incoming data items, such as flat files or relational tables, are sourced independently. To achieve this independence, there is no referential integrity implemented through foreign keys. Each staging table is a direct copy of the incoming data with only some system-generated attributes added. Figure 11.2 shows the template for loading a staging table.

The first step is to **truncate the staging tables**, if only one load should be kept. If the staging area should follow best practices and keep a limited history, the truncation has to take place once the data has been loaded into the Raw Data Vault. For performance reason, it might be advisable to **disable indexes** on the staging area, if there are any implemented. The next step is to perform a **bulk read on**

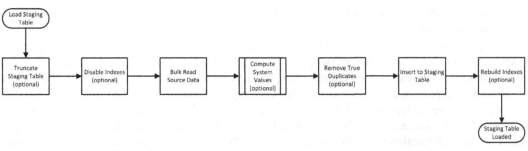

FIGURE 11.2

Template for staging area loading.

the source data from the source file or source database connection. As already mentioned, in order to achieve acceptable performance, the goal should be to read the data in chunks, not single records. If possible, complex APIs, such as the ones introduced by object-relational mapping (ORM), should be avoided. Instead, direct access to the relational tables or their raw data exported to flat files should be preferred. In Microsoft SQL Server, this can be achieved by executing the following T-SQL statement on the staging table [5]:

```
ALTER INDEX ALL ON StageArea.BTS.OnTimeOnTimePerformance
DISABLE;
```

Another purpose of the staging area is to **compute and add system-generated attributes** to the incoming data. By doing this, reuse of the attributes is possible. Figure 11.3 shows the subprocess in more detail. In some cases, true duplicates exist in the source data. If they are kept and loaded into the Raw Data Vault, they would only create additional workload, but no additional changes to hubs and links. Depending on the implementation of the satellite loading processes, they could cause additional problems during change detection. This is why **true duplicates should be removed** from the staging area. Finally, the data is **inserted into the staging table** and **indexes are rebuilt** again. The Microsoft SQL Statement is very similar to the previous one [5]:

```
ALTER INDEX ALL ON StageArea.BTS.OnTimeOnTimePerformance
REBUILD;
```

The following attributes are added in the **Compute System Values** subprocess, which is presented in Figure 11.3.

- **Load date:** the date and time when the batch arrived in the data warehouse (in the staging area). A batch includes all data that arrived as a set. In most cases, this includes all data in all flat files or relational tables from one source system.
- **Record source:** a readable string that identifies the source system and the module or source table where the data comes from. This is used for debugging purposes only and should help your team to trace errors.

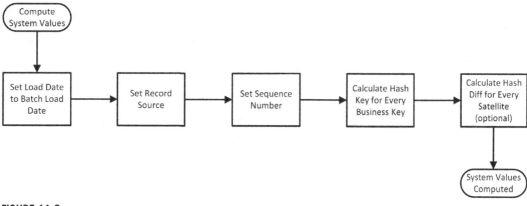

FIGURE 11.3

Compute system values subprocess.

- **Sequence number:** all records in a staging table are sequenced using a unique and ascending number. The purpose of this number is to recognize the order of the records in the source system and identify true duplicates, which are loaded to the staging area but not to downstream layers of the data warehouse. Note that the sequence number is not used for identification purposes of the record.
- **Hash keys:** every business key in the Raw Data Vault is hashed for identification purposes. This includes composite keys and key combinations used in Data Vault links. Chapter 4, Data Vault 2.0 Modeling, discusses how hash keys are used in hubs and links for identification purposes.
- **Hash diffs:** these keys are used to identify changes in descriptive attributes of satellite rows. This is also discussed in Chapter 4.

Because hash value computation consumes CPU power, there is an advantage of reusing the computed value. While the hash function that is used in this process is standardized (examples include MD5 and SHA-1), the input of the hash function has to follow organization-wide, defined standards. These standards have to be set by a governing body in the organization and should be based on the best practices as outlined in the next section.

11.2 HASHING IN THE DATA WAREHOUSE

Traditional data warehouse models often use sequence numbers to identify the records in other tables in the data warehouse and reference them in dependent tables. These numbers are generated in the data warehouse instead of being sourced from operational systems in order to use an independent sequence number that is controlled by the data warehouse.

There are multiple drawbacks with sequence numbers [6]:

- **Dependencies in the loading processes:** in order to load a destination, every dependency has to be loaded first. For example, loading a table that stores the customer addresses requires the loading of the customer table first, in order to look up the sequence number which identifies a particular customer.

- **Waiting on caches for parent lookups:** assuming sequence numbers instead of hashes would be applied. In this situation, Link and Satellite loads must "wait" for parent table lookup caches (particularly in ETL engines) to load with the cross-maps of business keys to sequence numbers. Hubs and links often contain large sets of rows that need to be cached before the ETL processing can begin. This causes a bottleneck in the loading processes. This can be alleviated or removed by switching the model to Data Vault 2.0 Hash Keys – eliminating the need for lookup caching altogether.
- **Dependencies on serial algorithms:** sequence numbers are often used as surrogate keys but they are what they are: sequences that are serial numbers. In order to generate such a sequence number, a sequence generator is often used, which presents a bottleneck because it needs to be synchronized in order to prevent two sequence numbers with the same value. In Big Data environments, the required synchronization can become a problem because data is coming at high speed and/or volume.
- **Complete restore limitations:** when restoring a parent table (e.g. the customer table from the previous example), the sequence numbers need to be the same as before the restore. Otherwise, the customer references in dependent tables become invalid (in the best case) or wrong (in the worst case).
- **Required synchronization of multiple environments:** if sequence numbers have to be unique across nodes or heterogeneous environments, synchronization of the sequence number generation is required. This synchronization can become a bottleneck in Big Data environments.
- **Data distribution and partitioning in MPP environments:** in MPP environments, the sequence number should not be used for data distribution or partitioning because queries can cause hot spots when getting data out of the MPP environment [7].
- **Scalability issues:** sequence numbers are easy to use but are limited when it comes to scalability. When using sequence numbers in large data warehouses with multiple terabytes or even petabytes of data, the sequence generation can become a bottleneck when loading large amounts of data. Sequences have an upper limit (usually), and in large data sets, or with repeated "restarts" due to error processing, the sequence generators can "run-out" of sequence numbers, and must then be cycled back to one. This is called roll-over, and isn't a preferred situation – nor is it advisable to have this situation in a Big Data system to begin with. The other side of this situation is performance. With Big Data, many times the loading processes need to be run in parallel. Sequence generators, when "partitioned" so they can run in parallel, assign groups of sequences – and can hit the upper limits of the sequence number faster. Why? Each group of sequences (one per partitioned process) requires a block of sequences, and often leaves holes in the sequencing as it loads, thus eating up sequences much quicker than expected.
- **Difference of NoSQL engines:** in many cases, NoSQL engines use hash keys instead of sequence numbers because of the limitations regarding MPP data distribution and scalability, described in the previous bullet points.

Due to these drawbacks and limitations, hash keys are used as primary keys in the Data Vault 2.0 model, thus replacing sequence numbers as surrogate keys. Hash functions ensure that (exactly) the same input (on a bit level) produces the same hash value. The following sections discuss how to use this characteristic of hash functions for generating nonsequential surrogate keys that can be used in data warehousing.

Chapter 4 has outlined some benefits of using hash keys in the Data Vault 2.0 model: because hash keys are calculated independently in loading processes, there are no lookups into other Data Vault 2.0 entities required in order to get the surrogate key of a business key. In general, a lookup into another table requires I/O performance in order to retrieve the sequence number for a given business key. On the other hand, computing a hash key only requires CPU performance, which is often favored over I/O performance because of better parallelization and better resource consumption in general.

The alternative to hash keys is to use business keys as identifying elements in the data warehouse. However, using hash keys provides the advantage that the primary keys (and the referencing columns) can always use a fixed length data type, which has performance advantages in Microsoft SQL Server. This is due to the fixed-length column value that can be stored directly in the data page, requiring no lookups in additional database pages (text/image page) when performing table joins. Similar advantages are seen in other relational database management systems. While business keys in hubs might be shorter than hash keys, hash keys tend to be shorter in link tables (where multiple business keys are combined), a factor often overlooked when discussing the storage requirements of hash keys versus business keys.

But it's not only the identification of business keys that can take advantage of introducing hash calculations in the data warehouse. Another advantage is the use of hash diff values, which can help to speed up column compares on descriptive attributes when loading satellites. This is of special interest for loading large amounts of raw data into satellites and is described in more detail in section 11.2.5.

While the benefits outweigh the drawbacks, the goal of the data warehouse is to reduce the number of hash key calculations in order to reduce CPU computations. Therefore, most hash values (hash keys and hash diffs) are calculated when loading the data from source systems into the stage area. This is not possible in every case, but is a desired strategy that should be achieved in 80% or more of the cases. Figure 11.4 shows potential locations in the loading process where hash values can be calculated if it is not possible to calculate and store the hash keys and hash diff values in the staging area.

Calculating the hash values upstream to the data warehouse increases the reusability of the values in downstream processes towards the business user and prevents recomputation of the same hash key or hash diff value. On the other hand, the reusability of hash diff values is limited because they are only used in one satellite.

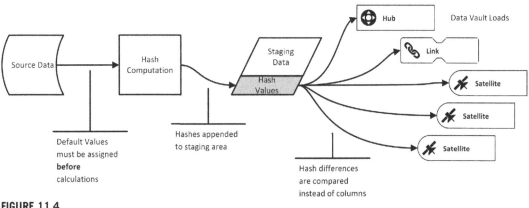

FIGURE 11.4

Stage load hash computation.

11.2.1 HASH FUNCTIONS REVISITED

There are multiple options available when applying hash functions in data warehousing. When selecting the hash function it is important to understand that hashing in the data warehouse doesn't have any intention of encrypting or securing the business key. The only goal is to replace sequential surrogate keys by a hash key alternative [8]. Hash functions have a desired set of characteristics, including [8]:

- **Deterministic:** for a given block of input data, the hash function will always generate the same hash value whenever called.
- **Irreversible:** a hash function is an irreversible, one-way function. It is not possible to derive the source data from the hash value.
- **Avalanche effect:** if the input data is changed only slightly, the hash value should change drastically. Also known as a cascading effect.
- **Collision-free:** any two different blocks of input data should always produce different hash values. The unlikely event of two input blocks generating the same hash value is called a collision. These hash collisions is discussed in more detail in section 11.2.3.

The most common and recommended options for the purpose of hashing business keys include MD5 and SHA-1:

- **MD5 message-digest algorithm (MD5):** The MD5 algorithm was introduced in 1992 as a replacement of MD4. It takes a message of arbitrary length as an input and produces a 128-bit (16-byte) hash value, called a message digest or "signature" of the input. In cryptography, it was commonly used to digitally sign the input, such as an email message or file download to prevent later modifications [9].
- **Secure hash algorithm (SHA):** In 1995, SHA-1 was published as an industry standard for secure hash algorithms and should replace MD5 due to security concerns. SHA-1 is a U.S. Federal Information Processing Standard [10].

Table 11.1 shows some key statistics about the generated hashes of both algorithms and, with SHA-256, an implementation of the secure hash algorithm with a larger message digest size:

The different output lengths are due to the fact that a character in hexadecimal representation can represent only 4 bits. For that reason, the space is doubled when using hexadecimal characters to represent the hash value. Section 11.2.2 discusses the advantages of the hexadecimal hash representation. Section 11.2.3 discusses the advantages of all three hash functions in more detail.

Note that both algorithms are used in cryptography, but they are not encryption algorithms. The hash result is typically encrypted with a private key, as used in public-key cryptosystems, for example

Table 11.1 Key Statistics for Selected Hash Algorithms			
	MD5	**SHA-1**	**SHA-256**
Max. Input Length	Unlimited	2^{64}-1 bits	2^{64}-1 bits
Output Length (binary)	128 bits (16 bytes)	160 bits (20 bytes)	256 bits (32 bytes)
Output Length (hex)	32 characters/bytes	40 characters/bytes	64 characters/bytes

RSA [11]. By doing so, a signature is created that is associated with the public key of the sender, which can be validated.

Unencrypted MD5 and SHA-1 hashes are often used to validate whether a download has not been compromised or accidentally modified due to transmission errors after downloading the file from the Web site of origin. For that reason, hashes are often seen next to downloads on Web sites, as shown in Figure 11.5.

In this case, there are multiple hash values provided using hexadecimal representation, including MD5, SHA-1 and SHA-256. By using hexadecimal characters, it is possible to include the hash value as a "readable" text directly into the Web site. Otherwise, the hash keys would have to be provided as additional binary file downloads. It is possible to validate the integrity of the downloaded file with a tool such as File Checksum Integrity Verifier (FCIV) from Microsoft [12]. The tool takes the downloaded file as input and reports the MD5 hash for the downloaded file:

```
FCIV -md5 LibreOffice_4.3.5_MacOS_x86-64.dmg
```

If there is no difference between the bits of the file on the server and the bits of the downloaded file on the client, the output of the File Checksum Integrity Verifier should be the same as stated on the Web site in Figure 11.5.

11.2.2 APPLYING HASH FUNCTIONS TO DATA

The approach described in the previous section uses an important characteristic of hash functions: the same input (on a bit level) produces the same, fixed-length hash value. In addition, the hash function produces a "random-like" value for each input. If only one bit changes in the input, the resulting hash value is not even close to the hash value without the changed bit. As described in the previous section, this characteristic is called the avalanche effect [13]. Consider the following examples:

Table 11.2 shows three example inputs and their respective MD5 and SHA-1 hash keys (note that MD5 outputs and SHA-1 outputs cannot be compared due to the different algorithms). Notice the inputs: the first two values are "Data Vault 2.0" and "DataVault 2.0": a space between the first two words was removed. While this change seems to be minimal, it is actually not. The character length is

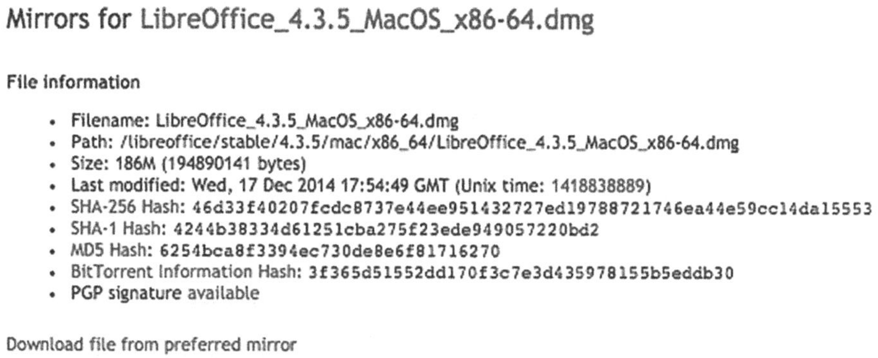

Mirrors for LibreOffice_4.3.5_MacOS_x86-64.dmg

File information

- Filename: LibreOffice_4.3.5_MacOS_x86-64.dmg
- Path: /libreoffice/stable/4.3.5/mac/x86_64/LibreOffice_4.3.5_MacOS_x86-64.dmg
- Size: 186M (194890141 bytes)
- Last modified: Wed, 17 Dec 2014 17:54:49 GMT (Unix time: 1418838889)
- SHA-256 Hash: 46d33f40207fcdc8737e44ee951432727ed19788721746ea44e59cc14da15553
- SHA-1 Hash: 4244b38334d61251cba275f23ede949057220bd2
- MD5 Hash: 6254bca8f3394ec730de8e6f81716270
- BitTorrent Information Hash: 3f365d51552dd170f3c7e3d435978155b5eddb30
- PGP signature available

Download file from preferred mirror

FIGURE 11.5

LibreOffice download with hash values for verification purposes.

different (from 14 characters down to 13) and therefore, the bit representation after the fourth character is completely different, as all following bits shift by eight characters to the left (Table 11.3).

Given their positions, all bold bits have changed, because they have been removed or shifted to the left. Therefore, we would expect this drastic change in the input to be reflected in their hash keys (which is the case in Table 11.2). And the same is true for an actual small change on the bit level (Table 11.4).

Here, only the first character case changes from an upper-case D to a lower-case d. Bitwise, the difference is just one bit that changes in the input, as indicated bold in Table 11.4: the bit on position 3 has changed from 0 to 1. However, even in this case of minor change, the hash values between example 2 and 3 in Table 11.2 are completely different, yet not randomly generated. The hash looks random, but it follows an algorithm that has the goal of ensuring that small changes have a high impact on the output – a desired characteristic in cryptography.

This characteristic is also desired when distributing the data in MPP environments such as Microsoft Analytics Platform System (formerly Microsoft SQL Server Parallel Data Warehouse). The distribution relies on a distribution column (other vendors call this a primary index). The data in this distribution column should be evenly distributed because all rows in a table are distributed according to this data in the column. If the data is skewed, the records will not be evenly distributed across the nodes, which will cause hot spots when answering queries [14]. Because the calculated hash value is "random-like," it is a good candidate for a distribution column. Even similar data is distributed evenly on the nodes, thus ensuring that the maximum possible number of nodes answers queries.

Hash values can be calculated in a number of locations, for example directly in the database (using T-SQL functions), in SSIS, or in a third-party application. However, while the implementation of the hash algorithm should be the same (in the case of SHA-1, this can be ensured through a validation program by the NIST [15]), the resulting hash value depends heavily on the input to the function.

Table 11.2 Hash Examples			
#	Input	Output (MD5)	Output (SHA-1)
1	Data Vault 2.0	CCD04E26434D844C002CF7B0914F61EB	47014AD9CAEA430A925F98FF21D7CD420F0E219A
2	DataVault 2.0	D234C1DA50518AC45A432D24AD756553	C11A059BBFD5DAA5A9E7ED594353CCDA13BA9151
3	dataVault 2.0	61CA9F6B4F747C5F09BAAB093FE21AF2	06495EEE633A19F30319457A39CEBD89B275A48B

Table 11.3 Binary Representation of Examples 1 and 2	
Input (ASCII)	Binary Representation
Data Vault 2.0	01000100 01100001 01110100 01100001 **00100000 01010110 01100001 01110101 01101100 01110100 00100000 00110010 00101110 00110000**
DataVault 2.0	01000100 01100001 01110100 01100001 **01010110 01100001 01110101 01101100 01110100 00100000 00110010 00101110 00110000**

Table 11.4 Binary Representation of Examples 2 and 3	
Input (ASCII)	Binary Representation
DataVault 2.0	01000100 01100001 01110100 01100001 01010110 01100001 01110101 01101100 01110100 00100000 00110010 00101110 00110000
dataVault 2.0	01100100 01100001 01110100 01100001 01010110 01100001 01110101 01101100 01110100 00100000 00110010 00101110 00110000

Even the same sentence can produce different hash values if the input on the bit level is not exactly the same. Raw data types (integers, floats, etc.) make things worse, as the binary representation might differ from system to system. In order to calculate a re-usable hash value, that is a hash value that is the same for the same data input, all raw data types are converted into a string before hashing. That reduces the complexity of the approach to hash the data. The following requirements have to be met by the input string:

1. **Character set:** the character set defines how bits of a string or varchar are interpreted into readable characters. Or in other terms: how bits represent characters. Because commonly available hash functions work with bits instead of characters, the character set plays an important role to ensure that the same characters end up with the same bit representation. This includes Unicode vs. non-Unicode choices.

2. **Leading and trailing spaces:** in many cases, any leading and trailing spaces don't play an important role for the business user of a data warehouse. For example, business keys usually don't include leading or trailing spaces and descriptive data is often trimmed from them as well before presented to the user. Because they don't change the meaning of the input and only the binary representation, they should not be included in the input to the hash function.

3. **Embedded or unseen control characters:** the same applies for any embedded or unseen control characters. Examples for this might be bell codes (BC) [16], carriage return (CR), new line (LF) or backspace sign, which often have no difference to the semantics of the text. Many of these control characters are inserted into text files or databases due to interoperability issues between operational systems.

4. **Data type, length, precision and scale:** the use of different data types, their length, and precision and scale settings produce different binary representations. For example, values stored in a decimal(5,2) or in a decimal(6,2) might be represented as the same characters, but are stored as different binary values. Therefore, one of the recommendations is to convert all data types to strings before hashing them.

5. **Date format:** when converting dates to strings, the question is how to represent dates in a common manner. It is recommended to cast all dates and timestamps into a standardized ISO8601 format [17].

6. **Decimal separator:** another problem when converting data types to strings concerns different regional settings. Depending on the current locale, different decimal and thousands separators are used. For example, the number 1,000.99 (in US format) is represented as 1.000,99 in Germany and 1'000.99 in Switzerland.

7. **Case sensitivity:** as already shown from the previous examples, the character case changes the binary representation of the string. Therefore, the character case has to be taken into consideration when hashing data. Depending on your data, case sensitivity needs to be turned on or off for your input data. For example, in most cases, business keys are case insensitive. Customer DE00042 is the same as de00042. There are exceptions to this rule, for example when business keys are actually case sensitive. The same applies to descriptive data that is often case sensitive, as well. We will discuss such examples in sections 11.2.4 and 11.2.5, respectively. Note that case sensitivity applies to the output as well. Some hash functions (or the accompanying conversion from binary values to a hexadecimal representation) produce a lower-case hex string, while others produce an upper-case hexadecimal string. The best practice is to convert all outputs from hash functions to upper-case.

8. **NULL values:** depending on the system where the hash value is calculated, the binary representation of a NULL value might be different, especially when converting NULL values to varchars or strings. Note that hash values are not always generated in a database but in other software environments such as the .NET framework, a Java Virtual Machine or in a Unix Shell. The recommended approach when dealing with NULL values is to always replace them by empty strings and use delimiters when concatenating multiple fields (for example, when calculating the hash key of a composite business key or the hash diff value of descriptive data).

9. **Lack of delimiters for concatenated fields:** because the recommendation is to replace NULL values by an empty string, there might be examples when different data becomes the same input after converting to strings and concatenating the individual elements of the input. Therefore the use of delimiters is required. This is described in more detail in section 11.2.4.

10. **Order of concatenated fields:** when concatenating fields, the order of the fields plays a vital role. If it is changed, the hash values become different.

11. **Endianness:** the architecture of software and hardware plays another significant role in how bytes are stored in memory. This can become an issue when not all hashes are generated on the same system, for example because some data is being hashed on other systems than the primary data warehouse system. For example, the .NET Framework is using little endian [18] (storing the least-significant byte (LSB) at the lowest memory address), while the Java Virtual Machine is using big endian [19] (storing the most significant byte (MSB) at the lowest memory address) as does Hadoop [20]. Microsoft SQL Server uses big endian in most cases [21]. On the hardware side, Intel® in its 80×86 architecture uses little endian [22].

12. **Everything else:** whenever the bit representation of the input string is changed, the hash value changes.

In order to deal with these issues and requirements, a first thought is to create a central function, such as a reusable user-defined function or SSIS script component that calculates the hash value by preparing the input and calling the appropriate hash function. However, this approach is often not enough, because today data is loaded into the data warehouse with various tools, for example an ETL tool such as SSIS, directly in the database (for example the stored procedure created in Chapter 10, Metadata Management) or in tools external to the data warehouse team. Other data is stored in NoSQL environments such as Hadoop and never touches the data warehouse until it is joined when building the information marts. However, if both parties use different approaches for dealing with these requirements, the join will fail, because the hash keys in hubs and links will be completely different from each other, preventing the joining of data across systems. For that reason, the first task when starting the data warehouse initiative is to create a standards document for hash value generation. The document should not only define which hashing function should be used to calculate the hash values, but also how the input is generated to ensure the same output for the same data. Table 11.5 reviews the standards that need to be established by this document and gives best practices for each.

Note that the recommendation for Endianess and SQL Server is to use Little Endian because the HashBytes function appears to use Little Endian. Refer to section 11.6.3 for a discussion related to SQL Server and SSIS.

Addressing these requirements in the design phase and throughout the whole data warehouse lifecycle is the first step in dealing with technological risks regarding the use of hashes in data warehousing. However, there are additional risks, which are covered in the next section, that need to be mitigated.

11.2.3 RISKS OF USING HASH FUNCTIONS

When using hash keys and hash diff values in the data warehouse, there are some additional issues that need to be considered in the design phase of the project. Ignoring these risks will sooner or later hit back on the data warehouse team.

Table 11.5 Best Practices for Hashing Standards Document

Standard	Best Practice
Hashing Function	MD5
Character set	UTF-8
Leading and trailing spaces	Strip
Control characters	Remove or change to blank (space)
Data type, length, precision and scale	Standardize to regional settings of organization's headquarters
Date format	Standardize to regional settings of organization's headquarters
Decimal separator	Standardize to regional settings of organization's headquarters
Case sensitivity	Business keys: all upper-case; descriptive data: it depends
NULL values	Remove by changing to empty string or other default value
Delimiters for concatenated fields	Semicolon or comma
Endianness	Little Endian (due to SQL Server and the Java Virtual Machine which is used for Hadoop)

11.2.3.1 Hash Collisions

Section 11.2.1 introduced **collision freedom** as a desired characteristic of hash functions. When hashing business keys while loading a hub, we want to prevent the hash function producing the same hash for two different business keys. Such a collision would represent a problem for a data warehouse built with Data Vault 2.0 modeling, because other entities, such as links or satellites, reference the business key using its hash value. If two business keys are using the same hash key, the reference would not be unique.

Because hash functions compress data from a theoretically unlimited input to a fixed-length hash value, it is not possible to prevent a hash collision, which is the same hash value for two arbitrary long inputs. And in fact, there are *random inputs* with the same hash key for any given *meaningful input*. For example, the 128-bit inputs (expressed in hexadecimal notation) shown in Table 11.6 produce the same MD5 hash value.

The common MD5 hash value is `008EE33A9D58B51CFEB425B0959121C9`. This type of hash collision is called a general hash collision. It is not possible to prevent this problem if compression takes place. If all input is random, which means binary blocks of random input, there are various levels of risks, depending on the selected hash function. Figure 11.6 shows a comparison of risks (the odds of a hash collision) for CRC-32, MD5 and SHA-1.

CRC-32 is not a recommended option for a hash function in data warehousing. However, it is included in Figure 11.6 to exemplify why this is the case: the risk of collisions is just too high. If a single hub or a single link contains only 77163 hashed records (a small-sized hub), the risk of a hash collision is 1 in 2 (50%). Using MD5, at least 5.06 billion (5.06×10^9) records need to be included in the hub to get such a risk for collisions. Compare this to SHA-1: in order to reach a risk of 50%, the number of 1.42×10^{24} records have to be added into the *same* hub first. Note that if a collision happens in another Data Vault entity (two different inputs, the same hash value, but different hubs), the collision is not a problem at all because no data is referenced erroneously. Does it mean that there is no risk of hash collisions when only a small number of records to be hashed is involved? No. The risk is just negligible: if a hub contains only ~200 business keys, hashed with MD5, the risk that a meteor would hit your data center is higher than that of a collision. The problem is that there is still a minor risk involved.

It is possible to reduce the risk even further by using the SHA-1 hash function. However, SHA-1 might not be available in all tools used in the data warehousing infrastructure. In these cases, the hashing function might be coded manually if that is possible.

Table 11.6 Example Single-Block Collision [23]

```
4d c9 68 ff 0e e3 5c 20 95 72 d4 77 7b 72 15 87
d3 6f a7 b2 1b dc 56 b7 4a 3d c0 78 3e 7b 95 18
af bf a2 00 a8 28 4b f3 6e 8e 4b 55 b3 5f 42 75
93 d8 49 67 6d a0 d1 55 5d 83 60 fb 5f 07 fe a2

4d c9 68 ff 0e e3 5c 20 95 72 d4 77 7b 72 15 87
d3 6f a7 b2 1b dc 56 b7 4a 3d c0 78 3e 7b 95 18
af bf a2 02 a8 28 4b f3 6e 8e 4b 55 b3 5f 42 75
93 d8 49 67 6d a0 d1 d5 5d 83 60 fb 5f 07 fe a2
```

Figure adapted by author from "Example single-block collision," by Marc Stevens. Copyright Marc Stevens. Reprinted with permission.

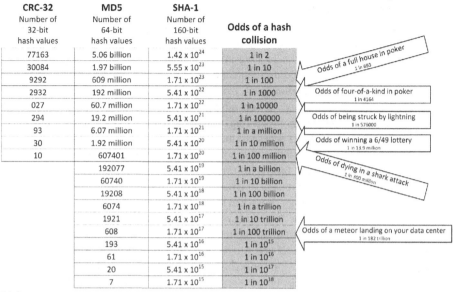

| CRC-32 | MD5 | SHA-1 | |
Number of 32-bit hash values	Number of 64-bit hash values	Number of 160-bit hash values	Odds of a hash collision
77163	5.06 billion	1.42×10^{24}	1 in 2
30084	1.97 billion	5.55×10^{23}	1 in 10
9292	609 million	1.71×10^{23}	1 in 100
2932	192 million	5.41×10^{22}	1 in 1000
027	60.7 million	1.71×10^{22}	1 in 10000
294	19.2 million	5.41×10^{21}	1 in 100000
93	6.07 million	1.71×10^{21}	1 in a million
30	1.92 million	5.41×10^{20}	1 in 10 million
10	607401	1.71×10^{20}	1 in 100 million
	192077	5.41×10^{19}	1 in a billion
	60740	1.71×10^{19}	1 in 10 billion
	19208	5.41×10^{18}	1 in 100 billion
	6074	1.71×10^{18}	1 in a trillion
	1921	5.41×10^{17}	1 in 10 trillion
	608	1.71×10^{17}	1 in 100 trillion
	193	5.41×10^{16}	$1 \text{ in } 10^{15}$
	61	1.71×10^{16}	$1 \text{ in } 10^{16}$
	20	5.41×10^{15}	$1 \text{ in } 10^{17}$
	7	1.71×10^{15}	$1 \text{ in } 10^{18}$

Annotations in figure:
Odds of a full house in poker — 1 in 693
Odds of four-of-a-kind in poker — 1 in 4164
Odds of being struck by lightning — 1 in 576000
Odds of winning a 6/49 lottery — 1 in 13.9 million
Odds of dying in a shark attack — 1 in 300 million
Odds of a meteor landing on your data center — 1 in 182 trillion

FIGURE 11.6

Probabilities of hash collisions [24].

Figure adapted by author from "Hash Collision Probabilities," by Jeff Preshing. Copyright Jeff Preshing. Reprinted with permission.

However, for data warehousing purposes, the inputs for potential collisions are not random nor binary as in Table 11.6. Instead, they are meaningful: business keys follow a (limited) string format; even descriptive data in satellites has only a limited input to be meaningful. Therefore, the chance for a collision between two meaningful inputs is even lower as presented in Figure 11.6.

In reality, while the risk of a hash collision tends to be very low for MD5 and SHA-1, there is no way to guarantee that there will be no collisions in the operational lifetime of the data warehouse. But it is possible to check for the direct opposite: when designing the data warehouse, it is possible to check if there is already a collision in the initial load. By hashing all business keys of a source file, we can find out if there are already collisions using a given hash function (such as MD5). If that is the case, we can move to a hash function (such as SHA-1) with a larger hash value output (bit-wise) before making the choice of hash function permanently. But having no hash collisions in the initial load has no meaning for the future. The first collision could still occur on the first operational day, by chance.

While it is not possible to prevent collisions, it is possible to detect them at least. When loading hub tables, we can ensure that there is no other business key in the hub having the same hash key. The same applies to link tables where we check for existing business key combinations with the same hash key. It will slow down the loading patterns a little, but ensure that no data becomes corrupted in the data warehouse. There are also techniques to detect a hash diff collision, but the chances for such collision are very low, much lower than on hash keys in hubs and links. Both techniques are described in full detail in Chapter 12, Loading the Data Vault.

11.2.3.2 Storage Requirements

Another consideration includes the required additional storage to keep the hash keys and hash diffs. Using SHA-1 instead of MD5 increases the storage requirements from 32 bytes (MD5 in hexadecimal representation) to 40 bytes (SHA-1). Compare this to a big-integer sequence number that only requires 8 bytes.

Generally, the additional storage requirements are not a real problem in the enterprise data warehouse layer (modeled in Data Vault 2.0 notation). In our experience, the advantages (such as the loading performance) outweigh this disadvantage of consuming more storage.

However, most data warehouse teams prefer (big) integer surrogate keys in information marts, for two reasons: first, business users have direct access to the information mart and might be confused by hash keys in dimension and fact tables. In addition, the storage requirements for using hash keys in fact tables are a concern for many teams. Because fact tables usually refer to multiple dimension tables and contain many rows, the additional storage requirement of a hash key becomes an issue. Consider the example of a fact table that refers to 10 dimension tables. Each fact requires 320 bytes for referencing the 10 dimensions if MD5 is used. If the fact table contains 10 million rows, around 3 GB are required to store only the references. Using SHA-1 requires 3.8 GB for storing the references to the dimension tables. Compare this to 762 MB when using 8-byte integers. If you decide to avoid MD5 in favor of a SHA algorithm, it is recommended to use SHA-1 over SHA-256 (or higher) because of storage requirements. SHA-1 already provides superior resistance against collisions, which makes SHA-256 in most if not all cases irrelevant.

For that reason, information marts are typically modeled using sequence number instead of hash keys (refer to Chapter 7, Dimensional Modeling, for a detailed description).

When storing hashes, avoid using the varchar datatype. Columns that use a varchar datatype might be stored in text pages instead of the main data page under some circumstances. Microsoft SQL Server moves columns with variable length out of the data page if the row size grows over 8,060 bytes [26]. Because hash keys are used for joining, the join performance will greatly benefit from having the hash key in the data page. If the hash key is stored in the text page, it has to be de-referenced first. Columns using a fixed-length datatype are guaranteed to be included in the data page.

On some occasions, data warehouse teams try to save storage by using binary(16) for MD5 hashes or binary(20) for SHA-1 hashes. Doing so limits the interoperability with other systems, such as Hadoop or BizTalk. Therefore, this is not a recommended practice. If you decide to do it anyway, avoid using the varbinary datatype for the same reasons as avoiding the varchar datatype. More interoperability issues are discussed in the next section.

11.2.3.3 Tool and Platform Compatibility

One of the reasons why hash keys have been introduced is that they improve the interoperability between different platforms, such as the relational database and NoSQL environments. By using hash keys in hubs and links, it is possible to integrate data on various platforms, structured in the relational database and unstructured data in NoSQL environments such as Hadoop. For that reason, the recommended data type to store hash keys is varchar because it is easy to read and write by external applications. If other datatypes are used, an on-the-fly conversion might be required which slows down the read/write process and makes it more complex.

Compatibility with other tools and platforms is also the reason to recommend MD5 for hash keys. Many systems, such as ETL tools, are capable of calculating MD5 hash keys. While SHA-1 is the newer algorithm and the recommended hashing function for encryption purposes nowadays, not all tools typically used in the business intelligence domain support it. On the other hand, most ETL tools and database systems support the MD5 hashing function out of the box. For the same reason, it is not recommended to use MD6 (the direct successor of MD5), SHA-256 or any other hashing algorithm that doesn't have widespread support compared to MD5 or SHA-1.

Before making a decision regarding the choice of hash function, the available tools and their hashing capabilities should be carefully reviewed to avoid surprises in later phases of the project.

11.2.3.4 Maintenance

In the rare case that a collision has occurred, the resolution includes increasing the bit-size of the hash value (hash key or hash diff) by changing the hash function. For example, if MD5 was used when a collision occurred, the recommendation is to move to SHA-1. This upgrade requires increasing the length of the hash key column (for example from 32 characters to 40) and to recalculate the hash values based on the business keys in the hub or link or the descriptive data in the satellites. Consider the recalculation of a hub's hash keys. Because other links and satellites reference these hash keys in order to reference the hub (for example to describe the business key in a satellite), at a minimum, all hash keys in dependent entities have to be recalculated, as well. Theoretically, all other hash keys could be left at the smaller size.

But leaving some hash keys in the smaller hash size would increase the maintenance costs because more management is required. It also hinders any automation efforts or requires more complex metadata to accomplish this task. Therefore, the recommendation is to use only one hash function for calculating all the hashes in the data warehouse.

For the same reason, it should be avoided to use different hash algorithms in the relational data warehouse and unstructured NoSQL environments, such as Hadoop (Figure 11.7).

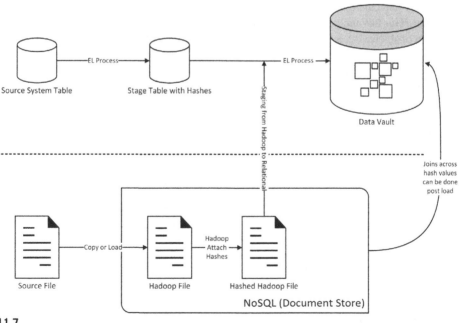

FIGURE 11.7

Integrating distinct parallel load operations.

Figure 11.7 shows that both environments independently calculate hashes for the data stored in both worlds because the data is sourced independently. Both systems identify business keys and their relationships for the purpose of hashing. In addition, whole documents in Hadoop can be linked to the data warehouse by a Data Vault 2.0 link that references the hash key of the Hadoop document. It is also possible to join across both systems when building the information marts.

In order to make this approach work, make sure that all systems use the same hash function and the same approach to apply it to the input data (refer to section 11.2.2 for details).

11.2.3.5 Performance

From a theoretical standpoint, it requires more CPU power to calculate one hash value than to generate one sequence value. The previous chapters have already discussed the reason why hash values are favored over sequence values (with regards to performance):

- **Easy to distribute hash key calculation:** the hash key calculation depends only on the availability of the hash function (which might be a tool problem) and the business key that needs to be hashed. For that reason, the hashing can be distributed very easily, for example to other environments or to multiple cluster nodes.
- **Hash key calculation is CPU not I/O intensive:** calculating the hash key is a CPU intensive operation (consider the calculation of a large number of hash keys) but doesn't require much I/O (the only I/O workload required is when storing the hash keys in the stage area for reusability). Because CPU workload can be easily and cheaply distributed over multiple CPUs, it is generally favored over I/O workload.
- **Loading of dependent tables doesn't require lookups:** the biggest performance gain comes from the fact that calculating the hash key requires only the business key, as described in the first bullet point. This advantage makes the lookup to retrieve the business key's sequence number from a hub obsolete. Because lookups cost a high amount of I/O, this is a popular advantage with high performance benefits.
- **Reduce the need for column comparing:** another intensive operation in data warehousing is to detect a change in descriptive data for versioning. In Data Vault, this happens when loading new rows into satellites because only deltas are stored in satellites. In order to detect if the new row should be stored in the satellite (which requires that at least one column be changed in the source system), every column between the source system (in the staging table) and the satellite has to be compared for a change. It also requires dealing with possible NULL values. Hash diff values can reduce the necessary comparisons to only one comparison: the hash diff value itself. Section 11.2.5 will show how to take advantage of the hash diff value.

In summary, hash keys provide a huge performance gain in most cases, especially when dealing with large amounts of data. For these reasons (and the additional ones regarding the integration with other environments), sequence numbers have been replaced by hash keys in Data Vault 2.0.

The previous sections have shown some advantages of hash functions in data warehousing, but they are no silver bullets [26]. Depending on how they are used, new problems might be introduced that need to be dealt with. However, the advantages of hash keys outweigh their drawbacks.

11.2.4 HASHING BUSINESS KEYS

The purpose of hash keys is to provide a surrogate key for business keys, composite business keys and business key combinations. Hash keys are defined in parent tables, which are hubs and links in Data

FIGURE 11.8

Hub with hash key (physical design).

Vault 2.0. They are used by all dependent Data Vault 2.0 structures, including links, satellites, bridges and PIT tables. Consider a hub example from Chapter 4 (Figure 11.8).

The hash key **FlightHashKey** is used for identification purposes of the business keys **Carrier** and **FlightNum** in the hub. All other attributes are metadata columns that are described later in this chapter. For link structures, the hash key that is used as an identifying element of the link is based on the business keys from the referenced hubs (Figure 11.9).

Note that there are a total of five hash keys in the **LinkConnection** link. Four of them are referencing other hubs. Only the **ConnectionHashKey** element is used as the primary key. This key is not calculated from the four hash values, but from the business keys they are actually based on. When loading the link structure, these business keys are usually available to the loading process.

Calculating a hash from other hash values is not recommended because it requires cascading hash operations. In order to calculate a hash based on other hashes, these hashes have to be calculated in the link loading process first. Because this operation might involve multiple layers of hashes, many unnecessary hash operations are introduced. Because they are CPU intensive operations, the primary goal of the loading patterns is to reduce them as much as possible.

In order to calculate hash key for hubs and links, it is required to concatenate all business key columns (think about composite business keys) and apply the guidelines from section 11.2.2 before the hash function is applied to the input. The following pseudo code shows the operation with n individual business keys in the composite key of the hub:

$$HashKey = Hash(UpperCase(Trim(BK_1) + d + Trim(BK_2) + \cdots + Trim(BK_n)))$$

BK_i represents the individual business key in the composite key and d the chosen delimiter. The order of the business keys should follow the definition of the physical table and should be part of the documentation. If the business key is not a composite business key, n equals to 1 and the above function is applied without delimiters. It assumes that all other standards, especially the endianness and character set, are taken care of. This also includes any control characters in the business keys and common conversion rules for various data types, for example floating values or dates and timestamps.

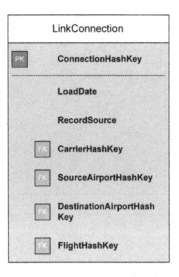

FIGURE 11.9

Link with hash keys (physical design).

The approach is the same for hubs and links: in the case of links, each BK_i represents a business key from the referenced hubs (see Figure 11.10). If hubs with composite business keys are used, all individual parts of the composite business key are included. For degenerated links, all degenerated fields have to be included as well. These weak hub references are part of the identifying hash key as any other hub reference.

While not intended on purpose, some of the individual business keys might be NULL. Because most database systems return NULL from string concatenations if one of the operators is a NULL value, NULL values have to be replaced by empty strings. Without the delimiter, the meaning of the business key combination would change in an erroneous way. Consider the example rows in Table 11.7.

After concatenating the four business keys without a delimiter, the string becomes in both cases "ABCDEFGHI". Because the input to the hash function is the same, the resulting hash value is the same as well. But it is obvious that both rows are different and should produce different hash values. This is achieved by using a semicolon (or any other character sequence) as a delimiter. The first row

	BK 1	BK 2	BK 3	BK 4	Hash Result (without Delimiters)	Hash Result (with Delimiters)
Table 11.7 Importance of Delimiters						
Row 1	ABC	(null)	DEF	GHI	6FEB8AC01A4400A7 28B482D0506C4BEB	D9D33F7E6E80D174 7C45465025E9E6AF
Row 2	ABC	DEF	(null)	GHI	6FEB8AC01A4400A7 28B482D0506C4BEB	FD4D58C47B5C343A 4A9E23922ABE4C46

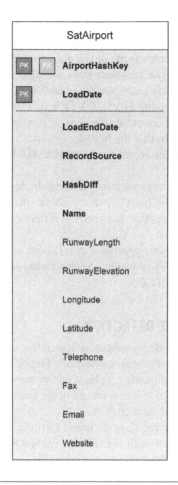

FIGURE 11.10

Satellite with multiple hub references (physical design).

is concatenated to "ABC;;DEF;GHI" and the second row to "ABC;DEF;;GHI". After sending the data through the hashing function, the desired output is achieved by retrieving different hash values.

In the previous chapter, a statement similar to the following T-SQL statement was used to perform the operation:

```
SELECT UPPER(CONVERT(char(32),HASHBYTES('MD5',
        UPPER(CONCAT(
            RTRIM(LTRIM(COALESCE(@event, ''))), ';',
            RTRIM(LTRIM(COALESCE(@computer, ''))), ';',
            RTRIM(LTRIM(COALESCE(@operator, ''))), ';',
            RTRIM(LTRIM(COALESCE(@sourceid, ''))), ';',
            RTRIM(LTRIM(COALESCE(@id, '')))
        ))
)),2));
```

This statement implements the previous pseudocode using Microsoft's MD5 implementation in SQL Server 2014 and takes care of potential NULL values in addition. Note that each individual business key (the variables, such as **@event**, in the above statement) is checked for NULL values using the **COALESCE** function. The business keys are also removed from leading and trailing spaces on an individual basis. In this example, a semicolon is used to separate the business keys before they are being hashed using the **HASHBYTES** function. The result of this function is a varbinary value. This varbinary is converted to a char(32) value. The last **UPPER** function around the **CONVERT** function makes sure that the hexadecimal hash key is using only uppercase letters. If SHA-1 should be used instead, the result from the **HASHBYTES** function has to be converted to a char(40) instead.

Note that, in rare cases, business keys are case-sensitive. In this case, the upper case function has to be avoided in order to generate a valid hash key that is able to distinguish between the different cases. Keep in mind that the goal is to differentiate between the different semantics of each key, not to follow the rules at all cost.

It is also possible to implement this approach in ETL, for example by using a SSIS community component **SSIS Multiple Hash** [27] or using a **Script Component** (standard component in SSIS). The latter is demonstrated in section 11.6.3.

11.2.5 HASHING FOR CHANGE DETECTION

Hash functions can also be used to detect changes in descriptive attributes. As described in Chapter 4, descriptive attributes are loaded from the source systems to Data Vault 2.0 satellites. Satellites are delta-driven and store incoming records only when at least one of the source columns has changed. In this case, the whole (new) record is loaded to a new record in the satellite. The loading process of satellites (and other entities) is discussed in the next chapter.

In order to detect a change that requires an insert into the target satellite, the columns of the source system have to be compared with the current record in the target satellite. If any of the column values differ, a change is detected and the record is loaded into the target. To perform the change detection, every column in the source must be compared with its equivalent column in the target. Especially when loading large amounts of data, this process can become too slow in some cases. For such cases, there is an alternative that involves hash values on the column values to be compared. Instead of comparing each individual column values, only two hash values (the hash diffs) are compared, which can improve the performance of the change detection process and therefore the satellite loading process.

The basic idea of the hash diff is the same as the hash key in the previous section: it uses the fact that, given a specific input, the hash function will always return the same hash value. Instead of comparing individual columns, only the hash diff on these columns is used (Table 11.8).

Table 11.8 shows data in a stage table and the current record in the target satellite. Both records are hashed using a MD5 hash function, which results in a 32-character-long hash diff. Because the descriptive data is the same in the stage table as in the satellite table, both sides share the same hash diff value. After comparing the **hash diff** column (instead of the individual columns **title**, **first name** and **last name**) no change is detected and, as a result, no row is inserted into the satellite. If the data changes only a little, the hash diff value becomes different (Table 11.9).

Table 11.8 Example Data Compared by Hash Diff (without a Change)

Attribute Name	Stage Table Value	Satellite Table Value
Title	Mrs.	Mrs.
First Name	Amy	Amy
Last Name	Miller	Miller
Hash Diff	CADAB1708BF002A85C49FF78DCFD9A65	CADAB1708BF002A85C49FF78DCFD9A65

Table 11.9 Example Data Compared by Hash Diff (with Change)

Attribute Name	Stage Table Value	Satellite Table Value
Title	Mrs.	Mrs.
First Name	Amy	Amy
Last Name	Freeman	Miller
Hash Diff	66C17DF4D91EE9F0CF39490BFCC20B60	CADAB1708BF002A85C49FF78DCFD9A65

As a result of the changed data, the hash diff is completely different. Because of this different value, it is easy to detect changes in the stage table without comparing the values itself. While both hash diffs have to be calculated, the hash from the satellite can be reused whenever data is loaded, because it is stored with the descriptive data in the satellite, as Figure 11.10 shows.

The satellite **SatAirport** contains a number of descriptive attributes. The **HashDiff** attribute stores the hash diff over the descriptive attributes and can be reused whenever a record in the stage table is present that describes the parent airport (identified by **AirportHashKey**).

The hash diff is calculated in a similar manner to the hash keys in the previous section. All descriptive attributes are concatenated using a delimiter before the hash diff is calculated. Before concatenating the attributes, leading and trailing spaces are removed and the data is formatted in a standardized format. Especially the data type, date formats, and decimal separators are of importance, because all descriptive data, including dates, decimal values and all other data types have to be converted to strings before the data is hashed. The following pseudocode is used within the first, yet incomplete, approach:

$$HashDiff = Hash(Trim(Data_1) + d + Trim(Data_2) + \cdots + Trim(Data_n))$$

$Data_i$ indicates descriptive attributes, d a delimiter. The only difference between the pseudocode in this section and the previous section (to calculate hash keys on business keys) is that the upper case function has been removed: in many cases, change detection should trigger a new satellite entry if the case of a character is changing. However, this depends on the requirements given by the organization. In other cases, case-sensitive descriptive data is set on a per-satellite basis or even a per-attribute basis. How case-sensitivity is implemented depends on the definition of the source system and the data warehouse, as well.

Table 11.10 Different Parents with the Same Descriptive Data						
Passenger HashKey	LoadDate	LoadEndDate	Record Source	Title	First Name	Last Name
9d4ef8a...	2014-06-03	9999-12-31	DomesticFlight	Mrs.	Amy	Miller
12af89e...	2014-06-05	9999-12-31	DomesticFlight	Mrs.	Amy	Miller

The above pseudocode is not complete yet. In order to increase the uniqueness among different parent values, the business keys of the parent are added to the hash diff function. Consider the example shown in Table 11.10.

In this case, there are two passengers Mrs. Amy Miller. They are distinguished by different hash keys, which result from different inputs, the business keys. If only the descriptive data is included in the hash diff calculation, both records would share the same hash diff value. This might not be very dangerous, but if the hash diffs were different, yet correct, we could use the hash diff to find a specific version of the descriptive data for one individual parent without using a combination of both the parent hash key and the hash diff. It is desired to have a hash diff that is unique over all satellite records, because then it would be sufficient to use only the hash diff to locate a particular version, which might improve the query performance for loading patterns in some circumstances.

We achieve this uniqueness of the hash key by adding the business keys of the parent to the hash diff calculation:

$$HashDiff = Hash(UpperCase(Trim(BK_1) + d + Trim(BK_3) + \cdots + Trim(BK_n)) + d$$
$$+ Trim(Data_1) + d + Trim(Data_2) + \cdots + Trim(Data_n))$$

The business keys of the parent are just added in front of the descriptive data, delimited by the same delimiter and following the same guidelines as outlined in the previous section. Both groups, the business keys and the descriptive data, must follow a documented order. A good practice is to use the column order of the table definition. In many cases, the business keys are uppercased while descriptive data remains case sensitive. Keep this in mind when standardizing and developing the hash diff function. Note that it's not the hash that is added to the front of the descriptive data but the business keys themselves. This follows the recommendation to avoid hashing hashes (hash-a-hash) in order to avoid cascaded calculations (refer to the previous section for more details).

The input to the hash function for the examples in Table 11.10 is presented in Table 11.11.

Because the input to the hash function is different (due to the included business key), the hash value for both inputs is different. When loading the satellites, it is ensured that this hash diff can be regained

Table 11.11 Example Input to Hash Diff Function	
Input to Hash Function	Hash Diff
7878;Mrs.;Amy;Miller	9DA0891434B92DF529B8CCCD86CC140B
2323;Mrs.;Amy;Miller	E890EE7980D5B13449704293A1BB4CCA

at any time because both the descriptive data as well as the business keys are available. Therefore, this is the recommended practice.

11.2.5.1 Maintaining the Hash Diffs

Using the hash diff can improve the performance of the satellite loading processes, especially on tables with many columns. However, it incurs a maintenance cost or effort in addition to the calculation in the stage area. The reason for this additional maintenance is that satellite tables might change. Consider the following example, presented in Table 11.12 to Table 11.14, which adds a column **academic title** to the example provided previously:

The first table shows the old satellite structure, with three descriptive attributes, namely **title**, **first name** and **last name**. Because the source system has changed, a new descriptive attribute is added in Table 11.13, called **academic title**. Because the source systems never delivered any data for this new column in the past, it is set to NULL, or any other value representing this fact.

Once the new column has been added to the source table, it can capture incoming data. In this case, a new record is being added to the table that overrides the first record (Amy Miller marries Mr.

Table 11.12 Initial Satellite Structure

Passenger HashKey	LoadDate	LoadEndDate	Record Source	Title	First Name	Last Name
8473d2a...	1991-06-26	9999-12-31	DomesticFlight	Mrs.	Amy	Miller
9d8e72a...	2001-06-03	9999-12-31	DomesticFlight	Mr.	Peter	Heinz

Table 11.13 Satellite Structure After Adding a New Column

Passenger HashKey	LoadDate	LoadEndDate	Record Source	Title	Academic Title	First Name	Last Name
8473d2a...	1991-06-26	9999-12-31	DomesticFlight	Mrs.	(null)	Amy	Miller
9d8e72a...	2001-06-03	9999-12-31	DomesticFlight	Mr.	(null)	Peter	Heinz

Table 11.14 New Records are being Added to the New Satellite Structure

Passenger HashKey	LoadDate	LoadEndDate	Record Source	Title	Academic Title	First Name	Last Name
8473d2a...	1991-06-26	2003-03-03	DomesticFlight	Mrs.	(null)	Amy	Miller
9d8e72a...	2001-06-03	9999-12-31	DomesticFlight	Mr.	(null)	Peter	Heinz
8473d2a...	2014-06-20	9999-12-31	DomesticFlight	Mrs.	Dr.	Amy	Freeman

Freeman). In addition, the source system provides an academic title for Mrs. Freeman. It is unclear if she always held this title, but from a data warehousing perspective, it makes no difference. For audit reasons, the old records will not be updated because at the time when they have been loaded (indicated by the load date), the source system did not deliver an academic title for her (or any other record).

The issue arises when hash diffs are used in this satellite. Tables 11.15,11.16 and 11.17 show the hash diffs for the above examples (in the same order as previously).

The numbers in the curly brackets indicate the corresponding business keys. The first table shows the MD5 values for the descriptive data. Note that the hash diffs are different to the ones provided in Table 11 because the example was slightly different: other business keys were used in that example.

The semantic meaning of the data behind the hash diffs in Table 11.15 and Table 11.16 did not change (compare this to Table 11.12 and Table 11.13). However, the hash diffs changed, indicating to the change detection that the rows have changed. The only difference between these tables is the introduction of a new column, **academic title**. But the new column has changed everything because it influenced the input to the hash diff function (Table 11.18).

Table 11.15 Hash Diffs for Initial Satellite Structure

Passenger HashKey	LoadDate	LoadEndDate	Hash Diff
8473d2a... {4455}	1991-06-26	9999-12-31	BDD9DD9208611F2A8CF3670053634FF0
9d8e72a... {6677}	2001-06-03	9999-12-31	B3B1724EF449DA9D9521FA95A88A82A3

Table 11.16 Hash Diffs for Satellite Structure After Adding a New Column

Passenger HashKey	LoadDate	LoadEndDate	Hash Diff
8473d2a... {4455}	1991-06-26	9999-12-31	4F860465EB585FABF3CBD28E7A29AEC0
9d8e72a... {6677}	2001-06-03	9999-12-31	FFCF6191C583F5B77273D4CABF3EB98F

Table 11.17 Hash Diffs After New Records Have Been Added to the New Satellite Structure

Passenger HashKey	LoadDate	LoadEndDate	Hash Diff
8473d2a... {4455}	1991-06-26	2003-03-03	4F860465EB585FABF3CBD28E7A29AEC0
9d8e72a... {6677}	2001-06-03	9999-12-31	FFCF6191C583F5B77273D4CABF3EB98F
8473d2a... {4455}	2014-06-20	9999-12-31	1C1E8C1799E39E567F746F720800B0E5

The first row presents the input for Amy Miller before the structural change to the satellite, and the second row the input after the column has been added. Notice the added semicolon in the input on the left side, between the title and the first name. This semicolon is due to the fact that a NULL column was introduced and changed to an empty string. The advantage of the semicolon that it allows for NULL values now becomes a disadvantage.

However, we actually need the new hash diff value because, otherwise, we're unable to detect any changes in the source system. If we leave the old hash diffs in the satellite table, all current source records (modified or unmodified) are interpreted as modified, due to the different hash diff value. Therefore, we need to update all hash diffs in the satellite table to prevent unnecessary (and unwanted) inserts into the satellite table.

It is possible to avoid this maintenance overhead of the hash diff by following a simple strategy. The first idea is to update only the current records in the satellite. They are indicated by having no load end date (or in the examples of this book, an end-date of 9999-12-31), because only those records are required for any regular comparison during satellite loading. All end-dated satellite entries have been replaced by newer records already and are not required to compare with. This approach reduces the number of records to be updated after structural changes but still incurs many updates, especially when there are many different parent entries.

But it is actually possible to further reduce the maintenance overhead to zero: by making sure that the hash diffs remain valid, even after structural changes. However, there are some conditions to make this happen:

1. Columns are only added, not deleted.
2. All new columns are added at the end of the table.
3. Columns that are NULL and at the end of the table are not added to the input of the hash function.

The first condition is required because of auditability reasons in any case. The goal of the data warehouse is to provide all data that was sourced at a given time. If columns are deleted, the auditability is not achieved anymore.

Meeting the second and the third condition is best explained by an example (Table 11.19, modified from Table 11.18):

Table 11.18 Modified Example Input to Hash Diff Function

Input to Hash Function	Hash Diff
4455;Mrs.;Amy;Miller	BDD9DD9208611F2A8CF3670053634FF0
4455;Mrs.;;Amy;Miller	4F860465EB585FABF3CBD28E7A29AEC0

Table 11.19 Improving the Hash Diff Calculation

Input to Hash Function	Hash Diff
4455;Mrs.;Amy;Miller	BDD9DD9208611F2A8CF3670053634FF0
4455;Mrs.;Amy;Miller;	D64074FE047165874481A7B299C4A766
4455;Mrs.;Amy;Miller	BDD9DD9208611F2A8CF3670053634FF0

The first line shows the input to the hash function before the structural change. The second line shows the input after the structural change, meeting the first two conditions, but not the third. Instead of adding the new column in the middle between the title and the first name, the academic title is added at the end of the table. Without meeting the last condition, a semicolon is added and the NULL value is added after the semicolon as an empty string. Because the input has changed by the addition of the semicolon character, the hash diff has changed, indicating a change.

If the third condition is met in addition, all empty columns at the end of the input are removed before the hash function is called. It means that all trailing semicolons are being removed. That way, the input becomes the same again and the hash diffs indicate no change because they have to be the same. This approach works with multiple NULL columns at the end.

How does it improve the satellite loading process? First, the old hash diffs are still valid. There is no semantic difference between the rows in Table 11.19. The only difference is a structural change that should not have an impact on the satellite loading process by triggering an insert operation into the satellite. This is achieved by this improved hash diff calculation.

However, if a new column is added to the satellite and the source system provides a value for the new column, a new hash diff is being calculated (Table 11.20).

Because the input to the hash function has changed between the two loads, the hash function will return two different hash diffs. This is in line with the requirements of the satellite loading process because the satellite should capture the change in Table 11.20.

The biggest advantage of the presented approach is that the hash diff values are always valid if the conditions listed earlier are met. On the other hand, the disadvantage is that the satellite columns might be in a different order than the source table, for example when new columns are added to the source table after it was initially sourced into the data warehouse. However, because this approach doesn't affect the auditability at all, we recommend this approach in most cases.

11.3 PURPOSE OF THE LOAD DATE

The **load date** identifies "*the date and time at which the data is physically inserted directly into the database*" [6]. In the case of the data warehouse, this might be the staging area, the Raw Data Vault or any other area where the data arrives. Once the data has arrived in the data warehouse, the load date is set and is part of the auditable metadata. Except for satellites, the load date is primarily a metadata attribute that helps when debugging the data warehouse. However, because it is part of the satellite's primary key, it is in fact an essential part of the model that needs to be taken special care of.

If the database system that is used for the data warehouse supports it, the **load date** should represent the instant that the data is inserted to the database. The time of arrival should be accurately

Table 11.20 Changing the Semantic Meaning

Input to Hash Function	Hash Diff
4455;Mrs.;Amy;Miller	BDD9DD9208611F2A8CF3670053634FF0
4455;Mrs.;Amy;Miller;Dr.	0044E798C5586E931A604D1E0CD09FA1

identified down to a millisecond level in order to support potential real-time ingestion of data. If the database system doesn't support timestamps but only dates, the alternative is to add a sub-sequence number to the load date that represents pseudo millisecond counters. This is required for satellites in order to make the primary key (which consists of the parent hash key and the load date) unique. This uniqueness requires milliseconds because data might be delivered multiple times a day (in batches or in real time).

The data warehouse has to be in control of the load date. Again, this is especially important for the Data Vault satellites because the load date is included in the satellite's primary key. If the load date breaks for any reason, the model will break and stop the loading process of the data warehouse. A load date typically breaks if two different batches are identified by the same load date. In this case, the satellite loading process would try to insert records (due to a detected change) with a duplicate key. For example, if a create date or export date from the source system that is not controlled by the data warehouse is used as a load date, the following issues are implicated:

- **Mixed arrival latency:** not all data arrives at the same batch window timeframe. There is often some form of ongoing mixed arrival schedule for source data. When the load date is generated during the insert into the data warehouse, this mixed arrival date time can be assigned gracefully. The inserts to the Raw Data Vault (in this case) occur at the time of arrival. In one case, the business needs to be updated every 5 seconds with live feed data; in another case, the EDW needs to show a time-lineage of arrival to an auditor for traceability reasons.
- **Mixed time zones for source data:** not all data is being created in the same time zone. Some source systems are located in the USA, some in India, and so on. If a create date were to be used as a load date, these time zones have to be aligned on the way into the data warehouse. Any conversion, no matter how simple, slows down the loading process of the data warehouse and increases the complexity. Increased complexity will not only increase the maintenance effort but also the chance that errors happen.
- **Missing dates on sources:** not all source systems provide a create date or another candidate to be used as a load date. Dealing with these exceptions requires conditions in the loading procedures, which should be avoided because it adds complexity again. Instead, apply the same logic to all sources to keep the loading procedures as simple as possible.
- **Trustworthiness of dates on sources:** not all source systems run correctly. In some cases, the time of the source system has an offset due to a wrong configuration or hardware failures (consider a defunct motherboard battery). In other cases, the date and time configuration of the source system is changed between loads (for example to fix an erroneous configuration or after replacing the motherboard battery). This actually makes things worse as it complicates the matters when times now overlap.

If the data warehouse team decides to use an external timestamp as the load date, the data warehouse loading process will fail in the following scenarios:

- **Create date is modified by source system:** the data warehouse team has no control over the create date from the external system. If the source system owner or the source system application decides to change the create date for any reason, it has to be handled by the data warehouse. However, how should this change be handled if the load date is part of the immutable primary key within satellites? Changing it is not possible for auditing reasons.

- **Loading history with create date as load date:** in other cases, the data warehouse team has to source historical data that might or might not have create dates. For example, if the source system has introduced the create date in a later version, historical data from earlier versions don't provide the create date.

For all these reasons, the load date has to be created by the data warehouse and not sourced from an external system. This also ensures the auditability of the data warehouse system because it allows auditors to reconcile the raw data warehouse data to the source systems. The load date further helps to analyze errors by loading cycles or inspecting the arrival of data in the data warehouse. It is also possible to analyze the actual latency between time of creation and time of arrival in the data warehouse.

System-driven load dates (system-driven by the data warehouse) can be used to determine the most recent / most current data set available for release downstream to the business users. While it doesn't provide complete temporal information, it provides the technical view on the most recent raw data or at any given point in time.

But what should be done with the dates and timestamps from the source system? Typically, the following timelines exist in source systems:

- Data creation dates
- Data modified dates
- Data extract dates
- Data applied dates such as
  - Effective start and end dates
  - Built dates
  - Scheduled dates
  - Executed dates
  - Deleted dates
  - Planned dates
  - Financed dates
  - Cancelled dates

None of these dates or any other date from the source system qualify as load dates. However, they provide value to the business. As such, they should be included in the data warehouse as descriptive data and loaded to Data Vault satellites.

11.4 PURPOSE OF THE RECORD SOURCE

The record source has been added for debugging purposes only. It can and should be used by the data warehousing team to trace where the row data came from. In order to achieve this, the record source is a string attribute that provides a technical name of the source system, as detailed as it is required. In most cases, data warehouse teams decide to use some hierarchical structure to indicate not only the source system, but also the module or table name. If accessing a relational Microsoft SQL Server source, the record source should use the following format:

```
[Source Application Name].[Schema Name].[Table Name]
```

For example, the following record source would indicate a table from the **CRM** application, in the **Cust** schema:

```
CRM.Cust.Customers
```

Avoid using only the name of the source system because following this approach can be very helpful when tracing down errors. When analyzing the data warehouse due to a run-time error, either in development or production, it is helpful to have detailed information available.

The record source is added to all tables in the staging area, the Raw Data Vault, the Business Vault and probably the information marts. But what if data from multiple sources is combined or aggregated? In this case, the record source is not clear anymore. The recommended practice is to set the record source to the technical name of the business rule that generated the record. The technical name can be found in the metadata of the data warehouse (refer to Chapter 10, Metadata Management). If there is no business rule, the record source should be set to SYSTEM. Examples include the ghost record in satellites (see Chapter 6, Advanced Data Vault Modeling) or any other system-driven records.

Use of record sources that are dependent on a specific load should be avoided. For example, the file name is often not a good candidate for a record source, especially if it contains a date. The record source should group all data together that comes from the same origin of data. Having a date in the record source prevents this. The same applies for physical database or server names: what if the location of the data changes? The file name, the database name or the server name might be changed in the future, even if the source where the records came from remains the same.

11.5 **TYPES OF DATA SOURCES**

The data warehouse can source the raw data from a variety of data sources, including structured, semistructured and unstructured sources. Data can also come from operational systems in batch loads or in real time, through the Enterprise Service Bus (ESB). Typical examples for source systems in data warehousing include [28]:

- **Relational tables:** operational systems often work with a relational database backend, such as Microsoft SQL Server, Oracle, MySQL, PostgreSQL, etc. This data can be directly accessed using OLE DB or ADO.NET sources in SSIS [29].
- **Text files:** if direct access of the relational database is not permitted, operational systems often export data into text files, such as comma-separated files (CSV) or files with fixed-length fields [29].
- **XML documents:** in other cases, operational systems also provide XML files that can be processed in SSIS [29].
- **JSON documents:** similar to XML documents, JSON documents provide semi-structured files that can be processed by SSIS using additional third-party components.
- **Spreadsheets:** a lot of business data is stored in spreadsheets, such as Microsoft Excel files, which can be directly sourced from SSIS [29] and Google Sheets, which can be sourced with third-party components.
- **CRM systems:** customer data is often stored in customer relationship management (CRM) systems, such as Microsoft Dynamics CRM, Salesforce CRM or SAP. Third-party data sources allow sourcing this data.

- **ERP systems:** organizations use ERP systems to store data from business activities, such as product planning, manufacturing, marketing and sales, inventory management or shipping and payment. Examples for ERP systems include Microsoft Dynamics ERP, Microsoft Dynamics GP, SAP ERP, and NetSuite. There are third-party data sources available for sourcing data from ERP systems.
- **CMS systems:** content management systems (CMS) provide the ability to create intranet applications for unstructured or semi-structured content. Third-party connectors allow connecting to CMS systems such as Microsoft SharePoint.
- **Accounting software:** this type of software is used to manage general ledger and perform other financial activities, such as payroll management. Examples include QuickBooks and Xero. Third-party components allow sourcing of data from these systems.
- **Unstructured documents:** include Word documents, PowerPoint presentations and other unstructured documents.
- **Semi-structured documents:** include emails, EDI messages, and OFX financial data formats which can be sourced with third-party components.
- **Cloud databases:** more and more data is stored in the cloud, for example in Microsoft Azure SQL Database, Amazon SimpleDB, or Amazon DynamoDB. Microsoft Azure SQL Database is supported by the OLE DB data source; other cloud databases are supported by third-party vendors.
- **Web sources:** the Internet provides a rich set of third-party data that can be added to the data warehouse in order to enrich the data from operational systems. The same applies to data from Intranet locations. Examples for file formats used typically in such settings include RSS feeds (for news syndication), OData and JSON (for standardized access to data sets) in addition to general XML documents. Some of these formats can be sourced by SSIS with built-in capabilities. Others require a third-party data driver.
- **Social networks:** social networks present another, yet more advanced, Web source. There are SSIS data sources to process data from social networks such as Twitter and Facebook.
- **Mainframe copybooks:** a lot of operational data is managed by mainframe systems and will be in the future. EBCDIC files are one of the standards and can be handled by SSIS with additional components.
- **File systems:** not all documents are stored in local file systems. Instead, some data resides on FTP servers, can be copied using secure copy (SCP) commands or is in the cloud, for example Amazon S3. Third-party components can assist in retrieving data from such remote stores.
- **Remote terminals:** In other cases, the data is on remote servers, but only accessible via remote terminals, such as telnet or secure shell (SSH). Again, third-party vendors extend SSIS if that is required.
- **Network access:** even TCP ports on the network might provide data that is sourced into the data warehouse.

In order to load the data using ETL tools, the access methods have to be supported by the tool itself. Not all tools support all data sources, but it is possible to extend them by custom components. Microsoft SSIS is such an example where the base functionality can be extended by custom components from third-party vendors. It is also possible to add generic data sources from the Web, especially by accessing REST or XML Web Services. Additional SSIS components can be found on CodePlex [30].

The remaining sections discuss how to source typical data sources, including the sample airline data that is used throughout the book.

11.6 **SOURCING FLAT FILES**

The first example loads flat files into the data warehouse. These flat files are typically exported from operational systems, which often use a relational database. Flat files include several of the previously listed formats, including comma-separated files (CSV), fixed-length files and Microsoft Excel Sheets.

When sourcing text-based files, such as CSV or fixed-length files, all data is formatted as strings. In order to convert the raw data during the export in the source system, which also uses other data types, such as integers, or decimal values, a format is applied to build the string text that is exported into the text file. By doing so, the source application defines, for example for decimal values, how many positions after the decimal point should be included and how many should be rounded off.

11.6.1 **CONTROL FLOW**

The companion Web site provides three CSV files from the BTS database, introduced in the opening of this chapter. In order to run the following example in SSIS, you have to extract the Zip file and place the CSV files into one folder. The final SSIS control flow will traverse through the folder and load all data from all CSV files in the folder into the staging area.

In order to traverse through the folder, drag a **Foreach Loop Container** on the canvas of the control flow. Double-click to edit it and set the following parameters as shown in Figure 11.11.

Change the **Enumerator** type to **Foreach File Enumerator**. Configure the file enumerator by setting the **Folder** to the location where the CSV files from the companion Web site are located. Change the **Files** wildcard to ***.csv** and **Retrieve file name** to **Name and extension**.

The last option defines how the file name of the traversed file should be stored in a variable. It is possible to store:

- the **name and extension:** only the file name and the file extension are stored in the variable.
- the **fully qualified name:** this includes the file location and the file name including the extension of the file.
- the **name only:** only the file name, without the file extension, is stored.

Select the option to store the **fully qualified name** because the full name is required by the data flow that will be created in the next step.

The variable that stores the file name of the currently traversed file is set on the next tab **Variable Mappings** (Figure 11.12).

To store the file name in a variable, either choose a pre-existing variable or create a new variable by focusing the cell in the **Variable** column of the grid and selecting <**New Variable...**>. The dialog as shown in Figure 11.13 will appear.

Set the **container** of the variable to **package**. For the purpose of this example, it would also be sufficient to set it to the foreach loop container itself to reduce the scope of the variable. Set the **name** of the variable to **sFileName**. We will later reference the variable using this variable name. The **namespace** should be set to **User** or a defined namespace of your choice that is used to store such variables. Set the **value type** to **String**, as it will store the file name and extension of the traversed file. The default **value** should be set to **default** or something similar. Make sure **read only** is not selected.

After selecting the **OK** button, the variable is added to the previous variable mapping dialog and shown in the table with index 0 (Figure 11.14).

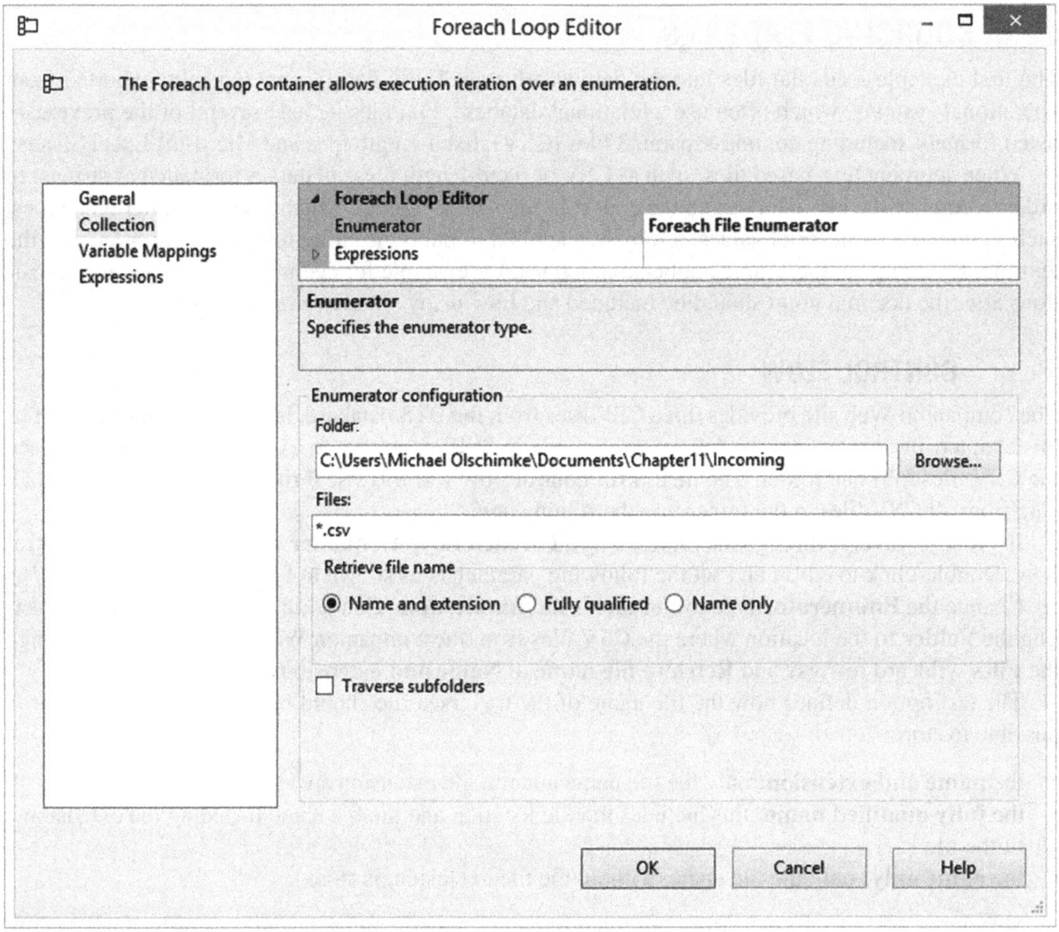

FIGURE 11.11

Configuring the collection of the foreach loop container.

Confirm the foreach loop editor by selecting **OK**. The next task ensures a consistent load date over all records in each file. For this purpose, the current timestamp is set to a SSIS variable using a Microsoft Visual C# script: whenever the container loops over a file, it first sets the current timestamp into the variable **User::dLoadDate** and then starts the data flow, which is discussed next. The data flow will use the timestamp in the variable to set the **load date** in the staging area. Follow the earlier approach and create a new SSIS variable by selecting the **Variables** menu entry in the context menu of the control flow. Create a new variable with name **dLoadDate** and the settings as shown in Table 11.21.

Close the dialog and drag a **Script Task** into the container. Open the editor as shown in Figure 11.15.

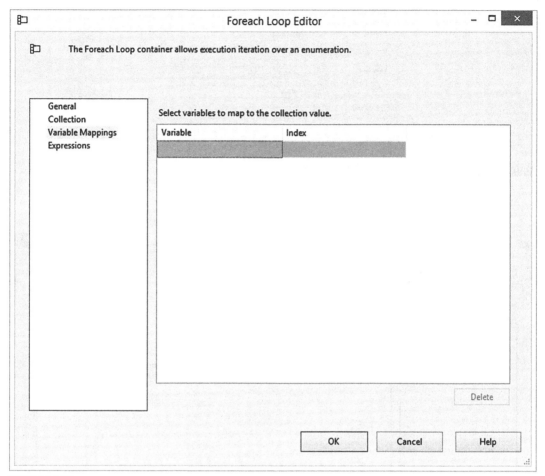

FIGURE 11.12

Map variable of foreach loop container.

Table 11.21 Variable dLoadDate Settings	
Parameter	**Value**
Name	dLoadDate
Scope	Package
Data type	DateTime
Value	12/30/1899

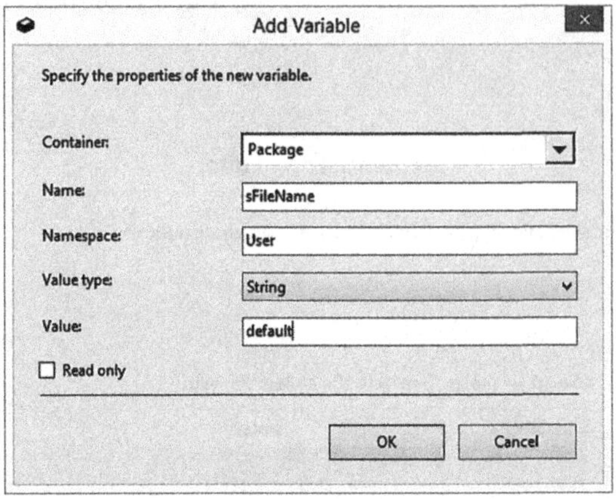

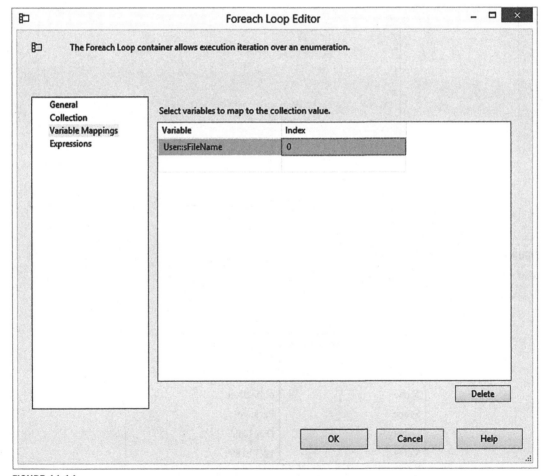

FIGURE 11.13

Add variable to store file name from foreach loop container.

FIGURE 11.14

Added variable to the foreach loop container.

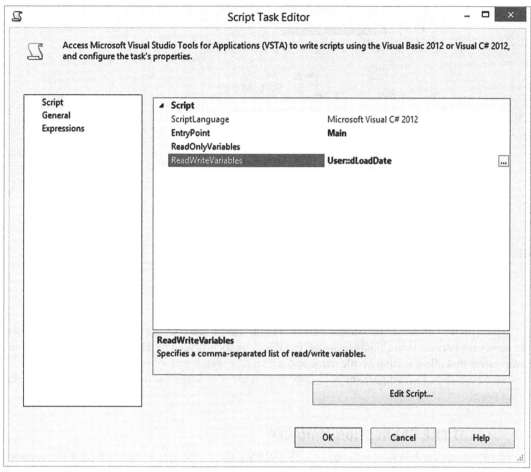

FIGURE 11.15

Script task editor to set the load date.

Add the variable **User::dLoadDate** to the **ReadWriteVariables** by using the dialog available after pressing the button with the … caption. Check the variable in the dialog and close it. Edit the script and enter the following code in the **Main** function:

```
Dts.Variables["User::dLoadDate"].Value = DateTime.Now;
Dts.TaskResult = (int)ScriptResults.Success;
```

This code writes the current timestamp of the system into the variable and reports a successful completion of the function to SSIS.

Add a **Data Flow Task** to the container and rename it to **Stage BTS On Time On Time Performance**. The final control flow is presented in Figure 11.16.

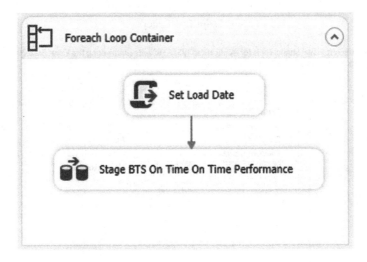

FIGURE 11.16

Control flow to source flat files.

The foreach loop container will enumerate over all files in the configured folder. Sort order of the file names appears to be in alphabetic order, but this is undocumented by Microsoft. There are custom components that allow sorting by file name and date among other options [31].

The next step is to configure the data flow task in order to stage the data in the flat files into the target tables.

11.6.2 FLAT FILE CONNECTION MANAGER

In order to set up the data flow for staging CSV flat files, the first step is to set up the **flat file connection manager**. Open the **Stage BTS On Time On Time Performance** data flow in the previous SSIS control flow. Drag a **Flat File Source** to the data flow (Figure 11.17).

Create a new flat file connection by selecting the **New...** button. In the following **Flat File Connection Manager Editor**, select one of the flat files in the source folder (Figure 11.18).

Make sure the **locale** is set to **English (United States)** and **Unicode** is not selected. The **format** should be set to **Delimited**, double quotes (") should be used as **text qualifier** and **header row delimiter** is set to **{CR}{LF}** as usual under Microsoft Windows. The column names are provided in the first data row of the source file; therefore activate the corresponding check box.

The data from the source file can be previewed on the **columns** tab. Switch to the **advanced** tab to configure the data types and other characteristics of the columns (Figure 11.19).

This configuration is required because the CSV file doesn't provide any metadata or description of the data, except the column headers. All data is formatted as strings only. While it is possible to manually configure the columns, it is also possible to use a wizard that analyzes the source data. Select the Suggest Types... button to start the wizard in Figure 11.20 (Figure 11.20).

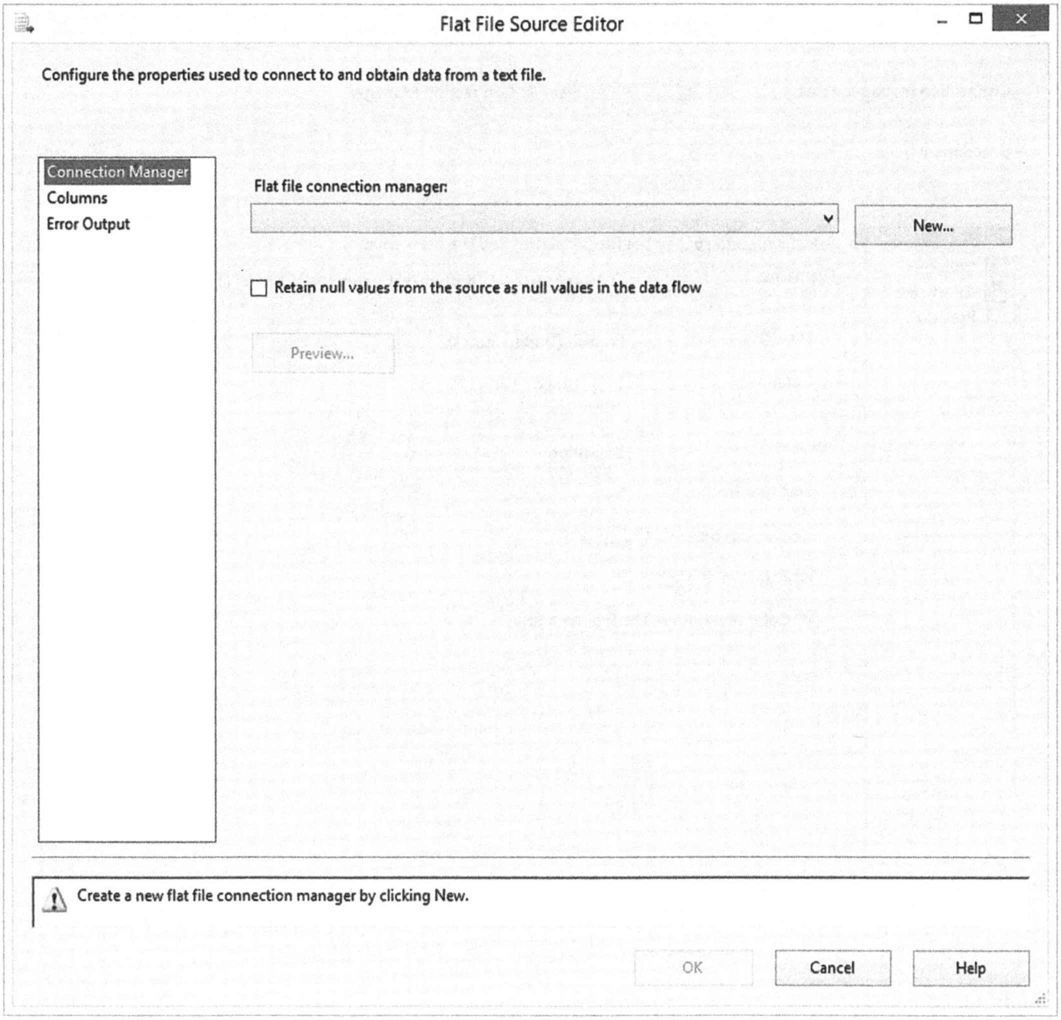

FIGURE 11.17

Flat file source editor.

The wizard analyzevs the source data by looking at a sample size only. This sample size should be large enough to capture all types of different characteristics of the data. Turn on the first two options and identify Boolean columns by 1 and 0. This follows the recommendation to use the actual data types of the raw data. Columns such as **delayed** are Boolean fields, which are formatted as 0 and 1. Make sure that **pad string columns** is turned off. After selecting the **OK** button, review the definitions of the source columns in the previous dialog. Note that some of the columns might have been incorrectly

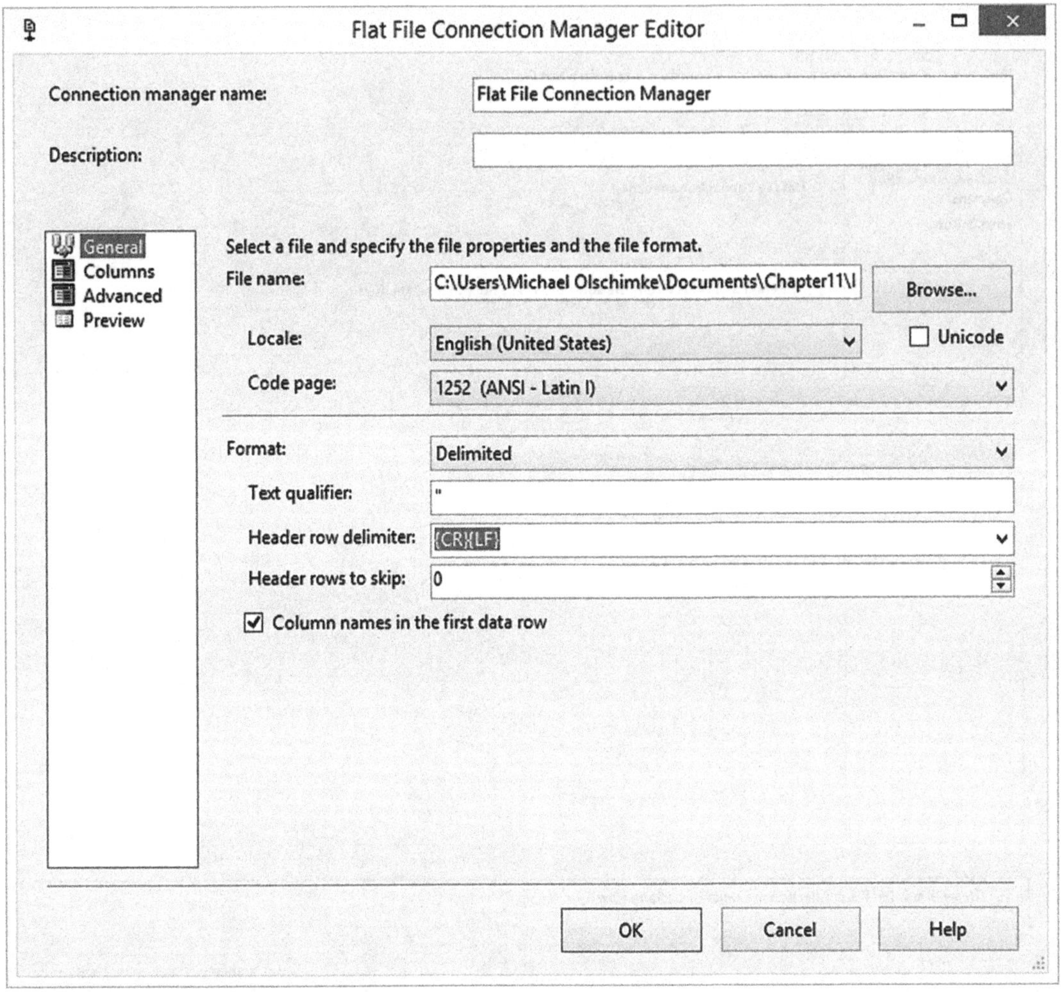

FIGURE 11.18

Setting up the flat file connection.

classified as Boolean because the data contains only records from January, which is in quarter 1 and month 1. Change them to better data types, such as two-byte signed integer. Also, you should increase some of the output column width of the string columns to allow longer city names, for example. Change all string columns from strings to Unicode strings. More information about the source columns can be found in the readme.html file that accompanies the source files.

After completion of the **flat file connection manager editor**, select **retain null values from the source as null values in the data flow** in the **flat file source editor**. Close the editor by selecting the **OK** button.

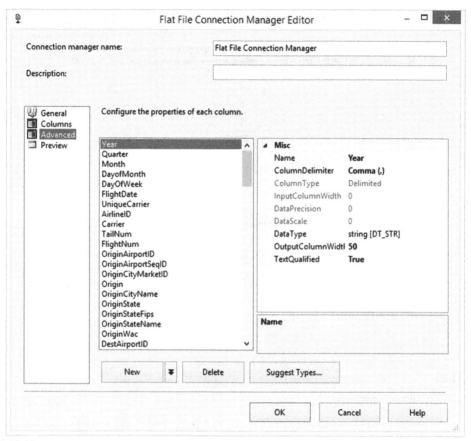

FIGURE 11.19

Configure columns of the flat file connection.

So far, the filename in the **Flat File Connection Manager** was configured using a static file name. This allows easy configuration of the columns and previewing data. In order to successfully traverse over all files in the source folder, we need to change the file name programmatically. Select the **Flat File Connection Manager** in the Connection Managers pane at the bottom of **Microsoft Visual Studio** and set the **DelayValidation** property to **True**. Open the expressions editor by clicking the ellipse button. The dialog in Figure 11.21 is shown.

Set the **ConnectionString** property by the following expression: **@[User::sFileName]**. This will set the file name to the file name stored in the SSIS variable obtained in the control flow.

11.6.3 DATA FLOW

After having configured the flat file connection, the next step is to add the system-generated attributes in the control flow and load the data into the destination.

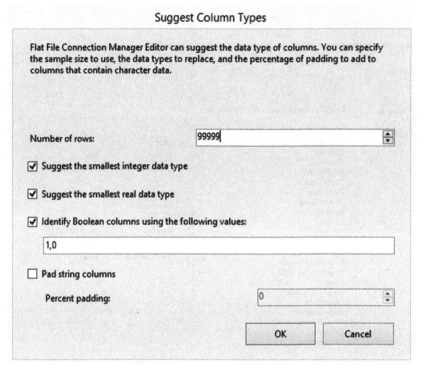

FIGURE 11.20

Suggest column types configuration.

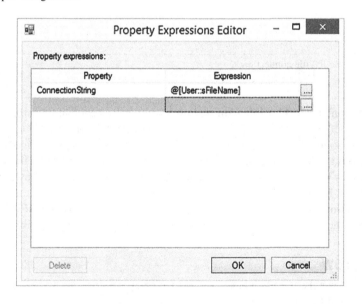

FIGURE 11.21

Property expression editor for flat file connection manager.

The following system-generated attributes should be added to the stage table:

- **Sequence number:** a number that is used to maintain the order of the source file in the relational database table.
- **Record source:** the source of origin of the data.
- **Load date:** the date and time when the record was loaded into the data warehouse. This should be consistent for all records in one file but different to other files.
- **Hash keys:** surrogate keys for each business key and their relations, based on a hash function.
- **Hash diffs:** hash values used to speed up column comparisons when loading descriptive data.

The primary key of the staging table consists of the sequence number and the load date. The combination of both fields must be unique for this reason.

The first step is to add the sequence number to the data flow. Microsoft SSIS doesn't provide a sequence generator. If the sequence should be created within SSIS, a **Script Component** is used. An alternative is to create an IDENTITY column in the Microsoft SQL Server table. The script component allows fully customized transformations, written in C# or Visual Basic.NET, to extend SSIS. Drag the component to the data flow canvas. The dialog in Figure 11.22 will be shown.

It is possible to use the script component in three different ways:

- **Source:** the script component acts as a source and sends records into the data flow. This is useful when loading data from data sources not directly supported by SSIS.
- **Destination:** the script component acts as a destination and supports writing records from the data flow into third-party locations such as custom APIs.
- **Transformation:** the script component transforms the input records from the data flow into different outputs and writes them back to the data flow.

FIGURE 11.22

Select script component type.

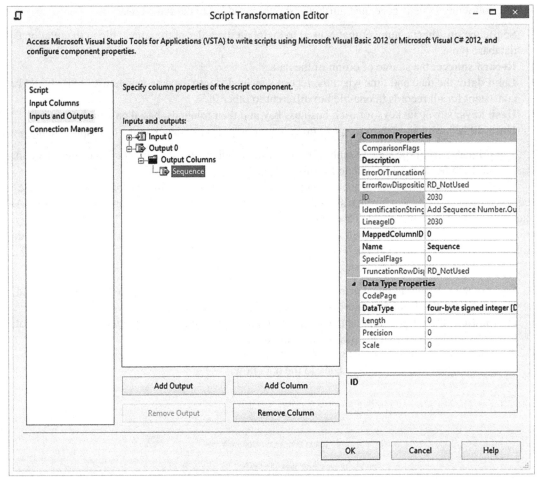

FIGURE 11.23

Script transformation editor to create a sequence output.

Because the goal of this step is to attach a sequence number to the data flow, select **transformation** before pressing the **OK** button. Connect the data flow of the **flat file source** to the script component. Open the **Script Transformation Editor** and add a new column on the **Inputs and Outputs** tab (Figure 11.23).

Select the folder **Output Columns** of the first output called **Output 0**. Select the **Add Column** button below the tree view. Name the output column **Sequence** and set the **DataType** property to

four-byte signed integer [DT_I4]. Switch back to the **Script** tab and select the **Edit Script...** button on the bottom right of the dialog. Replace the **Input0_ProcessInputRow** function by the following code:

```
private int seq = 1;
public override void Input0_ProcessInputRow( Input0Buffer Row)
{
    Row.Sequence = this.seq++;
}
```

This code introduces a new **seq** field that is increased for each row and returned into the data flow. Close the script and the script transformation editor.

The next step is to add the **record source** and the **load date**. Adding them is fairly simple: a **Derived Column** component can be added to the data flow. This is due to the simplicity of the required calculations. Drag a **Derived Column** component on the data flow canvas and connect it to the previous script component. Add the derived columns as shown in Table 11.22.

The first derived column creates a **LoadDate** column in the data flow. This column retrieves the load date from the variable, which was set in the control flow before the data flow was started. The **RecordSource** column is set statically to a detailed string that can be used for debugging purposes.

In addition, the same component can be used to prepare the hash calculations. For each hub and link in the target Data Vault model as shown in Figure 11.1, a hash key is required that is based on the business key or business key relationship in the model. There are five hubs and two links in the model. But the source file provides multiple columns that are mapped to the same target entity. For example, both **origin** and **dest**ination airports are mapped to the **HubAirport**. For that reason, multiple columns have to be hashed. Add the derived columns as shown in Table 11.23, which will represent the various inputs for the hash function.

Note that some of the input columns are converted to Unicode strings by the expression (**DT_WSTR,X**) where X is the configured length of the output string. All elements in the business key (BK) or the satellite payload (PL) for descriptive data are checked for NULL values by using the **REPLACENULL** function. Note the combination of case-insensitive business keys and case-sensitive payload in the last two derived columns.

The delimiter is hard-coded into the derived column because it can only be changed later with much effort. Changing the delimiter from semicolon to another character requires full reloading of the data warehouse. Also, it might be required to improve the expressions to support additional data types (such

Table 11.22 Derived Columns Required for Staging Process

Derived Column Name	Expression	Data Type
LoadDate	@[User::dLoadDate]	date
RecordSource	"BTS.OnTimeOnTimePerformance"	Unicode string

Table 11.23 Additional Derived Columns Required for Hashing in the Staging Process

Derived Column Name	Expression
FlightNumHubBK	UPPER(TRIM(REPLACENULL(Carrier,""")) + ";" + TRIM((DT_WSTR,5)REPLACENULL(FlightNum,""")))
OriginHubBK	UPPER(TRIM(REPLACENULL(Origin,""")))
CarrierHubBK	UPPER(TRIM(REPLACENULL(Carrier,""")))
TailNumHubBK	UPPER(TRIM(REPLACENULL(TailNum,""")))
DestHubBK	UPPER(TRIM(REPLACENULL(Dest,""")))
Div1AirportHubBK	UPPER(TRIM(REPLACENULL(Div1Airport,""")))
Div2AirportHubBK	UPPER(TRIM(REPLACENULL(Div2Airport,""")))
Div3AirportHubBK	UPPER(TRIM(REPLACENULL(Div3Airport,""")))
Div4AirportHubBK	UPPER(TRIM(REPLACENULL(Div4Airport,""")))
Div5AirportHubBK	UPPER(TRIM(REPLACENULL(Div5Airport,""")))
FlightLinkBK	UPPER(TRIM(REPLACENULL((DT_WSTR,2)Carrier,""")) + ";" + TRIM((DT_WSTR,5)REPLACENULL(FlightNum,""")) + ";" + TRIM(REPLACENULL((DT_WSTR,10)TailNum,""")) + ";" + TRIM(REPLACENULL((DT_WSTR,3)Origin,""")) + ";" + TRIM(REPLACENULL((DT_WSTR,3)Dest,""")) + ";" + TRIM((DT_WSTR,27)REPLACENULL(FlightDate,""")))
Div1FlightLinkBK	UPPER(TRIM((DT_WSTR,5)REPLACENULL(FlightNum,""")) + ";" + TRIM((DT_WSTR,10)REPLACENULL(Div1TailNum,""")) + ";" + TRIM((DT_WSTR,3)REPLACENULL(Origin,""")) + ";" + TRIM((DT_WSTR,3)REPLACENULL(Div1Airport,""")) + ";" + "1" + ";" + TRIM((DT_WSTR,27)REPLACENULL(FlightDate,""")))
Div2FlightLinkBK	UPPER(TRIM((DT_WSTR,5)REPLACENULL(FlightNum,""")) + ";" + TRIM((DT_WSTR,10)REPLACENULL(Div2Tailnum,""")) + ";" + TRIM((DT_WSTR,3)REPLACENULL(Origin,""")) + ";" + TRIM((DT_WSTR,3)REPLACENULL(Div2Airport,""")) + ";" + "2" + ";" + TRIM((DT_WSTR,27)REPLACENULL(FlightDate,""")))
Div3FlightLinkBK	UPPER(TRIM((DT_WSTR,5)REPLACENULL(FlightNum,""")) + ";" + TRIM((DT_WSTR,10)REPLACENULL(Div3TailNum,""")) + ";" + TRIM((DT_WSTR,3)REPLACENULL(Origin,""")) + ";" + TRIM((DT_WSTR,3)REPLACENULL(Div3Airport,""")) + ";" + "3" + ";" + TRIM((DT_WSTR,27)REPLACENULL(FlightDate,""")))
Div4FlightLinkBK	UPPER(TRIM((DT_WSTR,5)REPLACENULL(FlightNum,""")) + ";" + TRIM((DT_WSTR,10)REPLACENULL(Div4TailNum,""")) + ";" + TRIM((DT_WSTR,3)REPLACENULL(Origin,""")) + ";" + TRIM((DT_WSTR,3)REPLACENULL(Div4Airport,""")) + ";" + "4" + ";" + TRIM((DT_WSTR,27)REPLACENULL(FlightDate,""")))
Div5FlightLinkBK	UPPER(TRIM((DT_WSTR,5)REPLACENULL(FlightNum,""")) + ";" + TRIM((DT_WSTR,10)REPLACENULL(Div5TailNum,""")) + ";" + TRIM((DT_WSTR,3)REPLACENULL(Origin,""")) + ";" + TRIM((DT_WSTR,3)REPLACENULL(Div5Airport,""")) + ";" + "5" + ";" + TRIM((DT_WSTR,27)REPLACENULL(FlightDate,""")))

Table 11.23 Additional Derived Columns Required for Hashing in the Staging Process *(cont.)*

Derived Column Name	Expression
FlightNumCarrierLinkBK	UPPER(TRIM(REPLACENULL(Carrier,""))) + ";" + TRIM((DT_WSTR,5)REPLACENULL(FlightNum,"")) + ";" + TRIM(REPLACENULL(Carrier,"")))
OriginAirportSatPL	UPPER(TRIM(REPLACENULL(Origin,""))) + ";" + TRIM(REPLACENULL(OriginCityName,"")) + ";" + TRIM(REPLACENULL(OriginState,"")) + ";" + TRIM(REPLACENULL(OriginStateName,"")) + ";" + TRIM((DT_WSTR,5)REPLACENULL(OriginCityMarketID,"")) + ";" + TRIM((DT_WSTR,3)REPLACENULL(OriginStateFips,"")) + ";" + TRIM((DT_WSTR,3)REPLACENULL(OriginWac,""))
DestAirportSatPL	UPPER(TRIM(REPLACENULL(Dest,""))) + ";" + TRIM(REPLACENULL(DestCityName,"")) + ";" + TRIM(REPLACENULL(DestState,"")) + ";" + TRIM(REPLACENULL(DestStateName,"")) + ";" + TRIM((DT_WSTR,5)REPLACENULL(DestCityMarketID,"")) + ";" + TRIM((DT_WSTR,3)REPLACENULL(DestStateFips,"")) + ";" + TRIM((DT_WSTR,3)REPLACENULL(DestWac,""))

as Boolean and float values) and to standardize on the date format to be used: it is recommended to use ISO-8601 for converting date timestamps into character strings.

The Div1FlightLinkBK to Div5FlightLinkBK columns include a constant value that helps to un-pivot the incoming data. If the flight was diverted multiple times, the diversion information is provided in up to five sets of columns. When loading the data into the Raw Data Vault, it is loaded into a single link table with up to five records per incoming row.

The final setup is shown in Figure 11.24.

The new columns are shown in the grid on the bottom of the dialog. Select **OK** to close the dialog. The next step is to calculate the hash values for all business keys, their relationships and for descriptive attributes that should be added to the same satellites. Multiple options have been discussed in section 11.2. This section describes how to use a **Script Component** for hashing the inputs.

Drag another **Script Component** to the data flow canvas and connect it to the previous **Derived Column** transformation. Switch to the **Input Columns** tab and check all available input columns in the default input **Input 0**. Switch to the **Inputs and Outputs** tab. For each derived column that ends with **HubBK**, **LinkBK** or **SatPL**, add a corresponding **HashKey** or **HashDiff** column. For example, for **FlightNumHubBK**, add an output column **FlightNumHashKey** with a string (non-unicode) of length 32 and code page 1252. Because the hash value is based only on characters from 0 to 9 and A to F, a Western European code page, such as 1252 or even ASCII, is sufficient. The important step here is to define the one to be used and implement it consistently.

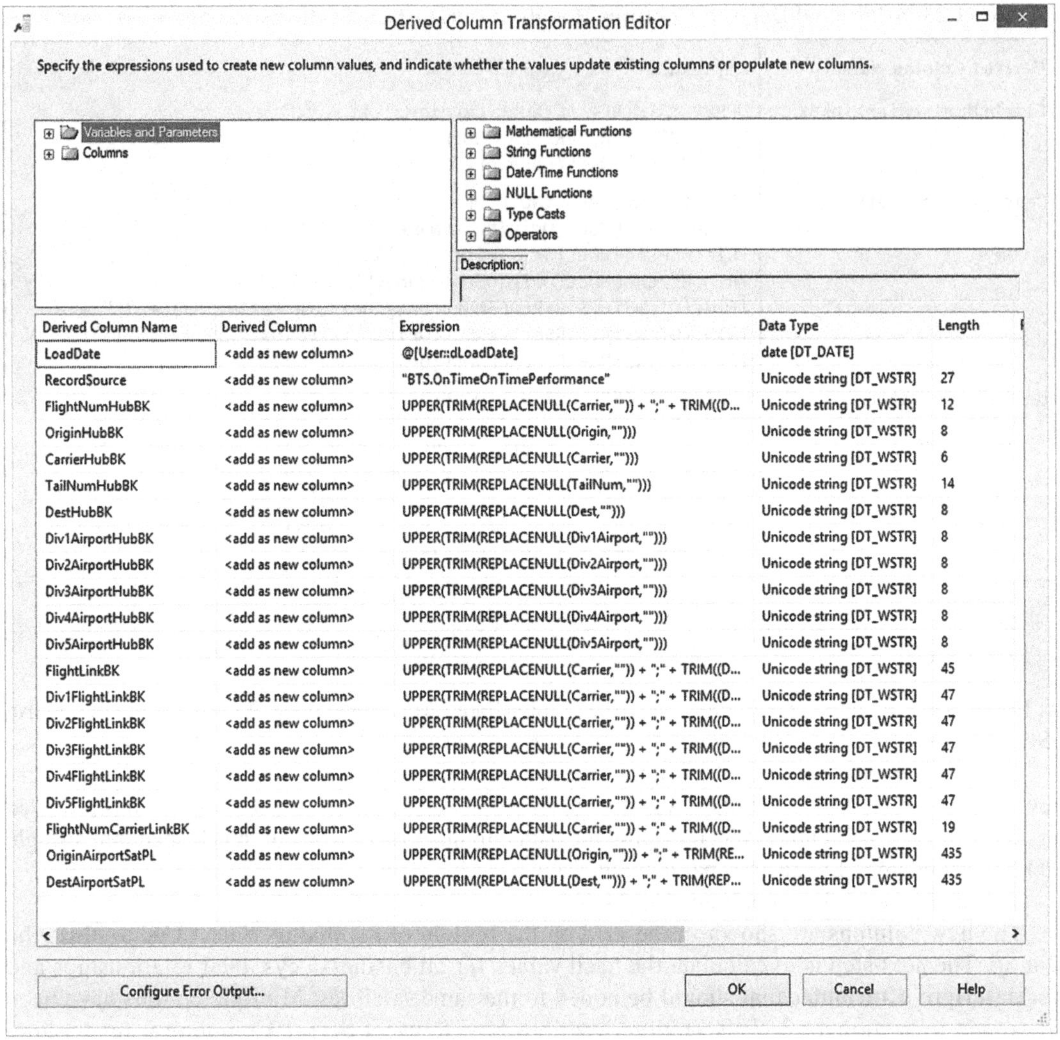

FIGURE 11.24

Derived column transformation editor to setup the system-generated columns.

Following this naming convention is important for the following script to work, because it hashes all input columns ending with either **HubBK**, **LinkBK** or **SatPL** and writes them into an output column with exactly the same name, ending with **HashKey** or **HashDiff** instead. This approach requires no programming at all; all configuration is done graphically in the Script Transformation Editor (Figure 11.25).

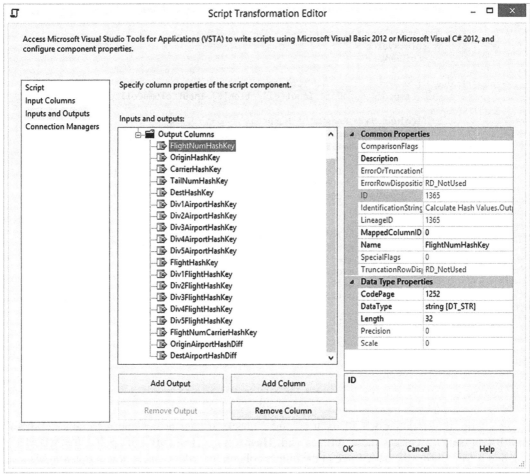

FIGURE 11.25

Output columns in the script transformation editor for applying the hash function.

Switch back to the **Script** tab and enter the following script using the **Edit Script...** button:

```
[Microsoft.SqlServer.Dts.Pipeline.SSISScriptComponentEntryPointAttribute]
public class ScriptMain : UserComponent
{
    MD5 md5 = System.Security.Cryptography.MD5.Create();
    System.Text.UnicodeEncoding encoding = new System.Text.UnicodeEncoding(false, false);

    /// <summary>
    /// This method is called once for every row that passes through the
    /// component from Input0.
    /// </summary>
    /// <param name="Row">The row that is currently passing through the
    /// component</param>
```

```
public override void Input0_ProcessInputRow(Input0Buffer Row)
{
    Type rowType = Row.GetType();
    String columnValue = "";
    String oColumnName = "";

    foreach (IDTSInputColumn100 iColumn in
        this.ComponentMetaData.InputCollection[0].InputColumnCollection) {

        if (iColumn.Name.EndsWith("HubBK")
            || iColumn.Name.EndsWith("LinkBK")
            || iColumn.Name.EndsWith("SatPL"))
        {
            oColumnName = iColumn.Name.Replace("HubBK", "HashKey");
            oColumnName = oColumnName.Replace("LinkBK", "HashKey");
            oColumnName = oColumnName.Replace("SatPL", "HashDiff");

            columnValue =
                rowType.GetProperty(iColumn.Name).GetValue(Row, null).ToString();
            columnValue = BitConverter.ToString(
                md5.ComputeHash(encoding.GetBytes(columnValue)));
            columnValue = columnValue.Replace("-", "");
            if (rowType.GetProperty(oColumnName) != null)
                rowType.GetProperty(oColumnName).SetValue(Row, columnValue, null);
        }
    }
}
```

This script traverses through all input columns, checks if their names end with either **HubBK**, **LinkBK** or **SatPL**, replaces these suffixes with **HashKey** or **HashDiff** and applies the MD5 hash function before storing the hash value in the output column. In order to make this script compile successfully, a reference to the assembly **System.Security** is required.

Note that this script implements a simplified hash diff calculation. It has not implemented the improved strategy to support changing satellite structures as described in section 11.2.5 with zero maintenance. In order to do so, any delimiters at the end of the input strings for hash diffs (columns ending with "SatPL") have to be removed from the input.

The last step is to set up the OLE DB destination to write the data flow into a staging table. Before doing so, create the target table in the staging area by executing the following script:

```
CREATE TABLE [bts].[OnTimeOnTimePerformance](
    [Sequence] [int] NOT NULL,
    [Year] [smallint] NULL,
    [Quarter] [smallint] NULL,
    [Month] [smallint] NULL,
```

```
[DayofMonth] [smallint] NULL,
[DayOfWeek] [smallint] NULL,
[FlightDate] [datetime] NULL,
[UniqueCarrier] [nvarchar](2) NULL,
[AirlineID] [smallint] NULL,
[Carrier] [nvarchar](2) NULL,
[TailNum] [nvarchar](6) NULL,
[FlightNum] [smallint] NULL,
[OriginAirportID] [smallint] NULL,
[OriginAirportSeqID] [int] NULL,
[OriginCityMarketID] [int] NULL,
[Origin] [nvarchar](3) NULL,
[OriginCityName] [nvarchar](100) NULL,
[OriginState] [nvarchar](2) NULL,
[OriginStateFips] [smallint] NULL,
[OriginStateName] [nvarchar](100) NULL,
[OriginWac] [smallint] NULL,
[DestAirportID] [smallint] NULL,
[DestAirportSeqID] [int] NULL,
[DestCityMarketID] [int] NULL,
[Dest] [nvarchar](3) NULL,
[DestCityName] [nvarchar](100) NULL,
[DestState] [nvarchar](2) NULL,
[DestStateFips] [smallint] NULL,
[DestStateName] [nvarchar](100) NULL,
[DestWac] [smallint] NULL,
[CRSDepTime] [smallint] NULL,
[DepTime] [smallint] NULL,
[DepDelay] [smallint] NULL,
[DepDelayMinutes] [smallint] NULL,
[DepDel15] [bit] NULL,
[DepartureDelayGroups] [smallint] NULL,
[DepTimeBlk] [nvarchar](9) NULL,
[TaxiOut] [smallint] NULL,
[WheelsOff] [smallint] NULL,
[WheelsOn] [smallint] NULL,
[TaxiIn] [smallint] NULL,
[CRSArrTime] [smallint] NULL,
[ArrTime] [smallint] NULL,
[ArrDelay] [smallint] NULL,
[ArrDelayMinutes] [smallint] NULL,
[ArrDel15] [bit] NULL,
[ArrivalDelayGroups] [smallint] NULL,
[ArrTimeBlk] [nvarchar](9) NULL,
[Cancelled] [bit] NULL,
[CancellationCode] [nvarchar](10) NULL,
[Diverted] [bit] NULL,
[CRSElapsedTime] [smallint] NULL,
[ActualElapsedTime] [smallint] NULL,
[AirTime] [smallint] NULL,
[Flights] [smallint] NULL,
[Distance] [int] NULL,
[DistanceGroup] [int] NULL,
[CarrierDelay] [smallint] NULL,
```

```
[WeatherDelay] [smallint] NULL,
[NASDelay] [smallint] NULL,
[SecurityDelay] [smallint] NULL,
[LateAircraftDelay] [smallint] NULL,
[FirstDepTime] [smallint] NULL,
[TotalAddGTime] [smallint] NULL,
[LongestAddGTime] [smallint] NULL,
[DivAirportLandings] [smallint] NULL,
[DivReachedDest] [bit] NULL,
[DivActualElapsedTime] [smallint] NULL,
[DivArrDelay] [smallint] NULL,
[DivDistance] [int] NULL,
[Div1Airport] [nvarchar](3) NULL,
[Div1AirportID] [smallint] NULL,
[Div1AirportSeqID] [smallint] NULL,
[Div1WheelsOn] [smallint] NULL,
[Div1TotalGTime] [smallint] NULL,
[Div1LongestGTime] [smallint] NULL,
[Div1WheelsOff] [smallint] NULL,
[Div1TailNum] [nvarchar](6) NULL,
[Div2Airport] [nvarchar](3) NULL,
[Div2AirportID] [smallint] NULL,
[Div2AirportSeqID] [smallint] NULL,
[Div2WheelsOn] [smallint] NULL,
[Div2TotalGTime] [smallint] NULL,
[Div2LongestGTime] [smallint] NULL,
[Div2WheelsOff] [smallint] NULL,
[Div2TailNum] [nvarchar](6) NULL,
[Div3Airport] [nvarchar](3) NULL,
[Div3AirportID] [smallint] NULL,
[Div3AirportSeqID] [smallint] NULL,
[Div3WheelsOn] [smallint] NULL,
[Div3TotalGTime] [smallint] NULL,
[Div3LongestGTime] [smallint] NULL,
[Div3WheelsOff] [smallint] NULL,
[Div3TailNum] [nvarchar](6) NULL,
[Div4Airport] [nvarchar](3) NULL,
[Div4AirportID] [smallint] NULL,
[Div4AirportSeqID] [smallint] NULL,
[Div4WheelsOn] [smallint] NULL,
[Div4TotalGTime] [smallint] NULL,
[Div4LongestGTime] [smallint] NULL,
[Div4WheelsOff] [smallint] NULL,
[Div4TailNum] [nvarchar](6) NULL,
[Div5Airport] [nvarchar](3) NULL,
[Div5AirportID] [smallint] NULL,
[Div5AirportSeqID] [smallint] NULL,
[Div5WheelsOn] [smallint] NULL,
[Div5TotalGTime] [smallint] NULL,
[Div5LongestGTime] [smallint] NULL,
[Div5WheelsOff] [smallint] NULL,
[Div5TailNum] [nvarchar](6) NULL,
```

```
      [LoadDate] [datetime] NOT NULL,
      [RecordSource] [nvarchar](27) NOT NULL,
      [FlightNumHashKey] [char](32) NOT NULL,
      [OriginHashKey] [char](32) NOT NULL,
      [CarrierHashKey] [char](32) NOT NULL,
      [TailNumHashKey] [char](32) NOT NULL,
      [DestHashKey] [char](32) NOT NULL,
      [Div1AirportHashKey] [char](32) NOT NULL,
      [Div2AirportHashKey] [char](32) NOT NULL,
      [Div3AirportHashKey] [char](32) NOT NULL,
      [Div4AirportHashKey] [char](32) NOT NULL,
      [Div5AirportHashKey] [char](32) NOT NULL,
      [FlightHashKey] [char](32) NOT NULL,
      [Div1FlightHashKey] [char](32) NOT NULL,
      [Div2FlightHashKey] [char](32) NOT NULL,
      [Div3FlightHashKey] [char](32) NOT NULL,
      [Div4FlightHashKey] [char](32) NOT NULL,
      [Div5FlightHashKey] [char](32) NOT NULL,
      [FlightNumCarrierHashKey] [char](32) NOT NULL,
      [OriginAirportHashDiff] [char](32) NOT NULL,
      [DestAirportHashDiff] [char](32) NOT NULL,
 CONSTRAINT [PK_OnTimeOnTimePerformance] PRIMARY KEY NONCLUSTERED
(
      [Sequence] ASC,
      [LoadDate] ASC
) ON [INDEX]
) ON [DATA]
```

In this script, all strings are configured as nvarchar to allow other languages to be added later on. It is also in line with the flat file source in the data flow, because the input columns have been configured as Unicode strings. The table is created in a schema called **bts**. The schemas as used in this chapter follow the convention that each source system uses its own schema.

The final step is to set up the destination. Drag an **OLE DB Destination** component to the data flow canvas and connect it to the **Script Component** that calculates the hash values. In the **OLE DB Destination Editor**, create a new connection manager. Set up the new connection to the **StageArea** database as shown in Figure 11.26.

After selecting the OK button, make sure the connection is taken over to the **OLE DB destination editor** and select the **OnTimeOnTimePerformance** table in the **bts** namespace as the destination (Figure 11.27).

Make sure to **keep null** values by activating the option. You might want to configure the other options, such as **rows per batch**. Switch to the **Mappings** tab and make sure that all columns from the data flow are mapped correctly to the destination (Figure 11.28).

Scroll down and make sure that the **HubBK**, **LinkBK** and **SatPL** columns have not found a destination column. They are only used in the data flow but not written to the destination. Instead, the corresponding hash key or hash diff value is written.

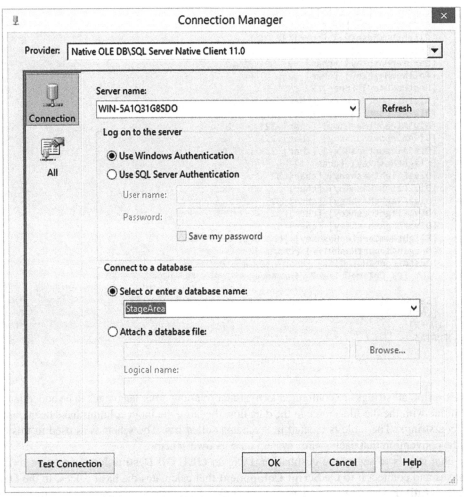

FIGURE 11.26

Setup connection manager.

Run the control flow by pressing the start button in the toolbar. After moving the data, open Microsoft SQL Server Management Studio and execute the following SQL statement to compare the hash calculation in TSQL with the one performed in SSIS:

```
SELECT TOP 10
    OriginHashKey AS OriginHashKey_SSIS,
    UPPER(CONVERT(char(32),HASHBYTES('MD5',
        UPPER(RTRIM(LTRIM(COALESCE(Origin, ''))))
    ),2)) AS OriginHashKey_TSQL,

    OriginAirportHashDiff AS OriginAirportHashDiff_SSIS,
    UPPER(CONVERT(char(32),HASHBYTES('MD5',
```

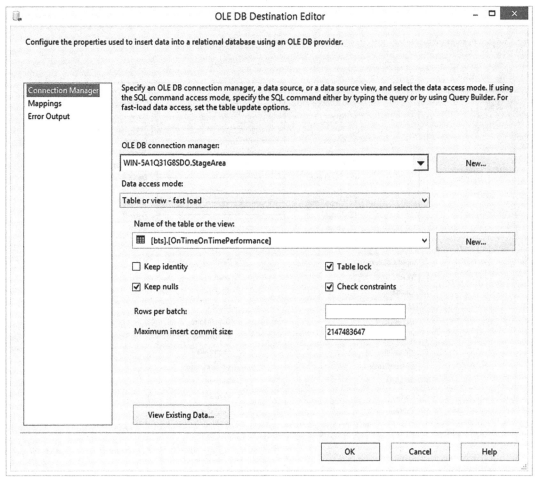

FIGURE 11.27

Set up OLE DB destination.

```
CONCAT(
        UPPER(RTRIM(LTRIM(COALESCE(Origin, '')))), ';',
        RTRIM(LTRIM(COALESCE(OriginCityName, ''))), ';',
        RTRIM(LTRIM(COALESCE(OriginState, ''))), ';',
        RTRIM(LTRIM(COALESCE(OriginStateName, ''))), ';',
        RTRIM(LTRIM(COALESCE(OriginCityMarketID, ''))), ';',
        RTRIM(LTRIM(COALESCE(OriginStateFips, ''))), ';',
        RTRIM(LTRIM(COALESCE(OriginWac, '')))
        )
    ),2)) AS OriginAirportHashDiff_TSQL
FROM
    [StageArea].[bts].[OnTimeOnTimePerformance]
```

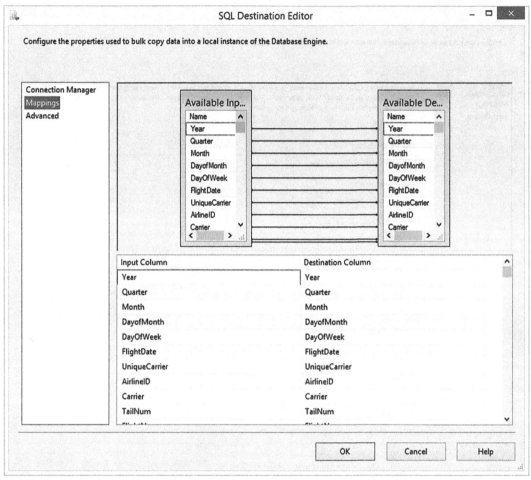

FIGURE 11.28

Map input columns to destination.

The statement should return four columns. The first two columns should return the **OriginHash-Key** and provide exactly the same result. The last two columns should produce the same **OriginAir-portHashDiff** value.

Note that there are two options to convert the columnValue variable in line 32 of the script used in the script component to calculate the hash values. This option is set in line 5 when the **System.Text. UnicodeEncoding** class is initialized:

```
System.Text.UnicodeEncoding encoding = new System.Text.UnicodeEncoding(false, false);
```

The first parameter in the constructor allows to set little endian (false) or big endian (true) for the conversion. When using big endian, the hash values produced in SSIS are different from those produced in T-SQL. Also make sure that the byte-order mark (the second parameter is set to false).

The control and data flows to source flat files into the staging area are now complete. Note that the Metrics Mart and Error Mart have been left out of the discussion by intention, due to space restrictions. In order to go productive, redirect errors into the Error Mart as shown in Chapter 10, Metadata Management, and capture base metrics in the same manner as discussed in Chapter 10 as well.

11.7 **SOURCING HISTORICAL DATA**

The previous section described the loading of flat file data sources. However, one special case remains that needs some thought. Before the data warehouse is put into production and loads data on a regular schedule, historical data is often loaded. The historical data often comes from the source application itself, from the archive or from a legacy data warehouse. Sourcing historical data allows the business to analyze trends that have started before the data warehouse has been put in place. Therefore, loading historical data is a common task in data warehousing.

Section 11.3 has described how the load date is applied to incoming data in order to identify the batch that loaded the data. When using this approach without modifications for loading historical data, a problem is incorporated into the loading process. Because all historical data is loaded in one batch, or at least in multiple batches around the same time, there is a risk that historical data cannot be loaded into the Data Vault any longer. If the same load date is used for all historical data, it would actually become impossible to load the data. The reason behind this problem is that the load date is part of the Data Vault 2.0 model because it is included in the primary key of satellites. Consider the three historical source files in Figure 11.29.

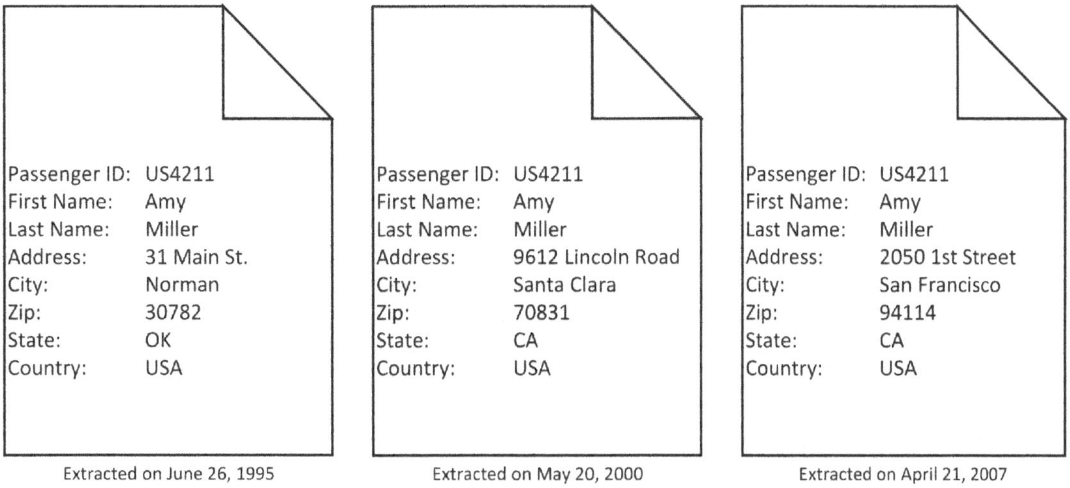

Passenger ID: US4211	Passenger ID: US4211	Passenger ID: US4211
First Name: Amy	First Name: Amy	First Name: Amy
Last Name: Miller	Last Name: Miller	Last Name: Miller
Address: 31 Main St.	Address: 9612 Lincoln Road	Address: 2050 1st Street
City: Norman	City: Santa Clara	City: San Francisco
Zip: 30782	Zip: 70831	Zip: 94114
State: OK	State: CA	State: CA
Country: USA	Country: USA	Country: USA
Extracted on June 26, 1995	Extracted on May 20, 2000	Extracted on April 21, 2007

FIGURE 11.29

Historical source files generated on various dates.

All three files contain address data for the same passenger. The passenger has moved over time. Because this historical data is of interest for the business users, it needs to be loaded into the data warehouse before going into production. If the initial data load, based on the historical data, is performed on January 1, 2015, the load dates for all three documents would be set to this date. Consider the effects on the satellite **SatPassengerAddress** shown in Table 11.24.

The problem is that the load date in Table 11.24 has been set to the same date. In fact, loading this data into the satellite table will not work, because the primary key is made up of the passenger hash key column and the load date column (refer to Chapter 4). This combination has to be unique to meet the requirements of the primary key. These records would be in violation with these requirements because the combination is always the same for all three rows.

To resolve this issue, there are two options: either load the data in three different batches, or set an artificial load date. The first solution would work from a technical perspective, but from a design perspective, there should be no difference between historical data and actual data. The data warehouse should pretend that the historical data was loaded just as the actual data on the day it was generated (or at least near the date). In the case of the example shown in Table 11.24, all historical data seems to be loaded on January 1, 2015. This is true, but not the desired view of the business.

The second approach is to set the load date to an artificial date. This is the preferred solution when loading archived historical data. The load date is set to the date it would have received if the historical data had been loaded in the past. By doing so, it simulates that the data warehouse would have been in place and the loading procedures would have sourced the file in the past. This is the only exception to the rule that the load date should not be a source-system generated date, because we're using the date of generation, in many cases the extract date. On the other hand, this is a one-off historical load and the load date is only derived from the historical date of generation, but under full control of the data warehouse. For example, the data warehouse team might decide to override a load date derived from the historic date of generation during the initial node when required. For all these reasons, the date of generation could be used as the load date (Table 11.25).

Note that the time part of the load date has been set to 00:00:00.000. There are two reasons for this decision: first, in many cases, the actual time when the historical data has been extracted from the source system is unknown because the file name or some log file provides only the date of extraction. The second reason is that the convention to set the time part of the load date for historical data helps to distinguish the historical data from the actual data which is still desired in some cases, for example

Table 11.24 Erroneous SatPassengerAddress Satellite

Passenger HashKey	Load Date	Load End Date	Record Source	Address	City	Zip	State	Country
8473d2a...	2015-01-01 08:34:12	2015-01-01 08:34:12.999	Domestic Flight	31 Main St.	Norman	30782	OK	USA
8473d2a...	2015-01-01 08:34:12	2015-01-01 08:34:12.999	Domestic Flight	9612 Lincoln Road	Santa Clara	70831	CA	USA
8473d2a...	2015-01-01 08:34:12	9999-12-31 24:59:59.999	Domestic Flight	2050 1st street	San Francisco	94114	CA	USA

Table 11.25 Corrected Satellite Data for SatPassengerAddress

Passenger HashKey	Load Date	Load End Date	Record Source	Address	City	Zip	State	Country
8473d2a...	1995-06-26 00:00:00.000	2000-05-20 23:59:59.999	Domestic Flight	31 Main St.	Norman	30782	OK	USA
8473d2a...	2000-05-20 00:00:00.000	2007-04-21 23:59:59.999	Domestic Flight	9612 Lincoln Road	Santa Clara	70831	CA	USA
8473d2a...	2007-04-21 00:00:00.000	9999-12-31 23:59:59.999	Domestic Flight	2050 1st street	San Francisco	94114	CA	USA

for debugging purposes. Following this recommendation is a compromise between the ability to distinguish the data from each other and the desire to load the historical data as it would have been loaded in the past.

11.7.1 SSIS EXAMPLE FOR SOURCING HISTORICAL DATA

Because the load date is set in the staging area, it has to be overridden in its loading processes when historical data should be loaded. In section 11.6, the current date was set as the load date by writing the timestamp into a SSIS variable using a script task. This script task needs to be modified for loading historical data. The goal is to develop a SSIS package that is able to handle both types of data (historical data for the initial load and daily loads).

The first step is to allow read-only access to the current file name in the forloop container. Open the **Script Task Editor** and select the ellipsis button to modify the **ReadOnlyVariables** (Figure 11.30).

In the following dialog, add the **Users::sFileName** variable which holds the current file name of the container that traverses over all files in the source directory.

The second step is to modify the source code of the script task. Instead of setting the current date, the following source is used to extract the date of extraction from the filename:

```
public partial class ScriptMain : VSTARTScriptObjectModelBase
    {
    private static string pattern =
        @".*On_Time_On_Time_Performance_(\d{4})_(\d{1,2})_(\d{1,2}).*";
    private Regex r = new Regex(pattern, RegexOptions.IgnoreCase);

    /// <summary>
    /// This method is called when this script task executes in the control flow.
    /// Before returning from this method, set the value of Dts.TaskResult to indicate
    /// success or failure.
    /// </summary>
    public void Main()

    {
        Match m = r.Match(Dts.Variables["User::sFileName"].Value.ToString());
        if (m.Success && m.Groups.Count >= 4)
```

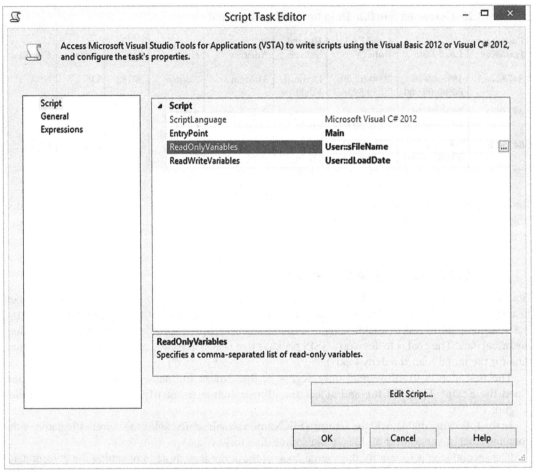

FIGURE 11.30

Script task editor to add ReadOnlyVariables.

```
        {
            int year = int.Parse(m.Groups[1].Value);
            int month = int.Parse(m.Groups[2].Value);
            int day = int.Parse(m.Groups[3].Value);

            Dts.Variables["User::dLoadDate"].Value = new DateTime(year, month, day);
        }
        else
        {
            // report error to the Error Mart
        }

        Dts.TaskResult = (int)ScriptResults.Success;
    }
}
```

The year, month and day are extracted from the source file name using a regular expression that captures dates from file names with YYYY_MM_DD formatted dates included in the file name. These expressions search for patterns within strings and are useful to extract information from semi-structured text such as the file names. If an error occurs, the error is reported to the Error Mart.

11.8 SOURCING THE SAMPLE AIRLINE DATA

The BTS data is provided as Google Sheets on Google Drive. The folder is accessible by the general public under the following link: http://goo.gl/TQ1R63. We will load the data from the Google Sheet files into the staging area of the local data warehouse.

Microsoft SSIS does not provide a component for easy access to files on Google Drive. However, it is possible to extend SSIS by Google Sheets components that can directly access live Google Sheets. In order to do so, download the following products from CData.com:

- **CData ADO.NET Provider for Google Apps:** The CData ADO.NET Provider for Google Apps gives developers the power to easily connect .NET applications to popular Google Services including Google Docs, Google Calendar, Google Talk, Search, and more. We will use the components to load all Google Sheets from the public folder on Google Drive [32]. The product can be found here: http://www.cdata.com/drivers/google/ado/
- **CData SSIS Components for Google Spreadsheets:** Powerful SSIS Source & Destination Components that allows you to easily connect SQL Server with live Google Spreadsheets through SSIS Workflows. We will use the Google Spreadsheets Data Flow Components to source the airline data from Google Sheets [33]. The product can be downloaded from http://www.cdata.com/drivers/gsheets/ssis/

The vendor provides an extended free trial for the purpose of this book. Use the given trial subscription codes when installing the software on your development machine (Table 11.26).

Note: If you decide to buy the components for your projects, you can use the coupon code **DVAULT10** to receive a 10% discount on the software.

As an alternative, you can also download the files as zipped CSV files manually from Google Drive, store them unpacked in a local folder and load the files using the procedure described in the previous section.

The next sections describe how to traverse over Google Drive in order to find the location and name of the airline data spreadsheets. It then sources each spreadsheet into the staging area. Before doing so, access to the Google Drive account has to be granted using OAuth 2.0. Otherwise traversing files on Google Drive is not allowed due to security concerns.

Table 11.26 License Keys for CData Components Required to Download the Sample Data
Product Name: CData SSIS Components for Google Spreadsheets 2015 [RLSAA] License: EVALUATION COPY Product Key: XRLSA-ASPST-D4FFD-2841W-MRREM
Product Name: CData ADO.NET Provider for Google Apps 2015 [RGRAA] License: EVALUATION COPY Product Key: XRGRA-AS1SR-V4FFD-2851T-ZWAFZ

11.8.1 AUTHENTICATING WITH GOOGLE DRIVE

Before the control flow is modified in the next section, Google Drive has to be set up in order to provide the data to SSIS. This requires two steps:

1. Import the folder under http://goo.gl/TQ1R63 into your personal Google Drive account.
2. Allow SSIS to connect to your Google Drive account by registering it as a Desktop application.

The second step requires setting up a project under https://console.developers.google.com/project in order to enable authorized access for desktop applications. Sign-in to the console and create a new project (Figure 11.31).

Provide a unique project name and project id. Select **Create** to create the project in your account. Wait until the project has been created. Once the project dashboard shows up, configure the **consent screen** by selecting the corresponding menu item under **APIs & auth** (Figure 11.32).

The consent screen is presented to the end-user in order to grant access to the personal Google Drive account. No worries: this user will just be you and nobody else.

Enter some information that identifies the application to the user and select the **Save** button.

OAuth 2.0 authorization is required to access the entities on Google Drive that we need to access in order to traverse all the airline data spreadsheets. Without it, the SSIS job described in the next sections cannot find out which spreadsheets are available. Therefore, select the **Create new Client ID** button to advance to the next screen (Figure 11.33).

Depending on the application type, different mechanisms are used to authenticate the application to the user. There are different settings for Web applications, service accounts and applications installed on local desktops or handheld devices. From a cloud provider point-of-view, SSIS is an installed desktop application. Therefore, select the **Installed application** option and **Other** as the application type. Create the client ID by pressing the default button on the screen. The client ID will be created and presented to you (Figure 11.34).

The first items, the client ID and the client secret, are required to allow your local SSIS control flow to access your Google Drive account. Write down both pieces of information or keep your Web browser open. Also, make sure to keep this information secret. When entering the information in the control or data flow, the consent screen will be opened in the default Web browser. When that happens, log into your Google account and confirm the application.

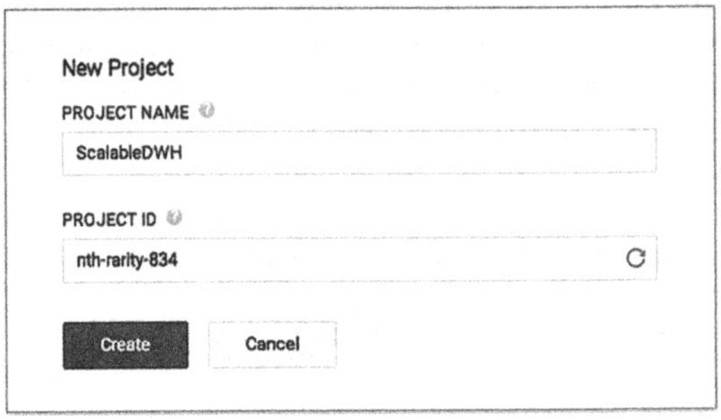

New Project

PROJECT NAME

ScalableDWH

PROJECT ID

nth-rarity-834

Create   Cancel

FIGURE 11.31

Create new project in Google Drive.

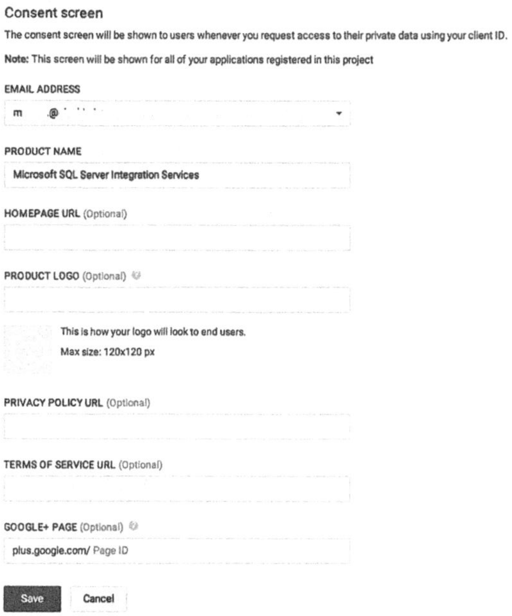

Consent screen

The consent screen will be shown to users whenever you request access to their private data using your client ID.

Note: This screen will be shown for all of your applications registered in this project

EMAIL ADDRESS

m   .@ · · · ·   ▾

PRODUCT NAME

Microsoft SQL Server Integration Services

HOMEPAGE URL (Optional)

PRODUCT LOGO (Optional) ⓘ

This is how your logo will look to end users.
Max size: 120x120 px

PRIVACY POLICY URL (Optional)

TERMS OF SERVICE URL (Optional)

GOOGLE+ PAGE (Optional) ⓘ

plus.google.com/ Page ID

[Save]   [Cancel]

FIGURE 11.32

Setup Consent screen.

Create Client ID

APPLICATION TYPE

◯ **Web application**
Accessed by web browsers over a network.

◯ **Service account**
Calls Google APIs on behalf of your application instead of an end-user.
Learn more

● **Installed application**
Runs on a desktop computer or handheld device (like Android or iPhone).

INSTALLED APPLICATION TYPE

◯ Android Learn more

◯ Chrome Application Learn more

◯ iOS Learn more

◯ PlayStation 4

● Other

[Create Client ID]   [Cancel]

FIGURE 11.33

Create client ID for desktop application.

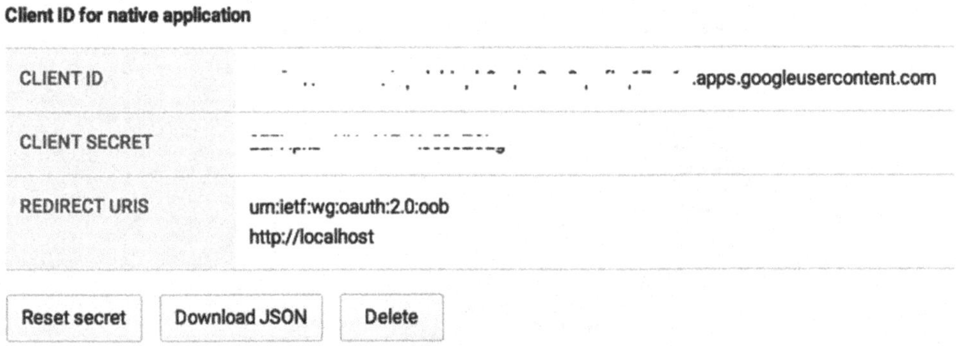

Client ID for native application

CLIENT ID	` .. . , ' ' , ' . ' . . , ' . ' . ` .apps.googleusercontent.com
CLIENT SECRET	` .--. .-- .-- .- .-- .---`
REDIRECT URIS	urn:ietf:wg:oauth:2.0:oob http://localhost

Reset secret	Download JSON	Delete

FIGURE 11.34

Client ID for native application.

Lastly, make sure to enable the **Drive API** and the **Drive SDK** under APIs.

11.8.2 CONTROL FLOW

The first step is to find out the Google Spreadsheets that are available on the Google Drive account. The basic idea is to use the ADO.NET provider for Google Apps to search for all spreadsheets with a name similar to "On_Time_On_Time" by performing a SELECT operation against the provider.

Drag an **Execute SQL Task** to the control flow, outside of the existing **Foreach Loop Container** (Figure 11.35).

Set the ConnectionType property to ADO.NET and create a new connection (Figure 11.36).

Set the properties as shown in Table 11.27 for the connection.

The first four properties are related to the authentication process. Note that there is also another authentication method available, based on user and password credentials. However, Google requires OAuth 2.0 for the operations performed by this SSIS control flow.

The pseudo columns setting activates all pseudo columns in all tables. The pseudo columns are required in order to perform a search on Google Drive. This is discussed next. Set timeout to 0 in order to avoid SSIS errors due to timeouts when selecting a large number of Google Spreadsheets.

Once the connection has been set up completely, select the **OK** button and finish the configuration of the Execute SQL Task: set the **ResultSet** property to **Full Result Set** and enter the following query in the **SQLStatement** property:

```
SELECT
      Title,
      CONCAT('https://spreadsheets.google.com/feeds/worksheets/',
            Id, '/private/full') AS FeedLink
FROM
      GDrive
WHERE
      Title LIKE '%TestCase%'
      AND Trashed=False
      AND MIMEType='application/vnd.google.apps.spreadsheet'
      AND Starred=true
```

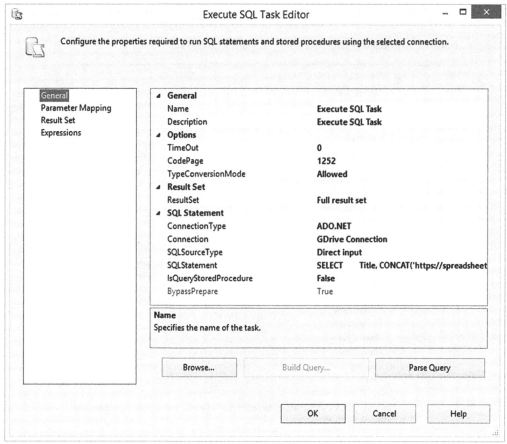

FIGURE 11.35

Execute SQL task editor for the Google Drive connection.

Table 11.27 Property Values for the Google Drive Connection

Property	Value
Initiate OAuth	True
OAuth Settings Location	A folder on the local file system accessible by SSIS
OAuth Client Id	Your client ID created in the previous section
OAuth Client Secret	Your client secret created in the previous section
Pseudo Columns	*=*
Readonly	True
Timeout	0

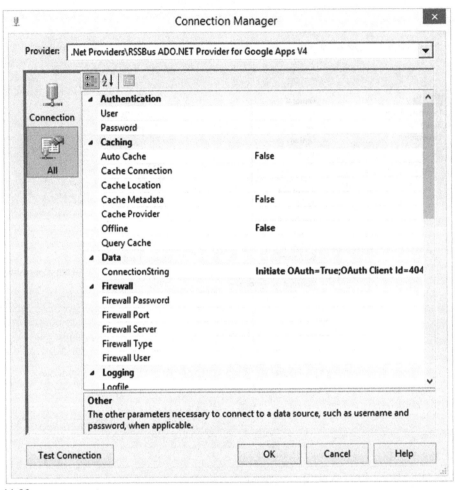

FIGURE 11.36

Connection manager for the Google Drive connection.

The statement selects the title and the spreadsheet ID of those files from Google Drive that meet the following conditions:

1. The title starts with "On_Time_On_Time": this makes sure that only files are selected that provide airline data.
2. The file is not trashed.
3. The file is a Google Spreadsheet.
4. The file is starred (optional).

The last condition reduces the number of spreadsheets returned by this query to a manageable number of documents: it only returns spreadsheets that have been starred. Remove this WHERE condition to retrieve all spreadsheets for the airline data. If you leave this option in, make sure you have actually starred some of the airline spreadsheets.

The conditions are provided to Google Drive by a pseudo column called Query. This pseudo column doesn't exist in the source sheet but is used by the CData ADO.NET source for Google Apps to provide the query in a SQL friendly format. Additional search parameters can be found under the following URL: https://developers.google.com/drive/web/search-parameters.

Note that the Id returned by Google Drive is used to build the feed link of the spreadsheet. It follows the following format: https://spreadsheets.google.com/feeds/worksheets/[id]/private/full.

Both the title and the feed link are required: the title is used to extract the load date as described in section 11.7. The feed link is used to access the data from the spreadsheet in the data flow.

Because the ADO.NET provider returns one row per spreadsheet, the result set has to be stored in an object variable. This can be configured on the **Result Set** tab of the **Execute SQL Task Editor** (Figure 11.37).

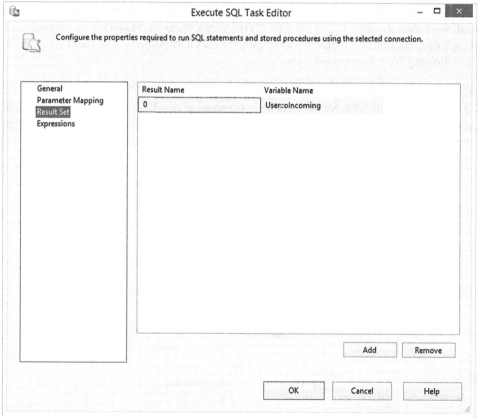

FIGURE 11.37

Configure the result set.

Create a new variable in the **User** namespace. Set the value type to **Object** because it will be used to store the whole dataset returned by the ADO.NET provider. Associate it to the result with name 0 as shown in Figure 11.37.

Close the editor and connect the Execute SQL Task to the Foreach Loop Container in the control flow (Figure 11.38).

The next step is to change the foreach loop container because it should no longer traverse over the local file system. Instead, it should traverse over the ADO.NET result set stored in the object variable. Open the editor of the container and switch to the **Collection** tab (Figure 11.39).

Change the enumerator to a **Foreach ADO Enumerator**. Set the **ADO object source variable** to the one that was configured in Figure 11.38. Make sure that the **enumeration mode** is set to **Rows in the first table**. Switch to the Variable Mappings tab in order to map from the columns in the result set to SSIS variables that can be used in the control and data flow (Figure 11.40).

The first column contains the title of the spreadsheet. This is the clear name that is also shown when viewing the Google Drive folder online. Make sure it is mapped to the sFileName variable created in section 11.6. The second column in the result set contains the feed link, which is required by the data flow to access the spreadsheet data. Create a new variable in the User namespace called sFeedLink with a value type of String and set the default value to a valid feed link, such as https://spreadsheets.google.com/feeds/worksheets/1gsbCxxTmfSZnoZQxCN1hoSZfnXFNgu-79JMwn35iVNc/private/full.

Setting this default value is required to configure the data flow properly. The feed link can be copied from the following Web site to avoid typing it in:

http://www.datavault.guru/2015/01/22/feedlink-for-sample-airline-data/.

You should also set the **sFileName** variable to the name of the sheet within the spreadsheet behind the feed link to avoid issues in the data flow later. Therefore, set the default value to "On_Time_On_Time_Performance_2006_2_27_DL".

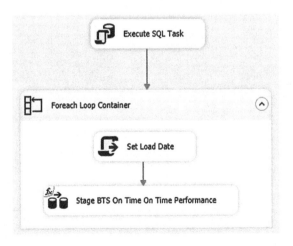

FIGURE 11.38

Control flow to source the sample airline data.

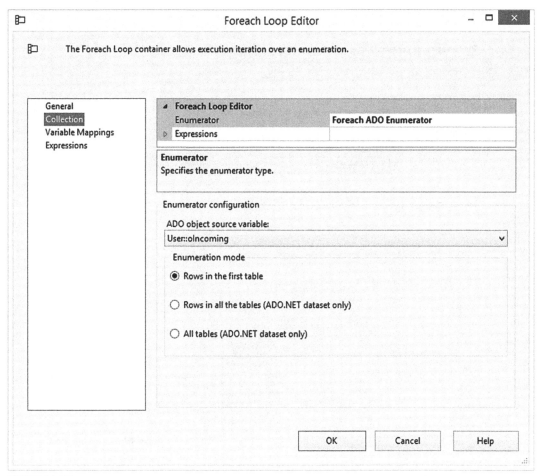

FIGURE 11.39

Modifying the enumerator of the foreach loop container.

Setting up the variables completes the setup of the control flow. The next step is to configure the data flow by changing the source.

11.8.3 GOOGLESHEETS CONNECTION MANAGER

After installation of both software packages, you will notice two new components in the SSIS Toolbox when switching to the Data Flow tab, as shown in Figure 11.41.

You can move the components into the **Other Source** or **Other Destination** folder by opening their context menu and selecting the respective menu item.

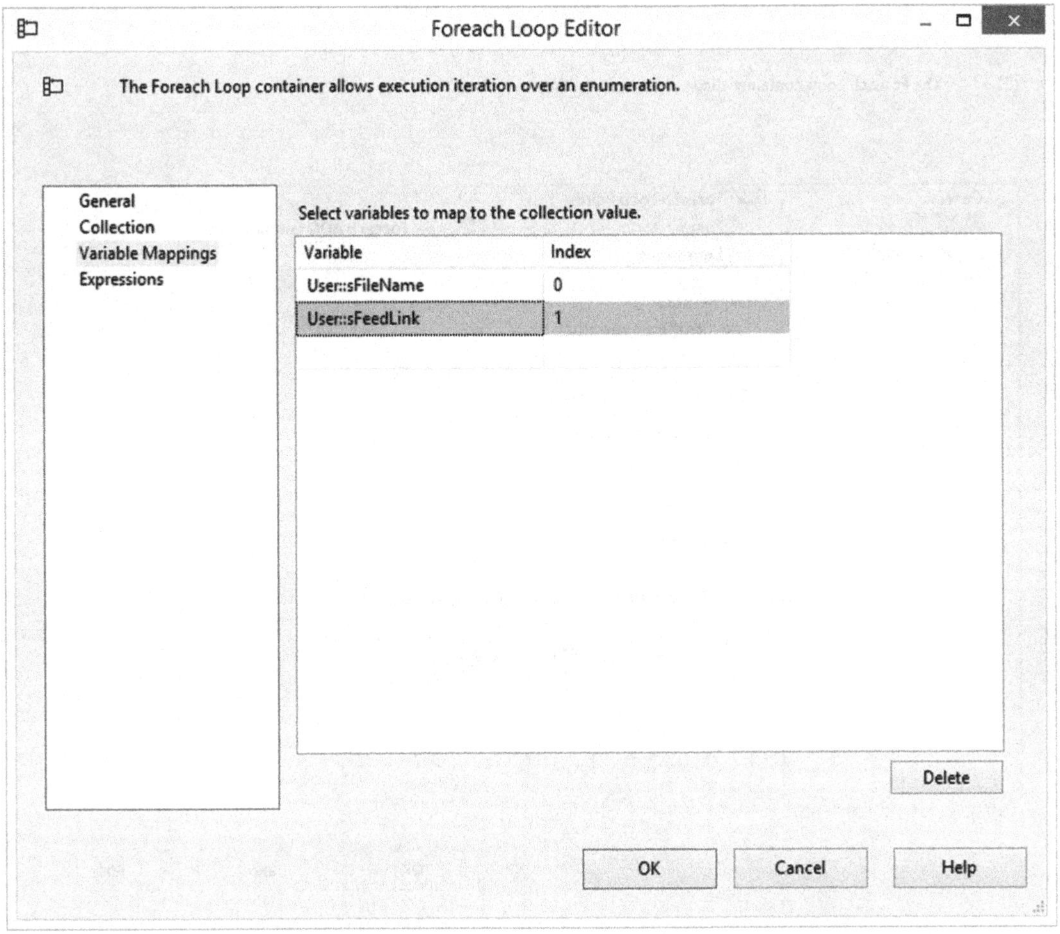

FIGURE 11.40

Variable mappings to map the columns in the result set to variables.

Drag a **CData GoogleSheets Source** to the data flow created in the previous section. It will replace the **Flat File Source** that was used before. Open the editor by double clicking the source and create a new connection using the **New...** button. The dialog shown in Figure 11.42 will appear.

Enter the information shown in Table 11.28 to set up the connection to a sample Google Sheets document.

The spreadsheet value should be set to the feed link that will be obtained in the control flow. It uniquely identifies a spreadsheet. For now, it is set as a constant value and replaced in an expression later. It is also possible to provide the name of the spreadsheet. However, because the API is limited

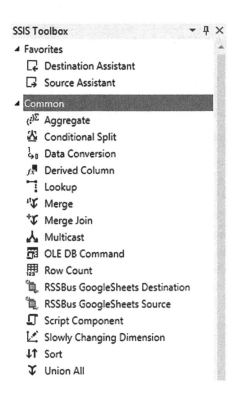

FIGURE 11.41

SSIS Toolbox with CData components.

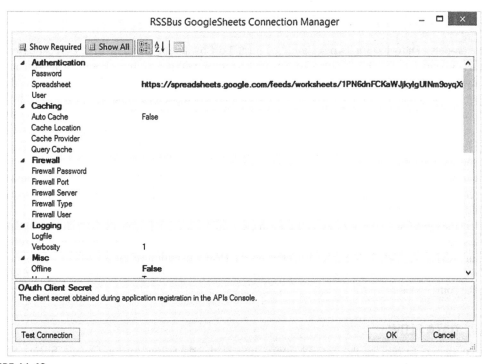

FIGURE 11.42

Connection manager to set up the Google Sheets connection.

Table 11.28 Required Property Values to Set Up the Google Sheets Connection

Property	Value
Initiate OAuth	True
OAuth Settings Location	A folder on the local file system accessible by SSIS. Make sure to use another folder than the one configured in the previous section.
OAuth Client Id	Your client ID created in section 11.8.1
OAuth Client Secret	Your client secret created in section 11.8.1
Spreadsheet	https://spreadsheets.google.com/feeds/worksheets/1gsbCxxTmfSZnoZQxCN1hoSZ fnXFNgu-79JMwn35iVNc/private/full
Readonly	True
Timeout	0
Header	True
Detect Data Types	0

to a small number of spreadsheets that can be accessed by name (there is an API limit that allows only 500 spreadsheet names to return), providing the feed link is a more secure way. To avoid typing in the feed link, copy it from the following Web site:

http://www.datavault.guru/2015/01/22/feedlink-for-sample-airline-data/

The property **Detect Data Types** should be turned off by setting its value to 0. In most cases, this option is quite useful, because it automatically detects the data types of the columns in the spreadsheet by analyzing a number of records. The number of records it uses for this analysis can be provided here. The more records it analyzes, the more secure the data type detection becomes [34]. However, because not all the airline data uploaded to Google Drive has diversions (the columns towards the right), the data type detection might fail. In order to avoid any such problems, we have decided to completely turn off the feature and force the source component to set all data types to varchar(2000) instead. This will affect the staging table as well.

Close the dialog by selecting the **OK** button. The connection is taken over as the active connection manager in the previous dialog. Because each spreadsheet has multiple tabs, select the corresponding tab from the **Table or View** box (Figure 11.43).

Select the table On_Time_On_Time_Performance_2006_2_27_DL from the list. The **Spreadsheets** view is a virtual view that returns a list of available spreadsheets (but it is limited to the 500 records). You can preview the data in the spreadsheet using the **Preview** button (Figure 11.44).

Also, make sure that switching to the **columns** tab in the editor retrieves the columns in the source. Close the source editor.

11.8.4 DATA FLOW

The next step is to replace the flat file connection in the data flow by the Google Sheets Source (Figures 11.45 and 11.46).

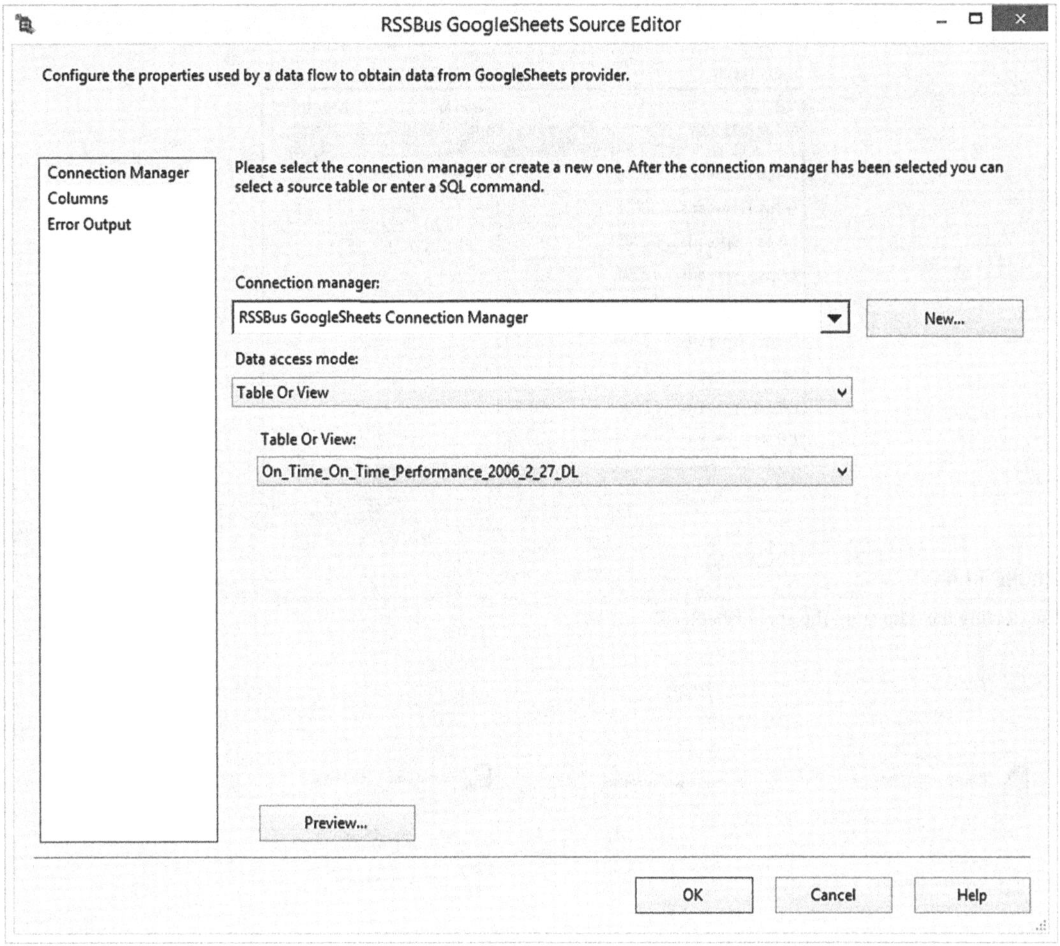

FIGURE 11.43

Setting up the connection in the CData GoogleSheets source editor.

Delete the old data flow path and connect the Google spreadsheet source to next component in the data flow (**Add Sequence Number**). After both components are connected, error messages are shown on two of the components.

The first error is on the script component that calculates the hash values. This is because the input column definition has changed and requires a rebuild of the script. Open the editor, open the script and rebuild it. After closing the script editor and the dialog, the error should be gone.

The second issue is a warning that indicates a column truncation. This warning appears because the destination table in the staging area is modeled after actual data types from the source file. Because the

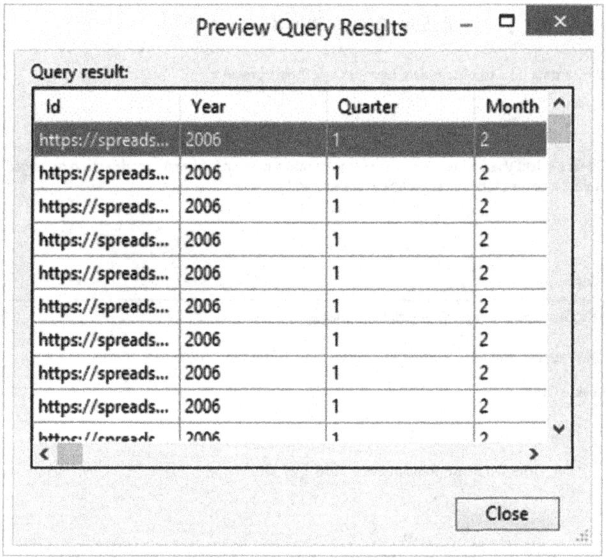

Preview Query Results   —   ☐   ✕

Query result:

Id	Year	Quarter	Month
https://spreads...	2006	1	2
https://spreads...	2006	1	2
https://spreads...	2006	1	2
https://spreads...	2006	1	2
https://spreads...	2006	1	2
https://spreads...	2006	1	2
https://spreads...	2006	1	2
https://spreads...	2006	1	2
https://spreads...	2006	1	2
httpc://cnreadc	2006	1	2

Close

FIGURE 11.44

Previewing the data from the spreadsheet.

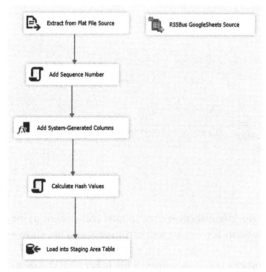

FIGURE 11.45

Data flow utilizing the flat file source.

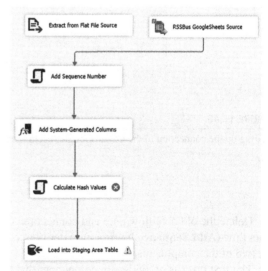

FIGURE 11.46

Data flow utilizing the Google spreadsheet.

Google Sheets Source only provides strings, another staging table is required. Use the following T-SQL script to create a new staging table*:

```sql
CREATE TABLE [bts].[OnTimeOnTimePerformanceGD](
    [Id] [nvarchar](255) NULL,
    [Year] [nvarchar](2000) NULL,
    [Quarter] [nvarchar](2000) NULL,
    [Month] [nvarchar](2000) NULL,
    [Dayofmonth] [nvarchar](2000) NULL,
    [Dayofweek] [nvarchar](2000) NULL,
    [Flightdate] [nvarchar](2000) NULL,
    [Uniquecarrier] [nvarchar](2000) NULL,
    [Airlineid] [nvarchar](2000) NULL,
    [Carrier] [nvarchar](2000) NULL,
    [Tailnum] [nvarchar](2000) NULL,
    [Flightnum] [nvarchar](2000) NULL,
    [Originairportid] [nvarchar](2000) NULL,
    [Originairportseqid] [nvarchar](2000) NULL,
    [Origincitymarketid] [nvarchar](2000) NULL,
    [Origin] [nvarchar](2000) NULL,
    [Origincityname] [nvarchar](2000) NULL,
    [Originstate] [nvarchar](2000) NULL,
    [Originstatefips] [nvarchar](2000) NULL,
    [Originstatename] [nvarchar](2000) NULL,
    [Originwac] [nvarchar](2000) NULL,
    [Destairportid] [nvarchar](2000) NULL,
    [Destairportseqid] [nvarchar](2000) NULL,
    [Destcitymarketid] [nvarchar](2000) NULL,
    [Dest] [nvarchar](2000) NULL,
    [Destcityname] [nvarchar](2000) NULL,
    [Deststate] [nvarchar](2000) NULL,
    [Deststatefips] [nvarchar](2000) NULL,
    [Deststatename] [nvarchar](2000) NULL,
    [Destwac] [nvarchar](2000) NULL,
    [Crsdeptime] [nvarchar](2000) NULL,
    [Deptime] [nvarchar](2000) NULL,
    [Depdelay] [nvarchar](2000) NULL,
    [Depdelayminutes] [nvarchar](2000) NULL,
    [Depdel15] [nvarchar](2000) NULL,
    [Departuredelaygroups] [nvarchar](2000) NULL,
    [Deptimeblk] [nvarchar](2000) NULL,
    [Taxiout] [nvarchar](2000) NULL,
    [Wheelsoff] [nvarchar](2000) NULL,
    [Wheelson] [nvarchar](2000) NULL,
    [Taxiin] [nvarchar](2000) NULL,
    [Crsarrtime] [nvarchar](2000) NULL,
    [Arrtime] [nvarchar](2000) NULL,
    [Arrdelay] [nvarchar](2000) NULL,
    [Arrdelayminutes] [nvarchar](2000) NULL,
    [Arrdel15] [nvarchar](2000) NULL,
    [Arrivaldelaygroups] [nvarchar](2000) NULL,
    [Arrtimeblk] [nvarchar](2000) NULL,
    [Cancelled] [nvarchar](2000) NULL,
    [Cancellationcode] [nvarchar](2000) NULL,
    [Diverted] [nvarchar](2000) NULL,
    [Crselapsedtime] [nvarchar](2000) NULL,
    [Actualelapsedtime] [nvarchar](2000) NULL,
```

*The file name of the source code file is provided on the companion site, please refer the site for more details: http://booksite.elsevier.com/9780128025109

```
[Airtime] [nvarchar](2000) NULL,
[Flights] [nvarchar](2000) NULL,
[Distance] [nvarchar](2000) NULL,
[Distancegroup] [nvarchar](2000) NULL,
[Carrierdelay] [nvarchar](2000) NULL,
[Weatherdelay] [nvarchar](2000) NULL,
[Nasdelay] [nvarchar](2000) NULL,
[Securitydelay] [nvarchar](2000) NULL,
[Lateaircraftdelay] [nvarchar](2000) NULL,
[Firstdeptime] [nvarchar](2000) NULL,
[Totaladdgtime] [nvarchar](2000) NULL,
[Longestaddgtime] [nvarchar](2000) NULL,
[Divairportlandings] [nvarchar](2000) NULL,
[Divreacheddest] [nvarchar](2000) NULL,
[Divactualelapsedtime] [nvarchar](2000) NULL,
[Divarrdelay] [nvarchar](2000) NULL,
[Divdistance] [nvarchar](2000) NULL,
[Div1airport] [nvarchar](2000) NULL,
[Div1airportid] [nvarchar](2000) NULL,
[Div1airportseqid] [nvarchar](2000) NULL,
[Div1wheelson] [nvarchar](2000) NULL,
[Div1totalgtime] [nvarchar](2000) NULL,
[Div1longestgtime] [nvarchar](2000) NULL,
[Div1wheelsoff] [nvarchar](2000) NULL,
[Div1tailnum] [nvarchar](2000) NULL,
[Div2airport] [nvarchar](2000) NULL,
[Div2airportid] [nvarchar](2000) NULL,
[Div2airportseqid] [nvarchar](2000) NULL,
[Div2wheelson] [nvarchar](2000) NULL,
[Div2totalgtime] [nvarchar](2000) NULL,
[Div2longestgtime] [nvarchar](2000) NULL,
[Div2wheelsoff] [nvarchar](2000) NULL,
[Div2tailnum] [nvarchar](2000) NULL,
[Div3airport] [nvarchar](2000) NULL,
[Div3airportid] [nvarchar](2000) NULL,
[Div3airportseqid] [nvarchar](2000) NULL,
[Div3wheelson] [nvarchar](2000) NULL,
[Div3totalgtime] [nvarchar](2000) NULL,
[Div3longestgtime] [nvarchar](2000) NULL,
[Div3wheelsoff] [nvarchar](2000) NULL,
[Div3tailnum] [nvarchar](2000) NULL,
[Div4airport] [nvarchar](2000) NULL,
[Div4airportid] [nvarchar](2000) NULL,
[Div4airportseqid] [nvarchar](2000) NULL,
[Div4wheelson] [nvarchar](2000) NULL,
[Div4totalgtime] [nvarchar](2000) NULL,
[Div4longestgtime] [nvarchar](2000) NULL,
[Div4wheelsoff] [nvarchar](2000) NULL,
[Div4tailnum] [nvarchar](2000) NULL,
[Div5airport] [nvarchar](2000) NULL,
[Div5airportid] [nvarchar](2000) NULL,
[Div5airportseqid] [nvarchar](2000) NULL,
[Div5wheelson] [nvarchar](2000) NULL,
[Div5totalgtime] [nvarchar](2000) NULL,
[Div5longestgtime] [nvarchar](2000) NULL,
[Div5wheelsoff] [nvarchar](2000) NULL,
[Div5tailnum] [nvarchar](2000) NULL,
[Sequence] [int] NOT NULL,
[LoadDate] [datetime] NOT NULL,
[RecordSource] [nvarchar](27) NOT NULL,
[FlightNumHashKey] [char](32) NOT NULL,
[OriginHashKey] [char](32) NOT NULL,
```

```
        [CarrierHashKey] [char](32) NOT NULL,
        [TailNumHashKey] [char](32) NOT NULL,
        [DestHashKey] [char](32) NOT NULL,
        [Div1AirportHashKey] [char](32) NOT NULL,
        [Div2AirportHashKey] [char](32) NOT NULL,
        [Div3AirportHashKey] [char](32) NOT NULL,
        [Div4AirportHashKey] [char](32) NOT NULL,
        [Div5AirportHashKey] [char](32) NOT NULL,
        [FlightHashKey] [char](32) NOT NULL,
        [Div1FlightHashKey] [char](32) NOT NULL,
        [Div2FlightHashKey] [char](32) NOT NULL,
        [Div3FlightHashKey] [char](32) NOT NULL,
        [Div4FlightHashKey] [char](32) NOT NULL,
        [Div5FlightHashKey] [char](32) NOT NULL,
        [FlightNumCarrierHashKey] [char](32) NOT NULL,
        [OriginAirportHashDiff] [char](32) NOT NULL,
        [DestAirportHashDiff] [char](32) NOT NULL,
 CONSTRAINT [PK_OnTimeOnTimePerformanceGD] PRIMARY KEY NONCLUSTERED
(
        [Sequence] ASC,
        [LoadDate] ASC
) ON [INDEX]
) ON [DATA]
```

Notice the nvarchar(2000) data types used for most columns (except the system-generated columns and the Id column that identifies each row in the Google Spreadsheets document). The alternative to convert all columns to the data types used in section 11.6.2 is too complicated in the staging process. Also, it would hinder automation efforts. Remember that another purpose for the staging area is to allow easy retrieval of the data from the source system. The data will be converted into the actual data types when it is loaded into the next layer, which is the Enterprise Data Warehouse (EDW) layer, modeled as a Data Vault 2.0 model.

Once the table has been created, it can be set as the target in the **OLE DB Destination Editor** (Figure 11.47).

Select the new staging table **[bts].[OnTimeOnTimePerformanceGD]** from the list of tables in the staging area. All other options should remain the same. However, make sure that the columns from the data flow are still mapped to the target columns because the name of the columns has changed. It follows the convention of the Google API to change the column name to lower-case, except the first letter. For example, the column name **DestAirportID** becomes **Destairportid**. Therefore, a remap of the columns is required. Change to the **Mappings** tab and select the **Map Items by Matching Names** menu item (Figure 11.48).

Make sure that all columns have been mapped. After selecting the OK button, start the process to load some data into the target table in the staging area. Generate and compare some of the hash values as described in section 11.6.3 to validate the process. If the hash values (either the hash keys or the hash diffs) are different, a problem has occurred in the SSIS process.

Finally, the configuration of the data flow needs to be adjusted in order to make use of the variables from the control flow. In the control flow, select the **CData GoogleSheets Connection Manager** and open the property expressions editor from its properties (Figure 11.49).

Set the expression of the **Spreadsheet** property to @[User::sFeedLink].

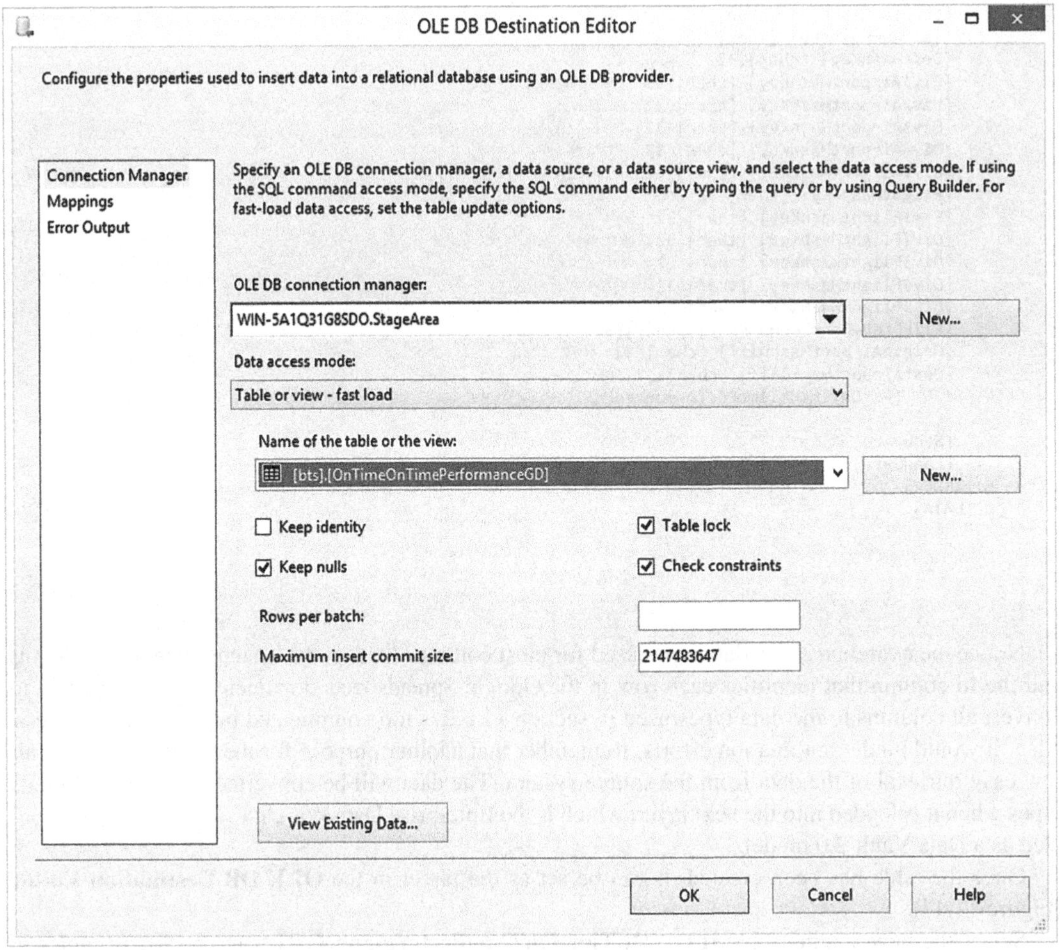

FIGURE 11.47

Configure OLE DB destination editor to use the new staging table.

Close the expression editor and set **DelayValidation** to **True**.

Select the canvas of the data flow and open the expression editor in its properties (Figure 11.50).

Select the property **[CData GoogleSheets Source].[TableOrView]** to dynamically set the name of the table (which is the sheet name within Google Sheets). Set it to the variable sFileName by adding the expression **@[User::sFileName]**. Confirm the dialog.

Finally, set the property **ValidateExternalMetadata** of the **CData GoogleSheets Source** to **False** in order to prevent validation of the variable at design-time.

To make this SSIS control flow less resource consuming (especially storage in the staging area), you could introduce command line parameters to the SSIS package and stage individual files, load them into the Raw Data Vault and truncate the staging tables before loading the next Google Sheet from the cloud.

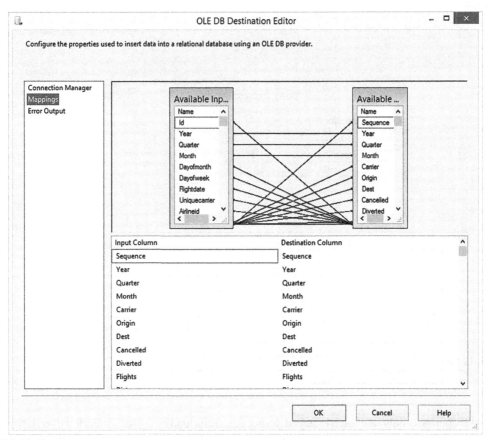

FIGURE 11.48

Remapping the columns after changing the data source.

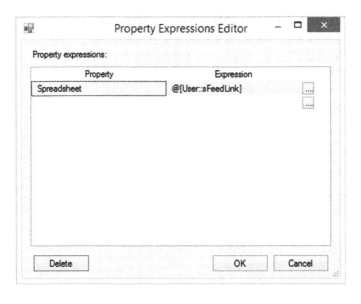

FIGURE 11.49

Property expression editor for GoogleSheets connection manager.

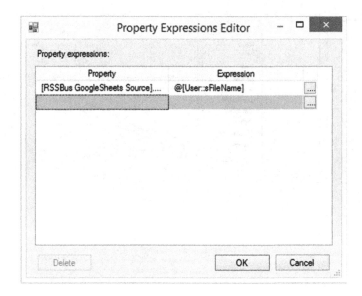

FIGURE 11.50

Property expression editor for data flow task.

Using this approach, only one batch is staged during this initial load at a given time. However, it requires that the Raw Data Vault be loaded just after staging an individual file. This is covered in the next chapter.

11.9 SOURCING DENORMALIZED DATA SOURCES

In some cases, source files are provided in a hierarchical or denormalized format. Examples for such files include XML files and COBOL copybooks. The flat file that was sourced in section 11.6 was also a denormalized flat file because it contained multiple diversions in the same row as the actual flight. This data was joined into the parent table.

The following code presents such a hierarchical XML file:

```xml
<?xml version="1.0" encoding="utf-8"?>
<flight id="DL1234">
  <passenger id="US4211">
    <title>Mrs.</title>
    <name>
      <firstname>Amy</firstname>
      <lastname>Miller</lastname>
    </name>
    <preferred-dish>Vegetarian</preferred-dish>
    <address-line-1>2050 1st Street</address-line-1>
    <address-line-2/>
    <city>San Francisco</city>
    <zip>94114</zip>
    <state>CA</state>
```

```
            <country>USA</country>
        </passenger>
    <passenger id="DE4949">
        <title>Mr.</title>
        <name>
            <firstname>Peter</firstname>
            <lastname>Heinz</lastname>
        </name>
        <preferred-dish>Meat</preferred-dish>
        <address-line-1>Auf dem Hofe 9</address-line-1>
        <address-line-2/>
        <city>Stadt Oldendorf</city>
        <zip>98472</zip>
        <state/>
        <country>Germany</country>
    </passenger>
</flight>
```

The XML file above contains two records in the following conceptual hierarchy:

- `flight` (id = DL1234)
    - `passenger` (id = US4211)
        - name (Amy Miller)
    - `passenger` (id = DE4949)
        - name (Heinz Peter)

XML files are not limited to three levels. The number of levels is unlimited. It is also possible to create an unbalanced XML file, which uses a different number of levels in each sub-tree.

In order to successfully load these formats into a relational staging area, they need to be normalized first. Otherwise, dealing with hierarchical tables becomes too complex when loading the data into the Enterprise Data Warehouse. Also, normalizing the data prepares the data for the Data Vault model, which requires that the data be normalized even further (Figure 11.51).

The normalization supports the divide-and-conquer approach of the Data Vault 2.0 System of Business Intelligence: instead of tackling the whole source file in its hierarchical format at once, in a complex staging process, the individual levels are sourced using the same approach as ordinary files. The only difference is that the source file is accessed multiple times and loaded into multiple target tables in the staging area.

To capture the data from the XML file in the beginning of this section, the following E/R model can be used (Figure 11.52).

There are three targets required: a flights table that covers flight information, a passenger table that covers the second level and a name table. Not only has the parent sequence been added, but also the respective business keys (**PassengerID** or **FlightID**) and their hash keys. The latter are required when loading the Data Vault model; the business keys are optional merely for debugging purposes. The **Passenger** staging table also includes an optional hash diff attribute on the descriptive attributes.

Note that only three entities are required because each level follows the same structure. If the structure of each sub-tree were different, as it is in XHTML (a XML derivative for presenting rich formatted information from Web servers using Web browsers, similar to HTML), this approach might not be

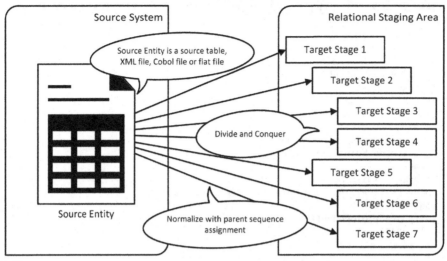

FIGURE 11.51

Normalizing source system files.

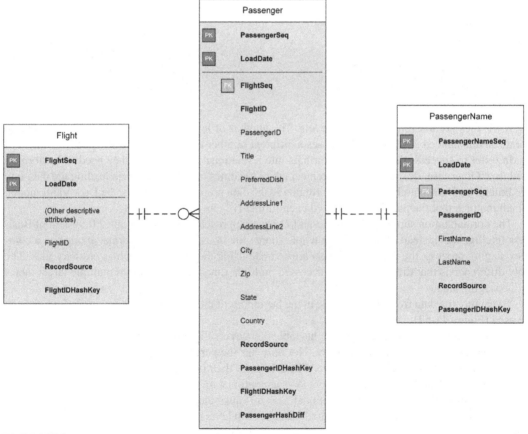

FIGURE 11.52

Normalized staging tables (physical design).

sufficient. If the input file doesn't use a common structure for all sub-trees, consider an approach using unstructured databases for staging, for example Hadoop or another NoSQL database.

Because the number of diversions in the flat file used in section 11.6 is limited to five and all columns from the child table (the diversions) are pivoted into the parent table, the normalization process is optional. If the number of diversions were unlimited and the structure in a hierarchical format, the normalization would be strongly suggested.

11.10 **SOURCING MASTER DATA FROM MDS**

Compared to data from flat files, relational data, such as master data from Microsoft Master Data Services (MDS), can be sourced much easier. The reason is that there is typically no need to source historical master data because the source only provides the current master data. In general, there is no difference from sourcing master data stored in Microsoft MDS to sourcing any other relational database for any kind of data.

However, if MDS houses analytical master data (refer to Chapter 9, Master Data Management), it is often located on the same infrastructure as the data warehouse. In this case, there is no need to actually load the data into the staging area because the primary reason of the staging area is to reduce the workload on the operational systems when loading the data warehouse. But if MDS is used to maintain only analytical master data, the additional workload on MDS is often negligible. Especially if the data warehouse team controls MDS, it is possible to make sure that data warehouse loads will not affect the business user.

For that reason, it is often possible to stage the master data using virtual views instead of materializing the data using ETL. But it is still required to attach the system-generated fields, including the sequence number, load date, record source and hashes. To virtually stage a master data entity, the following statement creates a stage area view in the **mds** schema on the **BTS_Region_DWH** subscription view of MDS (refer to Chapter 9 for instructions on creating the view in MDS):

```
CREATE VIEW [mds].[BTS_Region_DWH] AS
SELECT [ID]
      ,[MUID]
      ,[VersionName]
      ,[VersionNumber]
      ,[VersionFlag]
      ,[Name]
      ,[Code]
      ,[ChangeTrackingMask]
      ,[Abbreviation]
      ,[Sort Order]
      ,[External Reference]
      ,[Record Source]
      ,[Record Owner_Code]
      ,[Record Owner_Name]
      ,[Record Owner_ID]
      ,[Comments]
      ,[EnterDateTime]
      ,[EnterUserName]
      ,[EnterVersionNumber]
```

```sql
    ,[LastChgDateTime]
    ,[LastChgUserName]
    ,[LastChgVersionNumber]
    ,[ValidationStatus]

    -- Sequence ID
    ,ROW_NUMBER() OVER(ORDER BY ([Sort Order])) AS [Sequence]

    -- Load Date
    ,GETDATE() AS [LoadDate]

    -- Record Source
    ,'MDS.BTS.Region' AS [RecordSource]

    -- Hash key on region code
    ,UPPER(CONVERT(char(32),HASHBYTES('MD5',
        UPPER(RTRIM(LTRIM(COALESCE([Code], ''))))
    ),2)) AS RegionHashKey

    -- Hash key on record owner
    ,UPPER(CONVERT(char(32),HASHBYTES('MD5',
        UPPER(RTRIM(LTRIM(COALESCE([Record Owner_Name], ''))))
    ),2)) AS RecordOwnerHashKey

    -- Hash key on user name who created the record (optional)
    --,UPPER(CONVERT(char(32),HASHBYTES('MD5',
    --UPPER(RTRIM(LTRIM(COALESCE([EnterUserName], ''))))
    --),2)) AS EnterUserNameHashKey

    -- Hash key on user name who changed it the last time (optional)
    --,UPPER(CONVERT(char(32),HASHBYTES('MD5',
    --UPPER(RTRIM(LTRIM(COALESCE([LastChgUserName], ''))))
    --),2)) AS LastChgUserNameHashKey

    -- Hash diff on descriptive attributes
    ,UPPER(CONVERT(char(32),HASHBYTES('MD5',
        CONCAT(
            UPPER(RTRIM(LTRIM(COALESCE([Code], '')))), ';',
            RTRIM(LTRIM(COALESCE([ID], ''))), ';',
            RTRIM(LTRIM(COALESCE([MUID], ''))), ';',
            RTRIM(LTRIM(COALESCE([VersionName], ''))), ';',
            RTRIM(LTRIM(COALESCE([VersionNumber], ''))), ';',
            RTRIM(LTRIM(COALESCE([VersionFlag], ''))), ';',
            RTRIM(LTRIM(COALESCE([Name], ''))), ';',
            RTRIM(LTRIM(COALESCE([ChangeTrackingMask], ''))), ';',
            RTRIM(LTRIM(COALESCE([Abbreviation], ''))), ';',
            RTRIM(LTRIM(COALESCE([Sort Order], ''))), ';',
            RTRIM(LTRIM(COALESCE([External Reference], ''))), ';',
            RTRIM(LTRIM(COALESCE([Record Source], ''))), ';',
            RTRIM(LTRIM(COALESCE([Comments], ''))), ';',
            RTRIM(LTRIM(COALESCE([EnterDateTime], ''))), ';',
            RTRIM(LTRIM(COALESCE([EnterUserName], ''))), ';',
            RTRIM(LTRIM(COALESCE([EnterVersionNumber], ''))), ';',
            RTRIM(LTRIM(COALESCE([LastChgDateTime], ''))), ';',
            RTRIM(LTRIM(COALESCE([LastChgUserName], ''))), ';',
            RTRIM(LTRIM(COALESCE([LastChgVersionNumber], ''))), ';',
            RTRIM(LTRIM(COALESCE([ValidationStatus], '')))
        )
    ),2)) AS RegionHashDiff

FROM [MDS].[mdm].[BTS_Region_DWH]
```

The view first selects all columns from the source system. It then generates the sequence number, load date and record source. The sequence number is generated using the **ROW_NUMBER** function and is just a sequence on the **sort order**. Avoid using the sort order or any other numerical value (such as the ID) because they don't have to be unique. However, uniqueness is a requirement for the sequence number. The ID might be unique, but using it means losing control over the generation process.

The hash keys are generated in a similar manner to that discussed before. Note that MDS provides two attributes that identify the member in the region entity: code and name. In many cases, the code column is an appropriate business key that should be hashed. But in other cases, it is just a sequence number without meaning to the business. In this case, the business key might be located in the name. Another business key in the entity identifies the record owner. This column is part of a domain attribute in MDS. Domain attributes are always represented in subscription views by three columns: the code, the name, and the ID of the referenced entity. In the case of the record owner, the name column provides the business key because the code column is a sequence number without meaning to the business. Therefore, the name is used as the input to the hash function.

If the data warehouse contains detailed user information, for example from the Active Directory of the organization, users might become business objects that should be modeled in the EDW. In this case, the two columns **EnterUserName** and **LastChgUserName** become business keys that need to be hashed. For the purpose of this chapter (and the remainder of this book), these attributes are considered as descriptive data.

The descriptive data is hashed to obtain the hash diff in the last step. The input to the hash function contains the case-insensitive business key of the proposed parent and the case-sensitive descriptive attributes. The columns, which are part of the referenced record owner entity, are not included in the descriptive data because they will not be included in the target satellite.

The query only implements a simplified hash diff calculation. In order to support the improved strategy to support changing satellite structures (additional columns at the end of the satellite table, as described in section 11.2.5), any trailing delimiters have to be removed from the concatenated hash diff input.

Note that, in many cases, the hash key is actually not required for master data sources; many master data tables are modeled as reference tables in the EDW. We have included the hash diff primarily for demonstration purposes.

Creating virtual views for master data provides a valid approach to quickly sourcing master data into the data warehouse. Using a virtual approach enables the data warehouse team to provide the master data within only one iteration in the Data Vault 2.0 methodology. If MDS or a similar master data management solution is located on the same hardware infrastructure as the data warehouse, the business users should not recognize any performance issues. However, it is also possible to source the master data using ETL processes, for example in SSIS. It follows a similar approach to that described in section 11.6 but with an OLE DB source instead of a flat file source.

REFERENCES

[1] http://www.rita.dot.gov/bts/.
[2] http://www.dot.gov/.
[3] http://www.transtats.bts.gov/DatabaseInfo.asp?DB_ID=120.

[4] http://www.swiss.com/corporate/en/company/about-us/facts-and-figures.

[5] http://msdn.microsoft.com/en-us/library/ms177456.aspx.

[6] Daniel Linstedt: DV2.0 and Hash Keys: Hash Keys and Architecture Changes, pp. 1, 2, 9.

[7] http://www.b-eye-network.com/blogs/linstedt/archives/2014/08/data_vault_20_b.php.

[8] Michael Coles, Rodney Landrum: Expert SQL Server 2008 Encryption, p. 151.

[9] Network Working Group: The MD5 Message-Digest Algorithm, http://tools.ietf.org/pdf/rfc1321.pdf.

[10] Information Technology Laboratory, National Institute of Standards and Technology: Secure Hash Standard (SHS), http://csrc.nist.gov/publications/fips/fips180-4/fips-180-4.pdf.

[11] RSA Laboratories: "PKCS #1: RSA Cryptography Standard," http://www.emc.com/emc-plus/rsa-labs/pkcs/files/h11300-wp-pkcs-1v2-2-rsa-cryptography-standard.pdf.

[12] http://support.microsoft.com/kb/889768.

[13] http://www.apprendre-en-ligne.net/crypto/bibliotheque/feistel/index.html.

[14] Microsoft: SQL Server to SQL Server PDW Migration Guide (AU2), p. 14.

[15] http://csrc.nist.gov/groups/STM/cavp/documents/shs/shaval.htm.

[16] http://www.ecma-international.org/publications/files/ECMA-ST/Ecma-006.pdf.

[17] http://www.iso.org/iso/catalogue_detail?csnumber=40874.

[18] http://blogs.msdn.com/b/jeremykuhne/archive/2005/07/21/441247.aspx.

[19] http://docs.oracle.com/javase/specs/jvms/se7/html/jvms-4.html.

[20] https://hbase.apache.org/apidocs/org/apache/hadoop/hbase/util/ByteBufferUtils.html.

[21] Alastair Aitchison: "Beginning Spatial with SQL Server 2008," p. 93.

[22] Intel: Endianness White Paper, http://www.pascal-man.com/navigation/faq-java-browser/jython/endian.pdf

[23] Marc Stevens: Single-block collision attack on MD5, http://marc-stevens.nl/research/md5-1block-collision/md5-1block-collision.pdf.

[24] http://preshing.com/20110504/hash-collision-probabilities/.

[25] http://technet.microsoft.com/en-us/library/ms190969%28v=sql.105%29.aspx.

[26] Frederick P. Brooks Jr.: "The Mythical Man-Month: Essays on Software Engineering, Anniversary Edition (2nd Edition)", p. 179.

[27] http://ssismhash.codeplex.com/.

[28] Ralph Kimball, Joe Caserta: The Data Warehouse ETL Toolkit, p. 353f.

[29] Brian Knight, et al.: Professional Microsoft SQL Server 2014 Integration Services, pp. 101ff, 105ff, 110, 104f.

[30] https://ssisctc.codeplex.com/.

[31] http://microsoft-ssis.blogspot.de/2012/01/custom-ssis-component-foreach-sorted.html.

[32] http://www.cdata.com/drivers/google/ado/.

[33] http://www.cdata.com/drivers/gsheets/ssis/.

[34] http://cdn.CData.com/help/RL1/rssis/RSBGSheets_p_DetectDataTypes.htm.

LOADING THE DATA VAULT

12

This chapter focuses on the loading templates for the Raw Data Vault. These templates are built on some basic rules and best practices that have been accumulated over multiple years of experience. The patterns have evolved because of multiple performance issues with legacy ETL code. The top issues that affect the performance of the ETL loads are:

1. **Complexity:** the performance is affected by the variety of the data structures that need to be loaded into the data warehouse, but also by the data type alignment and the conformance of the data to set definitions. This is becoming a significant problem when dealing with highly unstructured data where the data structure changes from one record (or document) to the next.
2. **Data size:** volume also plays an important role regarding data warehouse loads. The more data is loaded, the more exposed are performance problems in the loading architecture and design.
3. **Latency:** the velocity of the data sources influences the frequency of the incoming data. If data needs to be loaded with high frequencies, small problems in the data flow will be exaggerated, leading to many more issues than before. Fast-arriving data also prohibits complexity in the processing stream because, depending on the infrastructure used, data might be lost if processing takes too long.

The complexity of the loading patterns is often additionally influenced by business rules that need to be processed upstream of the data warehouse. While the intention is to reduce the complexity of the data, the actual effect is that these business rules make the processes more complex because they change. The effect of the changed business rule has to be taken into consideration in later stages, which represents the majority of the increase in complexity.

When analyzing the fundamental issue of the ETL performance in many data warehouse projects, findings based on set logic (shown in Figure 12.1) are important to understand.

When dealing with a specific number of records that are loaded into the staging area, only about 60 to 80% are inserted records that have never been seen by the data warehouse before; 10 to 20% are updates of descriptive data to keys that are already in the data warehouse. And 5% of the incoming data describe deletes in the source system that should be tracked by the data warehouse as soft-deletes.

If only 20% of, e.g., 10 million rows (that is, 2 million rows) were identified by key, to be updates, then the aggregations of those 2 million rows would be even less – especially by month, quarter, and year. Those updates will identify specific sets of denormalized keys to be updated, along with a specific point in time. It would then be easy to meet performance objectives in a well-tuned relational database management system (RDBMS) environment.

However, many data warehouse developers construct their ETL routines to deal with the whole dataset in staging. If the problem were separated, each resulting individual process would have to deal with a decreasing process complexity, which makes it possible to increase performance, as we will learn a little later.

Please refer the companion site for more details — http://booksite.elsevier.com/9780128025109

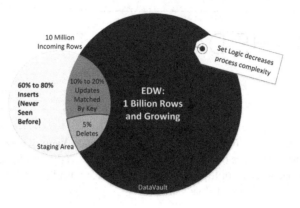

FIGURE 12.1

Set logic for data warehouses.

The key to improving the performance of data warehouse loading processes is based on two ideas:

1. **Divide and conquer the problem:** separate the processing of the loading procedures into separate groups in order to deal with smaller problems using a focused approach. In data warehousing, there are two different goals that should be reached individually: data warehousing and information processing.
2. **Apply set logic:** reduce the amount of data each process deals with by separating the data into different processes and reducing the amount of data as it is being processed.

The first idea is depicted in Figure 12.2: the two major goals are further divided into two separate activities each.

Data warehousing is different from sourcing of data because it has different issues:

- **Latency issues:** the performance of subsequent processes is affected by the latency of the source. Because the latency of the actual source system is not stable and varies over time, the staging area is used during sourcing to provide a stable latency of the incoming data. In other cases, data arrives in real-time which has to be taken into consideration by the sourcing application as well.
- **Arrival issues:** not all data arrives at the same time. The staging area is used to buffer the incoming data and makes sure that all dependencies are met if actually required.

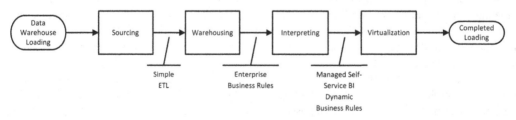

FIGURE 12.2

Overall loading process of the data warehouse.

- **Network issues:** the network could be the source of errors as well, for example when the network connection is too slow or important network devices or servers are unavailable.
- **Security issues:** in other cases, the data warehouse doesn't have access to the source system because the password was changed or expired.

This is the reason why the data is "dumped" into the staging area in order to separate these problems from the actual data warehousing. Each activity in Figure 12.2 deals with a separate problem. Some of these problems are also neutralized by using a NoSQL environment such as Hadoop or a similar technology.

In order to ensure the performance of the loading processes, the following rules should be followed:

1. **Decrease process complexity:** simplicity beats complexity. Simple loading processes are not only easier to maintain and administrate, they are also superior regarding performance.
2. **Decrease the amount of data:** reduce the amount of data that needs to be touched in order to load the target. This can also be achieved by using parallel processes where each process or thread is dealing with a smaller amount of data than the unparallelized process.
3. **Increase process parallelism:** the server is able to process multiple execution paths at the same time. For this reason, the intraoperation (inside one process) and interoperational (multiple processes) parallelism should be increased to take advantage of these capabilities.
4. **Combine all three:** to achieve superior performance, combine all three rules by reducing the complexity of the loading processes, decreasing the amount of data, and increasing the process parallelism, all at the same time. The best way to achieve this goal is to tackle one rule at a time.

Note that parallelism is **last** on the list, and should be avoided as long as possible, because any time a process is partitioned or parallelism is added, maintenance costs are increased. Instead, data warehouse teams should focus first on decreasing the complexity of the loading processes, yet many organizations don't even deal with this first rule. Also note that the parallelization requires that referential integrity be turned off in the Raw Data Vault, at least during load.

The overall loading process of the data warehouse implements these recommendations (Figure 12.3).

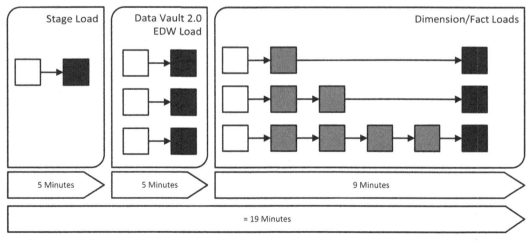

FIGURE 12.3

High-performance processes for the data warehouse.

Each phase of the loading process deals with a separate problem. By doing so, each phase also deals with progressively less data. Data is only loaded into the enterprise data warehouse (EDW) layer if it is new and unknown to the layer. And only data that is required for incrementally building the information mart is pushed into the next layer. This is also due to the fact that set logic has been applied to further reduce the amount of data to be dealt with. The separation of loading processes also favors highly simplified and focused loading patterns because each layer has a specific focus that is reflected in the loading patterns. The time each simplified phase requires is short due to high parallelization. Because of this short required time-frame, the overall process is short as well.

However, parallelization is not limited to one source system. The goal of the data warehouse loading processes is to load source systems as soon as they are ready to be loaded into the data warehouse. Waiting until a specific time in the night when all source systems are ready to be loaded into the data warehouse should be avoided. Instead, once a source system has provided its data to the data warehouse, it is staged, loaded to the data warehouse and, if possible, all information marts that directly depend on this data are processed. Figure 12.4 depicts this staggered approach.

In the figure, the data from multiple source systems is provided to the data warehouse at different times. Once the data is available to the data warehouse, it is staged immediately. It is also possible to load the data into the Raw Data Vault because there are no dependencies that require any waiting. In the case of Figure 12.4, all information marts depend on only one data source, which is a simplified example. In reality, there are synchronization points that have to be taken care of.

However, some of the dimension and fact tables that only depend on the one source system or have all other dependencies met (all other source systems loaded already) can be processed. This approach helps to take advantage of the available data warehouse infrastructure and increases the load window of the data warehouse because the peak in the loading process is reduced. It disperses the load of the engine over time and makes it possible to increase the number of loads for some of the source systems. Instead of loading the data only once a day, the data can be sourced multiple times a day because the loading processes are independent from each other and computing power remains available. Loading the data from a single source system multiple times a day also has the advantage that each single run can deal with less data if delta loading is used. However, it also requires that the data warehouse meet more operational requirements, such as a better uptime and more resiliency and elasticity of the data warehouse infrastructure.

This chapter presents the recommended templates for loading patterns of many Data Vault 2.0 entities. These templates are based on experience and optimization from projects and take full advantage of the Data Vault 2.0 model and the rules and recommendations outlined earlier in this chapter. Examples in T-SQL and SSIS are also provided for each presented template. It is easy to adapt the examples to ANSI SQL or other ETL engines.

12.1 LOADING RAW DATA VAULT ENTITIES

Similar to the staging area, the enterprise data warehouse layer has to be materialized. This EDW layer is responsible for storing the single version of the facts, at any given time. Therefore, virtualization is not an option for most entities in the EDW layer (some exceptions are discussed in section 12.2.1) and the Business Vault, which is discussed in Chapter 14, Loading the Dimensional Information Mart.

Implementing the loading processes for the Raw Data Vault only requires simple SQL statements, such as INSERT INTO <target> SELECT FROM <source> statements. However, organizations often

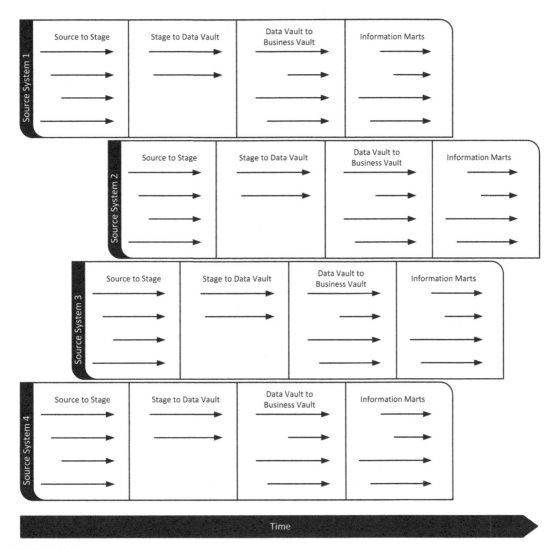

FIGURE 12.4

Staggering the load process of multiple source systems.

prefer to implement loading processes in ETL to more easily offload the required processing power to their existing ETL infrastructure, leveraging their ETL investments. For this reason, both options using SSIS and T-SQL are demonstrated in the next sections: each section focuses on one target entity, such as hubs, links, and satellites, including their special cases. The goal of the Raw Data Vault is to store raw data, so all patterns move raw data only. The data is extracted from the staging table and loaded into the target entity in the Raw Data Vault without modifications.

Note that the loading patterns use the load date from the staging area. However, it is also possible to create a new load date within the loading processes (for example, using GETDATE() or a similar function). The key is to control the load date within the data warehouse and not rely on a third-party system such as an operational source application.

The performance of the loading patterns is not only due to the design principles for data warehouse loading, as outlined in the previous section. It is also due to the use of hash keys instead of sequence numbers. The hash keys are used to overcome lookups into parent tables, which hinder parallelization and reduce performance due to higher I/O requirements. The characteristics of using hash keys in data warehousing have been discussed in the Chapter 11, Data Extraction. The loading templates presented in this chapter take direct advantage of these characteristics.

12.1.1 HUBS

When loading data from the staging area into the enterprise data warehouse layer, the Data Vault hubs are supposed to store the business keys of the source systems. This list has to be updated only in a single regard: in each load cycle new keys that have been added to the source system are added to the target hub. If keys get deleted in the source system, they remain in the target hub. The template for loading hub tables is presented in Figure 12.5.

The first step is to retrieve all business keys from the source. This step is not as trivial as it sounds. In many cases, there are multiple source tables within one source system that provide the same business keys because they are shared across the system. For example, a passenger table provides a list of passenger identification numbers and a table holding ticket information references the passenger using its business key (see Figure 12.6).

In order to guarantee that all passenger identification numbers have been sourced to the target hub table **HubPassenger**, the keys from all source tables have to be sourced using a UNION operation, as shown in this figure, or by running the template in Figure 12.5 multiple times, for each source table. In many cases, the second approach is the most favorable because it makes automation of the loading processes more feasible, for example by allowing a metadata driven definition of the loading patterns (refer to Chapter 10, Metadata Management, for more details).

In both cases, the question becomes which record source is set in the target hub table. The record source in the target reflects the detailed source system table that has provided the business key to the data warehouse for the first time. If multiple tables (or even multiple source systems) provide the business key at the same time, a predefined master system table is set as the record source. This master system table

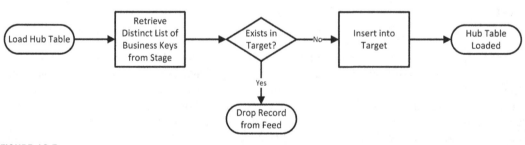

FIGURE 12.5

Template for loading hub tables.

FIGURE 12.6

Combining business keys from multiple sources.

is usually identified in the metadata and has the highest priority. If multiple patterns are used to load the same target hub table, the source table with the highest priority (as defined in the metadata) is sourced first. This way, the key found in the source tables with the highest priority will set the record source, because the duplicates in other sources will not be sourced anymore.

This behavior is guaranteed by the second step in Figure 12.5, which checks if the business key already exists in the target. This is done by performing a lookup into the target table to find out if the business key from the source already exists. Only new keys are processed further. Because this lookup should be performed only once per business key, only a distinct list of business keys were sourced from the source table in the staging area in the first step. This follows the approach of reducing the amount of data processed by the data flow as soon as possible.

Because the staging area contains both the business key and the hash key, both keys are sourced from the staging table and become available in the data flow. The lookup is performed using the business key and not the hash key. This is because of the rare risk of hash collisions described in the previous chapter. If two business keys produce the same hash key, a lookup on the hash key would return that the hash key already exists in the target. But due to the hash collision, this would mean a different business key. Performing the lookup on the business key will return a hit only if the business key already exists in the target table, regardless of the hash key. However, in the case of a hash collision, this will result in a primary key constraint violation when inserting the record in the next step. This is not the preferred solution, but it is the desired one, because we'd like to be notified in case of collision. Despite the low risk of a hash collision, the impact is high: if a collision happens, the hash function should be upgraded as described in Chapter 11, Data Extraction.

If a business key already exists in the target, the record is dropped from the data flow. Only if the business key doesn't exist in the target hub table, it is inserted into the target table. As already stated, the hash key is not calculated in this process because it is sourced from the staging table. If the business key consists of multiple parts, a so-called composite key, the process remains the same. The only difference is that the lookup has to include the whole composite key when performing the lookup operation.

Because the hub table stores all business keys that have been in the source systems in any point of time, this process doesn't delete any business keys or updates them for any reason. Once a business key has been inserted to the hub table, it remains there forever (not quite true if data has to be destructed for legal or other reasons).

12.1.1.1 T-SQL Example

The following DDL creates a target hub for the airport code found in the BTS performance data:

```
CREATE TABLE [raw].[HubAirportCode](
        [AirportCodeHashKey] [char](32) NOT NULL,
        [LoadDate] [datetime2](7) NOT NULL,
        [RecordSource] [nvarchar](50) NOT NULL,
        [AirportCode] [nvarchar](3) NULL,
 CONSTRAINT [PK_HubAirportCode] PRIMARY KEY NONCLUSTERED
(
        [AirportCodeHashKey] ASC
) ON [INDEX],
 CONSTRAINT [UK_HubAirportCode] UNIQUE NONCLUSTERED
(
        [AirportCode] ASC
) ON [INDEX]
) ON [DATA]
```

Throughout this book, the **raw** schema is used to store the tables and other database objects of the Raw Data Vault. The hub contains a hash key, which is based on the airport code columns from the source. In addition, it contains a load date and a record source column. The defining column is the **AirportCode** column at the end of the table definition. The use of a nonclustered primary key is strongly recommended because the hash key is used as the primary key. Because the hash key has a random distribution, the keys will not arrive in any order. If a clustered primary key were used, Microsoft SQL Server would rearrange the data rows on disk whenever a new record arrived. This would slow down INSERT performance and provide no value to the retrieval of data from the table. Therefore, we always use nonclustered primary keys, except for very small tables with a small number of inserts. In addition to the primary key on the hash key column, an alternate key is added in order to speed up lookups on the business key.

In order to load newly arrived airport codes from the source table in the staging area, the following T-simplified SQL command can be used:

```
INSERT INTO DataVault.[raw].HubAirportCode (
        AirportCodeHashKey, LoadDate, RecordSource, AirportCode
)
SELECT DISTINCT
        OriginHashKey, LoadDate, RecordSource, Origin
FROM
        StageArea.bts.OnTimeOnTimePerformanceGD
WHERE
        Origin NOT IN (SELECT AirportCode FROM DataVault.[raw].HubAirportCode)
        AND LoadDate = '1995-10-18 00:00:00.000'
```

Note that if the hub is defined by a composite business key, the NOT IN statement might not work, depending on the selected database management system. Microsoft SQL Server only supports one column in a NOT IN condition. However, it is possible to use a NOT EXISTS condition to overcome this limitation. This is done in the link loading statement in section 12.1.2.

The diversion airports are NULL if no flight diversion happened. This special case might be wrong from a business perspective, but nonetheless the NULL business key is also sourced into the hub because some links and satellites might use it as well (for example, see the link loading process in section 12.1.2).

Only keys which are unknown to the target hub should be inserted to avoid errors: if duplicate business keys or hash keys are inserted into the hub table, either the table's primary key on the hash key column or the alternate key on the business key column will raise a duplicate value error. To avoid the error, the first check in the WHERE clause is to check whether the business key is already in the target hub. This approach is the safest, because it detects hash collisions (refer to Chapter 11). But it also requires an index on the business key for faster lookups.

Hashing the business keys is not required because this task was performed when loading the staging area. The loading process for hubs uses these hash keys. Other entities, such as links and hubs, which are hanging off this hub, will use the same hash key as well.

The **LoadDate** is included in each WHERE clause because the staging area could contain multiple loads. This is not the desired state, but if an error happened over the weekend, there might be multiple batches in the staging area that have not been processed yet. The goal of the loading process is to stage each batch in the order it was loaded into the staging area: the Friday batch comes before the Saturday batch, the batch at 08:00 comes before the batch at 10:00. Therefore, the previous statement should be executed for one load date only, not multiple. This is also important when loading the other Data Vault entities, especially links (due to the required change detection). Trying to load everything at once is possible, but complicates the loading process.

The previous statement is simplified because it loads the business keys only from the **Origin** column and not the other business key columns available in the source staging table **bts.OnTimeOn-TimePerformance**. In order to load business keys from all source columns that provide airport codes, the following statements should be executed in parallel:

```
INSERT INTO DataVault.[raw].HubAirportCode (
        AirportCodeHashKey, LoadDate, RecordSource, AirportCode
)
SELECT DISTINCT
        OriginHashKey, LoadDate, RecordSource, Origin
FROM
        StageArea.bts.OnTimeOnTimePerformanceGD
WHERE
        Origin NOT IN (SELECT AirportCode FROM DataVault.[raw].HubAirportCode)
        AND LoadDate = '1995-10-18 00:00:00.000';
GO

INSERT INTO DataVault.[raw].HubAirportCode (
        AirportCodeHashKey, LoadDate, RecordSource, AirportCode
)
SELECT DISTINCT
        DestHashKey, LoadDate, RecordSource, Dest
FROM
        StageArea.bts.OnTimeOnTimePerformanceGD
WHERE
        Dest NOT IN (SELECT AirportCode FROM DataVault.[raw].HubAirportCode)
        AND LoadDate = '1995-10-18 00:00:00.000';
GO

INSERT INTO DataVault.[raw].HubAirportCode (
        AirportCodeHashKey, LoadDate, RecordSource, AirportCode
)
SELECT DISTINCT
        Div1AirportHashKey, LoadDate, RecordSource, Div1Airport
FROM
        StageArea.bts.OnTimeOnTimePerformanceGD
WHERE
        Div1Airport NOT IN (SELECT AirportCode FROM DataVault.[raw].HubAirportCode)
        AND LoadDate = '1995-10-18 00:00:00.000';
```

```
GO

INSERT INTO DataVault.[raw].HubAirportCode (
        AirportCodeHashKey, LoadDate, RecordSource, AirportCode
)
SELECT DISTINCT
        Div2AirportHashKey, LoadDate, RecordSource, Div2Airport
FROM
        StageArea.bts.OnTimeOnTimePerformanceGD
WHERE
        Div2Airport NOT IN (SELECT AirportCode FROM DataVault.[raw].HubAirportCode)
        AND LoadDate = '1995-10-18 00:00:00.000';
GO

INSERT INTO DataVault.[raw].HubAirportCode (
        AirportCodeHashKey, LoadDate, RecordSource, AirportCode
)
SELECT DISTINCT
        Div3AirportHashKey, LoadDate, RecordSource, Div3Airport
FROM
        StageArea.bts.OnTimeOnTimePerformanceGD
WHERE
        Div3Airport NOT IN (SELECT AirportCode FROM DataVault.[raw].HubAirportCode)
        AND LoadDate = '1995-10-18 00:00:00.000';
GO

INSERT INTO DataVault.[raw].HubAirportCode (
        AirportCodeHashKey, LoadDate, RecordSource, AirportCode
)
SELECT DISTINCT
        Div4AirportHashKey, LoadDate, RecordSource, Div4Airport
FROM
        StageArea.bts.OnTimeOnTimePerformanceGD
WHERE
        Div4Airport NOT IN (SELECT AirportCode FROM DataVault.[raw].HubAirportCode)
        AND LoadDate = '1995-10-18 00:00:00.000';
GO

INSERT INTO DataVault.[raw].HubAirportCode (
        AirportCodeHashKey, LoadDate, RecordSource, AirportCode
)
SELECT DISTINCT
        Div5AirportHashKey, LoadDate, RecordSource, Div5Airport
FROM
        StageArea.bts.OnTimeOnTimePerformanceGD
WHERE
        Div5Airport NOT IN (SELECT AirportCode FROM DataVault.[raw].HubAirportCode)
        AND LoadDate = '1995-10-18 00:00:00.000';
GO
```

Because there are multiple columns that might provide an airport code, namely Origin, Dest, Div1Airport, Div2Airport, Div3Airport, Div4Airport and Div5Airport, all of these source columns and their corresponding hash keys have to be sourced. Because these statements insert into the same target table, a locking or synchronization mechanism might be required. Locking on the table level is most efficient and better from a performance standpoint, but requires that only one process at a time inserts rows. Thus, the tables could either be executed in sequence or should recover from a deadlock by automatically restarting the process. Locking on the row-level and executing (and committing) only micro-batches enable the use of full-parallelized execution without further handling.

12.1.1.2 SSIS Example

It is also possible to utilize SSIS for loading the business keys into the target hubs. Using SSIS also requires that only one batch be loaded into the Raw Data Vault at a time. For this reason, the SSIS variable shown in Figure 12.7 is created.

This variable is used to select only the data for one batch in the data flow. After this batch has been loaded to the Raw Data Vault, the end-date is calculated for the records and the next batch is loaded into the target.

Note that it is also possible to load all batches in one job, but this requires a more complex loading process, especially for satellites. On the other hand, loading multiple batches at the same time is often done during initial loads, which is not the everyday case. An exception to this rule is real-time loading of data, which is out of the scope of this book. If the staging area doesn't provide multiple loads, the use of this variable can be omitted. It is only required for loading historical data or multiple batches from the staging area into the enterprise data warehouse layer.

To implement the hub loading statement from the previous section in SSIS, each statement is implemented as its own data flow. Before configuring the source components, create a new OLE DB connection manager to set up the database connection into the staging area (Figure 12.8).

Select the **StageArea** database from the list of available databases. Once all required settings are made, select the **OK** button to close the dialog. Drag an **OLE DB source** component to the canvas of the dataflow. Open the editor and configure the source component as shown in Figure 12.9.

Use the following SQL statement to set up the SQL command text:

```
SELECT DISTINCT
        OriginHashKey AS AirportCodeHashKey,
        LoadDate,
        RecordSource,
        CONVERT(nvarchar(3), Origin) AS AirportCode
FROM
        StageArea.bts.OnTimeOnTimePerformanceGD
WHERE
        LoadDate = ?
```

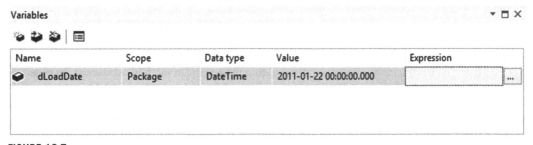

FIGURE 12.7

Adding load date variable to SSIS.

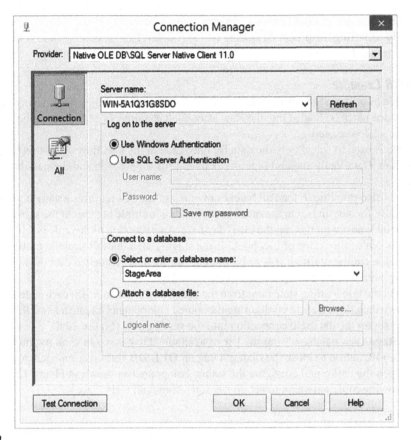

FIGURE 12.8

Setup connection to staging area.

Table 12.1 lists the other SQL statements that should be used in the data flows for additional columns from the source table in the staging area. Each SQL statement overrides the name of the incoming field to match the field name of the column in the destination hub table, which is not required but makes automation (or copy and paste) easier. It also makes the handling of the individual streams easier later on. Other than that, there are only two filters applied: the first filter is the DISTINCT in the SELECT clause that ensures that no duplicate business keys are retrieved from the source. The second filter is implemented in the WHERE clause to load only one batch from the staging area, based on the variable defined earlier. The parameter is referenced using a quotation mark in the SQL statement. In order to associate it with the variable, use the **Parameters...** button. The dialog in Figure 12.10 is presented.

Select the variable that was previously created and associate it with the first parameter. Select the **OK** button to complete the operation. Close the OLE DB Source Editor to save the SQL statement in the source component.

This completes the setup of the OLE DB source transformation. Close the dialog and drag a lookup transformation into the data flow. Connect the output of the OLE DB source transformation to the lookup and open the editor (Figure 12.11).

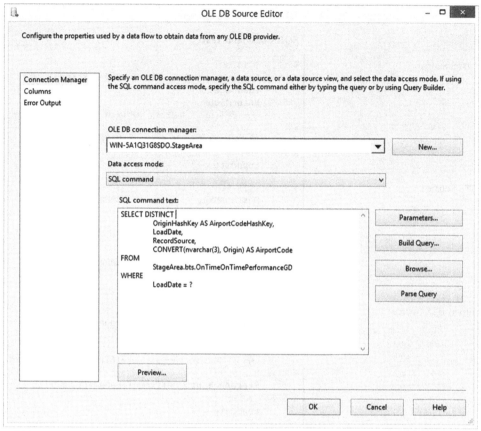

FIGURE 12.9

OLE DB source editor for retrieving the business keys from the staging area

The lookup is required to filter out the business keys that are already in the target hub from the data flow. After the lookup is performed, the records in the data flow are provided in two output paths:

- **Lookup match output:** this output contains all the business keys from the sources that are already known to the target hub. We are not interested in these business keys for further processing.
- **Lookup no match output:** this output provides all the business keys that have not been found in the target hub by this lookup. These keys should be added to the target.

This means that we are actually interested in those keys that haven't been found by the lookup. For this reason, it is important to **redirect rows to no match output** if the business key cannot be found in the destination. This setting can be set in the dialog page shown in Figure 12.11.

Switch to the next page, by selecting **Connection** from the list on the left. The dialog page is shown in Figure 12.12.

Table 12.1 SQL Statements for OLE DB Source Components

Name	SQL Command Text

Origin BTS Source	```sql
	SELECT DISTINCT
	        OriginHashKey AS AirportCodeHashKey,
	        LoadDate,
	        RecordSource,
	        CONVERT(nvarchar(3), Origin) AS AirportCode
	FROM
	        StageArea.bts.OnTimeOnTimePerformanceGD
	WHERE
	        LoadDate = ?
	``

Dest BTS Source	```sql
	SELECT DISTINCT
	        DestHashKey AS AirportCodeHashKey,
	        LoadDate,
	        RecordSource,
	        CONVERT(nvarchar(3), Dest) AS AirportCode
	FROM
	        StageArea.bts.OnTimeOnTimePerformanceGD
	WHERE
	        LoadDate = ?
	``

Div1Airport BTS Source	```sql
	SELECT DISTINCT
	        Div1AirportHashKey AS AirportCodeHashKey,
	        LoadDate,
	        RecordSource,
	        CONVERT(nvarchar(3), Div1Airport) AS AirportCode
	FROM
	        StageArea.bts.OnTimeOnTimePerformance
	WHERE
	        LoadDate = ?
	``

Div2Airport BTS Source	```sql
	SELECT DISTINCT
	        Div2AirportHashKey AS AirportCodeHashKey,
	        LoadDate,
	        RecordSource,
	        CONVERT(nvarchar(3), Div2Airport) AS AirportCode
	FROM
	        StageArea.bts.OnTimeOnTimePerformance
	WHERE
	        LoadDate = ?
	``

Div3Airport BTS Source	```sql
	SELECT DISTINCT
	        Div3AirportHashKey AS AirportCodeHashKey,
	        LoadDate,
	        RecordSource,
	        CONVERT(nvarchar(3), Div3Airport) AS AirportCode
	FROM
	        StageArea.bts.OnTimeOnTimePerformance
	WHERE
	        LoadDate = ?
	``

Table 12.1   SQL Statements for OLE DB Source Components *(cont.)*

Name	SQL Command Text

Div4Airport BTS Source	SELECT DISTINCT
	            Div4AirportHashKey AS AirportCodeHashKey,
	            LoadDate,
	            RecordSource,
	            CONVERT(nvarchar(3), Div4Airport) AS AirportCode
	FROM
	            StageArea.bts.OnTimeOnTimePerformance
	WHERE
	            LoadDate = ?

Div5Airport BTS Source	SELECT DISTINCT
	            Div5AirportHashKey AS AirportCodeHashKey,
	            LoadDate,
	            RecordSource,
	            CONVERT(nvarchar(3), Div5Airport) AS AirportCode
	FROM
	            StageArea.bts.OnTimeOnTimePerformance
	WHERE
	            LoadDate = ?

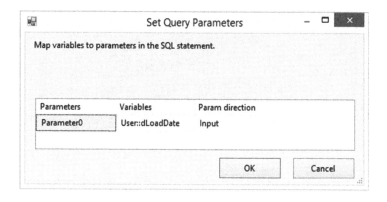

FIGURE 12.10

Set query parameters dialog.

Select the **DataVault** database connection and the **HubAirportCode** as the lookup table from the list of tables. You can use the **Preview…** button to check the data in the target. Select the **Columns** entry from the list on the left to switch to the columns page of the dialog (Figure 12.13).

This page actually influences whether the process is able to detect hash collisions. If the business key is used for the equi-join, hash collisions would be detected when inserting a new business key with an already existing hash key into the target hub, because it would violate the primary key on the hash key. If the hash key were used for the equi-join, duplicates wouldn't be detected because they share the same hash key. In fact, the new business key wouldn't be loaded into the target because the hash key on the business key is already present (has been found by the lookup). This would violate the definition of the hub, which is defined as a distinct list of business keys (and not hash keys). Therefore, the best choice is to use the business key

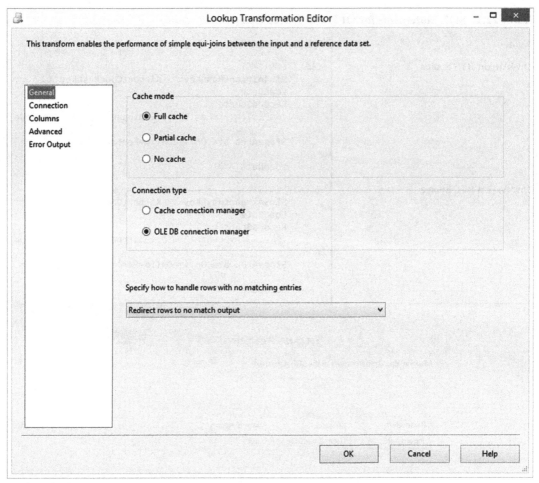

FIGURE 12.11

Lookup transformation editor to find out which business keys already exist.

in the equi-join operation of the lookup. It is not required to load any columns from the lookup into the data flow, because the only thing we're interested in is whether the business key is in the target hub table or not.

The last step in the process is to set up the destination. First, set up the OLE DB connection manager (Figure 12.14).

Once the connection manager has been set up, insert an OLE DB destination to the data flow canvas and connect the output from the lookup to the destination (Figure 12.15).

Once the path is connected, SSIS asks for the selection of the output (from the lookup transformation) that should be connected to the input of the OLE DB destination. This is because the lookup provides two outputs (plus the error output). Because we're interested in loading unknown business keys to the destination, select the **lookup no match output** in this dialog. Close the dialog and open the editor of the OLE DB destination (Figure 12.16).

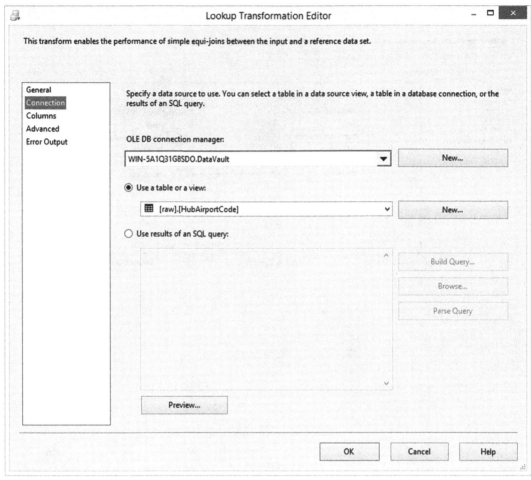

FIGURE 12.12

Setup lookup connection in the lookup transformation editor.

Because Data Vault 2.0 is based on hash keys, no identities are used. Therefore, **keep identity** is turned off. The option **keep nulls** should be checked in order to load a potential NULL business key, which is in line with the INSERT statement from the previous section. The table lock speeds up the loading process of the target table. However, it might require putting individual data flows with the same target table into a sequence in the control flow to avoid having to deal with deadlocks. Check constraints should be turned off as well. It is not recommended to use check constraints in the Raw Data Vault for two reasons: first, they reduce the performance of the loading process, and second, they often implement soft business rules, which should not be implemented at this point. Instead, they should be moved into the loading processes of the Business Vault or the information marts, which is covered in Chapter 14, Loading the Dimensional Information Mart.

Switch to the mapping page of the dialog by selecting the corresponding entry on the left side. The page shown in Figure 12.17 will appear.

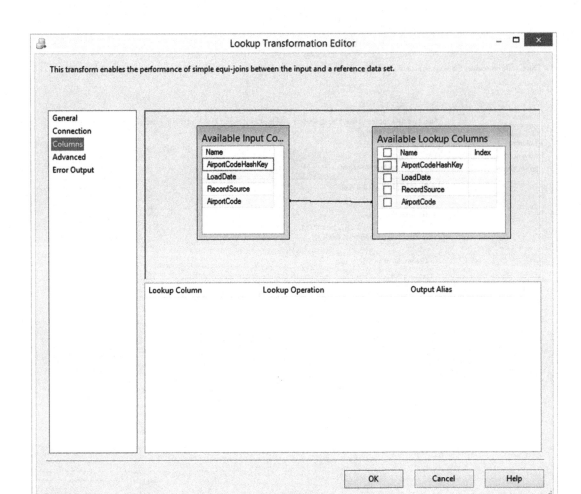

FIGURE 12.13

Configuring lookup columns in the lookup transformation editor.

Make sure that each column in the destination has been mapped to an input column. Select OK to close the dialog.

This completes the data flow for loading hub tables with SSIS. The final data flow is presented in Figure 12.18.

12.1.2 LINKS

The loading template for link tables in the Data Vault is actually very similar to the loading template of hub tables, especially if the hash keys are already calculated in the staging area, as is the recommended practice. The similarity of both templates is due to the fact that no lookups into the hubs referenced by the link are required. The loading template for links is completely independent of hub tables or any other tables (see Figure 12.19).

FIGURE 12.14

Configuring the OLE DB connection manager for the destination.

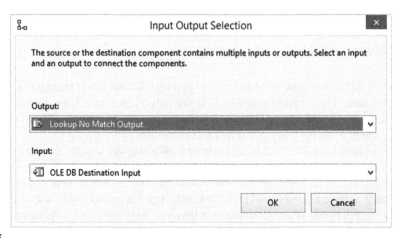

FIGURE 12.15

Output selection for destination component.

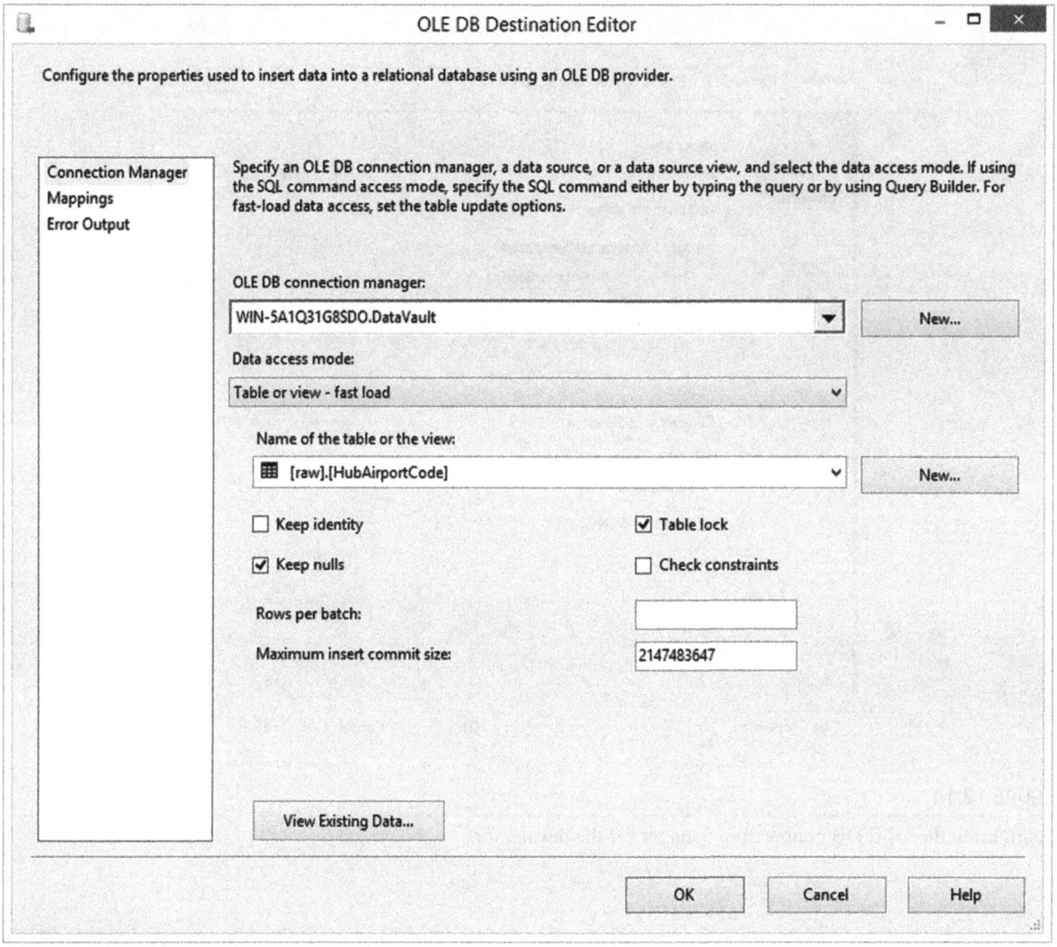

FIGURE 12.16

Setting up the connection in the OLE DB destination editor.

The first step in the loading process of links is to retrieve a distinct list of business key relationships from the source system. These relationships include not only the business keys; they also include the individual hash keys for the referenced hubs (where the business keys are defined) and the hash key of the relationship, which is the hash key of the link table structure.

Because only the hash keys are stored in the target link table, they are used to perform the lookup in the next step. This is sufficient in order to detect hash collisions in the link table. If the hash key of the input business key combination is the same for different inputs, the individual hash keys of the hub references will also be the same as the colliding record in the link table. For that reason, the lookup in the second step would return that the link combination doesn't exist in the target link table, but the subsequent insert would fail, due to the fact that both links (with different business key references, thus different hash keys used to reference the hubs in the link relationship) share the same link hash key which is used as the primary key of the table.

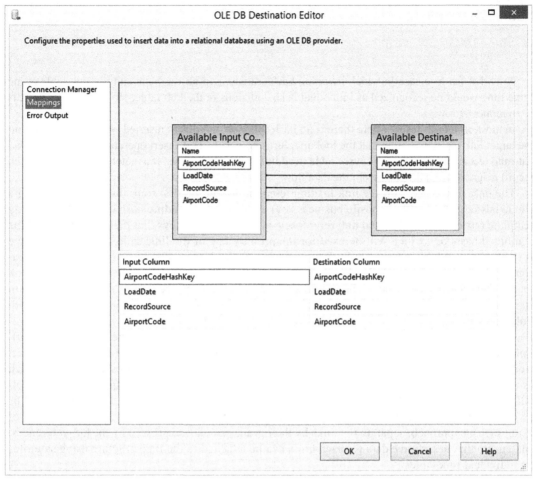

FIGURE 12.17

Mapping the columns from the data flow to the destination.

FIGURE 12.18

Data flow for loading Data Vault 2.0 hubs.

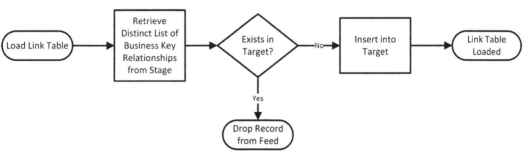

FIGURE 12.19

Template for loading link tables.

Note that the rare case in which there are hash collisions in all the hubs and the link table at the same time would be recognized as individual hash collisions in the hub table. However, such a risk is astronomically low.

In most, if not all, cases, where there is no hash collision, the link is inserted without any error into the target link table, assuming that the lookup returns no match. This insert operation includes the load date and record source from the source table in addition to the hash keys. If a match is returned, the link record is ignored and dropped from the data flow.

The only difference with the link loading template lies in the first step: instead of retrieving a single business key (or a composite business key) with its corresponding hash key, the link loading template retrieves the individual hub references: not the business keys, but their hash keys and the combined hash key, which will be used for the primary key of the link table. Another difference is the lookup, which does not use business keys but the hash keys of the hub references. The reason lies in the fact that the link table doesn't contain any business keys. Other than that, the link loading template is the same as the hub loading template. For this reason, it's a good practice to start implementing the hub loads first, and then adopt the hub loading template to be used with link tables.

Another similarity with the hub loading template is that the links might be sourced from multiple source tables, which might be spread over multiple source systems. In this case, the links from the various sources are combined into one target link table. This requires a similar approach as with hub loads: either the links are sourced in sequence or using the same approaches for parallelization. Note that combining links with different grain into the same target link table should be avoided. This leads to hub references that are NULL and is called "link overloading." Instead of using such an approach, separate the links by their grain, which is expressed by the hub references, and ensure that descriptive data for each grain can be attached to the link structure using satellites on individual link tables.

12.1.2.1 T-SQL Example

Because of the similarity of the loading templates for hubs and links, the T-SQL statement for loading link tables is very similar to the hub loading statement. It loads a standard link table that was created with the following statement:

```
CREATE TABLE [raw].[LinkFlightNumCarrier](
        [FlightNumCarrierHashKey] [char](32) NOT NULL,
        [LoadDate] [datetime2](7) NOT NULL,
        [RecordSource] [nvarchar](50) NOT NULL,
        [FlightNumHashKey] [char](32) NOT NULL,
        [CarrierHashKey] [char](32) NOT NULL,
 CONSTRAINT [PK_LinkFlightNumCarrier] PRIMARY KEY NONCLUSTERED
(
        [FlightNumCarrierHashKey] ASC
) ON [INDEX],
 CONSTRAINT [UK_LinkFlightNumCarrier] UNIQUE NONCLUSTERED
(
        [FlightNumHashKey] ASC,
        [CarrierHashKey] ASC
) ON [INDEX]
) ON [DATA]
```

This table is also created in the **raw** schema, as are all other tables of the Raw Data Vault throughout this book. Following the definition outlined in Chapter 4, Data Vault 2.0 Modeling, the table contains a hash key, which is used as the table's primary key and identifies each link entry uniquely. The table contains the load date and record source in the same manner, and for the same purpose, as the hub table. The difference in the definition lies in the following hash keys, namely **FlightNumHashKey** and **CarrierHashKey**, which store the parent hash keys of the referenced hubs.

The primary key is on the hash key of the link again and is nonclustered. In addition, the link table contains an alternate key on the hub references to ensure uniqueness of the link combination. The implicit index on this unique key is also used as an index for a lookup required in the loading process.

The loading process for links should only load newly arrived business key relationships from the source table in the staging area. For this reason, the insert statement is comparable to the hub statement, but is based on the hash keys from the referenced hubs and not on the business keys found in the source:

```
INSERT INTO DataVault.[raw].LinkFlightNumCarrier (
      FlightNumCarrierHashKey, LoadDate, RecordSource, FlightNumHashKey, CarrierHashKey
)
SELECT DISTINCT
      FlightNumCarrierHashKey, LoadDate, RecordSource, FlightNumHashKey, CarrierHashKey
FROM
      StageArea.bts.OnTimeOnTimePerformance s
WHERE
      NOT EXISTS (SELECT
                          1
                  FROM
                          DataVault.[raw].LinkFlightNumCarrier l
                  WHERE
                          s.FlightNumHashKey = l.FlightNumHashKey
                          AND s.CarrierHashKey = l.CarrierHashKey
                  )
      AND LoadDate = '2015-01-22 09:51:56.000'
```

The SELECT part in this statement uses a DISTINCT clause again, in order to avoid checking the same business key relationship multiple times. All hash keys have been calculated in the staging area again, which is used to simplify the actual loading and increase the reusability of the hash computation. Only relationships that don't exist in the target link table are inserted. Because link tables use more than one referenced hub, the statement uses a NOT EXISTS condition in favor to a NOT IN statement. The sub-query searches for relationships that consist of the same hash keys.

Similar to the use of the load date in the statement for loading hubs (refer to section 12.1.1), the previous statement is filtering the data to one specific load date. This is done in order to sequentially load the batches in the staging area to ensure that the deltas are correctly loaded into the data warehouse. Therefore, another statement is required to find out the available load dates in the staging area first, order them (the batch with the oldest load date should be loaded into the data warehouse first) and then execute the above statement per load date found in the staging area.

The statement doesn't check the validity of the incoming links. For example, in some cases, the source system provides a NULL value instead of a business key. In this case, the above statement maps NULL business keys to a hash key, which is the result of the hash function on an empty string. In order to maintain the data integrity, this key has to be added to the hub, as well. However, there are two cases that might happen when loading business key relationships:

1. **At least one expected business key was not provided:** in this case, the source system provided erroneous data because an expected business key, which was used in a foreign key reference, was not provided and is NULL.
2. **At least one optional business key was not provided:** the business key in the source system is optional and was not provided. This is not an actual error.

It is important to cover both cases in order to analyze both errors and design issues. If only one extra hub record is used to cover the NULL business keys, it is not possible to distinguish between these cases. For that reason, there should be actually two extra records in the target hub (see Table 12.2).

The first record indicates the first option: the expected business key was not provided by the source. This is an actual error. The business key is set to an artificial, system-generated value, in this case −1. The hash key is set statically as well, because it makes the identification easier. It could also be derived from the artificial business key.

The second record is used for business keys that are optional and not provided. For this case, the business key −2 was artificially set. The hash key is set to 22222222222222222222222222222222 (32 times the character "2"). This way, it is easy to identify records in the source system that are attached to the missing key for some reason. The third record in the table is a valid business key.

When data is loaded from the source and cannot be associated with a business key, for example because the business key column in a source flat file is left empty, the data in the satellite is associated with one of these entries in the hub table. If a business key is missing in satellites on hubs, many of these cases are attached to the first option that covers missing business keys.

However, especially when loading link tables from foreign key references in the source system, both cases are very common. If a NULL reference is found in the source system, this information is added to the link table (Table 12.3).

The first line describes a connection between Denver and an unknown destination airport. Because the record was expected but not provided by the source system, the hash reference into the airport hub is set to the hash key reserved for erroneous data.

The last record in Table 12.3 references the second reserved record in the airport hub, reserved for cases when an optional business key is not provided. This is not perfect, but also not an error.

In both cases, the incoming NULL value is replaced by the artificial business key from the hub, with the artificial hash key (or the hash key derived from the artificial business key). Once the link is loaded into the Raw Data Vault, it is possible to load satellite data that describes the erroneous or weird data. This descriptive data is typically found next to the foreign key reference, in the same source table.

By following this process, the data warehouse integrates as much data as possible and allows the data warehouse team and the business user to analyze any issues with the source system directly in the Raw Data Vault. The data will later be "cleansed" by business logic, when loaded into the information marts.

Table 12.2 Ghost Records in Airport Hub Table			
Airport Hash Key	**Load Date**	**Record Source**	**Airline ID**
1111...	0001-01-01 00:00:00.000	SYSTEM	-1
2222...	0001-01-01 00:00:00.000	SYSTEM	-2
1aab...	2013-07-13 03:12:11.000	BTS	JFK

Table 12.3 Linkconnection With Expected and Unexpected Null References

Connection Hash Key	Load Date	Record Source	Carrier Hash Key	Source Airport Hash Key	Destination Airport Hash Key	Flight Hash Key
87af...	2013-07-13 03:12:11	BTS	8fe9... {UA}	3de7... {DEN}	1111... {-1}	a87f... {UA942}
28db...	2013-07-13 03:12:11	BTS	8fe9... {UA}	3de7... {DEN}	1aab... {JFK}	8df7... {UA4711}
9de7...	2013-07-14 02:11:10	BTS	8fe9... {UA}	3de7... {DEN}	1aab... {JFK}	9eaf... {UA123}
9773...	2013-07-15 03:14:12	BTS.x	8fe9... {UA}	2222... {-2}	9bbe... {SFO}	821a... {UA883}

12.1.2.2 SSIS Example

Loading Data Vault 2.0 links in SSIS follows a similar approach to loading hubs. Because links can also be provided by multiple source tables (within the same source system), each source that provides link records desires its own data flow. After adding an OLE DB source transformation to the newly created data flow, open the OLE DB source editor (Figure 12.20).

Select the **StageArea** database from the list of databases and set the **data access mode** to **SQL command**. Insert the following SQL statement into the editor for the **SQL command text**:

```
SELECT DISTINCT
        FlightNumCarrierHashKey,
        LoadDate,
        RecordSource,
        FlightNumHashKey,
        CarrierHashKey
FROM
        StageArea.bts.OnTimeOnTimePerformanceGD
WHERE
        LoadDate = ?
```

This statement selects all links for a given batch from the source table in the staging area. The batch is indicated by the load date. This approach follows the hub loading process and requires using the variable defined in section 12.1.1 (Figure 12.21).

Map the parameter in the SQL command text to a SSIS variable by selecting the variable in the second column. The **param direction** should be set to **input** as it is the default. Close the dialog. This completes the configuration of the source component. Drag a lookup component into the data flow and connect its input to the default output from the OLE DB source. Open the lookup transformation editor, which is shown in Figure 12.22.

Similar to the hub loading process, the process shown in this section is interested in links that don't exist in the target table. That is why this lookup is performed against the target. To prevent a failure of the SSIS process, select **redirect rows to no match output** in the selection box. This will open another output that provides the unknown link structures that should be loaded into the target. Those that are already found in the target link table are ignored. This follows the link loading template outlined in section 12.1.2.

Switch to the **connection** page of this dialog by selecting the corresponding entry on the left side (Figure 12.23).

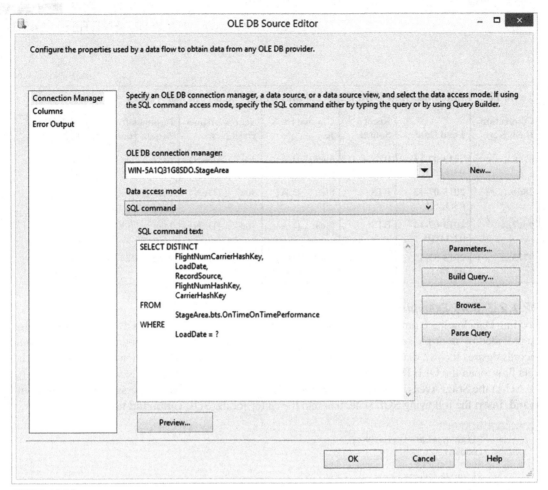

FIGURE 12.20

OLE DB source editor for loading links.

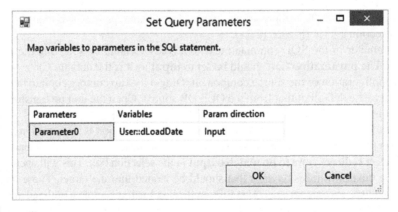

FIGURE 12.21

Set query parameter for load date timestamp.

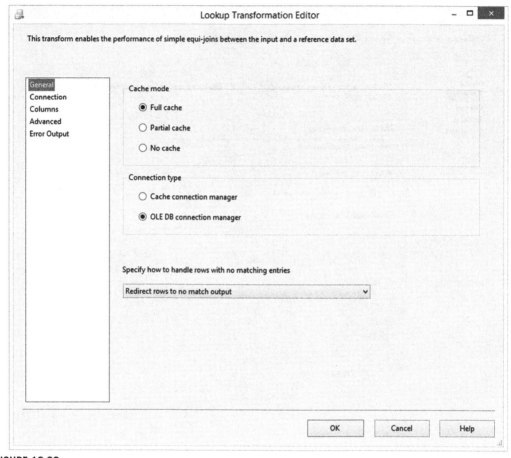

FIGURE 12.22

Set up the lookup transformation editor to find existing links.

This page sets up the connection to the lookup table. Because the goal of the lookup is to find out which links don't exist in the target table, select the **DataVault** database and the target table **Link-FlightNumCarrier**.

To complete the configuration of the lookup transformation, select the **columns** page on the left side of the dialog. The page shown in Figure 12.24 allows the configuration of the lookup columns and the columns that should be returned by the transformation.

Instead of using the hash key of the link (which is the primary key of the link table), the lookup should be performed on the hash keys of the referenced hubs. This improves the detection of hash key collisions. Because we're only interested in finding out which links are not in the target table yet, no columns are returned from the lookup table.

Select **OK** to close the lookup transformation editor. Insert an OLE DB destination and connect the output from the lookup to the destination. Because there are multiple outputs due to the redirection of unknown links in Figure 12.22, a dialog (Figure 12.25) is shown to map the output to the input.

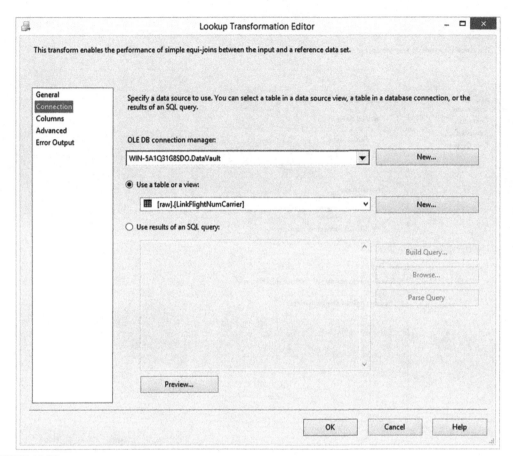

FIGURE 12.23

Setting up the connection in the lookup transformation editor for link tables.

The **lookup no match output** provides the link records from the source table in the staging area that have not been found in the target link table yet. Therefore, select this output and map it to the OLE DB destination input in order to load unknown link records to the target. The other output provides only link records that are already known to the target and will be ignored.

Close the dialog and open the **OLE DB destination editor**, shown in Figure 12.26.

Select the connection manager for the **DataVault** database and select the **LinkFlightNumCarrier** link table in the **raw** schema. Make sure that **keep nulls** and the **table lock** option are checked. **Keep identity** and **check constraints** should be unchecked for the same reasons as in the hub loading process. Consider changing the **rows per batch** and **maximum insert commit size** in order to adjust the SSIS load to your infrastructure.

Switch to the **mappings** page by selecting the entry in the list on the left of the dialog. The page shown in Figure 12.27 is presented.

Make sure that each column from the destination is mapped to a corresponding column in the source. Close the dialog. The final data flow is presented in Figure 12.28.

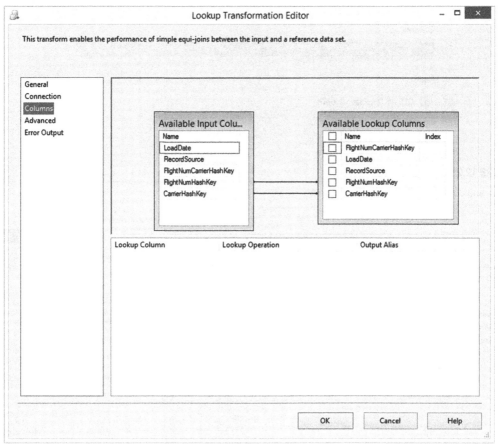

FIGURE 12.24

Configuring the columns of the link lookup.

This data flow might be extended by capturing errors in the error mart. Such an approach would follow the approach outlined in Chapter 10, Metadata Management.

12.1.3 NO-HISTORY LINKS

The loading pattern for no-history links (also known as transactional links) is even simpler than the loading template for standard links (described in section 12.1.2). The only difference is that the lookup in the loading template becomes optional (Figure 12.29).

Because no-history links are typically used for transactions or sensor data, one record needs to be loaded per transaction or event. It is not a distinct list of relationships. The lookup ensures that no duplicate transactions or events are loaded in the case of restarts.

This approach can be implemented in a fully recoverable approach, without the need to delete the partially loaded records in the target link table before restarting this process. While the process runs

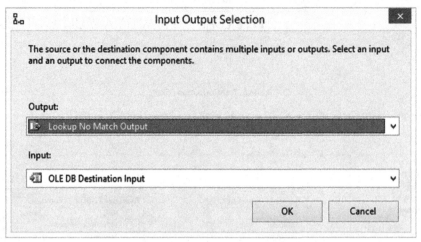

FIGURE 12.25

Input output selection for link loading process.

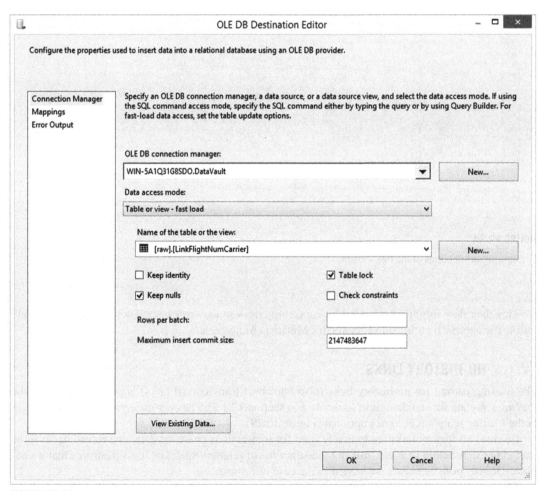

FIGURE 12.26

OLE DB destination editor for the link table destination.

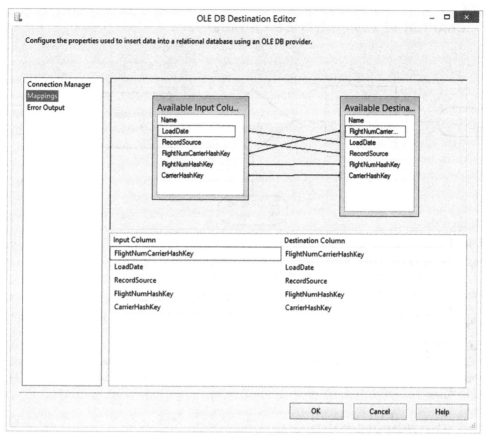

FIGURE 12.27

Mapping the columns in the OLE DB destination editor.

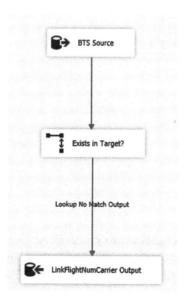

FIGURE 12.28

Data flow to load Data Vault 2.0 links.

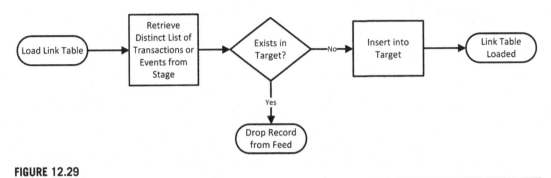

FIGURE 12.29

Template for loading nonhistorized link tables.

slower in the case of restarting the loading process (due to the lookup), it doesn't need any special handling. The ETL process is just restarted and loads the remaining records into the target table.

12.1.3.1 T-SQL Example

From a structural perspective, the no-history link target to be loaded in this section is not different to any other link table in the Raw Data Vault. The only difference is the name, which starts with "TLink" instead of "Link":

```
CREATE TABLE [raw].[TLinkFlight](
        [FlightHashKey] [char](32) NOT NULL,
        [LoadDate] [datetime2](7) NOT NULL,
        [RecordSource] [nvarchar](50) NOT NULL,
        [CarrierHashKey] [char](32) NOT NULL,
        [FlightNumHashKey] [char](32) NOT NULL,
        [TailNumHashKey] [char](32) NOT NULL,
        [OriginHashKey] [char](32) NOT NULL,
        [DestHashKey] [char](32) NOT NULL,
        [FlightDate] [datetime2](7) NOT NULL,
  CONSTRAINT [PK_TLinkFlight] PRIMARY KEY NONCLUSTERED
(
        [FlightHashKey] ASC
) ON [INDEX],
  CONSTRAINT [UK_LinkFlight] UNIQUE NONCLUSTERED
(
        [CarrierHashKey] ASC,
        [FlightNumHashKey] ASC,
        [TailNumHashKey] ASC,
        [OriginHashKey] ASC,
        [DestHashKey] ASC,
        [FlightDate] ASC
) ON [INDEX]
) ON [DATA]
```

The no-history link consists of **FlightHashKey** as an identifying hash key (used in the primary key), a load date and record source and the hash keys of the referenced hubs: **HubFlightNum**, **HubTailNum**, **HubAirport**. The latter was referenced twice and two hash keys are stored: one for the origin airport and the other for the destination airport.

The source data provides no unique event or transaction number: the flight data itself is not a good candidate to be used as a transaction or event number in the non-historized link. But such a number is required to achieve the proper grain, which fits the grain of the actual flights. Using only the hub references is not enough, because the flight number is reused from one day to the other. The goal is to achieve two goals for the loading process of no-history links:

1. **Same grain as transactions or events:** each transaction or event should have one record in the no-history link table in order to easily source fact tables from this table.
2. **Unique hash key for primary key:** the hash key in a link table is based on the referenced business keys. In order to achieve the first goal, another identifying element is required because, in most cases, the hub references alone have another grain than the transactions themselves (think of reoccurring customers, buying the same product in the same store).

Because no such transaction number is available in the source data, the flight date is added. It is not unique by itself, but fits the purpose of achieving the required grain and producing a unique hash key for the link when the date is included in the hash key calculation. The underlying elements, that is the hash keys of the referenced hubs and the flight date, are included in the alternate key for uniqueness and to speed up (optional) lookups.

Because the flight date was already included when calculating the hash key in the staging area, it is possible to simply load the data from the staging area into the no-history link:

```
INSERT INTO DataVault.[raw].TLinkFlight (
        FlightHashKey,
        LoadDate,
        RecordSource,
        CarrierHashKey,
        FlightNumHashKey,
        TailNumHashKey,
        OriginHashKey,
        DestHashKey,
        FlightDate
)
SELECT
        FlightHashKey,
        LoadDate,
        RecordSource,
        CarrierHashKey,
        FlightNumHashKey,
        TailNumHashKey,
        OriginHashKey,
        DestHashKey,
        FlightDate
FROM
        StageArea.bts.OnTimeOnTimePerformanceGD s
WHERE
        NOT EXISTS (SELECT
                        1
                FROM
                        DataVault.[raw].TLinkFlight l
                WHERE
                        s.CarrierHashKey = l.CarrierHashKey
                        AND s.FlightNumHashKey = l.FlightNumHashKey
                        AND s.TailNumHashKey = l.TailNumHashKey
                        AND s.OriginHashKey = l.OriginHashKey
                        AND s.DestHashKey = l.DestHashKey
                        AND s.FlightDate = l.FlightDate
                )
```

Also, the order in which the data is loaded into the link table doesn't matter, that's why there is no filter for a specific load date. All the data is simply loaded into the target table. To achieve a recoverable process, a lookup is required that checks whether the record to be loaded is already in the target table. The NOT EXISTS condition in the WHERE clause is taken from the statement to load standard link tables. Note that the flight date was included in this condition to make sure that duplicates are filtered out accordingly.

12.1.3.2 SSIS Example

To implement the T-SQL based loading process from the previous section in SSIS, a similar data flow is required to the previous SSIS example for loading Data Vault 2.0 links. Drop an OLE DB source transformation to a new data flow and open the editor (Figure 12.30).

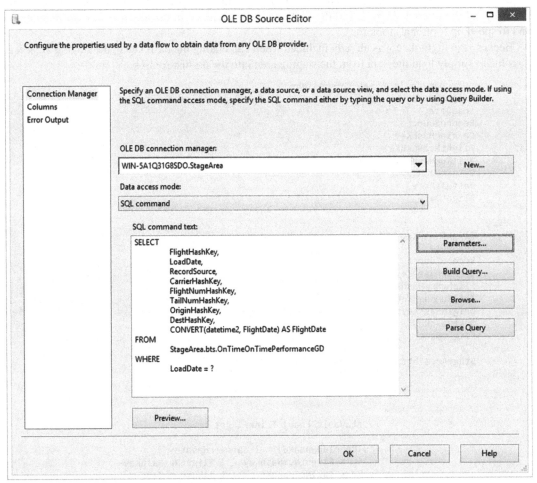

FIGURE 12.30

OLE DB source editor for no-history links.

The OLE DB source transformation loads the data from the source table in the staging area by using the following SQL command text:

```
SELECT
        FlightHashKey,
        LoadDate,
        RecordSource,
        CarrierHashKey,
        FlightNumHashKey,
        TailNumHashKey,
        OriginHashKey,
        DestHashKey,
        CONVERT(datetime2, FlightDate) AS FlightDate
FROM
        StageArea.bts.OnTimeOnTimePerformanceGD
WHERE
        LoadDate = ?
```

Because the **flight date** in the source table is stored as an nvarchar, it is converted into the correct data type on the way out of the staging area and into the Raw Data Vault no-history link table. This is the latest point that it should be done. If possible, it should already be done in the staging area, but in some cases (refer to Chapter 11, Data Extraction), it has to be done on the way out. The **load date** is also included in this statement to process only one batch at a time. As usual, use the **Parameters...** button to map the parameter to a SSIS variable (Figure 12.31).

Once the load date variable has been mapped to the parameter, close the dialog and the OLE DB source editor. Insert a lookup transformation into the data flow and connect it to the output of the OLE DB source. Open the lookup transformation editor, shown in Figure 12.32.

Again, make sure that **redirect rows to no match output** has been selected in the combo box on the first page. After that, switch to the next page by selecting **connection** from the list on the left of the dialog. The page is used to set up the target transaction link as the lookup table (Figure 12.33).

Make sure that **TLinkFlight** in the **raw** schema of the **DataVault** database is used for the connection and switch to the **columns** page of the dialog (Figure 12.34).

Similar to the standard link, the hash keys of the referenced hubs are used to perform the lookup. However, because the hash keys alone are not enough to correctly identify the link, the **flight date** is added into the equi-join of the lookup as well. No columns from the lookup table are returned because we're only interested in finding out if the no-history link already exists in the target or not.

Close the dialog and add an OLE DB destination to the data flow. Connect the output path from the lookup transformation to the destination transformation. Because unknown links are redirected into another output, the dialog shown in Figure 12.35 appears.

Select the **lookup no match output** because it contains all the records where no corresponding link record has been found in the target link table.

Close the dialog and open the OLE DB destination editor, as shown in Figure 12.36.

Select the target table, **TLinkFlight** in the **raw** schema of the **DataVault** database, and make sure that **keep nulls** and **table lock** are checked. The other options (**keep identity** and **check constraints**) should not be checked. **Rows per batch** and the **maximum insert commit size** should be adjusted to your data warehouse infrastructure. Check that the column mapping of the data flow to the destination table is correct by switching to the **mappings** page of the dialog (Figure 12.37).

Each destination column should have a corresponding input column. Select **OK** to confirm the changes to the dialog.

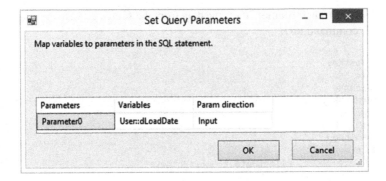

FIGURE 12.31

Set query parameter for nonhistorized link.

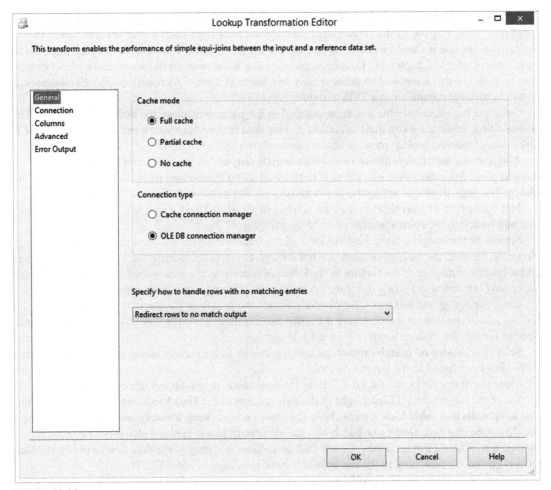

FIGURE 12.32

Lookup transformation editor for no-history links.

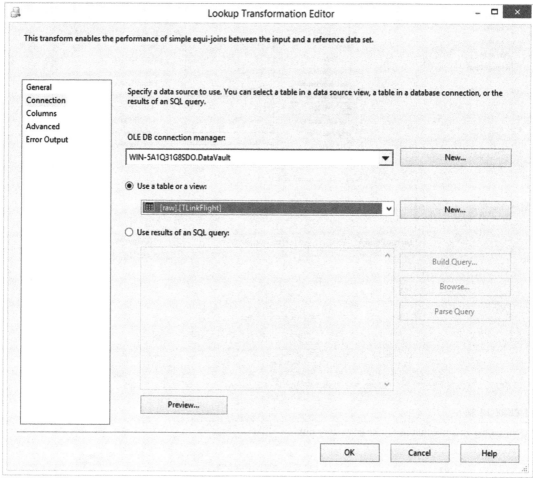

FIGURE 12.33

Setting up the connection in the lookup transformation editor for no-history links.

Figure 12.38 presents the final SSIS data flow for loading no-history links.

In addition to this link table, no-history links often have nonhistorized descriptive data stored in no-history satellites. Their loading process is covered in one of the coming sections on loading satellite entities.

12.1.4 SATELLITES

While the loading templates for hubs and links, even for special cases such as no-history links, are fairly simple, satellites are a little more complicated. However, the loading template for satellites follows the same design principles as discussed in the introduction to this chapter, thus becoming a fairly simple template as well.

The goal of the satellite loading process is to source the data from the staging area, find changes in the data and load these changes (and only these changes) into the target satellite. The default loading template for satellites is presented in Figure 12.39.

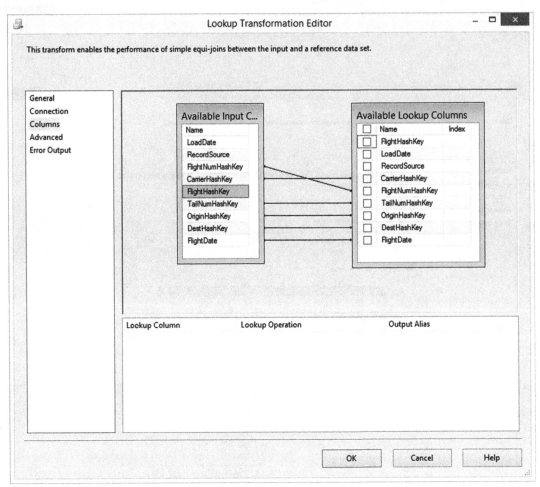

FIGURE 12.34

Configuring lookup columns for the no-history link.

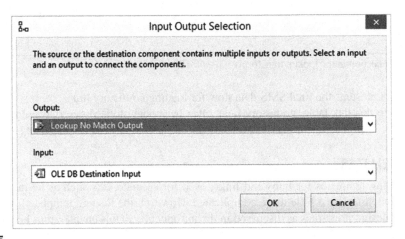

FIGURE 12.35

Input output selection for no-history links.

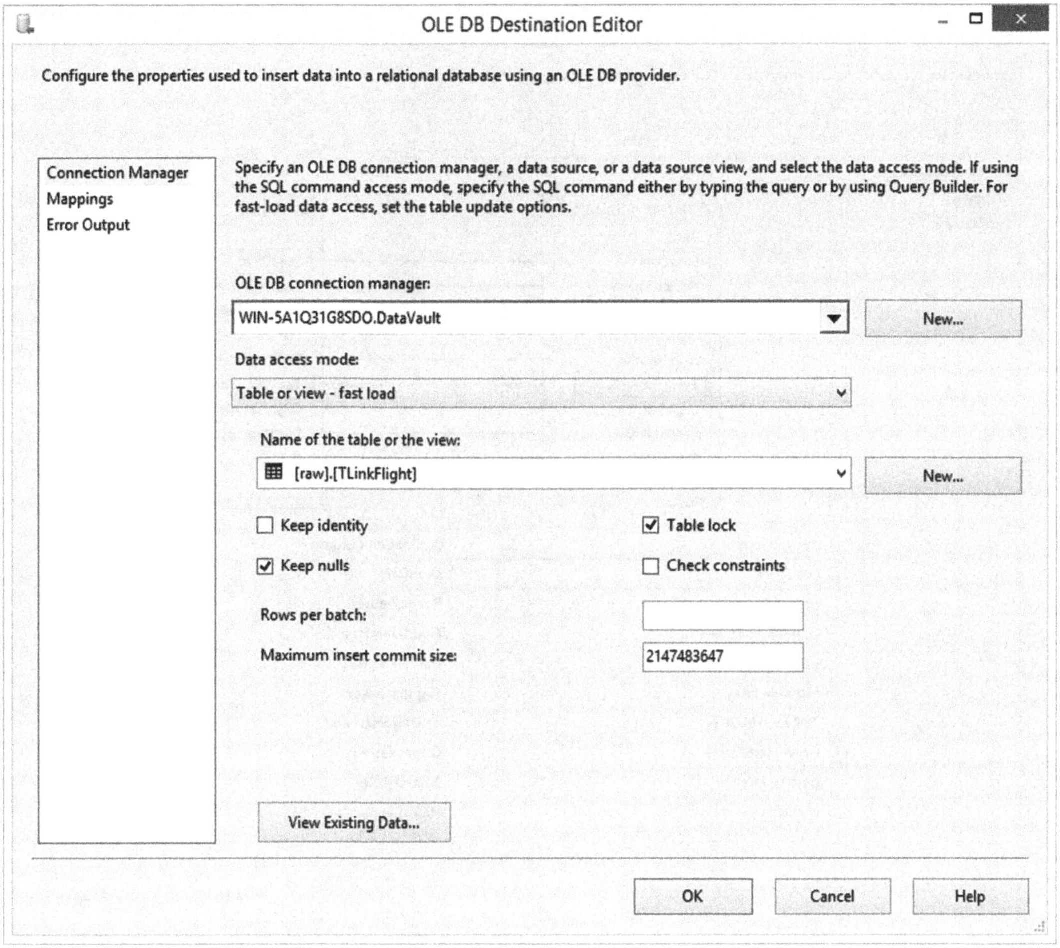

FIGURE 12.36

OLE DB destination editor of the no-history link.

The first step is to retrieve a distinct list of records from the staging table that might be changes. This step should omit **true** duplicates in the source because the satellite wouldn't capture them anyway. By doing so, the data flow reduces the amount of data early in the process, following the design principles for the loading templates.

Note that we define true duplicates as actual duplicates that are added to the staged data due to technical issues and provide no value to the business. We assume that these records should not be loaded into the Raw Data Vault and are filtered out in the loading process. If duplicates should be loaded, consider using a multi-active satellite for this purpose (refer to Chapter 5, Intermediate Data Vault Modeling, for more details).

Once the data (which contains both the descriptive data as well as the hash key of the parent hub or link table) has been sourced from the staging area, the latest record from the target satellite table that

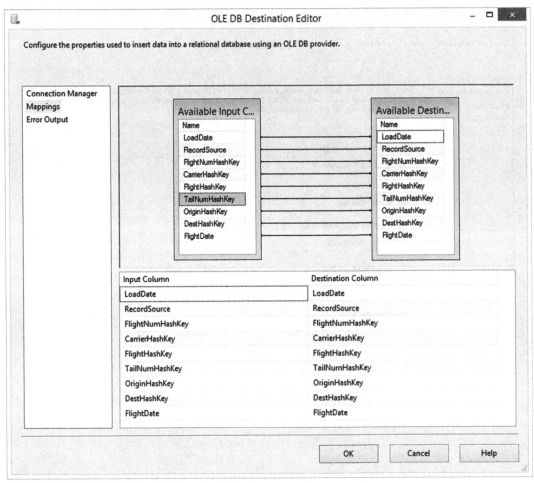

FIGURE 12.37

Mapping columns in the OLE DB destination editor of the no-history link.

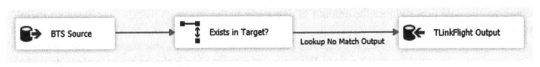

FIGURE 12.38

Complete SSIS data flow for loading no-history links.

matches the hash key is retrieved. This step is easy, because the latest record should have the latest load date of all the records for this hash key and a NULL or maximum load end date.

Both records, the record from the staging area and the latest satellite record obtained in the previous step, are compared column-wise. If all columns match, that means that no change has been detected, and the record is dropped from the feed because the satellite should not capture it. Remember that Data Vault satellites capture only deltas (new or changed records). If a record has not changed, it is not loaded into the satellite table.

If there is a change in at least one of the columns, the record is added to the target satellite table. Note that, in most cases, the change detection relies on all columns. However, there might be cases where some of the columns are ignored during column comparison. This would result in undetected changes. If all other columns were unmodified, no record would be added. Therefore, such a limited column comparison should be used only in specific and rare cases. Another thing to consider is if the column comparison should be case sensitive or case insensitive. Depending on the source data, both options make sense and are frequently used.

The major issue with the column comparison is that satellites sometimes contain a large number of columns that are required to be compared. This comparison can take time, especially if the number of records in the stage area that might contain changes to be captured is high as well. In order to speed up the performance of the loading template presented in Figure 12.39, hash diffs can be used. The hash diffs have been introduced as optional attributes to satellites in Chapter 4 and explained in great detail in the previous chapter.

Once the hash diff has been added to the satellite entity, it can be used to compare the input record with the target record with a comparison on one column only. When loading the Data Vault satellite, both required hash diffs from the source and the target are already calculated. The source data has already been hashed in the staging area, while the target satellites have the hash diffs included for each row by design.

Because of this preparatory work, the modified loading process doesn't require any hashing and is merely a simplified version of the standard loading template for satellites (Figure 12.40).

The difference between both loading patterns is only in the comparison step that either drops the record from the feed or loads it into the target table. This comparison is reduced to compare the hash diffs instead of all individual columns. It also removes the need to account for NULL values as this has been done in the hash diff calculation already by replacing the NULL values with empty strings in conjunction with delimiters. Other than the changed comparison, the template is the same as in Figure 12.39.

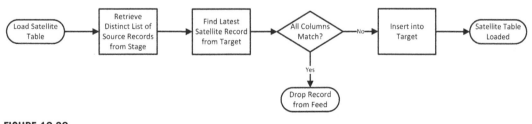

FIGURE 12.39

Template for loading satellite tables.

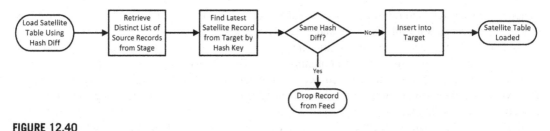

FIGURE 12.40

Template for loading satellite tables using hash diffs.

12.1.4.1 T-SQL Example

This section loads the descriptive data for the airports. However, there are two different sets of columns, each describing either the airport of origin or airport of destination. This data could be merged into one satellite, but aligning it might require additional business logic: what happens if data from both sets of columns contradict each other, e.g., using different descriptive data for the same airport and the same load date time? The load processes of the Raw Data Vault should not depend on any conditional business logic. Therefore, both sets of descriptive data are distributed to different satellites, each hanging off **HubAirport**. The first satellite captures the descriptive data for the originating airport and is created using the following DDL statement:

```
CREATE TABLE [raw].[SatOriginAirport](
        [AirportHashKey] [char](32) NOT NULL,
        [LoadDate] [datetime2](7) NOT NULL,
        [LoadEndDate] [datetime2](7) NULL,
        [RecordSource] [nvarchar](50) NOT NULL,
        [OriginCityName] [nvarchar](100) NOT NULL,
        [OriginState] [nvarchar](2) NOT NULL,
        [OriginStateName] [nvarchar](100) NOT NULL,
        [OriginCityMarketID] [int] NOT NULL,
        [OriginStateFips] [smallint] NOT NULL,
        [OriginWac] [smallint] NOT NULL,
  CONSTRAINT [PK_SatOriginAirport] PRIMARY KEY NONCLUSTERED
(
        [AirportHashKey] ASC,
        [LoadDate] ASC
) ON [INDEX]
) ON [DATA]
```

The satellite contains the parent hash key and the load date in its primary key. The load end date is NULLable and indicates if and when the record has been replaced by a newer version. The descriptive "payload" of the satellite is defined by the columns **OriginCityName**, **OriginState**, **OriginStateName**, **OriginCityMarketID**, **OriginStateFips** and **OriginWac**. Because the primary key contains a randomly distributed hash key, a nonclustered index should be used.

Note that this satellite does not use the hash diff value calculated in the staging area for demonstrative purposes. The next satellite, also presented in this section, uses the hash diff value.

It is easily possible to implement the template shown in Figure 12.39 in T-SQL only:

```
INSERT INTO DataVault.[raw].SatOriginAirport (
        AirportHashKey,
        LoadDate,
        LoadEndDate,
        RecordSource,
        OriginCityName,
        OriginState,
        OriginStateName,
        OriginCityMarketID,
        OriginStateFips,
        OriginWac
)
SELECT DISTINCT
        stg.OriginHashKey,
        stg.LoadDate,
        NULL,
        stg.RecordSource,
        stg.OriginCityName,
        stg.OriginState,
        stg.OriginStateName,
        stg.OriginCityMarketID,
        stg.OriginStateFips,
        stg.OriginWac
FROM
        StageArea.bts.OnTimeOnTimePerformanceGD stg
LEFT OUTER JOIN
        DataVault.[raw].SatOriginAirport sat
        ON (stg.OriginHashKey = sat.AirportHashKey AND sat.LoadEndDate IS NULL)
WHERE
        (ISNULL(stg.OriginCityName, '') != ISNULL(sat.OriginCityName, '')
        OR ISNULL(stg.OriginState, '') != ISNULL(sat.OriginState, '')
        OR ISNULL(stg.OriginStateName, '') != ISNULL(sat.OriginStateName, '')
        OR ISNULL(stg.OriginCityMarketID, 0) != ISNULL(sat.OriginCityMarketID, 0)
        OR ISNULL(stg.OriginStateFips, 0) != ISNULL(sat.OriginStateFips, 0)
        OR ISNULL(stg.OriginWac, 0) != ISNULL(sat.OriginWac, 0))
        AND stg.LoadDate = '1995-10-14 00:00:00.000'
```

This statement selects the data, including the parent hash key, the load date, the record source and the descriptive data from the source table in the staging area. The select is a DISTINCT operation because the airport is used in multiple flights (most airports serve multiple flights per day). If the DISTINCT option is left out, duplicate entries would be sourced and the subsequent insert operation would violate the primary key constraint of the target satellite. The load end date is explicitly set to NULL for demonstration purposes. As an alternative, it could also be removed from the list of columns and set implicitly. Because only changed data should be sourced into the target satellite, each column from the source stage table needs to be compared with its corresponding column in the target satellite table including a check for NULL values in the descriptive columns. This check could also be implemented using the ANSI-SQL standard function COALESCE. This column comparison is implemented in the WHERE clause of the statement. It requires that the target satellite be joined into the statement in order to have the current target values available. For this reason, a LEFT OUTER JOIN is used to join the data into the source dataset. The join condition compares both hash keys of the parent and requires that the record should be active. The latter is checked by selecting only records from the target with a load end date of NULL. When comparing the records, only new and active records with a load end date of NULL are interesting.

The additional filter on the source load date ensures that only one batch is loaded. This is very important in the loading process of satellites because the delta detection depends on the fact that only one batch is evaluated at the same time. Changing this is possible but complicates the process. Also, it is important to run the batches in the staging area in the right order, to make sure that the final satellite has captured the changes as desired.

The second satellite, **SatDestAirport**, which captures the descriptive data for the flight's destination airport, uses the hash diff value to improve the performance of the column comparison. Therefore, the hash diff column was added to a structure similar to the **SatOriginAirport**:

```
CREATE TABLE [raw].[SatDestAirport](
        [AirportHashKey] [char](32) NOT NULL,
        [LoadDate] [datetime2](7) NOT NULL,
        [LoadEndDate] [datetime2](7) NULL,
        [RecordSource] [nvarchar](50) NOT NULL,
        [HashDiff] [char](32) NOT NULL,
        [DestCityName] [nvarchar](100) NOT NULL,
        [DestState] [nvarchar](2) NOT NULL,
        [DestStateName] [nvarchar](100) NOT NULL,
        [DestCityMarketID] [int] NOT NULL,
        [DestStateFips] [smallint] NOT NULL,
        [DestWac] [smallint] NOT NULL,
  CONSTRAINT [PK_SatDestAirport] PRIMARY KEY NONCLUSTERED
(
        [AirportHashKey] ASC,
        [LoadDate] ASC
) ON [INDEX]
) ON [DATA]
```

The technical metadata of the satellite, including the parent hash key **AirportHashKey**, the load and end date and the record source, are exactly the same as in the previous satellite table. In addition, the hash diff column was added and the names of the descriptive columns are slightly different, due to different names in the source table.

To load the data from the source table in the staging area into the target satellite table, the following statement is used:

```
INSERT INTO DataVault.[raw].SatDestAirport (
        AirportHashKey,
        LoadDate,
        LoadEndDate,
        RecordSource,
        HashDiff,
        DestCityName,
        DestState,
        DestStateName,
        DestCityMarketID,
        DestStateFips,
        DestWac
)
```

```
SELECT DISTINCT
        stg.DestHashKey,
        stg.LoadDate,
        NULL,
        stg.RecordSource,
        stg.DestAirportHashDiff,
        stg.DestCityName,
        stg.DestState,
        stg.DestStateName,
        stg.DestCityMarketID,
        stg.DestStateFips,
        stg.DestWac
FROM
        StageArea.bts.OnTimeOnTimePerformanceGD stg
LEFT OUTER JOIN
        DataVault.[raw].SatDestAirport sat
        ON (stg.DestHashKey = sat.AirportHashKey AND sat.LoadEndDate IS NULL)
WHERE
        (sat.HashDiff IS NULL OR stg.DestAirportHashDiff != sat.HashDiff)
        AND stg.LoadDate = '1995-10-26 00:00:00.000'
```

The only difference from the previous INSERT statement, apart from the fact that it loads the table **SatDestAirport** instead of **SatOriginAirport** (thus sourcing different columns from the staging table), is that the column compare was simplified: only one column is compared instead of all descriptive columns. If the hash diff in the target is different from the one in the stage area, or if there is no record in the target satellite that fits to the hash key (which leads to a hash diff of NULL), the record is loaded into the target.

Both INSERT statements rely on an OUTER JOIN in order to join the data into one result set. This is required in order to compare the incoming data with the existing data or produce NULL values if there is no satellite entry with the same parent hash key as the incoming record. If another join type is used, the column compare would not compare a wrong record or data would be lost on the way from the staging table to the Raw Data Vault. If the performance of the loading process is too slow due to the OUTER JOIN, the best approach is to divide both datasets (the new and the changed records from the staging area) and process them separately. This is covered in section 12.1.6.

The descriptive data in both satellites can be combined later in the Business Vault, for example using PIT tables or computed satellites. These approaches are covered in Chapter 14, Loading the Dimensional Information Mart.

12.1.4.2 SSIS Example

It is also possible to implement the loading template for satellites using SSIS. This approach also requires the load date variable in the SSIS package to ensure that only one batch is loaded into the Raw Data Vault during a single SSIS execution.

The first step is to set up the source components in the SSIS data flow. Unlike the SSIS processes for hubs and links, the SSIS data flow presented in this example uses two different source components from different layers of the data warehouse:

1. **The source staging table:** this table provides the new and changed records along with unchanged records.
2. **The target satellite table:** this table provides the current version of the data in the target.

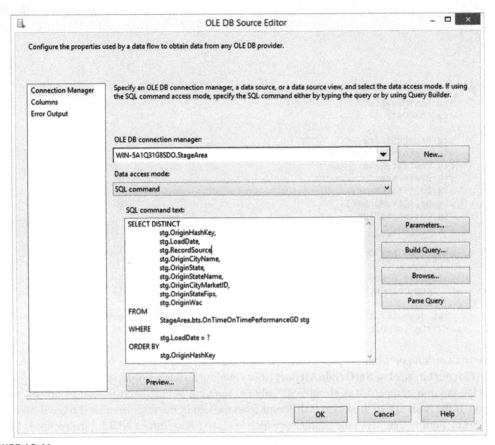

FIGURE 12.41

Set up the source component for the staging area data source.

The data from both sources will be merged in the data flow and compared during column comparison. Essentially, this approach implements a JOIN operation instead of a lookup (sub-query in T-SQL) for performance reasons. The first source component, an **OLE DB Source**, is set up using a SQL command, as Figure 12.41 shows.

The following SQL statement is used as SQL command text:

```
SELECT DISTINCT
        stg.OriginHashKey,
        stg.LoadDate,
        stg.RecordSource,
        stg.OriginCityName,
        stg.OriginState,
        stg.OriginStateName,
        stg.OriginCityMarketID,
        stg.OriginStateFips,
        stg.OriginWac
FROM
        StageArea.bts.OnTimeOnTimePerformanceGD stg
WHERE
        stg.LoadDate = ?
ORDER BY
        stg.OriginHashKey
```

There are two lines noteworthy: first, the ORDER BY clause is required for the merge operation of both data sources because it improves performance if the key that is used for merging the data streams already sorts both data flows. In this case, this will be the hash key. The second interesting line is the use of the WHERE clause to load only one batch from the staging area, based on the variable defined earlier. The parameter is referenced using a quotation mark in the SQL statement. In order to associate it with the variable, use the **Parameters...** button. The dialog shown in Figure 12.42 is presented.

Select the variable previously created and associate it with the first parameter. Select the **OK** button to complete the operation. Close the OLE DB Source Editor to save the SQL statement in the source component. However, the component is not completely set up yet. While the incoming data is ordered by the hash key to optimize merging the data flows, this setting has to be indicated to the output columns of the source component in addition.

Open the advanced editor from the context menu of the source component (Figure 12.43).

Select the **OLE DB Source Output** node in the tree view from the left. Set the **IsSorted** property of the output to true. The last setting is to indicate the actual column that was used for sorting. Select the column from the **Output Columns** folder in the tree view, as shown in Figure 12.44.

Set the **SortKeyPosition** property to the column number of the hash key in the source query. Because the hash key is the first column in the SQL statement used in Figure 12.41, the position value 1 is set.

This completes the setup of the staging table source. The next dialog shows the setup of the source component that sources the data from the target satellite, which is required to compare the incoming values with the existing values (Figure 12.45).

The following SQL statement is used as the SQL command text:

```
SELECT
        AirportHashKey,
        OriginCityName,
        OriginState,
        OriginStateName,
        OriginCityMarketID,
        OriginStateFips,
        OriginWac
FROM
        [raw].[SatOriginAirport]
WHERE
        LoadEndDate IS NULL
ORDER BY
        AirportHashKey
```

The statement loads all records from the target satellite, which are currently active (having a **load date** of NULL). The data is also ordered to enable merging the data flows in the next step. Because the data is ordered, this has to be indicated to the SSIS engine using the same approach by setting the **IsSorted** property of the output and the **SortKeyPosition** of the hash key output column as described in Figure 12.43 and Figure 12.44.

Once the data from both sources is available in the data flow, the next step is to merge both data streams in order to be able to compare the values from both the staging area and the target satellite. Drag a **Merge Join Transformation** to the data flow canvas and open the editor (Figure 12.46).

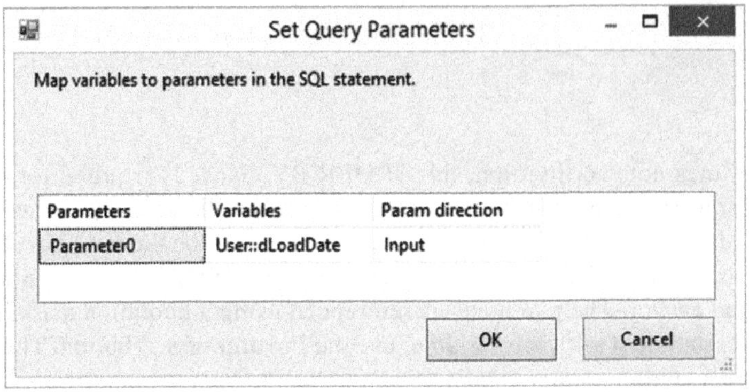

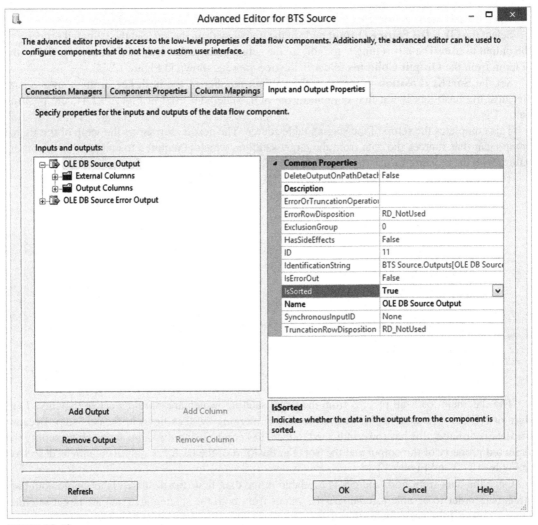

FIGURE 12.42

Set query parameters dialog.

FIGURE 12.43

Advanced editor of source component.

FIGURE 12.44

Setting the SortKeyPosition in the advanced editor.

There are two tasks to complete in this dialog: first, the columns that are used for the merge operation have to be connected. In this case, this is the hash key from each data stream because the streams are merged on this value. Drag the **OriginHashkey** column over the **AirportHashKey** in order to connect both columns. Also, make sure that the **join type** is set to **left outer join**. The second task is to select the columns that should be included in the merged data stream. This should include all columns from the staging area and the descriptive data from the target satellite because all of this data is required for either the column compare or the loading of the target satellite table. Because the descriptive columns are named the same in both the source and the target, rename one or both sides as in Figure 12.46.

Close the dialog and drag a conditional split transformation to the canvas of the data flow. This component is used to filter the records from the staging area source that don't represent a change from the data that is already in the target satellite (Figure 12.47).

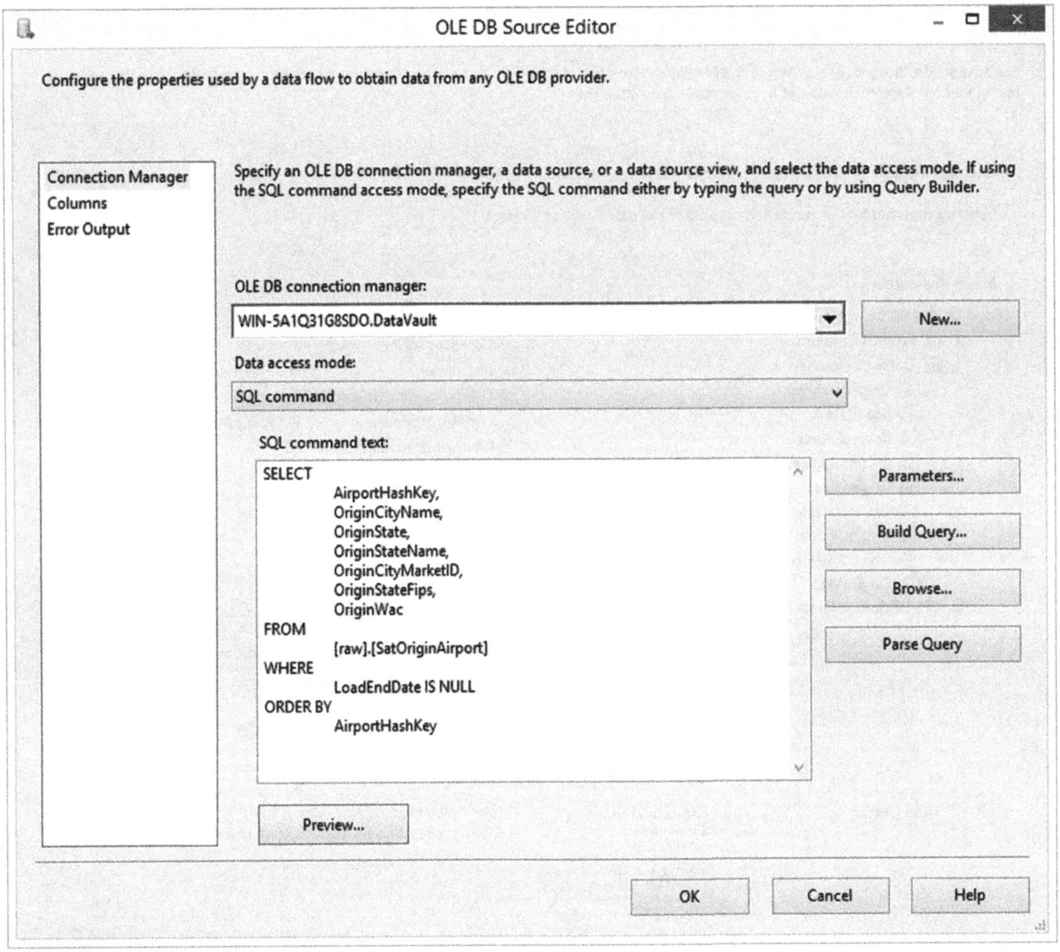

FIGURE 12.45

Source Editor for target data.

There should be two outputs configured in this dialog: one output for records that are new or changed and should be loaded into the target satellite and another output for the records that do not represent a change and should be ignored. The first is configured by adding another output to the list of outputs in the center of the dialog and setting the following condition:

```
REPLACENULL(OriginCityName,"") != REPLACENULL(TgtOriginCityName,"")
|| REPLACENULL(OriginState,"") != REPLACENULL(TgtOriginState,"")
|| REPLACENULL(OriginStateName,"") != REPLACENULL(TgtOriginStateName,"")
|| REPLACENULL((DT_I4)OriginCityMarketID,0) != REPLACENULL(TgtOriginCityMarketID,0)
|| REPLACENULL((DT_I2)OriginStateFips,0) != REPLACENULL(TgtOriginStateFips,0)
|| REPLACENULL((DT_I2)OriginWac,0) != REPLACENULL(TgtOriginWac,0)
```

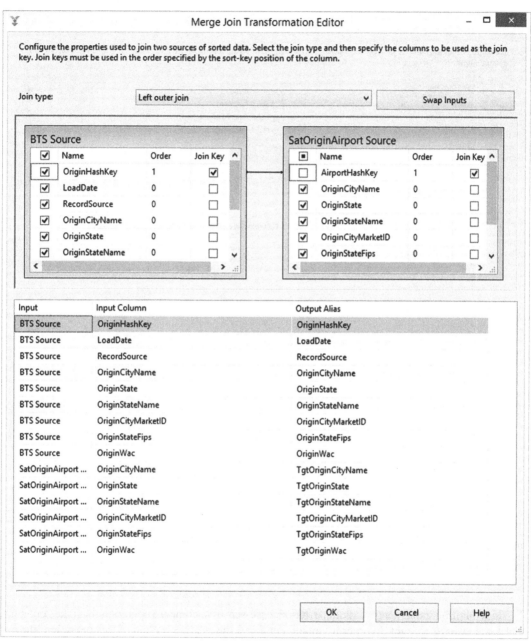

FIGURE 12.46

Merge join transformation editor.

FIGURE 12.47

Conditional split transformation editor.

This condition implements a columnar-based, case-sensitive compare operation that takes potential NULL values into account. In order to implement a case-insensitive version of this operation, the expression should be extended by **UPPER** functions on all columns from both the staging area and the target satellite. It is also important to take special care for columns with a float data type. If any of the fields in the payload are flow, then converting them to a string zero without a forced numeric (fixed decimal point) may actually fail the comparison for equality.

The default output is left as is and is responsible for dealing with the records that are already known to the target satellite. These records will be ignored.

Close the dialog and drag an OLE DB destination to the canvas. Connect the conditional split transformation to the destination component by dragging the data flow output of the conditional split transformation to the destination. The dialog in Figure 12.48 will be shown to let you select the desired output that should be written into the destination.

Select the **changed records** output from the conditional split transformation and the **OLE DB destination input** from the OLE DB destination component. Select the OK button to close the dialog. Open the OLE DB destination editor to set up the target (Figure 12.49).

On the first tab, select the target satellite table. Because NULL values should be written into the target, it is important to check the **keep null** option. To ensure highest performance, **table lock** should be turned on. Parallel loading of the same satellite table should not be required because the recommendation is to load only data from one source system into a satellite (separate data by source system). The other options should be adjusted; especially the **rows per batch** and the **maximum insert commit size** option. **Check constraints** should not be necessary as they often implement soft business rules, which should be implemented later.

Select mappings from the left to edit the column mappings from the columns in the data stream to the destination table columns (Figure 12.50).

Because the columns in the data flow and in the destination table use the same name, the mapping editor should have mapped most columns already. Make sure that each destination column except the **load end date** has a source column. The load end date is left NULL for now because end-dating is separated from this process and is covered in section 12.1.5. In most cases, the hash key needs to be mapped, because the name often differs in the source and the target table.

This completes the setup of the loading process for satellites. The complete data flow is presented in Figure 12.51.

The final loading process presented in the figure can be optimized by comparing the source data with the target data based on the hash diff value instead of each individual column value. In order to do so, the hash diff values have to be included in the data flow and used in the conditional split transformation instead of the individual column values. Therefore, a couple of modifications are required to the data flow presented before. In the following example, the previous data flow has been copied and adopted for another target satellite **SatDestAirport**.

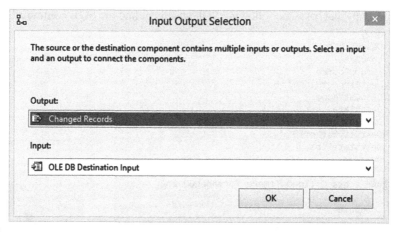

FIGURE 12.48

Input output selection dialog.

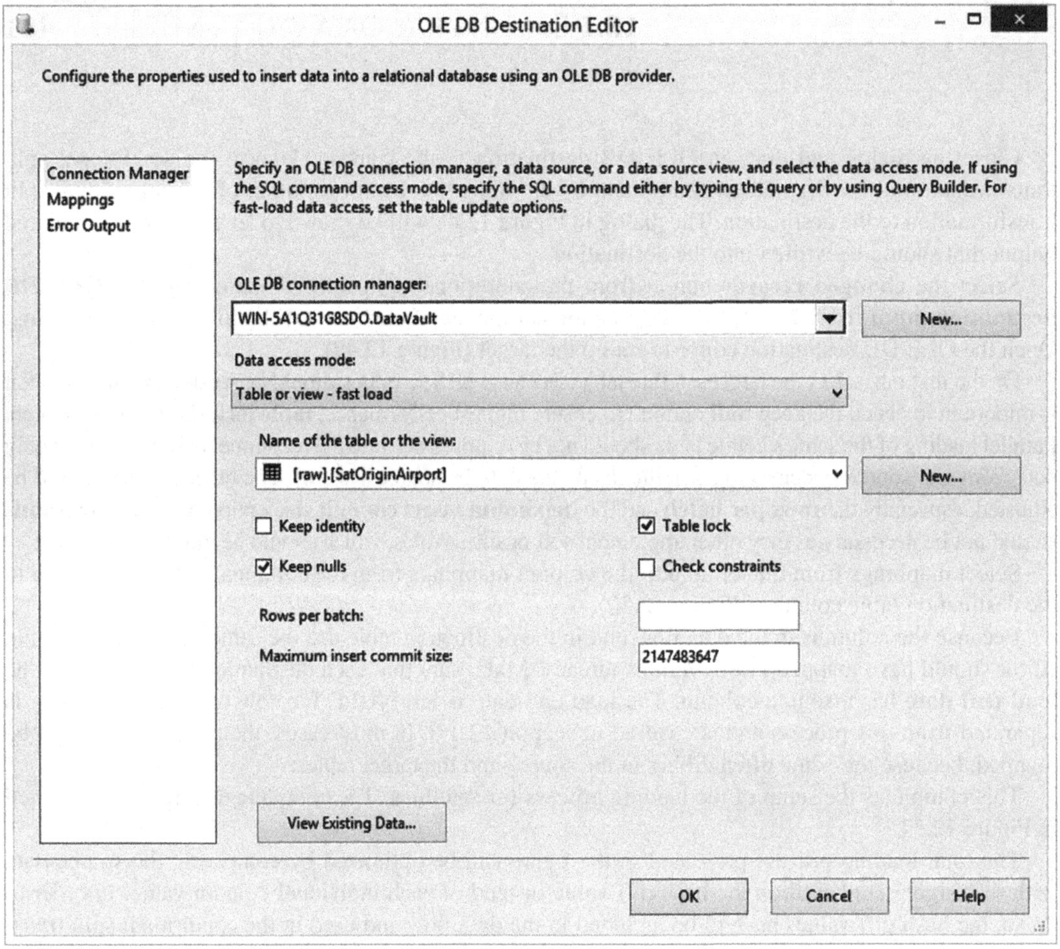

FIGURE 12.49

OLE DB destination editor.

Open the OLE DB source editor for the source table in the staging area (Figure 12.52).
In this dialog, copy and paste the following SQL statement into the **SQL command text** editor:

```
SELECT DISTINCT
        stg.DestHashKey,
        stg.LoadDate,
        stg.RecordSource,
        stg.DestAirportHashDiff,
        stg.DestCityName,
        stg.DestState,
        stg.DestStateName,
        stg.DestCityMarketID,
        stg.DestStateFips,
        stg.DestWac
FROM
        StageArea.bts.OnTimeOnTimePerformanceGD stg
WHERE
        stg.LoadDate = ?
ORDER BY
        stg.DestHashKey
```

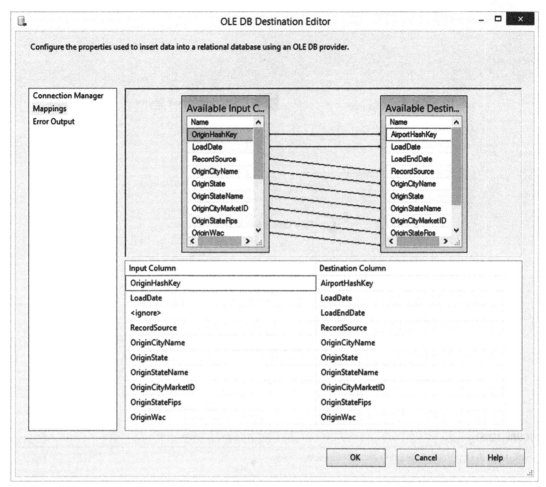

FIGURE 12.50

Mapping the columns from the data stream to the destination.

Make sure that the parameter is still bound to the **load date** variable previously created. Notice that the metadata of the output is out of sync when closing the dialog. Double-click the path in the data flow and select **delete unmapped input columns** to fix the issue.

Open the editor for the second source on the target satellite table (Figure 12.53).

Because the payload of the target satellite is not required for the delta checking, remove all descriptive columns from the SQL command text and add the **hash diff** column:

```
SELECT
        AirportHashKey,
        HashDiff
FROM
        [raw].[SatDestAirport]
WHERE
        LoadEndDate IS NULL
ORDER BY
        AirportHashKey
```

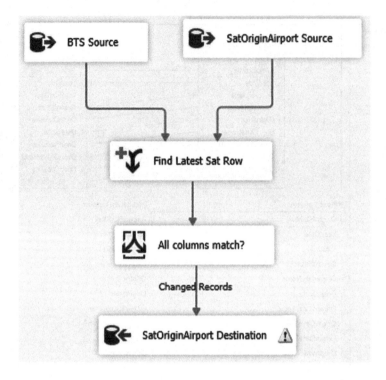

FIGURE 12.51

Satellite loading process based on column compare.

No other columns except the parent hash key and the hash diff values are required from the target. However, make sure that only active records are returned by limiting the result to records with a **load end date** of NULL.

After closing the dialog, fixing the metadata of the path in the data flow might be required for this source as well. Also make sure that both sources have **IsSorted** set to true for their output and the **SortKeyPosition** of the respective hash key column is set to 1.

The next task is to fix the merge join by using the merge join transformation editor, shown in Figure 12.54.

Make sure that the hash key from the staging area is mapped to the hash key in the target satellite table. In Figure 12.54, the **DestHashKey** is mapped to the **AirportHashKey**. In addition, select all columns from the staging area, because they contain the descriptive data that should be loaded into the target satellite. In order to check if any columns have changed, add the **hash diff** column from the target satellite to the data flow.

Close the dialog and open the editor of the **conditional split transformation** (Figure 12.55).

Replace the condition in the dialog shown in Figure 12.55 by the following expression:

ISNULL([HashDiff]) || ([DestAirportHashDiff]!=[HashDiff])

This expression only uses the hash diffs from the source and the target to perform the delta checking. It takes possible NULL values in the target hash diff into consideration to ensure that new records

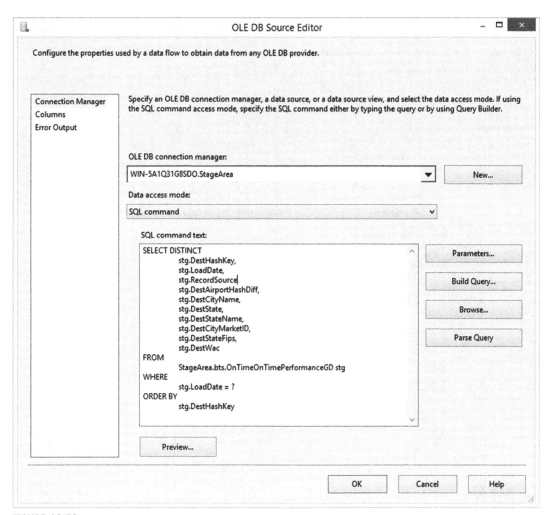

FIGURE 12.52

OLE DB source editor for destination airport staging data.

are loaded as well (they don't have a corresponding record in the target, thus their target hash diff is NULL).

Finally, the OLE DB destination has to be set up. Figure 12.56 shows the first page that sets up the table.

Change the name of the target to **SatDestAirport**. Make sure that keep nulls are enabled and switch to the mappings pane (Figure 12.57).

Make sure that all descriptive columns are mapped to the target and that the hash diff value from the source table in the staging area is mapped to the hash diff column of the target satellite. This is important to ensure that the hash diff is available when running this process another time.

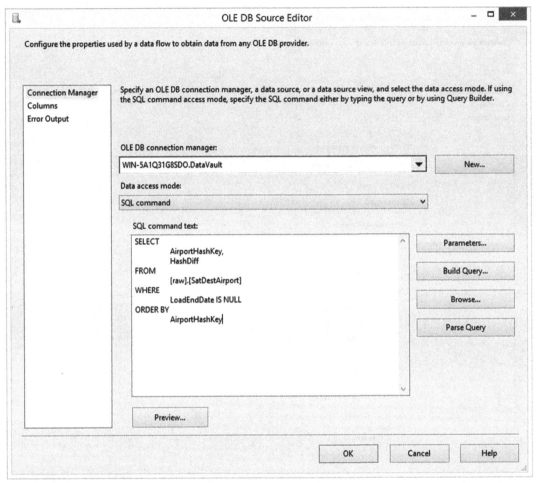

FIGURE 12.53

OLE DB source editor of the target satellite table.

The final data flow is presented in Figure 12.58.

In addition to the presented setup, a production-ready loading process would write erroneous data from the source into the error mart if it fails to load the data. In order to add the error mart to the data flows presented in this section, send error outputs to OLE DB destinations for the error mart as described in Chapter 10, Metadata Management.

12.1.5 END-DATING SATELLITES

The standard loading process of satellites is not complete yet. After the loading process for a satellite has been completed, there are multiple satellite entries active: two or more records have a load end date of NULL or 9999-12-31. This is invalid because there should be only one record active in a consistent

FIGURE 12.54

Merge join transformation editor for hash diff column compare.

Data Vault satellite (except for multi-active satellites). Therefore, an end-dating process is required after having loaded the data of one batch (one load date) from the staging table into the target satellite. The overall process is presented in Figure 12.59.

The first step in this process is to retrieve the data from the satellite table. Once the records have been retrieved, the records are sorted per group and per load date (descending) in the second step.

Within each group, the first record needs to be calculated (step 3) because this record should remain active. Therefore, the process sets the load end date to NULL for this record (or makes sure that this record keeps its NULL or future load end date). After that, the load end-dates of the remaining records

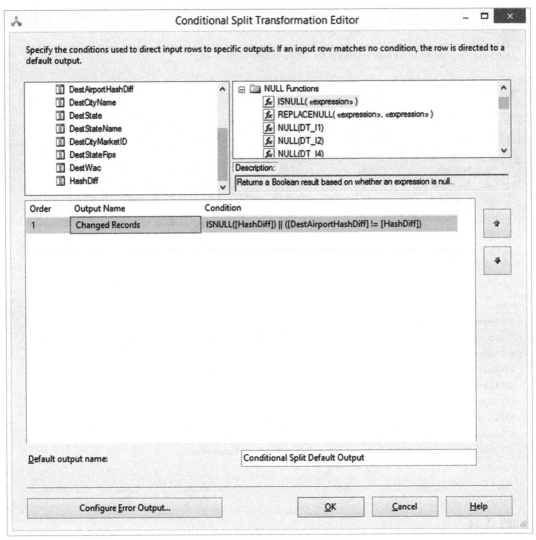

FIGURE 12.55

Conditional split transformation editor for delta checking based on hash diff.

are calculated for each group. This process is described next. Once all load end-dates are calculated, the target satellite is updated with the new load end-dates and the process completes.

Note that the sort operation in the second step of this process forces the use of the tempdb database in Microsoft SQL Server if the process is implemented in SQL Server. If implemented in SSIS, the sort operation will release the lock on the source component's connection of the satellite table.

The subprocess to calculate the load end-dates is shown in Figure 12.60.

In the first step, the incoming record set is reduced to those groups of data per parent hash key which have more than one active record per group. Active records are defined by records with a load end date

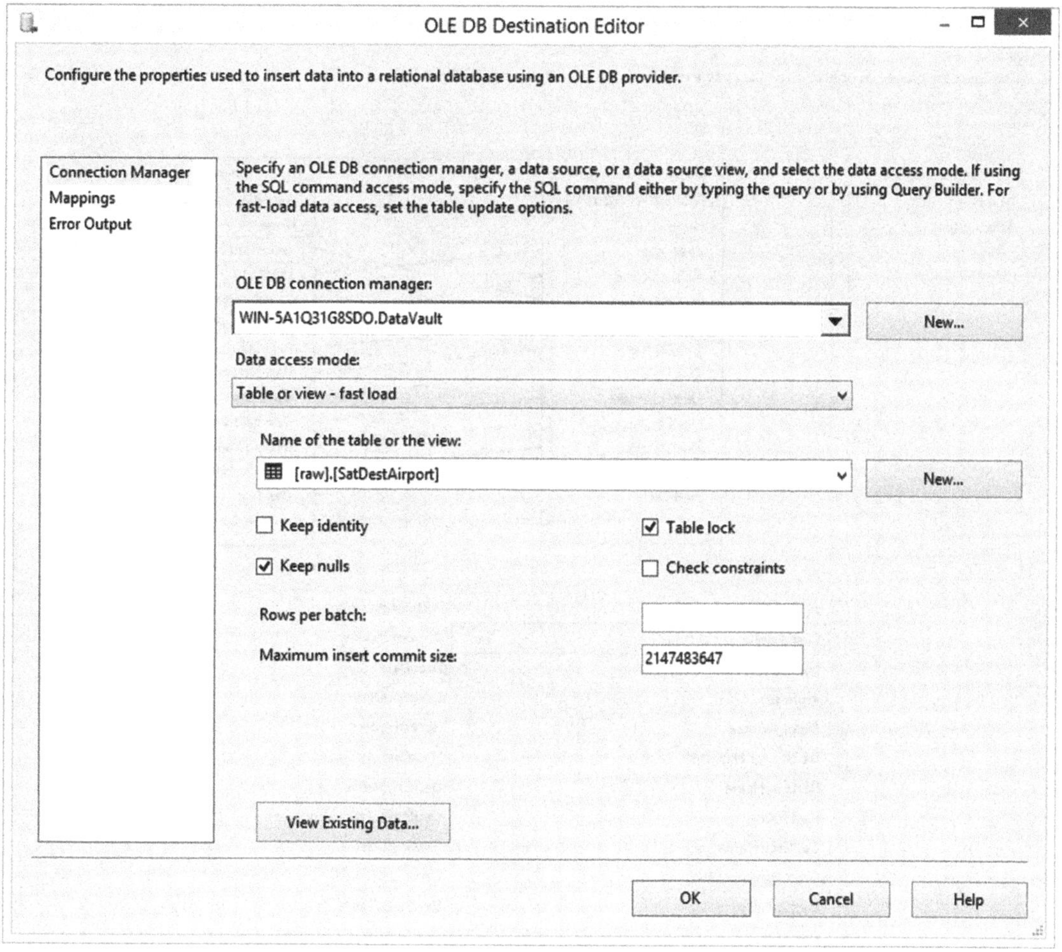

FIGURE 12.56

OLE DB destination editor for SatDestAirport.

of NULL or 9999-12-31 (the future date). All other records are not of interest for this process, because if there are not at least two active records per parent hash key, the single record has to remain open and, therefore, remains untouched.

After these records have been removed, each group is ordered by load date. This is achieved by ordering the whole data flow by hash key (to group all records belonging to one parent hash key together) and load date (descending). Ordering the load dates in a descending order is important because the process has to calculate "carry over" values for each record. This process is shown in Figure 12.61.

The first table on the left includes four parent hash keys. Only the data that belongs to the hash keys 2abcff… and 4444dd… are processed by this template because the other two hash keys don't have more than two active records in the satellite. For example, the data for the parent hash key 1bef79…

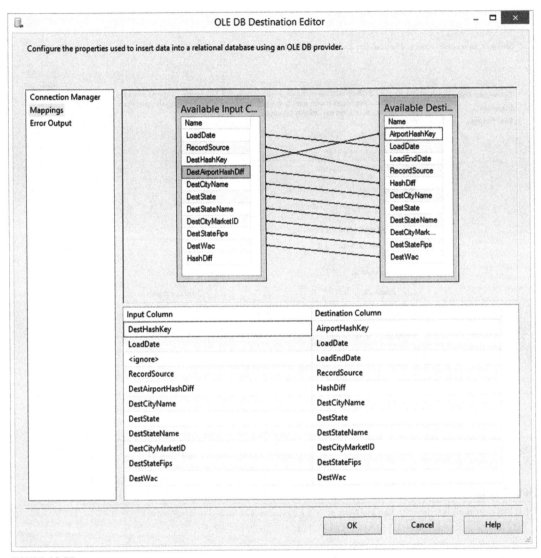

FIGURE 12.57

OLE DB destination editor for mapping the source columns to the target.

consists of one active record and one record already end-dated in the past. Once the data has been filtered out, the data is sorted by hash key and load end-date in the second step. The result is shown in the upper-right table.

Then, the "carry-over" value is calculated for each record within the group, except the first one (which should remain active). Each record except the first in the group should have a load end-date set to the load date of the next record in the group (ordered on a time-scale). Because of that, the load date of the newer record is copied over to the next older record, as shown in the lower-right table of Figure 12.61. Once all load end-dates have been set, the data is sent as updates to the target satellite.

The following T-SQL statement can be used to perform the end-dating process:

```
UPDATE SatPreferredDish SET
       LoadEndDate = (
            SELECT
                  DATEADD(ss,-1,MIN(z.LoadDate))
            FROM
                  SatPreferredDish z
            WHERE
                  z.PassengerHashKey = a.PassengerHashKey
            AND
                  z.LoadDate > a.LoadDate
       )
FROM
       SatPreferredDish a
WHERE
       LoadEndDate IS NULL AND PassengerHashKey = ?
```

This statement end-dates the satellite **SatPreferredDish**. It assumes open satellite entries (records which are not end-dated yet) to be are indicated by a NULL **LoadEndDate**. The sub-query in the statement retrieves the **LoadDate** of the next entry for each **PassengerHashKey**. By doing so, it implements the process as outlined in Figure 12.61.

The previous statement should be executed for each parent hash key individually, in order to ensure that it scales to higher amounts of data. While the statement is not a fast approach, the statement scales linearly on the number of parent hash keys. If the load end-dates of all hash keys are updated at once, in a single transaction, the resource requirements could become too high and the database server may start to swap data out of memory to disk in order to deal with the amounts of data. Depending on the database management system used, other approaches than the one presented in the previous statement are more feasible as well.

The process of end-dating the satellite data has been separated from the loading process in order to deal with each problem separately. This simplifies the loading process and ensures that the performance remains high. Another important issue is that the statement deals with all the whole group of data per parent hash key at once, in order to make sure that previously loaded data becomes end-dated as well. This is important because a previous loading process might have been aborted and may left the satellite data in an inconsistent state. Therefore, this separation becomes part of the restartability characteristics of the Data Vault 2.0 loading patterns.

12.1.6 SEPARATE NEW FROM CHANGED ROWS

The performance of the templates shown in the previous section relied on the separation of duties to some extent. For example, several operations have already been conducted in the staging area, such as hashing. Other operations are performed once the data have been loaded, such as setting the load end-date but also performing any recalculations.

The performance of the above templates can be improved further by more separation. This relies on the fact that the column comparisons are only required for parent hash keys that are already known to the satellite, i.e., potential updates to the same hash key. If the source system contains a record that describes a business key or business key relationship that is already known to the data warehouse, the column comparison is used to find out if the source system has changed between the loads.

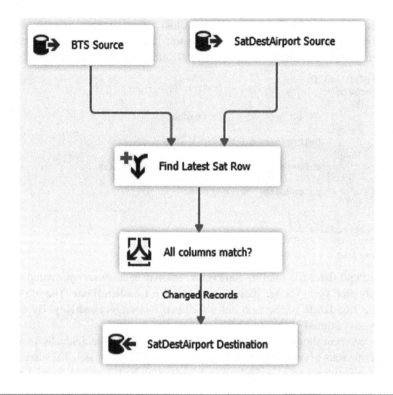

FIGURE 12.58

Complete data flow for loading satellites using hash diffs.

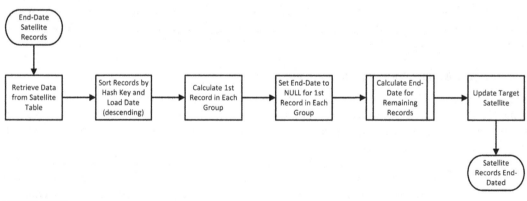

FIGURE 12.59

Template for setting the load end-date in satellite rows.

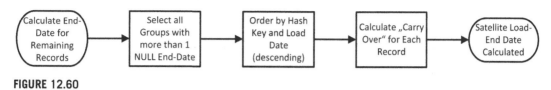

FIGURE 12.60

Calculate load end-date for remaining records subprocess.

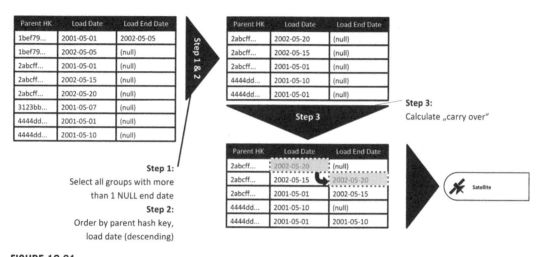

FIGURE 12.61

Calculate load end-date walkthrough.

But if the source system described a business key that is unknown to the satellite, the column comparison is not required: there will be no record available in the target that could be used in the update detection process. The new record has to be loaded into the target satellite in any case.

The previous templates always perform the column comparison. If SQL is used to implement the template, the compare might require an outer join because changed rows are detected using direct index match. But even if ETL is used, the column comparison is not required and reduces performance of the overall load. Therefore, it is possible to improve the performance of the satellite loads by separating new and changed records. This is especially useful if the number of new records in the source system outweighs the number of changed records. The programming logic that is required to detect changes should not be applied to new records because it reduces the performance of the loading pattern.

The first resulting template, which loads changed rows from the staging table only, remains mostly unchanged to the default satellite loading template in section 12.1.4 (Figure 12.62).

The only difference is in the first step because it only loads changed records from the staging tables. But implementing this step requires the identification of records that have potentially changed directly in the staging area. However, this is easy to do if the staging area is on the same infrastructure as the rest of the data warehouse. In this case, it is possible to do the source query on the staging area

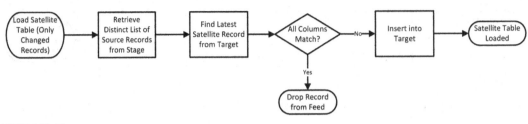

FIGURE 12.62

Template for loading only changed records into satellite tables.

and perform a look-ahead into the target to identify which hash keys are already known to the data warehouse:

```
SELECT DISTINCT
        stg.OriginHashKey,
        stg.LoadDate,
        NULL,
        stg.RecordSource,
        stg.OriginCityName,
        stg.OriginState,
        stg.OriginStateName,
        stg.OriginCityMarketID,
        stg.OriginStateFips,
        stg.OriginWac
FROM
        StageArea.bts.OnTimeOnTimePerformanceGD stg
INNER JOIN
        DataVault.[raw].SatOriginAirport sat
        ON (stg.OriginHashKey = sat.AirportHashKey AND sat.LoadEndDate IS NULL)
WHERE
        (
        (CASE WHEN (stg.OriginCityName IS NULL AND sat.OriginCityName IS NULL
            OR stg.OriginCityName = sat.OriginCityName)
            THEN 1 ELSE 0 END) = 0
        OR (CASE WHEN (stg.OriginState IS NULL AND sat.OriginState IS NULL
            OR stg.OriginState = sat.OriginState)
            THEN 1 ELSE 0 END) = 0
        OR (CASE WHEN (stg.OriginStateName IS NULL AND sat.OriginStateName IS NULL
            OR stg.OriginStateName = sat.OriginStateName)
            THEN 1 ELSE 0 END) = 0
        OR (CASE WHEN (stg.OriginCityMarketID IS NULL AND sat.OriginCityMarketID IS NULL
            OR stg.OriginCityMarketID = sat.OriginCityMarketID)
            THEN 1 ELSE 0 END) = 0
        OR (CASE WHEN (stg.OriginStateFips IS NULL AND sat.OriginStateFips IS NULL
            OR stg.OriginStateFips = sat.OriginStateFips)
            THEN 1 ELSE 0 END) = 0
        OR (CASE WHEN (stg.OriginWac IS NULL AND sat.OriginWac IS NULL
            OR stg.OriginWac = sat.OriginWac)
            THEN 1 ELSE 0 END) = 0
        )
        AND stg.LoadDate = '2011-01-22 00:00:00.000'
```

This statement shows that the staging area is not only used to reduce the workload on the source systems, but it can also be used to perform intermediate tasks that improve the performance of the data warehouse loading processes. And it shows the additional value of having calculated the hash keys in the staging area: it does not only improve the reusability of the hash computations, but can also be used to improve the loading processes even further (as described in this section).

In order to load the new records only, the loading template in Figure 12.62 can be greatly simplified because no change detection is required by the loading process anymore (Figure 12.63).

Not only is the column compare removed, but also the retrieval of the latest record from the target satellite table. New records are just loaded into the target. This template also requires that the source query on the staging area provides only new records with hash keys unknown to the target satellite:

```sql
SELECT DISTINCT
        stg.OriginHashKey,
        stg.LoadDate,
        NULL,
        stg.RecordSource,
        stg.OriginCityName,
        stg.OriginState,
        stg.OriginStateName,
        stg.OriginCityMarketID,
        stg.OriginStateFips,
        stg.OriginWac
FROM
        StageArea.bts.OnTimeOnTimePerformanceGD stg
LEFT OUTER JOIN
        DataVault.[raw].SatOriginAirport sat
        ON (stg.OriginHashKey = sat.AirportHashKey AND sat.LoadEndDate IS NULL)
WHERE
        (
        (CASE WHEN (stg.OriginCityName IS NULL AND sat.OriginCityName IS NULL
                OR stg.OriginCityName = sat.OriginCityName)
                THEN 1 ELSE 0 END) = 0
        OR (CASE WHEN (stg.OriginState IS NULL AND sat.OriginState IS NULL
                OR stg.OriginState = sat.OriginState)
                THEN 1 ELSE 0 END) = 0
        OR (CASE WHEN (stg.OriginStateName IS NULL AND sat.OriginStateName IS NULL
                OR stg.OriginStateName = sat.OriginStateName)
                THEN 1 ELSE 0 END) = 0
        OR (CASE WHEN (stg.OriginCityMarketID IS NULL AND sat.OriginCityMarketID IS NULL
                OR stg.OriginCityMarketID = sat.OriginCityMarketID)
                THEN 1 ELSE 0 END) = 0
        OR (CASE WHEN (stg.OriginStateFips IS NULL AND sat.OriginStateFips IS NULL
                OR stg.OriginStateFips = sat.OriginStateFips)
                THEN 1 ELSE 0 END) = 0
        OR (CASE WHEN (stg.OriginWac IS NULL AND sat.OriginWac IS NULL
                OR stg.OriginWac = sat.OriginWac)
                THEN 1 ELSE 0 END) = 0
        )
        AND sat.AirportHashKey IS NULL --new records only
        AND stg.LoadDate = '2011-01-22 00:00:00.000'
```

Both processes for new and changed records can run in parallel, because they operate on different sets of input data which are loaded into nonoverlapping primary keys of the target table (again, because the processed hash keys of each ETL process are different).

FIGURE 12.63

Template for loading only new records into satellite tables.

12.1.7 NO-HISTORY SATELLITES

The approach described in the previous section can also be used to load nonhistorized satellites. The reason is that the no-history satellite does not track changes in the source system. Instead, there are only new records that need to be loaded into the target table. Because of that, the same template as presented in Figure 12.63 can be used for loading satellites with no history.

The following DDL statement creates a no-history satellite in the Raw Data Vault:

```
CREATE TABLE [raw].[TSatFlight](
        [FlightHashKey] [char](32) NOT NULL,
        [LoadDate] [datetime2](7) NOT NULL,
        [RecordSource] [nvarchar](50) NOT NULL,
        [Year] [smallint] NULL,
        [Quarter] [smallint] NULL,
        [Month] [smallint] NULL,
        [DayOfMonth] [smallint] NULL,
        [DayOfWeek] [smallint] NULL,
        [CRSDepTime] [smallint] NULL,
        [DepTime] [smallint] NULL,
        [DepDelay] [smallint] NULL,
        [DepDelayMinutes] [smallint] NULL,
        [DepDel15] [bit] NULL,
        [DepartureDelayGroups] [smallint] NULL,
        [DepTimeBlk] [nvarchar](9) NULL,
        [TaxiOut] [smallint] NULL,
        [WheelsOff] [smallint] NULL,
        [WheelsOn] [smallint] NULL,
        [TaxiIn] [smallint] NULL,
        [CRSArrTime] [smallint] NULL,
        [ArrTime] [smallint] NULL,
        [ArrDelay] [smallint] NULL,
        [ArrDelayMinutes] [smallint] NULL,
        [ArrDel15] [bit] NULL,
        [ArrivalDelayGroups] [smallint] NULL,
        [ArrTimeBlk] [nvarchar](9) NULL,
        [Cancelled] [bit] NULL,
        [CancellationCode] [nvarchar](10) NULL,
        [Diverted] [bit] NULL,
        [CRSElapsedTime] [smallint] NULL,
        [ActualElapsedTime] [smallint] NULL,
        [AirTime] [smallint] NULL,
        [Flights] [smallint] NULL,
        [Distance] [int] NULL,
        [DistanceGroup] [int] NULL,
        [CarrierDelay] [smallint] NULL,
        [WeatherDelay] [smallint] NULL,
        [NASDelay] [smallint] NULL,
        [SecurityDelay] [smallint] NULL,
```

```
        [LateAircraftDelay] [smallint] NULL,
        [FirstDepTime] [smallint] NULL,
        [TotalAddGTime] [smallint] NULL,
        [LongestAddGTime] [smallint] NULL,
 CONSTRAINT [PK_TSatFlight] PRIMARY KEY NONCLUSTERED
(
        [FlightHashKey] ASC,
        [LoadDate] ASC
) ON [INDEX]
) ON [DATA]
```

There is no **load end date** in the satellite structure because changes are not tracked. For the same reason, the **load date** has been degraded to technical field without any importance for the model. The primary application is to be used during debugging: it exists in order to understand when data was loaded into the target. However, there is a secondary application to it: when incrementally loading subsequent information marts, it is helpful to load only new records into the information mart layer. This is why the load date was included in the primary key constraint: by doing so, the field is used for indexing, which improves the load performance of the information mart.

Before the data can be loaded to the information mart, which is described in Chapter 14, the data has to be loaded from the staging area into the no-history satellite. The following statement can be used for this purpose:

```
INSERT INTO DataVault.[raw].TSatFlight (
        [FlightHashKey]
       ,[LoadDate]
       ,[RecordSource]
       ,[Year]
       ,[Quarter]
       ,[Month]
       ,[DayOfMonth]
       ,[DayOfWeek]
       ,[CRSDepTime]
       ,[DepTime]
       ,[DepDelay]
       ,[DepDelayMinutes]
       ,[DepDel15]
       ,[DepartureDelayGroups]
       ,[DepTimeBlk]
       ,[TaxiOut]
       ,[WheelsOff]
       ,[WheelsOn]
       ,[TaxiIn]
       ,[CRSArrTime]
       ,[ArrTime]
       ,[ArrDelay]
       ,[ArrDelayMinutes]
       ,[ArrDel15]
       ,[ArrivalDelayGroups]
       ,[ArrTimeBlk]
       ,[Cancelled]
       ,[CancellationCode]
       ,[Diverted]
       ,[CRSElapsedTime]
       ,[ActualElapsedTime]
```

```
    ,[AirTime]
    ,[Flights]
    ,[Distance]
    ,[DistanceGroup]
    ,[CarrierDelay]
    ,[WeatherDelay]
    ,[NASDelay]
    ,[SecurityDelay]
    ,[LateAircraftDelay]
    ,[FirstDepTime]
    ,[TotalAddGTime]
    ,[LongestAddGTime]
    )
SELECT
        stg.[FlightHashKey]
        ,stg.[LoadDate]
        ,stg.[RecordSource]
        ,stg.[Year]
        ,stg.[Quarter]
        ,stg.[Month]
        ,stg.[DayOfMonth]
        ,stg.[DayOfWeek]
        ,stg.[CRSDepTime]
        ,stg.[DepTime]
        ,stg.[DepDelay]
        ,stg.[DepDelayMinutes]
        ,stg.[DepDel15]
        ,stg.[DepartureDelayGroups]
        ,stg.[DepTimeBlk]
        ,stg.[TaxiOut]
        ,stg.[WheelsOff]
        ,stg.[WheelsOn]
        ,stg.[TaxiIn]
        ,stg.[CRSArrTime]
        ,stg.[ArrTime]
        ,stg.[ArrDelay]
        ,stg.[ArrDelayMinutes]
        ,stg.[ArrDel15]
        ,stg.[ArrivalDelayGroups]
        ,stg.[ArrTimeBlk]
        ,stg.[Cancelled]
        ,stg.[CancellationCode]
        ,stg.[Diverted]
        ,stg.[CRSElapsedTime]
        ,stg.[ActualElapsedTime]
        ,stg.[AirTime]
        ,stg.[Flights]
        ,stg.[Distance]
        ,stg.[DistanceGroup]
        ,stg.[CarrierDelay]
        ,stg.[WeatherDelay]
        ,stg.[NASDelay]
        ,stg.[SecurityDelay]
        ,stg.[LateAircraftDelay]
        ,stg.[FirstDepTime]
        ,stg.[TotalAddGTime]
        ,stg.[LongestAddGTime]
```

```
FROM
        StageArea.bts.OnTimeOnTimePerformanceGD stg
LEFT OUTER JOIN
        DataVault.[raw].TSatFlight sat ON (stg.FlightHashKey = sat.FlightHashKey)
WHERE
        sat.FlightHashKey IS NULL
```

This statement implements a simple copy process. Restartability is guaranteed by adding a LEFT OUTER JOIN that checks if the hash key of the parent no-history link is already in the target satellite. If this is the case, the record from the staging area is ignored, otherwise loaded. The load date is not required for this join, because there should only be one record per parent hash key in the target satellite.

12.1.8 **SOFT-DELETING DATA IN HUBS AND LINKS**

The processes presented in sections 12.1.1 and 12.1.2 load business keys or relationships between business keys into the data warehouse that have been inserted into the operational source system since the last batch. However, business keys are not only inserted into the data warehouse; they are also changed or deleted. Changing business keys is more of a business problem and requires special care up to the extent of asking the question whether the business key that is loaded into the hub is actually the right business key. Review the requirements for business keys in Chapter 4.

However, deleting keys is a common and valid operation and happens frequently. A product is removed from the catalog and not offered anymore, users lose access and their user account is removed from the operational system, etc. The same applies for relationships: employees quit and hire on with a new organization, products are moved into another category, and so on. In all these cases, the business demands that these changes be loaded into the data warehouse to be available for analysis. But the data warehouse doesn't only reflect the current state of the data, but also the complete, nonvolatile history of the business keys, their relationships and all the descriptive data. For this reason, historic data usually cannot be deleted from the data warehouse.

Hubs and links play a vital role in the Data Vault 2.0 model to integrate the data of the data warehouse. If business keys are deleted from hubs or business key relationships are deleted from links, this integration breaks because descriptive data is stored in dependent satellites and references these business keys or relationships. Therefore, deleting records from hubs or links is not an option if the model is to remain intact.

The same applies to end-dating hubs and links. This approach would require a **load end date** in hub and link tables and could be used to end the employment of an employee with a specific company, for example. However, this approach introduces another problem (among others): what if the employee realizes that the new company was a bad choice and returns to the old organization? The HR people in the organization don't care that hiring back the employee would break the Data Vault model due to duplicate keys in link tables.

The solution is to use effectivity satellites, introduced in Chapter 5, Intermediate Data Vault Modeling, to model such effectivity dates. The hub only provides information as to which business keys ever existed in the source systems and the link table provides the information about all relationships that ever existed. The corresponding effectivity satellite on the table provides the information about the effectivity that is the start and the end date of the business key existence or relationship validity.

Actually deleting data from the data warehouse is only performed when legal or privacy requirements have to be met, for example in a data destruction strategy.

12.1.8.1 T-SQL Example

The following DDL creates an effectivity satellite which is used to track the validity of an airline ID:

```
CREATE TABLE [raw].[SatAirlineIDEffectivity](
        [AirlineIDHashKey] [char](32) NOT NULL,
        [LoadDate] [datetime2](7) NOT NULL,
        [LoadEndDate] [datetime2](7) NULL,
        [RecordSource] [nvarchar](50) NOT NULL,
        [Year Start] int NOT NULL,
        [Year End] int NOT NULL,
        [ValidFrom] [datetime2](7) NOT NULL,
        [ValidTo] [datetime2](7) NULL,
 CONSTRAINT [PK_SatAirlineIDEffectivity] PRIMARY KEY NONCLUSTERED
(
        [AirlineIDHashKey] ASC,
        [LoadDate] ASC
) ON [INDEX]
) ON [DATA]
```

Because the satellite is dependent on the **HubAirLineID**, it includes the hash key from its parent hub and the **load date** of the record in the primary key. In addition, the table definition includes a **load end date** and the **record source** as technical fields. By doing so, it follows the definition of a standard Data Vault 2.0 satellite and treats the dates in the payload (**ValidFrom** and **ValidTo**) as ordinary descriptive fields, which can be changed by the source system at any time. This is called bi-temporal modeling [1].

The other two fields in the payload of the satellite, year start and year end, are the actual raw data fields from the source table. They have been used to calculate the **ValidFrom** and **ValidTo** fields in the loading statement of the effectivity satellite:

```
INSERT INTO DataVault.[raw].SatAirlineIDEffectivity (
        AirlineIDHashKey,
        LoadDate,
        LoadEndDate,
        RecordSource,
        [Year Start],
        [Year End],
        ValidFrom,
        ValidTo
)
SELECT DISTINCT
        stg.AirlineIDHashKey,
        stg.LoadDate,
        NULL,
        stg.RecordSource,
        stg.[Year Start],
        stg.[Year End],
        DATEFROMPARTS(stg.[Year Start], 1, 1),
        DATEFROMPARTS(stg.[Year End], 12, 31)
FROM
        StageArea.my.CarrierHistory stg
LEFT OUTER JOIN
        DataVault.[raw].SatAirlineIDEffectivity sat
        ON (stg.AirlineIDHashKey = sat.AirlineIDHashKey AND sat.LoadEndDate IS NULL)
WHERE
        ISNULL(stg.[Year Start], 0) != ISNULL(sat.[Year Start], 0)
        AND ISNULL(stg.[Year End], 9999) != ISNULL(sat.[Year End], 9999)
```

This statement aligns the data type of the integer-based year data in the source system to the required timestamp by applying the **DATEFROMPARTS** function on both **year start** and **year end** columns. Because this is a data type alignment only without recalculating the value, it counts as a hard rule and can be applied when loading the Raw Data Vault. However, in order to be able to trace errors, the original values are stored along with the aligned values, as well. Other recalculations should be avoided to include in the loading procedures of the Raw Data Vault and moved into the Business Vault or the loading processes of the Information Marts. If the source data changes, the satellite captures this change just as it does any other descriptive data.

Note that the above example relies on a table that has been artificially created and is based on the carrier history entity in the example MDS entity on the companion Web site. The MDS table contains multiple entries per carrier, which was simplified for demonstration purposes. The resulting table was placed in a custom schema.

12.1.9 DEALING WITH MISSING DATA

The problem with deleted business keys and relationships is that it is not always possible to detect actual deletes properly: under some circumstances, the source feed might not provide a business key that is actually in the source system. There are various reasons why a business key or other data is missing from the source:

- **Source system not in scope:** the source system simply isn't being loaded to the data warehouse, for example when the source system did not deliver its exported source files to the data warehouse (due to a different schedule, for example).
- **Technical error:** in other cases the data exists in the source system, but is not exported, for technical reasons. The export could fail because there is no disk space left on the target disk for the export.
- **Source filter:** a source filter could have prevented the export of the data into the source file, even though the data is in the source system. When using delta loads, for example, only new data is exported into the file. Data that hasn't changed at all is not being exported in such settings.
- **ETL loading error:** sometimes, data is not loaded into the staging area, even if the data is in the source files. This could be due to implementation errors in the ETL loading routines.

For these reasons, it is not guaranteed that a business key has been deleted from the source system just because it is not loaded into the stage area. However, we'd like to know which records have been actually deleted in order to mark them as such (so called "soft deletes") in the data warehouse. Typically, this happens in effectivity satellites on hubs and links, as described in the previous section. In order to do so, we need to distinguish between data that has been left out of the source file for accidental reasons or by user action: that is, the record has been actually deleted from the source system.

In the best case, the source system provides an audit trail that tells the data warehouse what has happened to the source data between loads. This is the case when change data capture (CDC) has been activated in the source system and the CDC data is provided to the data warehouse as an audit trail. In such a case, the approach as outlined in section 12.1.8 can be used to load effectivity satellites from these sources.

However, in many cases, such an audit trail is not provided by the source system. Instead, a deleted record just disappears from the source data. It is not possible to distinguish between data that has been not provided by the source system and truly deleted data.

In order to solve this issue, the naïve approach is to retrieve all keys from the hub table and check if the hub keys are provided by the staging area (Figure 12.64).

This assumes that the staging area provides a full load and not a delta load of the incoming data. If this is the case, the business key still exists in the source system and it is clear that it hasn't been deleted. On the other hand, if the staging area doesn't provide the key, it could be assumed that the key doesn't exist in the source system anymore and therefore marked as deleted in the accompanying effectivity satellite.

The problem with this approach is that it requires many lookups, especially if the hub table contains a lot of business keys. For each key, the lookup into the source table has to be executed. In order to detect a deleted business key in hubs or deleted relationship in links, the process has to find the data that meets the following criteria:

1. The business key from the hub (or the relationship from the link) is not available in the source
2. The business key is not already soft-deleted in the target hub or link.

However, because of the full-scan on the target table, this process becomes unsustainable when the data grows. Instead of checking to see whether each hub key is still in the source table, the process should avoid the full-scan on the target table.

There is no solution to distinguish the missing and deleted business keys with 100% security. The best approach is to make an educated guess. The **last seen date** helps to make such a guess. This column is added to hubs (and links) where needed and used to build an inverted index tree. It is used only when CDC or an audit trail is not available from the source system (Figure 12.65).

The last seen date is used to track when the business key stopped appearing on the feed to the data warehouse. By using this system-driven attribute, it is possible to minimize the data set that is required to scan. This approach works only on hubs and links. It is not intended to be used with satellite tables.

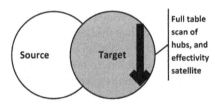

FIGURE 12.64

Full table scan required to detect deletes in the source system.

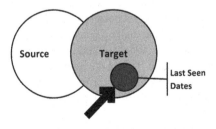

FIGURE 12.65

Introducing the last seen date in the loading process.

12.1.9.1 Data Aging

The last seen date helps to manage or reduce the table scan to a maintainable and viable set by introducing data aging (Figure 12.66).

There are four data sources in Figure 12.66: flights, passengers, carriers, and airports. No source provides an audit trail and might have missing data. To simplify the problem, each source provides only one business key in this example. In the first week, the flight system, the carriers and the airports system provide "their" business key to the data warehouse. In the second week, flights and airports keep providing the key, but the carrier key is gone. Instead, the passenger key is provided. In the third week, only the carrier key is provided, and all others are missing. In week four, only the airport key is delivered to the data warehouse.

The data warehouse needs to find out which of the keys have been deleted and disappeared from further loads and which business keys are only missing from some loads. The carrier and airport keys are such examples, but also the passenger key that will appear in week five again. The flight key, on the other hand, seems to be deleted, because it doesn't appear anymore. However, what if it appears in week eight?

The answer to this question cannot be given from the data warehouse team. Instead, the business has to answer this question. For each key, there might be different requirements. For example, the carrier key might be considered as deleted if it doesn't appear for three weeks. This is due to the fact that the source system is relatively unreliable delivering the data to the data warehouse. On the other hand, the flights system is very reliable and whenever a key has not been delivered in a load, it can be considered as being deleted from the source. It is also important if the source data is provided in full loads or delta loads. However, the same logic can be applied to delta loads: if a delta does not provide any data for a business key for several weeks, it can be assumed that the business key has been deleted (Figure 12.67).

In this figure, the business stated that flight numbers, which did not appear for three weeks, should be marked as deleted in the data warehouse in week 5. Such rules are only applied if the business decides to do so. Each key and each source system requires its own definition for data aging. The definition for each one should be provided by the business user and put into writing in the service level agreement between the data warehouse team and the business user.

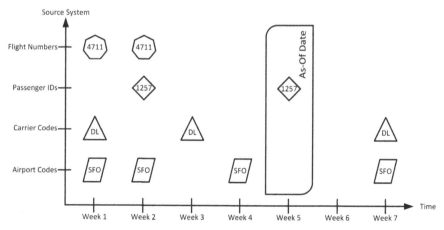

FIGURE 12.66

Data aging.

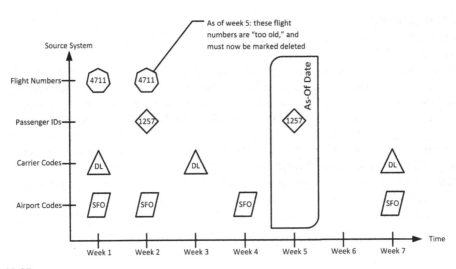

FIGURE 12.67

Mark business keys deleted.

If the business wants to avoid this discussion or cannot make a statement, the only alternative is to provide an audit trail to the data warehouse in order to detect deletes.

Using a load end represents a pragmatic approach to detect deltas on large data sets. However, it is a form of soft rule and therefore this approach violates the general recommendation that soft business rules should not be considered when loading the Raw Data Vault. If this should be avoided, status-tracking satellites could be used. They have been described in Chapter 5 and increase the performance by changing the update into an insert statement.

12.1.9.2 T-SQL Example

The last seen date is added to the hub structure as shown in the following DDL statement:

```
CREATE TABLE [raw].[HubFlightNum](
        [FlightNumHashKey] [char](32) NOT NULL,
        [LoadDate] [datetime2](7) NOT NULL,
        [RecordSource] [nvarchar](50) NOT NULL,
        [LastSeenDate] [datetime2](7) NOT NULL,
        [Carrier] [nvarchar](2) NULL,
        [FlightNum] [smallint] NULL,
 CONSTRAINT [PK_HubFlightNum] PRIMARY KEY NONCLUSTERED
(
        [FlightNumHashKey] ASC
) ON [INDEX],
 CONSTRAINT [UK_HubFlightNum] UNIQUE NONCLUSTERED
(
        [Carrier] ASC,
        [FlightNum] ASC
) ON [INDEX]
) ON [DATA]
```

The **last seen date** has been added to the system-generated attributes of the hub table. Other than that, the table follows the DDL for hubs, presented in section 12.1.1. In some cases, it might be recommended to create an index on the last seen date (first element of the index) and the hash key (second element of the index) to increase the performance of the table. This depends on the volume of data and if any partitioning schemes are used.

The following statement inserts new keys into the target hub:

```
INSERT INTO DataVault.[raw].HubFlightNum (
        FlightNumHashKey, LoadDate, RecordSource, LastSeenDate, Carrier, FlightNum
)
SELECT DISTINCT
        FlightNumHashKey, LoadDate, RecordSource, LoadDate, Carrier, FlightNum
FROM
        StageArea.bts.OnTimeOnTimePerformanceGD s
WHERE
        NOT EXISTS (SELECT
                        1
                FROM
                        DataVault.[raw].HubFlightNum h
                WHERE
                        s.Carrier = h.Carrier
                        AND s.FlightNum = h.FlightNum
                )
        AND LoadDate = '2003-10-01 00:00:00.000'
```

The last seen date for new keys, which are loaded to the hub, is set to the current load date. The WHERE clause is more complex than the statement for loading hubs presented in section 12.1.1, because of the composite business key.

After executing the previous statement, the following statement is executed in order to update the last seen date for those records that are already in the hub and are provided in the staging table:

```
UPDATE DataVault.[raw].HubFlightNum SET
        LastSeenDate = stg.LoadDate
FROM
        DataVault.[raw].HubFlightNum hub
INNER JOIN
        StageArea.bts.OnTimeOnTimePerformanceGD stg
ON
        stg.Carrier = hub.Carrier AND stg.FlightNum = hub.FlightNum
        AND hub.LastSeenDate < stg.LoadDate
WHERE
        stg.LoadDate = '2003-10-01 00:00:00.000'
```

This statement updates all records that have a last seen date that is older than the current load date (the load date currently loaded into the data warehouse). This is to reduce the number of updates on the target table.

Updating the last seen date is a separate process that doesn't affect the process that inserts new business keys into the target hub (which follows the standard process outlined in section 12.1.1).

12.2 LOADING REFERENCE TABLES

The purpose of reference tables is not only to simplify the Raw Data Vault 2.0 model but also the processes that deal with loading the data or using the data later on. The next sections describe multiple approaches to load reference data from the staging area into reference tables in the Raw Data Vault.

12.2.1 NO-HISTORY REFERENCE TABLES

If reference data should be loaded without taking care of the history, the loading process can be drastically simplified by using SQL views to create virtual reference tables. A similar approach was described in Chapter 11, Data Extraction, when staging master data from Microsoft Master Data Services (MDS) or any other master data management solution that is under control of the data warehouse team and primarily used for analytical master data. This approach can be used under the following conditions:

1. **History not required:** again, this solution is applicable for cases of nonhistorized reference tables only.
2. **Full load in staging area:** the source table in the staging area provides a full load and not a delta load.
3. **Same infrastructure:** the staging area is located on the same infrastructure as the data warehouse. If a different database server is used to house the staging area, the performance of the virtual reference tables could be impacted.
4. **Full control over staging area:** the staging area is under full control of the data warehouse team and the team decides about structural changes. The last thing that should happen in production is an uncontrolled update to the staging area that breaks a virtual reference table.
5. **Reference data in staging area is virtualized as well:** this condition rules out most applications but is important because the staging area should not be used as the central storage location. If reference data in the data warehouse layer is virtually depending on data in the staging area, the Data Vault 2.0 architecture has been violated.
6. **All required data is available:** in some cases, the source system loses old records (e.g., old countries). If this is OK, because old records are not required in the reference table, then this condition is negligible. However, because the data warehouse provides historic data, all codes referenced in satellites have to be dissolved by the reference table in the data warehouse layer.
7. **No data transformation required:** the data in the staging area is already in a format that requires no processing of soft business rules in order to prevent the execution of conditional logic when loading the Raw Data Vault.

If all these conditions are met, a virtual SQL view can be created in order to virtually provide the reference data to the users of the Raw Data Vault. This approach is typically used when providing reference data from an analytical MDM solution that is under control and managed by the data warehouse team. Such data is also staged virtually and centrally stored in the MDM application. The following DDL creates an example view that implements a nonhistorized reference table in the Raw Data Vault:

```
CREATE VIEW [raw].[RefRegion]
AS
SELECT
    [Code]
    ,[Name]
    ,[Abbreviation]
    ,[Sort Order]
    ,[External Reference]
    ,[Comments]
FROM
    [StageArea].[mds].[BTS_Region_DWH]
```

The view selects data from the table in the staging area, which is also a virtually provided staging view (refer to Chapter 11 for details). All columns are provided explicitly to avoid taking over unrequired columns but also to prevent taking over unforeseen changes to the underlying structure into the data warehouse. The view doesn't implement any soft business rules, but might implement hard business rules, such as data type alignment. It does however, brings the reference data from the staging area into the desired structure of a reference table, as discussed in Chapter 6, Advanced Data Vault Modeling.

This approach is most applicable for loading analytical master data from a master data management application such as Microsoft Master Data Services. Virtual reference tables are especially used in the agile Data Vault 2.0 methodology to provide the reference data as quickly as possible. If the business user agrees with the implemented functionality and materialization is required, the reference data can be materialized in a subsequent sprint, stretching the actual implementation of new functionality over multiple sprints.

12.2.1.1 T-SQL Example

In many other cases, especially if the data is already staged in the staging area, it should be materialized into the data warehouse layer to ensure that data is not spread over multiple layers. This decoupling from the staging area prevents any undesired side-effects if other parties change the underlying structure of the staging area. In such cases, the reference table is created in the data warehouse layer, for example by a statement such as the following:

```
CREATE TABLE [raw].[RefRegion](
        [Code] [nvarchar](2) NOT NULL,
        [Name] [nvarchar](250) NOT NULL,
        [Abbreviation] [nvarchar](2) NOT NULL,
        [Sort Order] [int] NOT NULL,
        [External Reference] [nvarchar](255) NULL,
        [Comments] [nvarchar](max) NULL,
 CONSTRAINT [PK_RefRegion] PRIMARY KEY CLUSTERED
(
        [Code] ASC
) ON [DATA]
) ON [DATA] TEXTIMAGE_ON [DATA]
```

The structure of the reference table follows the definition for nonhistorized reference tables outlined in Chapter 6. The primary key of the reference table consists of the **Code** column. Because this column holds a natural key instead of a hash key, the primary key uses a clustered index. There are multiple options for loading the reference table during the loading process of the Raw Data Vault. The most commonly used adds new and unknown reference codes from the staging area into the target reference table and updates records in the target that have changed in the source table. This way, no codes that could be used in any one of the satellites is lost. While it is not recommended to use the MERGE statement in loading the data warehouse, it is possible to load the reference table this way:

```
MERGE DataVault.[raw].RefRegion AS ref
USING (
        SELECT
                [Code],
                [Name],
                [Abbreviation],
                [Sort Order],
                [External Reference],
                [Comments]
```

```
        FROM
                [StageArea].[mds].[BTS_Region_DWH]
) AS stg ([Code], [Name], [Abbreviation], [Sort Order], [External Reference], [Comments])
ON (ref.[Code] = stg.[Code])
WHEN MATCHED THEN
        UPDATE SET
                ref.[Name] = stg.[Name],
                ref.[Abbreviation] = stg.[Abbreviation],
                ref.[Sort Order] = stg.[Sort Order],
                ref.[External Reference] = stg.[External Reference],
                ref.[Comments] = stg.[Comments]
WHEN NOT MATCHED THEN
        INSERT (
                [Code],
                [Name],
                [Abbreviation],
                [Sort Order],
                [External Reference],
                [Comments]
        )
        VALUES (
                stg.[Code], stg.[Name],
                stg.[Abbreviation],
                stg.[Sort Order],
                stg.[External Reference],
                stg.[Comments]
        );
```

Because the code column identifies the reference table, it becomes the search condition of the MERGE statement. If the code from the staging table is found in the target, the record in the reference table is updated. If it is unknown, it is inserted. If codes are deleted from the source system, they are ignored in order to preserve all codes in the reference table. Deletes are implemented by adding a WHEN NOT MATCHED BY SOURCE clause:

```
MERGE DataVault.[raw].RefRegion AS ref
USING (
        SELECT
                [Code],
                [Name],
                [Abbreviation],
                [Sort Order],
                [External Reference],
                [Comments]
        FROM
                [StageArea].[mds].[BTS_Region_DWH]
) AS stg ([Code], [Name], [Abbreviation], [Sort Order], [External Reference], [Comments])
ON (ref.[Code] = stg.[Code])
WHEN MATCHED THEN
        UPDATE SET
                ref.[Name] = stg.[Name],
                ref.[Abbreviation] = stg.[Abbreviation],
                ref.[Sort Order] = stg.[Sort Order],
                ref.[External Reference] = stg.[External Reference],
                ref.[Comments] = stg.[Comments]
```

```
WHEN NOT MATCHED BY TARGET THEN
       INSERT (
               [Code],
               [Name],
               [Abbreviation],
               [Sort Order],
               [External Reference],
               [Comments]
       )
       VALUES (
               stg.[Code], stg.[Name],
               stg.[Abbreviation],
               stg.[Sort Order],
               stg.[External Reference],
               stg.[Comments]
       )
WHEN NOT MATCHED BY SOURCE THEN DELETE;
```

The MERGE statement is generally not recommended to use in the loading processes of the data warehouse because of performance reasons and other issues with the MERGE statement on SQL Server [2]. Instead, the operations should be separated into individual statements to maintain performance. On the other hand, reference tables often have a relatively small size and performance doesn't become an issue. Therefore, using the MERGE statement might be simpler in some cases. If the reference table is large or performance becomes an issue, the statement should be separated.

12.2.2 HISTORY-BASED REFERENCE TABLES

History-based reference tables consist of two tables in fact (refer to Chapter 6, Advanced Data Vault Modeling, for more details about their definitions). The first table has the same structure as the no-history reference table and provides a list of codes and optionally some nonhistorized attributes of the codes in the list. The loading process is the same as described in the previous section.

12.2.2.1 T-SQL Example

The second table is a satellite that hangs off the reference table. The following statement creates a satellite on a reference table:

```
CREATE TABLE [raw].[RefSatRegion](
       [Code] [nvarchar](2) NOT NULL,
       [LoadDate] [datetime2](7) NOT NULL,
       [LoadEndDate] [datetime2](7) NULL,
       [RecordSource] [nvarchar](50) NOT NULL,
       [HashDiff] [char](32) NOT NULL,
       [ID] [int] NOT NULL,
       [MUID] [uniqueidentifier] NOT NULL,
       [VersionName] [nvarchar](50) NOT NULL,
       [VersionNumber] [int] NOT NULL,
       [VersionFlag] [nvarchar](50) NULL,
       [Name] [nvarchar](250) NULL,
       [ChangeTrackingMask] [int] NOT NULL,
       [Abbreviation] [nvarchar](2) NULL,
       [Sort Order] [decimal](38, 0) NULL,
```

```
        [External Reference] [nvarchar](255) NULL,
        [Record Source] [nvarchar](100) NULL,
        [Comments] [nvarchar](4000) NULL,
        [EnterDateTime] [datetime2](3) NOT NULL,
        [EnterUserName] [nvarchar](100) NULL,
        [EnterVersionNumber] [int] NULL,
        [LastChgDateTime] [datetime2](3) NOT NULL,
        [LastChgUserName] [nvarchar](100) NULL,
        [LastChgVersionNumber] [int] NULL,
        [ValidationStatus] [nvarchar](250) NULL,
 CONSTRAINT [PK_RefSatRegion] PRIMARY KEY CLUSTERED
(
        [Code] ASC,
        [LoadDate] ASC
) ON [DATA]
) ON [DATA]
```

Instead of a hash key, this satellite uses the code to reference its parent table. This is because there is no hash key in the parent reference table due to the goal of reference tables to increase readability of the data. Because the hash key is not used, a clustered index is used for the primary key to improve performance during reads. This satellite uses a hash diff column to improve the column comparison when inserting new records.

Many of the satellite columns are already in the parent reference table. However, this example shows how to track the changes to the source system data in addition to the simple reference table without history, which is provided for the business users. In other cases, only the attributes, which are not used in the parent reference table, are added to the historizing satellite. The best approach is left to the data warehousing team.

In order to load the satellite table on the reference table, the following statement can be used:

```
INSERT INTO DataVault.[raw].RefSatRegion (
        Code,
        LoadDate,
        LoadEndDate,
        RecordSource,
        HashDiff,
        ID,
        MUID,
        VersionName,
        VersionNumber,
        VersionFlag,
        Name,
        ChangeTrackingMask,
        Abbreviation,
        [Sort Order],
        [External Reference],
        [Record Source],
        Comments,
        EnterDateTime,
        EnterUserName,
        EnterVersionNumber,
        LastChgDateTime,
        LastChgUserName,
        LastChgVersionNumber,
        ValidationStatus
    )
```

```
SELECT DISTINCT
        stg.Code,
        stg.LoadDate,
        NULL,
        stg.RecordSource,
        stg.RegionHashDiff,
        stg.ID,
        stg.MUID,
        stg.VersionName,
        stg.VersionNumber,
        stg.VersionFlag,
        stg.Name,
        stg.ChangeTrackingMask,
        stg.Abbreviation,
        stg.[Sort Order],
        stg.[External Reference],
        stg.[Record Source],
        stg.Comments,
        stg.EnterDateTime,
        stg.EnterUserName,
        stg.EnterVersionNumber,
        stg.LastChgDateTime,
        stg.LastChgUserName,
        stg.LastChgVersionNumber,
        stg.ValidationStatus
FROM
        StageArea.mds.BTS_Region_DWH stg
LEFT OUTER JOIN
        DataVault.[raw].RefSatRegion sat
        ON (stg.Code = sat.Code AND sat.LoadEndDate IS NULL)
WHERE
        (sat.HashDiff IS NULL OR stg.RegionHashDiff != sat.HashDiff)
        AND stg.LoadDate = '2015-02-16 11:31:22.537'
```

This statement uses the same loading approach as standard Data Vault satellites, described in section 12.1.4. The **left outer join** is based on the satellite's parent key, consisting of the reference **code** and the **load date**. The column compare in this statement is based on the **hash diff** to improve loading performance. The statement has to be executed for each load date in the staging area, replacing the hard-coded load date in the shown SQL statement by a variable.

This satellite also requires being end-dated afterwards, similar to the process described in section 12.1.5.

12.2.3 CODE AND DESCRIPTIONS

A code and descriptions reference table provides a convenient method to deal with a large number of reference code groups. Typically, source systems provide various groups with only a couple of codes (refer to Chapter 6). The number of code groups that a source system provides can go to several hundreds with large systems. To avoid creating many reference tables with only a small number of codes, a common practice is to use only one reference table to capture code and descriptions. This table is a generalized table that provides only standard attributes, such as descriptions, sort orders, etc. The standard attributes are defined by the data warehouse team and provided for each group. If additional, nonstandard attributes are required for a code group, an individual reference table is required (see sections 12.2.1 and 12.2.2).

If the code and descriptions table should provide no history, it is possible to provide the table as a virtual SQL view, as standard, nonhistory reference tables. The DDL for such a virtual code and descriptions table is presented here:

```
CREATE VIEW [raw].[RefCodes] AS
SELECT
        'BTS.Region' AS [Group]
        ,[Code]
        ,[Name]
        ,[Abbreviation]
        ,[Sort Order]
        ,[External Reference]
        ,[Record Source]
        ,[Comments]
    FROM [StageArea].[mds].[BTS_Region_DWH]
    UNION ALL
    SELECT
        'FAA.AircraftCategory' AS [Group]
        ,[Code]
        ,[Name]
        ,[Abbreviation]
        ,[Sort Order]
        ,[External Reference]
        ,[Record Source]
        ,[Comments]
    FROM [StageArea].[mds].[FAA_AircraftCategory_DWH]
    UNION ALL
    SELECT
        'FAA.AircraftType' AS [Group]
        ,[Code]
        ,[Name]
        ,[Abbreviation]
        ,[Sort Order]
        ,[External Reference]
        ,[Record Source]
        ,[Comments]
    FROM [StageArea].[mds].[FAA_AircraftType_DWH]
```

In this example, the view creates a UNION ALL over multiple staging tables to create a code and descriptions table. In other cases, the source system provides the table including all available groups. The problem with the union is that adding many staging tables increases the complexity of the view. The **record source** is not required but might be helpful to trace the source of reference data in the resulting view. Again, the **record source** column is used by the data warehouse team for debugging purposes.

Note that the reference table should not consolidate reference codes from multiple sources. This would require business logic, which is applied after loading the raw data. Instead, it should provide descriptive information for codes used in the raw data that can be used to create business rules that transform the incoming raw data into useful information. Therefore, it is possible that similar groups exist in this table. If the codes in the group are not changed across multiple source systems, for example due to modifications to the group, multiple groups are used to keep all possible reference codes from the source systems. Therefore, an integration doesn't take place at this point.

12.2.3.1 T-SQL Example

The approach to virtually providing code and description tables has the same requirements as outlined in section 12.2.1. If any of these conditions are not met, or if the complexity of the view is becoming too high, the table could be materialized using the following DDL statement:

```
CREATE TABLE [raw].[RefCodes](
        [Group] [nvarchar](50) NOT NULL,
        [Code] [nvarchar](250) NOT NULL,
        [Name] [nvarchar](250) NOT NULL,
        [Abbreviation] [nvarchar](2) NULL,
        [Sort Order] [int] NOT NULL,
        [External Reference] [nvarchar](255) NULL,
        [Comments] [nvarchar](max) NULL,
        [Record Source] [nvarchar](100) NOT NULL,
  CONSTRAINT [PK_RefCodes] PRIMARY KEY CLUSTERED
(
        [Group] ASC,
        [Code] ASC
) ON [DATA]
) ON [DATA] TEXTIMAGE_ON [DATA]
```

As all other reference tables, the code and descriptions table relies on a clustered primary key because of the natural key in the **group** and **code** columns. It is possible to load the code and descriptions table using a MERGE statement again, but it becomes much more complex, due to the multiple source tables in the staging area:

```
MERGE DataVault.[raw].RefCodes AS ref
USING (
        SELECT
          'BTS.Region' AS [Group]
        ,[Code]
        ,[Name]
        ,[Abbreviation]
        ,[Sort Order]
        ,[External Reference]
        ,[Record Source]
        ,[Comments]
   FROM [StageArea].[mds].[BTS_Region_DWH]
   UNION ALL
   SELECT
           'FAA.AircraftCategory' AS [Group]
        ,[Code]
        ,[Name]
        ,[Abbreviation]
        ,[Sort Order]
        ,[External Reference]
        ,[Record Source]
        ,[Comments]
   FROM [StageArea].[mds].[FAA_AircraftCategory_DWH]
   UNION ALL
   SELECT
```

```
                  'FAA.AircraftType' AS [Group]
                ,[Code]
                ,[Name]
                ,[Abbreviation]
                ,[Sort Order]
                ,[External Reference]
                ,[Record Source]
                ,[Comments]
        FROM [StageArea].[mds].[FAA_AircraftType_DWH]
      ) AS stg ([Group], [Code], [Name], [Abbreviation], [Sort Order], [External Reference],
      [Record Source], [Comments])
      ON (ref.[Group] = stg.[Group] AND ref.[Code] = stg.[Code])
      WHEN MATCHED THEN
            UPDATE SET
                    ref.[Name] = stg.[Name],
                    ref.[Abbreviation] = stg.[Abbreviation],
                    ref.[Sort Order] = stg.[Sort Order],
                    ref.[External Reference] = stg.[External Reference],
                    ref.[Record Source] = stg.[Record Source],
                    ref.[Comments] = stg.[Comments]
      WHEN NOT MATCHED BY TARGET THEN
            INSERT (
                    [Group],
                    [Code],
                    [Name],
                    [Abbreviation],
                    [Sort Order],
                    [External Reference],
                    [Record Source],
                    [Comments]
            )
            VALUES (
                    stg.[Group], stg.[Code],
                    stg.[Name],
                    stg.[Abbreviation],
                    stg.[Sort Order],
                    stg.[External Reference],
                    stg.[Record Source],
                    stg.[Comments]
            );
```

This MERGE statement does not delete any codes in the target code and description table. The UNION ALL is still included in the SELECT clause in order to avoid dealing with parallel running of INSERT statements on the same table, for example by adding locks on the target table in the loading processes.

12.2.4 CODE AND DESCRIPTIONS WITH HISTORY

The last reference table example in this chapter is focused on historized code and description tables. The implementation follows the same approach as standard reference tables and involves a satellite on the code and description table for keeping historized attributes.

12.2.4.1 T-SQL Example

The following DDL is used to create such a satellite on the code and descriptions table:

```
CREATE TABLE [raw].[RefSatCodes](
        [Group] [nvarchar](50) NOT NULL,
        [Code] [nvarchar](2) NOT NULL,
        [LoadDate] [datetime2](7) NOT NULL,
        [LoadEndDate] [datetime2](7) NULL,
        [RecordSource] [nvarchar](50) NOT NULL,
        [HashDiff] [char](32) NOT NULL,
```

```
      [ID] [int] NOT NULL,
      [MUID] [uniqueidentifier] NOT NULL,
      [VersionName] [nvarchar](50) NOT NULL,
      [VersionNumber] [int] NOT NULL,
      [VersionFlag] [nvarchar](50) NULL,
      [Name] [nvarchar](250) NULL,
      [ChangeTrackingMask] [int] NOT NULL,
      [Abbreviation] [nvarchar](2) NULL,
      [Sort Order] [decimal](38, 0) NULL,
      [External Reference] [nvarchar](255) NULL,
      [Record Source] [nvarchar](100) NULL,
      [Comments] [nvarchar](4000) NULL,
      [EnterDateTime] [datetime2](3) NOT NULL,
      [EnterUserName] [nvarchar](100) NULL,
      [EnterVersionNumber] [int] NULL,
      [LastChgDateTime] [datetime2](3) NOT NULL,
      [LastChgUserName] [nvarchar](100) NULL,
      [LastChgVersionNumber] [int] NULL,
      [ValidationStatus] [nvarchar](250) NULL,
 CONSTRAINT [PK_RefSatCodes] PRIMARY KEY CLUSTERED
(
      [Group] ASC,
      [Code] ASC,
      [LoadDate] ASC
) ON [DATA]
) ON [DATA]
```

The DDL closely follows the DDL in section 12.2.2 but includes the **group** column in the primary key of the satellite, in addition to the **code** and **load date**. The satellite is loaded similarly using the following INSERT statement:

```
INSERT INTO DataVault.[raw].RefSatCodes (
      [Group],
      Code,
      LoadDate,
      LoadEndDate,
      RecordSource,
      HashDiff,
      ID,
      MUID,
      VersionName,
      VersionNumber,
      VersionFlag,
      Name,
      ChangeTrackingMask,
      Abbreviation,
      [Sort Order],
      [External Reference],
      [Record Source],
      Comments,
      EnterDateTime,
      EnterUserName,
      EnterVersionNumber,
      LastChgDateTime,
      LastChgUserName,
      LastChgVersionNumber,
      ValidationStatus
)
```

```sql
SELECT DISTINCT
      'BTS.Region' AS [Group],
        stg.Code,
        stg.LoadDate,
        NULL,
        stg.RecordSource,
        stg.RegionHashDiff,
        stg.ID,
        stg.MUID,
        stg.VersionName,
        stg.VersionNumber,
        stg.VersionFlag,
        stg.Name,
        stg.ChangeTrackingMask,
        stg.Abbreviation,
        stg.[Sort Order],
        stg.[External Reference],
        stg.[Record Source],
        stg.Comments,
        stg.EnterDateTime,
        stg.EnterUserName,
        stg.EnterVersionNumber,
        stg.LastChgDateTime,
        stg.LastChgUserName,
        stg.LastChgVersionNumber,
        stg.ValidationStatus
FROM
        StageArea.mds.BTS_Region_DWH stg
LEFT OUTER JOIN
        DataVault.[raw].RefSatCodes sat
        ON ('BTS.Region' = sat.[Group] AND stg.Code = sat.Code AND sat.LoadEndDate IS
NULL)
WHERE
        (sat.HashDiff IS NULL OR stg.RegionHashDiff != sat.HashDiff)
        AND stg.LoadDate = '2015-02-16 11:31:22.537'
UNION ALL
SELECT DISTINCT
        'FAA.AircraftCategory' AS [Group],
        stg.Code,
        stg.LoadDate,
        NULL,
        stg.RecordSource,
        stg.AircraftCategoryHashDiff,
        stg.ID,
        stg.MUID,
        stg.VersionName,
        stg.VersionNumber,
        stg.VersionFlag,
        stg.Name,
        stg.ChangeTrackingMask,
        stg.Abbreviation,
        stg.[Sort Order],
        stg.[External Reference],
        stg.[Record Source],
        stg.Comments,
        stg.EnterDateTime,
        stg.EnterUserName,
        stg.EnterVersionNumber,
        stg.LastChgDateTime,
        stg.LastChgUserName,
        stg.LastChgVersionNumber,
        stg.ValidationStatus
```

```
FROM
        StageArea.mds.FAA_AircraftCategory_DWH stg
LEFT OUTER JOIN
        DataVault.[raw].RefSatCodes sat
        ON ('FAA.AircraftCategory' = sat.[Group] AND stg.Code = sat.Code AND
sat.LoadEndDate IS NULL)
WHERE
        (sat.HashDiff IS NULL OR stg.AircraftCategoryHashDiff != sat.HashDiff)
        AND stg.LoadDate = '2015-02-16 11:31:22.537'
UNION ALL
SELECT DISTINCT
        'FAA.AircraftType' AS [Group],
        stg.Code,
        stg.LoadDate,
        NULL,
        stg.RecordSource,
        stg.AircraftTypeHashDiff,
        stg.ID,
        stg.MUID,
        stg.VersionName,
        stg.VersionNumber,
        stg.VersionFlag,
        stg.Name,
        stg.ChangeTrackingMask,
        stg.Abbreviation,
        stg.[Sort Order],
        stg.[External Reference],
        stg.[Record Source],
        stg.Comments,
        stg.EnterDateTime,
        stg.EnterUserName,
        stg.EnterVersionNumber,
        stg.LastChgDateTime,
        stg.LastChgUserName,
        stg.LastChgVersionNumber,
        stg.ValidationStatus
FROM
        StageArea.mds.FAA_AircraftType_DWH stg
LEFT OUTER JOIN
        DataVault.[raw].RefSatCodes sat
        ON ('FAA.AircraftType' = sat.[Group] AND stg.Code = sat.Code AND sat.LoadEndDate
IS NULL)
WHERE
        (sat.HashDiff IS NULL OR stg.AircraftTypeHashDiff != sat.HashDiff)
        AND stg.LoadDate = '2015-02-16 11:31:22.537'
```

Again, this statement uses the precalculated hash diff attribute to improve the performance of the column comparisons. It should be run for every load date in the staging area as it is required by all loading statements presented in this chapter.

This satellite requires being end-dated as described in section 12.1.5.

12.3 TRUNCATING THE STAGING AREA

Once the data has been loaded into the Raw Data Vault, the staging area should be cleaned up. This is because the storage consumption of the staging area should be kept to a minimum to reduce maintenance overhead and in order to improve the performance of subsequent loads of the data warehouse.

If the staging area contains only data that needs to be loaded into the data warehouse, no additional processes are required to manage which batches have been loaded into the data warehouse.

There are two options to truncate the staging area. Depending on the frequency of the incoming batches, it is feasible to use a TRUNCATE TABLE statement or it requires deleting only data with specific load dates only:

- **Truncate table:** the TRUNCATE TABLE statement can be used if it is guaranteed that all data from the staging table has been loaded into the Raw Data Vault and no new data has arrived between the load of the Raw Data Vault and the TRUNCATE TABLE statement. This is often the case when data is delivered only on a daily schedule but not more often.
- **Delete specific records:** if the staging area receives multiple batches over the day and the data warehouse team cannot guarantee that all data has been loaded into the Raw Data Vault, the TRUNCATE TABLE statement might accidentally delete data that is already in the staging area but not in the Raw Data Vault yet. Consider a delivery schedule of 15 minutes: the staging process loads the data from a source system in intervals of 15 minutes, for example by loading it directly off a relational database. In most cases, the data is loaded into the Raw Data Vault within this 15-minute cycle. But the data warehouse team cannot guarantee that this is the case in all loads. For example, during peak hours when other data sources are loaded as well, the loading process into the Raw Data Vault might take more time. If a TRUNCATE TABLE statement is used each time the loading process of the Raw Data Vault completes, data loss might occur in such cases. Therefore, only the records with the load date that has been loaded into the Raw Data Vault should be deleted.
- **Delete specific partitions:** because the DELETE statement is much slower than the TRUNCATE TABLE statement, data warehouse teams often rely on table partitioning to delete old records from the staging area. The tables in the staging area are partitioned on the load date. Whenever a batch has been completed, the partition with the corresponding load date is deleted as a whole.

These three options are typical examples of how to delete the data that has been processed by the Raw Data Vault loading processes from the staging area. By doing so, the staging area is kept smaller and more manageable.

REFERENCES

[1] Date C. An introduction to database systems. 7th ed. Reading, Menlo Park, New York: Addison-Wesley-Longman; 2000.
[2] Bertrand A. Use caution with SQL Server's MERGE statement, 2013, MSSQLTips.com website, available from http://www.mssqltips.com/sqlservertip/3074/use-caution-with-sql-servers-merge-statement/.

IMPLEMENTING DATA QUALITY

13

The goal of Data Vault 2.0 loads is to cover all data, regardless of its quality ("the good, the bad, and the ugly"). All data that is provided by the source systems should be loaded into the enterprise data warehouse, every time the source is in scope. In particular, these should be avoided:

- **Load bad data into an error file:** if data cannot be accepted into the Raw Data Vault for any reason, load it into the error mart.
- **Filter data because of technical issues:** duplicate primary keys (in the source system), violated NOT NULL constraints, missing indices or problems with joins should not prevent the raw data from being loaded into the Raw Data Vault. Adjust your loading procedures for these issues.
- **Prohibit NULL values:** instead of preventing NULL values in the Raw Data Vault, make sure to remove NOT NULL constraints from the Data Vault tables or set a default value.

With all the rules for acceptance of data relaxed, what if bad or ugly data is loaded into the data warehouse? At the very least, it should not be presented without further processing to the business user to be used in the decision-making process. This chapter covers the best practices for dealing with low data quality.

13.1 BUSINESS EXPECTATIONS REGARDING DATA QUALITY

Business users expect that the data warehouse will present correct information of high quality. However, data quality is a subjective concept. Data that is correct for one business user might be wrong for another with different requirements or another understanding of the business view. There is no "golden copy" or "single version of the truth" in data warehousing [1]. Just consider the business user who wants to compare reports from the data warehouse with the reports from an operational system, including all the calculations, which might differ. In many cases, data warehouse projects divert from the calculations and aggregations in operational systems due to enterprise alignment or to overcome errors in the source system. This is not a desired solution, but is reality grounded in the fact that the data warehouse often fixes issues that should have been fixed in the source system or the business processes. In any case, the data warehouse should provide both "versions of the truth." That's why Data Vault 2.0 focuses on the "single version of the facts."

The expectations regarding data quality should be distinguished by two categories [1]:

- **Data quality expectations:** these are expressed by rules, which measure the validity of the data values. This includes the identification of missing or unusable data, the description of data in conflict, the determination of duplicate records and the exploration of missing links between the data [1].
- **Business expectations:** these are measures related to the performance, productivity, and efficiency of processes. Typical questions raised by the business are focused on the throughput

decreased due to errors, the percentage of time that is spent in order to rework failed processes, and the loss in value of transactions that failed because of wrong transactions [1].

In order to meet the business expectations regarding data quality, both expectations have to be brought in line. The conformance to business expectations and its corresponding business value should be set in relation to the conformance to data quality expectations. This can provide a framework for data quality improvements [1].

Another question is where these data quality improvements should take place. Typically, there are different types of errors in a data warehouse and there are recommended practices for fixing and creating an alignment between the expectations of the business and the data quality expectations:

- **Data errors:** the best approach is to fix data errors in the source application and the business process that generates the data. Otherwise, the root cause of the error has not been fixed and more errors will emerge and need to be fixed later in a more costly approach.
- **Business rule errors:** this is an error that actually needs to be fixed in the data warehouse because the business rules, which are implemented in the Business Vault or in the loading routines for the information marts, are erroneous.
- **Perception errors:** if the business has a wrong perception of the data produced by the business process, the requirements for the data warehouse should be changed in most cases.

Because the data is owned by the business and IT should only be responsible for delivering it back to the business in an aggregated fashion, the IT should reduce the amount of work dedicated to implementing business rules. Instead, this responsibility should be given to business users as much as possible. This concept, called managed self-service BI, has been introduced in Chapter 2, Scalable Data Warehouse Architecture. If this approach is followed, then IT only governs the process, and provides the raw data for the business user to implement their business rules. The responsibility to fix business rule errors moves to the business user, in effect.

13.2 THE COSTS OF LOW DATA QUALITY

When data of low quality is loaded into the data warehouse, it incurs costs often overseen by business users. These costs can be put into several categories:

- **Customer and partner satisfaction:** in some cases, especially if external parties also use the data warehouse, low data quality can affect customer satisfaction [2]. For example, in some cases, the data warehouse is used to create quarterly invoices or financial statements to external partners. If the data on these statements is wrong, it can seriously damage the business relationship between customers or partners.[3]
- **Regulatory impacts:** in other cases, the data warehouse is used to generate statements required by government regulations or the law, industry bodies or internal units to meet self-imposed policies [1]. If these reports are wrong, and if you know it, you might end up in court. There are industries that have a large number of regulations to be met, for example the USA PATRIOT Act, Sarbanes-Oxley Act and the Basel II Accords in the financial industry [1].
- **Financial costs:** improving the data quality might cost substantial amounts of money. However, not improving the data quality and making wrong decisions will cost multiple times more [2]

This includes increased operating costs, decreased revenues, reduction or delays in cash flow, increased penalties, fines or other charges [1].

- **Organizational mistrust:** if end-users know that a data warehouse provides erroneous reports, they try to avoid the system by using the operational system to pull the reports or build their own silo data warehouse instead of using the enterprise data warehouse system [2] Therefore, providing reports with high data quality is a requirement for any successful enterprise data warehouse strategy.
- **Re-engineering:** if the data warehouse provides reports with low data quality and the organization cannot fix the issues (either in the source system or the data warehouse itself), many organizations decide to fail the project and start from the beginning [2].
- **Decision-making:** delivering bad data, even temporarily, provides a serious problem for business managers in meeting their goals. Many of their decisions are based on the information provided by the data warehouse. If this information is wrong, they cannot make the right decisions and lose time in meeting the goals set by higher management. Even if the data warehouse provides corrected information some months later in the year, the time is gone for the managers to fix the decisions made in the past, which were based on wrong assumptions [2].
- **Business strategy:** in order to achieve organizational excellence, top management requires outstanding data [2].

The cost of low data quality outweighs the cost of assessments, inspection and fixing the issue by multiple times. Therefore, it is advisable to improve the data quality before information in reports is given to business users. The best place for such improvements lies in the business processes and the operational systems to achieve total quality. However, if this is not possible, the data warehouse can be used for fixing bad data as well.

13.3 **THE VALUE OF BAD DATA**

In legacy data warehousing, bad data is fixed before it is loaded into the data warehouse. The biggest drawback of this approach is that the original data is not available for analysis anymore, at least not easily. This prevents any analysis for understanding the gap between business expectations, as outlined in the previous section, and the data quality of the source systems (Figure 13.1).

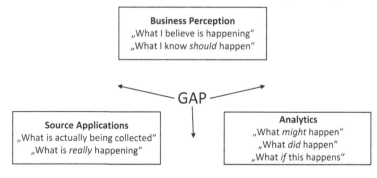

FIGURE 13.1

Gap analysis.

During the gap analysis presented in Figure 13.1, the business users explain to the data warehouse team what they believe happens in the business and what they think should happen in a perfect process. They also tell the data warehouse team how the data used in the business processes should be collected from the source systems.

But when the data warehouse team actually loads the data from the source systems, they often find these expectations to be broken because the source systems provide the truth about the data being collected and what is really happening from a data perspective. In addition, the source application provides insights into the process layer of the enterprise and often shows which processes are broken from a business perspective.

These are the two "versions of the truth." Both sides are right: the business has an expectation about the business processes that should be in place and the source systems are right because they show what kind of data (and of what quality) is actually being tracked, because of the actual business processes in place. Between both versions is a gap that should be closed.

A good data warehouse solution should assist the business in this gap analysis. It should be possible to discover where the requirements for the current business views or beliefs don't match what is being collected or being run. If the data warehouse team wants to help the business see the gaps, it is required to show them the bad data and help the business to see problems in their applications in order to correct them. Therefore, the gap analysis involves multiple layers, which are presented in Figure 13.2.

The business requirements represent the business expectations, while the raw data represents the source system data. The information layer provides altered, matched and integrated information in the enterprise data warehouse and in the information marts.

Sourcing raw data, including bad and ugly data, provides some values to the data warehouse:

- If problems are found (now or in the future) it is possible to handle them when the raw data is available.
- If the data is translated or interpreted before loaded into the data warehouse, a lot of gaps are sourced. These gaps are represented by the "fixed" data.
- Self-service BI isn't possible without IT involvement which is required to take back some of the interpretations of the raw data.
- It is possible to push more business rules into front-end tools for managed self-service BI usage because all the raw data is still available.
- IT is not responsible for interpreting the raw data, except the programming that is required.

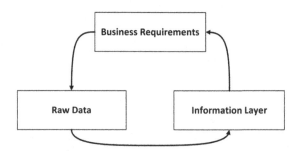

FIGURE 13.2

Layers of gap analysis.

Having the bad data in the data warehouse helps to reconcile integrated and altered data with the source systems and with business requirements. This is the reason why bad data, and ugly-looking data, is kept in the data warehouse and not modified, transformed or fixed in any sense on the way into the data warehouse.

13.4 DATA QUALITY IN THE ARCHITECTURE

Data quality routines correct errors, complete raw data or transform it to provide more business value. This is exactly the purpose of soft business rules. Therefore, data quality routines are considered as soft business rules in the reference architecture of Data Vault 2.0 (Figure 13.3).

Just like soft business rules, data quality routines change frequently: for example, if the data quality improvement is based on fixed translation rules, kept in a knowledge database, these rules evolve over time. And if a data mining approach is used to correct errors, inject missing data, or match entities, there are no fixed rules. Instead, the data-mining algorithm can adapt to new data and is often trained on a regular basis.

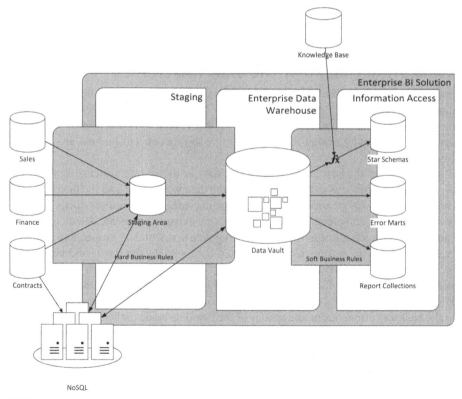

FIGURE 13.3

Data quality in the Data Vault 2.0 architecture.

Because soft business rules are implemented in the Business Vault or in the loading processes of the Information Marts, any data quality routines should be implemented in these places as well. By implementing data quality as soft business rules, the incoming raw data is not modified in any way and remains in the enterprise data warehouse for further analysis. If the data quality rules change, or new knowledge regarding the data is obtained, it is possible to adjust the data quality routines without reloading any previous raw data. The same is true if the business expectations change and with them, the understanding of high quality data.

The concept of multiple Information Marts is also helpful if there are multiple views of high quality data. In some cases, information consumers want to use information processed with enterprise-agreed data corrections. Other information consumers have their own understanding of data quality and the required corrections to the incoming data. And another type of user wants to use the raw data because they are interested in analyzing erroneous data from the operational system. In all these cases, individual information marts can be used to satisfy each type of information consumer and their individual requirements. It is also possible for information consumers in a self-service BI approach to mix and match the data quality routines as they see fit for their given task. This requires that data quality routines be implemented in the Business Vault if possible, so the cleansed results can be reused for multiple information marts. This is why the examples in this chapter are all based on the Business Vault. However, it is also valid to directly load the data (virtualized or materialized) into the target Information Mart.

13.5 CORRECTING ERRORS IN THE DATA WAREHOUSE

The correction of errors in the data warehouse represents only a suboptimal choice. The best choice is to fix data errors in the information processes of the business and in the operational systems. The goal is to eliminate not the errors, but the need to fix them. This can be achieved by improving the information processes and by designing quality into these processes to prevent any defects that require fixing [3].

While this represents the best choice, fixing the data in the source systems is often rejected as out-of-scope. Instead, erroneous data is loaded into the data warehouse and the business expects the errors to be fixed on the way downstream towards the end-user. This requires costly data correction activity, which cannot be complete. In many cases, not all existing errors are detected by data quality software and new errors are introduced. The resulting data set, which is propagated to the end-user, contains valid data from the source, along with fixed data, undetected errors and newly introduced errors [3].

Because of these limitations, the approach described in this chapter ensures that the raw data is kept in the data warehouse. By doing so, it is possible to fix additional issues that are found later in the process or to take back any erroneous modifications of the raw data made earlier. Typically, the following errors can be fixed in the business intelligence system [3]:

- **Transform, enhance, and calculate derived data:** the calculation of derived data is often necessary when the raw data is not in the form required by the business user. The transformation increases the value of the information and is considered to be an enhancement of the data [3].

- **Standardization of data:** standardized data is required by the business user to communicate effectively with peers. It also involves standardizing the data formats [3].
- **Correct and complete data:** in some cases, the data from the operational system is incorrect or incomplete and cannot be fixed at the root of the failure. In this suboptimal case, the data warehouse is responsible for fixing the issue on the way towards the business user [3].
- **Match and consolidate data:** matching and consolidating data is often required when dealing with multiple data sources that produce the same type of data and duplicate data is involved. Examples include customer or passenger records, product records and other cases of operational master data [3].
- **Data quality tagging:** another common practice is to provide information about the data quality to downstream users [4].

Note that these "corrections" are not directly applied on the raw data, i.e., in form of updates. Instead, these modifications are implemented after retrieving the raw data from the Raw Data Vault and loading the data into the Business Vault or information mart layers where the cleansed data is materialized or provided in a virtual form.

The next sections describe the best practices for each case and provide an example using T-SQL or SSIS (whatever fits best). However, understand that the best case is to fix these issues in the operational system or in the business process that generates the data. Fixing these issues in the data warehouse represents only a suboptimal choice. Too often, this is what happens in reality. Data quality tagging is shown in section 13.8.3.

13.6 **TRANSFORM, ENHANCE AND CALCULATE DERIVED DATA**

Raw data from source systems often have data quality issues, including [4,5]:

- **Dummy values:** the source might compensate for missing values by the use of default values.
- **Reused keys:** business keys or surrogate keys are reused in the source system, which might lead to identification issues.
- **Multipurpose fields:** fields in the source database are overloaded and used for multiple purposes. It requires extra business logic to ensure the integrity of the data or use it.
- **Multipurpose tables:** similarly, relational tables can be used to store different business entities, for example, both people and corporations. These tables contain many empty columns because many columns are only used by one type of entity and not the others. Examples include the first and last name of an individual person versus the organizational name.
- **Noncompliance with business rules:** often, the source data is not in conformance with set business rules due to a lack of validation. The values stored in the source database might not represent allowed domain values.

- **Conflicting data from multiple sources:** a common problem when loading data from multiple source systems is that the raw data might be in conflict. For example, the delivery address of a customer or the spelling of the customer's first name ("Dan" versus "Daniel") might be different.
- **Redundant data:** some operational databases contain redundant data, primarily because of data modeling issues. This often leads to inconsistencies in the data, similar to the conflicts from multiple source systems (which are redundant data, as well).
- **Smart columns:** some source system columns contain "smart" data, that is data with structural meaning. This is often found in business keys (review smart keys in Chapter 4, Data Vault 2.0 Modeling) but can be found in descriptive data as well. XML and JSON encoded columns are other examples of such smart columns, because they also provide structural meaning.

Business users often take advantage of transforming this data into more valuable data. Combining conflicting data might provide actionable insights to business users [1]. For example, when screening passengers for security reasons, context information is helpful: where did the passenger board the plane, where is the passenger heading to, what is the purpose of the trip, etc. It is also helpful to integrate information from other data sources, such as intelligence and police records about the passenger, to identify potential security threats. The value of the raw data increases greatly when such information is added in an enhancement process [1].

Because of this, organizations often purchase additional data from external information suppliers [6]. There are various types of data that can be added to enhance the data [7]:

- **Geographic information:** external information suppliers can help with address standardization and provide geo-tagging, including geographic coordinates, regional coding, municipality, neighborhood mapping and other kinds of geographic data.
- **Demographic information:** a large amount of demographic data can be bought, even on a personal or individual enterprise level, including age, martial status, gender, income, ethnic coding or the annual revenue, number of employees, etc.
- **Psychographic information:** these enhancements are used to categorize populations regarding their product and brand preferences and their organizational memberships (for example, political parties). It also includes information about leisure activities, vacation preferences and shopping time preferences.

There is also business value in precalculating or aggregating data for frequently asked queries [6].

13.6.1 T-SQL EXAMPLE

Computed satellites provide a good option for transforming, enhancing or calculating derived values. The following DDL creates a virtual computed satellite, which calculates derived columns based on the **Distance** column:

```sql
CREATE VIEW [biz].[TSatFlight] AS
SELECT
        [FlightHashKey]
        ,[LoadDate]
        ,'SR4711' AS RecordSource
        ,[Year]
        ,[Quarter]
        ,[Month]
        ,[DayOfMonth]
        ,[DayOfWeek]
        ,[CRSDepTime]
        ,[DepTime]
        ,[DepDelay]
        ,[DepDelayMinutes]
        ,[DepDel15]
        ,[DepartureDelayGroups]
        ,[DepTimeBlk]
        ,[TaxiOut]
        ,[WheelsOff]
        ,[WheelsOn]
        ,[TaxiIn]
        ,[CRSArrTime]
        ,[ArrTime]
        ,[ArrDelay]
        ,[ArrDelayMinutes]
        ,[ArrDel15]
        ,[ArrivalDelayGroups]
        ,[ArrTimeBlk]
        ,[Cancelled]
        ,[CancellationCode]
        ,[Diverted]
        ,[CRSElapsedTime]
        ,[ActualElapsedTime]
        ,[AirTime]
        ,[Flights]
        ,[Distance] AS DistanceM
        ,[Distance] * 0.87 AS DistanceNM
        ,[Distance] * 1.6 AS DistanceKM
        ,[Distance] / IIF([AirTime] = 0, NULL, [AirTime]*1.0) AS Speed
        ,[DistanceGroup]
        ,[CarrierDelay]
        ,[WeatherDelay]
        ,[NASDelay]
        ,[SecurityDelay]
        ,[LateAircraftDelay]
        ,[FirstDepTime]
        ,[TotalAddGTime]
        ,[LongestAddGTime]
FROM
        [DataVault].[raw].[TSatFlight];
```

Because the data was modified, a new **record source** is used. This approach follows the one in Chapter 14, Loading the Dimensional Information Mark, and helps to identify which soft business rule was implemented in order to produce the data in the satellite.

In addition to the raw data, which is provided for convenience to the power user, the **Distance** column is renamed and used to calculate the distance in nautical miles (**DistanceNM**), kilometers (**DistanceKM**) and the ground speed (column **Speed**).

13.7 STANDARDIZATION OF DATA

During standardization raw data is transformed into a standard format with the goal to provide the data in a shareable, enterprise-wide set of entity types and attributes. The formats and data values are standardized to further enhance the potential business communication and facilitate the data cleansing process because a consistent format helps to consolidate data from multiple sources and identify duplicate records [6]. Examples for data standardization include [1,6]:

- **Stripping extraneous punctuation or white spaces:** some character strings have additional punctuations or white spaces that need to be removed, for example by character trimming.
- **Rearranging data:** in some cases, individual tokens, such as first name and last name, are rearranged into a standard format.
- **Reordering data:** in other cases, there is an implicit order of the elements in a data element, for example in postal addresses. Reordering brings the data into a standardized order.
- **Domain value redundancy:** data from different sources (or even within the same source) might use different unit of measures. In some cases, airline miles might be provided in aeronautic miles, in other cases, ground kilometers.
- **Format inconsistencies:** phone numbers, tax identification numbers, zip codes, and other data elements might be formatted in different ways. Having no enterprise-wide format hinders efficient data analysis or prevents the automated detection of duplicates.
- **Mapping data:** often, there are mapping rules to standardize reference codes used in an operational system to enterprise-wide reference codes or to transform other abbreviations into more meaningful information.

The latter can often be implemented with the help of analytical master data, which are loaded into reference tables in Data Vault 2.0.

13.7.1 T-SQL EXAMPLE

Because the analytical master data has been provided as reference tables to the enterprise data warehouse, it is easy to perform lookups into the analytical master data, even if the Business Vault is virtualized. The following DDL statement is based on the computed satellite created in the previous section and joins a reference table to resolve a system-wide code to an abbreviation requested by the business user:

```
CREATE VIEW [biz].[TSatCleansedFlight] AS
SELECT
        [FlightHashKey]
        ,[LoadDate]
        ,'SR4711.DQ' AS RecordSource
        ,[Year]
        ,[Quarter]
        ,[Month]
        ,[DayOfMonth]
        ,[DayOfWeek]
        ,[CRSDepTime]
        ,[DepTime]
        ,[DepDelay]
        ,[DepDelayMinutes]
        ,[DepDel15]
        ,[DepartureDelayGroups]
        ,[DepTimeBlk]
        ,[TaxiOut]
        ,[WheelsOff]
        ,[WheelsOn]
        ,[TaxiIn]
        ,[CRSArrTime]
        ,[ArrTime]
        ,[ArrDelay]
        ,[ArrDelayMinutes]
        ,[ArrDel15]
        ,[ArrivalDelayGroups]
        ,[ArrTimeBlk]
        ,[Cancelled]
        ,[CancellationCode]
        ,[Diverted]
        ,[CRSElapsedTime]
        ,[ActualElapsedTime]
        ,[AirTime]
        ,[Flights]
        ,[DistanceM]
        ,[DistanceNM]
        ,[DistanceKM]
        ,[Speed]
        ,[DistanceGroup]
        ,[DataVault].[raw].[RefDistanceGroup].Abbreviation AS DistanceGroupText
        ,[CarrierDelay]
        ,[WeatherDelay]
        ,[NASDelay]
        ,[SecurityDelay]
        ,[LateAircraftDelay]
        ,[FirstDepTime]
        ,[TotalAddGTime]
        ,[LongestAddGTime]
FROM
        [DataVault].[biz].[TSatFlight] flight
LEFT JOIN
        [DataVault].[raw].[RefDistanceGroup]
        ON (flight.[DistanceGroup] = [DataVault].[raw].[RefDistanceGroup].Code)
```

The source attribute **DistanceGroup** is a code limited to the source system. It is not used organization-wide. Therefore, the business requests that the code should be resolved into an abbreviation known and used by the business. The mapping is provided in the analytical master data, which is loaded into the Data Vault 2.0 model as reference tables. The resolution of the system codes into known codes can be done by simply joining the reference table **RefDistanceGroup** to the computed satellite and adding the abbreviation as a new attribute, **DistanceGroupText**.

Because the computed satellite has modified the data, a new **record source** is provided.

Another use-case is to align the formatting of the raw data to a common format, for example when dealing with currencies, dates and times, or postal addresses.

13.8 CORRECT AND COMPLETE DATA

The goal of this process is to improve the quality of the data by correcting missing values, known errors and suspect data [6]. This requires that the data errors are known to the data warehouse team or can be found easily using predefined constraints. The first often replaces attribute values of specific records, while the latter is often defined by relatively open business rules involving domain knowledge [30]. Examples include [2]:

- **Single data fields:** this business rule ensures that all data values are following a predefined format, and are within a specific range or domain value.
- **Multiple data fields:** this business rule ensures the integrity between multiple data fields, for example by ensuring that passenger IDs and passenger's country (who issued the ID) match.
- **Probability:** flags unlikely combinations of data values, for example the gender of a passenger and the name.

There are multiple options for the correction of such data errors [7]:

- **Automated correction:** this approach is based on rule-based standardizations, normalizations and corrections. Computed satellites often employ such rules and provide the cleansed data to the next layer in the loading process. Therefore, it is possible to implement this approach in a fully virtualized manner without materializing the cleansed data in the Business Vault.
- **Manual directed correction:** this approach is using automated correction, but the results require manual review (and intervention) before the cleansed data is provided to the next layer in the loading process. To simplify the review process, a confidence level is often introduced and stored along the corrected data. This approach requires materialization of the cleansed data in the Business Vault and should include a confidence value and the result of the manual inspection process. The data steward might also overwrite the cleansed data in a manual correction process. In this case, an external tool is required in addition.
- **Manual correction:** in this case, data stewards inspect the raw data manually and perform their corrections. This approach is often combined with external tools and might involve MDM applications such as Microsoft Master Data Services when dealing with master data.

In some cases, it is not possible to correct all data errors in the raw data. It has to be determined by the business user how to handle such uncorrectable or suspect data. There are multiple options [6]:

- **Reject the data:** if the data is not being used in aggregations or calculations, it might be reasonable to exclude the data from the information mart.
- **Accept the data without a change:** in this case, the data is loaded into the information mart without further notice to the business user.
- **Accept the data with tagging:** instead of just loading the data into the information mart, the error is documented by a tag or comment that is presented to the business user.
- **Estimate the correct or approximate values:** in some cases, it is possible to approximate missing values. This can be used to avoid excluding the data but entails some risks if the estimates are significantly overstating or understating the actual value. The advantage is that this approach helps to keep all occurrences of the data, which is helpful when counting the data.

It is helpful to attach a tag to the resulting data that identifies the applied option. This is especially true for the last case, to indicate to the business user that they are not dealing with actual values but estimates [6].

13.8.1 T-SQL EXAMPLE

In order to reject data without further notice, the virtual satellite can be extended by a WHERE clause:

```
CREATE VIEW [biz].[TSatCleansedFlight2] AS
SELECT
        [FlightHashKey]
        ,[LoadDate]
        ,[RecordSource]
        ,[Year]
        ,[Quarter]
        ,[Month]
        ,[DayOfMonth]
        ,[DayOfWeek]
        ,[CRSDepTime]
        ,[DepTime]
        ,[DepDelay]
        ,[DepDelayMinutes]
        ,[DepDel15]
        ,[DepartureDelayGroups]
        ,[DepTimeBlk]
        ,[TaxiOut]
        ,[WheelsOff]
        ,[WheelsOn]
        ,[TaxiIn]
        ,[CRSArrTime]
        ,[ArrTime]
        ,[ArrDelay]
        ,[ArrDelayMinutes]
        ,[ArrDel15]
        ,[ArrivalDelayGroups]
        ,[ArrTimeBlk]
        ,[Cancelled]
        ,[CancellationCode]
        ,[Diverted]
        ,[CRSElapsedTime]
```

```
        , [ActualElapsedTime]
        , [AirTime]
        , [Flights]
        , [DistanceM]
        , [DistanceNM]
        , [DistanceKM]
        , [Speed]
        , [DistanceGroup]
        , [DistanceGroupText]
        , [CarrierDelay]
        , [WeatherDelay]
        , [NASDelay]
        , [SecurityDelay]
        , [LateAircraftDelay]
        , [FirstDepTime]
        , [TotalAddGTime]
        , [LongestAddGTime]
FROM
        [DataVault].[biz].[TSatCleansedFlight]
WHERE
        NOT ([Cancelled] = 0 AND [AirTime] = 0)
```

Some of the source data is erroneous and the business decided to exclude these records completely from further analysis. The WHERE clause filters these faulty records, which are actual flights that haven't been **cancelled** but which have no **airtime**. Because the data itself is not modified, the record source from the base satellite **TSatCleansedFlight** is used. However, this approach removes the ability to identify the soft business rule that is responsible for filtering the data.

13.8.2 DQS EXAMPLE

Correcting raw data can also be performed using data quality management software, such as Microsoft Data Quality Services (DQS), which is included in Microsoft SQL Server. DQS consists of three important components:

- **Server component:** this component is responsible for the execution of cleansing operations and the management of knowledge bases, which keep information about domains and how to identify errors.
- **Client application:** the client application is used by the administrator to set up knowledge bases and by data stewards to define the domain. Data stewards also use it to manually cleanse the data.
- **SSIS transformation:** in order to automatically cleanse the data, a SSIS transformation is available that can be used in SSIS data flows.

Before creating a SSIS data flow that uses DQS for automatic data cleansing, a knowledge base has to be created and domain knowledge implemented.

The following example uses an artificial dataset on passenger records required for security screening [8]. This dataset requires cleansing operations because some of the passenger names and other attributes are misspelled and the dataset contains duplicate records.

Open the DQS client application, connect to the DQS server and create a new knowledge base. The dialog in Figure 13.4 is shown.

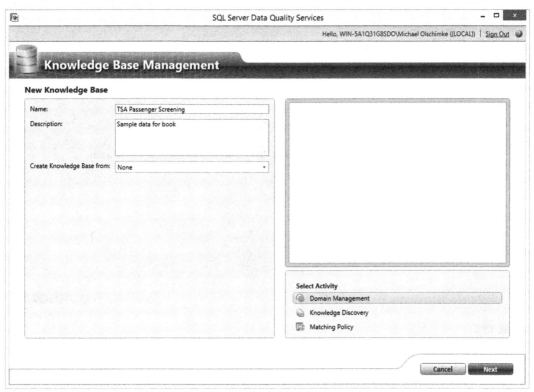

FIGURE 13.4

Create new knowledge base in DQS client.

Provide a name for the new knowledge base and an optional description. There are three possible activities available [9]:

- **Domain management:** this activity is used to create, modify and verify the domains used within the knowledge base. It is possible to change rules and reference values that define the domain. It is possible to verify raw data against the domains in the knowledge base in SSIS.
- **Knowledge discovery:** the definition of domain knowledge can be assisted using this activity where domain knowledge is discovered from source data.
- **Matching policy:** this activity is used to prepare the knowledge base for de-duplication of records. However, this activity is not yet supported by SSIS and only manual-directed correction is supported.

Select **domain management** and click the **next** button to continue. The knowledge base is shown and domains can be managed in the dialog, shown in Figure 13.5.

The dialog presents all available domains in the list on the left side. The right side is used to present the definitions, rules, and other properties of the selected domain. Because the knowledge base is empty, create a new domain by selecting the button on the top left of the left side (Figure 13.6).

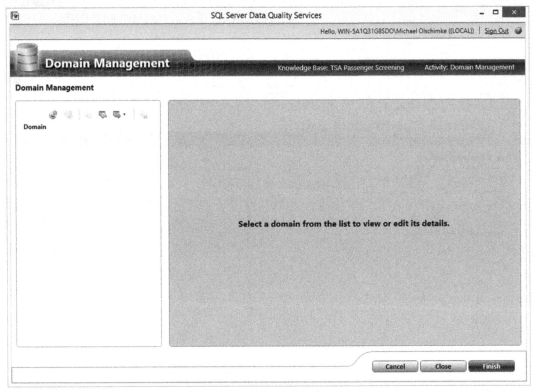

FIGURE 13.5

Domain management in the DQS client.

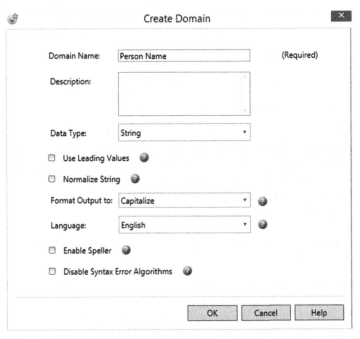

FIGURE 13.6

Create domain in DQS client.

Domains in DQS are defined by the following attributes:

- **Domain name:** the name of the domain.
- **Description:** an optional description of the domain.
- **Data type:** the data type of the domain.
- **Use leading values:** indicates that a leading value should be used instead of synonyms that have the same meaning.
- **Normalize string:** indicates if punctuation should be removed from the input string when performing data quality operations.
- **Format output to:** indicates the data format that should be used when domain values are returned.
- **Language:** the language of the domain's values. This is an important attribute for string domains, required by data quality algorithms.
- **Enable speller:** indicates if the language speller should be applied to the incoming raw data.
- **Disable syntax error algorithms:** this option is used in knowledge discovery activities to check for syntax errors.

Some of these options are only available when the **data type** has been set to **string**.

Close the dialog and switch to the **domain rules** tab (Figure 13.7).

Create a new domain rule that will be used to ensure the maximum string length of a name part. Give it a meaningful name and build the rule as shown in Figure 13.7. This completes the setup of the first domain. Use the dialog to set up the remaining domains in the knowledge database (Table 13.1).

Note that the other domains do not use domain rules (even though **Person DOB** contains some interesting errors in the test dataset). **Person sex** and **person name suffix** define domain values instead (Figure 13.8 and Figure 13.9).

Only the characters "F" and "M" are valid domain values for the domain **person sex**. All other values in raw data will be considered invalid. NULL values are corrected to empty strings.

The domain person name suffix contains a defined set of valid domain values, including "II", "III", "IV" and "Jr.". However, the raw data contains other values as well, for example "JR" which is corrected to "Jr.". In addition, after initial analysis, some errors in the data have been found, for example the suffix "IL" which is corrected to "II".

Whenever a correction is performed by DQS, a warning is provided to the user. It is possible to return this warning to SSIS as well for further processing.

Table 13.1 Domains to Set Up in the Knowledge Database

Domain Name	Data Type	Options	Format	Rule
Person Name	String		Capitalize	Length is less than or equal to <50>
Person DOB	Integer		None	none
Person Sex	String	Use Leading Values	Upper Case	None
Person Name Suffix	String	Use Leading Values Normalize String	None	none

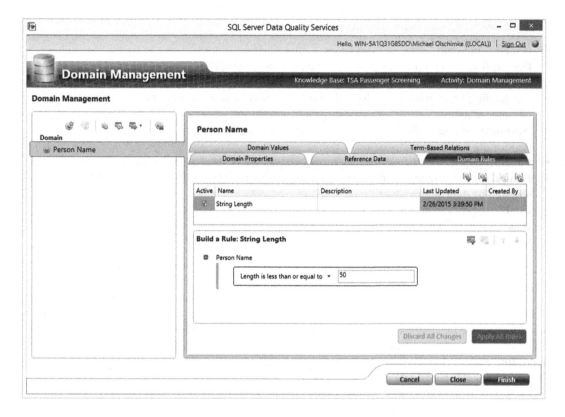

FIGURE 13.7

Defining domain rules for a domain in the DQS client.

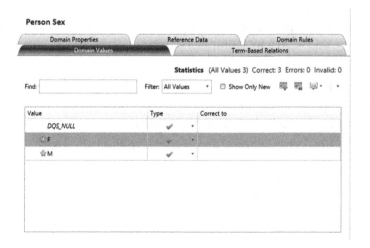

FIGURE 13.8

Domain values of the person sex domain.

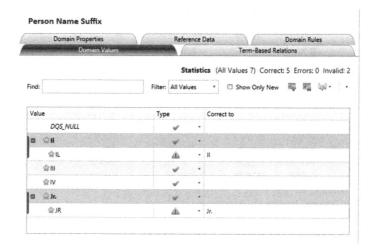

FIGURE 13.9
Domain values of the person name suffix domain.

The domain person name is used in multiple instances, for example as **person first name**, **person last name** and **person middle name**. Instead of creating multiple, independent domains with redundant definitions, it is possible to derive new domains from existing domains by creating a linked domain (Figure 13.10).

Create all three linked domains and derive them from the person name domain. Commit the changes to the knowledge base by selecting the **finish** button on the bottom right of the DQS client. The domains are published to the knowledge base and are available to data stewards or SSIS processes.

13.8.3 SSIS EXAMPLE

The next step is to use the DQS knowledge base in SSIS to retrieve descriptive data from a raw satellite, cleanse the data and write it into a new materialized satellite in the Business Vault. The source data is stored in the raw satellite SatPassenger. Figure 13.11 shows some descriptive data from the satellite.

FIGURE 13.10

Creating a linked domain in DQS.

LastName	FirstName	MiddleName	Suffix	DOB	Sex
GROSS	KAYLA	KATHY		19960619	F
JACKSON	DANIEL	ALLEN		20000326	M
HAYS	ISIAH	JORDAN	JR	19970612	M
JOHNSON	MAURICE			19961122	M
DE JESUS	LUIS			19970828	M
CARLSEN	AMY	LEEANN		19970728	F
CLARK	MIKE	SAMUEL		19970129	M
O BRYANT	SEAN			19970801	M
SHEPPARD	STEVEN	T		19970130	M
HUGHES	JOSEPH			19970609	M
KING	CHRISTY			19990920	F
HAYAKAWA	ATSUSHI			19960609	F
BARRON	ANTHONY	ALFONSO		19970801	M

FIGURE 13.11

Sample data from SatPassenger.

The following DDL statement is used to create the target satellite:

```
CREATE TABLE [biz].[SatCleansedPassenger](
        [PersonHashKey] [varchar](32) NOT NULL,
        [LoadDate] [datetime2](7) NOT NULL,
        [LoadEndDate] [datetime2](7) NULL,
        [RecordSource] [nvarchar](50) NOT NULL,
        [Sequence] [int] NOT NULL,
        [LastName] [nvarchar](50) NOT NULL,
        [LastName_Status] [nvarchar](100) NULL,
        [LastName_Confidence] [nvarchar](100) NULL,
        [LastName_Reason] [nvarchar](4000) NULL,
        [FirstName] [nvarchar](50) NOT NULL,
        [FirstName_Status] [nvarchar](100) NULL,
        [FirstName_Confidence] [nvarchar](100) NULL,
        [FirstName_Reason] [nvarchar](4000) NULL,
        [MiddleName] [nvarchar](50) NOT NULL,
        [MiddleName_Status] [nvarchar](100) NULL,
        [MiddleName_Confidence] [nvarchar](100) NULL,
        [MiddleName_Reason] [nvarchar](4000) NULL,
        [Suffix] [nvarchar](50) NULL,
        [Suffix_Status] [nvarchar](100) NULL,
        [Suffix_Confidence] [nvarchar](100) NULL,
        [Suffix_Reason] [nvarchar](4000) NULL,
        [DOB] [date] NULL,
        [DOB_Status] [nvarchar](100) NULL,
        [DOB_Confidence] [nvarchar](100) NULL,
        [DOB_Reason] [nvarchar](4000) NULL,
        [Sex] [varchar](1) NOT NULL,
        [Sex_Status] [nvarchar](100) NULL,
        [Sex_Confidence] [nvarchar](100) NULL,
        [Sex_Reason] [nvarchar](4000) NULL,
        [Record Status] [nvarchar](100) NULL,
        [Appended Data] [nvarchar](4000) NULL,
        [Appended Data Schema] [nvarchar](4000) NULL,
  CONSTRAINT [PK_SatCleansedPassenger] PRIMARY KEY NONCLUSTERED
(
        [PersonHashKey] ASC,
        [LoadDate] ASC
) ON [INDEX]
) ON [DATA]
```

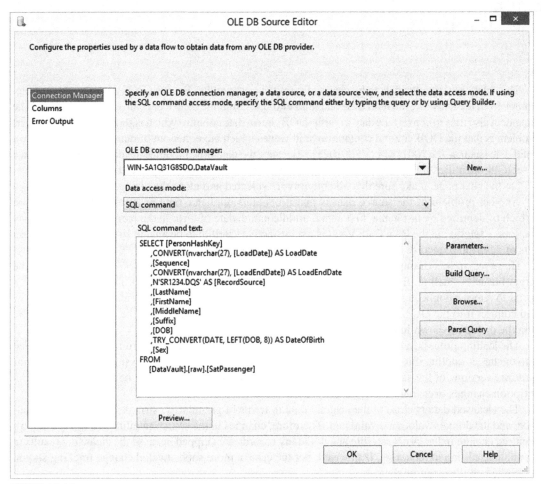

FIGURE 13.12

OLE DB source editor to retrieve raw data from source satellite.

Despite the existence of a sequence attribute, the previous satellite is a standard (computed) satellite and not a multi-active satellite. The sequence number is not included in the primary key definition. It is used for reference purposes only, in order to retrieve the raw data for a cleansed record.

Create a new data flow and add an OLE DB source to it. Open the editor to configure the source connection and columns (Figure 13.12).

Select the source database **DataVault** and choose **SQL command** as data access mode. Set the **SQL command text** to the following query:

```
SELECT [PersonHashKey]
      ,CONVERT(nvarchar(27), [LoadDate]) AS LoadDate
      ,[Sequence]
      ,CONVERT(nvarchar(27), [LoadEndDate]) AS LoadEndDate
      ,N'SR1234.DQS' AS [RecordSource]
      ,[LastName]
      ,[FirstName]
      ,[MiddleName]
      ,[Suffix]
      ,[DOB]
      ,TRY_CONVERT(DATE, LEFT(DOB, 8)) AS DateOfBirth
      ,[Sex]
FROM
      [DataVault].[raw].[SatPassenger]
```

This query retrieves the data to be cleansed from the raw satellite. Because DQS doesn't support time-stamps from the database, the **load date** and **load end date** from the source are converted into strings. The statement also tries to convert the date of birth (DOB) into a date column (which is supported by DQS). The problem is that the DOB column contains invalid values which are either out of range or do not specify a valid date (such as the 20011414 or 20010231). Because the data flow modifies the data, the record source is set to the identifier of the soft business rule definition in the meta mart (formatted as Unicode string).

On the next page, make sure that all columns are selected and close the dialog.

Another problem of the source data is that it contains duplicate data describing the same person (which is identified by last name, first name, middle name, date of birth in the parent hub). This is why the source satellite in the Raw Data Vault is a multi-active satellite to be able to store multiple different sets of descriptive records for the same (composite) business key.

However, in this example, the business has decided to store only one passenger description in the target business satellite. Because it doesn't really matter which one is chosen, it is possible to use a sorter to remove duplicates in a simple approach. Therefore, drag a sort transformation to the data flow and connect it to the OLE DB source transformation from the last step. Open the editor and configure it in the dialog as shown in Figure 13.13.

The loading process in this section follows a simple approach: each record from the source is loaded into the target satellite if it is not a duplicate of the same description within the same batch. That means multiple versions of the same record should be loaded into the target to show how the (cleansed) description changes over time.

The cleansed data is close to the original data in terms of granularity: strings are correctly capitalized, and the domain values are validated. Therefore, changes in the source satellite will likely lead to a required change in the target satellite and not many records are skipped because the cleansing results in an unchanged line in the target. If this were not the case, a more sophisticated change tracking should be applied on the cleansed data.

Because the approach used in this example is simplified, the data is sorted by the two columns **PassengerHashKey** and **LoadDate** only. When new entries are loaded in later batches, they are just taken over; however, duplicate records for the same passenger in the same batch are removed.

In order to ensure the restartability of the process, the data flow has to check if there is already a record with the same hash key and load date in the target satellite. This is done using a lookup component, especially because no descriptive data should be compared (because the data flow avoids true delta checking on the target). Add a lookup transformation to the data flow, connect it to the existing transformations and open the lookup transformation editor (Figure 13.14).

The setup is similar to other loading procedures, as rows without matching entries are redirected to a "no match output." The only difference is that the cache has been turned off: using the cache in this example makes no sense because the combination of hash key and load date is unique in the underlying data stream from the source (due to the de-duplication in the sort transformation from the last step) and, therefore, the lookup would not profit from an enabled cache. The lookup condition will be configured on the third page of this dialog (the **columns** page).

Select the next page to set up the connection (Figure 13.15).

Because the SQL command text used in the source has converted the load date to a string data type (due to DQS), the same has to be done in the lookup. Otherwise, the columns cannot be used in the lookup condition because of different data types. Connect to the **DataVault** database and use the following statement to retrieve the data for the lookup:

```
SELECT
    [PersonHashKey]
    ,CONVERT(nvarchar(27), [LoadDate]) AS LoadDate
FROM
    [DataVault].[biz].[SatCleansedPassenger]
```

Because no descriptive data is required from the lookup table, only the **hash key** and the converted **load date** are retrieved from the target satellite in the Business Vault. The lookup condition based on these two columns is configured on the next page, shown in Figure 13.16.

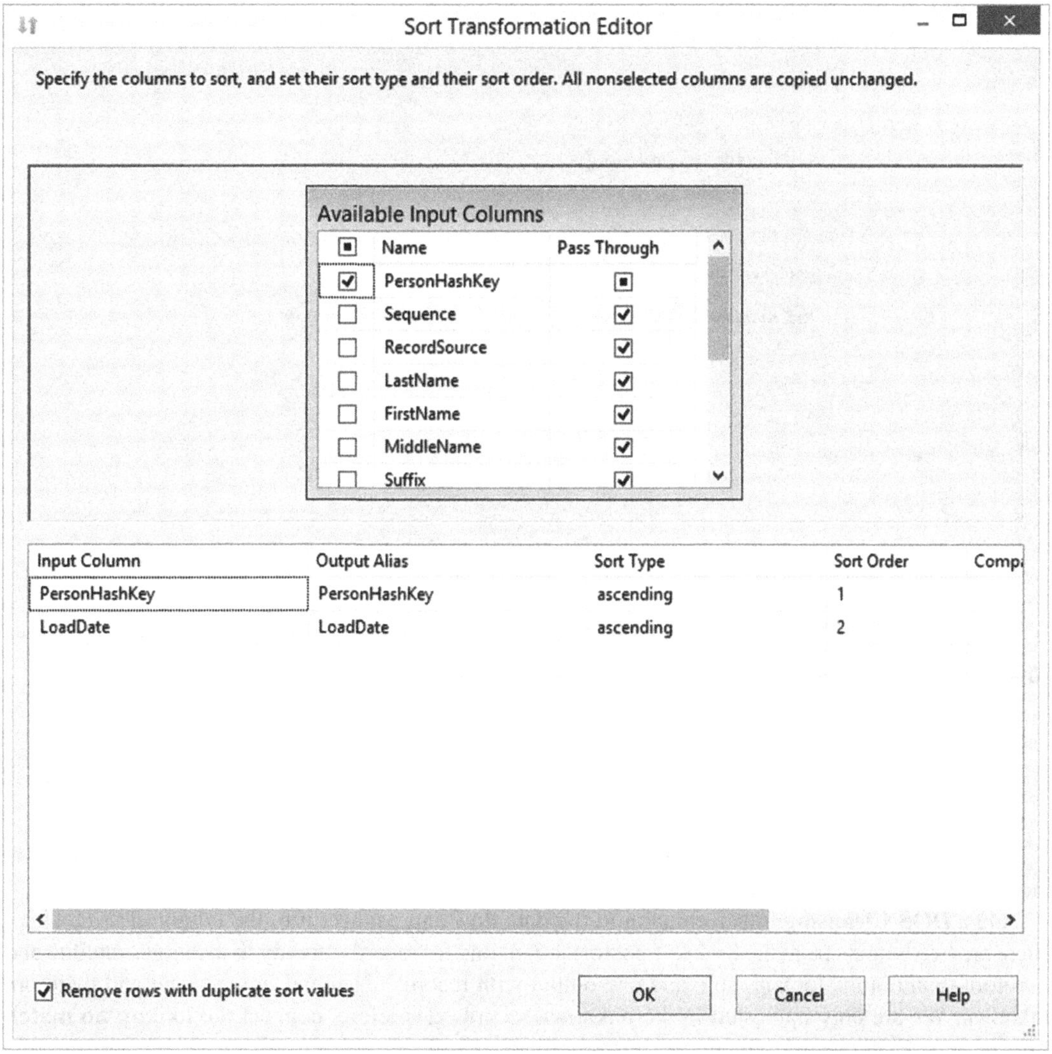

FIGURE 13.13

Sort transformation editor to remove duplicate passenger descriptions.

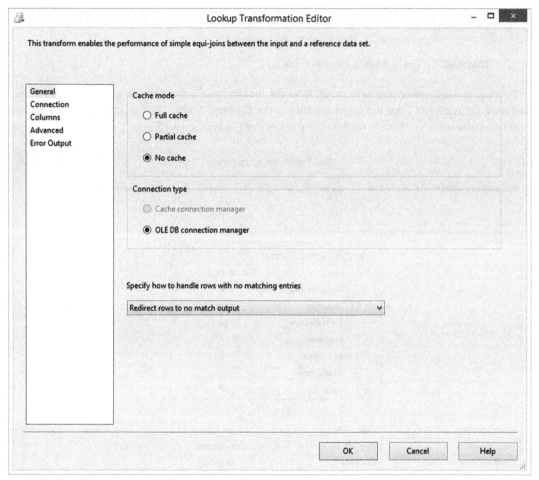

FIGURE 13.14

Lookup transformation editor to check if the key combination is already in the cleansed target satellite.

Connect the corresponding hash keys and load dates from both the source table and the lookup table and close the dialog by clicking the OK button.

Add a **DQS Cleansing** transformation to the data flow and connect it to the output of the lookup. There are two outputs from the lookup transformation: one for records already in the target satellite and therefore found in the lookup table and one output with records not found in the target and therefore unknown. We are only interested in the unknown records. Therefore, connect the **lookup no match output** to the DQS cleansing input, as shown in Figure 13.17.

After closing the dialog, the connection between components is configured. Open the configuration editor for the DQS cleansing transformation (Figure 13.18).

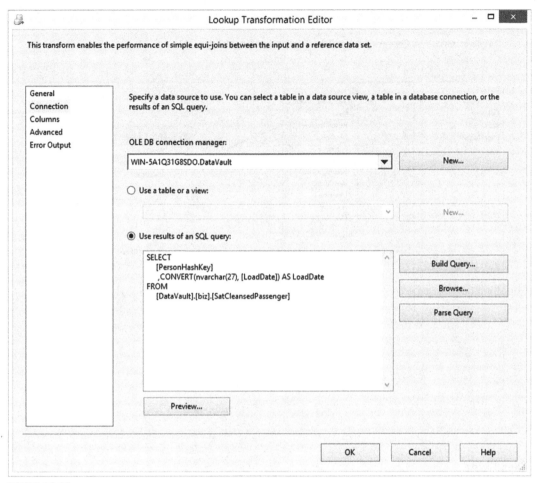

FIGURE 13.15

Set up the connection of the lookup transformation.

Create a new connection to the DQS server by using the **new** button. Once the connection is established, select the knowledge base configured in the previous section. The dialog will show domains found in the knowledge base.

Switch to the **mapping** tab to map the columns in the data flow to the domains in the knowledge base (Figure 13.19).

Select the columns from the data flow that should be cleansed in the grid on the upper half of the dialog. In order to cleanse a column, a corresponding DQS domain is required. If there are other columns in the data flow without a corresponding domain in the knowledge base, they have to be added in DQS first (as in the previous section).

Map each selected input column to a DQS domain. Leave all other options (source alias, output alias, status alias, confidence alias and reason alias), as they are. These columns will provide useful

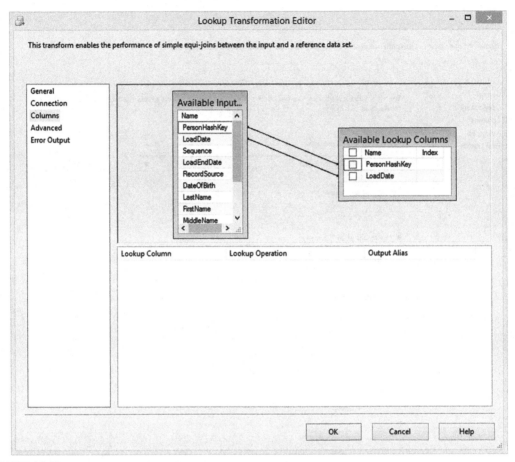

FIGURE 13.16

Configure lookup condition.

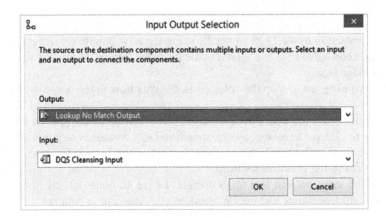

FIGURE 13.17

Connecting the lookup output to the DQS cleansing input.

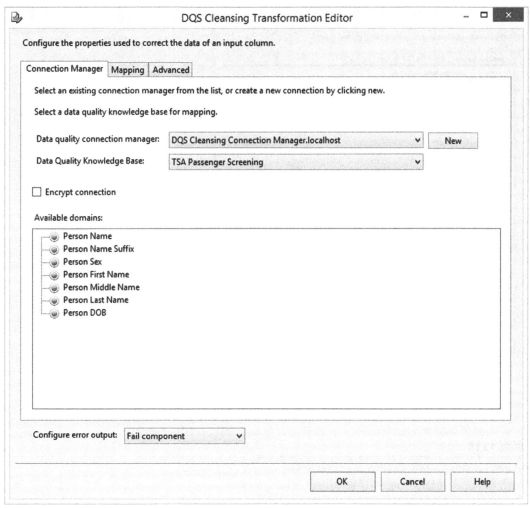

FIGURE 13.18

DQS cleansing transformation editor.

information about the data cleansing operations to the business user. However, in order to actually include these informative columns in the output of the DQS cleansing transformation, switch to the **advanced** tab (Figure 13.20).

Check all options to add all informative columns. The first option is used to standardize the output, which means that their standardized counterparts might replace domain values.

Close the dialog and add an OLE DB destination component to the data flow. Connect it to the DQS cleansing transformation. Open the editor of the OLE DB destination transformation to configure it (Figure 13.21).

Select the **DataVault** database and the target satellite in the Business Vault. Configure the column mapping between the data flow and the target table on the next page, shown in Figure 13.22.

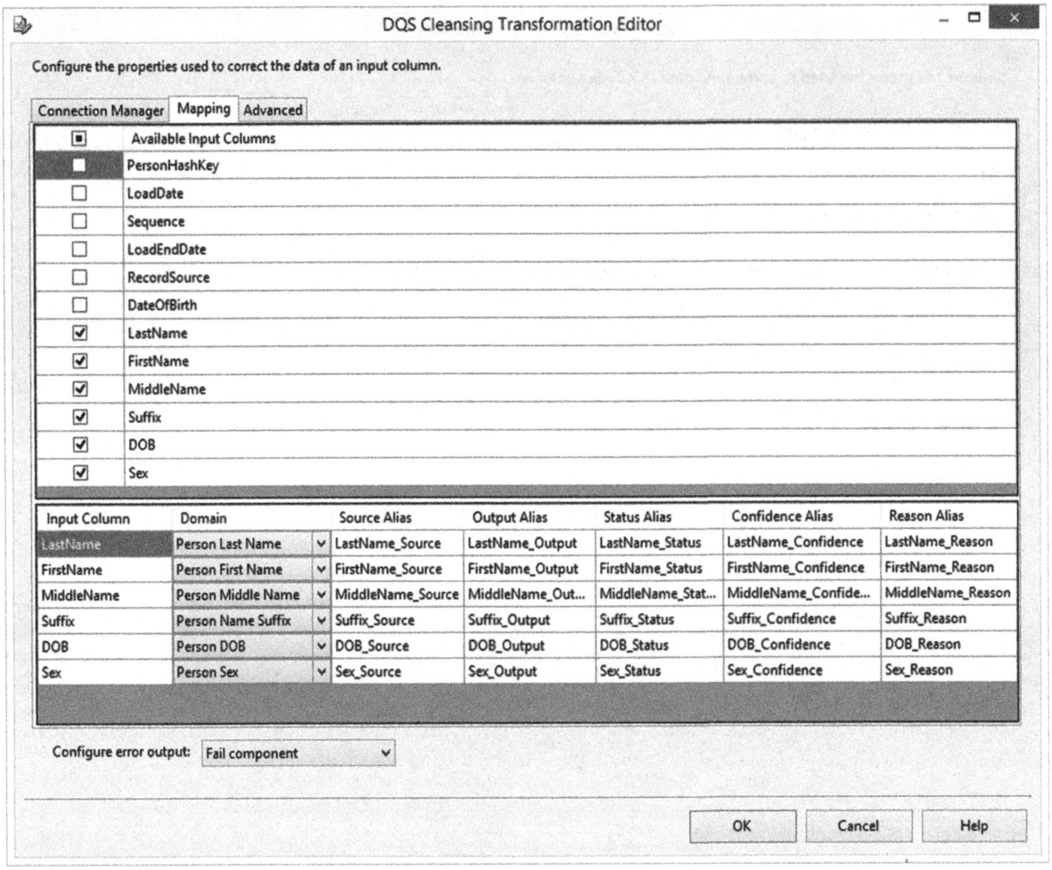

FIGURE 13.19

Mapping columns from the data flow to DQS domains.

The source columns from the DQS cleansing transformation are ignored because the same data is found in the raw satellite. The sequence from the source is added as a descriptive attribute to the target satellite (which is not a multi-active satellite) to retrieve the corresponding record from the source. The output columns are mapped to the cleansed attributes. All other attributes (status, confidence, and reason) are added and mapped to the target as well.

The final data flow is presented in Figure 13.23.

Because the lookup is executed before the DQS cleansing takes place, the data is reduced to the records that are unknown to the target satellite and actually require data cleansing: all known records have been cleansed in the past.

Note that the ETL process to build a business satellite often doesn't follow a prescribed template, as is the case when loading the Raw Data Vault as shown in Chapter 12, Loading the Data Vault. Instead, most business vault entities are loaded using individual processes, which is hard to automate.

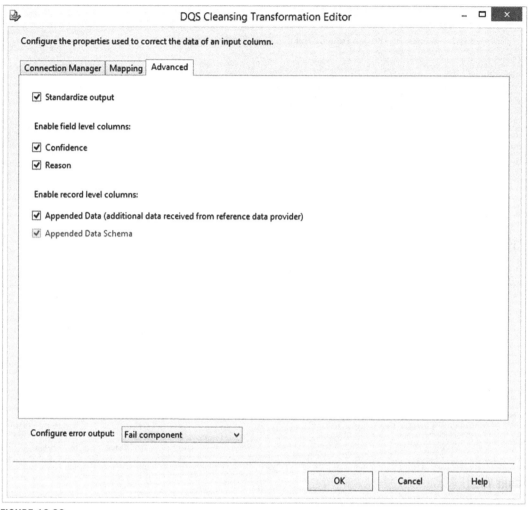

FIGURE 13.20

Advanced tab of DQS cleansing transformation editor.

To complete the process, it is required to end-date the target satellite. This approach, however, follows the standard end-dating process for satellites in the Raw Data Vault, outlined in Chapter 12.

To further improve the solution, the informative attributes from the DQS cleansing transformation could be loaded into a separate satellite instead of the same target. This would improve the usability and performance of the cleansed satellite.

The resulting satellite can be used as any other satellite in the Raw or Business Data Vault for loading the information marts.

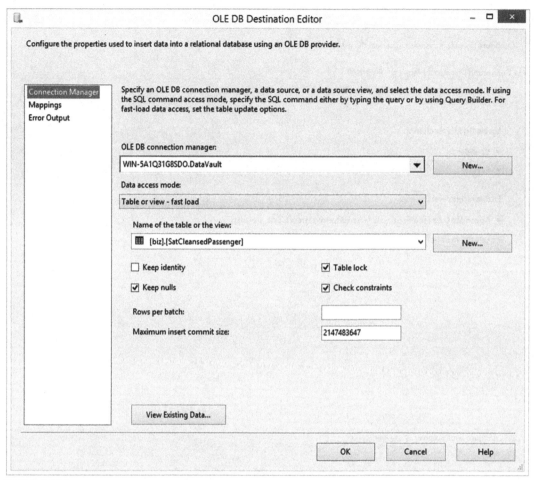

FIGURE 13.21

OLE DB destination editor for target satellite in Business Vault.

13.9 MATCH AND CONSOLIDATE DATA

A typical task in data warehousing is to resolve identities that [36]:

- **Represent the same entity:** here, duplicate business keys or relationships from the same or different source systems mean the same business entity. The typical goal is to merge the business entities into one and consolidate the data from both records or remove duplicate data in favor of a master record.
- **Represent the wrong entity:** there are cases where the business user thinks that a record is not in the system because of a slight variation in the descriptive data, which leads to an unfound (yet existing) record [10].

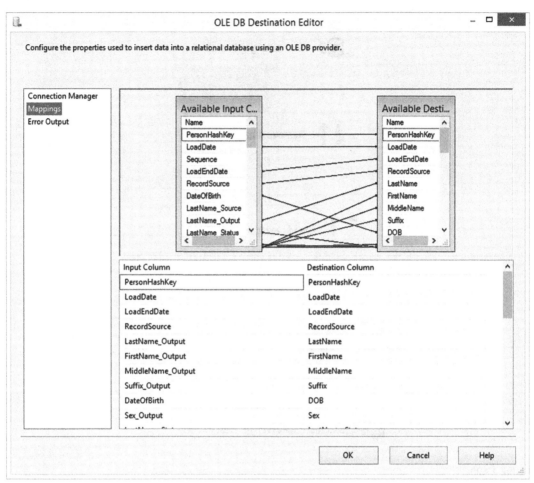

FIGURE 13.22

Column mapping in the OLE DB destination editor.

- **Represent the same household:** in other cases, there are different business entities (identified as such) that belong together. For example, they live in the same household or work in the same organization. The goal is to aggregate the data to the higher order entity.

For all cases, there are entities in the Data Vault 2.0 model that support each of them. The resolution of duplicate identifiers for the same business entities can be solved with a same-as-link (SAL) that was introduced in Chapter 5. Errors in descriptive data can be fixed using computed satellites, similar to the approaches discussed in section 13.8. The last case can be solved with a hierarchical link.

This approach can be supported by a variety of techniques and tools, for example [3]:

- **Data matching techniques:** it is possible to identify potential duplicates using matching techniques, such as phonetic, match code, cross-reference, partial text match, pattern matching, and fuzzy logic algorithms [6].

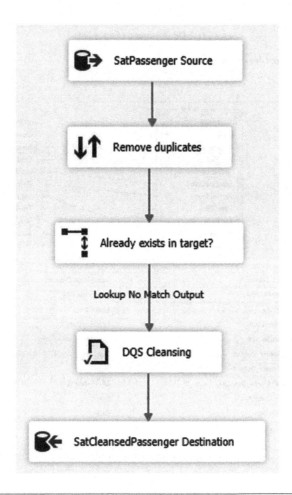

FIGURE 13.23

Data cleansing in SSIS.

- **Data mining software:** instead of relying on rules, data mining tools rely on artificial intelligence algorithms that find close matches.
- **Data correction software:** such software implements data cleansing and other algorithms to test for potential duplicate matches and merge the records.

The next section presents how to de-duplicate data using a fuzzy data matching algorithm included in SSIS.

13.9.1 SSIS EXAMPLE

Fuzzy logic represents a fairly easy approach for data de-duplication and is supported by SSIS. The example in section 13.8.3 has demonstrated how to cleanse descriptive attributes in satellites. The satellite also contained duplicate data, describing similar persons. However, in order to cleanse the data, the hub has to be cleansed first.

The recommended approach for data de-duplication in Data Vault 2.0 is to take advantage of a same-as link, introduced in Chapter 5. By doing so, the raw data is left untouched and the concept provides the most flexibility.

The **HubPerson** is defined using the following DDL:

```
CREATE TABLE [raw].[HubPerson](
        [PersonHashKey] [char](32) NOT NULL,
        [LoadDate] [datetime2](7) NOT NULL,
        [RecordSource] [nvarchar](50) NOT NULL,
        [LastName] [nvarchar](50) NOT NULL,
        [FirstName] [nvarchar](50) NOT NULL,
        [MiddleName] [nvarchar](50) NOT NULL,
        [DOB] [int] NOT NULL,
 CONSTRAINT [PK_HubPerson] PRIMARY KEY NONCLUSTERED
(
        [PersonHashKey] ASC
) ON [INDEX],
 CONSTRAINT [UK_HubPerson] UNIQUE NONCLUSTERED
(
        [LastName] ASC,
        [FirstName] ASC,
        [MiddleName] ASC,
        [DOB] ASC
) ON [INDEX]
) ON [DATA]
```

The business key of this hub is a composite key consisting of the attributes LastName, FirstName, MiddleName, and date of birth DOB, apparently because there was no passenger ID or person ID available in the source data. This is a weak way of identifying a person, with many possible false positive matches. The better approach is to use a business key for this identification purpose. However, the sample data doesn't provide such a business key and, in reality, there are some cases where no business key for persons is available.

Create the following same-as link so it can be used as the data flow's destination:

```
CREATE TABLE [biz].[SALPerson](
        [SALPersonHashKey] [char](32) NOT NULL,
        [LoadDate] [datetime2](7) NOT NULL,
        [RecordSource] [nvarchar](50) NOT NULL,
        [PersonMasterHashKey] [char](32) NOT NULL,
        [PersonDuplicateHashKey] [char](32) NOT NULL,
        [Score] [real] NOT NULL,
 CONSTRAINT [PK_SALPerson] PRIMARY KEY NONCLUSTERED
(
        [SALPersonHashKey] ASC
) ON [INDEX],
 CONSTRAINT [UK_SALPerson] UNIQUE NONCLUSTERED
(
        [PersonMasterHashKey] ASC,
        [PersonDuplicateHashKey] ASC
) ON [INDEX]
) ON [DATA]
```

The same-as link is defined by two hash keys, which point to the same referenced hub, **HubPerson**. One of the hash keys references the master record; the other hash key references the duplicate record that should be replaced by the master in subsequent queries.

Create a new data flow and drag an **OLE DB source** component to it. Open the editor (Figure 13.24).

Because only data is used as descriptive input for the following fuzzy group process, no other descriptive data needs to be joined to the source. Therefore, the **HubPerson** in the Raw Data Vault is selected. If additional descriptive data should be considered in the de-duplication process, for example data from dependent satellites, the data should be joined in a source SQL command.

Make sure that all columns from the hub are included in the OLE DB source and close the dialog. Add a **fuzzy grouping** transformation to the canvas of the data flow and connect it to the source.

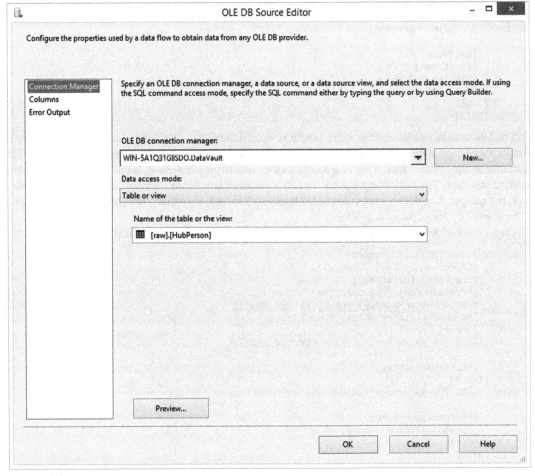

FIGURE 13.24

OLE DB source editor for HubPerson.

Because the fuzzy grouping algorithm is resource-intensive, it requires a database for storing temporary SQL Server tables. Create a new connection and specify the **tempdb** database (Figure 13.25).

The advantage of the **tempdb** database is that every user has access to the database and created objects are dropped on disconnect [11]. In most cases, it is also configured for such applications. As an alternative, it is also possible to use another database for storing these temporary objects. You should consult your data warehouse administrator for more information.

Make sure the created tempdb connection manager is selected on the first page of the fuzzy grouping transformation editor (Figure 13.26).

Select the **columns** tab to set up the descriptive columns that should be used in the de-duplication process (Figure 13.27).

Select all descriptive columns and set the match type. For string columns, this should be fuzzy. In some cases, it makes sense to enforce the exactness of other attributes, as this is the case for the DOB column. This domain knowledge is usually provided by the business user.

Make sure that all other columns that are not used in the fuzzy grouping algorithm are activated for pass-through and switch to the **advanced** tab, shown in Figure 13.28.

FIGURE 13.25

Configuring tempdb for fuzzy grouping.

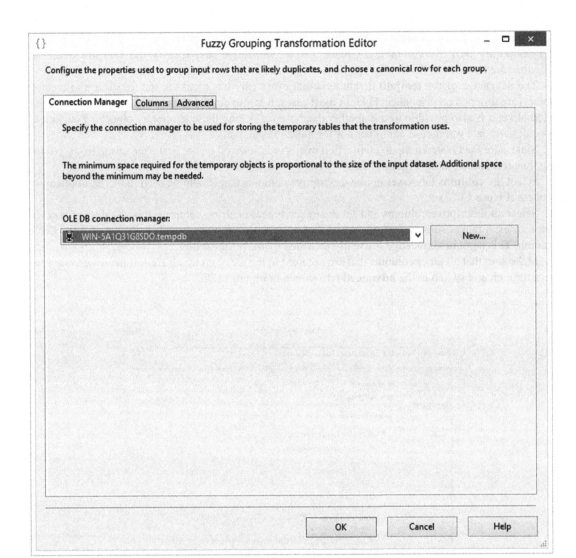

FIGURE 13.26

Configuring the connection manager of the fuzzy grouping transformation.

The similarity threshold influences which persons are considered as duplicates. The lower the threshold is, the more false-positive matches the algorithm will produce. On the other hand, keeping the value too high increases the number of false-negative matches:

- **False-positive match:** the fuzzy-grouping algorithm wrongly (false) thinks that two persons are the same (positive).
- **False-negative match:** the fuzzy-grouping algorithm wrongly (false) thinks that two persons are not the same (negative).

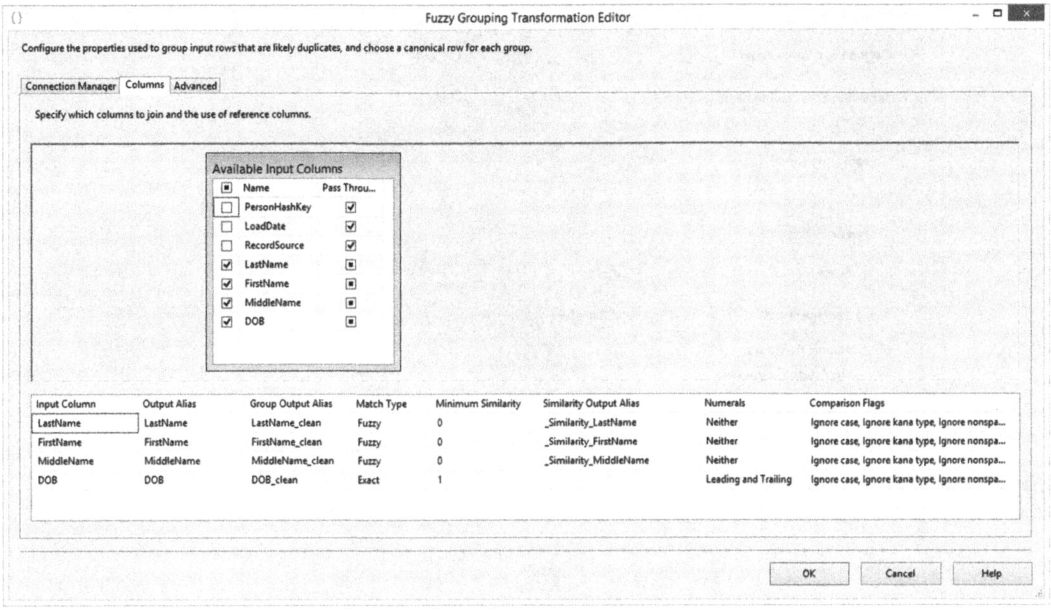

FIGURE 13.27

Setting up descriptive columns for de-duplication.

- **True-positive match:** the algorithms correctly (true) identified two persons as duplicates (positive).
- **True-negative match:** the algorithm correctly (true) classified both persons as different (negative).

While the default value of 0.80 is a good setting for most cases, the same-as link is capable of providing a better solution when setting this threshold to a lower value because it gives the user of the same-as link (the information mart or a power user) more choices. Therefore, set the threshold to a very low value of 0.05. This will produce a lot of false-negative matches, but section 13.10 will demonstrate that it doesn't matter (not from a storage or usage perspective) but allows the user to use a user-defined threshold instead of relying on this constant value. It is only recommended to set the threshold to a higher value when dealing with large volumes of business keys in the source hub (regardless of any descriptive data).

The result that will be produced by the fuzzy grouping transformation is shown in Figure 13.29. The transformation adds the columns defined in Figure 13.28 which are used as follows:

- **_key_in:** a surrogate key that identifies the original record. In the same-as link terminology, this is the duplicate key. The surrogate key was introduced by SSIS and is not coming from the source.
- **_key_out:** the surrogate key of the record that the record should be mapped to. This is the master key. If the record should not be mapped to another record, both surrogate keys are the same.
- **_score:** the similarity score of both records (the duplicate and the master record). If both are the same (and no mapping takes place), the similarity score is 1.0 (100% equal).

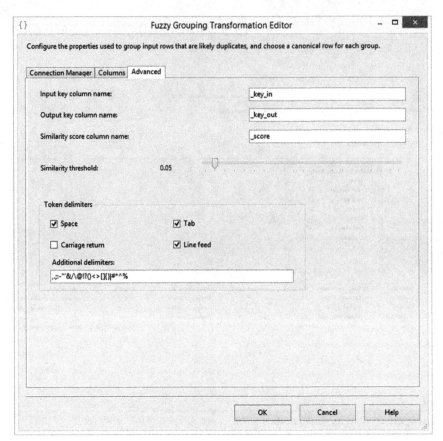

FIGURE 13.28

Configuring advanced options in the fuzzy grouping transformation editor.

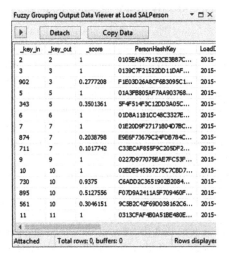

FIGURE 13.29

Output of fuzzy grouping transformation.

The problem with this output, which cannot be influenced much, is that the hash keys of the master and duplicate records are required for loading the target same-as link. The hash key that is in the data flow identifies the duplicate record. In order to add the hash key of the master, the easiest and probably the fastest way is to create a copy of the data and merge it back by joining over the surrogate keys.

Close the fuzzy grouping transformation editor, add a **multicast** transformation to the data flow and add two **sort** transformations, each fed from a path from the multicast transformation. The first sort transformation is configured to sort its own copy of the data flow by the surrogate key of the master record (Figure 13.30).

Select the column **_key_out** for sorting and pass through all other columns. Close the dialog and open the configuration dialog for the second sort transformation, which sorts its copy of the data flow by the surrogate key of the duplicate record (Figure 13.31).

Select the surrogate key of the duplicate, which is **_key_in**. Enable pass-through for all other columns. Close the dialog and add a **merge join** transformation. Connect it to the outputs of both sort transformations and open the transformation editor (Figure 13.32).

Connect **_key_in** from the duplicate data stream to **_key_out** from the master data stream with each other. This becomes the join condition. Select both hash keys and name them **MasterPersonHashKey** and **DuplicatePersonHashKey**. They will be written to the target link and reference the hub. Make sure to select all elements of the composite business key (LastName, FirstName, MiddleName, and DOB) from each stream. They are required in order to calculate the hash key for the same-as link. In addition, select the **_score** attribute from the duplicate data stream. It will be written to the target link as well.

Set the join type to inner join: there should be a matching master record in the second data flow.

Close the editor and connect the output of the **merge join** transformation to a new **derived column** transformation. It is used to calculate the hash key of the same-as link using the approach presented in Chapter 11, Data Extraction (see Figure 13.33).

Add a **load date** to the stream and retrieve the load date of the current batch from the SSIS variable **dLoadDate**. Set the **record source** to an identifier for the soft rule. Calculate the input to be used for the link hash key (SALPersonHashKey) calculation using the following expression:

```
UPPER(TRIM(REPLACENULL(DuplicateLastName,""")) + ";" + TRIM(REPLACENULL(DuplicateFirstName,"""))
+ ";" + TRIM(REPLACENULL(DuplicateMiddleName,"")) + ";" +
TRIM(REPLACENULL((DT_WSTR,8)DuplicateDOB,"")) + ";" + TRIM(REPLACENULL(MasterLastName,"")) +
";" + TRIM(REPLACENULL(MasterFirstName,"")) + ";" + TRIM(REPLACENULL(MasterMiddleName,"")) + ";"
+ TRIM(REPLACENULL((DT_WSTR,8)MasterDOB,"")))
```

Make sure the name of the input column ends with "LinkBK" so that the hash function can catch up the business key automatically. Drag a script component to the canvas and connect it to the existing data flow. Its purpose is to calculate the hash key based on the input created in the last step. It follows the same approach as in Chapter 11.

Open the script transformation editor and switch to the **input** columns page (Figure 13.34).

Select the input column created in the previous step. Switch to the **inputs and outputs** tab and create a new output (Figure 13.35).

Add a new output column to the existing output. Use the exact same name as the selected input column but ending with "HashKey" (refer to Chapter 11 for details). Use a string data type with a length

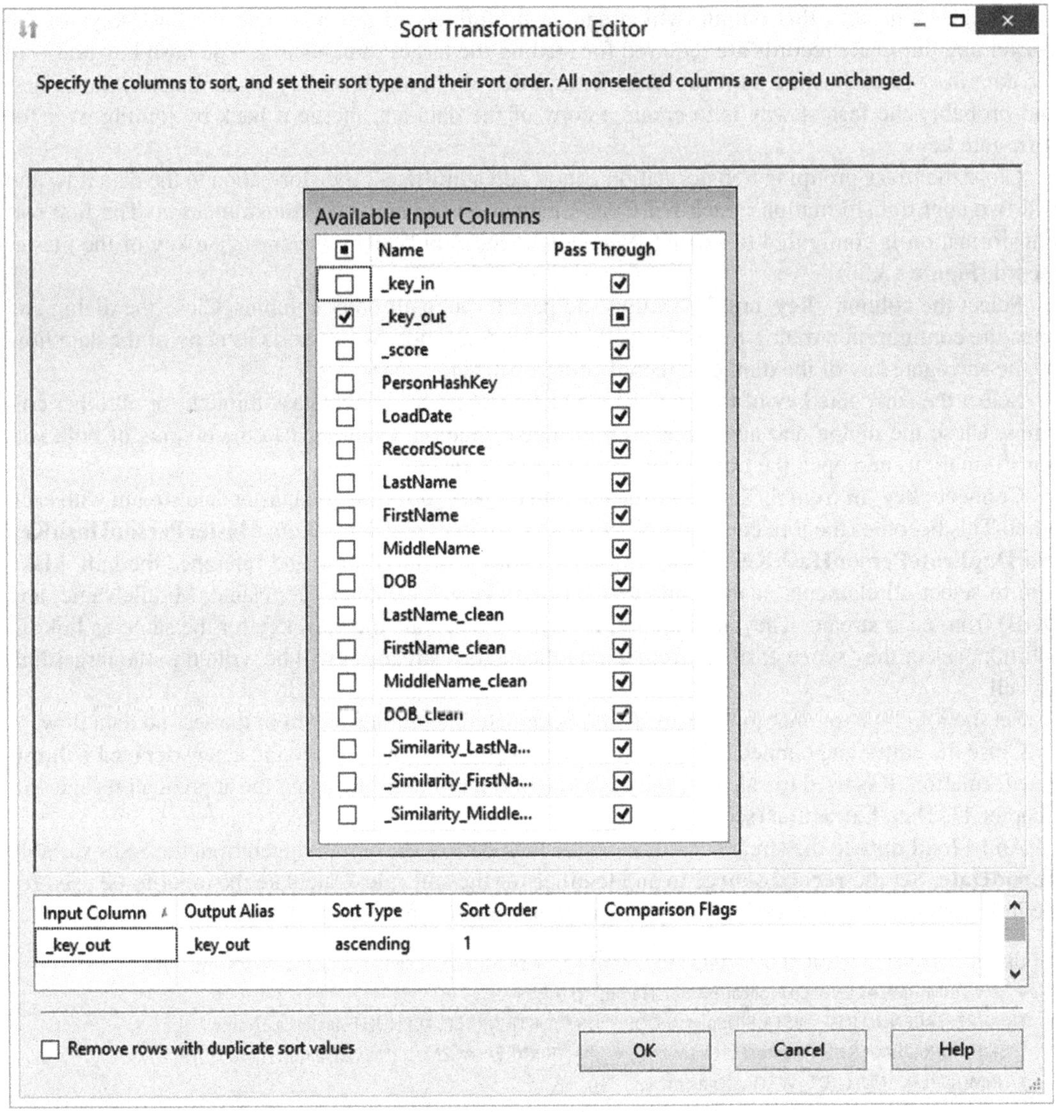

FIGURE 13.30

Configuration of the sort transformation of the master data flow.

of 32 characters and code page 1252 (or whatever code page is appropriate in your data warehouse environment). However, note that the hash key uses only characters from 0 to 9 and A to F. Switch to the script tab and add the script from Chapter 11.

Build the script and close both the script editor and the script transformation editor. Drag an **OLE DB destination** component to the data flow and connect it to the output of the script component. Open the editor to configure the target (Figure 13.36).

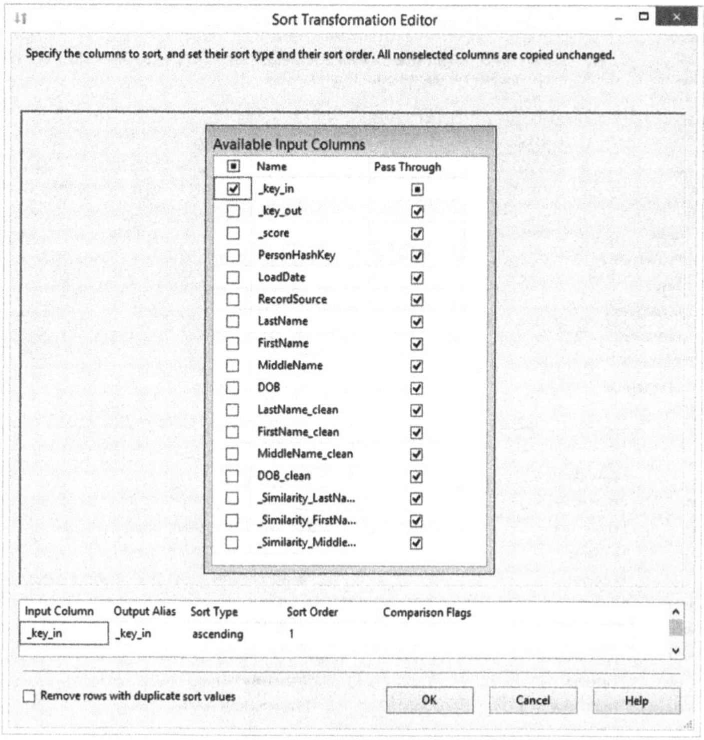

FIGURE 13.31

Configuration of the sort transformation of the duplicate data flow.

Select the target link SALPerson in the Business Vault. Check keep nulls and table lock. Switch to the mappings tab to configure the mapping between the data flow and the target table (Figure 13.37).

Make sure that each target column is sourced from the data flow. Close the dialog.

The final data flow is presented in Figure 13.38.

There are two options to run this data flow in practice:

1. Incremental load: this approach requires updating entries when the scores or the mapping (from duplicate to master) change.
2. Truncate target before full load: in order to avoid the update, the target is truncated and reloaded with every run.

In most cases, the second option is much easier to use while still feasible from a performance standpoint. Only if the hub contains many records is incremental loading required.

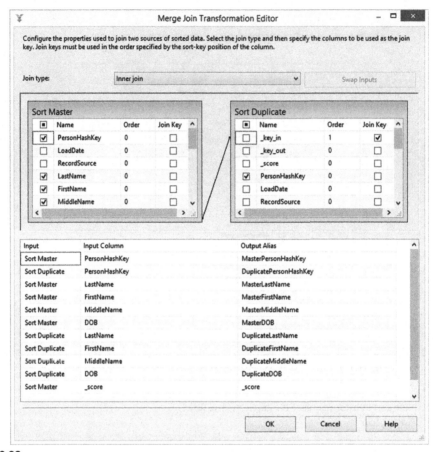

FIGURE 13.32

Merge join transformation editor for joining the master record to the duplicate record.

13.10 CREATING DIMENSIONS FROM SAME-AS LINKS

The same-as link created in the previous section can be used as the foundation for a de-duplicated dimension:

```
CREATE VIEW DimPassenger AS
SELECT
        src.PersonHashKey
        ,sat.FirstName
        ,sat.MiddleName
        ,sat.LastName
        ,sat.DOB
```

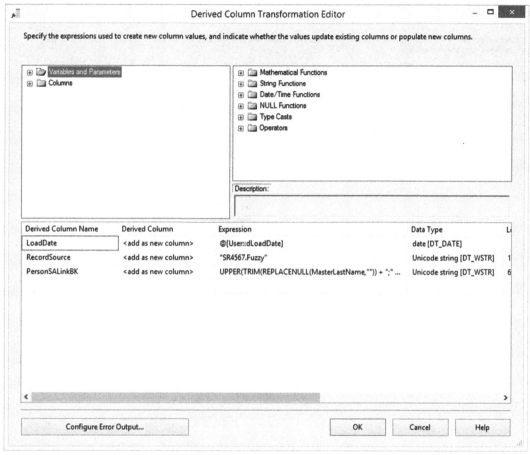

FIGURE 13.33

Derived column transformation editor.

```
FROM (
        SELECT DISTINCT PersonMasterHashKey AS PersonHashKey
        FROM [DataVault].[biz].[SALPerson]
        WHERE Score >= 0.5
        UNION ALL
        SELECT DISTINCT PersonDuplicateHashKey AS PersonHashKey
        FROM [DataVault].[biz].[SALPerson]
        WHERE Score < 0.5
) src
LEFT JOIN [DataVault].[biz].[SatCleansedPassenger] sat ON (
            sat.PersonHashKey = src.PersonHashKey AND sat.LoadEndDate IS NULL
)
WHERE
        sat.LoadEndDate IS NULL
        AND sat.PersonHashKey IS NOT NULL
```

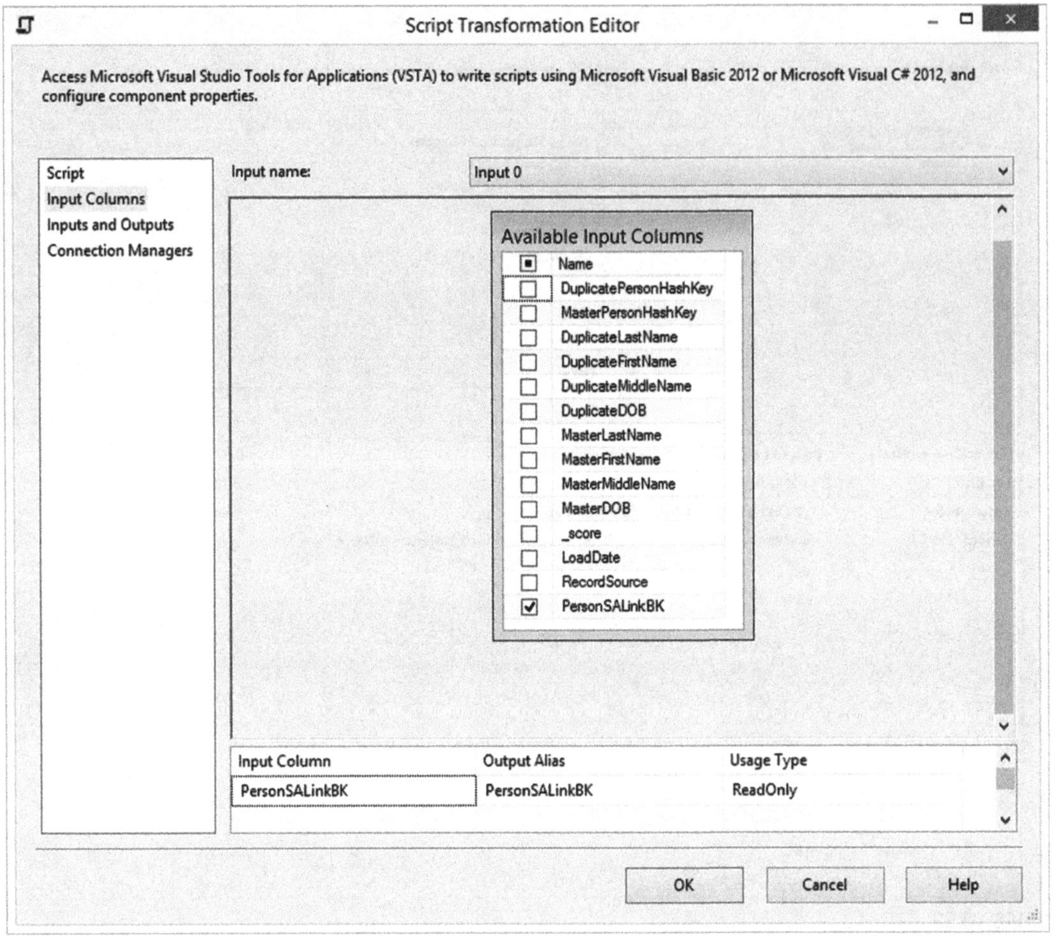

FIGURE 13.34

Configuring the input columns in the script transformation editor.

Instead of sourcing the virtual view from the actual hub and its satellites, the same-as link is used as the source and the satellites, which still hang off the hub, are joined to the same-as link to provide descriptive data.

The previous statement uses the score value from the fuzzy grouping transformation to dynamically select the mappings between the (potential) duplicate and the master record in the parent hub. By providing this score value, a power user can adjust this constant value (in the above statement 0.5) to include more or fewer mappings into the dimension: the lower the constant is set, the more business keys are mapped to a master in the dimension. A higher value means that the confidence of the algorithm should be higher before mapping takes place.

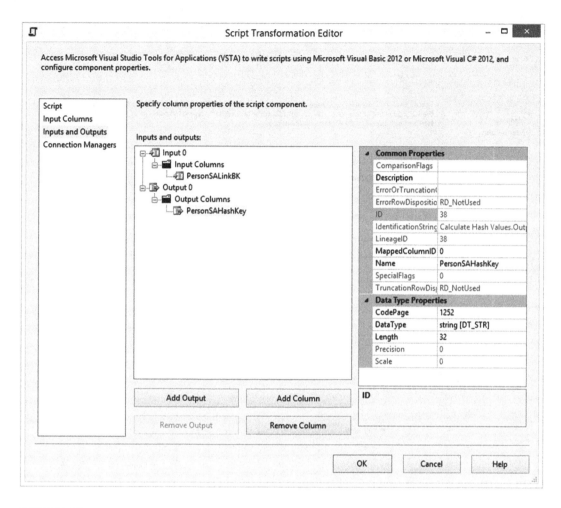

FIGURE 13.35

Configuring input and output columns in the script transformation editor.

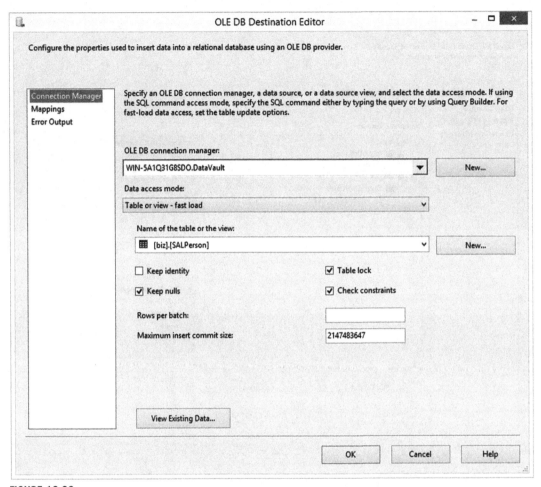

FIGURE 13.36

Configuring the same-as link target in the OLE DB destination editor.

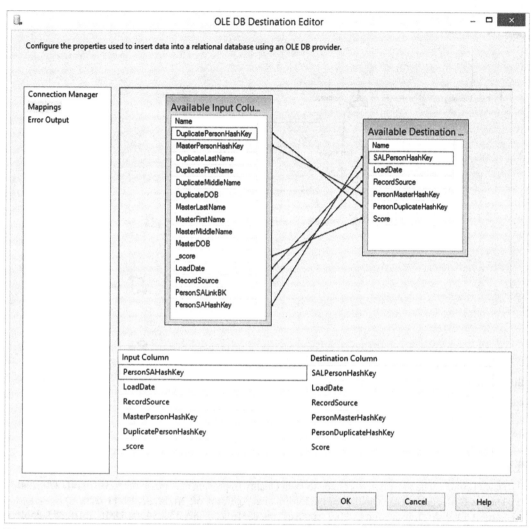

FIGURE 13.37

Configuring column mapping for the same-as link in the OLE DB destination editor.

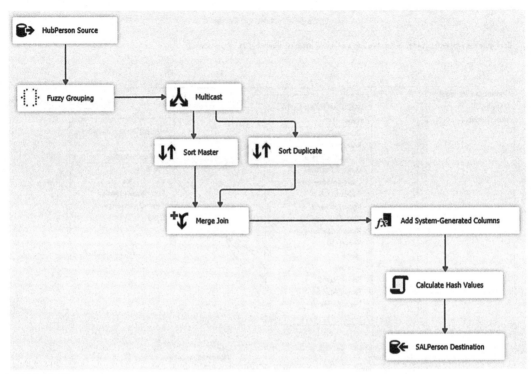

FIGURE 13.38

Data flow for de-duplication and loading same-as links.

REFERENCES

[1] David Loshin: "The Practitioner's Guide to Data Quality Improvement," pp. 4–6, 6f, 314, 314f, 270, 294f.

[2] Thomas C. Redman: "Data Quality for the Information Age", pp. 6f, 7ff, 8f, 9f, 10, 11, 22f.

[3] Larry P. English: "Information Quality Applied," pp. 251ff, 329, 332, 338, 345ff, 348ff, 351ff, 353, 356ff.

[4] Fisher et al. "Introduction to Information Quality," pp. 236f, 238f.

[5] Scott Ambler: "Refactoring Databases," p. 24f.

[6] Larry P. English: "Improving Data Warehouse and Business Information Quality," pp. 252, 260f, 261, 262, 267f, 274, 257ff.

[7] "DAMA Guide to the Data Management Body of Knowledge," pp. 305, 311.

[8] CDC Immunization Information Systems (IIS): "Deduplication Toolkit," retrieved from http://www.cdc.gov/vaccines/programs/iis/technical-guidance/deduplication.html.

[9] Leonard et al. "SQL Server 2012 Integration Services Design Patterns," p. 103f.

[10] "DAMA Guide to the Data Management Body of Knowledge," p. 310.

[11] https://msdn.microsoft.com/en-us/library/ms190768.aspx.

LOADING THE DIMENSIONAL INFORMATION MART

14

Once the raw data has been loaded from the operational source systems into the Raw Data Vault, the next step is to process the raw data and load the results from this processing into the information marts. This chapter covers both steps.

14.1 USING THE BUSINESS VAULT AS AN INTERMEDIATE TO THE INFORMATION MART

The Business Vault serves as an intermediate between the Raw Data Vault and information marts. By doing so, it stores intermediate results from processed (soft) business rules that are stored for reusability. The next sections provide examples for implementing reusable business logic and storing the results for later usage when loading one or multiple information marts.

14.1.1 COMPUTED SATELLITE

Computed satellites are one of the artifacts in the Data Vault architecture to implement soft business rules. They are also used a lot for data quality cleansing, as described in the next chapter.

In many cases, computed satellites are provided in a virtual manner, using SQL views. The following DDL creates a computed satellite that hangs off **HubAirport** and provides the cultural region of the airport's location:

```
CREATE VIEW [biz].[SatDestAirportCulturalRegion] AS
SELECT
      [AirportHashKey]
     ,[LoadDate]
     ,[LoadEndDate]
     ,'SR9376' AS [RecordSource]
     ,[HashDiff]
     ,[DestCityName]
     ,[DestState]
     ,[DestStateName]
     ,[DestCityMarketID]
     ,[DestStateFips]
     ,[DestWac]
     ,CASE
```

```
        WHEN DestState IN ('CT', 'ME', 'MA', 'NH', 'RI', 'VT') THEN 'New England'
        WHEN DestState IN ('DE', 'MD', 'NJ', 'NY', 'PA', 'DC') THEN 'Mid Atlantic'
        WHEN DestState IN ('AL', 'AR', 'FL', 'GA', 'KY', 'LA') THEN 'The South'
        WHEN DestState IN ('MS', 'NC', 'SC', 'TN', 'VA', 'WV') THEN 'The South'
        WHEN DestState IN ('IL', 'IN', 'IA', 'KS', 'MI', 'MN') THEN 'Midwest'
        WHEN DestState IN ('MO', 'NE', 'ND', 'OH', 'SD', 'WI') THEN 'Midwest'
        WHEN DestState IN ('AZ', 'NM', 'OK', 'TX') THEN 'The Southwest'
        WHEN DestState IN ('AK', 'CO', 'CA', 'HI', 'ID', 'MT') THEN 'The West'
        WHEN DestState IN ('NV', 'OR', 'UT', 'WA', 'WY') THEN 'The West'
        ELSE NULL
      END AS CulturalRegion
FROM
      [DataVault].[raw].[SatDestAirport] src
```

The example satellite is based on an already existing satellite in the Raw Data Vault and introduces a computed attribute **CulturalRegion** based on the airport's state [1]. Essentially, this computed attribute is based on a mapping between the state abbreviation and a hard-coded mapping rule. Note that there are better options to implement such mapping: the use of analytical master data allows the business user to take control over this mapping and change it without IT involvement if necessary.

Another consideration is the use of the **record source** attribute. Because the computed satellite has changed the data to some extent, the record source is not the original source system anymore. Instead, the identifier of the soft business rule in the meta mart is used because the computed satellite implements the soft business rule. To some extent, the data was generated by the soft business rule and not by the source system (however, the generation is based on the data from the source system). Using the soft rule identifiers is only one option for the record source. Chapter 4, Data Vault 2.0 Modeling, has already stated that the record source attribute is an attribute that serves a debugging purpose. The IT organization should use it in the best manner that serves this purpose. Another choice would be to set the record source to "SYSTEM" or leave the original record source value. Throughout the book, we will set a soft business rule identifier whenever data was changed only slightly. If data was only filtered, we'll leave the original record source (because data values haven't changed).

There are multiple advantages of implementing soft business rules using virtualized computed satellites:

- **The implementation is simple and comprehensible:** usually, for each soft business rule definition, there should be an implementation. By using virtual satellites, this implementation is very compact. The alternative is to use a more complex ETL process, especially if the business rule is too complex to be covered in a SQL statement.
- **Quick development:** developing a SQL view is certainly faster than developing an ETL process with similar functionality (however, it might depend on the tools used).
- **Quick deployment:** it is also often faster to deploy a new or modified SQL view than deploying ETL processes.

These advantages are especially helpful when developing the data warehouse using the agile Data Vault 2.0 methodology. However, there are also some disadvantages:

- **Limited complexity:** if the soft business rule definition requires a too complex implementation, it might be required to split the implementation into multiple computed satellites (or other entities in the Business Vault) or implement the soft business rule using an ETL tools such as SSIS.

- **Performance**: while virtualization works well in many cases, some soft business rules require too much computing power, for example because many calculations are required or many joins are involved. In this case, it might be better to materialize the computed satellite by using ETL tools.

Computed satellites are covered more extensively in Chapter 13, Implementing Data Quality, when they are used for more complex data quality cleansing operations.

14.1.2 BUILDING AN EXPLORATION LINK

In some cases, however, virtualization is not an option. This is the case if external tools are involved, for example data mining tools such as the data mining extensions within SQL Server Analysis Services or another external tool that produces output that is calculated based on the raw data and not sourced directly from the source system (such as the output from Data Quality Services, which is covered in the next chapter).

An exploration link is such an example. The entity, the definition of which is described in detail in Chapter 5, Intermediate Data Vault Modeling, is used to store links that are artificially generated and not found in the source system. One way to implement such exploration links is by using an **association rule** algorithm, such as **Apriori** or **FP Growth**. Microsoft SQL Server provides such an algorithm in the Data Mining extension of SQL Server Analysis Services.

The following example implements and uses a data mining model that provides airlines with information about frequent connections between airports. The main answer provided by this model is:

Which airport destinations should be provided given the current connections offered by my airline?

The goal of this example is to provide new destinations that fit the current offerings of the airline. The suggestions are based on the offerings of all airlines. However, the data mining example in this chapter is far from being completely realistic:

- No data cleansing has been performed
- The loaded data in this chapter might be incomplete and not all patterns are covered
- Trends in the data set are not accounted for
- Errors might exist in the following code and the setup of the algorithm

In the end, the example has been developed quickly to show how to use a data mining model to populate an exploration link and not how to provide such predictions. Keep this in mind when using the model.

In order to use the example from this section, it is required to create a new **Analysis Server** database on the data warehouse infrastructure and to modify two configuration settings (Figure 14.1).

Open the properties dialog of the **Analysis Server** database using the context menu of the database and **General** tab. Make sure to check the option **show advanced (all) properties**, because some of the options that need to be modified are hidden by default.

The first setting that needs to be set is the **Data Mining \ AllowAdHocOpenRowsetQueries** to make sure that the model can be loaded directly from a source entity in the Raw Data Vault. The other option is to set up the providers that can be used in such an open rowset query by setting the **Data Mining \ AllowedProvidersInOpenRowset** to "**sqloledb,MSDataShape**" which enables both data providers.

Once these configuration options are modified, it is possible to create and train a data mining model on the server without using SSIS. Without modifying these settings, model training requires loading

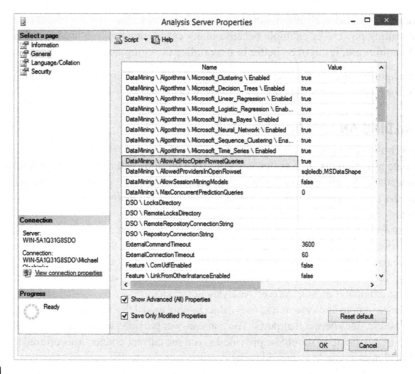

FIGURE 14.1

Analysis server properties.

the data using SSIS or another tool, and using the model for populating the exploration link becomes more complex as well.

Open a new **DMX query** in **Microsoft SQL Server Management Studio**. Enter the following statement to create a new data mining model using Microsoft's implementation of an association rule algorithm:

```
CREATE MINING MODEL ConnectionAssociation (
     CarrierOrigin text key,
     Origin text discrete predict,
     Connection table predict (
          Dest text key
     )
)
Using Microsoft_Association_Rules(Minimum_Support = 0.02, Minimum_Probability =
0.40);
```

This statement will create the model in the SQL Server Analysis Services database. The model will predict the destinations that are applicable for a given origin of the carrier. The parameters **minimum support** and **minimum probability** influence the number of frequent patterns that are accepted into the model. In the end, a pattern (here: flight connection) is considered as frequent if it is in at least 2%

of all flight connections in the source data (parameter **minimum support**). It will be included into the model if the pattern is able to predict a destination airport with at least 40% probability (parameter **minimum probability**) [2].

Once the model has been created, it needs to be trained using the existing connections of all airlines (this is actually realistic to do so, because all the data is available in public). The following DMX statement trains the model (finds frequent patterns) by inserting data into the data mining model:

```
INSERT INTO ConnectionAssociation (CarrierOrigin, Origin, Connection(Skip, Dest))
OPENROWSET('MSDataShape', 'data provider=SQLOLEDB;Server=localhost;UID=sa;PWD=datavault',
'Shape
{ SELECT DISTINCT
        carrier.Carrier+origin.AirportCode AS CarrierOrigin,
        origin.AirportCode AS Origin
  FROM
        [DataVault].[raw].[TLinkFlight] flight
INNER JOIN
        [DataVault].[raw].[HubCarrier] carrier ON carrier.CarrierHashKey =
flight.CarrierHashKey
INNER JOIN
        [DataVault].[raw].[HubAirportCode] origin ON origin.AirportCodeHashKey =
flight.OriginHashKey

        }
APPEND (
{       SELECT DISTINCT
        carrier.Carrier+origin.AirportCode AS CarrierOrigin,
        dest.AirportCode AS Dest
  FROM
        [DataVault].[raw].[TLinkFlight] flight
INNER JOIN
        [DataVault].[raw].[HubCarrier] carrier ON carrier.CarrierHashKey =
flight.CarrierHashKey
INNER JOIN
        [DataVault].[raw].[HubAirportCode] origin ON origin.AirportCodeHashKey =
flight.OriginHashKey
INNER JOIN
        [DataVault].[raw].[HubAirportCode] dest ON dest.AirportCodeHashKey =
flight.DestHashKey }
RELATE CarrierOrigin to CarrierOrigin) AS Connection');
```

Without going too much into detail, this command loads the data from the existing no-history link **TLinkFlight** in the Raw Data Vault. These connections are used to train the model.

After these two statements have been executed, the model is ready to use. It has found frequent patterns (flight connections). The next step is to create a SSIS data flow that uses these frequent patterns to predict additional destination airports for a given pair of carrier and origin airport ("if you are a carrier that operates out of X, you might be interested in offering flight connections to Y, based on the frequent patterns found").

Create a new data flow and insert an **OLE DB source** to the data flow. The data flow has to load all carrier and origin airport combinations from the Raw Data Vault source. Open the editor for the OLE DB source (Figure 14.2).

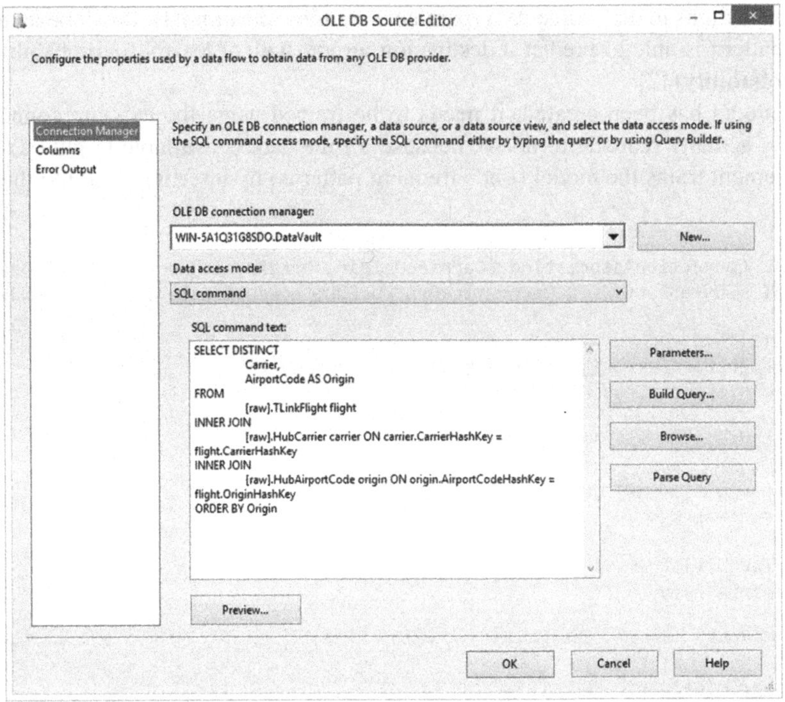

FIGURE 14.2

OLE DB source editor for the data mining source.

Enter the following SQL statement as SQL command text:

```
SELECT DISTINCT
        Carrier,
        AirportCode AS Origin
FROM
        [raw].TLinkFlight flight
INNER JOIN
        [raw].HubCarrier carrier ON carrier.CarrierHashKey = flight.CarrierHashKey
INNER JOIN
        [raw].HubAirportCode origin ON origin.AirportCodeHashKey = flight.OriginHashKey
ORDER BY
        Origin
```

This statement loads all combinations from the same no-history link in the Raw Data Vault. However, it doesn't take the current destination airports into account, because we're interested in retrieving additional destinations, currently not served by the carrier from this origin airport.

Add a **Data Mining Query** task to the data flow and connect it to the OLE DB source. Open the editor and create a new connection using the **New** button. The dialog is shown in Figure 14.3.

Connect to the Analysis Services database where the data mining model was created before. Close the dialog and select the mining structure in the data mining query transformation editor (Figure 14.4).

Make sure that the mining structure **ConnectionAssociation_Structure** and the mining model **ConnectionAssociation** are selected and switch to the query tab (Figure 14.5).

This statement loads all the connections of the carrier into the model and retrieves recommendations for additional flight destination for the currently offered set of flights. Enter the following SQL statement into the data mining query text box:

```
SELECT FLATTENED
  (PredictAssociation(ConnectionAssociation.Connection,3)) AS Recommendation
FROM
  ConnectionAssociation
NATURAL PREDICTION JOIN
SHAPE {
      @InputRowset
}
APPEND ({
      OPENROWSET(
              'SQLOLEDB',
              'Integrated Security=SSPI; Data Source=localhost;
              Initial Catalog=DataVault',
              'SELECT DISTINCT
                      origin.AirportCode AS Origin,
                      dest.AirportCode AS Dest
              FROM
                      [raw].TLinkFlight flight
              INNER JOIN
                      [raw].HubAirportCode origin ON origin.AirportCodeHashKey =
flight.OriginHashKey
              INNER JOIN
                      [raw].HubAirportCode dest ON dest.AirportCodeHashKey =
flight.DestHashKey
              ORDER BY
                      Origin'
      )
}
RELATE Origin TO Origin) AS Connection AS t
```

This statement basically provides the connections of the current carrier in @InputRowset to the trained model and asks for up to three recommended destinations based on the current connections of the carrier. For each carrier and origin, the data mining task returns the top three recommended destinations that the carrier should consider for the current origin airport. The recommendations are provided as records in the data flow.

Once the recommendations are in the data flow, the business keys should be hashed. The model was created with the business keys (instead of the hash keys) because the link is easier to produce afterwards: the primary hash key is calculated from the business key of the carrier, the origin airport and the recommended airport.

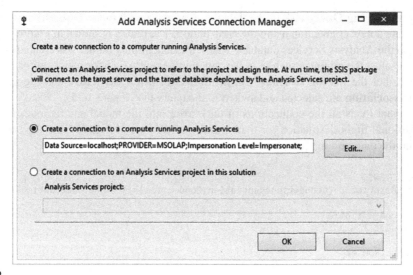

FIGURE 14.3

Add Analysis Services connection manager.

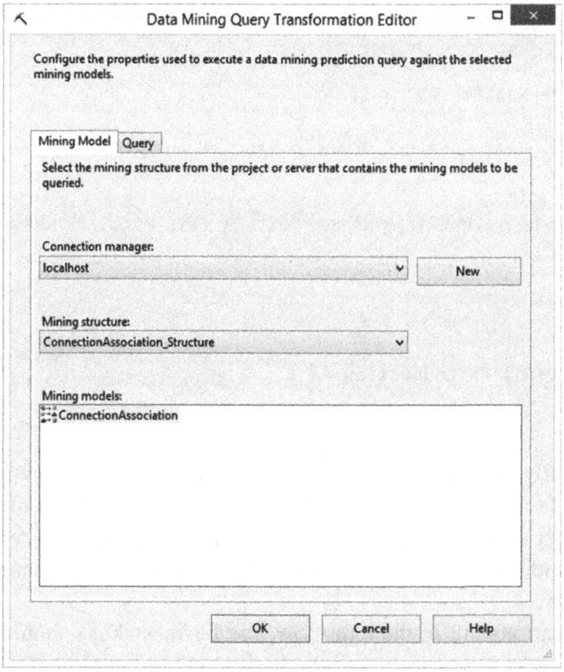

FIGURE 14.4

Data mining query transformation editor.

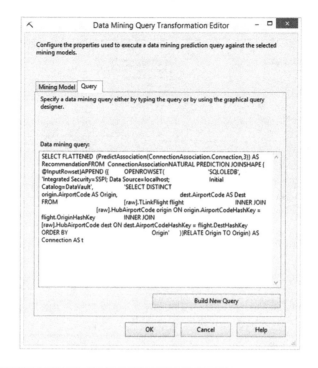

FIGURE 14.5

Editing the data mining query in the data mining query transformation editor.

The hashing approach follows the approach outlined in Chapter 11, Data Extraction: first, the columns are concatenated using a derived column transformation (Figure 14.6).

The derived columns are created using the provided expressions (Table 14.1).

Note the record source attribute, which is set to the identifier of the soft rule that defines the requirements and the process of the data mining task in the meta mart. The load date is retrieved from the SSIS variable dLoadDate in the User namespace. By doing so, all records in the target will use the same load date, which makes it easier to group the records in the target.

Because the hash key was used in the data mining model, the keys from the source data and the business key for the predicted destination airport are readily available for the hash key computation in the next step. Drag a **script transformation** to the data flow and connect it to the output path of the previous step (Figure 14.7).

This step also follows the process outlined in Chapter 11. Check all columns ending with HubBK or LinkBK as inputs to the script component. Copy the hashing script from Chapter 11 and compile the script. Create corresponding output columns on the next page, shown in Figure 14.8.

Ensure that each input column has a corresponding output column. Make sure that the data type is set to string and the length of the column is set to 32 characters (if MD5 hash keys are used). Close the script transformation editor and drag an OLE DB destination to the data flow. After connecting it to the existing components, open the editor (Figure 14.9).

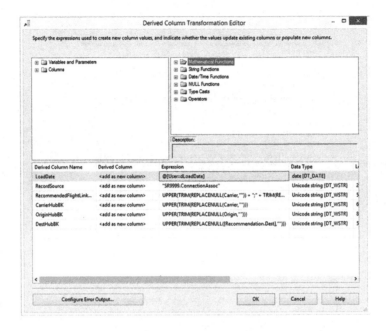

FIGURE 14.6

Derived column transformation editor.

FIGURE 14.7

Script transformation editor.

Table 14.1 Derived Columns and Their Expressions

Derived Column Name	Expression
LoadDate	@[User::dLoadDate]
RecordSource	"SR9999.ConnectionAssoc"
RecommendedFlightLinkBK	UPPER(TRIM(REPLACENULL(Carrier,""))) + ";" + TRIM(REPLACENULL(Origin,""))) + ";" + TRIM(REPLACENULL([Recommendation.Dest],"")))
CarrierHubBK	UPPER(TRIM(REPLACENULL(Carrier,"")))
OriginHubBK	UPPER(TRIM(REPLACENULL(Origin,"")))
DestHubBK	UPPER(TRIM(REPLACENULL([Recommendation.Dest],"")))

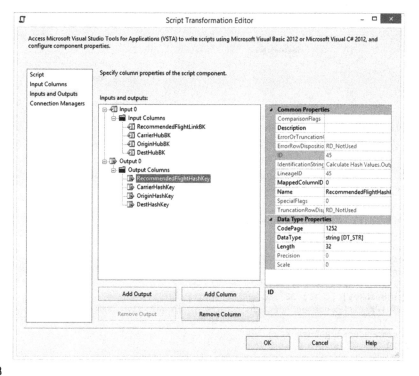

FIGURE 14.8

Input and output columns in the script transformation editor.

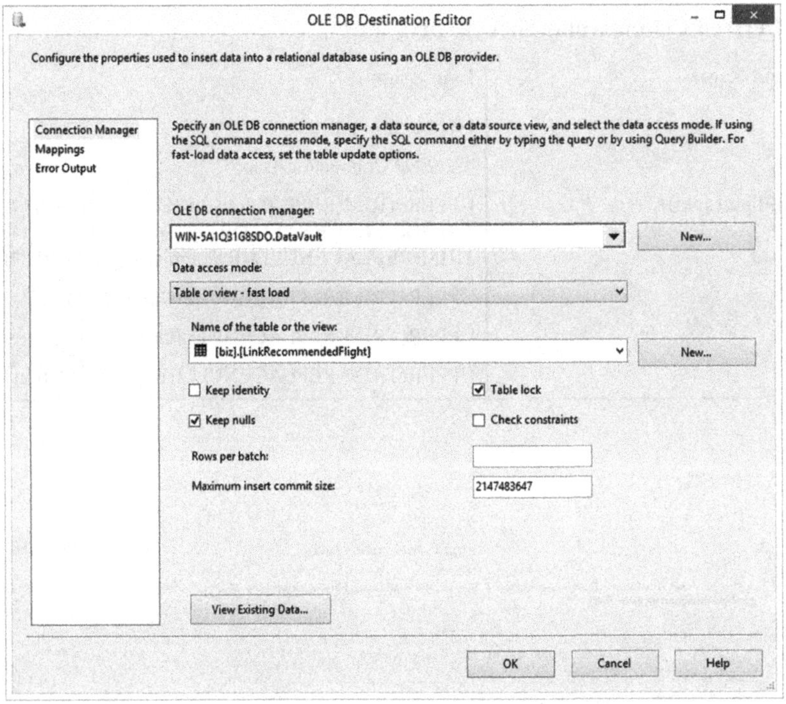

FIGURE 14.9

Setting up the OLE DB destination connection for exploration link.

The data is loaded into an exploration link table in the Business Vault. Create the table using the following DDL script:

```
CREATE TABLE [biz].[LinkRecommendedFlight](
        [RecommendedFlightHashKey] [char](32) NOT NULL,
        [LoadDate] [datetime2](7) NOT NULL,
        [RecordSource] [nvarchar](50) NOT NULL,
        [CarrierHashKey] [char](32) NOT NULL,
        [OriginHashKey] [char](32) NOT NULL,
        [DestHashKey] [char](32) NOT NULL,
 CONSTRAINT [PK_LinkRecommendedFlight] PRIMARY KEY NONCLUSTERED
(
        [RecommendedFlightHashKey] ASC
) ON [INDEX],
 CONSTRAINT [UK_LinkRecommendedFlight] UNIQUE NONCLUSTERED
(
        [CarrierHashKey] ASC,
        [OriginHashKey] ASC,
        [DestHashKey] ASC
) ON [INDEX]
) ON [DATA]
```

Select the table in the dialog and make sure that **keep nulls** and **table lock** options are selected. Switch to the **mappings** page (Figure 14.10).

Make sure that each destination column has a corresponding source column and close the dialog. The data flow is completed and shown in Figure 14.11.

Because the frequent patterns in the model change over time, it is advisable to run this data flow frequently, for example once a week or month. Before running this data flow, the best choice is to truncate the target table first. In many cases, the patterns, if they change, are too different to run an update on the data. Using this approach is absolutely valid from an auditing perspective: the Business Vault may not be auditable and its tables can be reloaded at any point in time.

14.2 **MATERIALIZING THE INFORMATION MART**

The previous examples have shown how to implement the Business Vault. The ultimate goal, however, is to build and populate the information marts that will be used by the business users. The Business Vault plays only an intermediate step towards this goal, as outlined as in section 14.1.

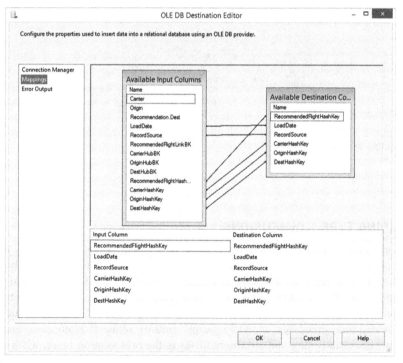

FIGURE 14.10

Mapping columns in the OLE DB destination editor.

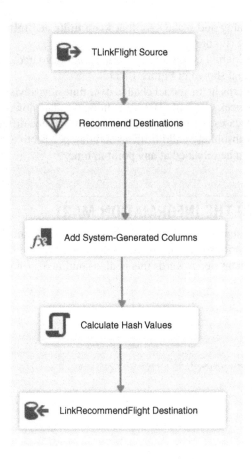

FIGURE 14.11

Data flow for loading an exploration link.

14.2.1 LOADING TYPE 1 DIMENSIONS

The first example creates and loads a Type 1 dimension, which provides no history of the dimension members but only the most current version of the descriptive data. In many cases, this involves all members ever loaded to the data warehouse, because historical data should be analyzed. For example, if a product has reached its end of line, it is still available in the product dimension because there might be historical data that depends on this now-outdated record. Or the product may be still active in the operational processes, for example in warranty requests from customers. Therefore, dimension members usually stay and are filtered later in the presentation layer, when not used by a specific data set.

The following DDL statement is used to create the dimension table in the information mart:

```
CREATE TABLE [dbo].[DimAirport](
      [AirportKey] [char](32) NOT NULL,
      [AirportCode] [nvarchar](3) NULL,
      [CityName] [nvarchar](100) NOT NULL,
      [State] [nvarchar](2) NOT NULL,
      [StateName] [nvarchar](100) NOT NULL,
      [CityMarketID] [int] NOT NULL,
      [StateFips] [smallint] NOT NULL,
      [Wac] [smallint] NOT NULL,
 CONSTRAINT [PK_DimAirport] PRIMARY KEY NONCLUSTERED
(
      [AirportKey] ASC
) ON [DATA]
) ON [DATA]
```

Note that **AirportCodeKey** identifies the rows of the dimension table, which is the hash key from the Data Vault 2.0 model. Using the hash key instead of a sequence number improves the provision of dimension tables because the hash key is already available in the Data Vault 2.0 model. This is described in more detail in Chapter 7, Dimensional Modeling.

In order to load this table for a Type 1 dimension, a simple INSERT statement in combination with a TRUNCATE TABLE statement is sufficient:

```
TRUNCATE TABLE FlightInformationMart.dbo.DimAirport;
GO

INSERT INTO FlightInformationMart.dbo.DimAirport
SELECT
      COALESCE(hub.AirportCodeHashKey, '') AS AirportKey
      ,IIF(hub.AirportCode IS NOT NULL AND hub.AirportCode <> '',
            hub.AirportCode, '?') AS AirportCode
      ,COALESCE(satd.[DestCityName], sato.[OriginCityName], 'Unknown') AS CityName
      ,COALESCE(satd.[DestState], sato.[OriginState], '?') AS [State]
      ,COALESCE(satd.[DestStateName], sato.[OriginStateName], 'Unknown') AS StateName
      ,COALESCE(satd.[DestCityMarketID], sato.[OriginCityMarketID], 0) AS CityMarketID
      ,COALESCE(satd.[DestStateFips], sato.[OriginStateFips], 0) AS StateFips
      ,COALESCE(satd.[DestWac], sato.[OriginWac], 0) AS Wac
FROM
      DataVault.[raw].HubAirportCode hub
LEFT JOIN
      DataVault.[raw].SatDestAirport satd ON (
            satd.AirportHashKey = hub.AirportCodeHashKey
      )
LEFT JOIN
      DataVault.[raw].SatOriginAirport sato ON (
            sato.AirportHashKey = hub.AirportCodeHashKey
      )
WHERE
      satd.LoadEndDate IS NULL AND sato.LoadEndDate IS NULL;
GO
```

The table is first truncated and then completely reloaded in order to avoid dealing with updates. Another option is to use a MERGE statement if there are not many members in the dimension.

While this approach is a naïve approach, it demonstrates an advantage and characteristic of the Data Vault 2.0 model: many if not most dimensions are built by querying the data from a hub and joining descriptive data from one or more satellites. Each satellite might come from different source systems and it is part of the business logic in the dimension load to decide which satellite is representing the leading system if multiple systems provide contradicting raw data. Since only the latest version of the descriptive data should be included in Type 1 dimensions, a WHERE condition is applied on the satellite data to select only the active (most current) records. If the dimension should contain only members that are not deleted in the source system, the effectivity satellite on the hub should be taken into consideration by joining it in the query and adding a filter to remove deleted members.

However, the sources for dimensions are not limited to hubs and satellites. In fact, the data can come from multiple source entities in the Data Vault 2.0 model, including links. Therefore, when building dimension tables in the information mart, the first step is to identify the table (or set of tables) that provides the desired grain for the destination table. From our experience, the grain for dimension tables comes from a hub table in 80% of the cases. Other typical sources for building dimensions are same-as links because they are the outcome of de-duplication efforts. This will be demonstrated in the next chapter.

The complexity of the statement is due to the COALESCE statements that deal with potential airports that are only described in one satellite. In such a case, there is no descriptive data available from all satellites and the columns are NULL. This is also the reason why a LEFT JOIN was used, which is not the most frequently performed join operation in most databases, including Microsoft SQL Server. Section 14.3 explains how to use PIT tables in conjunction with ghost records to achieve INNER JOINs with equi-join conditions.

14.2.2 LOADING TYPE 2 DIMENSIONS

Joining the data becomes a bigger problem when dealing with Type 2 dimensions. In this case, multiple if not all versions of the descriptive data from the satellites should be sourced into the target. Before looking at the loading statement, review the DDL statement for creating a Type 2 dimension table that can be used in the dimensional model:

```
CREATE TABLE [dbo].[DimAirport2](
        [AirportKey] [char](32) NOT NULL,
        [AirportCodeHashKey] [char](32) NOT NULL,
        [LoadDate] [datetime2](7) NOT NULL,
        [LoadEndDate] [datetime2](7) NULL,
        [AirportCode] [nvarchar](3) NULL,
        [CityName] [nvarchar](100) NOT NULL,
        [State] [nvarchar](2) NOT NULL,
        [StateName] [nvarchar](100) NOT NULL,
        [CityMarketID] [int] NOT NULL,
        [StateFips] [smallint] NOT NULL,
        [Wac] [smallint] NOT NULL,
```

```
CONSTRAINT [PK_DimAirport2] PRIMARY KEY NONCLUSTERED
(
        [AirportKey] ASC
) ON [INDEX],
 CONSTRAINT [UK_DimAirport2] UNIQUE NONCLUSTERED
(
        [AirportCodeHashKey] ASC,
        [LoadDate] ASC
) ON [INDEX]
) ON [DATA]
```

The table is an extended version of the same table used in the previous section. In Type 2 dimensions, the key column is not directly sourced from the hash key column in the Raw Data Vault 2.0 hub table. Instead, it is a value that is calculated from the business key and a date (for example the load date or a snapshot date introduced a little later). This way, every row gets a unique hash key assigned, which is required for identifying the record in the dimension.

Because the key by itself is not from the Raw Data Vault, additional attributes are required to identify not only the member (using **AirportCodeHashKey**) but also the right version (using **LoadDate**) when loading the fact table. Once both table types, the facts and the dimensions, are loaded, the key is used for joining the data.

Both the hash key and load date columns are also used when loading the Type 2 dimension table using the following, incremental approach:

```
INSERT INTO FlightInformationMart.dbo.DimAirport2
SELECT
    UPPER(CONVERT(char(32),
        HASHBYTES('MD5', CONCAT(
            UPPER(RTRIM(LTRIM(hub.AirportCode)))
            , ';'
            , CONVERT(NVARCHAR(30), src.LoadDate, 126)
        ))
    ,2)) AS AirportKey
    ,src.AirportHashKey AS AirportCodeHashKey
    ,src.LoadDate
    ,NULL AS LoadEndDate
    ,IIF(hub.AirportCode IS NOT NULL AND hub.AirportCode <> '',
      hub.AirportCode, '?') AS AirportCode
    ,COALESCE(satd.[DestCityName], sato.[OriginCityName], 'Unknown') AS CityName
    ,COALESCE(satd.[DestState], sato.[OriginState], '?') AS [State]
    ,COALESCE(satd.[DestStateName], sato.[OriginStateName], 'Unknown') AS StateName
    ,COALESCE(satd.[DestCityMarketID], sato.[OriginCityMarketID], 0) AS CityMarketID
    ,COALESCE(satd.[DestStateFips], sato.[OriginStateFips], 0) AS StateFips
    ,COALESCE(satd.[DestWac], sato.[OriginWac], 0) AS Wac
FROM
        (SELECT AirportHashKey, LoadDate FROM DataVault.[raw].SatOriginAirportMod
        UNION
        SELECT AirportHashKey, LoadDate FROM DataVault.[raw].SatDestAirportMod) src
```

```
INNER JOIN DataVault.[raw].HubAirportCode hub ON (
      src.AirportHashKey = hub.AirportCodeHashKey
)
LEFT OUTER JOIN DataVault.[raw].SatDestAirportMod satd ON (
      satd.AirportHashKey = src.AirportHashKey
      AND src.LoadDate BETWEEN
            satd.LoadDate AND COALESCE(satd.LoadEndDate, '9999-12-31 23:59:59.999')
)
LEFT OUTER JOIN DataVault.[raw].SatOriginAirportMod sato ON (
      sato.AirportHashKey = src.AirportHashKey
      AND src.LoadDate BETWEEN
            sato.LoadDate AND COALESCE(sato.LoadEndDate, '9999-12-31 23:59:59.999')
)
WHERE NOT EXISTS (
      SELECT
            1
      FROM
            FlightInformationMart.dbo.DimAirport2 tgt
      WHERE
            src.AirportHashKey = tgt.AirportCodeHashKey
                  AND src.LoadDate = tgt.LoadDate
)
```

New records from the Raw Data Vault source are loaded into the target, based on the hash key and the load date. Because the target is a Type 2 dimension table, all versions from the Raw Data Vault that are not currently in the destination should be loaded into the dimension table. The hub that provided the grain in the last section is not a good candidate for the FROM clause because it provides the wrong grain. Instead, the versions of descriptive data are stored in the satellites – actually, spread over all satellite tables that depend on the hub. Therefore, the grain for this statement is provided by a subquery in the FROM statement that returns the potential **load date** and **hash key** combinations. For each combination that is not yet in the target, which is checked by the WHERE condition, the corresponding descriptive data is sourced from each satellite using a LEFT OUTER JOIN. While the processing of the descriptive data in the SELECT clause is similar to the statement for Type 1 dimension loads in the previous section, the join condition is much more complex. This is true not only from a reader's perspective, but also from the perspective of the SQL optimizer.

To achieve higher performance of Type 2 dimension loads, an equi-join is the preferred solution. However, if performance is not an issue because there are not many joins involved in the actual loading statement or if the number of records is small, this approach might work very well (at least for the majority of dimension tables). However, note that, due to independent changes to the satellites and the naïve approach implemented for selecting the descriptive data from the source, it might happen that the Type 2 dimension provides two unchanged entries, for example if the secondary satellite (in the previous example, the source airport) changes but the primary satellite (destination airport) overrides this change. Depending on the technology used for the information mart (or dependent OLAP cubes), this might pose a problem.

To complete the loading process, the load end date needs to be maintained. This can be done using an end-dating SQL statement, similar to the one for end-dating Data Vault 2.0 satellite tables:

```sql
UPDATE DimAirport2 SET
        LoadEndDate = (
                SELECT
                        DATEADD(ss,-1,MIN(z.LoadDate))
                FROM
                        DimAirport2 z
                WHERE
                        z.AirportCodeHashkey = a.AirportCodeHashkey
                AND
                        z.LoadDate > a.LoadDate
        )
FROM
        DimAirport2 a
WHERE
        LoadEndDate IS NULL AND AirportCodeHashkey = ?
```

In order to maintain the performance of the statement, it should be applied per hash key in the dimension. Otherwise, the scalability of the statement could be limited if the number of records in the satellite table is large.

14.2.3 LOADING FACT TABLES

The following DDL statement creates a fact table with many columns and references to dimension tables:

```sql
CREATE TABLE [dbo].[FactFlight](
        [CarrierKey] [char](32) NOT NULL,
        [FlightNumKey] [char](32) NOT NULL,
        [TailNumKey] [char](32) NOT NULL,
        [OriginKey] [char](32) NOT NULL,
        [DestKey] [char](32) NOT NULL,
        [FlightDateKey] int NOT NULL,
        [FlightDate] [datetime2](7) NOT NULL,
        [Year] [smallint] NULL,
        [Quarter] [smallint] NULL,
        [Month] [smallint] NULL,
        [DayOfMonth] [smallint] NULL,
        [DayOfWeek] [smallint] NULL,
        [CRSDepTime] [smallint] NULL,
```

```
        [DepTime] [smallint] NULL,
        [DepDelay] [smallint] NULL,
        [DepDelayMinutes] [smallint] NULL,
        [DepDel15] [bit] NULL,
        [DepartureDelayGroups] [smallint] NULL,
        [DepTimeBlk] [nvarchar](9) NULL,
        [TaxiOut] [smallint] NULL,
        [WheelsOff] [smallint] NULL,
        [WheelsOn] [smallint] NULL,
        [TaxiIn] [smallint] NULL,
        [CRSArrTime] [smallint] NULL,
        [ArrTime] [smallint] NULL,
        [ArrDelay] [smallint] NULL,
        [ArrDelayMinutes] [smallint] NULL,
        [ArrDel15] [bit] NULL,
        [ArrivalDelayGroups] [smallint] NULL,
        [ArrTimeBlk] [nvarchar](9) NULL,
        [Cancelled] [bit] NULL,
        [CancellationCode] [nvarchar](10) NULL,
        [Diverted] [bit] NULL,
        [CRSElapsedTime] [smallint] NULL,
        [ActualElapsedTime] [smallint] NULL,
        [AirTime] [smallint] NULL,
        [Flights] [smallint] NULL,
        [Distance] [int] NULL,
        [DistanceGroup] [int] NULL,
        [CarrierDelay] [smallint] NULL,
        [WeatherDelay] [smallint] NULL,
        [NASDelay] [smallint] NULL,
        [SecurityDelay] [smallint] NULL,
        [LateAircraftDelay] [smallint] NULL,
        [FirstDepTime] [smallint] NULL,
        [TotalAddGTime] [smallint] NULL,
        [LongestAddGTime] [smallint] NULL,
 CONSTRAINT [PK_FactFlight] PRIMARY KEY NONCLUSTERED
 (
        [CarrierKey] ASC,
        [FlightNumKey] ASC,
        [TailNumKey] ASC,
        [OriginKey] ASC,
        [DestKey] ASC,
        [FlightDateKey] ASC
 ) ON [INDEX]
 ) ON [DATA]
```

The fact table itself is not identified by a key because no other tables depend on it, as described in Chapter 7. Instead, the primary key is based on the hash values of the dimension tables including the flight date key because they are defining the grain of the fact table.

Note that the FlightDateKey is an integer value for better readability of the date value. This approach follows the standard approach for building and using date dimensions (covered in the next chapter).

The following statement populates the data into the fact table:

```
INSERT INTO FlightInformationMart.dbo.FactFlight
SELECT
      link.CarrierHashKey AS CarrierKey
     ,link.FlightNumHashKey AS FlightNumKey
     ,link.TailNumHashKey AS TailNumKey
     ,UPPER(CONVERT(char(32), HASHBYTES('MD5',
        CONCAT(UPPER(RTRIM(LTRIM(hubOrigin.AirportCode))), ';', CONVERT(NVARCHAR(30),
        SatOrigin.LoadDate, 126))),2)) AS OriginKey
     ,UPPER(CONVERT(char(32), HASHBYTES('MD5',
        CONCAT(UPPER(RTRIM(LTRIM(hubDest.AirportCode))), ';', CONVERT(NVARCHAR(30),
        SatDest.LoadDate, 126))),2)) AS DestKey
     ,DATEPART(YEAR,
        link.FlightDate)*10000+DATEPART(MONTH, link.FlightDate)*100
        +DATEPART(DAY, link.FlightDate) AS FlightDateKey
     ,link.[FlightDate]
     ,sat.[Year]
     ,sat.[Quarter]
     ,sat.[Month]
     ,sat.[DayOfMonth]
     ,sat.[DayOfWeek]
     ,sat.[CRSDepTime]
     ,sat.[DepTime]
     ,sat.[DepDelay]
     ,sat.[DepDelayMinutes]
     ,sat.[DepDel15]
     ,sat.[DepartureDelayGroups]
     ,sat.[DepTimeBlk]
     ,sat.[TaxiOut]
     ,sat.[WheelsOff]
     ,sat.[WheelsOn]
     ,sat.[TaxiIn]
     ,sat.[CRSArrTime]
     ,sat.[ArrTime]
     ,sat.[ArrDelay]
     ,sat.[ArrDelayMinutes]
     ,sat.[ArrDel15]
     ,sat.[ArrivalDelayGroups]
     ,sat.[ArrTimeBlk]
     ,sat.[Cancelled]
     ,sat.[CancellationCode]
     ,sat.[Diverted]
     ,sat.[CRSElapsedTime]
     ,sat.[ActualElapsedTime]
     ,sat.[AirTime]
     ,sat.[Flights]
     ,sat.[Distance]
     ,sat.[DistanceGroup]
     ,sat.[CarrierDelay]
     ,sat.[WeatherDelay]
     ,sat.[NASDelay]
     ,sat.[SecurityDelay]
     ,sat.[LateAircraftDelay]
     ,sat.[FirstDepTime]
```

```
        ,sat.[TotalAddGTime]
        ,sat.[LongestAddGTime]
FROM
    [DataVault].[raw].[TLinkFlight] link
INNER JOIN [DataVault].[raw].[HubAirportCode] HubOrigin ON (
            HubOrigin.AirportCodeHashKey = link.OriginHashKey
)
INNER JOIN [DataVault].[raw].[SatOriginAirportMod2] SatOrigin ON (
            SatOrigin.AirportHashKey = link.OriginHashKey
            AND link.LoadDate BETWEEN
                    SatOrigin.LoadDate
                    AND COALESCE(SatOrigin.LoadEndDate, '9999-12-31 23:59:59.999')
)
INNER JOIN [DataVault].[raw].[HubAirportCode] HubDest ON (
            HubDest.AirportCodeHashKey = link.DestHashKey
)
INNER JOIN [DataVault].[raw].[SatDestAirportMod2] SatDest ON (
            SatDest.AirportHashKey = link.DestHashKey
            AND link.LoadDate BETWEEN
                    SatDest.LoadDate
                    AND COALESCE(SatDest.LoadEndDate, '9999-12-31 23:59:59.999')
)
INNER JOIN DataVault.[raw].TSatFlight sat ON (
            sat.FlightHashKey = link.FlightHashKey
)
WHERE
            NOT EXISTS (SELECT
                            1
                    FROM
                            FlightInformationMart.dbo.FactFlight tgt
                    WHERE
                            COALESCE(UPPER(CONVERT(char(32), HASHBYTES('MD5',

                            CONCAT(UPPER(RTRIM(LTRIM(hubOrigin.AirportCode))), ';',
        CONVERT(NVARCHAR(30), SatOrigin.LoadDate, 126))),2)),
        REPLICATE('0', 32)) = tgt.OriginKey
        AND COALESCE(UPPER(CONVERT(char(32), HASHBYTES('MD5',
        CONCAT(UPPER(RTRIM(LTRIM(hubDest.AirportCode))), ';',
        CONVERT(NVARCHAR(30), SatDest.LoadDate, 126))),2)),
        REPLICATE('0', 32)) = tgt.DestKey
        AND link.CarrierHashKey = tgt.CarrierKey
        AND link.FlightNumHashKey = tgt.FlightNumKey
        AND link.TailNumHashKey = tgt.TailNumKey
        AND link.FlightDate = tgt.FlightDate
)
```

The facts are loaded from the nonhistorized link **TLinkFlights**. Each Type 2 dimension that is used by the target requires the recalculation of the key, which is based on the business key and the load date in the above example with standard satellites. The key is then stored in the fact table to support later joins between the fact table and dimension tables. Section 14.3.2 introduces a method for reusing such calculations. Because the business key is required, the hub has to be joined.

The complex calculation is not necessary when using Type 1 dimensions because the **key** is the same as the hash key in the Raw Data Vault. Note the INNER JOIN, which requires that the dimension table provide a record, even in the NULL case. For this reason, the dimension table should include an unknown record.

Another approach to avoid the complex calculation is to retrieve the key from the dimension in the information mart. However, this would add additional and unnecessary dependencies to the loading processes, which should be avoided in order to improve the parallelization of the loading processes that load the information marts.

Joining the record from the satellite is based on the hash key from the hub. However, the hash key by itself is not sufficient for the join. Instead, the **LoadDate** and **LoadEndDate** from the satellite are used to find the active record for the fact record.

The WHERE clause is required to support incremental loading and includes all elements of the alternate key from the target table, which is based on the elements of the source table, in this case. It also includes the transaction date (**FlightDate**). In other cases, the transaction ID would be used because it is part of the alternate key. If a record with this combination is not found in the target, it is loaded from the source to the target. Note that the key for the originating and destination airports are recalculated again in order to support the condition. Again, section 14.3.2 introduces a method for reusing such calculations and avoiding this recalculation.

Additional descriptive data that is not included in the source link is sourced from the no-history satellite **TSatFlight** which hangs off **TLinkFlight**. This satellite is joined on the hash key only because there should be only one record per transaction, which eases the integration of both data sources in this loading statement.

The previously mentioned unknown record can be populated using the following statement into the dimension tables:

```
INSERT INTO [dbo].[DimCarrier]
        ([CarrierKey]
        ,[Carrier]
        ,[Code]
        ,[Name]
        ,[Corporate Name]
        ,[Abbreviation]
        ,[Unique Abbreviation]
        ,[Group_Code]
        ,[Region_Code]
        ,[Satisfaction Rank]
        ,[Sort Order]
        ,[External Reference]
        ,[Comments])
    VALUES (
            REPLICATE('0', 32)
            , '?'
            , 0
            , 'Unknown'
            , 'Unknown'
            , '?'
            , '?'
            , '?'
            , '?'
            , 9999
            , 0
            , ''
            , ''
        );
```

This unknown record is required due to the use of the REPLICATE('0', 32) statement when loading the fact table. If this record is missing, the integrity of the information mart is compromised.

14.2.4 LOADING AGGREGATED FACT TABLES

It is also possible to change the grain when loading the data from the Data Vault model into the information mart. For example, the following DDL creates a **FactConnection** fact table that removes carrier and tail number references and aggregates the measures of the source table:

```
CREATE TABLE [dbo].[FactConnection](
      [CarrierKey] [char](32) NOT NULL,
      [OriginKey] [char](32) NOT NULL,
      [DestKey] [char](32) NOT NULL,
      [FlightDateKey] [int] NOT NULL,
      [FlightDate] [datetime2](7) NOT NULL,
      [Year] [smallint] NOT NULL,
      [Quarter] [smallint] NOT NULL,
      [Month] [smallint] NOT NULL,
      [DayOfMonth] [smallint] NOT NULL,
      [DayOfWeek] [smallint] NOT NULL,
      [SumDepDelay] [int] NOT NULL,
      [SumDepDelayMinutes] [int] NOT NULL,
      [SumTaxiOut] [int] NOT NULL,
      [SumWheelsOff] [int] NOT NULL,
      [SumWheelsOn] [int] NOT NULL,
      [SumTaxiIn] [int] NOT NULL,
      [SumArrDelay] [int] NOT NULL,
      [SumArrDelayMinutes] [int] NOT NULL,
      [SumCancelled] [int] NOT NULL,
      [SumDiverted] [int] NOT NULL,
      [SumAirTime] [int] NOT NULL,
      [SumFlights] [int] NOT NULL,
      [SumDistance] [int] NOT NULL,
      [SumCArrierDelay] [int] NOT NULL,
      [SumWeatherDelay] [int] NOT NULL,
      [SumNASDelay] [int] NOT NULL,
      [SumSecurityDelay] [int] NOT NULL,
      [SumLateAircraftDelay] [int] NOT NULL,
CONSTRAINT [PK_FactConnection] PRIMARY KEY NONCLUSTERED
(
      [CarrierKey] ASC,
      [OriginKey] ASC,
      [DestKey] ASC,
      [FlightDateKey] ASC
) ON [INDEX]
) ON [DATA]
```

In order to incrementally load the data into the new aggregated fact table, the following statement is executed once a day:

```sql
INSERT INTO FactConnection
SELECT
      link.CarrierHashKey AS CarrierKey
      ,UPPER(CONVERT(char(32), HASHBYTES('MD5',
             CONCAT(UPPER(RTRIM(LTRIM(hubOrigin.AirportCode))), ';',
             CONVERT(NVARCHAR(30), SatOrigin.LoadDate, 126))),2)) AS OriginKey
      ,UPPER(CONVERT(char(32), HASHBYTES('MD5',
             CONCAT(UPPER(RTRIM(LTRIM(hubDest.AirportCode))), ';', CONVERT(NVARCHAR(30),
             SatDest.LoadDate, 126))),2)) AS DestKey
      ,DATEPART(YEAR, link.FlightDate)*10000
             +DATEPART(MONTH, link.FlightDate)*100
             +DATEPART(DAY, link.FlightDate) AS FlightDateKey
      ,link.[FlightDate]
      ,sat.[Year]
      ,sat.[Quarter]
      ,sat.[Month]
      ,sat.[DayOfMonth]
      ,sat.[DayOfWeek]
      ,SUM(sat.[DepDelay]) AS SumDepDelay
      ,SUM(sat.[DepDelayMinutes]) AS SumDepDelayMinutes
      ,SUM(sat.[TaxiOut]) AS SumTaxiOut
      ,SUM(sat.[WheelsOff]) AS SumWheelsOff
      ,SUM(sat.[WheelsOn]) AS SumWheelsOn
      ,SUM(sat.[TaxiIn]) AS SumTaxiIn
      ,SUM(sat.[ArrDelay]) AS SumArrDelay
      ,SUM(sat.[ArrDelayMinutes]) AS SumArrDelayMinutes
      ,SUM(CASE WHEN sat.Cancelled=1 THEN 1 ELSE 0 END) AS SumCancelled
      ,SUM(CASE WHEN sat.Diverted=1 THEN 1 ELSE 0 END) AS SumDiverted
      ,SUM(sat.[AirTime]) AS SumAirTime
      ,SUM(sat.[Flights]) AS SumFlights
      ,SUM(sat.[Distance]) AS SumDistance
      ,SUM(sat.[CarrierDelay]) AS SumCArrierDelay
      ,SUM(sat.[WeatherDelay]) AS SumWeatherDelay
      ,SUM(sat.[NASDelay]) AS SumNASDelay
      ,SUM(sat.[SecurityDelay]) AS SumSecurityDelay
      ,SUM(sat.[LateAircraftDelay]) AS SumLateAircraftDelay
FROM [DataVault].[raw].[TLinkFlight] link
INNER JOIN [DataVault].[raw].[HubAirportCode] HubOrigin ON (
             HubOrigin.AirportCodeHashKey = link.OriginHashKey
)
INNER JOIN [DataVault].[raw].[SatOriginAirportMod2] SatOrigin ON (
             SatOrigin.AirportHashKey = link.OriginHashKey
             AND link.LoadDate BETWEEN SatOrigin.LoadDate AND
                   COALESCE(SatOrigin.LoadEndDate, '9999-12-31 23:59:59.999')
)
INNER JOIN [DataVault].[raw].[HubAirportCode] HubDest ON (
             HubDest.AirportCodeHashKey = link.DestHashKey
)
INNER JOIN [DataVault].[raw].[SatDestAirportMod2] SatDest ON (
             SatDest.AirportHashKey = link.DestHashKey
             AND link.LoadDate BETWEEN SatDest.LoadDate AND
```

```
                COALESCE(SatDest.LoadEndDate, '9999-12-31 23:59:59.999')
    )
INNER JOIN DataVault.[raw].TSatFlight sat ON (
    sat.FlightHashKey = link.FlightHashKey
)
WHERE
            NOT EXISTS (SELECT
                    1
            FROM
                    FlightInformationMart.dbo.FactConnection tgt
            WHERE
                    COALESCE(UPPER(CONVERT(char(32), HASHBYTES('MD5',
                    CONCAT(UPPER(RTRIM(LTRIM(hubOrigin.AirportCode))), ';',
                    CONVERT(NVARCHAR(30), SatOrigin.LoadDate, 126))),2)),
                    REPLICATE('0', 32)) = tgt.OriginKey
                    AND COALESCE(UPPER(CONVERT(char(32), HASHBYTES('MD5',
                    CONCAT(UPPER(RTRIM(LTRIM(hubDest.AirportCode))), ';',
                    CONVERT(NVARCHAR(30), SatDest.LoadDate, 126))),2)),
                    REPLICATE('0', 32)) = tgt.DestKey
                    AND link.CarrierHashKey = tgt.CarrierKey
                    AND link.FlightDate = tgt.FlightDate
            )
GROUP BY
    link.FlightDate, sat.[Year], sat.[Quarter], sat.[Month], sat.[DayOfMonth],
    sat.[DayOfWeek], link.CarrierHashKey, hubOrigin.AirportCode, SatOrigin.LoadDate,
    hubDest.AirportCode, SatDest.LoadDate
```

This approach only works if the data is grouped over the date, among other dimensions (sourced from the hubs). If the data is aggregated on other dimensions or if the data is loaded multiple times over the day, this statement would fail to update the existing information in the target. However, there are advanced concepts that allow such incremental loads of aggregated fact tables, but this is out of the scope of this book.

14.3 LEVERAGING PIT AND BRIDGE TABLES FOR VIRTUALIZATION

The previous sections have shown some examples for providing materialized dimension and fact tables. Some of them are based on naïve approaches that require truncating the target first.

The major drawback of such materialization is that the data needs to be moved in order to support the materialization. However, it provides optimal performance when directly querying the relational information mart. Consider the following virtual view that provides an aggregated fact "table" which is based on the incremental loading of aggregated fact data in section 14.2.4:

```
CREATE VIEW dbo.FactConnection2 AS
SELECT
    link.CarrierHashKey AS CarrierKey
    ,UPPER(CONVERT(char(32), HASHBYTES('MD5',
            CONCAT(UPPER(RTRIM(LTRIM(hubOrigin.AirportCode))), ';',
            CONVERT(NVARCHAR(30), SatOrigin.LoadDate, 126))),2)) AS OriginKey
    ,UPPER(CONVERT(char(32), HASHBYTES('MD5',
```

```
                CONCAT(UPPER(RTRIM(LTRIM(hubDest.AirportCode))), ';', CONVERT(NVARCHAR(30),
                SatDest.LoadDate, 126))),2)) AS DestKey
       ,DATEPART(YEAR, link.FlightDate)*10000
                +DATEPART(MONTH, link.FlightDate)*100
                +DATEPART(DAY, link.FlightDate) AS FlightDateKey
       ,link.[FlightDate]
       ,sat.[Year]
       ,sat.[Quarter]
       ,sat.[Month]
       ,sat.[DayOfMonth]
       ,sat.[DayOfWeek]
       ,SUM(sat.[DepDelay]) AS SumDepDelay
       ,SUM(sat.[DepDelayMinutes]) AS SumDepDelayMinutes
       ,SUM(sat.[TaxiOut]) AS SumTaxiOut
       ,SUM(sat.[WheelsOff]) AS SumWheelsOff
       ,SUM(sat.[WheelsOn]) AS SumWheelsOn
       ,SUM(sat.[TaxiIn]) AS SumTaxiIn
       ,SUM(sat.[ArrDelay]) AS SumArrDelay
       ,SUM(sat.[ArrDelayMinutes]) AS SumArrDelayMinutes
       ,SUM(CASE WHEN sat.Cancelled=1 THEN 1 ELSE 0 END) AS SumCancelled
       ,SUM(CASE WHEN sat.Diverted=1 THEN 1 ELSE 0 END) AS SumDiverted
       ,SUM(sat.[AirTime]) AS SumAirTime
       ,SUM(sat.[Flights]) AS SumFlights
       ,SUM(sat.[Distance]) AS SumDistance
       ,SUM(sat.[CarrierDelay]) AS SumCArrierDelay
       ,SUM(sat.[WeatherDelay]) AS SumWeatherDelay
       ,SUM(sat.[NASDelay]) AS SumNASDelay
       ,SUM(sat.[SecurityDelay]) AS SumSecurityDelay
       ,SUM(sat.[LateAircraftDelay]) AS SumLateAircraftDelay
FROM [DataVault].[raw].[TLinkFlight] link
INNER JOIN [DataVault].[raw].[HubAirportCode] HubOrigin ON (
                HubOrigin.AirportCodeHashKey = link.OriginHashKey
)
INNER JOIN [DataVault].[raw].[SatOriginAirportMod2] SatOrigin ON (
                SatOrigin.AirportHashKey = link.OriginHashKey
                AND link.LoadDate BETWEEN SatOrigin.LoadDate AND
                        COALESCE(SatOrigin.LoadEndDate, '9999-12-31 23:59:59.999')
)
INNER JOIN [DataVault].[raw].[HubAirportCode] HubDest ON (
                HubDest.AirportCodeHashKey = link.DestHashKey
)
INNER JOIN [DataVault].[raw].[SatDestAirportMod2] SatDest ON (
                SatDest.AirportHashKey = link.DestHashKey
                AND link.LoadDate BETWEEN SatDest.LoadDate AND
                        COALESCE(SatDest.LoadEndDate, '9999-12-31 23:59:59.999')
)
INNER JOIN DataVault.[raw].TSatFlight sat ON (
        sat.FlightHashKey = link.FlightHashKey
)
GROUP BY
        link.FlightDate, sat.[Year], sat.[Quarter], sat.[Month], sat.[DayOfMonth],
        sat.[DayOfWeek], link.CarrierHashKey, hubOrigin.AirportCode, SatOrigin.LoadDate,
        hubDest.AirportCode, SatDest.LoadDate
```

14.3.1 FACTORS THAT AFFECT PERFORMANCE OF VIRTUALIZED FACTS

Because the produced fact "table" is based on a virtual view, the aggregation has to occur whenever data is sourced from the fact table. Depending on the number of records in the source table, these calculations can be resource intensive and hinder the deployment of virtualized fact tables. Also joining the data might become a problem if complex or a larger number of joins is required. Major factors that affect the performance are

- **Joins**, which might require complex join conditions
- **Aggregations and grain changes**, which require resource intensive computations to aggregate or recompute the data.

Once the source tables have been joined, selecting the measures that should be included in the virtualized fact table is not very resource intensive anymore and allows the customization of fact data for different information marts.

A similar problem exists if dimension tables should be provided in a virtual manner: instead of materializing the data in the destination, only a virtual view is provided that sources the data directly from the hub and the involved satellites:

```
CREATE VIEW DimCarrier2 AS
SELECT
        hub.CarrierHashKey AS CarrierKey
        , CASE WHEN hub.Carrier IS NOT NULL AND hub.Carrier <> ''
            THEN hub.Carrier
            ELSE '?'
          END AS Carrier
        , CASE WHEN sat.Code IS NOT NULL AND sat.Code <> ''
            THEN sat.Code
            ELSE '?'
          END AS Code
        , CASE WHEN sat.Name IS NOT NULL AND sat.Name <> ''
            THEN sat.Name
            ELSE 'Unknown'
          END AS Name
        , COALESCE(sat.[Corporate Name], '') AS [Corporate Name]
        , COALESCE(sat.Abbreviation, '') AS Abbreviation
        , COALESCE(sat.[Unique Abbreviation], '') AS [Unique Abbreviation]
        , COALESCE(sat.[Group_Code], '') AS [Group Code]
        , COALESCE(sat.[Region_Code], '') AS [Region Code]
        , COALESCE(sat.[Satisfaction Rank], 9999) AS [Satisfaction Rank]
        , COALESCE(sat.[Sort Order], 9999) AS [Sort Order]
        , COALESCE(sat.[External Reference], '') AS [External Reference]
        , COALESCE(sat.Comments, '') AS Comments
    FROM
        DataVault.[raw].HubCarrier hub
    LEFT JOIN
        DataVault.[raw].SatCarrier sat ON (
            sat.CarrierHashKey = hub.CarrierHashKey
        )
    WHERE
        sat.LoadEndDate IS NULL
```

```
UNION ALL
SELECT
        REPLICATE('0', 32)
      , '?'
      , '?'
      , 'Unknown'
      , 'Unknown'
      , '?'
      , '?'
      , '?'
      , '?'
      , 9999
      , 0
      , ''
      , ''
      ;
```

The above view for a Type 1 dimension is based on a SELECT statement that sources its grain from the hub and joins descriptive data from only one satellite (an easy case). The unknown record is also provided in a virtual manner by adding it using a UNION ALL clause.

There are multiple problems with this approach: first, the source query requires joins, which have to be resolved by the SQL optimizer. The joins also require complex conditions because the dependent satellites don't provide data for each snapshot date but only when changes have been detected in the source system. In addition, business logic is required to implement the soft business rule, for example to select between potentially contradicting raw data from multiple source systems or to recalculate raw data into the desired format. If multiple targets should be supported, we see that the joins are always the same and, in many cases, the most resource-intensive operations. Business logic depends on the target that should be produced and the specific requirements of the business users. In many cases, the soft business rule is not as resource intensive compared to the join operations.

14.3.2 ADVANTAGES OF VIRTUALIZATION

Despite the problems with providing virtualized dimension and fact tables, there are several advantages that drive the need for virtualization in the data warehouse, especially when providing multiple information marts [3]:

- **Simplified solution**: providing facts and dimensions using virtualized approaches is more agile and responsive to user requests than ETL-based integration. These approaches require no data moving or data materialization and are far easier to design and develop.
- **Agile development process**: because it is easy to create and modify virtual facts and dimensions, it is possible to use such an approach in an agile development process that provides the final solution in multiple iterations. This requires that the cost to modify an existing solution is low.
- **Ease of change**: because the cost to modify an existing virtualized fact or dimension table is low, it is also possible to react on changes from the business that occur later in the lifetime of the data warehouse, for example if new products are introduced or the market changes and requires new business logic.

- **Improved developer productivity**: instead of relying on complex ETL-based solutions that are hard to develop, test, and deploy and are prone to changes once deployed, developers can quickly build solutions and demonstrate them to the end-user. If they have produced the wrong solution, they will fail fast, and have the time to start from scratch without generating too much cost.
- **Lower total cost of ownership (TCO)**: in addition to lower development costs (due to higher developer productivity), organizations save storage costs because data doesn't need to be materialized, which consumes disk space. While materializing data, for example using index views or using ETL, improves query performance, it often introduces data inconsistencies that increase the overall costs of the data warehouse.

To take advantage of these characteristics of virtualized information delivery, the Data Vault 2.0 model uses PIT and bridge tables to maintain the desired performance requirements by the business users, despite the fact that joins are required to collect the data, grain shifts occur and aggregations and other resource-intensive computations are performed when delivering the information.

The next sections demonstrate how to leverage these standard entities to provide virtualized fact and dimension tables, customizable for multiple information marts with different requirements, while maintaining superior query performance.

14.3.3 LOADING PIT TABLES

The last section has introduced two activities with delivering dimension tables:

1. **Joining the data from multiple satellites**: the data that is required for information delivery is stored in multiple satellites, often dependent on the same hub.
2. **Implementing the business logic**: a specific dimension for an information mart is based on individual selection of descriptive data from specific satellites and the application of business logic to this data. The actual definition of the business logic depends on the actual target and is user driven (expressed by user requirements).

The first activity is the most resource-intensive operation in the majority of cases. However, it is also possible to separate both activities in an easy way. This separation can be used to reuse the joins by materializing the intermediate result and providing it in a way that optimizes the customization for different information mart targets. This is where the PIT table comes into play.

As outlined in Chapter 6, Advanced Data Vault Modeling, the PIT table is like an index used by the query and provides information about the active satellite entries per snapshot date. The goal is to materialize as much of the join logic as possible and end up with an equi-join only. This join type is the most performant version of joining on most (if not all) relational database servers, including Microsoft SQL Server.

In order to maximize the performance of the PIT table while maintaining low storage requirements, one and only one ghost record is required in each satellite used by the PIT table. This ghost record is used when no record is active in the referenced satellite and serves as the unknown or NULL case. By using the ghost record, it is possible to avoid NULL checks in general, because the join condition will always point to an active record in the satellite table: either an actual record which is active at the given snapshot date or the ghost record.

The following statement is used to create the ghost record in the satellite:

```
INSERT INTO [raw].[SatDestAirportMod]
            ([AirportHashKey]
            ,[LoadDate]
            ,[LoadEndDate]
            ,[RecordSource]
            ,[HashDiff]
            ,[DestCityName]
            ,[DestState]
            ,[DestStateName]
            ,[DestCityMarketID]
            ,[DestStateFips]
            ,[DestWac])
      VALUES
            (REPLICATE('0', 32)
            ,'0001-01-01 00:00:00.000'
            ,'9999-12-31 23:59:59.999'
            ,'SYSTEM'
            ,REPLICATE('0', 32)
            ,'Unknown City'
            ,'?'
            ,'Unknown State'
            ,0
            ,0
            ,0)
```

This statement is usually executed after the satellite table has been created using the CREATE TABLE DDL statement to make sure that each satellite has a ghost record. Because the record is calculated and not sourced from a source system, the record source has been set to "SYSTEM" and the record is not part of the auditable raw data from the source system. Therefore, the ghost record can be modified at any time, for example when new attributes are added to the satellite table. Note that the hash key and the hash diff values are set to 32 zero values and the load date set to the first day and timestamp of all times, while the load end date is set to the last date and timestamp of all times. All other descriptive columns are set to default values that should be shown if no better data is available.

The PIT table is usually loaded in an incremental approach, based on the snapshot date. Each ETL load inserts the data that is missing for the given snapshot date. The following DDL statement creates the PIT table in the Business Vault:

```
CREATE TABLE [biz].[PITAirportCode](
      [AirportKey] [char](32) NOT NULL,
      [AirportCodeHashKey] [char](32) NOT NULL,
      [SnapshotDate] [datetime2](7) NOT NULL,
      [OriginAirportHashKey] [char](32) NOT NULL,
      [OriginLoadDate] [datetime2](7) NOT NULL,
      [DestAirportHashKey] [char](32) NOT NULL,
      [DestLoadDate] [datetime2](7) NOT NULL,
```

```
    CONSTRAINT [PK_PITAirportCode] PRIMARY KEY NONCLUSTERED
(
        [AirportKey] ASC
) ON [INDEX],
    CONSTRAINT [UK_PITAirportCode] UNIQUE NONCLUSTERED
(
        [AirportCodeHashKey] ASC,
        [SnapshotDate] ASC
) ON [INDEX]
) ON [DATA]
```

The primary key **AirportKey** is of a hash value derived from the business key of the hub **HubAirport-Code** and the **snapshot date**, which is a rolling date, controlled by the ETL process. The alternate key of the PIT table is the **AirportCodeHashKey** from the parent hub and the **snapshot date**. All other columns are pointing to one satellite entry, identified by a hash key and a load date. There are two additional columns per referenced satellite. In this case, two satellites have been referenced; therefore, four additional columns are required. If satellites are added to the hub, the PIT has to be modified as part of the process.

There are multiple options to load the PIT table. One is to use an **Execute SQL Task** in the control flow that is executed whenever the Business Vault is populated. This is usually done just after the loading procedures for all satellites in the Raw Data Vault and in the Business Vault are completed. The Business Vault satellites are required, because they can be added to the PIT as well, which makes sense if they are load-date oriented and not based on a snapshot date.

Note that implementing this approach using only SQL is another option and uses similar statements to those used in the following description.

To implement a task to load a PIT table in SSIS, add an Execute SQL Task to the control flow of your SSIS package. Open the task editor (Figure 14.12).

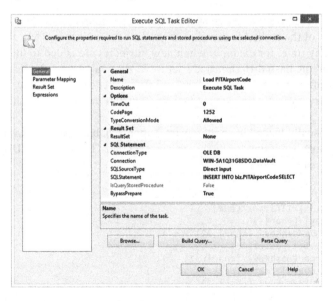

FIGURE 14.12

Execute SQL task editor for PIT table.

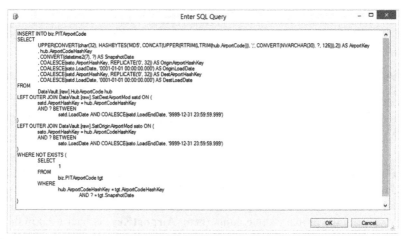

FIGURE 14.13

Enter SQL query dialog for PIT table.

Because the Business Vault is part of the EDW layer, set the connection of the **Execute SQL Task** to the **DataVault** connection manager used in other chapters. Open the SQL query editor by clicking the ellipse button in the properties value column. The dialog in Figure 14.13 is shown.

The following statement is used for loading one snapshot to the PIT. Set the query to the following SQL text:

```
INSERT INTO biz.PITAirportCode
SELECT
        UPPER(CONVERT(char(32),
                HASHBYTES('MD5', CONCAT(
                        UPPER(RTRIM(LTRIM(hub.AirportCode)))
                        , ';'
                        , CONVERT(NVARCHAR(30), ?, 126)
                ))
        ,2)) AS AirportKey
        , hub.AirportCodeHashKey
        , CONVERT(datetime2(7), ?) AS SnapshotDate
        , COALESCE(sato.AirportHashKey, REPLICATE('0', 32)) AS OriginAirportHashKey
        , COALESCE(sato.LoadDate, '0001-01-01 00:00:00.000') AS OriginLoadDate
        , COALESCE(satd.AirportHashKey, REPLICATE('0', 32)) AS DestAirportHashKey
        , COALESCE(satd.LoadDate, '0001-01-01 00:00:00.000') AS DestLoadDate
FROM
        DataVault.[raw].HubAirportCode hub
LEFT OUTER JOIN DataVault.[raw].SatDestAirportMod satd ON (
        satd.AirportHashKey = hub.AirportCodeHashKey
        AND ? BETWEEN
                satd.LoadDate AND COALESCE(satd.LoadEndDate, '9999-12-31 23:59:59.999')
)
LEFT OUTER JOIN DataVault.[raw].SatOriginAirportMod sato ON (
        sato.AirportHashKey = hub.AirportCodeHashKey
        AND ? BETWEEN
```

```
          sato.LoadDate AND COALESCE(sato.LoadEndDate, '9999-12-31 23:59:59.999')
)
WHERE NOT EXISTS (
    SELECT
            1
    FROM
            biz.PITAirportCode tgt
    WHERE
            hub.AirportCodeHashKey = tgt.AirportCodeHashKey
                AND ? = tgt.SnapshotDate
)
```

Similar to other statements in this chapter, the BETWEEN statement assumes that the **load date** and the **load end date** are not overlapping (the **load end date** of the previous record is the **load date** minus one nanosecond of the next record). The goal is to load the data from this statement into a target PIT table. This key value in the primary key column (here: **AirportKey**) is later used in the dimensional tables of the dependent information marts.

The source statement generates a record per hash key in the parent hub and the snapshot date (which is set by a variable in the statement and set by SSIS). Due to the WHERE condition, the approach is recoverable and could be used to ensure that new business keys are also populated into the target for past snapshot dates to ensure equi-joins at all points in time. This is optional and requires running past snapshot dates again in SSIS.

The snapshot date is stored in a variable **dSnapshotDate** in the SSIS control flow. In order to bind the variable to the parameters in this SQL statement, close the SQL query editor and switch to the **parameter mapping** page of the execute SQL task editor. The page in Figure 14.14 is shown.

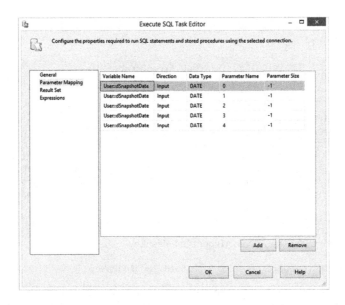

FIGURE 14.14

Parameter mapping in execute SQL task editor for the PIT table.

Because the snapshot date is used multiple times in the SQL statement, and the parameters are not named in OLE DB statements, the variable has to be bound multiple times. For each question mark, add a parameter mapping to the list and select the **dSnapshotDate** variable in the User namespace. Select the **DATE** data type and set each parameter to one instance of the parameter reference (from 0 to 4). Leave the parameter size as is.

Set the variable **dSnapshotDate** to a desired value (usually a date with a time of 00:00:00.000) and run the task. It is also possible to execute the task in a **for loop container** in order to insert multiple snapshot dates, for example during an initial load.

In some cases, the dimension tables should not include one entry per snapshot date but only when changes in the descriptive data occur. This is the actual case for Type 2 dimensions of SSAS OLAP cubes. In this case, it is possible to modify the WHERE condition of the above statement and load only changes into the PIT table. The load date of the referenced satellites is used for the change detection. This is a sufficient approach because the load date changes per change that is added to the satellite.

14.3.4 CREATING VIRTUALIZED DIMENSIONS

In order to implement the Type 2 dimension introduced in section 14.2.2 by using the PIT table from the previous section, the following T-SQL view is created:

```
CREATE VIEW [dbo].[DimAirport3] AS
SELECT
      pit.AirportKey
      ,pit.AirportCodeHashKey
      ,pit.SnapshotDate
      ,CASE
        WHEN hub.AirportCode IS NOT NULL AND hub.AirportCode <> '' THEN hub.AirportCode
        ELSE '?'
       END AS AirportCode
      ,COALESCE(satd.[DestCityName], sato.[OriginCityName], 'Unknown') AS CityName
      ,COALESCE(satd.[DestState], sato.[OriginState], '?') AS [State]
      ,COALESCE(satd.[DestStateName], sato.[OriginStateName], 'Unknown') AS StateName
      ,COALESCE(satd.[DestCityMarketID], sato.[OriginCityMarketID], 0) AS CityMarketID
      ,COALESCE(satd.[DestStateFips], sato.[OriginStateFips], 0) AS StateFips
      ,COALESCE(satd.[DestWac], sato.[OriginWac], 0) AS Wac
FROM
      DataVault.[biz].[PITAirportCode] pit
INNER JOIN DataVault.[raw].HubAirportCode hub ON (
      pit.AirportCodeHashKey = hub.AirportCodeHashKey
)
INNER JOIN DataVault.[raw].SatOriginAirportMod sato ON (
      sato.AirportHashKey = pit.OriginAirportHashKey
      AND sato.LoadDate = pit.OriginLoadDate
)
INNER JOIN DataVault.[raw].SatDestAirportMod satd ON (
      satd.AirportHashKey = pit.DestAirportHashKey
      AND satd.LoadDate = pit.DestLoadDate
)
```

This view implements the same business logic as in the original example: it provides a list of airports with descriptive information from the destination airport source or, if this primary source doesn't provide any data at that snapshot date, it alternatively loads descriptive data from the origin airport satellite.

The biggest difference from the original example is that the joins have changed from LEFT OUTER JOINs to INNER JOINs. In addition, all joins are equi-joins to further increase the performance of the join operations. Another advantage is that the query is based on the PIT table, instead of collecting load dates from multiple satellites, which provides further performance improvements. It joins the airport code hub, in order to retrieve the business key, which is stored in the hub only. It also joins both satellites that provide the descriptive data.

Note that the business logic is problematic, because the checks are based on individual fields. A better approach would check whether the leading satellite provides any useful data by performing a check on the referenced hash key in the PIT table:

```sql
CREATE VIEW [dbo].[DimAirport4] AS
SELECT
        pit.AirportKey
        ,pit.AirportCodeHashKey
        ,pit.SnapshotDate
        ,CASE
          WHEN hub.AirportCode IS NOT NULL AND hub.AirportCode <> ''
          THEN hub.AirportCode
          ELSE '?'
         END AS AirportCode
        ,CASE
          WHEN pit.DestAirportHashKey = '00000000000000000000000000000000'
          THEN sato.[OriginCityName]
          ELSE satd.[DestCityName]
         END AS CityName
        ,CASE
          WHEN pit.DestAirportHashKey = '00000000000000000000000000000000'
          THEN sato.[OriginState]
          ELSE satd.[DestState]
         END AS [State]
        ,CASE
          WHEN pit.DestAirportHashKey = '00000000000000000000000000000000'
          THEN sato.[OriginStateName]
          ELSE satd.[DestStateName]
         END AS StateName
        ,CASE
          WHEN pit.DestAirportHashKey = '00000000000000000000000000000000'
          THEN sato.[OriginCityMarketID]
          ELSE satd.[DestCityMarketID]
         END AS CityMarketID
        ,CASE
          WHEN pit.DestAirportHashKey = '00000000000000000000000000000000'
          THEN sato.[OriginStateFips]
          ELSE satd.[DestStateFips]
         END AS StateFips
```

```
        ,CASE
          WHEN pit.DestAirportHashKey = '00000000000000000000000000000000'
          THEN sato.[OriginWac]
          ELSE satd.[DestWac]
        END AS Wac
FROM
        DataVault.[biz].[PITAirportCode] pit
INNER JOIN DataVault.[raw].HubAirportCode hub ON (
        pit.AirportCodeHashKey = hub.AirportCodeHashKey
)
INNER JOIN DataVault.[raw].SatOriginAirportMod sato ON (
        sato.AirportHashKey = pit.OriginAirportHashKey
        AND sato.LoadDate = pit.OriginLoadDate
)
INNER JOIN DataVault.[raw].SatDestAirportMod satd ON (
        satd.AirportHashKey = pit.DestAirportHashKey
        AND satd.LoadDate = pit.DestLoadDate
)
```

If the referenced hash key is the ghost record, the data is retrieved from the other satellite. Implementing this change is relatively cheap because all the data is provided by virtual means while meeting the performance requirements of the business users.

The very same PIT table can be used to produce other virtual dimensions that implement different business logic. For example, the following view creates a virtual dimension that provides descriptive information from the destination airport source only:

```
CREATE VIEW [dbo].[DimAirportCalif] AS
SELECT
        pit.AirportKey
        ,pit.AirportCodeHashKey
        ,pit.SnapshotDate
        ,CASE
          WHEN hub.AirportCode IS NOT NULL AND hub.AirportCode <> '' THEN hub.AirportCode
          ELSE '?'
          END AS AirportCode
        ,satd.[DestCityName]
        ,satd.[DestState]
        ,satd.[DestStateName]
        ,satd.[DestCityMarketID]
        ,satd.[DestStateFips]
        ,satd.[DestWac]
FROM
        DataVault.[biz].[PITAirportCode] pit
INNER JOIN DataVault.[raw].HubAirportCode hub ON (
        pit.AirportCodeHashKey = hub.AirportCodeHashKey
)
INNER JOIN DataVault.[raw].SatDestAirportMod satd ON (
        satd.AirportHashKey = pit.DestAirportHashKey
        AND satd.LoadDate = pit.DestLoadDate
)
WHERE
        satd.DestState = 'CA'
```

The query statement only joins the satellites that are actually required for the purpose of the dimension. In this example, there is an additional filter on airports from California, which is part of the business rule implemented in this view.

The examples presented in this section should have given you an impression of the advantages that are achieved by separating the join operation from the rest of the business logic. Similar concepts are applied to fact tables in the following sections.

14.3.5 **LOADING BRIDGE TABLES**

The purpose of a bridge table is to ensure that the performance requirements of business users are met for virtual fact tables. The performance of fact tables, when sourced from a Data Vault 2.0 model, depends on three important factors:

1. **Joins between links**: because the desired grain is often not found in only one Data Vault 2.0 link, multiple links are joined in order to achieve the right grain. A prejoining improves the performance of this factor.
2. **Required aggregations and otherwise computed values**: other issues that limit the performance of virtual fact tables are required aggregations that have to be performed on the raw data, often involving a grain shift in addition. In other cases, measures are computed from raw data and added to the fact table. The latter might require complex business logic for the calculation.
3. **Applying additional customization**: a specific fact table includes a number of dimensions and measures that have to be derived from the raw data. The actual number and characteristic is defined by the individual business specification.

Joining and aggregating the data and running complex computational logic are the most resource-intensive operations of these activities. On the other hand, the results from these activities are often reusable for multiple targets (fact tables). Therefore, an approach that materializes the first two activities and separates it from the customization provides an advantage in the information delivery of fact tables, just as the PIT table does for dimension tables. Bridge tables are used for exactly this purpose: to provide the materialized basis for virtual fact tables that meet the performance requirements of the business users.

The following DDL statement creates a simple and minimal bridge table in the Business Vault schema of the EDW:

```
CREATE TABLE [biz].[BrDiversionFlight](
        [SnapshotDate] [datetime2](7) NOT NULL,
        [RecordSource] [nvarchar](50) NOT NULL,
        [FlightHashKey] [char](32) NOT NULL,
        [CarrierHashKey] [char](32) NOT NULL,
        [FlightNumHashKey] [char](32) NOT NULL,
        [TailNumHashKey] [char](32) NOT NULL,
        [OriginHashKey] [char](32) NOT NULL,
        [DestHashKey] [char](32) NOT NULL,
        [FlightDate] [datetime2](7) NOT NULL,
        [DivTailNumHashKey] [char](32) NOT NULL,
        [DivAirportHashKey] [char](32) NOT NULL,
        [Diversion] [int] NOT NULL,
```

```
CONSTRAINT [PK_BrDiversionFlight] PRIMARY KEY NONCLUSTERED
(
        [FlightNumHashKey]
        ,[FlightDate]
        ,[OriginHashKey]
        ,[Diversion]
) ON [INDEX],
INDEX IX_BrDiversionFlight_FlightHashKey ( FlightHashKey ASC ) ON [INDEX],
INDEX IX_BrDiversionFlight_DestHashKey ( DestHashKey ASC, SnapshotDate ASC ) ON [INDEX]
) ON [DATA]
```

The bridge table performs only a prejoining of the nonhistorized links **TLinkFlight** and **TDiversionFlight**, which is required to produce a later fact table that is used to analyze the flight diversions and should include information from the planned flight.

The grain defines the primary key of the bridge table. It is also used by the next SQL statement that incrementally loads the bridge table.

Note that the bridge table implements some indices on the hash keys in order to improve the performance of joins between the bridge table and hubs or satellites. This is necessary for those columns, which are heavily used by ad-hoc queries, because foreign keys are not implemented in the EDW and therefore the implied indices are missing from the table.

In order to load the bridge, the following incremental INSERT statement is used within SSIS:

```
INSERT INTO DataVault.biz.BrDiversionFlight
SELECT
        DATEADD(DAY, 1, CONVERT(date, DATEADD(MCS, -1, div.LoadDate))) AS SnapshotDate
        , div.RecordSource
        , flight.FlightHashKey
        , flight.CarrierHashKey
        , flight.FlightNumHashKey
        , flight.TailNumHashKey
        , flight.OriginHashKey
        , flight.DestHashKey
        , flight.FlightDate
        , div.DivTailNumHashKey
        , div.DivAirportHashKey
        , div.Diversion
FROM
        [DataVault].[raw].[TLinkFlight] flight,
        [DataVault].[raw].[TLinkDiversionFlight] div
WHERE
        flight.FlightNumHashKey = div.FlightNumHashKey
        AND flight.FlightDate = div.FlightDate
        AND flight.OriginHashKey = div.StartAirportHashKey
        AND NOT EXISTS (
                SELECT
                        1
                FROM
                        DataVault.biz.BrDiversionFlight tgt
                WHERE
                        flight.FlightNumHashKey = tgt.FlightNumHashKey
                                AND div.FlightDate = tgt.FlightDate
                                AND flight.OriginHashKey = tgt.OriginHashKey
                                AND div.Diversion = tgt.Diversion
        )
```

This example implements a bridge table based on nonhistorized links. However, the loading procedures for standard Data Vault 2.0 links are the same. This bridge joins both links together and avoids a Cartesian product by using appropriate conditions in the WHERE clause. The bridge actually "bridges" two links and multiple hubs. However, the hubs are not joined at this time, because the business keys are not prejoined into the bridge by default. Only the hash key is added to the bridge table, but this key is already available in the link structures.

The sub-select statement in the WHERE clause is required to support incremental loading and is based on the primary key of the bridge table.

The load date from the source is calculated to the next snapshot date. This is easy if the snapshot date follows a regular pattern because it can be calculated in this case. If the snapshot date follows a different pattern, a lookup into a reference table for the snapshots of the target might be required. Having calculated the snapshot date makes it easier when retrieving information from or via PIT tables in the virtual fact table, for example to retrieve additional descriptive information from dependent satellites of the PIT table. If there is a need for the (technical) load date in the target, it is possible to add it to the bridge in addition. But in most cases, other dates provide more business value, for example the flight date in our example.

Note that the calculation might differ in your case. The one provided in the previous statement requires daily snapshot dates and ensures that load dates without time are mapped to the same snapshot date.

However, the goal of the bridge table is to provide the basis for virtual fact tables with superior performance. If the overall query performance is improved by prejoining information from hubs and their dependent satellites, it should be done, for example by joining the business keys from hubs into the bridge table. However, keep in mind that the performance of the bridge table also drops if the table becomes too wide. In the end, it requires some experimentation to find the right mixes for every individual bridge table.

More performance gains are achieved by ensuring that the bridge table is in the same grain as the target fact table. For example, the following bridge table changes the grain of the previous bridge table:

```
CREATE TABLE [biz].[BrConnection](
        [SnapshotDate] [datetime2](7) NOT NULL,
        [RecordSource] [nvarchar](50) NOT NULL,
        [CarrierHashKey] [char](32) NOT NULL,
        [OriginHashKey] [char](32) NOT NULL,
        [DestHashKey] [char](32) NOT NULL,
        [FlightDate] [datetime2](7) NOT NULL,
        [Year] [smallint] NOT NULL,
        [Quarter] [smallint] NOT NULL,
        [Month] [smallint] NOT NULL,
        [DayOfMonth] [smallint] NOT NULL,
        [DayOfWeek] [smallint] NOT NULL,
        [SumDepDelay] [int] NOT NULL,
        [SumDepDelayMinutes] [int] NOT NULL,
        [SumTaxiOut] [int] NOT NULL,
        [SumWheelsOff] [int] NOT NULL,
        [SumWheelsOn] [int] NOT NULL,
        [SumTaxiIn] [int] NOT NULL,
        [SumArrDelay] [int] NOT NULL,
        [SumArrDelayMinutes] [int] NOT NULL,
        [SumCancelled] [int] NOT NULL,
```

```
    [SumDiverted] [int] NOT NULL,
    [SumAirTime] [int] NOT NULL,
    [SumFlights] [int] NOT NULL,
    [SumDistance] [int] NOT NULL,
    [SumCArrierDelay] [int] NOT NULL,
    [SumWeatherDelay] [int] NOT NULL,
    [SumNASDelay] [int] NOT NULL,
    [SumSecurityDelay] [int] NOT NULL,
    [SumLateAircraftDelay] [int] NOT NULL,
CONSTRAINT [PK_BrConnection] PRIMARY KEY NONCLUSTERED
(
    [CarrierHashKey]
    ,[OriginHashKey]
    ,[DestHashKey]
    ,[FlightDate]

) ON [INDEX],
) ON [DATA]
```

The grain was changed by removing a hub reference from the bridge table. This is also called a "grain shift" and there are two options for it:

- **Removing hub references**: reduces the granularity, for example, by using a GROUP BY clause in the INSERT statement.
- **Adding hub references**: increases the granularity, for example by joining additional links to the current set of used links.

The table is loaded with the following incremental statement that is typically used from an Execute SQL task in SSIS again:

```
INSERT INTO biz.BrConnection
SELECT
    link.FlightDate AS SnapshotDate
    ,'SR9483'
    ,link.CarrierHashKey
    ,link.OriginHashKey
    ,link.DestHashKey
    ,link.[FlightDate]
    ,sat.[Year]
    ,sat.[Quarter]
    ,sat.[Month]
    ,sat.[DayOfMonth]
    ,sat.[DayOfWeek]
    ,SUM(sat.[DepDelay]) AS SumDepDelay
    ,SUM(sat.[DepDelayMinutes]) AS SumDepDelayMinutes
    ,SUM(sat.[TaxiOut]) AS SumTaxiOut
    ,SUM(sat.[WheelsOff]) AS SumWheelsOff
    ,SUM(sat.[WheelsOn]) AS SumWheelsOn
    ,SUM(sat.[TaxiIn]) AS SumTaxiIn
    ,SUM(sat.[ArrDelay]) AS SumArrDelay
    ,SUM(sat.[ArrDelayMinutes]) AS SumArrDelayMinutes
    ,SUM(CASE WHEN sat.Cancelled=1 THEN 1 ELSE 0 END) AS SumCancelled
    ,SUM(CASE WHEN sat.Diverted=1 THEN 1 ELSE 0 END) AS SumDiverted
```

```
        ,SUM(sat.[AirTime]) AS SumAirTime
        ,SUM(sat.[Flights]) AS SumFlights
        ,SUM(sat.[Distance]) AS SumDistance
        ,SUM(sat.[CarrierDelay]) AS SumCArrierDelay
        ,SUM(sat.[WeatherDelay]) AS SumWeatherDelay
        ,SUM(sat.[NASDelay]) AS SumNASDelay
        ,SUM(sat.[SecurityDelay]) AS SumSecurityDelay
        ,SUM(sat.[LateAircraftDelay]) AS SumLateAircraftDelay
    FROM
            [DataVault].[raw].[TLinkFlight] link
    INNER JOIN DataVault.[raw].TSatFlight sat ON (
        sat.FlightHashKey = link.FlightHashKey
    )
    WHERE
                NOT EXISTS (SELECT
                        1
                    FROM
                        [DataVault].[biz].[BrConnection] tgt
                    WHERE
                        link.CarrierHashKey = tgt.CarrierHashKey
                        AND link.OriginHashKey = tgt.OriginHashKey
                        AND link.DestHashKey = tgt.DestHashKey
                        AND link.FlightDate = tgt.FlightDate
                    )

    GROUP BY
        link.CarrierHashKey, link.OriginHashKey, link.DestHashKey, link.FlightDate,
        sat.[Year], sat.[Quarter], sat.[Month], sat.[DayOfMonth], sat.[DayOfWeek]
```

The INSERT statement implements the grain shift by removing hub references (to **HubCarrier**, **HubTailNumber** and **HubFlightNumber**) and applying a GROUP BY clause on the data. It further improves the performance of virtualized fact tables by adding the results of required aggregations to the materialized bridge. Because the aggregations represent business logic that is implemented by this bridge, the **record source** is set to a fixed value in the load statement. The **snapshot date** was not calculated from the **load date** because it is not sufficient to do so (due to the aggregation). Instead, the **flight date** was used as a **snapshot date**, which is more appropriate for the target information mart.

These bridge tables can now be used as the basis to provide virtual fact tables.

14.3.6 CREATING VIRTUALIZED FACTS

The virtualized fact tables implement the additional customization that is required by individual fact tables in various information marts and can differ in the representation of the information. However, the grain of fact tables that depend on the same bridge table should be the same. If the grain differs between the virtual fact table and the bridge table, a new bridge should be introduced in the Business Vault to ensure that the performance meets the requirements of the business users.

The following DDL statement creates a virtual fact entity based on **BrDiversionFlight**:

```
CREATE VIEW FactDiversions AS
SELECT
        lflight.FlightDate
        ,DATEPART(YEAR, lflight.FlightDate)*10000
                +DATEPART(MONTH, lflight.FlightDate)*100
                +DATEPART(DAY, lflight.FlightDate) AS FlightDateKey
        ,c.Carrier
        ,CONCAT(fn.Carrier, fn.FlightNum) AS FlightNum
        ,tn.TailNum
        ,pitOrigin.AirportKey AS OriginAirportKey
        ,pitDest.AirportKey AS DestAirportKey
        ,dtn.TailNum AS DivTailNum
        ,pitDivAirport.AirportKey AS DivAirportKey
        ,br.Diversion
        ,sat.[CRSDepTime]
        ,sat.[DepTime]
        ,sat.[DepDelay]
        ,sat.[DepDelayMinutes]
        ,sat.[DepDel15]
        ,sat.[DepartureDelayGroups]
        ,sat.[DepTimeBlk]
        ,sat.[TaxiOut]
        ,sat.[WheelsOff]
        ,sat.[WheelsOn]
        ,sat.[TaxiIn]
        ,sat.[CRSArrTime]
        ,sat.[ArrTime]
        ,sat.[ArrDelay]
        ,sat.[ArrDelayMinutes]
        ,sat.[ArrDel15]
        ,sat.[ArrivalDelayGroups]
        ,sat.[ArrTimeBlk]
        ,sat.[Cancelled]
        ,sat.[CancellationCode]
        ,sat.[Diverted]
        ,sat.[CRSElapsedTime]
        ,sat.[ActualElapsedTime]
        ,sat.[AirTime]
        ,sat.[Flights]
        ,sat.[Distance]
        ,sat.[DistanceGroup]
        ,sat.[CarrierDelay]
        ,sat.[WeatherDelay]
        ,sat.[NASDelay]
        ,sat.[SecurityDelay]
        ,sat.[LateAircraftDelay]
        ,sat.[FirstDepTime]
        ,sat.[TotalAddGTime]
        ,sat.[LongestAddGTime]
```

```
FROM
        [DataVault].[biz].[BrDiversionFlight] br
INNER JOIN [DataVault].[raw].[TLinkFlight] lflight ON (
        lflight.FlightHashKey = br.FlightHashKey
)
INNER JOIN DataVault.[raw].TSatFlight sat ON (
            sat.FlightHashKey = br.FlightHashKey
)
INNER JOIN [DataVault].[raw].[HubCarrier] c ON (
    c.CarrierHashKey = br.CarrierHashKey
)
INNER JOIN [DataVault].[raw].[HubFlightNum] fn ON (
    fn.FlightNumHashKey = br.FlightNumHashKey
)
INNER JOIN [DataVault].[raw].[HubTailNum] tn ON (
    tn.TailNumHashKey = br.TailNumHashKey
)
INNER JOIN [DataVault].[biz].[PITAirportCode] pitOrigin ON (
    pitOrigin.AirportCodeHashKey = br.OriginHashKey
        AND pitOrigin.SnapshotDate = br.SnapshotDate
)
INNER JOIN [DataVault].[biz].[PITAirportCode] pitDest ON (
    pitDest.AirportCodeHashKey = br.DestHashKey
        AND pitDest.SnapshotDate = br.SnapshotDate
)
INNER JOIN [DataVault].[raw].[HubTailNum] dtn ON (
    dtn.TailNumHashKey = br.DivTailNumHashKey
)
INNER JOIN [DataVault].[biz].[PITAirportCode] pitDivAirport ON (
    pitDivAirport.AirportCodeHashKey = br.DivAirportHashKey
        AND pitDivAirport.SnapshotDate = br.SnapshotDate
)
```

At first glance, the statement looks large. But for the SQL optimizer, most activities required to execute this statement are relatively cheap (performance-wise). The statement joins measures from the nonhistorized satellite **TSatFlight**. This join, as all the other joins in this statement, is based on an inner join with an equi-join condition. If a business key is required in the fact table (for example, because not all dimensions are provided via dimension tables in this example), the hub is joined on the hash key only in order to retrieve the business key or composite key from the hub. This statement concatenates the composite key from hub **HubFlightNum** into a format that the user is familiar with. This business logic could be extended to serve other requirements by the end-user, which might differ per information mart or fact table.

Note that the **flight date** could be easily sourced from the bridge table source. This statement joins **TLinkFlight** for demonstrative purposes: because the grain is the same, it is easily possible to join the original source of the bridge table in order to include additional or missing data into the fact table. In order to support such joins, the link hash key, in this example **FlightHashKey**, should be included.

If dimension tables should be provided for some dimensions, it is easy to retrieve the required key values for the dimension entry. This hash value comes from the PIT table. However, because the PIT table provides multiple snapshots for the same hash key, the equi-join condition for the PIT table is extended to include the snapshot date of the fact. This snapshot date was calculated from the technical load date and helps us to retrieve the appropriate entry in the PIT table. We could also use the PIT table to retrieve a load date for satellites included in the PIT table to retrieve additional descriptive data from dependent satellites:

```
CREATE VIEW FactDiversions2 AS
SELECT
      lflight.FlightDate
      ,DATEPART(YEAR, lflight.FlightDate)*10000
            +DATEPART(MONTH, lflight.FlightDate)*100
            +DATEPART(DAY, lflight.FlightDate) AS FlightDateKey
      ,c.Carrier
      ,CONCAT(fn.Carrier, fn.FlightNum) AS FlightNum
      ,tn.TailNum
      ,oa.AirportCode
      ,soa.OriginCityName
      ,soa.OriginState
      ,soa.OriginStateName
      ,pitDest.AirportKey AS DestAirportKey
      ,dtn.TailNum AS DivTailNum
      ,pitDivAirport.AirportKey AS DivAirportKey
      ,br.Diversion
      ,sat.[CRSDepTime]
      ,sat.[DepTime]
      ,sat.[DepDelay]
      ,sat.[DepDelayMinutes]
      ,sat.[DepDel15]
      ,sat.[DepartureDelayGroups]
      ,sat.[DepTimeBlk]
      ,sat.[TaxiOut]
      ,sat.[WheelsOff]
      ,sat.[WheelsOn]
      ,sat.[TaxiIn]
      ,sat.[CRSArrTime]
      ,sat.[ArrTime]
      ,sat.[ArrDelay]
      ,sat.[ArrDelayMinutes]
      ,sat.[ArrDel15]
      ,sat.[ArrivalDelayGroups]
      ,sat.[ArrTimeBlk]
      ,sat.[Cancelled]
      ,sat.[CancellationCode]
      ,sat.[Diverted]
      ,sat.[CRSElapsedTime]
      ,sat.[ActualElapsedTime]
      ,sat.[AirTime]
      ,sat.[Flights]
      ,sat.[Distance]
      ,sat.[DistanceGroup]
      ,sat.[CarrierDelay]
      ,sat.[WeatherDelay]
      ,sat.[NASDelay]
      ,sat.[SecurityDelay]
```

```
        ,sat.[LateAircraftDelay]
        ,sat.[FirstDepTime]
        ,sat.[TotalAddGTime]
        ,sat.[LongestAddGTime]

FROM
        [DataVault].[biz].[BrDiversionFlight] br
INNER JOIN [DataVault].[raw].[TLinkFlight] lflight ON (
        lflight.FlightHashKey = br.FlightHashKey
)
INNER JOIN DataVault.[raw].TSatFlight sat ON (
        sat.FlightHashKey = br.FlightHashKey
)
INNER JOIN [DataVault].[raw].[HubCarrier] c ON (
        c.CarrierHashKey = br.CarrierHashKey
)
INNER JOIN [DataVault].[raw].[HubFlightNum] fn ON (
        fn.FlightNumHashKey = br.FlightNumHashKey
)
INNER JOIN [DataVault].[raw].[HubTailNum] tn ON (
        tn.TailNumHashKey = br.TailNumHashKey
)
INNER JOIN [DataVault].[biz].[PITAirportCode] pitOrigin ON (
        pitOrigin.AirportCodeHashKey = br.OriginHashKey
            AND pitOrigin.SnapshotDate = br.SnapshotDate
)
INNER JOIN [DataVault].[raw].[HubAirportCode] oa ON (
        oa.AirportCodeHashKey = br.OriginHashKey
)
INNER JOIN [DataVault].[raw].[SatOriginAirportMod] soa ON (
        soa.AirportHashKey = pitOrigin.OriginAirportHashKey
        AND soa.LoadDate = pitOrigin.OriginLoadDate
)
INNER JOIN [DataVault].[biz].[PITAirportCode] pitDest ON (
        pitDest.AirportCodeHashKey = br.DestHashKey
            AND pitDest.SnapshotDate = br.SnapshotDate
)
INNER JOIN [DataVault].[raw].[HubTailNum] dtn ON (
        dtn.TailNumHashKey = br.DivTailNumHashKey
)
INNER JOIN [DataVault].[biz].[PITAirportCode] pitDivAirport ON (
        pitDivAirport.AirportCodeHashKey = br.DivAirportHashKey
            AND pitDivAirport.SnapshotDate = br.SnapshotDate
)
```

In this example, the key value for the origin airport dimension is replaced by attributes directly joined into the fact table. However, the PIT is still used in order to retrieve the appropriate load date in the dependent satellite **SatOriginAirportMod**. Joining the satellite requires only INNER JOINs with equi-join condition, due to the available PIT table. Without the PIT, a more complex join would be required to find the appropriate delta record. It would involve a BETWEEN condition and a LEFT JOIN because it is not guaranteed that the satellite provides a record for the given snapshot date.

Another example implements a virtual fact table on the aggregated bridge **BrConnection**:

```
CREATE VIEW FactConnection3 AS
SELECT
      c.Carrier
     ,pitOrigin.AirportKey AS OriginAirportKey
     ,pitDest.AirportKey AS DestAirportKey
     ,DATEPART(YEAR, br.FlightDate)*10000
              +DATEPART(MONTH, br.FlightDate)*100
              +DATEPART(DAY, br.FlightDate) AS FlightDateKey
     ,br.[FlightDate]
     ,br.[Year]
     ,br.[Quarter]
     ,br.[Month]
     ,br.[DayOfMonth]
     ,br.[DayOfWeek]
     ,br.[SumDepDelay]
     ,br.[SumDepDelayMinutes]
     ,br.[SumTaxiOut]
     ,br.[SumWheelsOff]
     ,br.[SumWheelsOn]
     ,br.[SumTaxiIn]
     ,br.[SumArrDelay]
     ,br.[SumArrDelayMinutes]
     ,br.[SumCancelled]
     ,br.[SumDiverted]
     ,br.[SumAirTime]
     ,br.[SumFlights]
     ,br.[SumDistance]
     ,br.[SumCArrierDelay]
     ,br.[SumWeatherDelay]
     ,br.[SumNASDelay]
     ,br.[SumSecurityDelay]
     ,br.[SumLateAircraftDelay]
   FROM
        [DataVault].[biz].[BrConnection] br
   INNER JOIN [DataVault].[raw].[HubCarrier] c ON (
      c.CarrierHashKey = br.CarrierHashKey
   )
   INNER JOIN [DataVault].[biz].[PITAirportCode] pitOrigin ON (
      pitOrigin.AirportCodeHashKey = br.OriginHashKey
         AND pitOrigin.SnapshotDate = br.SnapshotDate
   )
   INNER JOIN [DataVault].[biz].[PITAirportCode] pitDest ON (
      pitDest.AirportCodeHashKey = br.DestHashKey
         AND pitDest.SnapshotDate = br.SnapshotDate
   )
```

This table includes no business logic for the aggregations, because these operations were already performed when loading the bridge table. Because these aggregated measures are included in the bridge table, no additional data from the no-history link or satellite are required as well. In addition to the measures, this fact table includes the key values to dimension tables for origin airport and destination airport. Additional descriptive data could be joined from hubs and satellites if required for a specific target.

14.4 IMPLEMENTING TEMPORAL DIMENSIONS

The examples from sections 14.2 and 14.3 have demonstrated how to provide Type 2 dimensions using joins between the hub table and dependent satellites or the PIT table and dependent satellites. All of these joins were based on the **load date** to find the record in the dependent satellite that is current for a given snapshot date. The load date was used because it provides information about the technical validity of a record in the history of the data: which data was current at a given point in time, from a technical perspective.

However, in some cases, business users don't want to analyze the data from a technical perspective. Instead, they are interested in a temporal perspective that is based on the effectivity dates, defined by the business. These effectivity dates come in various ways, for example **valid from** and **valid to** dates and **membership start** and **membership end** dates. Chapter 5, Intermediate Data Vault Modeling, has shown how to store such effectivity dates in effectivity satellites, which are added to hubs and links to indicate if business keys in hubs are deleted in the source system or have become invalid, and the validity of relationships between business keys in Data Vault 2.0 links. These satellites also ensure that changes to these effectivity dates are tracked in an auditable manner.

In order to create Type 2 dimensions that reflect the temporal perspective, a special form of a PIT table can be used. The following table implements such a temporal PIT:

```sql
CREATE TABLE [biz].[TPITAirportCode](
        [AirportKey] [char](32) NOT NULL,
        [AirportCodeHashKey] [char](32) NOT NULL,
        [SnapshotDate] [datetime2](7) NOT NULL,
        [OriginAirportHashKey] [char](32) NOT NULL,
        [OriginLoadDate] [datetime2](7) NOT NULL,
        [DestAirportHashKey] [char](32) NOT NULL,
        [DestLoadDate] [datetime2](7) NOT NULL,
 CONSTRAINT [PK_TPITAirportCode] PRIMARY KEY NONCLUSTERED
(
        [AirportKey] ASC
) ON [INDEX],
 CONSTRAINT [UK_TPITAirportCode] UNIQUE NONCLUSTERED
(
        [AirportCodeHashKey] ASC,
        [SnapshotDate] ASC
) ON [INDEX]
) ON [DATA]
```

Notice that there is no difference in the structure between a standard PIT and a temporal PIT. However, instead of prejoining the data based on load date, the effectivity date or any other descriptive date is used when loading the temporal PIT table:

```sql
INSERT INTO biz.TPITAirportCode
SELECT
        UPPER(CONVERT(char(32),
                HASHBYTES('MD5', CONCAT(
                        UPPER(RTRIM(LTRIM(hub.AirportCode)))
                        , ';'
                        , CONVERT(NVARCHAR(30), ?, 126)
                ))
        ))
```

```
        ,2)) AS AirportKey
        , hub.AirportCodeHashKey
        , CONVERT(datetime2(7), ?) AS SnapshotDate
        , COALESCE(sato.AirportHashKey, REPLICATE('0', 32)) AS OriginAirportHashKey
        , COALESCE(sato.LoadDate, '0001-01-01 00:00:00.000') AS OriginLoadDate
        , COALESCE(satd.AirportHashKey, REPLICATE('0', 32)) AS DestAirportHashKey
        , COALESCE(satd.LoadDate, '0001-01-01 00:00:00.000') AS DestLoadDate
FROM
        DataVault.[raw].HubAirportCode hub
LEFT OUTER JOIN DataVault.[raw].SatDestAirportMod2 satd ON (
        satd.AirportHashKey = hub.AirportCodeHashKey
        AND satd.LoadEndDate IS NULL
        AND ? BETWEEN
                satd.ValidFrom AND COALESCE(satd.ValidTo, '9999-12-31 23:59:59.999')
)
LEFT OUTER JOIN DataVault.[raw].SatOriginAirportMod2 sato ON (
        sato.AirportHashKey = hub.AirportCodeHashKey
        AND sato.LoadEndDate IS NULL
        AND ? BETWEEN
                sato.ValidFrom AND COALESCE(sato.ValidTo, '9999-12-31 23:59:59.999')
)
WHERE NOT EXISTS (
        SELECT
                1
        FROM
                biz.TPITAirportCode tgt
        WHERE
                hub.AirportCodeHashKey = tgt.AirportCodeHashKey
                    AND ? = tgt.SnapshotDate
)
```

The join conditions are based on the currently active record from the satellite, as indicated by a **load end date** of NULL, and the **snapshot date** from the PIT between the **valid from** and **valid to** dates from the descriptive satellite (not an effectivity satellite). However, if the effectivity dates change in the raw data, the PIT needs to be updated for past records or records are deleted from the PIT and the above statement inserts the current view requested by the business. Updating the table will be costly from a performance standpoint. Instead, add a load date to the temporal PIT table and partition over it and remove old partitions whenever the current partition was successfully loaded. By doing so, the temporal PIT table is turned into a rolling history of joins.

In order to present the data to the business user, a similar view can be used as in section 14.3.3:

```
CREATE VIEW [dbo].[DimAirport5] AS
SELECT
        pit.AirportKey
        ,pit.AirportCodeHashKey
        ,pit.SnapshotDate
        ,CASE
            WHEN hub.AirportCode IS NOT NULL AND hub.AirportCode <> '' THEN hub.AirportCode
            ELSE '?'
          END AS AirportCode
        ,COALESCE(satd.[DestCityName], sato.[OriginCityName], 'Unknown') AS CityName
```

```
        ,COALESCE(satd.[DestState], sato.[OriginState], '?') AS [State]
        ,COALESCE(satd.[DestStateName], sato.[OriginStateName], 'Unknown') AS StateName
        ,COALESCE(satd.[DestCityMarketID], sato.[OriginCityMarketID], 0) AS CityMarketID
        ,COALESCE(satd.[DestStateFips], sato.[OriginStateFips], 0) AS StateFips
        ,COALESCE(satd.[DestWac], sato.[OriginWac], 0) AS Wac
FROM
        DataVault.[biz].[TPITAirportCode] pit
INNER JOIN DataVault.[raw].HubAirportCode hub ON (
        pit.AirportCodeHashKey = hub.AirportCodeHashKey
)
INNER JOIN DataVault.[raw].SatOriginAirportMod sato ON (
        sato.AirportHashKey = pit.OriginAirportHashKey
        AND sato.LoadDate = pit.OriginLoadDate
)
INNER JOIN DataVault.[raw].SatDestAirportMod satd ON (
        satd.AirportHashKey = pit.DestAirportHashKey
        AND satd.LoadDate = pit.DestLoadDate
)
```

The only difference between the two views is the primary source of the fact table, which is the above temporal PIT table instead of the standard PIT. Other than that, the view definition is exactly as before. Therefore, it is also easy to use for power users who directly access the Data Vault 2.0 model, because they only need to change the PIT source in order to access a temporal view of the data instead of the technically historized view.

14.5 IMPLEMENTING DATA QUALITY USING PIT TABLES

Another application of PIT tables is to use it for data cleansing purposes. In some (rare) cases, it might be appropriate to use a PIT table for master and duplicate resolution and other data cleansing activities. The following DDL creates just another version of the PIT table used before:

```
CREATE TABLE [biz].[QPITAirportCode](
        [AirportKey] [char](32) NOT NULL,
        [AirportCodeHashKey] [char](32) NOT NULL,
        [SnapshotDate] [datetime2](7) NOT NULL,
        [OriginAirportHashKey] [char](32) NOT NULL,
        [OriginLoadDate] [datetime2](7) NOT NULL,
        [DestAirportHashKey] [char](32) NOT NULL,
        [DestLoadDate] [datetime2](7) NOT NULL,
    CONSTRAINT [PK_QPITAirportCode] PRIMARY KEY NONCLUSTERED
    (
        [AirportKey] ASC
    ) ON [INDEX],
    CONSTRAINT [UK_QPITAirportCode] UNIQUE NONCLUSTERED
    (
        [AirportCodeHashKey] ASC,
        [SnapshotDate] ASC
    ) ON [INDEX]
) ON [DATA]
```

Again, the only difference between this PIT table and the ones used before is the name. The column definitions remain the same. However, the loading statement differs:

```
INSERT INTO biz.QPITAirportCode
SELECT
        UPPER(CONVERT(char(32), HASHBYTES('MD5',
                CONCAT(UPPER(RTRIM(LTRIM(hub.AirportCode))), ';', CONVERT(NVARCHAR(30), ?,
        126))),2)) AS AirportKey
        , hub.AirportCodeHashKey
        , CONVERT(datetime2(7), ?) AS SnapshotDate
        , COALESCE(sato.AirportHashKey, REPLICATE('0', 32)) AS OriginAirportHashKey
        , COALESCE(sato.LoadDate, '0001-01-01 00:00:00.000') AS OriginLoadDate
        , CASE
            WHEN satd.DestCityName = 'Frisco, CA' THEN REPLICATE('0', 32)
            ELSE COALESCE(satd.AirportHashKey, REPLICATE('0', 32))
          END AS DestAirportHashKey
        , CASE
            WHEN satd.DestCityName = 'Frisco, CA' THEN '0001-01-01 00:00:00.000'
            ELSE COALESCE(satd.LoadDate, '0001-01-01 00:00:00.000')
          END AS DestLoadDate
FROM
        DataVault.[raw].HubAirportCode hub
LEFT OUTER JOIN DataVault.[raw].SatDestAirportMod satd ON (
        satd.AirportHashKey = hub.AirportCodeHashKey
        AND ? BETWEEN
                satd.LoadDate AND COALESCE(satd.LoadEndDate, '9999-12-31 23:59:59.999')
)
LEFT OUTER JOIN DataVault.[raw].SatOriginAirportMod sato ON (
        sato.AirportHashKey = hub.AirportCodeHashKey
        AND ? BETWEEN
                sato.LoadDate AND COALESCE(sato.LoadEndDate, '9999-12-31 23:59:59.999')
)
WHERE NOT EXISTS (
        SELECT
                1
        FROM
                biz.QPITAirportCode tgt
        WHERE
                hub.AirportCodeHashKey = tgt.AirportCodeHashKey
                        AND ? = tgt.SnapshotDate
)
```

The preceding statement loads the DQ PIT but cleanses the data by setting the **DestAirportHash-Key** and **DestLoadDate** to the ghost record in the case that the **DestCityName** is "Frisco, CA". Similarly any other business logic could be applied when loading the DQ PIT table. The business logic in the dependent dimension view would automatically pick a record from an alternate satellite if the ghost record is found. The advantage of this approach is that it is transparent to the user: similarly to temporal dimensions, power users could just use the DQ PIT to source cleansed dimension data. On the other hand, the business logic is hidden in the loading procedure of the PIT table. A similar approach could be achieved by adding a computed satellite with cleansed data that could also be added to the standard (or temporal) PIT table. If the power user wants to use cleansed information, this computed satellite is joined to the PIT table instead of the raw satellite.

However, this example shows the power of PIT tables (and similarly bridge tables) for delivering the data that is required by the business user.

14.6 DEALING WITH REFERENCE DATA

In many cases, reference codes are included in Raw Data Vault satellites. These codes vary from source system to source system but business users expect a conformed view on such codes in order to run analytical statements across source systems.

Instead of modifying the code in the Raw Data Vault satellite, which would compromise the auditability of the Raw Data Vault, the code from a specific source system is replaced or enriched by descriptive data from reference tables when the Business Vault or information marts are being built. The following DDL creates a simplified computed satellite in the Business Vault:

```
CREATE VIEW biz.TSatFlightDelay AS
SELECT
        [FlightHashKey]
        ,[LoadDate]
        ,[RecordSource]
        ,[DepDelay]
        ,[DepDelayMinutes]
        ,[DepDel15]
        ,[DepartureDelayGroups]
        ,[ArrDelay]
        ,[ArrDelayMinutes]
        ,[ArrDel15]
        ,[ArrivalDelayGroups]
        ,[CarrierDelay]
        ,[WeatherDelay]
        ,[NASDelay]
        ,[SecurityDelay]
        ,[LateAircraftDelay]
FROM
        [DataVault].[raw].[TSatFlight]
```

This computed satellite is directly based on the satellite **TSatFlight** in the Raw Data Vault. It is merely a selection of some columns without any filtering or computing of rows that only serves as the playground for the example in this section.

The next statement modifies this computed satellite by adding descriptive data from a reference table to the satellite:

```
CREATE VIEW biz.TSatFlightDelay2 AS
SELECT
        s.[FlightHashKey]
        ,s.[LoadDate]
        ,s.[RecordSource]
        ,s.[DepDelay]
        ,s.[DepDelayMinutes]
        ,s.[DepDel15]
        ,s.[DepartureDelayGroups]
```

```
        ,rd.Name AS DepDelayName
        ,rd.Abbreviation AS DepDelayAbbr
        ,s.[ArrDelay]
        ,s.[ArrDelayMinutes]
        ,s.[ArrDel15]
        ,s.[ArrivalDelayGroups]
        ,ra.Name AS ArrDelayName
        ,ra.Abbreviation AS ArrDelayAbbr
        ,s.[CarrierDelay]
        ,s.[WeatherDelay]
        ,s.[NASDelay]
        ,s.[SecurityDelay]
        ,s.[LateAircraftDelay]
FROM
        [DataVault].[raw].[TSatFlight] s
INNER JOIN
        [DataVault].[raw].[RefDelayGroup] rd ON (s.[DepartureDelayGroups] = rd.Code)
INNER JOIN
        [DataVault].[raw].[RefDelayGroup] ra ON (s.[ArrivalDelayGroups] = ra.Code)
```

The descriptive data is joined from the reference table **RefDelayGroup**, which is just a view on a master data table in MDS. The reference table is joined twice because it is used to describe two codes in the satellite (**DepartureDelayGroups** and **ArrivalDelayGroups**).

By doing so, the descriptive data is added to the computed satellite by adding some of the attributes from the joined reference table to the view. This approach is perfectly fine, especially for creating star schemas. Instead of joining the data in the computed satellite, it could also be joined when creating the dimension tables or fact tables.

However, it is also possible to create a dimension based on reference tables:

```
CREATE VIEW DimDelayGroup AS
SELECT
        [Code] AS DelayGroupKey
        ,[Name]
        ,[Abbreviation]
        ,[Sort Order]
FROM
        [DataVault].[raw].[RefDelayGroup]
```

In this case, the **code** is used as the dimension key because it is defined as a unique value that never changes. Because of simplicity, the code is not hashed when creating dimension tables for reference data. Once the dimension table is defined, the dimension key is referenced by a fact table (using the code). It is also possible to reference the dimension from another dimension, creating a snow-flake schema.

In many cases, there are mapping tables that help to map between codes from individual source systems to conformed codes for the data warehouse. The easiest approach is to create a master data entity with the code column used for the conformed code and individual columns per source system code. There are also options if multiple codes from the source system need to be mapped to the same conformed code in the data warehouse.

14.7 ABOUT HASH KEYS IN THE INFORMATION MART

The information mart uses hash keys to define the relationships between facts and dimensions. Because the information mart is provided virtually, this presents no problem in most cases. However, the OLAP cubes are often materialized and storage might become an issue. In other cases, performance might be affected to some extent.

The following sections provide recommended solutions and best practices to deal with storage and performance bottlenecks that might be due to hash keys.

14.7.1 ADVANTAGES OF USING HASH KEYS IN THE INFORMATION MART

The advantage of using hash keys in the information mart is the ease of use when sourcing the data. All other options require more complex solutions and loading processes. Chapter 15, Multidimensional Database, shows that the hash keys can be used when creating the multidimensional database without any problems from a structural perspective.

For Type 1 dimensions, the hash key from the hub is used to populate the key attribute in the dimension. If Type 2 dimensions should be provided, the key from the PIT table is used because it identifies each change in the PIT (and thus the dimension table) uniquely.

Using hash keys in the data warehouse, including in the dimensional model, is future-proof for all requirements regarding the volume, variety and velocity of data and thus the recommended approach for building information marts and multidimensional databases.

We truly believe that you should only deviate from this recommendation if you *really* need to.

14.7.2 REDUCE THE NUMBER OF DIMENSIONS IN CUBE

If you have a performance or storage issue in your solution, our first recommendation is to review the number of dimensions in your information mart and dependent cubes. In most cases, it is possible to reduce the number of dimensions by providing multiple cubes that are more tailored for specific business cases. This way, the required storage is reduced per cube, which improves the overall performance of the solution while maintaining ease of development and use.

14.7.3 USE FIXED BINARY DATA TYPE FOR HASH VALUES

If you still have an issue after reducing the number of dimensions in your solution or if reducing the dimensions is not an option, you should consider storing the hash keys using a binary datatype (but not a BLOB, CLOB, TEXT, or LOB data type if you're using other environments). For example, it is possible to store the result from the MD5 hash function in Microsoft SQL Server using a binary(16) column. Instead of storing it as a hexadecimal string, which requires 32 characters (thus 32 bytes), the hash value is stored in its binary format, requiring only 16 bytes.

The drawback of this solution is that some tools that are part of the BI stack of your organization might not support reading or writing to binary columns. This might become a problem if transparent access using views is also not possible. You should review the tools to be used in the future, including enterprise service buses (ESBs) (such as Microsoft BizTalk, which doesn't directly support binary datatypes) and the workarounds available (SQL views, stored procedures, etc.).

The advantage of storing the hash keys as character strings is that the string is supported in any tool.

14.7.4 **REDUCE THE SIZE OF THE HASH KEY**

Depending on the selected hash function, the size of the hash values might differ (refer to Chapter 11, Data Extraction, for a detailed discussion). If you're using SHA-1 (or higher) to hash your business keys, consider using MD5 because it provides an appropriate solution while maintaining a manageable hash value size. All other options require more storage and might affect performance in a more serious way. Avoid using anything higher than SHA-1 because you will probably not gain anything for the additional storage or reduced performance.

On the other hand, avoid using CRC or MD4 functions, due to increased risk for collisions. Our general recommendation is to use the MD5 hash function for calculating the hash keys.

14.7.5 **INTRODUCE ADDITIONAL SEQUENCE NUMBERS**

It is also possible to introduce sequence numbers in the PIT tables (for using them in Type 2 dimensions) or *close to hubs* (for example in hubs themselves or other structures). This should be your last choice, because it makes dealing with the data more complex.

Also note that such a solution requires that the sequence number be materialized (again, for example in the PIT table) to be stable for virtualization. If the sequence number is not materialized somewhere, it is not possible to incrementally load information marts and OLAP cubes. It is also not possible to perform cross-business queries that join multiple information marts or cubes.

This solution would require the replacement of the key column (the hash value that is calculated per parent business key and snapshot date) by an integer sequence value. This value can be used to identify Type 2 dimensions. Because the PIT table probably contains many records, a bigint data type is required. For Type 1 dimensions, a hash key should be introduced per business key in hubs.

REFERENCES

[1] U.S. Diplomatic Mission to Germany (website), 2015, "About the USA", available at http://usa.usembassy.de/travel-regions.htm.
[2] Microsoft, Microsoft Association Algorithm Technical Reference, 2015, available at https://msdn.microsoft.com/en-us/library/cc280428.aspx.
[3] Judith R. Davis, Robert Eve: "Data Virtualization," p. 47ff.

MULTIDIMENSIONAL DATABASE

The previous chapters of this book have described how to set up the relational part of the data warehouse. It provides the raw data and information for users to perform their analytical work, either using ad-hoc SQL queries or, more commonly, analytical applications, such as Microsoft SQL Server Reporting Services or spreadsheets, e.g., PowerPivot for Microsoft Excel.

However, most casual business users are not dealing with the relational data warehouse. Instead, many of them prefer multidimensional databases as their main interface for accessing the information for analytical purposes. These multidimensional databases are designed to support Online Analytic Processing (OLAP) and are an effective tool to consume information because it allows business users to formulate queries and get quick responses [1]. A multidimensional database is best suited when the end-user wants to work with aggregated information instead of raw facts.

Microsoft SQL Server Analysis Services (SSAS) provides an OLAP solution developed by Microsoft as part of their SQL Server Business Intelligence stack. SSAS also provides a Tabular mode that contains the detailed data [2]. It provides the presentation database that includes aggregations and indexes to provide high query performance [1]. SSAS has some interesting characteristics [1]:

- **User-defined metadata:** the multidimensional database consists of one or more OLAP cubes, which are based on facts and dimensions, closely following the definitions known from the information marts created in the previous chapter. SSAS also supports hierarchies, and the option to combine facts from multiple OLAP cubes. If the relational foundation was built using the principles in the previous chapter, it becomes possible to run queries across multiple OLAP cubes.
- **Query performance:** SSAS provides superior query performance when dealing with analytic queries. Such queries are characterized by grouping and aggregating when executed against a relational database.
- **Aggregation management:** one of the reasons why OLAP cubes provide superior performance for analytic queries is the fact that they precompute the data at different grain levels. This aggregation management is transparent to the business user.
- **Calculations:** in some cases, it is required to add calculations to the OLAP cube, for example when dealing with percentages. SSAS provides such calculated measures among other calculations.
- **Security provisions:** SSAS provides complex security rules to protect the aggregated data against unauthorized use.

As a summary, SSAS is best for providing aggregated information. It is not a good database to provide detailed information, typically dealt with in operational business processes. This is where a relational database or a NoSQL environment becomes more appropriate.

The goal of this last chapter is to complete the end-to-end discussion about how to build a scalable data warehouse. It is not going to replace an OLAP or SSAS book. It will, however, focus on some characteristics that are unique for information marts prepared and built during the previous chapters (even though there are only a few, mainly due to the fact that we're dealing with virtualized information marts).

15.1 ACCESSING THE INFORMATION MART

The information mart provides *all* the information that should be presented to the end-user. If this is not the case, because some data from the Raw Data Vault is missing, it should be included by the information mart first, before the SSAS database is being built. Accessing the Raw Data Vault or the Business Vault directly to retrieve additional information or raw data that is not available in the information mart should be avoided.

Also, there might be multiple information marts. Each OLAP cube should only access one information mart in most cases. If data is required from other information marts, this data should be added to the primary information mart. With virtualized facts and dimensions, this becomes very easy and doesn't require additional storage. In some cases, it requires that business logic needs to be moved upstream from the loading procedures of the second information mart into the Business Vault in order to be accessible for the primary information mart. This is the desired solution because the Business Vault should provide reusable business rules, not any one of the information marts.

15.1.1 CREATING A DATA SOURCE

Therefore, there should be only one information mart required to build the SSAS database. Create a new **Analysis Services Multidimensional and Data Mining Project** in Microsoft SQL Server Data Tools and add a new data source to the project.

Create a new data source in the **solution explorer**. The **data source wizard** is presented. After the initial welcome page, a page appears that is used to select the connection string. If the connection string for the information mart is not available yet, create one by selecting the **new** button. The dialog in Figure 15.1 is shown.

Enter the server name, your user credentials to the information mart and the database that provides the relational information mart entities. After selecting the OK button, the connection appears in the previous dialog, as shown in Figure 15.2.

Make sure that the connection to the information mart is selected and select the **next** button. The next dialog configures the impersonation information of Analysis Services (Figure 15.3).

The provided settings are used by Analysis Services to connect to the relational information mart. The following options are available [3]:

1. **Use a specific Windows user name and password:** this option allows a specific user account and its password to be provided, to access the relational information mart. It is a useful option if a dedicated Windows user account was created to access the information mart, for example with only read-only privileges.
2. **Use the service account:** the service account that is running the Analysis Services database is used to access the information mart. This is the default option. In order to use this option, a database login should be created for the service account. It also requires granting of access to the information mart.

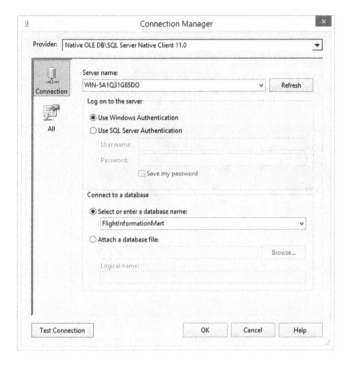

FIGURE 15.1

Create connection to information mart.

FIGURE 15.2

Select information mart connection in the data source wizard.

FIGURE 15.3

Impersonation information configuration.

3. **Use the credentials of the current user:** In some rare cases, the current user should be used for accessing the relational information mart. Note that this option is not available for multidimensional databases if they are located on the database backend.
4. **Inherit:** this option uses the impersonation options of the parent database (the Analysis Service database). It is helpful when setting the options centrally.

Select the appropriate setting and provide user credentials if necessary. If you don't know what option to choose, ask your database administrator or select the **use the service account** option as a best guess. It will require that the service account (the Windows account that is running Analysis Services) has access to the relational information mart.

Select the **next** button to continue. The data source wizard is completed with the page shown in Figure 15.4.

Make sure that the name of the data source is correct and select the **finish** button to complete the wizard.

15.1.2 CREATING DATA SOURCE VIEW

Once the data source for the information mart has been successfully configured, a data source view needs to be created which is used to access the relational database model in the information mart. From the solution explorer, select **new data source view** from the context menu of the **data source view**s folder. The **data source view wizard** appears. After the initial welcome page of the wizard, the page in Figure 15.5 is shown.

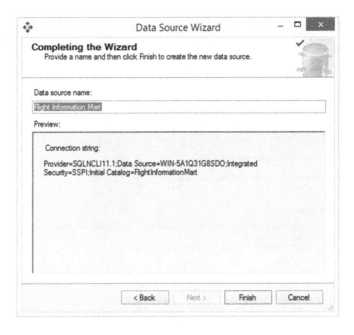

FIGURE 15.4

Complete the data source wizard.

FIGURE 15.5

Selecting a data source in the data source view wizard.

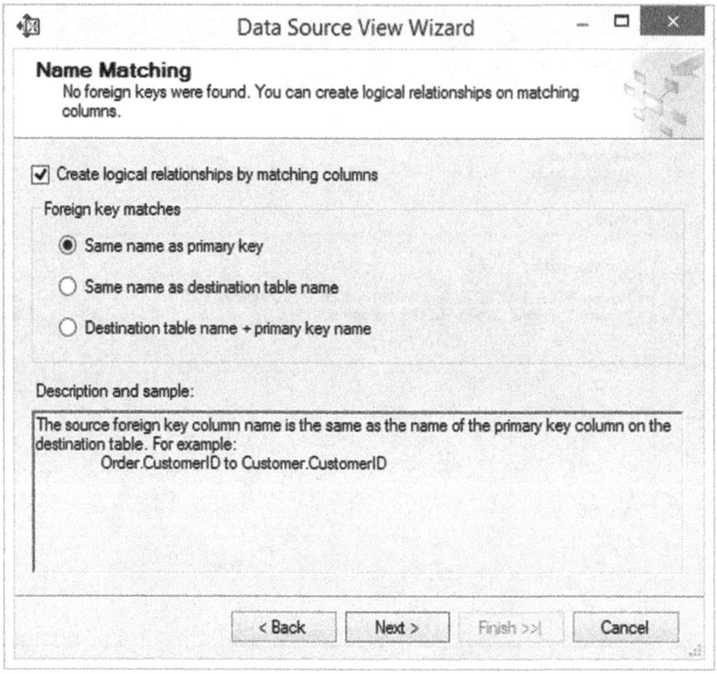

FIGURE 15.6

Configure name matching for the data source view.

Select the data source to the relational information mart that was just created and select the **next** button. The page presented in Figure 15.6 is shown.

In most cases, information marts don't use foreign key references. Therefore, Analysis Services offers the option to create logical relationships from the metadata of the tables found in the information mart. The relationships are found based on the column and table names. However, as shown in Figure 15.9, this matching is not 100% accurate, especially if naming conventions are not thoroughly followed. SSAS offers the following methods to detect the foreign key relationships in the information mart [4]:

1. **Same name as primary key:** the logical relationship is created based on the equality of the fact table column name and the name of the dimension's primary key.
2. **Same name as destination table name:** the logical relationship is created when the fact table column name matches the name of the dimension table.
3. **Destination table name + primary key name:** only if the fact table column name matches the dimension's table name concatenated with the name of the primary key column.

Select an appropriate matching method, based on your naming conventions and select the **next** button. The next dialog is presented in Figure 15.7.

FIGURE 15.7

Select tables and views from the information mart.

Select the tables and views (usually the facts and dimensions in the dimensional model) that should be included in the data source view. Make sure that there is at least one selected fact table and all required dimension tables on the right list of **included objects**. Select the **next** button. The next page shows the settings of the configured data source view (Figure 15.8).

Review the settings and make sure that the name of the data source view meets your expectations. Select the **finish** button to complete the wizard. The selected tables from the information mart are added to the data source view and presented as a logical model in the center of the application (Figure 15.9).

Note that there are some missing logical relationships. For example, the relationships between the fact table and the **airport** dimension are missing because the fact columns are not using the same name as the primary key column in the dimension. For this reason, the automatic mapping did not work. The same applies to **FlightNumKey** in **DimFlightNum**, which is not mapped to the column with the same name in the fact table. Drag the column from the fact table to the primary key of the corresponding dimension to create a logical relationship in both cases. Note that **DimAirport2** is referenced twice: once for **OriginKey** and **DestKey** in the fact table. The corrected data source view is presented in Figure 15.10.

This completes the first step to access the information mart that was created throughout the book. The next steps are creating dimensions based on the dimension tables and the cube itself, based on the fact table.

FIGURE 15.8

Complete the data source view wizard.

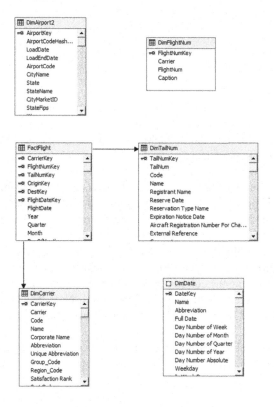

FIGURE 15.9

Initial data source view with missing logical relationships.

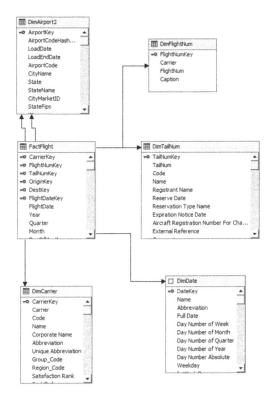

FIGURE 15.10

Data source view after logical relationships have been fixed.

15.2 CREATING DIMENSIONS

The data source view, created in section 15.1.2, provides SSAS access to and defines the relational information mart. The following sections of this chapter describe how the multidimensional database and the OLAP cubes are defined based on this data source view. The first step is to define the dimensions of the database and where the dimension data is being sourced.

To create a new dimension, select **new dimension** from the context menu of the **dimension** folder in the **solution explorer**. Click the **next** button on the welcome page of the dimension wizard. The page shown in Figure 15.11 is presented.

The page allows you to define the data source of the dimension or to create new data for some specific cases. The following options are available [5]:

1. **Use an existing table:** create a dimension from an existing table in the information mart. The information mart table will influence which attributes will be available for inclusion to the dimension.
2. **Generate a time table in the data source:** create a new time table in the information mart and use this table as the source for the dimension.

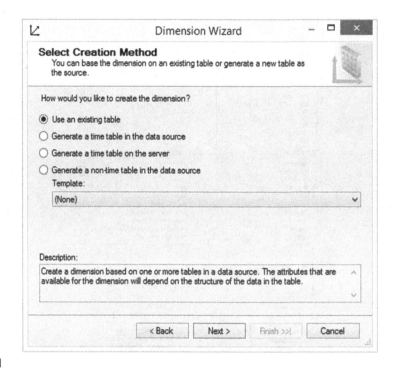

FIGURE 15.11

Selecting a creation method in the dimension wizard.

3. **Generate a time table on the server:** create a new time table on the SSAS server database and not the information mart.
4. **Generate a nontime table in the data source:** create a new table in the information mart, based on dimension attributes created in this wizard. An ETL job is required to load the dimension table created in this top-down approach.

Select the first option to create a new dimension in the multidimensional database based on data from the information mart. This is the recommended option for both standard dimensions and date dimensions. Refer to the next section which provides an alternate method to create a time table with more business-user involvement than the standard approach in SSIS.

After the **next** button is selected, the page in Figure 15.12 is shown.

This page asks for the table and columns information to source a new dimension from an existing table, as selected on the previous page. Select the data source view that was created in section 15.1.2 and one of the dimension tables.

Make sure that the **key column** was selected as key column. There should be only one key column per dimension table.

The **name column** defines the default caption for the member in the dimension. Select an appropriate and useful column that provides a distinguishable and understandable name for each member in the dimension.

FIGURE 15.12

Specify source information in the dimension wizard.

After setting up this configuration, select the **next** button to select the attributes of the dimension on the next page, as shown in Figure 15.13.

Select all the columns from the source table that should be usable by the business user and include them into the dimension. It is possible to set up various attribute types that change the behavior of SSAS for common use cases, such as currency and geography dimensions [6].

After setting up the attributes, click the **next** button to proceed to the next page, which completes the dimension wizard (Figure 15.14).

Review the settings for the dimension and make sure to provide a dimension name that is meaningful for the business user. Click **finish** to create the dimension in the multidimensional database.

Repeat the process for other dimensions in the dimensional model, such as **DimCarrier**, **DimFlightNum** and **DimTailNum**. The next section describes how to set up a date dimension, based on the **DimDate** entity in the information mart.

15.2.1 DATE DIMENSION

While Analysis Services provides the capability to set up a date dimension (time table) from the dimension wizard, there is some advantage of running the process on your own. Instead of using the time data provided by SSAS, the recommended managed self-service BI approach is to provide an analytical

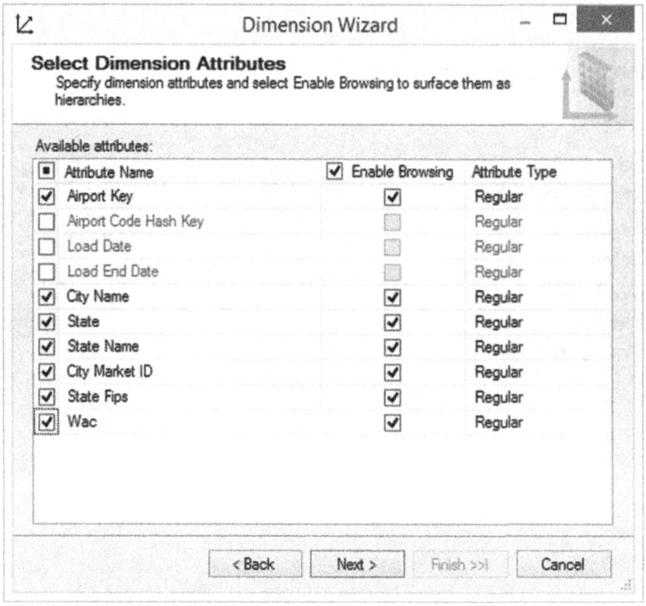

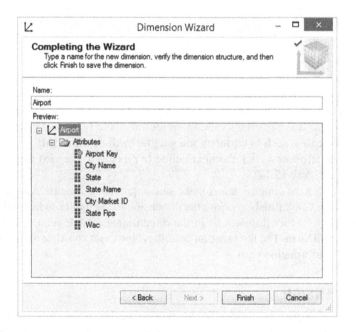

FIGURE 15.13

Select dimension attributes in the dimension wizard.

FIGURE 15.14

Complete the dimension wizard.

master data table with the dates that should be included in the date dimension and their corresponding descriptive fields. The advantage of this approach is that the descriptive fields can be modified by the business user, for example when changing date and months abbreviations or captions. The Microsoft Data Services (MDS) **DWH** model supplied with this book provides members for a date dimension with descriptive attributes that can be overwritten in MDS.

The information mart on the companion Web site includes a **DimDate** table that sources a limited number of descriptive attributes for the date dimension:

```
CREATE VIEW [dbo].[DimDate] AS
SELECT CONVERT(int, [Code]) AS DateKey
    ,[Name]
    ,[Abbreviation]
    ,[Full Date]
    ,[Quarter Number of Year]
    ,[Quarter Abbreviation]
    ,[Month Number of Year]
    ,[Month Abbreviation]
    ,[Day Number of Week]
    ,[Day Number of Month]
    ,[Day Number of Quarter]
    ,[Day Number of Year]
    ,[Day Number Absolute]
    ,[Year Number]
    ,[Weekday]
    ,[Is Week Day]
    ,[Is Last Day of Week]
    ,[Is Last Day of Month]
    ,[Is Last Day of Quarter]
    ,[Is Last Day of Year]
    ,[Sort Order]
    ,[External Reference]
    ,[Comments]
 FROM [DataVault].[raw].[RefDate]
```

This view in the information mart is directly based on a reference table in the Raw Data Vault and follows the approach for providing reference tables as dimensions outlined in Chapter 14, Loading the Information Mart. The reference table itself is a virtual view as well, because the analytical master data is under full control of the data warehouse and the other requirements for virtually providing reference data outlined in Chapter 12, Loading the Data Vault, are fully met.

In order to create a date dimension based on reference data from analytical master data, create a new dimension from the solution explorer and select the creation method (Figure 15.15).

Because the date dimension is sourced from reference data provided by the **DimDate** table in the information mart, select **use an existing table** again, following the approach in the previous section. Select **next** to continue (see Figure 15.16).

Select the **DateKey** dimension which is a code attribute (instead of a hash value, as in most other dimensions). Also, specify an appropriate **name** column before selecting the **next** button.

Set up the attributes of the date dimension on the page shown in Figure 15.17.

Select the attributes that should be provided by the date dimension. Also, consider setting the correct **attribute types**, which has been simplified in this example. After setting up the attributes, select

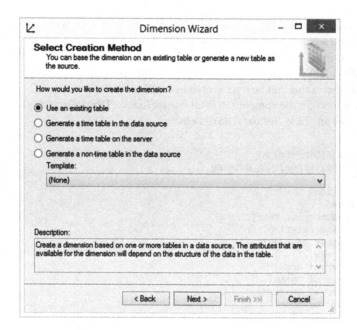

FIGURE 15.15

Select creation method for date dimension.

FIGURE 15.16

Specify source information for date dimension.

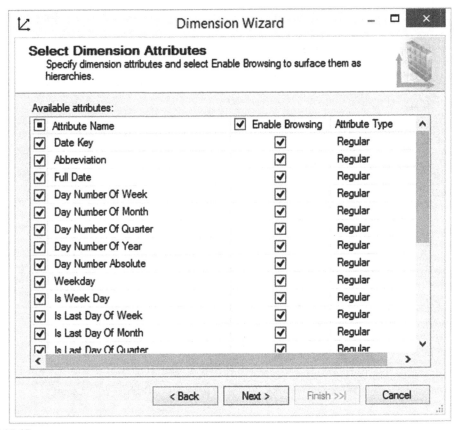

FIGURE 15.17

Select dimension attributes for date dimension.

the **next** button to proceed to the next page of the dimension wizard. The summary page will be shown as presented in Figure 15.18.

Review the settings and provide a meaningful dimension name before clicking the **finish** button. This completes the dimension wizard and adds the date dimension to the multidimensional database.

The final step is to define a date hierarchy that allows the end-user to analyze the data in the multidimensional table by different levels of grain, such as year, quarter, month or date. To define the hierarchy, open the **date** dimension in design mode (by using the context menu of the dimension in the solution explorer) and drag the **year number** attribute to the hierarchy canvas in the center of the screen. If you don't see the canvas shown in Figure 15.19, make sure that you're on the **dimension structure** tab. Add the following attributes to the hierarchy:

1. Year Number
2. Quarter Abbreviation
3. Month Abbreviation
4. Full Date

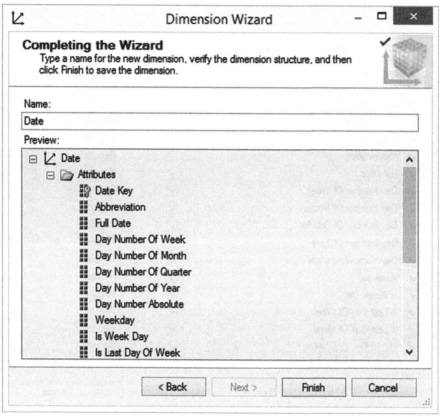

FIGURE 15.18

Completing the dimension wizard for the date dimension.

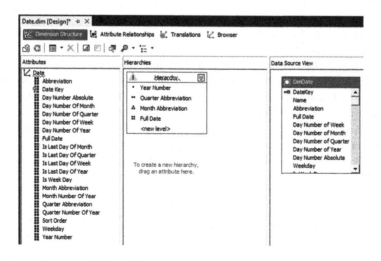

FIGURE 15.19

Defining the hierarchy of the date dimension.

The end result is shown in Figure 15.19.

It is also possible to set a hierarchy name to distinguish the hierarchy from other hierarchies, because it is possible to define multiple hierarchies per dimension. Save the dimension once your dimension structure is complete.

The example presented in this section provides an alternative to the standard date dimension in SSAS. Sourcing a date dimension from master data has the advantage that the business user has more control over the descriptive data but it also requires to create a relatively large table with analytical master data. This table is primarily intended for power users who know how to maintain the descriptive date information in the table and will not be managed by casual users.

15.3 **CREATING CUBES**

The dimensions created in this chapter are part of the multidimensional SSAS database and are used by multiple cubes. Each cube is based on one or more fact tables, but the recommendation is to create one virtual fact table in the information mart per cube. This way, it is possible to optimize the use of bridge tables for the final targets, because it improves the general performance as discussed in Chapter 14, Loading the Information Mart.

To create a new cube based on a fact table in the information mart, start the **cube wizard** by selecting **new cube** from the context menu of the **cubes** folder in the solution explorer. Click next on the welcome page of the wizard and select the creation method in the following page, shown in Figure 15.20.

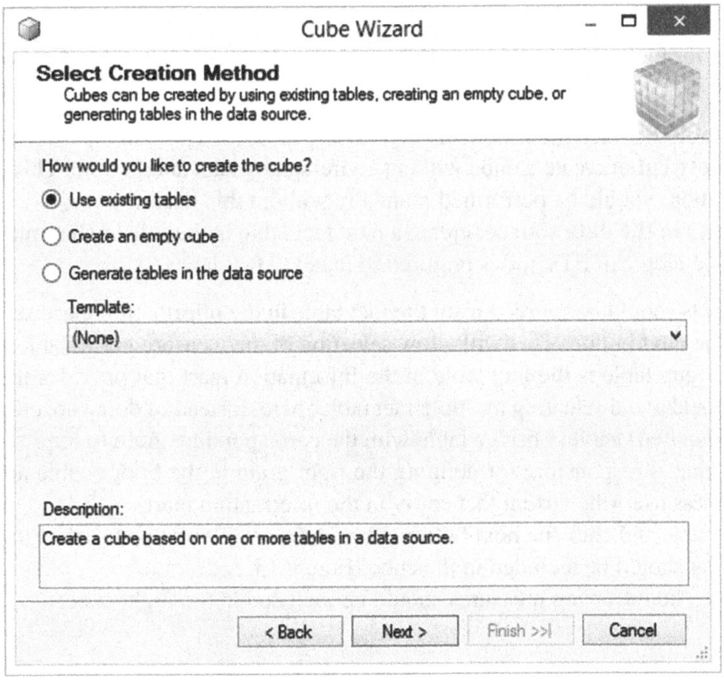

FIGURE 15.20

Selecting creation method in the cube wizard.

FIGURE 15.21

Select measure group tables in the cube wizard.

The page asks for the source of the data to be added as facts into the cube. The following options are available [7]:

1. **Use existing tables:** source the facts from an existing table (or view) in the information mart.
2. **Create an empty cube:** create a cube without sourcing any data at this time. This option is useful if all configurations should be performed manually without this wizard.
3. **Generate tables in the data source:** create a new fact table in the information mart based on the settings in this dialog. An ETL job is required to load the fact table.

Because the facts should be sourced from the fact table in the information mart, select **use existing tables** and click the **next** button. This will allow selection of the measure group table (Figure 15.21).

The measure group table is the fact table in the information mart that provides the facts and their measures. You should avoid selecting multiple fact tables here. Instead of doing so, create a new virtual fact table and (if required) another bridge table with the corresponding grain to improve the reusability of business logic that is responsible for defining the right grain in the bridge table and how it is presented to the business user (the virtual fact entity in the information mart).

Select the fact table and click the **next** button. The next page allows you to select the measures from the source table that should be included in the cube (Figure 15.22).

In this example, the following measures should be included in the flight cube:

- Dep Delay
- Dep Delay Minutes

- Taxi Out
- Taxi In
- Arr Delay
- Arr Delay Minutes
- CRS Elapsed Time
- Actual Elapsed Time
- Air Time

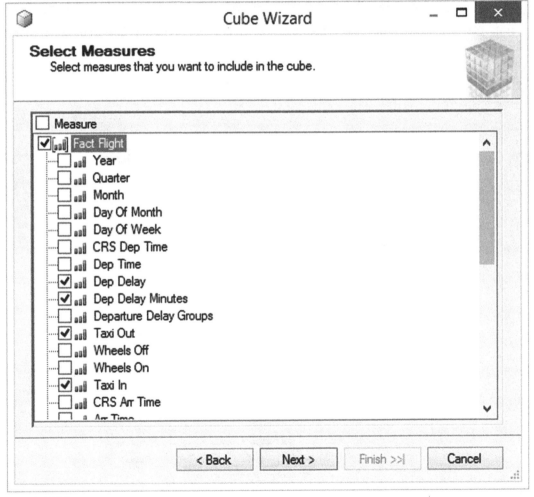

FIGURE 15.22

Select measures for the cube.

- Flights
- Distance
- Carrier Delay
- Weather Delay
- NAS Delay
- Security Delay
- Late Aircraft Delay
- Fact Flight Count

Select the above measures and click the **next** button. The next page is shown in Figure 15.23.

The page presented in Figure 15.23 allows you to include existing dimensions, which have been created in section 15.2. Select all required dimensions and select the **next** button to add additional dimensions (Figure 15.24).

If the fact table includes dimensional attributes which are not provided as dimension tables in the information mart, the dimensions can be set up using this page. Because there are no additional dimensions to be created in the **FactFlight** table, click the **next** button to continue. The next page, shown in Figure 15.25, presents the configuration of the cube for reviewing.

FIGURE 15.23

Select existing dimensions to be included in the cube.

FIGURE 15.24

Select new dimensions to be included in the cube.

FIGURE 15.25

Completing the cube wizard.

Review the cube configuration presented on the page and provide a meaningful **cube name** for the business user. Select the **finish** button to complete and close the cube wizard. The cube is put into design mode and the logical model of the cube should be shown (Figure 15.26).

The model should include the fact table **FactFlight** and all selected dimension tables. Review the logical model before starting the cube processing and deployment that is required for using it in the front-end tool of your choice.

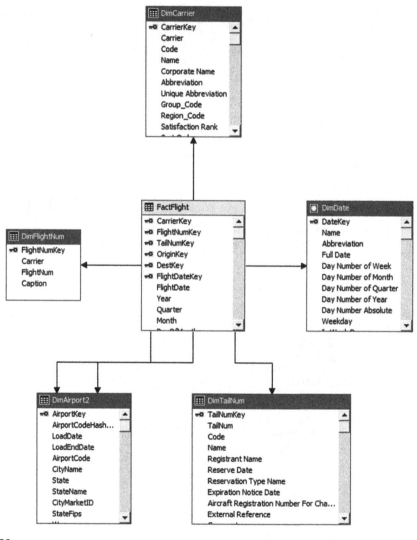

FIGURE 15.26

Logical model of the flight cube.

Note that the logical model for the cube, presented in Figure 15.26, provides only a simplified cube for flight information. There are many dimensions and measures missing from the cube that are required to put this cube into production. However, it serves as an appropriate final example for the information mart created in this book.

15.3.1 PROCESSING THE CUBE

Once the cube has been defined, it needs to be processed and deployed to the Analysis Services database on the database back-end. To process the cube, open the context menu of the cube in the solution explorer and select **process**. Make sure that the cube definition is saved. The dialog shown in Figure 15.27 appears on the screen.

FIGURE 15.27

Process flight information mart cube.

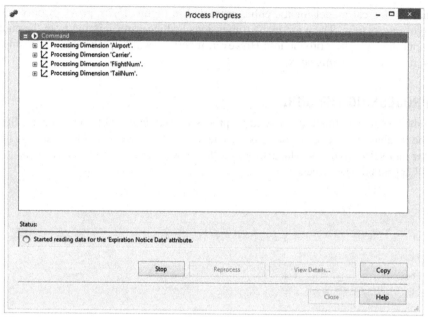

FIGURE 15.28

Process progress.

Click the **run** button in the dialog to initiate the cube processing. The next dialog, presented in Figure 15.28, shows the progress of the cube processing.

Wait until the cube processing completes and close the dialog using the **close** button. The cube is now ready for use.

15.4 ACCESSING THE CUBE

To retrieve aggregated information from the cube, open Microsoft SQL Server Management Studio, connect to the Analysis Services database and create a new MDX query on the database just created. Enter the following MDX statement:

```
SELECT
        CROSSJOIN([Date].[Full Date].members, [Measures].[Distance]) ON COLUMNS,
        [Carrier].[Carrier].[Carrier] ON ROWS
FROM
        [Flight Information Mart]
WHERE
        [Date].[Hierarchy].[Year Number].[2003].[Q4'03].[Oct'03]
```

This statement returns the distance flown in October 2003 by carrier. It is only one way of retrieving information from the cube, giving end-users full freedom to choose the measures and dimensions provided by the cube for ad-hoc access.

REFERENCES

[1] Joy Mundy and Warren Thornthwaite: The Microsoft Data Warehouse Toolkit, Second Edition, pp. 245, 247, 247ff.

[2] https://msdn.microsoft.com/en-us/library/hh212940.aspx.

[3] https://msdn.microsoft.com/en-us/library/ms187597.aspx.

[4] https://msdn.microsoft.com/en-us/library/ms186995.aspx.

[5] https://msdn.microsoft.com/en-us/library/ms178681.aspx.

[6] https://msdn.microsoft.com/en-us/library/ms175662.aspx.

[7] https://msdn.microsoft.com/en-us/library/ms187975.aspx.

Subject Index

A

Add analysis services connection manager, 573, 574
Add sequence number, 415, 416
AirlineID. *See* Airline identification number (AirlineID)
Airline identification number (AirlineID), 100
Airline industry software system, functional characteristics, 54
    external inputs (EI), 54
    external inquiries (EQ), 54
    external interface files (EIF), 54
    external outputs (EO), 54
AirportCode column, 436
AirportHashKey satellite, 365, 472
Airport hub table, 452
    ghost records in, 452
    null references, link connection with, 453
Analysis server database, 569, 570
API. *See* Application programming interface (API)
Application programming interface (API), 202, 343, 412, 419
Association rule algorithm, 569
    apriori, 569
    FP growth, 569
Audit transformation editor, 337, 338

B

Bad data, 26, 231, 521
Big Data, 7
    definition of, 7
    environments, 348
    performance issues, 7
Bill of material (BOM) hierarchy, 129
BOM. *See* Bill of material (BOM) hierarchy
BTS. *See* Bureau of Transportation Statistics (BTS)
Bureau of Transportation Statistics (BTS), 343
Business intelligence system, 19, 195, 345, 524
    correct and complete data, 525
    data quality tagging, 525
    data, standardization of, 525
    derived data, transforming of, 524
    match and consolidate data, 525
Business keys, 95, 307, 450
    composite, 95, 311
    hashing of, 350
    identification process, 96
    loading of, 451
    NULL, 436
    scope of, 97
    vs. surrogate keys, 97

Business logic, 45, 137, 199, 279, 335, 452
Business metadata, 284
    business column names, 285
    data elements, technical numbering of, 285
    definitions, 285
    ontologies and taxonomies, 285
    physical table and column names, 285
Business Vault, 28, 124, 151, 567
    computed aggregate links, 124
        FlightCount, 137
        HubAirport, 137
        HubCarrier, 137
        HubFlight, 137
        LinkFlight, 137
        LinkService, 137
        SatService, 137
    computed satellites, 124
    exploration links, 124

C

Capability maturity model integration (CMMI), 12, 33, 39, 231
    capability levels, 40
    Data Vault 2.0 methodology, integrating CMMI in, 41
    maturity level 5, advancing to, 41
    maturity levels, 40
CData
    components, 403
    GoogleSheets source, 412, 415
CDC. *See* Change data capture (CDC) systems
Change data capture (CDC) systems, 100, 143, 151, 501
    for employees, 144
CMMI. *See* Capability maturity model integration (CMMI)
CMS. *See* Content management systems (CMS)
COALESCE
    function, 364
    statements, 582
CodePlex, 288
Comma-separated values (CSV), 61, 324
Composite keys, 96
    bar codes, 96
    credit card numbers, 96
    email addresses, 96
    IMEI number, 96
    ISBN codes, 96
    ISSN codes, 96
    MAC numbers, 96
    phone numbers, 96